THE WORLD'S HISTORY

VOLUME ONE: PREHISTORY TO 1500

HOWARD SPODEK

THE WORLD'S HISTORY

VOLUME ONE: PREHISTORY TO 1500   FIFTH EDITION

PEARSON

Boston   Columbus   Indianapolis   New York   San Francisco
Hoboken   Amsterdam   Cape Town   Dubai   London
Madrid   Milan   Munich   Paris   Montréal   Toronto   Delhi   Mexico City
São Paulo   Sydney   Hong Kong   Seoul   Singapore   Taipei   Tokyo

Vice-President of Product Development:
Dickson Musslewhite
Senior Acquisitions Editor: Billy J. Grieco
Program Manager: Emily Tamburri
Project Manager: Gail Cocker
Senior Operations Supervisor: Mary Ann Gloriande
Media Director: Sacha Laustsen
Media Editor: Michael Halas
Media Project Manager: Elizabeth Roden

Printed and bound by Times Offset, Malaysia

Credits and acknowledgments borrowed from other sources
and reproduced, with permission, in this textbook appear
on the appropriate page within text or on the credits pages
in the back of this book.

Front cover: Two men with an ibex, Tanzoumaitak,
Tassili Mountains, Sahara, 7000–6000 B.C.E. Rock painting.
AKG Images.

This book was designed and produced by
Laurence King Publishing Ltd, London
www.laurenceking.com

Every effort has been made to contact the copyright holders,
but should there be any errors or omissions, Laurence King
Publishing Ltd would be pleased to insert the appropriate
acknowledgment in any subsequent printing of this
publication.

Commissioning editor: Kara Hattersley-Smith
Senior editor: Melissa Danny
Production: Simon Walsh
Designer: Nick Newton
Picture researcher: Peter Kent
Text permissions editor: Julie Kemp
Copy editor: Rosanna Lewis
Proofreader: Jessica McCarthy
Indexer: Pauline Hubner

Library of Congress Cataloging-in-Publication Data

Spodek, Howard
    The world's history / Howard Spodek. -- Fifth edition.
        pages cm
    Includes bibliographical references and index.
    ISBN 978-0-205-99612-4 -- ISBN 0-205-99612-4
    1. World history. I. Title.
    D20.S77 2015
    909--dc23
                            2014010924

10 9 8 7 6 5 4 3 2 1

Combined Volume
ISBN 10: 0-205-99612-4
ISBN 13: 978-0-205-99612-4

Volume 1 ISBN 10: 0-205-99607-8
ISBN 13: 978-0-205-99607-0

Volume 1 A La Carte ISBN 10: 0-205-98145-3
ISBN 13: 978-0-205-98145-8

Volume 2 ISBN 10: 0-205-99606-X
ISBN 13: 978-0-205-99606-3

Volume 2 A La Carte ISBN 10: 0-205-98137-2
ISBN 13: 978-0-205-98137-3

BRIEF CONTENTS

CONTENTS

MAPS

AT A GLANCE

CHARTS

Engage your students *beyond* the classroom . . .

. . . with **MyHistoryLab** and
THE WORLD'S HISTORY, Fifth Edition

Would your students get more out of their introductory history course if you could engage them with history *beyond* the classroom? Would class discussion go farther if they were reading and writing more, working with primary sources, studying maps, and mastering key topics . . . *before* class meetings begin?

If your answer to these questions is yes, then it's time to consider how MyHistoryLab can help you meet these challenges. MyHistoryLab offers immersive content, tools, and experiences to engage students and help them succeed, enabling you to craft a better learning experience for them in your introductory survey course.

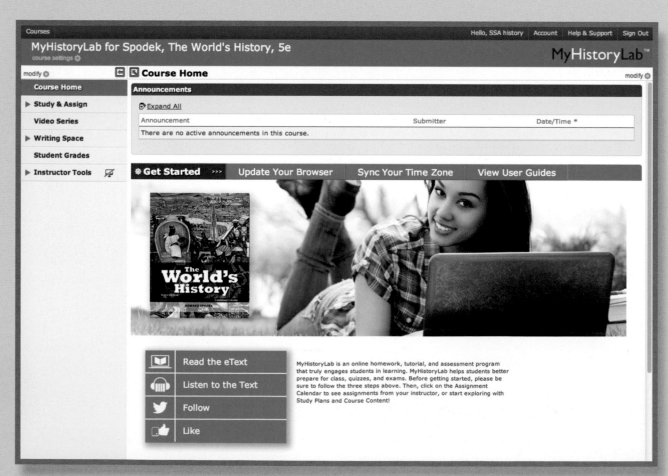

Prepare students on key topics with the MyHistoryLab Video Series

Are your introductory history students ready and eager to contend with a college textbook narrative? If not, help them get up to speed with the new MyHistoryLab Video Series: Key Topics in Western Civilization. Correlated to the chapters of *The World's History*, each video unit reviews key topics of the period, readying students to get the most from the text narrative. These engaging videos feature seasoned historians reviewing the pivotal stories of our past, in a lively format designed to demonstrate the power of historical narrative.

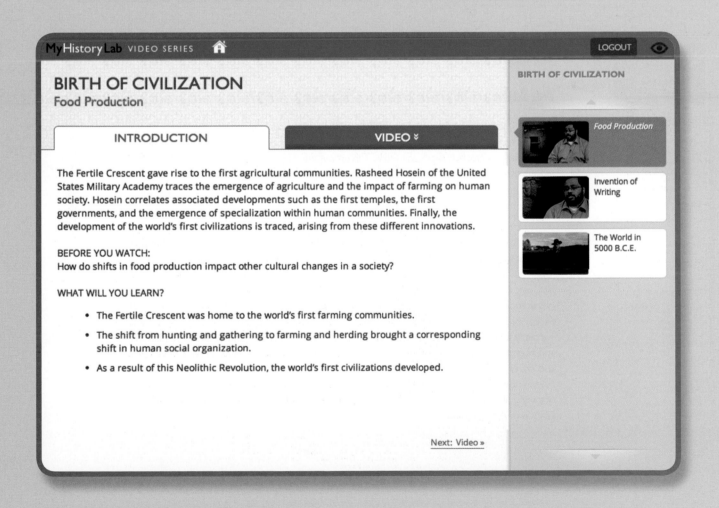

MyHistoryLab VIDEO SERIES   LOGOUT

BIRTH OF CIVILIZATION
Food Production

| INTRODUCTION | VIDEO ⌄ |

The Fertile Crescent gave rise to the first agricultural communities. Rasheed Hosein of the United States Military Academy traces the emergence of agriculture and the impact of farming on human society. Hosein correlates associated developments such as the first temples, the first governments, and the emergence of specialization within human communities. Finally, the development of the world's first civilizations is traced, arising from these different innovations.

BEFORE YOU WATCH:
How do shifts in food production impact other cultural changes in a society?

WHAT WILL YOU LEARN?

- The Fertile Crescent was home to the world's first farming communities.

- The shift from hunting and gathering to farming and herding brought a corresponding shift in human social organization.

- As a result of this Neolithic Revolution, the world's first civilizations developed.

Next: Video »

BIRTH OF CIVILIZATION

Food Production

Invention of Writing

The World in 5000 B.C.E.

Drive your students into primary sources with the new MyHistoryLibrary

Now your students can read dozens of the most commonly assigned primary-source documents, specially formatted in Pearson's powerful new eText. Students also have the option of listening to each reading in the accompanying Chapter Audio. Either way, students may access the text or the audio with various devices anytime they have access to the Internet.

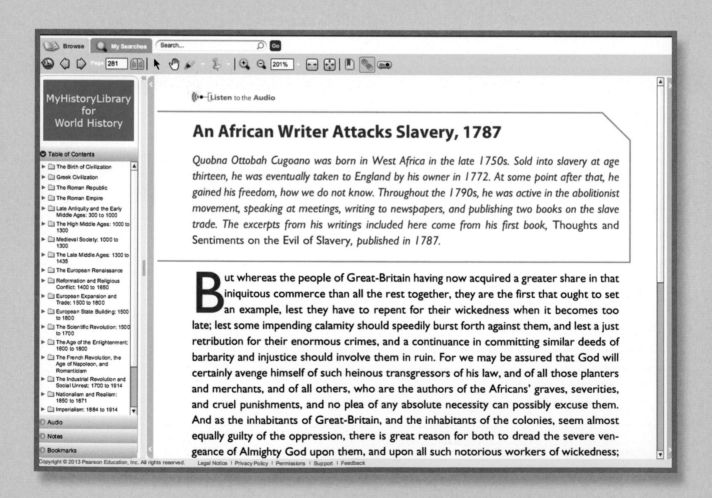

Browse   My Searches   Search...   Go

Page 281   201%

((•—|Listen to the Audio

An African Writer Attacks Slavery, 1787

Quobna Ottobah Cugoano was born in West Africa in the late 1750s. Sold into slavery at age thirteen, he was eventually taken to England by his owner in 1772. At some point after that, he gained his freedom, how we do not know. Throughout the 1790s, he was active in the abolitionist movement, speaking at meetings, writing to newspapers, and publishing two books on the slave trade. The excerpts from his writings included here come from his first book, Thoughts and Sentiments on the Evil of Slavery, published in 1787.

But whereas the people of Great-Britain having now acquired a greater share in that iniquitous commerce than all the rest together, they are the first that ought to set an example, lest they have to repent for their wickedness when it becomes too late; lest some impending calamity should speedily burst forth against them, and lest a just retribution for their enormous crimes, and a continuance in committing similar deeds of barbarity and injustice should involve them in ruin. For we may be assured that God will certainly avenge himself of such heinous transgressors of his law, and of all those planters and merchants, and of all others, who are the authors of the Africans' graves, severities, and cruel punishments, and no plea of any absolute necessity can possibly excuse them. And as the inhabitants of Great-Britain, and the inhabitants of the colonies, seem almost equally guilty of the oppression, there is great reason for both to dread the severe vengeance of Almighty God upon them, and upon all such notorious workers of wickedness;

Immerse your students in a powerful eText deeply integrated with MyHistoryLab

ntroductory survey teachers have long struggled to get students engaged in traditional textbooks. Now Pearson's MyHistoryLab offers a deeply immersive eText that transforms how students experience history. With a new pedagogically driven design, it highlights a clear learning path through the material and offers a visually stunning learning experience in print or on a screen. With the Pearson eText, students can transition directly to MyHistoryLab resources such as primary-source documents, videos, and Closer Look features. At last, history students can experience the eText they have been waiting for—one that comes alive on the screen.

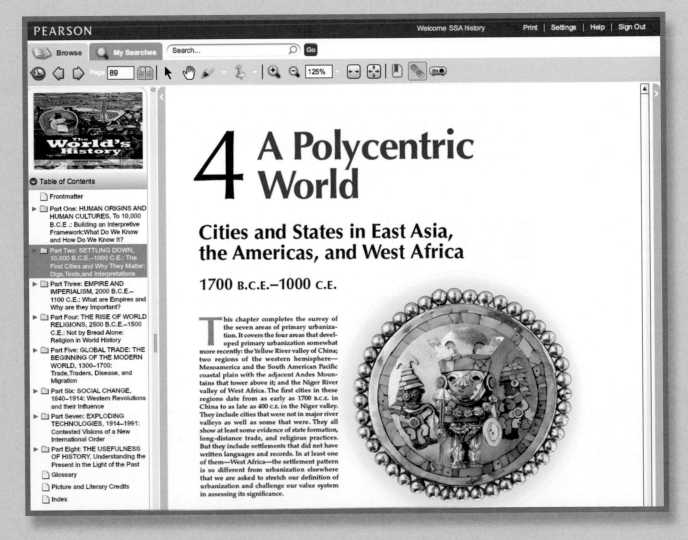

PEARSON

Welcome SSA history   Print | Settings | Help | Sign Out

Browse   My Searches   Search...   Go

Page 89   125%

4 A Polycentric World

Cities and States in East Asia, the Americas, and West Africa

1700 B.C.E.–1000 C.E.

This chapter completes the survey of the seven areas of primary urbanization. It covers the four areas that developed primary urbanization somewhat more recently: the Yellow River valley of China; two regions of the western hemisphere—Mesoamerica and the South American Pacific coastal plain with the adjacent Andes Mountains that tower above it; and the Niger River valley of West Africa. The first cities in these regions date from as early as 1700 B.C.E. in China to as late as 400 C.E. in the Niger valley. They include cities that were not in major river valleys as well as some that were. They all show at least some evidence of state formation, long-distance trade, and religious practices. But they include settlements that did not have written languages and records. In at least one of them—West Africa—the settlement pattern is so different from urbanization elsewhere that we are asked to stretch our definition of urbanization and challenge our value system in assessing its significance.

Writing Space

Better writers make great learners—who perform better in their courses. To help you develop and assess concept mastery and critical thinking through writing, we created the Writing Space in MyHistoryLab. It's a single place to create, track, and grade writing assignments, provide writing resources, and exchange meaningful, personalized feedback with students, quickly and easily. Plus, Writing Space includes integrated access to Turnitin, the global leader in plagiarism prevention.

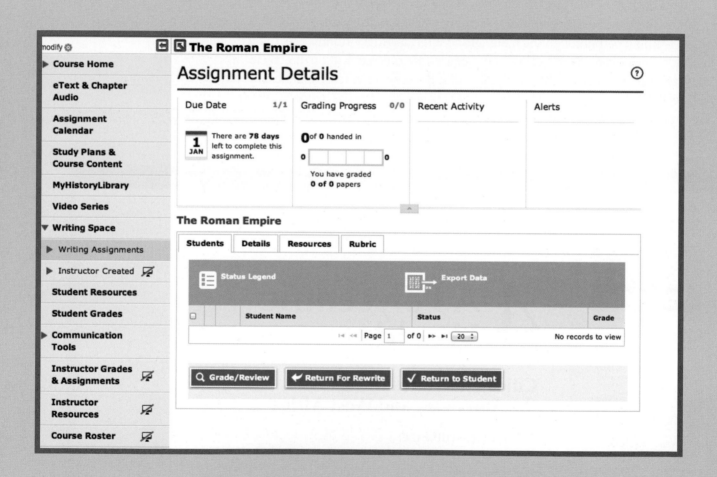

Key Supplements and Customer Support

Annotated Instructor's eText

Contained within MyHistoryLab, the *Annotated Instructor's eText* for your Pearson textbook leverages the powerful Pearson eText platform to make it easier than ever for you to access subject-specific resources for class preparation. The *AI eText* serves as the hub for all instructor resources, with chapter-by-chapter links to PowerPoint slides, content from the Instructor's Manual, and *MyHistoryLab's* ClassPrep engine, which contains a wealth of history content organized for classroom use.

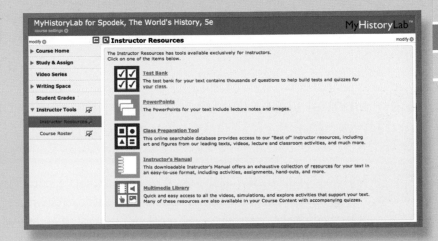

Instructor's Manual

The Instructor's Manual for *The World's History* contains learning objectives, a list of important themes discussed in the chapter, an annotated chapter outline with summaries of each section's content, suggestions for class activities, discussion questions, and suggestions for additional print and online resources for instructors. At the end of each chapter, MyHistoryLab Media Assignments catalog all of the MyHistoryLab resources for the chapter. The Instructor's Manual also contains a MyHistoryLab syllabus and suggestions for integrating MyHistoryLab into your course.

PowerPoint Presentations

Strong PowerPoint presentations make lectures more engaging for students. Correlated to the chapters of *The World's History*, each presentation includes a full lecture outline and a wealth of images, maps, and time lines from the textbook.

MyTest Test Bank

Containing a diverse set of multiple-choice, short-answer, and essay questions, the MyTest test bank supports a variety of assessment strategies. The large pool of multiple choice questions for each chapter includes factual, conceptual, and analytical questions, so that instructors may assess students on basic information as well as critical thinking.

Customer Support

Our dedicated team of local Pearson representatives will work with you not only to choose course materials but also to integrate them into your class and assess their effectiveness. Moreover, live support for MyHistoryLab users, both educators and students, is available 24/7.

Provide choices for your students through a variety of formats and price points

These alternatives to the traditional printed textbook are available for *THE WORLD'S HISTORY,* Fifth Edition.

>>> **MyHistoryLab with eTextbook** offers a full digital version of the print book and is readable on iOS and Android tablets. Students can get access to **MyHistoryLab** with the print book or save even more by purchasing on-line access at **www.myhistorylab.com**.

>>> **Books a la Carte** is a convenient, three-hole-punched, loose-leaf version of the traditional text at a discounted price—allowing students to carry only what they need to class. The Books a la Carte edition is also available with **MyHistoryLab** access.

>>> **CourseSmart eTextbooks** offer the same content as the printed text in a convenient online format—with highlighting, online search, and printing capabilities. Learn more at **www.coursesmart.com**. The **CourseSmart eTextbook** is also available with **MyHistoryLab** access.

>>> **Pearson Custom Library** helps instructors build the perfect course solution. For enrollments of at least 25, create your own textbook by combining chapters from best-selling Pearson textbooks and reading selections. To begin building your custom text, visit **www.pearsoncustomlibrary.com**.

PREFACE

Why History?

The professional historian and the student of an introductory course often seem to pass each other on different tracks. For the professional, nothing is more fascinating than history. For the student, particularly one in a compulsory course, the whole enterprise often seems a bore. This introductory text is designed to help the student to understand and share the fascination of the historian. It will also remind professors of their original attraction to history, before they began the specialization that has almost certainly marked their later careers. Furthermore, it encourages student and professor to explore together the history of the world and the significance of this study.

Professional historians love their field for many reasons. History offers perspective and guidance in forming a personal view of human development. It teaches the necessity of seeing many sides of issues. It explores the complexity and interrelationship of events and makes possible the search for patterns and meaning in human life.

Historians love to debate—the challenge of demonstrating that their interpretations of the pattern and significance of events are the most accurate and the most satisfying in their fit between the available data and theory. Historians also love the detective work of the profession, whether it is searching through old archives, uncovering and using new sources of information, or reinterpreting long-ignored sources. In recent years historians have turned, for example, to oral history, old church records, files of photographs, cave paintings, individual census records, and reinterpretation of mythology.

Historical records are not simply lists of events, however. They are the means by which historians develop their interpretation of those events. Because interpretation differs, there is no single historical record, but various narrations of events each told from a different perspective. Therefore the study of history is intimately linked to the study of values, the values of the historical actors, of the historians who have written about them, and of the students engaged in learning about them.

Professional historians consider history to be the king of disciplines. Synthesizing the concepts of fellow social scientists in economics, politics, anthropology, sociology, and geography, historians create a more integrated and comprehensive interpretation of the past. Joining with their colleagues in the humanities, historians delight in hearing and telling exciting stories that recall heroes and villains, the low-born and the high, the wisdom and the folly of days gone by. Increasingly, history also includes the history of science—its discoveries, its methods, and its implications for philosophy, technology, and human life. This fusion of the social sciences, humanities, and natural sciences gives the study of history its range, depth, significance, and pleasure. Training in historical thinking provides an excellent introduction to understanding change and continuity in our own day as well as in the past.

Why World History?

Why specifically world history? Why should we teach and study world history, and what should be the content of such a course?

First, world history is a good place to begin for it is a new field for professor and student alike. Neither its content nor its pedagogy is yet fixed. Many of the existing textbooks on the market still have their origins in the study of Western Europe, with segments added to cover the rest of the world. World history as the study of the interrelationships of all regions of the world, seen from the many perspectives of the different peoples of the earth, is still virgin territory.

Second, for citizens of multicultural, multiethnic nations such as the United States, Canada, South Africa, and India, and of many other countries, such as the United Kingdom, Australia, and most nations of the European Union, which are moving in that direction, a world history course offers the opportunity to gain an appreciation of the national and cultural origins of all their diverse fellow citizens. In this way, the study of world history may help to strengthen the bonds of national citizenship.

Third, as the entire world becomes a single unit for interaction, it becomes an increasingly appropriate subject for historical study. The new reality of global interaction in communication, business, politics, religion, culture, and ecology has helped to generate the new academic subject of world history.

Organization and Approach

The text, like the year-long course, links *chronology, themes,* and *geography* in eight units, or Parts, of study. The Parts move progressively along a time line from the emergence of early humans to the present day. Each Part emphasizes a single theme—for example, urbanization or religion or migration—and students learn to use them all to analyze historical events and to develop a grasp of the chronology of human development. The final chapter employs all the themes developed in the first seven Parts and adds an additional one, identity—personal, group, national, and global—as tools for understanding the history of our own times. Geographically, each Part covers the entire globe, although specific topics place greater emphasis on specific regions.

New to the Fifth Edition

Each chapter of the book has been reviewed and revised for this new edition, to accommodate new scholarship and in response to reviewer comments. The final two chapters, dealing with the contemporary world, have been extensively revised.

The pedagogical features have been carefully examined, and a completely new design makes it easy for students to find special features, such as the How Do We Know? boxes. The Turning Point boxes and Part openers have been revised, rewritten, and combined into one for all Parts.

Content Changes

Within each Part, material has been updated, revised, and added. Examples of some of the more notable changes and additions include: Substantial additions to the discussion of the DNA genetic record; additional material on the Aryans and the Indus valley settlers; discussion of recent archaeological discoveries in China; expanded coverage of agricultural villages; new material on Theodora, wife of the emperor Justinian; updated scholarship on the history of the Jewish people; new scholarship on the slave trade to the Americas; consideration of Russian migration to the west coast of the New World, via the Bering Straits and Alaska.

In updating the book to cover the events of contemporary history, we have added new materials to reflect new developments. These include: Breakthroughs in genetically modified crops; new ideas about the morality of using animals, especially chimpanzees, in research; coverage of the world economic collapse of 2008 and the nature of the recovery that began about 2012/13; discussion of the so-called Arab Spring; information on the Naxalite revolts in the tribal (*adivasi*) areas of India; material on globalization; updates in ecological technology and reliance on petrofuels; material on WikiLeaks, Julian Assange, Bradley Manning, and Edward Snowden; the public humanitarian activism of rock stars such as Bono; and the significance of the early influence of Pope Francis I on the Roman Catholic Church.

Chapter-by-Chapter Revisions

Chapter One, on human origins, substantially modifies and adds to the discussion of the DNA genetic record.

Chapter Two expands coverage of agricultural villages. Material has been added on family life, village life, treatment of graves, and the role of women. The discussion of Hammurabi's Code has been enhanced.

Chapter Three clarifies the significance of the New, Middle, and Old Kingdoms with additional information. Material has been added explaining the relationship between the Aryans and the Indus valley settlers.

Chapter Four adds material on recent archaeological discoveries at Huanbei and in the Anyang region of China. Coverage has been added on Eurasian immigrants to the New World and on the peoples in and urbanization of the Andes Mountains. A new excerpt from the *Popol Vuh* has been included.

Chapter Six includes new information on Theodora, wife of Emperor Justinian.

Chapter Ten includes updated scholarship on the history of the Jewish people and material on early Christian attitudes to sexuality, beginning with Jesus' early follower Paul, and leading to the later ban on priests marrying.

Chapter Eleven's section on the Crusades has been expanded and updated to reflect recent scholarship.

Chapter Twelve has been reorganized chronologically and geographically, and now moves from the general introduction to the specifics of trade in the Indian Ocean and Asia, then to Africa, and finally to the Americas. The section on the Mongol Empire has been revised and expanded, and indicates the reasons that many historians now call the Mongol Empire, and its trade routes, the marker of the beginning of the modern world.

Chapter Fourteen adds material on the inflation caused by the trans-Pacific silver trade. A new section discusses the Thirty Years War. Coverage has been added of the St. Bartholomew's Day Massacre and Cardinal Richelieu. Material has been added on the rule and achievements of Catherine the Great. The section on the Ottoman Empire has been expanded, and material has been added on the *millet* system.

Chapter Fifteen adds material on Russian expansion across the Bering Straits and into "Russian America." New scholarship has been included relating to the number of slaves transported to the Americas. New material covers the *janissary* system in the Ottoman Empire.

Chapter Sixteen expands on *Candide* and adds more coverage of the ideas of Adam Smith. Additional material is included on the "American school" of ethnography, as described by Samuel George Morton. The chapter now includes a discussion of the salons of Paris and an excerpt from Rousseau's *Emile*. Historiography of the French Revolution has been expanded with new scholarship.

The **Part Seven opener** and the **Turning Point** are restructured into one, reframing the discussion of the Olympics as a case study of what was happening in international relations at the time.

Chapter Eighteen now includes coverage of the German historian and philosopher Heinrich von Treitschke. The chapter covers the modernization program in Egypt, including *Aida*, the new opera commissioned from Verdi.

Chapter Nineteen has been restructured to show that while Latin America and China did not get involved in World War I, the war and the Great Depression did affect them, and the effects came about because of their decisions not to industrialize effectively.

Chapter Twenty contains an expanded discussion of the Italian preference for fascism over communism. Coverage of the Nuremberg Trials has been expanded, and material has been added on the Tokyo Tribunal.

Chapter Twenty-one has been tightened and reorganized. More has been added to the discussion of the beginning of the ecology movement.

Chapter Twenty-two shows a more comprehensive discussion of the importance of Mohandas Gandhi.

Chapter Twenty-three includes updated material on chimpanzee research, genetically modified plants, and infectious diseases that are transmitted from animals to humans. It includes coverage of China's plan, now being implemented, to move millions of people to cities built by the government for that purpose. Material on migration to cities has been added throughout, along with updated material on urban slums and the UN's Conferences on Human Settlements, Habitats I and II. Coverage of terrorism and world terrorist organizations and actions has been updated, with a section added on Boko Haram in Nigeria. The coverage of Barack Obama's presidency has been expanded, as has

the discussion of China's economy and its rise as a superpower. Discussion of world poverty has been updated with new research. The chapter includes coverage of the economic crash of 2008 and the global recession. The Arab Spring is analyzed and information brought up to date. In religion, there are updates on internal tension between secular and religious Israelis; on the Catholic Church and Pope Francis I; and on the significance of evangelical Christianity and of the religions of new immigrants in the United States.

Chapter Twenty-four has been much updated, with new data on population levels, the value of the global economy, the amount of goods shipped globally, and so on. New material covers globalization and the protests against it; social media; poverty and efforts to eradicate it worldwide; and growing income disparity. A new section covers the financial crisis that began in 2008 and the recovery that began in 2013. The chapter includes expanded coverage of nationalist and separatist movements from Ireland to Spain, to Canada, to Belgium, to several African nations. The Arab Spring is discussed for its political ramifications, somewhat distinct from its religious ramifications covered in Chapter Twenty-three. Gender issues, and especially changing family relationships, have gained expanded coverage. Coverage of the Naxalite revolts in India has been added, and that of migration and of refugees has been thoroughly updated with new facts and statistics. Updates to the cultural coverage include the additions of Kiran Ahluwalia and Bono. A new section discusses Bradley Manning, WikiLeaks, and Edward Snowden. Material has been added to update the information on ecological technology and reliance on petrofuels.

Special Features

● Learning Objectives now appear at the beginning of each chapter, and are repeated in question form under the relevant section headings and in tabs down the side of each page as reminders, before being answered at the end of each chapter, to encourage students to consider their own reading of the chapter.

LEARNING OBJECTIVES

8.1 ((	8.2 ((	8.3 ((	8.4 ((
Describe the important literature of the Aryan immigrants.	Understand the philosophy of the Maurya and Gupta Empires.	Describe the consequences of the Hunas invasion of India.	Compare India's empires with those of China and Rome.

((**Listen** on **MyHistoryLab**

8.1

8.2 What were the philosophies of the Maurya and Gupta empires?

8.3

8.4

A Golden Age of Learnin[g]
erature and Hindu philo[s]
composed two epic poer
Shakuntala, the first Sans
times. Much of the impor
transcribed into writing, i
emendations were made t
The Gupta Empire beg[a]
spondence. Panini (*fl. c. 40*
Astadhyayi (perhaps the m
but the Mauryas and mos
that was closer to the com[
as the *Laws of Manu*, and i
studied, revised, and fur[

Despite its military and cultural achievements, the Gupta dynasty's power began to wane in the late fifth century C.E. The subcontinent was once again politically divided and subject to one wave of invader-rulers after another. These internal divisions and conquests by outsiders—notably the Mughals in the sixteenth century and British in the eighteenth—continued until the modern independence of India and Pakistan in 1947 and of Bangladesh in 1971.

Huna Invasions End the Age of Empires

8.3 What were the consequences of the Hunas' invasion of India?

In the fifth century, new conquerors came through the passes of the nor[
throwing the Gupta Empire and establishing their own headquarters
Afghanistan. These invaders were the Hunas, a branch of the Xiongnu
Mongol tribes that roamed the regions north of the Great Wall of Chi[
times invaded. In previous expansions, they had driven other group[
into the Roman Empire, as we saw in the chapter "Rome and the
Domino-fashion, these groups pushed one another westward. The[

• The Introduction to the book describes the key themes of the text and the methods historians use to practice their craft.

• The introductions to each of the eight Parts now include more specific key references to the chapters that follow.

• **MyHistoryLab** links, to primary sources, videos, images, and maps, appear throughout the chapters.

was theirs. In the next 20 years they captured the Yucatán and most of Central America, although revolts continued in the region. Cortés became ruler of the Kingdom of New Spain, reorganized in 1535 as the Vice-Royalty of New Spain.

View the **Closer Look: The Meeting of Cortés and Moctezuma** on **MyHistoryLab**

Read the **Document: Excerpt from The Broken Spears, an Indian account of the conquest of Mexico** on **MyHistoryLab**

Read the **Document: Anonymous (Aztec): The Midwife Addresses the Woman Who Has Died in Childbirth** on **MyHistoryLab**

In South America, Vasco Nuñez de Balboa found a portage across the Isthmus of Panama in 1513. Now the Spanish could transport their ships from the Atlantic coast overland across the Isthmus and sail south along the Pacific Coast to Peru. Rumors of great stores of gold encouraged these voyages to the Inca Empire. Like the Aztecs, the Inca were divided. In 1525,

• Key Terms are listed at the end of each chapter for easy reference, and collected in the Glossary at the end of the book.

KEY TERMS

blood and iron Bismarck's policy of using warfare against enemies as a means of unifying his new nation. Subsequently the term has been used to designate the policy of any government committed to foreign warfare as a means of internal unification.

pogrom A murderous attack on a group of people—usually based on their ethnicity or religion—that is sanctioned by the government, either officially or unofficially.

• Turning Point essays, some completely new for this edition, illustrate visually the connections between one Part and the next. In some cases, the Turning Points tell their own story as well, notably in the bridge into the twenty-first century that uses the modern Olympic Games to illustrate and introduce many of the issues that are to follow. Turning Point Questions ask students to consider the material that has been presented.

PART SEVEN

TURNING POINT: EXPLODING TECHNOLOGIES

1914–1991

For Death and Life

The twentieth century began with great promise. The political and industrial revolutions of the previous two centuries encouraged Western Europeans to believe that they were mastering the secrets of securing a long, productive, comfortable, and meaningful life for the individual and the community. They believed that they were transmitting these benefits around the globe through their colonial policies, and that their colonial possessions would continue long into the foreseeable future. The Polish poet Wislawa Szymborska (1923–2012) captured this optimism in the opening of her poem "The Century's Decline" of 1986:

American atomic weapons test in the Marshall Islands, northern Pacific, 1950. Soon after World War II other nations besides America undertook to create atomic weapons: Russia, Britain, France, and somewhat later China, India, Pakistan, and North Korea. An international arms race had begun. Many began to believe that the mark of a powerful nation was the possession of nuclear weapons.

644

• The How Do We Know? features help the student to understand how historians use evidence, both textual and visual, to interpret the past.

HOW DO WE KNOW?

Evaluating the Legacy of Colonialism

As the colonial era ended, historians divided sharply in assessing the impact of colonial rule. Leften Stavrianos, who spent most of his career at the University of California, San Diego, presented a Marxist, primarily economic, critical perspective. Colonial rule created "an unprecedented increase in productivity" in commerce and industry, but no corresponding increase in pay for the workers nor in distribution of wealth to the colony. In many colonies, white settlers and plantation owners seized the best lands. Rural communities were disrupted as

> private property arrangements displaced the former communal ownership and cultivation of land ... Land now became a mere possession, food a mere commodity of exchange, neighbor a mere common property owner and labor a mere means of survival. (Stavrianos, p. 9)

As the Industrial Revolution matured into industrial capitalism, exploitation became more severe. The results were unfortunate and long lasting:

> All these global economic trends combined to produce the present division of the world into the developed West as against the underdeveloped Third World. But underdevelopment did not mean nondevelopment; rather it meant distorted development—development designed to produce only one or two commodities needed by the Western markets rather than overall development to meet local needs. In short, it was the familiar Third World curse of economic growth without economic development. (p. 11)

Theodore Von Laue, on the other hand, who studied Westernization, said very little about economic inequality. Deeply influenced by Judeo-Christian perspectives, he emphasized the cultural upheaval of colonialism and the paradoxical introduction by force of Western values of freedom: "The world revolution of Westernization, in short, carried a double thrust. It was freedom, justice, and peace—the best of the European tradition—on the one hand; on the other hand (and rather unconsciously) raw power to reshape the world in one's own image" (Von Laue, p. 16). The transformation to Western values was not complete, however:

> Underneath the global universals of power and its most visible supporting skills—literacy, science and technology, large-scale organization—the former diversities persist. The traditional cultures, though in mortal peril, linger under the ground floors of life. Rival political ideologies and ambitions clash head on. The world's major religions vie with each other as keenly as ever. Attitudes, values, life-styles from all continents mingle freely in the global marketplace, reducing in the intensified invidious comparison all former absolute truths to questionable hypotheses. (p. 7)

Von Laue looked forward to the day when all people "will be ready to fuse their personal egos with the egos of billions of other human beings, even in intimate matters like procreation and family size" (p. 9). It would appear that the common values on that day would be the Western values of the Enlightenment.

Dipesh Chakrabarty questioned this assumption that Western values would win out. Born in India after independence, trained in Australia and the United States, and later teaching there as well, Chakrabarty argued that the greatest (self-)deception of the colonizers was to project European values as the appropriate goals for the entire world, and to see history moving in that direction: "First in Europe, then elsewhere." He rejected the idea that the rest of the world exists in Europe's "waiting room." He did appreciate European, Enlightenment values, but he did not think they were the only valid ones, nor that they ought to or necessarily would become universal. Chakrabarty did not address economic issues. On cultural transformations brought by colonialism, however, he was not prepared to accept Von Laue's celebration of exclusively Western values, nor to look forward to the day when they alone would triumph.

- Which effects of colonialism do you think were more important, the economic and technological effects, or the cultural effects? Please be specific about the effects you are discussing.
- To the extent that the Cold War from the mid-1940s to the mid-1980s represents in part the values of the West, what values do you think colonized countries learned from the West?
- Do you think it is a good idea that some day the peoples of the world may share a similar set of values? Why or why not? If it is a good idea, then what should those values be? To what extent are they technological values?

• This edition also continues the emphasis on the use of primary sources, for this is the kind of material from which the historical record is argued and fashioned. Most chapters have two or more Source boxes, which have been colored purple in this edition to stand out.

SOURCE

The Journal of Columbus' First Voyage to the Americas

Columbus kept a day-by-day journal of his first voyage. The original has been lost, but fortunately the priest Bartolomé de Las Casas (1474–1566) prepared an abstract, which he used in writing his own *Historia de Las Indias* (1875). Columbus' leading biographer in English, Samuel Eliot Morison, calls the abstract "The most important document in the entire history of American discovery." This account of what Columbus saw and how he related to it is written sometimes in the first person of Columbus, and sometimes in the third person, as the voice of Las Casas. Note especially the overwhelming importance given to religion:

> **Prologue:** Your Highnesses, as Catholic Christians and Princes devoted to the Holy Christian Faith and the propagators thereof, and enemies of the sect of Mahomet and of all idolatries and heresies, resolved to send me, Christopher Columbus, to the said regions of India, to see the said princes and peoples and lands and the disposition of them and of all, and the manner in which may be undertaken their conversion to our Holy Faith, and ordained that I should not go by land (the usual way) to the Orient, but by the route of the Occident, by which no one to this day knows for sure that anyone has gone ...
>
> **12 October 1492:** At two hours after midnight appeared the land, at a distance of two leagues ... Presently they saw naked people, and the Admiral went ashore in his barge, and [others] followed. The Admiral broke out the royal standard, and the captains [displayed] two banners of the Green Cross, which the Admiral flew on all the vessels as a signal, with an F and a Y, one at one arm of the cross and the other on the other, and over each letter his or her crown ... and said that they should bear faith and witness how he before them all was taking, as in fact he took, possession of the said island for the King and Queen ...
>
> **15 October:** It was my wish to bypass no island without taking possession, although having taken one you can claim all ...
>
> **22 October:** All this night and today I was here, waiting to see if the king here or other people would bring gold or anything substantial, and many of this people came, like the others of the other islands, as naked and as painted, some of them white, others red, others black, and [painted] in many ways ... any little thing I gave them, and also our coming, they considered a great wonder, and believed that we had come from the sky ...
>
> **1 November:** It is certain that this is the mainland and that I am before Zayto [Zaytun] and Quisay [Hangzhou] [two great port cities of China], 100 leagues more or less distant the one from the other ...
>
> **6 November:** If they had access to devout religious persons knowing the language, they would all turn Christian, and so I hope in Our Lord that Your Highnesses will do something about it with much care ... And after your days (for we are all mortal) ... you will be well received before the eternal Creator ...
>
> **12 November:** Yesterday came aboard the ship a dugout with six young men, and five came on board; these I ordered to be detained and I am bringing them. Afterwards I sent to a house which is on the western bank of the river, and they brought seven women, small and large, and three boys. I did this because the [Indian] men would behave better in Spain with women of their country than without them ...
>
> **27 November:** Your Highnesses ought not to consent that any foreigner does business or sets foot here, except Christian Catholics, since this was the end and the beginning of the enterprise ...
>
> **22 December:** The Indians were so free, and the Spaniards so covetous and overreaching, that it was not enough that for a lace-tip or a little piece of glass and crockery or other things of no value, the Indians should give them what they asked; even without giving anything they [the Spaniards] wanted to get and take all, which the Admiral had always forbidden ...
>
> **23 December:** In that hour ... more than 1000 persons had come to the ship, and that all brought something that they owned, and that before they come within half a crossbow shot of the ship, they stand up in their canoes with what they brought in their hands, saying "Take! Take!" (cited in Morison, pp. 41–179)

• The Suggested Readings for each chapter have been thoroughly revised, updated, and expanded to reflect current scholarship. Films, videos, and online assets have been added. Each item in the bibliography is annotated to direct students with their reading.

• Each chapter text ends with a discussion of legacies to the future, namely, What Difference Does It Make?

• Each chapter concludes with a Chapter Review, where the reader is given answers to the Learning Objectives, essentially a summary of the most important material covered in each main heading.

THE MEIJI RESTORATION AND INDUSTRIALIZATION IN JAPAN

1853	Commander Perry sails into Edo Bay, ending 250 years' isolation
1854	Treaty of Kanagawa gives United States trading rights with Japan
1860s	Series of "unequal treaties" gives United States, Britain, France, Russia, and Netherlands commercial and territorial privileges
1868	*Daimyo* force Tokugawa shogun to abdicate. Executive power vested with emperor in Meiji restoration
1871	Administration is overhauled; Western-style changes introduced
1872	National education system introduced, providing teaching for 90 percent of children by 1900
1872	First railway opened
1873	Old order changed by removal of privileges of samurai class
1876	Koreans, under threat, agree to open three of their ports to the Japanese and exchange diplomats
1877	Satsuma rebellion represented last great (unsuccessful) challenge of conservative forces
1879	Representative system of local government introduced
1884	Western-style peerage (upper house) created
1885	Cabinet government introduced
1889	Adoption of constitution based on Bismarck's Germany
1889	Number of cotton mills has risen from three (1877) to 83
1894–95	War with China ends in Japanese victory
1895	Japan annexes Taiwan and Pescadores Islands
1902	Britain and Japan sign military pact
1904–05	War with Russia ends in Japanese victory
1910	Japan annexes Korea
1914	Japan joins World War I on side of Allies

AT A GLANCE: THE AGE OF REVOLUTIONS

DATE	EUROPE	NORTH AMERICA	LATIN AMERICA
1640	• Galileo dies; Newton is born (1642) • Civil wars in England (1642–46; 1647–49; 1649–51) • Execution of King Charles I of England (1649) • Hobbes' *Leviathan* (1651) • Restoration of English monarchy (1660) • Royal Society of London founded (1662)		• Portugal takes Brazil from the Dutch (1654)
1670	• The "Glorious Revolution" in England (1688) • The English Bill of Rights (1689) • John Locke's *Second Treatise on Government* (1689) • *Philosophes*: Diderot (1713–84); Voltaire (1694–1778); Rousseau (1712–78); Montesquieu (1689–1755)		
1760	• Tennis Court Oath (June 20, 1789) • French Revolution (1789–99) • "March of the Women" (1789) • "Great Fear" (1789)	• British levy taxes on Americans in the Stamp Act (1765) • American Declaration of Independence (1776); War of Independence (1775–81) • Constitution (1789)	• Revolts against European rule in Peru, Colombia, and Brazil (1780–98) • Tupac Amarú revolt, Peru (1780)
1790	• "Second French Revolution" (1791–99) • "Reign of Terror" (1793–95) • Napoleon seizes power (1799); Emperor (1804) • *Concordat* between Napoleon and Pope Pius VII (1801) • Napoleon issues Civil Code (1804) • Napoleon invades Russia; finally defeated (1812)	• Bill of Rights ratified (1791) • Louisiana Purchase from France (1803)	• Toussaint L'Ouverture leads slave revolt against French in Saint-Domingue (Haiti) (1791) • Haiti proclaims independence (1804) • Joseph Bonaparte, king of Spain (1808) • Bolívar and San Martín lead revolts against Spain (1808–28) • Paraguay declares independence (1810–11)
1820	• Congress of Vienna (1814–15) • Reform Act extends voting franchise in Britain (1832) • Britain abolishes slavery in its empire (1833)	• President Andrew Jackson evicts Cherokee Indian Nation: "Trail of Tears" (1838) • Warfare with Mexico ends in victory for America (1848) • United States abolishes slavery (1863, 1865)	• Mexico wins independence (1821) • Prince Pedro declares Brazil independent (1822)

New Layout and Design

Readers will notice cleaner design of box features. The format has reverted to the original taller page size so that the text and pictures have a little more room to breathe.

Maps and Illustrations

To aid the student, extensive, clear, and informative charts and maps represent information graphically and geographically. A wide range of illustrations, most in color, supplements the written word. For the fifth edition we have added more than 50 new illustrations.

Acknowledgments for the Fifth Edition

Each edition, each evolution of the text, brings new, indispensable colleagues who make the enterprise what it continues to become. This revision began once again at Laurence King Publishing in London, under the guidance of Kara Hattersley-Smith, and then Melissa Danny and, under her supervision, the illustrators, designers, proofreaders, and other personnel who have added their suggestions, based on a wealth of experience, and kept the project on track. Freelance editor Margaret Manos of New York and New Hampshire once again read the text—old and new—with great sensitivity and worked wonders in reorganizing, clarifying, streamlining, and improving readability. She sifted through the many external reviews and focused their key comments and criticisms into improving the revision process. She frequently sharpened perspectives, especially on issues of feminism and European and American history. In some important cases she helped to select artwork that added insight and aesthetics to the arguments of the book. At Pearson, Billy Grieco exercised overarching supervision of the entire project.

Kara Hattersley-Smith, Editorial Manager, assures me that this transoceanic venture has proceeded smoothly, aided by Melissa Danny, Senior Editor, Nick Newton, Designer, and Peter Kent, Picture Researcher. Without them, there would be no fifth edition, and I am grateful for their patient and firm guidance and wise diplomacy.

I have also benefitted immensely from the kindness of the many students (especially my own students at Temple University), colleagues, and teachers who have used this book and taken time to share with me their advice and suggestions. A surprising number of high-school teachers and students, who use this book as their text for AP World History, have written to me over the years with interesting questions that have kept me on my toes, and suggestions that have benefitted the text. I thank them all and hope that they will see the effects of their good counsel in this edition.

One element that has not changed in this new edition is the mental image I keep before me of my own children—albeit at a younger age, since by now their knowledge in so many fields far surpasses my own—and of my students. I write for them.

Grateful acknowledgments are also extended to the following reviewers of the fifth edition: Raymond Hylton, Virginia Union University; Robert Haug, University of Cincinnati; Cynthia Stephan, South Florida Bible College; Bruce Strouble, Bainbridge College; Walter Roberts, University of North Texas; James Brodman, University of Central Arkansas; Robert Hendershot, Grand Rapids Community College; Adrianna Lozano, Purdue University; Michele Louro, Salem State University; Maxim Matusevich, Seton Hall University; Jared Krebsbach, University of Memphis; Joseph Sramek, Southern Illinois University; Eleanor Aronstein, Marist College; Mark Tauger, West Virginia University; Faith Childress, Rockhurst University; Dandan Chen, Wells College.

About the Author

Howard Spodek received his B.A. degree from Columbia University (1963), majoring in history and specializing in Columbia's newly designed program in Asian Studies. He received his M.A. (1966) and Ph.D. (1972) from the University of Chicago, majoring in history and specializing in India. His first trip to India was on a Fulbright Fellowship, 1964–66, and he has spent a total of some twelve years studying and teaching in India. He has also traveled widely throughout the United States, Latin America, Asia, Africa, and Europe. He has been a faculty member at Temple University since 1972, appointed Full Professor in 1984. He was awarded Temple's Great Teacher designation in 1993.

Spodek's work in world history began in 1988 when he became Academic Director of a comprehensive, innovative program working with teachers in the School District of Philadelphia to improve their knowledge base in world history and facilitate a rewriting of the world-history program in the schools. Immediately following this program, he became principal investigator of a program that brought college professors and high-school teachers together to reconsider, revise, and, in many cases, initiate the teaching of world history in several of the colleges and universities in the Philadelphia metropolitan area. Those projects led directly to the writing of the first edition of the current text (1997).

Howard Spodek has published extensively on urbanization in India, including *Urban-Rural Integration in Regional Development* (1976); *Urban Form and Meaning in South-East Asia* (editor, with Doris Srinivasan, 1993); *Ahmedabad: Shock City of Twentieth-Century India* (2011); and a wide array of articles, including analyses of working women's organizations. In addition, he wrote and produced the documentary film *Ahmedabad* (1983), and was the executive producer and subject specialist for the documentary film *The Urban World: A Case Study of Slum Relocation in Ahmedabad, India* (2013). He organized and served on the three-person team that translated the six-volume *Autobiography of Indulal Yagnik* from Gujarati to English (2011). He has written on his experiences with world-history faculty at the college and high-school levels in articles in *The History Teacher* (1992, 1995). He has received funding for his research, writing, teaching, and film from Fulbright, the National Endowment for the Humanities, the National Science Foundation, the American Institute of Indian Studies, the Smithsonian Institution, and the World Bank.

Howard Spodek

INTRODUCTION:
The World Through Historians' Eyes

Themes and Turning Points

Most readers of this textbook have probably not taken many courses in history. Few are (thus far) planning to major in history, much less become professional historians. A lot therefore rides on this single text. It must present a general introduction to world history that interests, engages, and even fascinates the reader through its subject matter, its narrative, and its analysis. It must open the eyes, minds, and hearts of students who come to this course believing that history is only about the past, and mostly a matter of learning names, dates, and places. It must introduce them to the methods and "habits of mind" of the historian. It must demonstrate how knowledge of the contents and methods of world history—and of this book in particular—will broaden their horizons and also have practical usefulness.

"Usefulness" is a word not always associated with the study of history. Indeed, in everyday conversation, the phrase "that's history" means that an event is no longer significant. It may once have been important, but it is not now. From that point of view, "history" is a record of people and events that are dead and gone. For the historian, however, the opposite is true. The past has made us who we are, and continues to influence who we are becoming. In this sense, the past is not dead, just as people whom we have known personally and who have influenced our lives are not "dead," even though they may no longer be with us. This text will highlight ways in which the past continues to have a profound effect on the present and future. It will help us to understand who we have become.

History does not provide specific answers to today's problems, but it does provide examples and case studies that help us to improve our thinking. Generals study past wars to understand how modern battles may be fought; economists study past periods of growth and recession to understand how we can encourage the former and avoid the latter. Understanding the ways in which families and relationships have functioned in the past helps us find ways to make our own families and relationships more satisfying today.

World history gives us the largest possible canvas on which to carry out these studies. We cannot, however, study everything that ever happened. We must choose what to include and what to exclude. We must choose strategies that maximize our ability to understand our lives today in the context of the whole range of human experience.

In this text we choose two fundamental organizing principles as our framework for the study and teaching of world history. First, we choose a series of eight chronological turning points, each of which changed the patterns of human life. Second, we explain the importance of each of these changes in terms of the new themes they introduced into human experience. These two elements—chronological turning points and interpretive themes—go together.

This text is organized around eight turning points and themes. Others might also have been chosen, but these turning points represent some of the most important transformations in human life. The thematic analysis of these turning points encourages students to grapple with the origins and continuing presence of eight of the most significant themes in life: the biological and cultural qualities that make humans the special creatures we are; the settlements we create and live in; the political power we assemble and sometimes oppose; the religious systems through which many individuals and communities find meaning; the movement of trade and people that has linked the peoples of the world ever more closely, sometimes in cooperation, sometimes in competition, and sometimes in conflict; the political, industrial, and social revolutions, especially of the seventeenth through the twentieth

Learning about silkworms, from a book on the silk industry. Gouache on paper. Chinese school, nineteenth century. This painting suggests some of the concerns of modern world history that have previously received less attention: non-Western regions presented in their own right, and not only in their relationship to the West; daily activities and ordinary people; the human conditions of production and trade; the activities of women. Also, the use of art and illustration is a powerful tool in our becoming acquainted with the peoples of the world throughout time.

centuries, the era we now call "modern"; the technological developments that continue to reshape our world; and the quest for personal and group identity, so prevalent in our own times.

Because real life does not fit neatly into exact chronological periods, there will be significant overlap among the turning points. Readers may argue that the themes are also not limited to single chronological periods. For example, political regimes, religious systems, and economic organizations appear at all times in history. This argument is, of course, correct: "Everything is related to everything else," and in reality each chronological period will include several themes. We have chosen, however, to highlight particular themes in particular historical periods so that students will understand these themes more thoroughly and learn to employ them as tools of analysis in forming their own understanding of our world.

Chronological Turning Points and Part Themes

PART ONE Turning Point: Human Origins
To 10,000 B.C.E.
The emergence of the first humans. Biological and early cultural evolution.
THEME: Historians and anthropologists search for and interpret fossils, DNA biological materials, and artifacts to determine what is human about humans.

PART TWO Turning Point: Settlement Patterns
10,000 B.C.E.–1000 C.E.
Creating settlements, first agricultural villages and then cities.
THEME: Settlements—villages, towns, and cities—are created to meet community needs and, in the process, create new communities and new needs.

PART THREE Turning Point: From City-states to Empires
2000 B.C.E.–1100 C.E.
Creating empires, from Sargon of Assyria through Alexander the Great, Republican and Imperial Rome, Qin and Han China, and India of the Mauryas and Guptas.
THEME: Imperial political power is generated, expanded, consolidated, and resisted.

PART FOUR Turning Point: Creating World Religions
2500 B.C.E.–1500 C.E.
Creating global religions: Judaism, Christianity, Islam, Hinduism, and Buddhism.
THEME: Spiritual feelings are mobilized into powerful religious systems, some of which attain global scope.

PART FIVE Turning Point: Trade
1300–1700
The global movement of goods and people bridges the seas and links the continents.
THEME: The flow of goods and people is channeled into global networks, creating new knowledge, inspiring new outlooks, and challenging existing political and economic structures.

PART SIX Turning Point: Revolution
1640–1914
Revolutions: political, industrial, and social.
THEME: Vast, abrupt changes in political and economic systems create new social values and institutions, transforming the lives of individuals, families, and communities.

PART SEVEN Turning Point: Exploding Technologies
1914–1991
Technological change and its human control.
THEME: New technological systems, both simple and complex, are instituted that improve—and threaten—human life.

PART EIGHT Turning Point: From Past to Present to Future
1979–
The application of historical themes to an understanding of contemporary events.
THEME: A brief review of the seven themes developed until now, and an exploration of their applicability to the understanding of our own times, the last 30 to 40 years. Includes a final consideration of ways in which individuals and groups form their own identities in the space between past and future.

Global Scope

The scope of this text, and of each turning point and theme within it, is global. Often the method is comparative, especially in early times, as we compare early cities, early empires, and early global religions across regions of the world. For more recent times, the method is more interactive. For example, the study of the Industrial Revolution in Europe includes its funding—in part—from the wealth that poured into Europe from its New World conquests of people, land, gold, and silver, and from African slave labor; its global extensions in the form of imperialism in Asia, Africa, Australia, and Latin America; and the interaction of colonizers and colonized in response to the new opportunities and challenges.

Social Science Methods, Comparative History, and the Study of Values

Comparative History and the Methods of the Social Sciences

The global, interactive, and comparative format of this text provides also an introduction to social science methodology. The methods of the social sciences are embedded in the structure of the book. Because each part is built on relationships among different regions of the world, the reader will become accustomed to posing hypotheses based on general principles and to testing them against comparative data from around the world.

This method of moving back and forth between general theory and specific case study, testing the degree to which the general theory and the specific data fit each other, is at the heart of the social sciences. For example, in Part Two we will explore the general characteristics of cities, and then examine how well these generalizations hold up through case studies of various cities around the world. In Part Three we will seek general theories of the rise and fall of early empires based on comparisons of China, Rome, and India. In Part Four we will search for commonalities among religious systems through a survey of five world religions. In Part Eight we begin with an analysis of new issues of political and cultural identity and then examine their significance in a series of brief case studies in different regions of the world. These comparisons enable us more clearly to think about and understand the workings of cities, empires, and religions not only of the past, but also of our own time and place.

Multiple Perspectives

The text highlights the importance of multiple perspectives in studying and interpreting history. The answers we get—the narrative histories we write—are based on the questions we ask. Each Part suggests a variety of questions that can be asked about the historical event that is being studied and a variety of interpretations that can emerge in the process of answering them. Often there is more than one "correct" way of understanding change over time and its significance. Different questions will trigger very different research and very different answers. For example, in Part Five we ask about the stages and processes by which Western commercial power began to surpass that of Asia. This question presupposes the fact that at earlier times Asian power had been superior, and raises the additional questions of why it declined and why European power advanced. In Part Six we ask how the Industrial Revolution affected and changed relationships between men and women; this question will yield different research and a different narrative from questions about, for example, women's contributions to industrialization, which is a useful question, but a different one.

Through the systematic study of the past in this thematic, comparative framework, students will gain tools for understanding and making their own place in the world. They will not only learn how the peoples of the world have gotten to where we are, but also consider the possibility of setting out in new directions for new goals.

Assessing Values

This form of analysis will also introduce a study of values. In order to understand the choices made by people in the past, we must attempt to understand the values that informed their thinking and actions. These values may be similar to, or quite different from, our own. In order to understand the interpretation introduced by later historians, we must understand the historians' values as well. These, too, may be similar to, or different from, our own. Historians usually had personal perspectives from which they viewed the past, and these perspectives influenced their interpretation. Finally, in order for student-readers to form their own understanding of the past, and to make it more useful in their own lives, they must also see how their own values influence their evaluation of past events.

For most of the past century, social scientists spoke of creating "value-free" disciplines. Today, most scholars believe that this is impossible. We cannot be "value-free." On the contrary, we must attempt to understand the values that have inspired historical actors, previous historians, and ourselves. Coming to an understanding of the values of others—historical actors and the historians who have studied them—will help readers to recognize and formulate their own values, a central part of a liberal arts education.

History and Identity

History is among the most passionate and bitterly contentious of disciplines because most people and groups locate a large part of their identity in their history. Americans may take pride in their nationality, for example, for having created a representative, constitutional democracy that has endured for more than 200 years (see Part Six). Yet they may be saddened, shamed, or perhaps incensed by the existence of 250 years of slavery followed by inequality in race relations continuing to the present (see Part Five). Christians may take pride in 2,000 years of missions of compassion toward the poor and downtrodden, yet they may be saddened, shamed, or even incensed by an almost equally long record of religious warfare and of persecution of those whose beliefs differed from their own (see Part Four).

As various ethnic, religious, class, and gender groups represent themselves in public political life, they seek not only to understand the history that has made them what they are, but also to persuade others to understand that history in the same way, to create a new consciousness.

Feminist historians, for example, find in their reading of history that patriarchy, a system of male-created and male-dominated institutions, has subordinated women. From available data and their interpretation of them, they attempt to weave a persuasive argument that will win over others to their position.

Some will not be persuaded. They may not even agree that women have been subordinated to men, but argue that both genders have shared in a great deal of suffering (and joy) throughout history (see Parts One and Seven). The historical debates over the origins and evolution of gender relationships evoke strong emotions because people's self-image, the image of their group, and others' perceptions of them are all at stake. And the stakes can be high.

Control of Historical Records

From earliest times, control over historical records and their interpretation has been fundamental to control over people's thoughts. The first emperor of China, Qin Shi Huangdi (r. 221–210 B.C.E.)—the man who built the concept of a united China, an idea that has lasted until today—attempted to destroy all knowledge of the past:

> He then abolished the ways of ancient sage kings and put to the torch the writings of the Hundred Schools in an attempt to keep the people in ignorance. He demolished the walls of major cities and put to death men of fame and talent. (de Bary, I: 229)

So wrote Jia Yi (201–168? B.C.E.), poet and statesman of the succeeding Han dynasty. Qin Shi Huangdi wished that only his interpretation of China's past, and his place in it, be preserved. Later intellectuals condemned his actions—but the lost records were irretrievable (see Part Three).

In similar fashion, the first great historian of the Christian Church, Eusebius of Caesarea (c. 260–339), in his accounts of the early Christians in the Roman Empire, chose carefully to include elements that he considered of "profit" to his mission, and to exclude those that were not:

> It is not for us to describe their miserable vicissitudes [in persecution] … just as it is not a part of our task to leave on record their faction-fights and their unnatural conduct towards each other, prior to the persecution. That is why we have decided to say no more about them than suffices for us to justify God's Judgment … We shall rather set forth in our whole narrative only what may be of profit, first, to our own times, and then to later times. (MacMullen, p. 6)

Historical Revision

The interpretation of events may become highly contested and be revised even after several centuries have passed.

Colonial governments seeking to control subject peoples sometimes argued that the conquered people were so backward that they benefitted from the conquest. Later historians, with more distance and more detachment, were often less kind to the colonizers. Some 1,900 years ago, the historian Tacitus was writing bitterly of the ancient Romans in their conquest of England: "Robbery, butchery, rapine, the liars call Empire; they create a desolation and call it peace." (Agricola, p. 30)

In our own era, the many nations that have won their freedom from colonialism display similar resentment against their foreign rulers, and set out to revise the historical record in keeping with their newly won political freedom. Jawaharlal Nehru, the first prime minister of independent India (1947–64), wrote in 1944 from the prison cell in which he had been incarcerated for his leadership of his country's independence movement:

> British accounts of India's history, more especially of what is called the British period, are bitterly resented. History is almost always written by the victors and conquerors and gives their viewpoint; or, at any rate, the victors' version is given prominence and holds the field. (Nehru, p. 289)

Philip Curtin, historian of Africa and of slavery, elaborates an equally critical view of European colonial accounts of Africa's history:

> African history was seriously neglected until the 1950s … The colonial period in Africa left an intellectual legacy to be overcome, just as it had in other parts of the world. … The colonial imprint on historical knowledge emerged in the nineteenth and early twentieth centuries as a false perspective, a Eurocentric view of world history created at a time of European domination … Even where Europeans never ruled, European knowledge was often accepted as modern knowledge, including aspects of the Eurocentric historiography. (Curtin, p. 54)

Instead, Curtin continues, a proper historiography must

> … show the African past from an African point of view … For Africans, to know about the past of their own societies is a form of self-knowledge crucial to a sense of identity in a diverse and rapidly changing world. A recovery of African history has been an important part of African development over recent decades. (p. 54)

Religious and ethnic groups, too, may seek to control historical records. In 1542, the Roman Catholic Church established an Index of Prohibited Books to ban writings it considered heretical. (The Spanish Inquisition, ironically, stored away many records that later scholars used to recreate its history and the history of those whom it persecuted.) More recently, despite all the evidence of the Holocaust, the murder of six million Jews by the Nazi government of Germany during World War II, a few people have claimed that the murders never took place. They deny the existence

Indians giving Hernán Cortés a headband, from Diego Duran's Historia de las Indias, 1547. Bent on conquest and plunder, the bearded Spaniard Cortés arrived on the Atlantic coast of Mexico in 1519. His forces sacked the ancient city of Tenochtitlán, decimated the Aztec people, and imprisoned their chief, Moctezuma II, before proclaiming the Aztec Empire "New Spain." By stark contrast, this bland Spanish watercolor shows local tribesmen respectfully paying homage to the invader as if he were a god; in ignoring the brutality exercised in the colonization of South America, the artist is, in effect, "rewriting" history. (Biblioteca National, Madrid)

of such racial and religious hatred and its consequences, and ignore deep-seated problems in the relationships between majority and minority populations.

The significance of the voyages of Columbus was once celebrated uncritically in the United States in tribute both to "the Admiral of the Ocean Sea" himself and to the courage and enterprise of the European explorers and early settlers who brought their civilizations to the Americas. In South America, however, where Native American Indians are more numerous and people of European ancestry often form a smaller proportion of the population, the celebrations have been far more ambivalent, muted, and meditative.

In 1992, on the 500th anniversary of Columbus' first voyage to the Americas, altogether new and more sobering elements entered the commemoration ceremonies, even in the United States. The negative consequences of Columbus' voyages, previously ignored, were now recalled and emphasized: the death of up to 90 percent of the Native American Indian population in the century after the arrival of Europeans; the Atlantic slave trade, initiated by trade in Indian slaves; and the exploitation of the natural resources of a continent until then little touched by humans. The

ecological consequences, which are only now beginning to receive more attention, were not all negative, however. They included the fruitful exchange of natural products between the hemispheres. Horses, wheat, and sheep were introduced to the Americas; potatoes, tomatoes, and corn to Afro-Eurasia. Unfortunately, the spread of syphilis was another consequence of the exchange; scholars disagree on who transmitted this disease to whom (see Part Five).

Thugs sometimes gain control of national histories. George Orwell's satirical novel *Animal Farm* (published in 1945) presented an allegory in which pigs come to rule a farm. Among their many acts of domination, the pigs seize control of the historical records of the farm animals' failed experiment in equality, and impose their own official interpretation, which justifies their own rule. The rewriting of history and suppression of alternative records by the Communist Party of the former Soviet Union between 1917 and 1989 reveals the bitter truth underlying Orwell's satire (see Part Seven).

Although the American experience is much different, in the United States, too, records have been suppressed. Scholars are still trying to use the Freedom of Information Act to pry open sealed diplomatic archives. (Most official

Lenin addressing troops in Sverdlov Square, Moscow, May 5, 1920. The leaders of the Russian communist revolution crudely refashioned the historical record to suit the wishes of the winners. After Lenin's death in 1924, his second-in-command Leon Trotsky (pictured sitting on the podium in the top picture) lost to Joseph Stalin the bitter power struggle that ensued. Not only was Trotsky banished from the Soviet Union, but also his appearance was expunged from the official archives (see doctored picture, bottom).

archives everywhere have 20-, 30-, or 40-year rules governing the waiting period before certain sensitive records are opened to the public. These rules are designed to protect living people and contemporary policies from excessive scrutiny.)

What Do We Know? How Do We Know It? What Difference Does It Make?

So, historical records are not simply lists of events. They are the means by which individuals and groups develop their interpretation of these events. All people develop their own interpretation of past events; historians do it professionally. Because interpretation differs, there is no single historical record, but various narrations of events, each told from a different perspective. Therefore the study of history is intimately linked to the study of values.

To construct their interpretation, historians examine the values—the motives, wishes, desires, visions—of people of the past. In interpreting those values, historians must confront and engage their own values, comparing and contrasting them with those of people in the past. For example, they ask how various people viewed slavery, or child labor, or education, or art and music in societies of the past. In the back of their minds they compare and contrast those older values with values held by various people today, and especially with their own personal values. They ask: How and why have values changed—or remained the same—over the passage of time? Why, and in what ways, do my values compare with values of the past? By learning to pose such questions, students will be better equipped to discover and create their own place in the continuing movement of human history. This text, therefore, consistently addresses three fundamental questions:

What Do We Know?
How Do We Know It?
What Difference Does It Make?

Even when historians agree on which events are most significant, they may differ in evaluating why those events are significant. One historian's interpretation of events may be diametrically opposed to another's. For example, virtually all historians agree that part of the significance of World War II lies in its new policies and technology of destruction: nuclear weapons in battle and genocide behind the lines. In terms of interpretation, pessimists might stress the continuing menace of this legacy of terror, while optimists might argue that the very violence of the war and the Holocaust triggered a search for limits on nuclear arms and greater tolerance for minorities. With each success in nuclear arms limitation and in toleration, the optimists seem more persuasive; with each spread of nuclear weapons and each outbreak of genocide, the pessimists seem to prevail.

The study of history is thus an interpretation of significance as well as an investigation of facts. The significance of events is determined by their consequences. Sometimes we do not know what the consequences are; or the consequences may not have run their course; or we may differ in our assessment of the consequences. This play between past events and their current consequences is what the historian E.H. Carr had in mind in his famous description of history as "an unending dialogue between the present and the past" (Carr, p. 30).

Tools

The study of history requires many tools, and this text includes most of the principal ones:

- Primary sources are accounts that were produced at the time an event occurred. Those who produced them were eyewitnesses with direct knowledge of what happened. The core of historical study is an encounter with primary materials, usually documents, but including other artifacts—for example, letters, diaries, newspaper accounts, photographs, and artwork. Every chapter in this text includes representative primary materials.
- Secondary sources are interpretations of past events by later historians who re-examine the primary sources either from new perspectives, or with the addition of primary sources that had been lost or overlooked.
- Images, a strong feature of this book, complement the written text, offering non-verbal "texts" of the time. These are often central pieces of evidence. For example, in Chapter Nine we illustrate the influence of Hinduism and Buddhism in Southeast Asia through the temple architecture of the region.
- Maps place events in space and in geographical relationship to one another.
- Chronological time lines situate events in time and sequence.
- Brief charts supply summaries as well as contextual information on such topics as religion, science, and trade.

Suggested Readings

Basic, Comprehensive, Introductory Materials

Carr, E.H. *What Is History?* (Harmondsworth, Middlesex: Penguin Books, 1964). A classic introduction to the study of history and historiography from the point of view of a master.

Budd, Adam, ed. *The Modern Historiography Reader: Western Sources* (New York: Routledge, 2009). Presents 55 essays from about 1700 to the present, discussing major forms of historical inquiry and writing.

Cannadine, David, ed. *What is History Now?* (New York: Palgrave Macmillan, 2002). Revisits the question asked by Carr and presents nine different answers, each by a master of some form of history today: social, political, religious, cultural, etc.

Tosh, John. *The Pursuit of History: Aims, Methods, and New Directions in the Study of Modern History* (London: Longman, 4th ed., 2006). Excellent, comprehensive introduction to the study of history, with discussions of many different kinds of historical study, their methods and purposes.

——, ed. *Historians on History: Readings* (Harlow, England: Pearson, 2nd ed., 2009). Excellent selection of brief extracts from major historians who have given new direction to the field, mostly practicing in the last half-century.

For World History specifically, see the three volumes edited for the American Historical Association

Adas, Michael. *Agricultural and Pastoral Societies in Ancient and Classical History* (Philadelphia, PA: Temple University Press, 2001).

——. *Islamic and European Expansion: The Forging of a Global Order* (Philadelphia, PA: Temple University Press, 1993).

——. *Essays on Twentieth Century History* (Philadelphia, PA: Temple University Press, 2010).

More Specialized Materials

Bennett, Judith M. "Medieval Women, Modern Women: Across the Great Divide," in David Aers, ed., *Culture and History, 1350–1600: Essays on English Communities, Identities, and Writing* (New York: Harvester Wheatsheaf, 1992), pp. 147–75. Discusses continuity, in contrast to change, in women's history.

Curtin, Philip D. "Recent Trends in African Historiography and Their Contribution to History in General," in Joseph Ki-Zerbo, ed., *General History of Africa, Vol. I: Methodology and African Pre-History* (Berkeley: University of California Press, 1981), pp. 54–71. An excellent introduction to this fine series commissioned by the United Nations.

Dunn, Ross. *The New World History: A Teacher's Companion* (Boston, MA: Bedford/St. Martin's, 2000). Excellent selections both on what the new world history ought to be, and what it is as major historians write it.

de Bary, William Theodore, et al., comps. *Sources of Chinese Tradition*, 2 vols. (New York: Columbia University Press, 2nd ed., 1999, 2000). The anthology of materials on the subject.

Lerner, Gerda. *The Creation of Patriarchy* (New York: Oxford University Press, 1986). A controversial study of patriarchy in ancient Mesopotamia by a distinguished historian of the United States. Lerner retooled to study this fundamental feminist question.

MacMullen, Ramsay. *Christianizing the Roman Empire (A.D. 100–400)* (New Haven, CT: Yale University Press, 1984). Excellent analysis of the factors leading to Christianity's success in the Roman Empire. Gives a major role to government support.

Manning, Patrick. *Navigating World History: Historians Create a Global Past* (New York: Palgrave Macmillan, 2003). A major historian presents a magisterial, somewhat dense survey of the field.

Nehru, Jawaharlal. *Glimpses of World History* (New York: Penguin, 2004). A history of the world, written in jail during the struggle for freedom by the man who became India's first prime minister.

Orwell, George. *Animal Farm* (New York: Harcourt, Brace, 1946). A classic satire on government by thugs; aimed at the USSR.

Tacitus, Cornelius. *Tacitus' Agricola, Germany, and Dialogue on Orators*, trans. Herbert W. Benario (Norman: University of Oklahoma Press, 1991). One of ancient Rome's great historians who understood the cruelty underlying the power of empire.

THE WORLD'S HISTORY

FIFTH EDITION

PART ONE

TURNING POINT: HUMAN ORIGINS

To 10,000 B.C.E.

Humankind Begins

Historians ask some very big questions. Of course, the stereotype of the historian as a person who searches in dusty archives for tiny, concrete bits of data is often correct. Detail and accuracy are important. Beneath this search for details, however, lie profound questions of fundamental importance. In this chapter we address some of the biggest questions of all: Where did humans come from? How did our collective life on earth begin? How are we similar to other living species, and how are we unique?

When and where should we begin our search? This is one of the hottest questions in the study of world history today. It was not always so. (For non-historians it may be surprising, but historical questions are not settled once and for all.) Until the mid-nineteenth century, stories, often in the form of religious traditions, provided the answers to our questions about human origins and the meaning and purpose of human life. Then a reevaluation of religious and narrative traditions invited a search for alternative explanations.

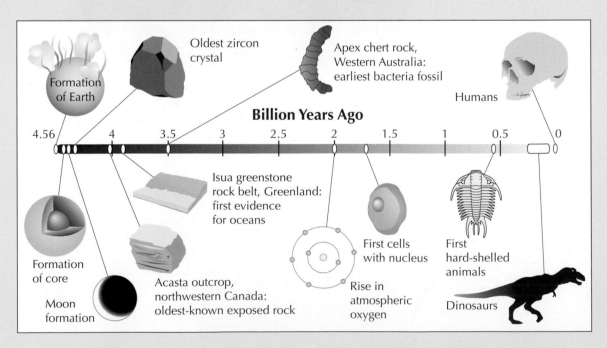

The timeline of Earth. Scientists now believe that the universe came into existence about 13.7 billion years ago, the earth about 4.5 billion years ago, cellular life forms about 1.7 billion years ago, and humans—*Homo sapiens*—only about 100,000 years ago.

Nevertheless, until perhaps fifty years ago, most historians would have begun their accounts of world history with Mesopotamia and Egypt, the first civilizations which created writing and written records, a little more than 5000 years ago. For these historians, "history" requires writing, for only with writing can we determine people's ideas and motives. Only with writing can we discover how we humans have understood our world. The study of the past without written records – through archaeology, for example – is "prehistory," less important and less valuable than the real thing.

At another extreme, in the last two decades, some historians have begun to speak of "big history"; these historians begin their accounts with the creation of the universe, perhaps 14 billion years ago, and continue on with the formation of the planet Earth, about 4.5 billion years ago, and the emergence of the first single-celled life forms, about 3.7 billion years ago. This perspective usually begins with the study of science and of the basic chemical, physical, and biological building blocks of the universe. Since modern humans appear very late in the history of the universe, only about 100,000 years ago, in these accounts, humans appear correspondingly late. Modern times may occupy only a very small proportion of these accounts.

We choose a middle path. We are concerned with human life, so we begin our account with the evolution of the first modern humans from their origins as primates, about 100,000 years ago, much later than the creation of the universe as a whole, but much earlier than the first writing. We ask: "What does it mean to be human?" This profound question leads us to the study of human creativity. Humans are what humans do. We travel and migrate, often out of sheer curiosity as well as to find food and shelter. As we shall see, by about 15,000 B.C.E., humans had traveled, mostly over land, and established themselves on all the continents of the earth except Antarctica. We also create and invent tools. Our account in this chapter begins with the simplest stone tools dating back millions of years and continues up to the invention of pottery and of sedentary farming some 10,000 years ago. Finally, we humans also express our feelings and ideas in art, music, dance, ritual, and literature. In this chapter we examine early evidence of this creativity in the forms of sculptures and cave paintings from 20,000 years ago.

For time periods more recent than 20,000 years ago, we usually adopt the notation "B.C.E." (Before the Common Era) and "C.E." (Common Era). These designations correspond exactly to the more familiar "B.C." (Before Christ) and "A.D." (Anno Domini, "in the year of our Lord"), but remove the specific reference to a single religion. For dates more than 20,000 years ago, "B.P." (Before the Present) is sometimes used.

A skeleton from Herculaneum, Italy, 2001. An archaeologist excavates the skeleton of an inhabitant from the Roman city of Herculaneum, which was buried by the eruption of Mount Vesuvius in 79 C.E.

1 The Dry Bones Speak

To 10,000 B.C.E.

The study of the earliest development of humans advances very quickly and often in sudden leaps forward. Because we know so little to begin with, each new discovery has a profound impact. Before Darwin, the entire religious and mythological literature of the Judeo-Christian-Islamic world assumed that humans had been created directly by God about 6,000 years ago. (Hindu and Buddhist mythology had a much deeper time frame, but little interest in exploring the distant past as history.) Darwin's theories, and a continuing array of fossil finds which supports them, propose a vastly longer time frame and a different interpretive framework for understanding human origins and early development. The discovery in 1953 of the structure of the DNA molecule, and our subsequent understanding of its role in determining the nature of each species and each individual, have further enriched our understanding of the evolution of humans. Discoveries of human cultural achievements beginning 35,000 years ago—sophisticated toolkits, cave paintings and small sculptures, long-distance migrations by land and sea—have added to our appreciation of the accomplishments of our ancestors, and of the people who study them so assiduously.

A skeleton from Herculaneum, Italy, 2001. An archaeologist excavates the skeleton of an inhabitant from Herculaneum.

LEARNING OBJECTIVES

1.1 ((	1.2 ((	1.3 ((
Understand how myths explain creation.	Describe the evolution of human beings.	Discuss the cultural creations of early humans.

((Listen on MyHistoryLab

Human Origins in Myth and History

1.1   How do myths explain the origins of human beings on the earth?

Where did we come from? How did humans come to inhabit the earth? These questions are difficult to answer because the earliest human beings left no written records or obvious oral traditions. For more than a century, we have sought the answer to these questions in the earth, in the records of the fossils that archaeologists and **paleoanthropologists** have discovered and interpreted. But before the diggers came with their interpretations, human societies from many parts of the world developed stories based on popular beliefs to explain our origins. Passed from generation to generation as folk wisdom, these stories give meaning to human existence. They not only tell how humans came to inhabit the earth, they also suggest why. Some of these stories, especially those that have been incorporated into religious texts such as the Bible, still inspire the imaginations and govern the behavior of hundreds of millions of people around the world.

Early Myths

As professional history developed, many historians dismissed these stories as **myths**, imaginative constructions that cannot be verified with the kinds of records historians usually use. However, myth and history share a common purpose—trying to explain how the world came to be as it is. Many historians and anthropologists now accept myths as important aids in understanding how different societies have interpreted the origins of the human world. Myths often contain important truths, and they can

KEY TERMS

paleoanthropology The study of the earliest humans and their environments.

myth An interpretive story of the past that cannot be verified historically but may have a deep moral message.

AT A GLANCE: EARLY HUMANS AND THEIR ANCESTORS

YEARS AGO	PERIOD	HOMINID EVOLUTION	MATERIAL CULTURE
6.5 million		• Toumai	
5 million	• Pliocene	• Fragments found in northern Kenya; possibly *Australopithecus*	
4.5 million		• *Ardipithecus ramidus*	
3.75 million	• Pleistocene	• *Australopithecus* genus, including Lucy (East and southern Africa) • *Homo habilis* (eastern and southern Africa) • *Homo erectus* (Africa) • *Homo erectus* thought to have moved from Africa into Eurasia	• Tools • Stone artifacts • Use of fire
500,000		• *Homo sapiens* (archaic form) • Remains of Beijing Man (*Sinanthropus*) found at Zhoukoudian	
130,000–80,000		• *Homo sapiens* (Africa and western Asia)	• Stone artifacts
100,000–33,000		• Neanderthals (Europe and western Asia)	
40,000	• Aurignacian		• Tools include long blades • First passage from Siberia to Alaska
30,000	• Gravettian	• Human remains of the Upper Paleolithic type, *Homo sapiens sapiens* (remains from 25,000) found in China	• Venus figures (25,000–12,000)
20,000	• Solutrean		• Chauvet cave, France (18,000)
17,000	• Magdalenian		• Lascaux cave paintings (c. 15,000) • Altamira cave paintings (c. 13,550)

1.1

1.2

1.3

How do myths
explain the
origins of human
beings on the
earth?

have powerful effects on people's values and behavior. Shared myths give cohesion to social relationships and provide people with a sense of shared community.

For thousands of years, various creation stories have presented people with explanations of their place in the world and of their relationship to the gods, to the rest of creation, and to one another. The narratives have similarities, but also significant differences. Some portray humans as the exalted crown of creation, others as reconfigured parasites; some depict humans as partners with the gods, others as their servants; some suggest the equality of all humans, others stress a variety of **caste**, race, and gender hierarchies. To some degree, surely, people transmit the stories as quaint tales told for enjoyment only, but they also provide guidance on how people should understand and live their lives.

One of the earliest known stories is the *Enuma Elish* epic of the people of Akkad in Mesopotamia. This account probably dates back to almost 2000 B.C.E. It tells of wars among the gods. Tiamat mates with Apsu and gives birth to younger gods. Later the parents seek to kill off this new generation of their children-gods. To save the god-children, the god Ea slays Apsu while Ea's son Marduk rallies the younger gods, and kills and dismembers Tiamat and her new husband, Kingu. From the blood of Kingu, Marduk creates humans (and all of earth's creatures), on condition that they are to be his servants. Written at a time when the competitive city-states of Mesopotamia were constantly at war, this myth elevated the importance of Babylon, the city that Marduk chooses as his capital; affirmed the authority of its powerful priests and rulers; and assigned purpose and direction to human life.

India, vast and diverse, has many different stories about the origin of humans. Two of the most widespread and powerful illustrate two principal dimensions of the thought and practice of Hindu religious traditions. The ancient epic *Rigveda*, which dates from about 1000 B.C.E., emphasizes the mystical, unknowable qualities of life and its origins:

> Who verily knows and who can here declare it, whence it was born and whence comes this creation?
>
> The Gods are later than this world's production. Who knows then whence it first came into being?
>
> He, the first origin of this creation, whether he formed it all or did not form it, whose eye controls this world in highest heaven, he verily knows it or perhaps he knows not.

In contrast to this reverent but puzzled view of creation, another of the most famous hymns of the *Rigveda*, the Purusha-sakta, describes the creation of the world by the gods' sacrifice and dismemberment of a giant man, Purusha:

> His mouth became the Brahmin; his arms were made into the Warrior, his thighs the People, and from his feet the Servants were born.
>
> The moon was born from his mind; from his eye the sun was born. Indra and Agni came from his mouth, and from his vital breath the Wind was born. (Ch. 10; v. 129)

In this account, humans are part of nature, subject to the laws of the universe, but they are not born equal among themselves. Several groups are created with different qualities and in different castes. This myth of creation supports the hierarchical organization of India's historic caste system.

KEY TERM

caste A hierarchical ordering of people into groups, fixed from birth, based on their inherited ritual status and determining whom they may marry and with whom they may eat.

Shiva Nataraja, or Dancing Shiva. Bronze from the Chola Dynasty, southern India, thirteenth century. The cosmic dance of the Hindu Lord Shiva brings about destruction, crushing evil underfoot, and prepares the way for rebirth in the cycle of existence. The bronze sculptures of the Cholas, and the architecture of their temples, are striking in their beauty and power. (Museum of Fine Arts, Houston)

How do myths explain the origins of human beings on the earth?

1.1
1.2
1.3

Perhaps the most widely known creation story is told in the Book of Genesis in the Hebrew Bible. Beginning from nothing, in five days God created heaven and earth; created light and separated it from darkness; created water and separated it from dry land; and created flora, birds, and fishes, and the sun, moon, and stars. God began the sixth day by creating larger land animals and reptiles, and then humans "in his own image."

The Book of Genesis assigns humans a unique and privileged place as the final crown and master of creation. Humans are specially created in God's own image, with dominion over all other living creatures. When the creation of humans is complete and their exalted position in nature is specified, God proclaims the whole process and product of creation as "good." Here humans hold an exalted position within, but also above, the rest of creation.

Until the late eighteenth century, these kinds of story were the only accounts we had of the origins of humans. No other explanations seemed necessary. In any case, no one expected to find actual physical evidence for the processes by which humans came to exist.

The Evolutionary Explanation

During the eighteenth century, some philosophers and natural scientists in Europe, who were most familiar with the creation story told in the Bible, began to challenge its belief in the individual, special creation of each life form. They saw so many similarities among different species that they could not believe that each had been created separately, although they could not demonstrate the processes through which these similarities and differences had developed. They saw some creatures change forms during their life cycle, such as the metamorphosis of the caterpillar into the moth, or the tadpole into the frog, but they could not establish the processes by which one species metamorphosed into another. They also knew the processes of breeding by which farmers encouraged the development of particular strains in farm animals and plants, but they lacked the conception of a time frame of millions of years that would allow for the natural evolution of a new species from an existing one.

Challenging the authority of the biblical account required a new method of inquiry, a new system for organizing knowledge. By the mid-eighteenth century, a new intellectual environment had begun to emerge. Scientific method called for the direct observation of nature, the recording and analysis of observation, and the discussion and debate of findings throughout an international community of scholars. It rejected the authority of religious texts that asserted truths without presenting substantiating evidence.

Charles Darwin (1809–82) and Alfred Russel Wallace (1823–1913), separately, formulated the modern theory of the biological evolution of species. They saw the mounting evidence of biological similarities among related species; they understood that these similar species were, in fact, related to one another, not separate creations; and they allowed a time frame adequate for major transformations of species to take place. They then went on to demonstrate the method by which small differences within a species were transmitted from generation to generation, increasing the differentiation until new forms were produced.

Both Darwin and Wallace reached their conclusions as a result of extensive travel overseas. Darwin carried out his observations on a scientific voyage around the world in 1831–36 aboard the British warship *Beagle*, and especially during his stay in the Galapagos Islands off the equatorial west coast of South America. Wallace traveled for many years in the islands of Southeast Asia. In 1855 he published a paper suggesting a common ancestor for primates and man. In 1858 Wallace and Darwin published a joint paper on the basic concepts of evolution.

In the isolated Galapagos Islands, Darwin had found various kinds of finches, all of which were similar to each other except in their beaks. He rejected the idea that

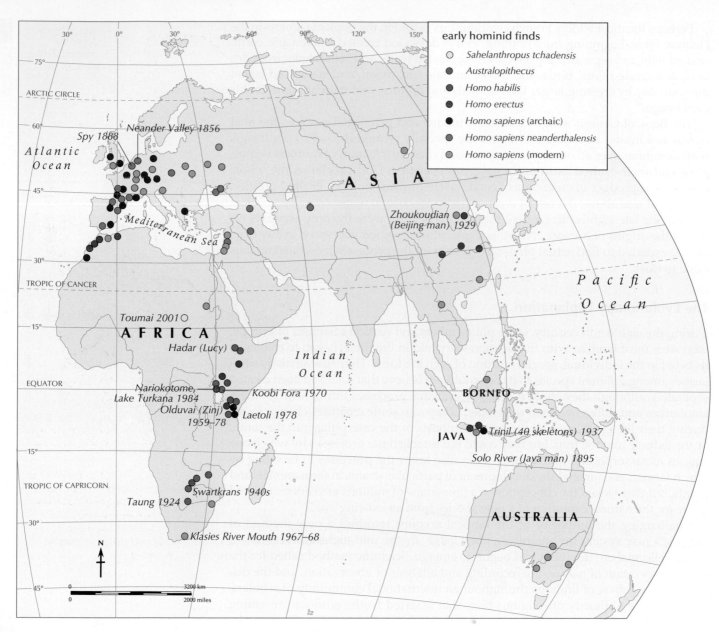

early hominid finds

○ *Sahelanthropus tchadensis*
● *Australopithecus*
● *Homo habilis*
● *Homo erectus*
● *Homo sapiens* (archaic)
● *Homo sapiens neanderthalensis*
● *Homo sapiens* (modern)

Human ancestors. Fossil remains of the earliest direct human ancestors, *Australopithecus* and *Homo habilis*, dating from one million to five million years ago, have been found only in tropical Africa. The unique soil and climatic conditions there have preserved the fossils. *Homo erectus* remains, from 1.5 million years ago, are the earliest to be found outside Africa. They, along with *Homo sapiens*, have been found throughout Eurasia.

1.1
1.2
1.3

How do myths explain the origins of human beings on the earth?

each kind of finch had been separately created. Rather, he argued, there must have been an ancestor common to them all throughout the islands. Because each island offered slightly different food sources, different beaks were better suited to different islands. The different ecological niches on each separate island to which the birds had immigrated had evoked slightly different evolutionary development. From a single, common ancestor, new species had evolved over time on the different islands.

Darwin compared natural selection to the selection process practiced by humans in breeding animals. Farmers know that specific traits among their animals can be exaggerated through breeding. Horses, for example, can be bred either for speed or for power by selecting those horses in which the desired trait appears. In nature the act of selection occurs spontaneously, if more slowly, as plants and animals with traits that are more appropriate to an environment survive and reproduce while others do not.

In 1859 Darwin published his findings and conclusions in *On the Origin of Species by Means of Natural Selection*, a book that challenged humankind's conception of life on earth and of our place in the universe. Darwin explained that the pressure for each organism to compete, survive, and reproduce created a kind of natural selection. The population of each species increased until its ecological niche was filled to capacity. In the face of this population pressure, the species that were better adapted to the niche survived; the rest were crowded out and tended toward extinction. Small differences always appeared within a species: some members were taller, some shorter; some more brightly colored, others less radiant; some with more flexible hands and feet, others less manipulable. Those members with differences that aided survival in any given ecological setting tended to live on and to transmit their differences to their descendants. Others died out. Darwin called this process "natural selection" or "survival of the fittest."

The New Challenges. Darwin's argument challenged two prevailing stories of creation, especially the biblical views. First, the process of natural selection had no goal beyond survival and reproduction. Unlike many existing creation myths, especially biblical stories, evolutionary theory postulated no **teleology**, no ethical or moral goals and purposes of life. Second, the theory of natural selection described the evolution of ever more "fit" organisms, better adapted to their environment, evolving from existing ones. The special, separate creation of each species was not necessary.

For Darwin, the process of natural selection of more complex, better adapted forms also explained the evolution of humans from simpler, less well-adapted organisms. Perhaps this was "the Creator's" method. Darwin concluded *On the Origin of Species*:

"That Troubles Our Monkey Again." Cartoon of Charles Darwin from *Fun*, November 16, 1872. As scientists and theologians struggled to come to terms with the implications of evolutionary theory, popular reaction was often hostile and derisive. In this cartoon from a contemporary British weekly, Darwin is caricatured as an ape checking the pulse of a woman—or, as the cartoonist ironically refers to her, a "female descendant of marine ascidian" (a tiny invertebrate).

> Thus, from the war of nature, from famine and death, the most exalted object which we are capable of conceiving, namely, the production of the higher animals, directly follows. There is grandeur in this view of life, with its several powers, having been originally breathed by the Creator into a few forms or into one; and that, whilst this planet has gone cycling on according to the fixed law of gravity, from so simple a beginning endless forms most beautiful and most wonderful have been, and are being, evolved.

Note, however, that the words "by the Creator" did not appear in the first edition. Darwin added them later, perhaps in response to criticisms raised by more conventional Christian religious thinkers, who continued to find the biblical story a credible explanation for the origins of human beings.

Within a decade, Darwin's ideas had won over the scientific community. In 1871, in *The Descent of Man*, Darwin extended his argument to the evolution of humans, concluding explicitly that "man is descended from some lowly organized form." Humans are a part of the order of primates, most closely related to great apes and chimpanzees.

The search now began for evidence of the "missing link" between humans and apes, for some creature, living or extinct, that stood at an intermediate point in the

How do myths explain the origins of human beings on the earth?

1.1

1.2

1.3

KEY TERM

teleology The philosophical study of final causes or purposes. Teleology refers especially to any system that interprets nature or the universe as having design or purpose. It has been used to provide evidence for the existence of God.

1.1

1.2   What do we
know about the
1.3   evolution of
human beings?

evolutionary process. In this search archaeology, and the adjunct field of paleoan-thropology, flourished.

Fossils and Fossil-hunters

1.2   What do we know about the evolution of human beings?

The search for the "missing link" began in Europe, because that is where the major scientific researchers lived and worked. Later, the search led to Java, Indonesia, and Beijing, China. Still more recently, Africa has yielded the earliest specimens of the human species, fulfilling Darwin's prediction of an African origin of human evolution, based on the abundance of nonhuman primates—apes and chimpanzees—living on that continent.

As archaeologists discovered a variety of kinds of **hominid**—creatures that exhibited some characteristics of humans as well as of earlier primates—they concluded that there was no single missing link, but rather a variety of evolutionary paths that led to the emergence of humans.

The Puzzling Neanderthals

In August 1856, workers quarrying for limestone in a cave in the Neander Valley near Düsseldorf, Germany, found a thick skullcap with a sloping forehead and several skeletal bones of limbs. Some speculated that it was a deformed human. Others thought it was a soldier lost in a previous war. Similar skeletal remains had been found before, but without any clearer understanding of their meaning.

In 1863, Thomas Henry Huxley (1825–95), a leading advocate of Darwin's theory of evolution, argued that the skull was part of a primitive human being who stood between nonhuman primates and *Homo sapiens*, our own species. He claimed that it was the "missing link." In 1864, scholars gave the fossil a name that signified this intermediate position: *Homo neanderthalensis*.

One of the first questions archaeologists asked themselves was: What did *Homo neanderthalensis* look like? Reconstructing the appearance of Neanderthals was difficult, because soft tissue—hair, flesh, and cartilage—does not survive as fossils. Scientists had to use their imaginations.

The earliest efforts to reconstruct the appearance of Neanderthals showed them walking like apes, with a spine that had no curves, and hunchbacked, with their heads pushed forward on top of their spines. Showing muscular but clumsy-looking creatures, with heavy jaws and low, sloping foreheads, these pictures strongly suggested that *Homo neanderthalensis* was brutish and lacking in intelligence. For many years this interpretation, and others similar to it, carried great weight. Museum representations carried the message to the general public. Over the years, however, archaeologists have discovered more about Neanderthals' ability to make tools and survive in challenging environments. Impressed with these accomplishments, anthropologists now create reconstructions that show Neanderthals looking much less "primitive" and more like modern humans.

Moving beyond the individual skeleton in isolation, teams of experts from such disciplines as biology, geology, and climatology cooperate to reconstruct the natural settings of human and hominid development. As Neanderthal skeletons have been found from northern Europe to Africa, from Gibraltar to Iran, these natural settings vary greatly. Remains from caves near Gibraltar suggest that Neanderthals in that area lived in a nuclear family. Elsewhere, evidence shows that many Neanderthals lived in larger bands of up to 20 to 30 individuals.

One recent discovery suggests that at least some Neanderthals were cannibals. The evidence comes from a cave in southern France. A total of 78 bones from at least

KEY TERMS

hominid Any of a family (*Hominidae*) of erect bipedal (two-legged) primate mammals, which includes humans and humanlike species.

Homo sapiens Homo, "human," is the genus in which modern humans are placed; *sapiens* means "wise."

Diorama of "bovine" Neanderthals. Displayed for decades in the Field Museum of Natural History in Chicago, this reconstruction suggests that Neanderthals were unintelligent and clumsy. More recent interpretations portray a more intelligent, more graceful creature.

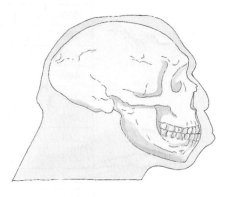

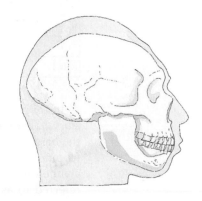

Alternate reconstructions from Neanderthal skull. Because soft tissues—hair, flesh, cartilage—do not survive as fossils, archaeologists must use their imaginations in adding these elements to the solid bone of excavated skeletons.

two adults, two teenagers, and two children aged about seven show that the flesh from all parts of the bodies was carefully removed. Bones were smashed with rocks to get at the inside marrow, and skulls were broken open. The Neanderthal bones and the bones of deer were tossed together into a heap and show similar marks from the same stone tools. On the other hand, there are many other examples of Neanderthals burying their dead carefully, suggesting that their cultural behavior differed from group to group.

Homo erectus: A Worldwide Wanderer

The next of these prehistoric hominid species to be unearthed—the most widespread, and the closest to modern humans—was *Homo erectus* ("upright human"). Examples of this species were discovered in widely dispersed locations throughout the eastern hemisphere and first named according to the locations in which they were found. Later, anthropologists recognized the similarities among them, named them collectively *Homo erectus*, and traced their migration patterns from their earliest home in Africa to new habitats across Asia.

1.1

1.2

1.3

What do we know about the evolution of human beings?

KEY TERM

Homo erectus The most widespread of all prehistoric hominids, and the most similar to humans. Evolved about two million years ago and became extinct 100,000 years ago.

1.1

1.2

1.3

What do we
know about the
evolution of
human beings?

LANDMARKS IN EARLY LIFE

Years ago (millions)	Geological period	Life form
2,500	Archaean	earliest living things
590	Cambrian	first fossils
505	Ordovician	first fish
438	Silurian	first land plants
408	Devonian	first amphibians
360	Carboniferous	first reptiles
286	Permian	reptiles expanded
248	Triassic	first mammals and dinosaurs
213	Jurassic	first birds
144	Cretaceous	heyday of dinosaurs
65	Cretaceous	mammals flourished; dinosaurs extinct
25	Tertiary	first hominoid (ancestor of apes and humans)
5	Tertiary	first hominid (human ancestor)
0.1	Quaternary	modern humans appeared

In 1891, Eugène Dubois (1858–1940), a surgeon in the Dutch army in Java, Indonesia, was exploring for fossils. Employing the labor of convicts in Dutch prisons, along the bank of the Solo River, he discovered a cranium with a brain capacity of 900 cc (compared to the modern human average of 1,400 cc), a molar, and a femur. Dubois claimed to have discovered *Pithecanthropus erectus,* or ape-man. This find, widely referred to as Java Man, was the first early hominid discovered outside Europe. Dubois' Java Man forced scholars to consider the theories of the evolution of humans more seriously and to understand the process in a global context.

In 1929, in the vast Zhoukoudian cave, 30 miles from Beijing, Chinese archaeologists discovered a 500,000-year-old skullcap. In the next few years, in this fossil-rich cave, they discovered 14 more fossil skulls and the remains of some 40 individuals, whom they dated to 600,000 to 200,000 years ago. The cave seems to have been the home of a band of hunters, who lived in a forested, grassy, riverine area and who ate plants as well as animals, such as bison and deer. Remaining bones and ash indicate their ability to use fire for light and cooking. With a brain capacity ranging from 775 to 1,300 cc and a height up to 5 feet 6 inches, anatomically Beijing Man was almost identical to Java Man. About a decade later, further excavations in Java turned up the nearly complete skull of one hominid and the skeletons of some 40 others who had lived 100,000 to 900,000 years ago. Anthropologists soon recognized similarities between Java Man and Beijing Man, and classified them collectively under the name *Homo erectus.* The 40 skeletons from Java represent one-third of all the *Homo erectus* skeletons uncovered to this day in the entire world. Those in the Zhoukoudian cave represent another third. The most complete skeleton we have of *Homo erectus* was discovered, however, in Africa, in 1984, on the shores of Lake Turkana, Kenya.

The Search Shifts to Africa

In 1924, a medical student in South Africa called the attention of his professor, Raymond Dart, to some fossils in a quarry near Taung. Dart investigated and proclaimed the Taung skull to be *Australopithecus africanus,* "southern apelike creature of Africa," a two-million-year-old ancestor of humans. Another medical doctor, Robert Broom, discovered additional hominid fossils, including some of *Homo erectus,*

1.1

What do we
know about the
evolution of
human beings?

1.2

1.3

similar to those discovered in Java and China. Between 1945 and 1955, Dart and his colleagues began to discover bone tools among the hominid fossils, as well as evidence of the first controlled use of fire, about a million years ago. Their research extended beyond the archaeology of individual hominid skeletons to paleoanthropology. Their ecological analyses included, for example, the fossils of hundreds of animals discovered near the hominids.

Archaeologist Louis Leakey (1903–72) began his excavations in East Africa in the 1930s, although his most important discoveries were achieved with his wife, Mary (1913–96), after 1959 in the Olduvai Gorge, where the Great Rift Valley cuts through northern Tanzania.

The Great Rift Valley runs from the Jordan River valley and the Dead Sea southward through the Red Sea, Ethiopia, Kenya, Tanzania, and Mozambique. The Rift is a fossil-hunter's delight. From at least seven million years ago until perhaps 100,000 years ago, it was a fertile, populated region; it is geologically still shifting and, therefore, has covered and uncovered its deposits over time. Rivers that run through the Rift Valley further the process of uncovering the fossils, and it is volcanic, generating lava and ash that preserve the fossils caught within it and provide the material for relatively accurate dating.

At Olduvai in 1959, the Leakeys discovered a hominid they called *Zinjanthropus boisei*, soon nicknamed "Zinj." At first they hoped that Zinj might be an early specimen of *Homo*, but its skull was too small, its teeth were too large, its arms were too long, and its face was too much like an ape's. Zinj, who was 1,750,000 years old, was another *Australopithecus*, a hominid closer to apes than to modern humans. The *Australopithecus* clan was thus extended to include a new cousin, *Australopithecus*

Louis and Mary Leakey examining the palate of the "Zinj" skull, 1959. This husband-and-wife team revolutionized our understanding of anthropology. Their excavations in the Olduvai Gorge in East Africa led to the generally accepted belief that hominids originally evolved in Africa.

13

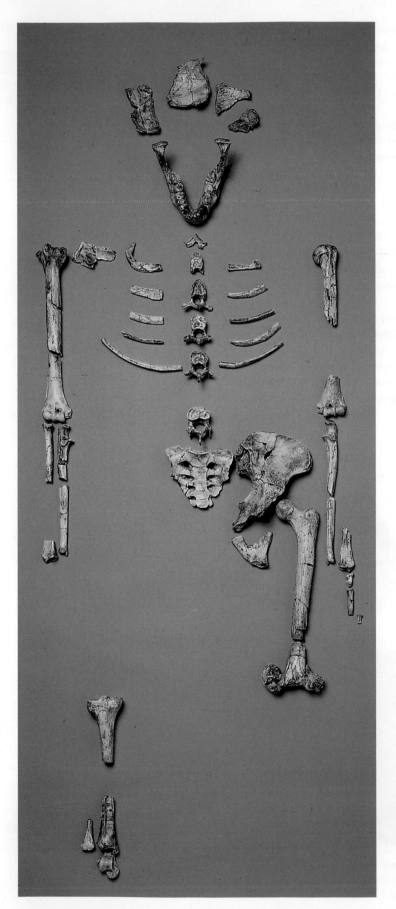

boisei. The australopithecine family tree—or "bush"—by now showed a number of branches, although the relationship among them and to us is not always clear. The chart later in this chapter represents these branches and relationships.

📖 **Read** the **Document: The Long Journey (5M BCE)** on **MyHistoryLab**

Homo habilis. The Leakeys' continued excavations at Olduvai turned up skull fragments of creatures with brain capacities of 650 cc, between the 400–500 cc of australopithecines and the 1,400 cc of modern humans. The Leakeys named this new type of hominid *Homo habilis*, "handy person," because of the stone tools they made and used in scavenging, hunting, and butchering food. Dating suggested that *Homo habilis* lived at about the same time as Zinj, demonstrating that *Homo* and *Australopithecus* had lived side by side about two million years ago.

The Leakeys' discoveries at Olduvai furthered the search for the ancestors of modern humans in several directions: they pushed back the date of the earliest known representative of the genus *Homo* to 1.5–2 million years ago; they indicated the extent of the tool-using capacity of these early *Homo* representatives; and they reconstructed the ecology of the region 2.5–1.5 million years ago, placing *Homo habilis* within it as hunter and scavenger. Together with earlier discoveries, the findings enabled the Leakeys to identify Africa as the home of the earliest hominids and the earliest representatives of the genus *Homo*.

In the 1970s, Louis and Mary's son, Richard Leakey (b. 1944), discovered additional bones of the species *Homo habilis* at Koobi Fora on the east side of Lake Turkana in Kenya. The finds confirmed the size of its brain at about 650 cc; its opposable thumb, which allowed it to grip objects powerfully and manipulate them precisely, and thus to make tools; and its upright, bipedal (two-legged) walk, evident from the form of its hip and leg bones.

Australopithecus afarensis. In 1974, at Hadar, Ethiopia, near the Awash River, Donald Johanson (b. 1943) discovered "Lucy," the first known representative of

"Lucy" skeleton, *Australopithecus afarensis*, found at Hadar, Ethiopia. "Lucy" is thought to have lived about 3.2 million years ago, and was at the time of her discovery in 1974 the earliest known hominid ancestor of modern man. She had humanlike hands and could walk upright; however, there is no evidence that she made or used tools, and her sturdy, curved arms are still consistent with tree-climbing. Until the discovery of *Ardipithecus* in 1994, Lucy was the most complete hominid skeleton from the period before two million years ago. (Natural History Museum, London)

Australopithecus afarensis, named for the local Afar people. (Lucy herself was named for the Beatles song "Lucy in the Sky with Diamonds," which was playing on a tape recorder just as the Johanson team was realizing the importance of their find.) This discovery pushed back the date of the earliest known hominid to about 3.2 million years ago.

Lucy's overall height was between 3 feet 6 inches and 4 feet, and Johanson and his team estimated her weight as 60 pounds. The archaeologists were able to uncover about 40 percent of her skeleton, making Lucy the earliest and most complete hominid skeleton known at the time. She had humanlike hands, but there is no evidence that she made or used tools, and her sturdy, curved arms are still consistent with tree-climbing. Later excavations at Hadar revealed numerous additional skeletons of *Australopithecus afarensis*, including the first complete skull, discovered by Johanson in 1992.

The cranial capacity of Lucy and her fellow *Australopithecus afarensis* was only 400 cc, too small for her to be a *Homo*. Her pelvis was too small to allow the birth of offspring with a larger skull, but the form of that pelvis and the fit of her knee joints characterized Lucy as a two-legged hominid. Lucy had walked upright. She was a kind of bipedal ape, and, in her bipedalism, an ancestor of modern humans.

Further evidence of the bipedalism of these apelike creatures came from Laetoli, Tanzania. There, in 1978, Mary Leakey discovered the footprints of two *Australopithecus afarensis* walking side by side. In volcanic ash, she found 70 footprints walking a distance of 80 feet. The ash provided material for dating the prints; they were 3.5 million years old. The tracks suggest that *Australopithecus afarensis* had a slower, more rolling gait than modern man, although the prints reveal well-defined feet. Mary Leakey saw in them a slight sideward turn, a hesitation in direction, which she interpreted as the first evidence of human doubt.

In 1994, some 17 fossils of a new genus, *Ardipithecus ramidus*, "ground ape," were discovered in Aramis, Ethiopia, in the bed of the Awash River, not far from the Lucy find. An international team of archaeologists analyzed them. Ten of the fossils were teeth, two were cranial fragments, and the remainder were bones from the left arm. Later, the team recovered about 80 percent of an *Ardipithecus ramidus* skeleton. It dated to 4.4 million years, pushing back the date of the earliest apelike hominid by half a million years.

Then, in 2001, a team working in Chad, Africa, under the French paleoanthropologist Michel Brunet (b. 1940), discovered a six- to seven-million-year-old skull, nicknamed "Toumai," which means "hope of life" in the Goran language. Toumai is at least 2.5 million years older than any previously discovered hominid skull, and, remarkably, it is nearly complete. On the cusp between ape and human, it displays human characteristics that include a relatively thick and continuous brow ridge, a relatively flat nose and face, and canine teeth that are shorter and more thickly enameled than those of chimpanzees. On the other hand, its cranial capacity is about the size of a chimp's, about one-fourth of a modern human's. It is not clear if Toumai was bipedal, but its spine entered its cranium in a pathway consistent with bipedalism.

Hominid footprints, Laetoli, northern Tanzania. These footprints in ash at Laetoli confirmed that hominids were walking upright 3.5 million years ago. The tracks reveal well-defined feet and suggest that *Australopithecus afarensis* had a slower, more rolling gait than modern man. Mary Leakey (pictured) discovered the prints.

1.1

1.2

What do we know about the evolution of human beings?

1.3

15

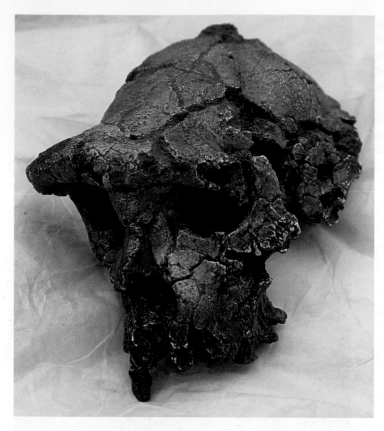

"Toumai," the oldest prehuman fossil, Chad, Africa, 2001. This skull was discovered in Chad by an international team of paleoanthropologists. It is from the earliest member of the prehuman family so far discovered, dating back six to seven million years. "Toumai" is the name given to children in Chad born near the dry season.

1.1

1.2   What do we know about the evolution of human beings?

1.3

"Toumai" fits the dominant theories of evolution as to the time at which and the pattern by which the hominid line of evolution separated from the chimpanzee line, taking on its own distinct characteristics. It challenges most current beliefs, however, in suggesting that hominids evolved not only in the difficult, harsh, arid climate of the Rift Valley, where all the earlier hominids had been uncovered, but also in the more accommodating lush forests that covered western Chad six million years ago.

As paleoanthropologists assembled this record of the earliest human ancestors, they also found more recent skeletons that more closely resemble our own. The earliest known anatomically modern *Homo sapiens* fossil also appeared in Africa. It was discovered in 1967–68 in caves at the Klasies River mouth on the coast of South Africa. These fossil remains of the oldest known example of the species *Homo sapiens* date to 75,000 to 115,000 years ago. They include lower and upper jaws, skull fragments, teeth, and bones of limbs. With them fossil-hunters found thousands of stone quartzite tools, an abundance of bones from numerous land mammals, and the remains of hundreds of thousands of shellfish, suggesting a diet rich in meat and seafood. The Klasies River mouth discovery raised most provocatively the question of where the first *Homo sapiens* emerged, and how they spread.

The Debate over African Origins

Almost all paleoanthropologists and archaeologists now believe that *Homo erectus* appeared first in Africa and spread from there to Asia and, perhaps, to Europe between one and two million years ago. But then the scholars split into two camps: the "multiregionalists" and the "out-of-Africa" camp. The multiregionalists argue that *Homo erectus* evolved into *Homo sapiens* in each region of migration. The out-of-Africa group argues that *Homo erectus* evolved into *Homo sapiens* only once—in Africa. Then, about 100,000 years ago, the new humans emigrated to the rest of the world from Africa.

Both groups of scholars agree that the varieties of racial development—differences in physical characteristics such as skin color, characteristics of hair, bone structure, and minor genetic modification—are responses to different ecological niches. They differ, however, on the time and place of the development. If the evolution from *Homo erectus* to *Homo sapiens* began in several different locations up to two million years ago, then racial differentiation is very old. Even so, the groups did not remain entirely separate from one another, and over time substantial interbreeding took place among the different regional groups despite their geographic distances. No race remained "pure. If, according to the alternative theory, all modern *Homo sapiens* share a common origin until just 100,000 years ago, and began to differentiate by race only after emigrating from Africa to new locations, then these differences are much more recent and even more superficial.

At present, the supporters of the "out-of-Africa" theory are in the majority. They point out that it is more common for just one branch of any particular species to evolve into another and ultimately to displace all the other branches than for all the different branches to evolve simultaneously. They minimize the biological significance of race based on skin color as a relatively recent, and only "skin-deep,"

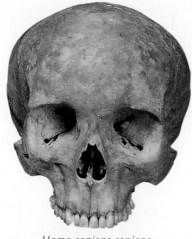

Homo sapiens sapiens
present day

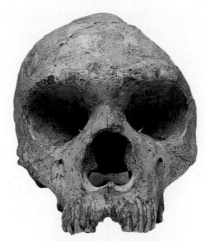

Homo (sapiens) neanderthalensis
50,000 B.P.

Homo erectus
1.4 million B.P.

Homo habilis
1.8 million B.P.

Australopithecus boisei
1.9 million B.P.

Australopithecus africanus
2.7 million B.P.

difference among the peoples of the earth. The advocates of both the multiregional and the out-of-Africa schools of thought agree that at deeper levels, such as blood types and the ability to interbreed, race has no significance. ➥

Reading the Genetic Record

In the search for the time and place of the origins of *Homo sapiens*, a different kind of discovery, based on genetics rather than fossils, on laboratory research rather than field excavations, emerged in the 1960s. Scientists began to study the DNA (deoxyribonucleic acid) record of human and animal genes. DNA is each cell's chemical code of instructions for building proteins, and the DNA research reveals the degrees of similarity and difference among the creatures studied. While the fossil record relied on comparing form and function among the relatively few specimens that have been discovered, DNA research relied on comparison of the arrangement of the basic building blocks of existence from the single-cell organism through the most complex animal form.

Because DNA is inherited, differences and similarities in the proteins and DNA of animals (including humans) living today suggest the date up to which they might have shared common ancestors before separating into different streams of evolution.

Skull reconstructions of some of the ancestors of modern man in chronological order. The generalized dates attached to each species imply that one followed the other, but actually some earlier species lived on for some time alongside more recent ones. By about 35,000 B.C.E., however, all except *Homo sapiens* were extinct. (Natural History Museum, London)

1.1

What do we know about the evolution of human beings?

1.2

1.3

17

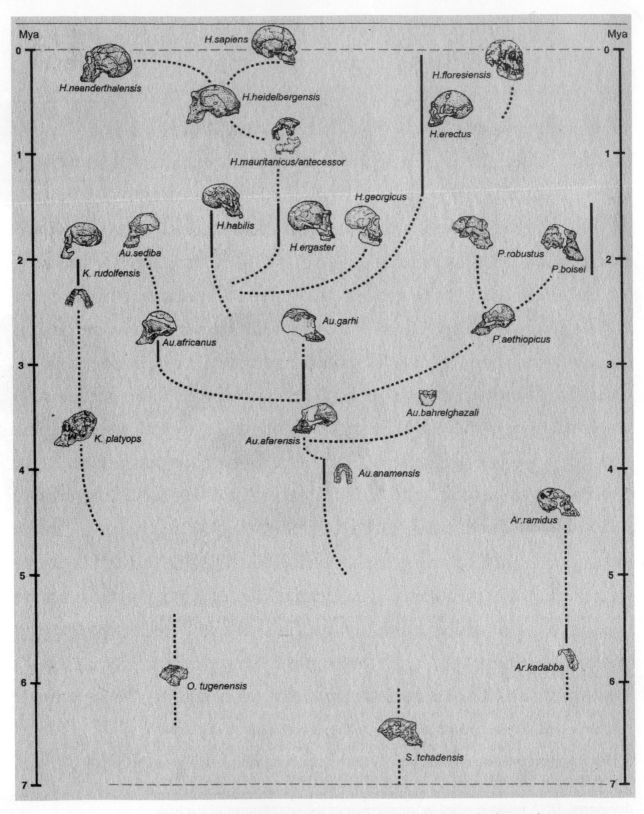

The human "bush." Popular thought usually imagines a straight-line development from apes to humans, but anthropologists speak of a human "bush," a variety of interacting and interbreeding species that finally produced *Homo sapiens*. Most anthropological models see *Ardipithecus ramidus* and *Australopithecus afarensis* as the first steps in the branching-apart of humans from apes about five million years ago. One line of further evolution led toward modern *Homo sapiens*. All the other hominid forms, those in our own line and those in other lines, subsequently became extinct.

1.1

1.2 What do we
know about the
evolution of
1.3 human beings?

1.1
1.2
1.3

What do we
know about the
evolution of
human beings?

In 1970, for example, biochemists first analyzed the protein albumin and the DNA of apes and humans and found that, genetically, modern humans are 97 percent the same as chimpanzees and 96 percent the same as gorillas. These data suggest that chimpanzees, gorillas, and humans shared common ancestors until five to seven million years ago, when evolutionary separation occurred. This genetic dating matches and reinforces the fossil record.

Extending the method further, researchers have analyzed the mitochondrial DNA (genetic material found outside the cell nucleus and passed only from mother to daughter) of thousands of women living today, and conclude that *Homo sapiens sapiens* emerged solely from Africa around 120,000 years ago, and that all of us today are descendants of a single woman living in Africa about 200,000 years ago. They often call her "mitochondrial Eve" or "the African Eve." This does not mean that she was the only woman alive at the time, but she is the only one who has descendants still living today in an unbroken female line: that is, in every generation there was a mother who gave birth to at least one daughter. Similarly, analysis of the Y-chromosomes (structures containing DNA, and passed only from father to son) of thousands of men living today shows that the earliest ancestor who contained this chromosome lived in Africa about 150,000 years ago, "Y-chromosomal Adam" or "the African Adam." Again, he was not the only man alive at the time, but the only one who has descendants alive today in an unbroken male, father-to-son, line.

The Theory of Scientific Revolution

We have given a lengthy introduction to various explanations for the emergence of the first humans. Many historians would choose to move more quickly toward the present, although, of course, in covering six million years in one chapter we are moving swiftly! We have chosen to elaborate this account not only for its intrinsic interest but also because it helps to demonstrate most clearly our concern with "how we know" as well as with "what we know," since we believe that historians and paleoanthropologists share in the traditions of social science.

Paleoanthropologists maintain a lively debate about each of their findings and interpretations. They present their views and situate them within the ongoing debates in their field. They present the historical record as an ongoing search and argument. Existing data may be reevaluated; new data may be added; interpretations may be revised; new questions may arise. The historical record is never complete.

Amendments to the historical record, however, are usually minor additions to, or revisions of, a pattern already well known. Thomas Kuhn, in his path-breaking study of the history of science, *The Structure of Scientific Revolutions*, wrote that

> normal science [like history] … is a highly cumulative enterprise, eminently successful in its aim, the steady extension of the scope and precision of scientific knowledge. Normal science does not aim at novelties of fact or theory and, when successful, finds none. (Kuhn, p. 52)

The history of the evolution of hominids usually follows this pattern of "normal science." Thus the discoveries of 4.5-million-year-old *Ardipithecus ramidus* in 1994, of six- to seven-million-year-old Toumai in 2001, and of *Homo floresiensis*, discovered in 2003 and dating to as recently as 13,000 years ago, did not surprise paleoanthropologists. The new fossils fit neatly into the expected time frame for the process of evolution from apes to hominids (although the geographical location of Toumai in Chad was unexpected, and *Homo floresiensis* was a very late survival of pre-*Homo sapiens sapiens*). This was normal science filling in an existing model, or paradigm, with new detail.

Sometimes, however, new discoveries challenge existing paradigms. At first the new discoveries are discounted as exceptions to the rule. But when the exceptions

1.1

1.2

1.3

What do cultural creations tell us about the lives of early humans?

KEY STAGES IN HUMAN DEVELOPMENT

4.5 million B.P.	First appearance of bipedalism. (First clear appearance; Toumai of Chad, 6 million B.C.E., was apparently bipedal.)
2 million B.P.	Change in structure of forelimbs—bipedalism is perfected. Gradual expansion and reorganization of the brain. Hunting, scavenging, and gathering cultures stimulate production of stone tools.
500,000 B.P.	Rapid brain growth.
120,000 B.P.	*Homo sapiens sapiens*, anatomically modern humans. Fire now in use.
40,000 B.P.	Interglacial period. Existence of modern humans, with fully developed brain and speech. Tools constructed from component parts. Cave art and portable art in Europe. Human migration begins from Asia into America.
10,000 B.C.E.	Invention of bow and arrows. Domestication of reindeer and dog (north Eurasia). Settled food production.
8000–4000 B.C.E.	Increase of human population by 1,500 percent. Domestication of sheep and goats (Near East). Earliest pottery (Japan). Farming spreads to Western Europe. Rice cultivation starts in Asia.
3000 B.C.E.	Writing, metals.

increase, scientists seek new explanatory paradigms. Darwin's breakthrough followed this second pattern of scientific revolution. His discoveries on the voyage of the *Beagle* and his subsequent analyses of his findings challenged the existing concepts of creation that were based on biblical narratives. Darwin provided a radically different scientific explanation of the mechanisms of evolution that displaced the biblical paradigm. Both Darwin's scientific analysis and the Book of Genesis in the Bible, however, postulate the creation of an entire cosmos and world, replete with flora and fauna, before humans achieve their place in the universe and begin to name the other species.

Major revisions of the historical record often follow this trajectory. A general pattern of explanation is followed, until new research raises new questions and new theoretical paradigms provide more fitting explanations for all the available data and information. Throughout this text we shall continue to see changes in historical explanation over time. A "paradigm shift" may occur not only as a result of the discovery of new data, or of new interpretations that better fit the available data, but also as a response to new questions being raised that may not have been asked before. The historical record, like the scientific record on evolution, is always subject to reevaluation. Readers of this textbook may want to keep up with the latest research through such popular journals as *Archaeology* or *Scientific American*, or the online record of the Human Origins project at the Smithsonian Institution in Washington, DC. More specialized journals include *Nature* and *Science*. For example, see on the Smithsonian website the record of the discovery in 2003 and the continuing interpretation of the fossil *Homo floresiensis*, sometimes known as "The Hobbit" because of its small size. Or see the research on the presence of Neanderthal genes in modern *Homo sapiens sapiens* on the online version of *Archaeology*.

Humans Create Culture

1.3 What do cultural creations tell us about the lives of early humans?

Until now we have been examining biological evolution, "natural selection." Those organisms best able to survive did survive. By the time of *Homo habilis*, the *Homo* biological genus was creating simple tools through which it could shape nature to meet its needs. *Homo habilis* sculpted stone tools of increasing sophistication. They apparently hunted, scavenged, gathered in groups, and shared their booty. Throughout the intervening two million years, up to our own day, *Homo* has continued to increase its sophistication in creating tools, art, rituals, settlements, concepts, and language, and in domesticating plants and animals—the basic elements of what anthropologists call culture. By the time *Homo sapiens* had evolved, cultural creativity had superseded biology as the principal method by which humans coped with nature. Humans were no longer content to exist in nature. They sought to control it.

Cultural evolution seems to have been encouraged by biological evolution. As the *Homo* brain continued to develop and get bigger, it became impossible for the genus *Homo*, with its relatively narrow birth canal, to give birth to a child with a fully formed brain in a fully formed cranium. The brain capacity of human young must continue to develop for some time after birth (in fact, the brain of a human reaches its adult size only at the age of six or seven). Within the genus *Homo*, therefore, parents must devote significant time to nurturing and teaching their young children. In addition, in female *Homo sapiens* the *oestrus* cycle, the alternating period of fertility and infertility, occurs each month rather than seasonally, allowing them to bear children more frequently than other primates. Increased childbearing further increases the time and energy devoted to nurturing the young. Because of the greater attention to nurturing, cultural life could flourish—and it did.

Our species has not changed anatomically since the earliest known appearance of *Homo sapiens* in the archaeological record about 200,000 years ago. The skeletons unearthed at the Klasies River mouth are no

Two Aurignacian implements, France, Mesolithic era (c. 30,000 B.P.). Stone Age cultures first appeared in Western Europe in 33,000 B.P. and underwent constant changes in technology—implying a gradual evolution in human behavior. By the Aurignacian era, flint-end scrapers (right) were employed in processing skins, woodworking, and carving artifacts like this bone spearpoint (left). (Natural History Museum, London)

different from our own. About 120,000 years ago, however, a new creativity appeared in the cultural and social life of *Homo sapiens*, perhaps the result of a modification in the internal structure of the brain. The people who lived before this development are called "archaic" *Homo sapiens*; those with the new cultural capabilities are considered a new subspecies, **Homo sapiens sapiens** (wise, wise human). They are us. Unlike their predecessors, *Homo sapiens sapiens* developed forms of symbolic expression, apparently spiritual and cultural in nature, including burial rituals and artwork that is sometimes stunningly beautiful and creative.

Seven creative behaviors mark the arrival of *Homo sapiens sapiens*. First, we persisted. We are the lone survivor from among all the hominids of the last six million years. Second, we continued to spread to all parts of the globe in waves of migration that had begun even earlier. Third, we built small, temporary settlements to serve as base camps for hunting and gathering. Fourth, we continued to craft more sophisticated tools. Fifth, we elaborated more sophisticated use of language. Sixth, by about 25,000 B.C.E., on cave walls and in stone, we began to paint and sculpt magnificent works of art and symbolism. Seventh, by 15,000–10,000 B.C.E., we began to domesticate plants and animals, introducing the art and science of agriculture.

How Did We Survive While Others Became Extinct?

While Neanderthals appeared to be *a* link between apes and humans, continuing excavations demonstrated that they were not *the* link. In fact, as researchers have

1.1
1.2
1.3

What do cultural creations tell us about the lives of early humans?

KEY TERMS

B.P. Before the Present. Archaeologists frequently use this notation, especially for dates before about 20,000 B.C.E.

Homo sapiens sapiens The first human being of the modern type.

HOW DO WE KNOW?

Dating Archaeological Finds

Continuous improvements in dating techniques have changed our understanding of the relationships among the early *Homo sapiens*, and even among the earlier hominids, and their relationships to their environment. The most common technique, since its discovery in 1949, is radiocarbon dating, sometimes called the carbon 14 (C14) method. Living organisms breathe in air, and so they contain the same percentage of atoms of radioactive carbon as the earth's atmosphere. When an organism dies, its radiocarbon atoms disintegrate at a steady, known rate. By measuring the amount of radiocarbon remaining in a fossil skeleton, scientists can calculate backward to the date of death. Because the total amount of radiocarbon in any organism is small, little is left after 40,000 years, and the method does not work at all beyond 70,000 years into the past.

For a broader spectrum of dates, scientists use a technique called thermoluminescence, developed in 1987. This technique was applied to burned flints discovered in the caves where early humans had lived. Radioactivity occurring in nature releases electrons in flint and clay, but they can finally escape only when the substance is heated. When the flints were first burned by the people of the caves, the electrons freed up to that time were released. Reheating the flints in the laboratory today releases the electrons stored up since the first burning. Scientists calculate the date of the first burning by measuring the light of those electrons.

This technique works not only for burned flint of 50,000–300,000 years of age, but also for burnt clay, enabling scientists to date pottery from the last 10,000 years.

For much earlier dates, such as those of the earliest hominid fossils that go back as much as six million years, scientists measure the decay of the radioactive element potassium 40 into argon 40, a process that takes place in volcanic rocks and soils. Potassium-argon dating, in use since the 1950s, was invaluable in estimating the age of the soil in which stone tools and hominid remains were found in the Olduvai Gorge. This dating method was the clue to determining the deep antiquity of these fossils, and in shifting the search for the earliest hominids to Africa.

- Biochemists and physicists have their contribution to make in understanding—and dating—the evolution of the earliest humans. What have been the contributions of other academic specialists encountered in this book?
- What are the similarities between radiocarbon, thermoluminescence, and potassium-argon dating? Why is each limited to a particular time period?
- Which of these methods directly dates fossil remains? Which dates the soil in which fossils are found? What might be the problems with dating fossils by the soil in which they are found?

1.1
1.2
1.3

What do cultural creations tell us about the lives of early humans?

continued to find additional examples of early hominids all over the world, it has become increasingly clear that there is no single chain leading directly from apes to humans. Rather, anthropologists now believe that many hominids contributed to a formation better described as a "bush" of various hominids, with many branches, and that our species evolved from the various interbreedings of these hominids. All the other intervening species died out. As a result, it might appear that first there were apes and then, in a direct chain, there were humans. But the fossils of many different species in between show that the evolutionary path was not so direct.

For example, from our first appearance in the archaeological record, about 120,000 years ago, until about 35,000 years ago, anatomically modern *Homo sapiens sapiens* seem to have coexisted alongside Neanderthals and other archaic *Homo sapiens* in several sites. The best studied are in the Middle East. Caves near Haifa, Israel, have yielded skeletons and tools of both Neanderthals and modern humans from almost that entire time period. They shared similar types of tool. Neanderthals seem to have used slightly simpler, smaller Mousterian stone tools (named for the village of Le Moustier in southwestern France, where they have been most clearly documented). Their modern human neighbors used the thinner, longer, more precisely crafted Aurignacian tools (named for another hunter-gatherer site in southern France). The differences were marked but not huge.

How, then, did modern *Homo sapiens sapiens* eventually displace all other hominids? Three principal interpretations, in various combinations, have been suggested. The first is that modern humans defeated all the other hominids through warfare and murder. This theory suggests a violent streak in the earliest humans. The second theory suggests that modern humans successfully filled up the ecological niche available, outcompeting archaic *Homo sapiens* for the available resources. Modern humans did not directly confront the archaic forms but displaced them—in a sense, we ate them out of house and home. The third, related theory argues that in some cases,

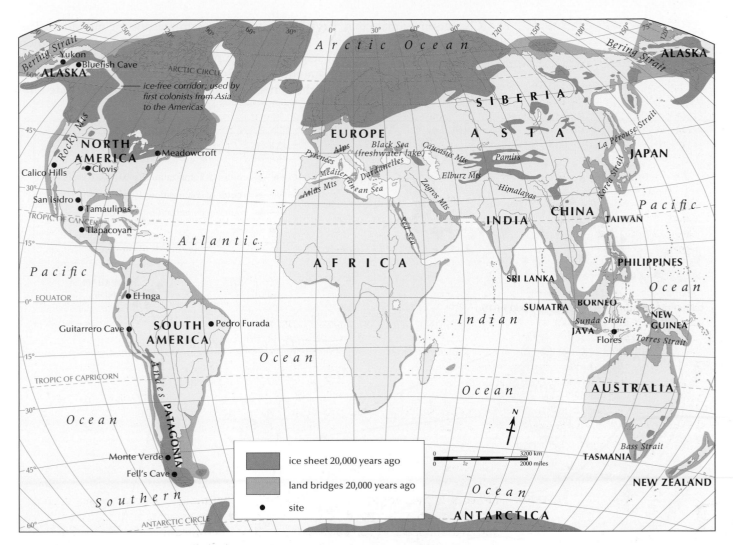

Early humans in the Ice Age. By 20,000 years ago, when ice covered much of Europe and much of Canada, almost the whole world (except Polynesia) had been colonized. Early humans were able to spread north because water frozen into ice sheets reduced sea levels so much that land bridges appeared, linking most major areas. The cold was intense, and the migrants' survival depended on their ability to stitch together animal hides into primitive clothing, control fire, and hunt large mammals.

1.1

1.2

1.3

What do cultural creations tell us about the lives of early humans?

modern humans and Neanderthals mated. Research published in 2010, using DNA from Neanderthal bones dating from 45,000 to 34,000 years ago, discovered in caves in Croatia, argues that the genes of human beings today are composed of between 1 and 4 percent Neanderthal genes. At least once, and presumably more frequently, our immediate ancestors made love, not war, and we contain a Neanderthal heritage. Because *Homo sapiens sapiens* was better adapted to nature as the ice ages ended, it was mostly their (our) genes that survived and persisted.

Global Migration

Homo sapiens sapiens appeared in Africa no later than 120,000 years ago, evolving from *Homo erectus*. Within 30,000 years the species began to appear throughout Europe and Asia. Anthropologists suspect that early human migrations were not aimless wanderings, but were purposeful and specific. From earliest prehistory, people weighed their options and opportunities and then chose appropriate actions. Global migration was the ultimate outcome.

Changes in climate may have been one of the main reasons for migration. The Sahara, now a desert, provides one example. Until about 90,000 years ago, when the earth was in a warm, wet stage, the Sahara region was fertile and attractive to human settlement. People and animals from southern Africa migrated there. But then began an "ice age," one of the periods of global cooling that have affected the

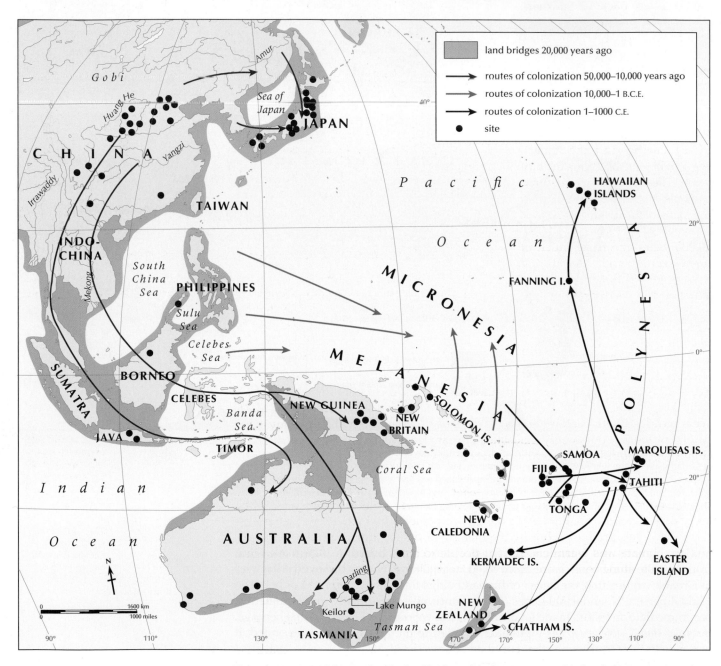

The colonization of the Pacific. The land bridges of the last Ice Age enabled early humans to spread south from China to Java and Borneo. There, some knowledge of navigation was required to cross the Banda Sea to New Guinea and Australia. The most spectacular voyages were undertaken by the Polynesians, who journeyed hundreds and thousands of miles by canoe into the uncharted Pacific waters.

🔎 View the **Interactive Map**: **Intercontinental Migration Patterns in Pre-History** on **MyHistoryLab**

🔎 View the **Map**: **The Spread of Human Populations** on **MyHistoryLab**

1.1

1.2

1.3   What do cultural creations tell us about the lives of early humans?

earth's climate over millions of years. Much of the earth's water froze. The Sahara dried up, turning to desert, and people and animals emigrated. Some may have turned back to southern Africa; some may have journeyed toward the North African coast; still others may have followed the Nile valley into western Asia. So began one wave in a global process of migration.

To reach the most distant areas, such as Australia, the islands of the Pacific, and the Americas, took tens of thousands of years. These migrations required changes in climate as well as in the skills of *Homo sapiens sapiens*. The successive ice ages of 90,000–10,000 years ago froze much of the water of the oceans, reducing sea levels, extending the coasts of the continents, and creating land bridges that linked modern China with Japan, Southeast Asia with the Philippines and Indonesia, and Siberia with Alaska.

"Navigation in Van Diemen's Land," Charles Alexandre Lesueur, plate 14 from *Voyage of Discovery to Australian Lands*, 1807. Engraving. When Europeans began settling Van Diemen's Land, now called Tasmania, in Australia, they found people who had arrived there some 40,000 years before, having crossed over from southeastern China.

People reached Southeast Asia apparently via land bridges about 50,000 years ago. Reaching Australia, however, required the sailing knowledge and skill to cover hundreds of miles of open water, and the continent was reached only about 45,000 years ago. The Pacific islands known as Polynesia, thousands of miles from any major landmass, were peopled only thousands of years later. Only in 1000 B.C.E. did New Guineans, performing extraordinary feats of navigation in simple canoes, colonize Polynesia.

North America was reached about 14,000–16,000 years ago. Until then, Siberia and the north of the continent may have been too cold for human passage. But by about 16,000 years ago, the last of the great ice sheets had retreated. Despite the rising sea levels brought about by the melting of the ice, a land bridge remained, and the climate was warm enough for people to cross over into North America. In the 1920s, stone tools were discovered near Clovis, New Mexico. Similar tool kits were subsequently discovered across North America, suggesting that the Clovis immigrants were the first humans to inhabit the Americas, about 13,000 years ago. In the 1970s, however, discoveries at Monte Verde, Chile, suggested an arrival 1,000–1,500 years before that. It also raised the question—not answered—of how a settlement so far south could precede those in North America: could the immigrants have used ships for at least part of their journey? Beginning in about 2008, findings relating to mastodon hunts in what is now Washington State, and tool kits in what is now Texas and elsewhere, and the DNA testing of remains of human feces in several additional locations suggest three waves of arrival slightly earlier, perhaps 15,000 years ago. The search for even earlier settlements continues, although none are expected before about 16,000 years ago, the end of the last major ice age.

1.1
1.2
1.3

What do cultural creations tell us about the lives of early humans?

View the **Closer Look: Mammoth Hut** on **MyHistoryLab**

What do cultural creations tell us about the lives of early humans?

Increased Population and New Settlements

Gradually, as human population expanded, so, too, did the number of human groups and the closeness or "density" of their relationships to one another. Such increasing density and population pressure became a staple of human history. Frequently, the result was conflict among groups for the best lands and resources. Some groups chose to stand and fight for their territory, others reached accommodation with newcomers, and yet others emigrated, either by choice or by force, following losses in battle. (These patterns have repeated themselves for tens of thousands of years. Today there are some 17 million refugees in the world.)

How large were these groups? They had to include enough members to provide security in defense and cooperation in work, yet be small enough to subsist on the natural resources available and to resolve the interpersonal friction that threatened the cohesion of the group and the safety of its members.

Calculated from the experience of modern hunter-gatherers, such as the Khoisan of the African Kalahari Desert, and theoretical mathematical models of group process, a five-family group of 25 people seems the ideal balance. Mating and marriage rules

HOW DO WE KNOW?

Man the Hunter or Woman the Gatherer?

Every human society has established its own patterns of gender relationships between males and females. In recent years especially, historians have turned their attention to discovering and analyzing these patterns. Their research is often determined both by the historical materials available and, to some degree, by their own biases.

In 1971 anthropologist Sally Slocum, writing under the pseudonym Sally Linton, published one of the first feminist critiques of the current understanding of hominid evolution. She was responding to a set of papers published in 1968 entitled *Man the Hunter*. One of the papers asserted: "The biology, psychology, and customs that separate us from the apes—all these we owe to the hunters of time past." This argument, Slocum replied, put too much emphasis on aggressive behavior, the tools and organized planning required for hunting, the importance of fresh meat in the hominid diet, and male activities generally.

In "Woman the Gatherer: Male Bias in Anthropology," Slocum pointed out that gathering contributed more to group nutrition than hunting, as studies of modern hunter-gatherers showed. She also pointed out that tools usually linked to hunting might have been used for gathering instead, and she urged anthropologists to look afresh at the whole idea of tools:

> Bones, sticks, and hand-axes could be used for digging up tubers or roots, or to pulverize tough vegetable matter for easier eating. If, however, instead of thinking in terms of tools and weapons, we think in terms of cultural inventions, a new aspect is presented. I suggest that two of the earliest and most important cultural inventions were containers to hold the products of gathering, and some sort of sling or net to carry babies.

Further, Slocum argued, the skills of raising and nurturing young children, usually women's tasks, evoked more innovation and perhaps more development of the brain than did hunting:

I suggest that longer periods of infant dependency, more difficult births, and longer gestation periods also demanded more skills in social organization and communication—creating selective pressure for increased brain size without looking to hunting as an explanation. The need to organize for feeding after weaning, learning to handle the more complex social-emotional bonds that were developing, the new skills and cultural inventions surrounding more extensive gathering—all would demand larger brains. Too much attention has been given to the skills required by hunting, and too little to the skills required for gathering and the raising of dependent young.

Slocum concluded that anthropologists needed to confront their own assumptions about male dominance. As she put it, "The basis of any discipline is not the answers it gets, but the questions it asks."

- Sally Slocum suggests that our historical searches are determined by the questions we ask. Are there questions about the paleoanthropological record that you want to ask that have not been addressed thus far? Can you suggest methods to find answers to these questions?
- Sally Slocum wrote of "Male Bias in Anthropology." Do you think that the different experiences of men and women influence the questions they ask in historical time as well as in prehistory? Give examples. Keep this list at hand as you read this book to determine whether you seem to be correct.
- How do the resources available for answering questions—such as stone tools as compared with fibers and cloths, or tools for hunting compared with tools for child-raising—determine the agendas for scholarly research?

1.1

1.2

1.3

What do cultural
creations tell us
about the lives of
early humans?

might well have required, as they often do today, choosing a mate from outside the immediate band. For such an exogamous, or external, marriage pattern to function, a tribe would theoretically require at least 19 bands of 25 members each, a total of 475 people, a figure reasonably close to the 500 found in modern hunter-gatherer societies.

How much territory did such bands require to support themselves? Anthropologists have calculated that an individual using the technology of Upper Paleolithic times (150,000–12,000 years ago) would have required 77 square miles of relatively unproductive land or 7–8 square miles of fertile land to meet survival needs. At such densities, the area of the United States (excluding Alaska and Hawaii) might have supported a maximum of 600,000 people; and the entire world ten million at most, although actual populations were less. As populations grew, bands began to stake out their own territories and to mark out boundaries. They began to work out formal relationships with the occupants of neighboring areas.

Groups began to establish small settlements. The Neanderthals had occupied upland sites, but the later Cro-Magnons (named for the region in France where this subspecies was originally discovered) moved down into the more valuable valleys and riverbeds. About half their sites are within 1,100 yards of a river, and all are near fords or shallows. These sites not only allow easy crossing, but also are at the points of animal crossings and therefore good for hunting. Tools took on regional patterns both in processes of manufacture and in styles of aesthetic appearance. These local patterns differentiated each group from its neighbors. Each group may have begun to develop a language, or a dialect, of its own.

Changes in the Toolkit

Even as the pace of exploration, migration, and trade increased, the clearest changes in human development appeared in our stone toolkits. The steady improvements in tool technology give this period its archaeological names. The entire period is called the Paleolithic or Old Stone Age. Tools show a slow progression from the Lower Paleolithic, ending about 150,000 years ago, to the Upper Paleolithic, which continued to about 10,000 B.C.E.

From about 2.5 million years ago until about 150,000 years ago, the dominant technology of *Homo erectus* had been Acheulian hand-held axes and cleavers made of stone (named for St. Acheul in northern France, but actually developed first in Africa and only later throughout Europe and Asia). Some sites from about 250,000 years ago reveal a more sophisticated technique, the Levallois (named for a suburb in Paris where the first examples were discovered). The Levallois technique produced more precise tools, including side-scrapers and backed knives, fashioned by more consistent patterns of preparing flakes from the stone, and a more standardized final shape and size. This technique marked the emergence of archaic *Homo sapiens*.

The technology of *Homo sapiens sapiens* developed much more rapidly. By about 40,000 years ago, Aurignacian tools were being produced in or near a cave close to the present-day village of Aurignac in the Pyrenees. This technology included narrow blades of stone as well as tools crafted from bone, ivory, and antler. Four additional styles followed, each named for the region in France in which it was discovered. Gravettian styles appear about 30,000 to about 20,000 years ago. Then came Solutrean styles, 20,000–17,000 years ago, which included the production of the first known needles. Magdalenian tools, about 17,000–12,000 years ago, included barbed harpoons carved from antlers. Finally, Azilian tools, 12,000–8000 B.C.E. (from the border between France and Spain), completed the Paleolithic sequence. Each location and time period had its own aesthetic style, and each produced an increasing variety of tools. Tool patterns began to differ from one region to another, suggesting the formation of new communities among small hunter-gatherer bands, and a greater sense of separation and distinction between groups.

1.1

1.2

1.3   What do cultural creations tell us about the lives of early humans?

Not all tools were directly related to food production, nor even to work. As early as 35,000 B.P., flutes made from the bones of birds, reindeer, and bears suggest that creating and performing instrumental music had already become part of the human repertoire. Aesthetics and play already had their roles.

The tools we have found represent only a small fraction of the daily objects that early humans probably made and used. Tools made of stone have endured; those of wood have not. Those made from natural fibers have, of course, disintegrated, which means we know little about clothing or basketry or food preparation. In most hunter-gatherer societies, making clothing and preparing food are usually women's work. So a whole area of technological development, most likely in the hands of women, was long overlooked through the focus on stone tools.

Language, Music, and Communication

Language is an intangible innovation, invisible in the archaeological record. It must be inferred from more solid evidence: global migration, fixed settlement sites, new tools and new materials, regional differences in production, trade across long distances, social hierarchies often marked by personal adornment and ritual burials, and the creation of art and instrumental music. Many of these activities would have been difficult, if not impossible, without some kind of language.

Exactly when a system of spoken language emerged is much debated, especially because we can only infer the answer. The craniums of archaic *Homo sapiens* were as large as, or even larger than, our own, and they seem to have indentations indicating

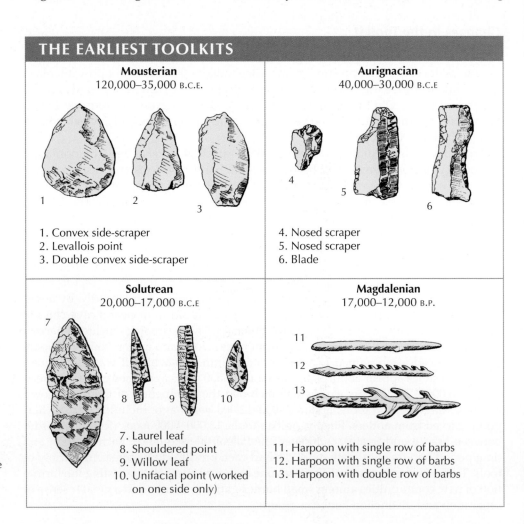

THE EARLIEST TOOLKITS

Mousterian
120,000–35,000 B.C.E.

1. Convex side-scraper
2. Levallois point
3. Double convex side-scraper

Aurignacian
40,000–30,000 B.C.E

4. Nosed scraper
5. Nosed scraper
6. Blade

Solutrean
20,000–17,000 B.C.E

7. Laurel leaf
8. Shouldered point
9. Willow leaf
10. Unifacial point (worked on one side only)

Magdalenian
17,000–12,000 B.P.

11. Harpoon with single row of barbs
12. Harpoon with single row of barbs
13. Harpoon with double row of barbs

Early tools. Many of the earliest human tools were crafted from stone and show increasing sophistication. The "toolkits" shown here are named for the four different locations in which they were found. At first, humans simply chipped away at stone until edges and points were exposed. Later, they began to carve the stone to meet more specific needs. The development took 100,000 years.

1.1

1.2

1.3

What do cultural
creations tell us
about the lives of
early humans?

Bone flute, found in the Dordogne, France, c. 35,000 B.P.
Simple wind instruments like this 4½-inch-long flute were made
from the hollowed-out bones of birds, reindeer, and bears.
They date back to as long ago as 35,000 B.P. (British Museum,
London). To hear a 9,000-year-old flute from China actually
played, go to: http://www.bnl.gov/bnlweb/pubaf/pr/1999/
bnlpr092299.html.

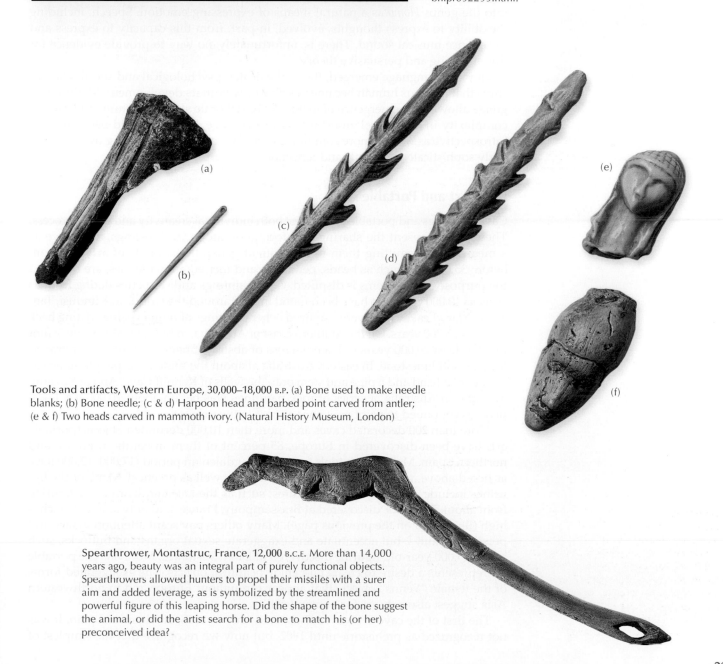

(a)

(b)

(c)

(d)

(e)

(f)

Tools and artifacts, Western Europe, 30,000–18,000 B.P. (a) Bone used to make needle
blanks; (b) Bone needle; (c & d) Harpoon head and barbed point carved from antler;
(e & f) Two heads carved in mammoth ivory. (Natural History Museum, London)

Spearthrower, Montastruc, France, 12,000 B.C.E. More than 14,000
years ago, beauty was an integral part of purely functional objects.
Spearthrowers allowed hunters to propel their missiles with a surer
aim and added leverage, as is symbolized by the streamlined and
powerful figure of this leaping horse. Did the shape of the bone suggest
the animal, or did the artist search for a bone to match his (or her)
preconceived idea?

What do cultural creations tell us about the lives of early humans?

the presence of areas in the brain that influence speech capacity. Archaic *Homo sapiens* probably possessed a larynx that had descended sufficiently low in the throat to produce the sounds of modern human language.

The dispute arises here. Some anthropologists believe that with this biological equipment, humans began to develop modern language and speech slowly, through cultural evolution. Others, notably the linguist Noam Chomsky (b. 1928), believe that a change took place within the organization of the brain that gave humans a new capacity for language. Chomsky draws his conclusion from analyzing similarities in the "deep structure" of languages around the world. These universal similarities suggest that the rules of syntax of human language are embedded in the brain. Chomsky argues that just as humans are born to walk, so they are born to talk. Bipedalism is not a learned cultural capacity, but has evolved biologically; talking, too, is not culturally learned but has biologically evolved. (The use of individual languages is, of course, culturally specific.) The archaeologist Steven Mithen goes farther, and argues that before there was language, there was music and rhythm, also "hardwired' into the genus *Homo* as a natural means of expressing emotion. Speech, including the ability to express thoughts, evolved, in part, from this capacity to express and experience musical sound. There is, unfortunately, no way to provide evidence for this engaging and persuasive theory.

However language emerged, the sophisticated psychological and social relationships that make us human became possible only with its development. Modern language allowed the emergence of increasingly elaborate social structures and greater complexity in human relationships. With language, humans could become more introspective as well as more communicative with others, deliberating over increasingly sophisticated thoughts and reflections.

Cave Art and Portable Art

Cave paintings and portable art suggest both individual creativity and group process. They may represent the sharing of information, hope, and feelings, and serve as a means of transmitting them to subsequent generations. Finds of artwork from before 35,000 B.P., such as beads, pendants, and incised animal bones, are rare, and the purpose of such items is disputed. Cave paintings and statuettes dating from as early as 40,000 years ago have been found in sites around the world. At Kundusi, Tanzania, Mary Leakey discovered stylized ocher paintings of human beings dating back perhaps 25,000 years. On the southern coast of Australia, in the Koonalda Cave, a flint mine at least 20,000 years old, a crisscross of abstract finger patterns was engraved into the soft limestone. In eastern Australia at about the same time, people stenciled images of a hand and a pipe and stem onto the walls of Kenniff Cave. And at Kakadu, in northern Australia, a series of rock paintings was begun about 20,000 B.P. Local peoples continued to paint new ones almost to the present.

More than 200 decorated caves and more than 10,000 decorated objects (portable art) have been discovered in Europe, 85 percent of them in southern France and northern Spain. Many of the tools from the Magdalenian period (17,000–12,000 B.P.), as noted above, were fashioned to be beautiful as well as practical. Many of the figurines include delicately carved features, such as the face and hair on the figurine from about 22,000 B.P. discovered at Brassempouy, France, and only about 1½ inches high (illustrated on the previous page). Many others pay scant attention to face and personal features, but accentuate and exaggerate sexual organs and buttocks, such as the 25,000-year-old figurine discovered at Dolní Vestonice, Moravia. The portable art represents a desire to create and enjoy beautiful objects. The exaggerated forms of the female "Venus" objects that appear throughout Europe and in northwestern Asia suggest also a desire for human fertility.

The first of the cave art was rediscovered only in 1868, at Altamira, Spain. It was not recognized as prehistoric until 1902, but now we recognize that the simplest of the paintings—red disks, lines, dots—date back 40,000 years. They probably evolved from an artistic tradition 10,000 years older than that. We do not know if the tradition began in Africa and was brought to Europe, or if it originated in Europe, shortly after the first humans arrived. By now, 200 caves decorated with artworks have been discovered in Europe, most of them in the river valleys of southwest France and the adjacent Pyrenees and the Cantabrian Mountains of northern Spain. The most recent discoveries, stunning in the variety of animal life depicted and the artistry employed, include the Cosquer Cave in 1991 and the Chauvet Cave in 1994, both in southern France.

The painters used natural pigments, such as ocher, that produced reds, browns, and yellows, and manganese oxides that made black and violet. (So far, blues and greens have not been found.) Over time, the subject matter—which began as simple abstract forms—became more figurative. The depiction of humans is rare in the European caves. The usual representations are of large animals, such as bison, deer, wild oxen, and horses. Occasionally there are mammoths, lions, and fish, as well as fantasy figures, such as unicorns. Clay sculptures of bison have been found at caves such as Le Tuc d'Audoubert, France. In many caves, the outlines of human hands have been stenciled onto the walls by projecting pigment around the hands. No one knows how the pigments were applied, but the most common guess is that they were chewed and then either spat directly or blown through a pipe onto the walls.

Some of the cave art was abstract, some representational, some painted, some in relief. This rich artistic tradition did not continue past the Magdalenian period, about 12,000 B.P. Many of the techniques of the cave paintings, such as perspective and the feeling of movement, did not reappear in Western art until the Renaissance, about 1400 C.E.

What do cultural creations tell us about the lives of early humans?

1.1
1.2
1.3

Clay bison, from Le Tuc d'Audoubert, Ariège, France, after 15,000 B.C.E. Most cave art owes its survival to the very particular atmospheric conditions formed in the limestone caves in which it was sealed thousands of years ago. Only a very small number of sculptures have survived. The one reproduced here—in high relief—shows a female being pursued by a male bison.

"Venus" figurine, found at Dolní Vestonice, Moravia, c. 23,000 B.P. Several hundred early female figures have been recovered, but no male figures. This seems to support the thesis that these statuettes were created not so much as representations of ideal feminine beauty, but as fertility charms Notice how the breasts, buttocks, and thighs are emphasized to the exclusion of any individualizing facial traits. (Moravian Museum, Brno)

📖 Read the **Document**: Early Art: Religion and Worship? (25,000 BCE) on **MyHistoryLab**

1.1

1.2

1.3 What do cultural creations tell us about the lives of early humans?

Ever since the cave art was rediscovered, people have wondered about its function and meaning. The first interpretation to gain widespread acceptance argued that the paintings represented a kind of magic designed to bring good fortune to the hunters of the animals represented on the cave walls. The seemingly abstract geometrical patterns, some said, represented hunting equipment, such as traps, snares, and weapons. The mural paintings of animals may represent a hope for their fertility so that the hunters might find abundant prey. Another interpretation suggested that the caves were meeting grounds to which neighboring bands of people returned each year to arrange marriages and to cement political and social alliances. The different styles of painting in each cave represent the artistic production of many different groups.

The art is often located not at the mouth of the cave, where it would have been in daily view of the campsites, but deep in the inner recesses. Why were so many images—about one-third of the total—painted so deep inside the caves? Some scholars of prehistoric art have suggested that they were not simply decorative, but were links to ancient spirits, which were remembered and invoked in the dark depths of the cave through shamanistic rituals. Among the San people of the Kalahari Desert, **shamans** are thought to communicate with spirits by means of trances induced through the use of drugs, breathing exercises, singing, dancing, and rhythmic clapping. They enter into trance states of increasing intensity in which they "see" first geometric patterns, then images from nature, and finally creatures not found in nature at all. Sometimes they see these various images as projections on the wall. Supporters of this theory believe that the Upper Paleolithic cave paintings represent such shamanistic hallucinations or visions from trance states.

The cave art and portable art of 25,000–10,000 B.P. begin the known record of human aesthetic creation. For the first time we have examples of what humans regarded as beautiful and therefore worth creating and preserving. From this time onward, the desire to create and appreciate beauty is part of the human story. The cave creations also give us insight into their creators' search for meaning and purpose in life. Our art gives outward expression to our understanding of, and our deepest feelings about, our place in the world. In our art we express our fears and our hopes for ourselves, our loved ones, our communities, our world. Through our art we attempt to connect with larger forces in the world and to communicate with one another. By studying the form and meaning of ancient art, historians attempt to understand the external aesthetics and the inner world of the people who produced it.

Agriculture: From Hunter-gatherer to Farmer

Some hunter-gatherers began to stay for longer periods at their temporary campsites. They noted the patterns of growth of the wild grains they gathered and the migration habits of the animals they hunted. They began to experiment with planting the seeds of the largest, most nutritious cereals in the Middle East and Europe, maize in the Americas, and root crops in Southeast Asia. In addition to pursuing animals as prey, people may have tried to restrict their movements to particular locations, or hunters may have built their own campsites at points frequented by the animals, adjusting human movements to those of the animals. They learned to domesticate dogs, and domesticated dogs may have accompanied the first Americans on their travels across Beringia (the land bridge between easternmost Asia and westernmost North America, today the Bering Strait). In the Middle East, the sheep was the first species to be domesticated, perhaps 10,000 years ago.

Chauvet Cave, Rhône-Alpes region, France, 18,000 B.C.E. On Christmas Day 1994, a team of archaeologists led by Jean-Marie Chauvet discovered a cave 1,640 feet deep in the Ardèche River Canyon. The cave's 300-plus Paleolithic wall paintings of horses, buffalo, and lions are the earliest known examples anywhere in the world.

📖 Read the Document: **A Need to Remember (13,000 BCE)** on **MyHistoryLab**

1.1

1.2

1.3

What do cultural creations tell us about the lives of early humans?

By 15,000–10,000 B.C.E., humans had the biological and cultural capacity to farm and raise animals. But first they had to want to do so. Otherwise why give up hunting and gathering? Why settle down? Perhaps the transformation took place at sites with especially valuable and accessible natural resources, such as the fishing sites of the Jomon people of Japan, or the quarries of obsidian stone, used for making sharp cutting tools, around Çatal Hüyük in modern Turkey. A permanent source of food to eat or materials to trade might have outweighed the desire to shift with the seasons and travel with the herds.

Perhaps rising population pressures left no alternative. The press of neighbors may have restricted scope for travel. On limited land, hunter-gatherers would have found that planting their own crops and domesticating their own animals could provide them with more food than hunting and gathering. Despite the risks of weather and of plant and animal diseases that left agricultural settlements vulnerable, some groups began to settle. Ten thousand years ago, almost all humans lived by hunting and gathering. Two thousand years ago, most were farmers or herders. This transformation created not only the first agricultural villages, but also cities. Cities grew up as the central administrative, economic, and religious centers of their regions. A new era was beginning. It is the subject of the next chapter and Part Two.

📖 Read the **Document**: **From Hunter-gatherers to Food-producers—Overcoming Obstacles** on **MyHistoryLab**

KEY TERM

shaman In the religious beliefs of some African, Asian, and American tribal societies, a person capable of entering into trances and believed to be endowed with supernatural powers, with the ability to cure the sick, find lost or stolen property, predict the future, and protect the community from evil spirits. A shaman may act as judge or ruler, and, as a priest, a shaman directs communal sacrifices and escorts the souls of the dead to the next world.

The Story of Prehistory:
What Difference Does It Make?

The materials of this chapter, which are largely based on the research of paleoanthropologists, make us aware of different ways of knowing and their different kinds of usefulness. They lead us to be open-minded, yet skeptical, for example, of the uses of creation stories as a way of explaining the significance of human life, and to note that different myths and stories encourage different behaviors. Myths that are widely accepted within a society are not merely quaint stories; they are powerful explanatory messages that speak deeply to people's understanding of the world.

Similarly, these materials lead us to be open-minded, yet skeptical, of the powers of science to explain the world. Scientific research does not exist in a vacuum, but responds to the questions we ask. The process of evolution was not immediately evident until scientists began asking the right questions; the role of women in cultural evolution was not considered until feminist researchers began asking questions that had not been asked before; Africa as a location for the earliest hominids and humans was ignored until racial prejudices were put aside. Scientific enquiry is an enormously powerful tool in unlocking the mysteries of the world, but it addresses only those questions that we ask.

We have also learned to distinguish between "ordinary" science, which builds on what is already known and accepted, and revolutionary science, which puzzles over new information and anomalies, elements that do not fit into already existing patterns, until it may create "paradigm shifts," new ways of understanding the world.

We have seen that from the very earliest times human behavior has been characterized by migration; the creation of tools; the formation of ever-larger groups, which nevertheless apparently create distinctions between members and "others"; communication through language; self-expression through art; and oscillation between accepting nature as it is and trying to control it. These are the principal legacies of the earliest hominids and humans, and they are the record of our success in finding methods of understanding our world more clearly through historiography and through paleoanthropology.

CHAPTER REVIEW

HUMAN ORIGINS IN MYTH AND HISTORY

1.1 How do myths explain the origins of human beings on the earth?

Each culture has its own myths and creation stories that it passes down from generation to generation. Such narratives tell us a great deal about the values of the culture that created them.

FOSSILS AND FOSSIL-HUNTERS

1.2 What do we know about the evolution of human beings?

Beginning in the mid-1800s, fossil-hunters sought a "missing link" between human beings and apes. Today, DNA analysis demonstrates a wide variety of evolutionary paths that led to the emergence of human beings. Evolutionary biologists join paleoanthropologists in studying the relationship between humans, Neanderthals, chimpanzees, and apes.

HUMANS CREATE CULTURE

1.3 What do cultural creations tell us about the lives of early humans?

From the earliest times, humans have migrated from place to place, crafted tools, organized into groups, communicated through language, and expressed themselves in art. Today we examine their creations to understand how they survived, flourished, and understood their place in the universe.

Suggested Readings

PRINCIPAL SOURCES

Adas, Michael, ed. *Agricultural and Pastoral Societies in Ancient and Classical History* (Philadelphia: Temple University Press, 2001). Ten diverse, expert, readable essays provide invaluable guides to relatively recent research.

Barber, Elizabeth Wayland. *Women's Work: The First 20,000 Years: Women, Cloth, and Society in Early Times* (New York: W.W. Norton & Co., 1994). Fascinating account of the earliest known production of cloth, and women's role in producing it.

Charlesworth, Brian and Deborah. *Evolution: A Very Short Introduction* (New York: Oxford University Press, 2003). Excellent. Covers theories, fossils, and DNA.

Darwin, Charles. *Darwin*, ed. Philip Appleman (New York: W.W. Norton & Co., 2nd ed., 1979). Excellent anthology of works by and about Darwin.

Fagan, Brian M. *People of the Earth* (Upper Saddle River, NJ. Prentice Hall, 13th ed., 2010). Outstanding textbook introduction to prehistoric human life around the globe.

Johanson, Donald, Lenora Johanson, and Blake Edgar. *Ancestors: In Search of Human Origins* (New York: Villard Books, 1994). An account of the work of one of the greatest paleoanthropologists, and of its significance.

Leakey, Richard, and Roger Lewin. *Origins Reconsidered* (New York: Doubleday, 1992). A great paleoanthropologist, continuing and expanding the accomplishments of his even more famous parents, presents his account of the fossil record of evolution.

Lewin, Roger. *The Origin of Modern Humans* (New York: Scientific American Library, 1993). Remarkably lucid presentation of the story of evolution and early humans.

Mithen, Steven. *After the Ice: A Global Human History, 20,000–5000 B.C.* (Cambridge: Harvard University Press, 2004). A global tour emphasizing patterns of living, with special emphasis on the effects of climate.

Past Worlds: The (London) Times Atlas of Archaeology (London: Times Books Ltd., 1988). Text, maps, pictures are all superb on all aspects of archaeological understanding and accomplishment.

Renfrew, Colin. *The Making of the Human Mind* (New York: Modern Library, 2007). A scholarly review of archaeological and anthropological studies of early *Homo sapiens*, especially on the evolution of the mind.

Stringer, Chris, and Peter Andrews. *The Complete World of Human Evolution* (London: Thames and Hudson, 2nd ed., 2012). Brief, clear, concise, authoritative account of human evolution, beautifully illustrated, presented in neatly packaged, readable, discrete topical sections.

Tattersall, Ian. *The World from Beginnings to 1000 B.C.E.* (New York: Oxford University Press, 2008). Brief, clear, concise, authoritative account from the genetic and fossil study of earliest humans through the beginning of agriculture.

——. *Masters of the Planet: The Search for Our Human Origins* (New York: Palgrave Macmillan, 2012). Emphasizes more recent discoveries and lays out the framework for understanding the theory of a "bush" of human ancestors rather than a linear progression.

ADDITIONAL SOURCES

Brown, Judith. "Note on the Division of Labor by Sex," *American Anthropologist* LXXII (1970), pp. 1075–76. Argues that, historically, women's work has been compatible with child-care responsibilities.

Chauvet, Jean-Marie, Eliette Brunel Deschamps, and Christian Hillaire. *Dawn of Art: The Chauvet Cave, the Oldest Known Paintings in the World* (New York: Abrams, 1996). Gorgeous presentation of this recently discovered cave art.

Darwin, Charles. *The Origin of Species by Means of Natural Selection or the Preservation of Favored Races in the Struggle for Life*, reprinted from the Sixth Edition, ed. Edmund B. Wilson (New York: Macmillan, 1927). The classic, revolutionary work.

——. *On the Origin of Species 1859* (New York: New York University Press, 1988). The first edition, without mention of "the Creator."

Dawkins, Richard. *The Selfish Gene* (New York: Oxford University Press, 30th anniversary edition, 2006). Classic work identifying genes as the units "selected" by nature to survive and reproduce.

Fedigan, Linda. "The Changing Role of Women in Models of Human Evolution," *Annual Review of Anthropology* XV (1986), pp. 22–66. Comprehensive introduction to feminist perspectives on evolution.

Gamble, Clive. *Timewalkers: The Prehistory of Global Colonization* (Cambridge, MA: Harvard University Press, 1994). Ponders the migrations of humans from earliest times to all corners of the earth.

Gould, Stephen Jay. *The Structure of Evolutionary Theory* (Cambridge, MA: Harvard University Press, 2002). A comprehensive summary of all that we know of evolution today, by a master scholar-writer, published just months before his death.

Holm, Jean, with John Bowker, eds. *Myth and History* (London: Pinter Publishers, 1994). Analysis of the functions of myth and of history in human understanding.

Kuhn, Thomas S. *The Structure of Scientific Revolutions* (Chicago, IL: University of Chicago Press, 1970).

Lewis-Williams, David. *The Mind in the Cave: Consciousness and the Origins of Art* (London: Thames and Hudson, 2002). Argues that in prehistoric caves "image-making," religion, and social discriminations were a "package deal," as humans realized a new capability for higher-order thought.

Lewontin, Richard. *It Ain't Necessarily So: The Dream of the Human Genome and Other Illusions* (New York: New York Review of Books, 2000). Social nurture is more important than genetic nature argues this leading evolutionary biologist.

Linton, Sally (pseud. for Sally Slocum). "Woman the Gatherer: Male Bias in Anthropology," in Sue-Ellen Jacobs, ed., *Women in Perspective: A Guide for Cross-Cultural Studies* (Urbana, IL: University of Illinois Press, 1971). Asking new questions from a feminist perspective, Linton demonstrates a much enhanced role of women in early cultural evolution.

McNeill, William H. *Mythistory and Other Essays* (Chicago, IL: University of Chicago Press, 1986). A master historian discusses the difference between myth and the professional study of history, and how the two perspectives intersect in the public mind.

Mithen, Steven. *The Singing Neanderthals: The Origins of Music, Language, Mind and Body* (Cambridge, MA: Harvard University Press, 2006). Differentiates between the evolution of the emotional, musical capacities of humans, and of our linguistic, informational abilities.

Nature. Interdisciplinary scientific journal related to biological concerns. Volume 418 (2002) contained numerous articles on the discovery of Toumai, and reprinted several classic articles on earlier archaeological discoveries, from Dart's in 1925 to the present.

The New English Bible (New York: Oxford University Press, 1976). For clarity and simple, basic annotation, my favorite edition.

Pfeiffer, John. *The Creative Explosion* (Ithaca, NY: Cornell University Press, 1982). Argues for a dramatic leap in human intellectual and artistic capacities about 35,000 years ago in Europe. Very well written. Now more controversial than ever.

Scott, Joan W. "Gender: A Useful Category of Historical Analysis," *American Historical Review* XCI (1986), pp. 1053–76. A classic article in helping to bring feminist perspectives into mainstream historical research.

Stearns, Peter. *Sexuality in World History* (New York: Routledge, 2009). The understanding and regulation of sexuality in various societies around the world through time.

Wilson, E.O. *Sociobiology* (Cambridge, MA: Harvard University Press, 25th anniversary edition, 2000). Classic presentation of the importance of genetic inheritance in human behavior.

FILMS

Video on molecular evolution by Prof. Robert Weinberg of MIT (2004; 50 minutes) http://ocw.mit.edu/courses/biology/7-012-introduction-to-biology-fall-2004/video-lectures/lecture-32-molecular-evolution

Video on the ethics of using genetics to determine the future of individuals by Prof. Robert Weinberg of MIT (2004;50 minutes) http://ocw.mit.edu/courses/biology/7-012-introduction-to-biology-fall-2004/video-lectures/lecture-35-human-polymorphisms-and-cancer-classification

PART TWO

TURNING POINT: SETTLEMENT PATTERNS

10,000 B.C.E.–1000 C.E.

Settling Down: Villages and Cities

As human populations grew, hunting and gathering alone could not produce enough to feed them all. People had to travel ever greater distances, which brought them into direct conflict with their neighbors—who were also hard pushed to hunt and gather adequate food and were also expanding in number. Settled agriculture was the solution. Careful attention to plant and animal patterns on the part of hunter-gatherers had already set the stage.

The Agricultural Village

As they settled down, humans began to domesticate not only food crops but also animals, which served for food, for power and energy in carrying goods and pulling plows, and for products such as milk, wool, fur, and leather. Village dwellers produced tools that were increasingly sophisticated in usefulness and aesthetic beauty. Some of these tools were made of organic materials, such as bone and fiber, but many were made of stone. Villagers became skilled at grinding and polishing the stone tools, and this new era is called the Neolithic or New Stone Age.

Settled agriculture began about 12,000 years ago in the Fertile Crescent—that is, Mesopotamia, the valley between the Tigris and Euphrates rivers—and in the Nile valley. However, one of the best preserved early villages was discovered in China at Banpo, near Xi'an. The residents of Banpo cultivated millet and domesticated pigs and dogs. They practiced slash-and-burn agriculture, and pollen samples show distinct alternating periods of cultivation and fallow.

Farming in China, c. 5000 B.C.E. Evidence of the earliest established agriculture in East Asia is found in the arid but fertile regions of north central China, along the central reaches of the Huang He (Yellow River). Villages such as Banpo grew up on the flood plain, rich in alluvial and loess deposits, where drought-resistant plants such as millet could be cultivated. (Xi'an and Luoyang are included for placement purposes.)

Model reconstruction of Banpo. The Banpo site has been made into a museum open to the public. Visitors can walk on special paths through the ancient ruins. This on-site model provides an archaeological reconstruction of what the entire village looked like in its time.

The most ancient layers of the excavation, which date to about 6000 B.C.E., give a clear idea of the physical form of an early agricultural village.

Immediately adjacent to the excavation, archaeologists have reconstructed a model of the entire prehistoric village. It represents Banpo's three housing styles: square, round, and an oblong, split level, part underground and part above. Banpo villagers stored their grain in some 200 underground pits, which were dug throughout the village. A moat surrounds the entire residential settlement.

North of the village was a pottery production center with six kilns, and next to them was a public cemetery where some 250 graves have been excavated. The bodies of children were placed in urns and buried in the main residential area. Archaeologists do not know why adults and children were buried separately.

In the center of the settlement was a large square building. What was its function? Presumably it had political and social significance for the entire village. Was it a ruler's palace? A priest's shrine? A place for the Banpo inhabitants to discuss public affairs? We do not know.

Agriculture was the basis of most early villages, but there were exceptions. In southern Japan, the Jomon people supported themselves by fishing and hunting deer and wild boar with bows and arrows, and by gathering and storing acorns, nuts, and seeds. Some of the Jomon lived in caves, but others built villages with individual pit-houses and central, communal buildings. They may have also cultivated root crops and cereals, but they were not primarily agricultural. They created stone tools but they are most famous for their distinctive pottery, some of the world's earliest and most beautiful, dating to as early as 10,500 B.C.E. It was made by forming clay into cords and wrapping the cords by hand into pots. Their pots were both functional and artistic (see image of a Jomon vase in the chapter entitled "From Village Community to City-state").

Another non-agricultural development in villages occurred in eastern Anatolia (modern Turkey), on the shores of Lake Van. The presence of volcanic obsidian stone gave

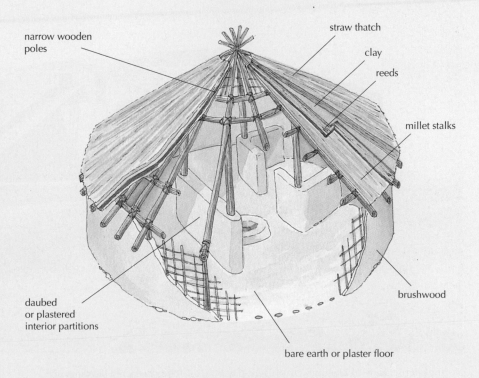

straw thatch
clay
reeds
millet stalks
narrow wooden poles
brushwood
daubed or plastered interior partitions
bare earth or plaster floor

Typical Banpo dwelling. Three forms of residence have been reconstructed at Banpo—round, square, and oblong with part underground. Here, archaeologists provide an illustration of the round form.

Obsidian blades, Çatal Hüyük, c. 3000 B.C.E. Çatal Hüyük carried on trade in these obsidian tools, exchanging them with villages near and far for food and agricultural commodities. It was taking on the commercial characteristics of a small town.

Northeastern façade of Ziggurat, Ur, present-day Iraq, c. 2100 B.C.E. Sacred buildings and temples dominated the center of Ur and this three-story-high ziggurat was the most famous of them. Each major Mesopotamian city had a ziggurat dedicated to its deity. Ur's was dedicated to Nanna, the moon God.

villagers a substance they could craft into blades of extraordinary sharpness, which they used themselves and also traded to villages hundreds of miles away on the eastern shores of the Mediterranean and the Persian Gulf. For most of these Anatolian villages, the trade in obsidian was complementary to agriculture. But one site, Çatal Hüyük, grew into a 32-acre town, with an economy based on the manufacture and trade of obsidian tools. Çatal Hüyük stands out as a new kind of settlement, one that combined agriculture with industry and trade. It was a transitional form in the development of early cities.

The First Cities

The construction of cities, with impressive buildings and crowds of inhabitants, along with other, less tangible, developments, brought a revolution in human settlement patterns. Cities were nodes in the regional networks of exchange of goods and culture, and they encouraged the production of sophisticated arts, the specialization of labor, and the elaboration of a social hierarchy. Most significantly, cities signaled the emergence of a state organization for guiding and administering the city and its surrounding area. The new state, hand-in-glove with the new city, provided leadership, organization, and official control of

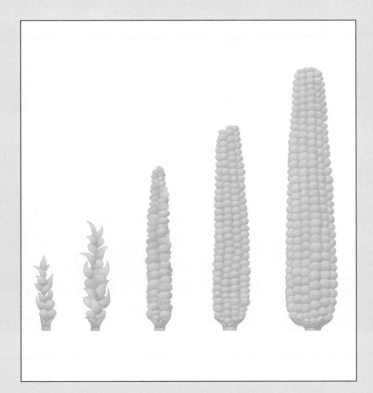

Evolution of maize. The steady evolution of maize, from the rather stunted cob of wild corn from the valley of Mexico (about 5000 B.C.E.) to the more productive and nutritious plant of about 1 B.C.E., reveals the benefits that came with the creation of agricultural villages.

armed power. It governed the people of the city, sometimes with their consent, often without it. The state enforced and helped to create the conditions of hierarchy that emerged among the people of the new cities. In all these characteristics, the ancient city reminds us of our own.

Unlike modern cities, however, almost all early cities were relatively small. The largest contained perhaps 100,000 people in eight square miles; most had only a few thousand inhabitants. Until the Industrial Revolution in the late nineteenth century, a few thousand people concentrated in 100 acres might have constituted a city, for cities held only a tiny percentage of the total population of any region.

Most of the world's population were farmers or hunter-gatherers when the first cities developed. The multiplication of cities and urban residents that we see today took place only after the Industrial Revolution created new urban factories, transportation hubs, and mass labor forces. Moreover, many of the early cities, although small, were centers of independent city-states; most cities today are single points in much larger national and even international networks. Finally, the earliest cities emerged in each of seven regions around the world. Mostly, they took root along the banks of great rivers, reflecting the importance of water, irrigation, and agriculture to their development. The world's earliest cities emerged between the Tigris and Euphrates rivers in what is now modern Iraq. They developed along the Nile River in Egypt and in the Indus valley of modern Pakistan. In China the earliest cities flourished in the flood plain of the Yellow River. Finally, early cities appeared in West Africa near the great bed of the Niger River. The Americas provide some exceptions, with the growth of great civilizations in the valleys and jungles of Mexico and on the heights of the Andes Mountains.

Many of these early cities were dedicated to gods and were built on the foundations of existing shrine centers. As the cities grew, the shrines grew with them, providing a more profound meaning to the lives of their inhabitants by linking their mundane existence to transcendent and powerful supernatural forces.

Turning Point Questions

1. Why was the development of agriculture essential to the growth of the city?
2. What is the difference between a village and a city?
3. In what ways did settling down and abandoning nomadism change people's lives?
4. Cities brought together larger numbers of people in a relatively smaller geographic space than villages had. In addition, they marked the creation of political states. What was the significance of the new states to the way people lived?

2 From Village Community to City-state

Food First: The Agricultural Village

10,000 B.C.E.–750 B.C.E.

Until about 12,000 years ago humans hunted and gathered their food, following the migrations of animals and the seasonal cycles of the crops. They established temporary base camps for their activities, and caves served them for homes and meeting-places, but they had not established permanent settlements. They had begun to domesticate some animals, especially the dog and the sheep, but they had not yet begun the systematic practice of agriculture. Then, about 10,000 B.C.E., people began to settle down, constructing the first agricultural villages.

Sumerian ruins, Uruk, present-day Iraq, c. 2100 B.C.E. A man and child stand amid what is left of the ancient city of Uruk.

LEARNING OBJECTIVES

2.1 ((•
Describe the world's first villages.

2.2 ((•
Discuss the creation and contributions of the earliest cities.

2.3 ((•
Tell the story of the world's first urban revolution.

2.4 ((•
Distinguish between cities and villages in size and organization.

((• Listen on **MyHistoryLab**

Why did they do it? Is food production through agriculture easier than hunting and gathering? Surprisingly, the answer seems to be "no." Research suggests that, with the technology available at that time, adult farmers had to work an equivalent of 1,000–1,300 hours a year for their food, while hunter-gatherers needed only 800–1,000 hours. Moreover, agricultural work was more difficult.

Why did they change? An appealing, although unproved, answer is that increasing population pressure, perhaps accompanied by centuries of unfavorable climates, such as the droughts in Mesopotamia, forced people to take on the more productive methods of irrigated agriculture. Scientists estimate that even in a lush tropical environment, 0.4 square miles of land could support only nine people through hunting and gathering; under organized, sedentary agricultural techniques, the same area could support 200–400 people. In the less fertile subtropical and temperate climates into which the expanding populations were moving at the end of the last ice age, after about 13,000 B.C.E., hunting and gathering were even less productive. For humankind to survive, sedentary agriculture became a necessity.

The memory of this transition survives in myth. For example, the myth of Shen Nung, whom the ancient Chinese honored as the inventor of agriculture and its wooden tools (and of poetry), captures the transformation:

> The people of old ate the meat of animals and birds. But in the time of Shen Nung, there were so many people that there were no longer enough animals and birds to supply their needs. So it was that Shen Nung taught the people how to cultivate the earth. (Bairoch, p. 6)

In addition to increasing agricultural productivity, villages facilitated an increase in activities of all kinds. It may have taken longer to raise food than to hunt and gather it, but the sedentary farmers did not stop work when they had secured their food supply. In their villages they went on to create textiles, pottery, metallurgy,

AT A GLANCE: VILLAGE COMMUNITIES AND CITY-STATES

DATE	POLITICS	RELIGION AND CULTURE	SOCIAL DEVELOPMENT
4500 B.C.E.	● Ubaid people in Mesopotamia		
3500 B.C.E.	● Sumerians (3300–2350) ● Ziggurats built	● Cuneiform writing ● Sumerian pantheon	● Urbanization in Mesopotamia
3000 B.C.E.	● Hereditary kings emerge		● Invention of the wheel ● Bronze casting ● Sumerian city-states (2800–1850)
2500 B.C.E.	● Ur, First Dynasty (2500–2350) ● Akkadian kingdoms (2350–2150); Sargon of Akkad (2334–2279) ● Third Dynasty of Ur (c. 2112–2004)	● Akkadian language used in Sumer ● *The Epic of Gilgamesh* (c. 2113–1991)	● Sumerian Laws
2000 B.C.E.	● Semitic rulers gain control of Mesopotamia ● First dynasty of Babylon (c. 1894–1595) ● Hammurabi (1792–1750) ● Hittites in Asia Minor		● Mycenaean traders in Aegean 1800–1000 B.C.E. ● Hammurabi's Code of Law
1500 B.C.E.	● Hittite Empire (c. 1460–1200)	● "Golden age" of Ugarit	
1000 B.C.E.	● Assyrian Empire (900–612)	● Hebrew Scriptures recorded	
750 B.C.E.	● Sargon II (d. 705) ● Sennacherib (c. 705–681) ● Ashurbanipal (d. 627) ● Fall of Nineveh (imperial capital) (612) ● Nebuchadnezzar (605–562)	● *Gilgamesh* (complete version) ● Homer (*fl.* 8th century) ● Hesiod (*fl.* 700)	
600 B.C.E.	● Neo–Babylonian Empire	● Library at Nineveh	
500 B.C.E.	● Persian Empire in control of Mesopotamia		

2.1

2.2

2.3

2.4

What was life
like in the world's
first agricultural
villages?

architecture, tools, and objects of great beauty, especially in sculpture and painting. Did agriculturists work harder than hunter-gatherers simply to survive under greater population pressure, or because they craved the added rewards of their extra labor, or both? We can never know for sure, but the agricultural village opened new possibilities for economic, social, political, and artistic creativity. The very act of domesticating plants and animals put humans in charge of directing evolution. The village changed forever humanity's concepts of life's necessities and potentials.

The Agricultural Village

2.1   What was life like in the world's first agricultural villages?

The first agricultural villages that archaeologists have discovered date to about 10,000 B.C.E. They are located in the "Fertile Crescent," which curves from the Persian Gulf and the Zagros Mountains in the east and south, on the border of today's Iraq and Iran, northwest into present-day Turkey, and then turns south and west through present-day Syria, Lebanon, and Israel on the Mediterranean Sea, and on into the Nile valley. In this region, wild grasses—the ancestors of modern wheat and barley—provided the basic grains, first for gathering, and later for cultivation. By 8000 B.C.E. the Natufians, named for their valley in northern Israel, and the peoples immediately to the south, in the Jordan River valley near Jericho, were growing fully domesticated cereals. Peas and lentils and other legumes followed. Irrigation enabled this agriculture. Villagers developed additional new skills: sewing, basket weaving, textile manufacture, pottery making. Some trade linked the villages, and small boats began to appear on the Nile, the Tigris, and the Euphrates by about 3500 B.C.E. There had already been some limited sea-borne trade in the Aegean Sea, off the coast of modern Greece, by 6000 B.C.E.

The peoples of the Fertile Crescent hunted gazelles and goats. Later, they domesticated the goat and the sheep. (Dogs were domesticated three millennia earlier, in several different regions of the world.) In Turkey they added pigs; around the Mediterranean, there were cattle. Life in settled villages, with domesticated animals living as neighbors, or even residing in villagers' homes, brought new problems of sanitation and hygiene. New diseases flourished, including smallpox, flu, measles, mumps, whooping cough, bubonic plague, malaria, yellow fever, tuberculosis, and rabies. Diseases became increasingly endemic as villages grew in size and density, and, later, as cities emerged. Nevertheless, birth rates were high and population continued to increase.

In other parts of the world, agriculture and animal domestication focused on other varieties. In the western hemisphere, these included maize, especially in Mesoamerica, and root crops such as manioc and sweet potatoes in South America. Amerindians domesticated the llama, the guinea pig, and the turkey. Domesticated dogs probably accompanied their migrant masters across the Bering Strait about 15,000 years ago. Perhaps the process of domestication was then repeated with the dogs found in the Americas.

In Southeast Asia and tropical Africa, wild roots and tubers, including yams, were the staple crops. In the Vindhya Mountain areas of central India, rice was among the first crops to be cultivated, about 5000 B.C.E. Anthropologists are uncertain when rice was first cultivated in Southeast and East Asia, rather than just being harvested from the wild, but a date similar to India's seems likely. From earliest times, as today, China's agriculture seems to have favored rice in the south and millet in the north. Some crops, including cotton and gourds, were brought under cultivation in many locations around the globe.

Our knowledge of early agriculture continues to grow as the archaeological record is expanded and revised. European sedentary agriculture, for example, which was once thought to have been borrowed from the Near East, may have been a local response to changing climate conditions.

The era in which villages took form is usually called **Neolithic**, or New Stone Age, named for its tools rather than its crops. Farming called for a different toolkit from hunting and gathering. For cutting, grinding, chopping, scraping, piercing, and digging, village artisans fashioned new tools from stone. Archaeological digs from Neolithic villages abound with blades, knives, sickles, adzes, arrows, daggers, spears, fish hooks and harpoons, mortars and pestles, and rudimentary plows and hoes.

As villages expanded their economic base, these stone tools became valued as items of trade. Obsidian—a kind of volcanic glass with very sharp edges—was traded from Anatolia and is found in hundreds of digs from central Turkey to Syria and the Jordan valley. Among other items of trade, recognized by their appearance in digs a long distance away from their point of origin, are seashells, jade, turquoise, and ceramics. Metallurgy in bronze formed one of the major technological accomplishments that would later usher in the transition from village to city. By 7000 B.C.E., craftsmen were working with raw copper in southeastern Turkey; three thousand years later, craftsmen with far more experience learned to smelt the copper with alloys and transform it into bronze.

Although ceramics occasionally appear among nomadic populations, the weight and fragility of clay make pottery essentially a creation of the established Neolithic village. As a vessel for storage, pottery further reflected the sedentary character of the new village life. The fine designs and colors decorating its pottery became the most distinctive identifying mark of the Neolithic village, and archaeologists often designate eras, locations, and groups of people by descriptions of their pottery—the "grayware," the "red glazed," or the "cord-marked," for example.

Simple pottery is easy to make and accessible to anyone, but specialized craftspeople developed ceramics into a medium of artistic creativity. Fine ceramic jewelry, statuary, and figurines attained great beauty and were frequently used in religious rituals.

Village life created and required several new social adaptations that paved the way for later urbanization. Increased size and stability of residence required more organizational leadership and brought about some degree of hierarchy, as leaders and followers sorted themselves out. The Natufians, for example, a people of the eastern Mediterranean, buried their dead in cemeteries with stone slab grave covers and mortar markers. Seashells and stone bowls found in some of the graves suggest an early hierarchical ranking system. Sedentary life also led to demarcating possessions, especially possessions of land. In place of the shared community responsibilities of the roaming bands of hunter-gatherers, newly settled villagers staked their claims on their own fields, and the idea of private property was born.

Family life also underwent a transformation. Settling down led to the development of more formalized family structures in both nuclear (father-mother-children) and extended families (including also grandparents, spouses of married children, and their children). Before the advent of writing, it is difficult to know how women were valued as compared to men, but most scholars now agree that women were decisive in the transition to agriculture in most regions:

> On the basis of anthropological evidence for societies still living traditional foraging lifestyles and those living by simple, non-mechanical farming, taken in conjunction with direct archaeological evidence, it seems probable that it was women who made the first observations of plant behavior, and worked out, presumably by long trial and error, how to grow and tend crops. (Ehrenberg, p. 78)

Women probably also had the major responsibility for cooking, carrying water, producing clothing—weaving is the most studied of their early arts—and, of course, most important of all, they gave birth to children and probably had the major responsibility for nurturing and raising them. Still, we do not know the degree to which agricultural,

What was life like in the world's first agricultural villages?

2.1
2.2
2.3
2.4

KEY TERM

Neolithic "New Stone Age," the last division of the Stone Age, immediately preceding the development of metallurgy and corresponding to the ninth to fifth millennia B.C.E. It was characterized by the increasing domestication of animals and cultivation of crops, established agricultural communities, and the appearance of such crafts as pottery and weaving.

Jomon vase, Kanto province, Japan. Earthenware. Jomon pottery dates to as early as *c.* 10,000 B.C.E., making it (among) the oldest in the world. Jomon means "cord marking" because the village potter formed the work from the bottom, without the use of a wheel, adding coil upon coil of soft clay. (Musée Guimet, Paris)

village societies valued women as compared to men. As we shall see below, once societies became literate and urban—and we have written records—we find women valued less than men.

Some villages did form on an economic base of hunting and gathering. In southern Japan, for example, a non-agricultural village society appeared among the Jomon people along with some of the earliest and most beautiful pottery (see the introduction to Part Two). Jomon pottery, which is marked by distinctive cord lines, dates back to 10,500 B.C.E. and spread from the southern island of Kyushu northward through Honshu, reaching Hokkaido by 6500 B.C.E. The Jomon villagers supported themselves by fishing, hunting deer and wild boar, and gathering and storing nuts. They created stone tools and lived in caves and in pit-houses in settled villages with central, communal buildings. Yet the Japanese did not develop agricultural cultivation for another several thousand years. Similar villages without agricultural bases were established in a few other regions with similar availability of food supplies in nature. The native Americans of the Pacific coast, from today's California to Canada, found abundant fish; deer, elk, and bear; and berries, acorns, and hazelnuts. They ate well with no need for farming. Seafood from the Pacific also enabled the area of Norte Chico, not far from modern Lima, Peru, to establish villages without an agricultural base. In Denmark and southern Sweden, too, the sea provided adequate food, so while the people along these coasts did build villages, they did not begin farming until about 3200 B.C.E.

📖 **Read** the **Document**: **A Visitor from the Neolithic Age: The Iceman (3300 BCE)** on **MyHistoryLab**

What was life like in the world's first agricultural villages?

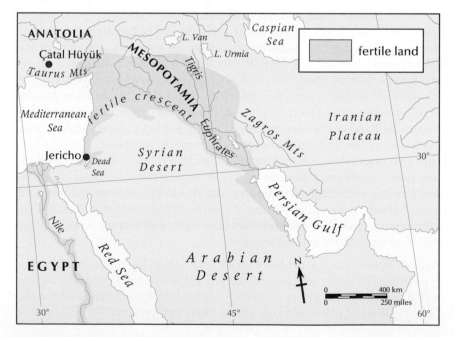

The Fertile Crescent. The Tigris and Euphrates rivers gave life to the first known agricultural villages, about 10,000 years ago, and the first known cities in human history, about 5000 years ago. Fertile land extended to the Mediterranean and some contact apparently continued to the Nile valley. Its borders were defined to the south by arid regions receiving less than 10 inches of rainfall per year, and to the north by mountains and semi-arid plateaux.

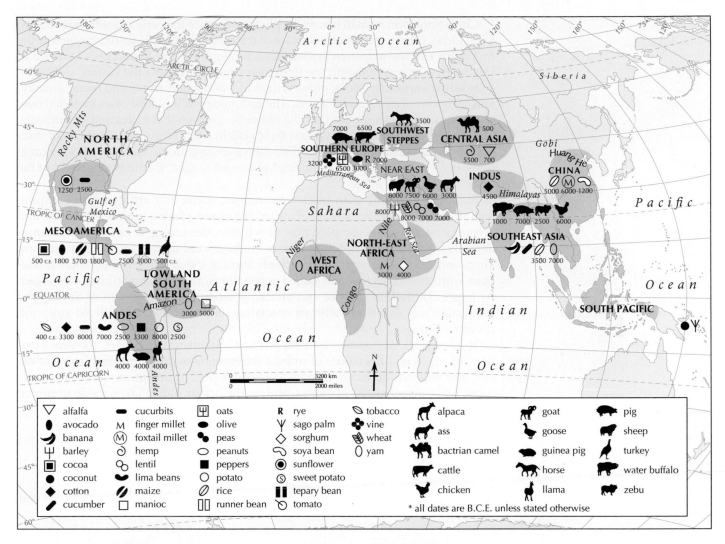

The origins of agriculture and domestic animals. The development of agriculture and the domestication of animals took place independently in different parts of the world, but the Near East, Mesoamerica, Southeast Asia, and China were among the first and most significant regions.

The First Cities

| 2.2 | In what way were cities new creations, different from villages? |

The first cities were constructed on the economic base of sedentary village agricultural communities. In excavating these earliest cities around the globe, archaeologists ask which city forms were invented indigenously, by their own inhabitants, and which were borrowed from earlier examples or, perhaps, imposed from outside on local rural populations. Technically, the question is one of **innovation** versus **diffusion**. Thus far, most experts agree that innovative primary urbanization, not borrowed or imposed from outside, occurred in seven places: five river valleys in the eastern hemisphere—Mesopotamia, the Nile, the Indus, the Huang He, and the Niger—and, in the western hemisphere, in Mexico and in the Andes Mountains. The birth of primary urbanization took place in these seven locations at very different times, with Mesopotamia the oldest, at about 3300 B.C.E., and the Niger the most recent, at about 400 C.E.

KEY TERMS

innovation The explanation that similar cultural traits, techniques, or objects found among different groups of people were invented independently rather than spread from one group to another.

diffusion The spread of ideas, objects, or traits from one culture to another.

In what way were cities new creations, different from villages?

2.1
2.2
2.3
2.4

In what way
were cities
new creations,
different from
villages?

Cities transform human life, as the physical form of the early cities shows vividly. Even today we can trace on the surface of the earth the 5,500-year-old designs of the first cities and the irrigation systems that supported them. Remnants of walls and fragments of monuments still rise from their sites. From under the surface archaeologists salvage artifacts: bricks; pottery; tools of wood, bone, stone, and metal; jewelry; and skeletons of citizens and slaves. The technology of the early cities included new means of transportation; we find the remains of wheeled vehicles and of sailboats. The earliest city dwellers advanced their skill in metallurgy, and products of their craftsmanship in copper, tin, and their alloys abound in the archaeological excavations. In recognition of these technological breakthroughs, we often call the era of the first cities the Bronze Age.

But cities are more than bricks and mortar, metal and artifacts. They require institutions for their larger scale of organization and administration. As society and economy became more complex, new class hierarchies emerged. Professional administrators, skilled artisans, long-distance traders, local merchants, and priests and kings enriched the diversity and sophistication of the growing cities. External relations with other cities required skilled negotiations, and a diplomatic corps emerged. Armies mobilized for defense and attack. In short, with the growth of the city the early state was also born, with its specialized organization, centralized rule, and powerful armies.

To keep track of business transactions and administrative orders, the proclamations of rulers and the rituals of priests, the legends of gods and the history of the city, new methods of record-keeping were developed. At first these were tokens, pictures, seals, personalized markings, and, in the Andes, *quipu*, knots made in special

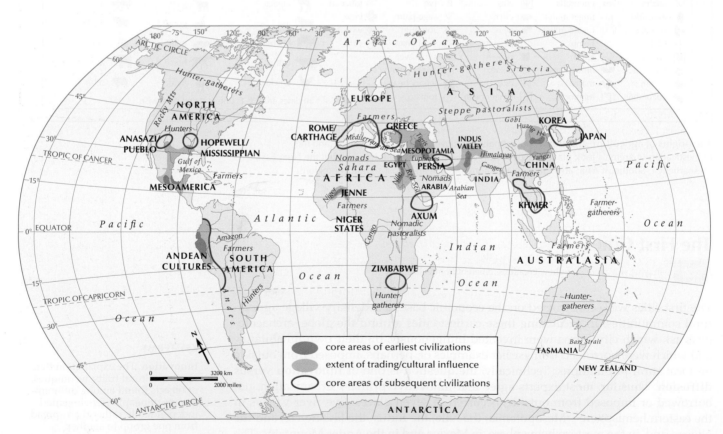

The spread of civilizations. The first civilizations developed where unique local climatic and soil conditions, favorable to settled agriculture, occurred, mostly in major river basins. With the development of an agricultural surplus came the growth of urban centers, trade, and population. Related civilizations tended to develop in regions adjacent to these heartlands, or along trade routes between them.

lengths of string. By about 3300 B.C.E., in Sumer, which is geographically equivalent to today's southern Iraq, the world's first system of writing had evolved. This was one of the most revolutionary inventions in human history. The prestigious occupation of scribe was born, and schoolteachers soon followed.

📖 **Read** the **Document**: **Redefining Self—From Tribe to Village to City (1500 BCE)** on **MyHistoryLab**

Sumer: The Birth of the City

2.3   Who pioneered the world's first urban revolution and how did it change human life?

A people called the Sumerians pioneered the world's first urban revolution in Mesopotamia, literally "between the rivers"—that is, the region between the Tigris and Euphrates rivers, approximately modern Iraq. They migrated into southern Mesopotamia about 4000 B.C.E., perhaps from around the Caspian Sea, but no one knows for sure. They faced uncertain odds. While the area between the Tigris and Euphrates became known as the Fertile Crescent for its high agricultural productivity, high temperatures and unpredictable floods constantly challenged the Sumerians. To succeed in building cities in the region, peoples had to construct irrigation ditches and intricate canals.

The Sumerians were not the first to inhabit this land. Archaeological excavation of pottery shows the earlier presence in Mesopotamia of the Ubaidians, a people who spoke the Semitic languages of northern Africa and the Middle East, and spread throughout Mesopotamia from south to north, from about 5300 B.C.E. to about 4000 B.C.E.. The Ubaidians drained marshes, developed an early irrigation system, domesticated plants and animals, and settled into agricultural villages, which show marks of social hierarchy. The Ubaidian village societies came to an end about 3800 B.C.E., apparently because the water levels of the Mesopotamian rivers and lakes dropped, and the land became too arid for farming.

Several centuries later, the Sumerians began to dominate the region, supplanting the Semitic-speaking populations. They dug better canals for irrigation, improved roads, and expanded urban developments. For a millennium, from 3300 B.C.E. until 2350 B.C.E., the Sumerians lived in warring city-states—Kish, Uruk, Ur, Nippur, Lagash, Umma, and dozens of smaller ones. Each of these city-states included a central city with a temple, and the agricultural region surrounding it. The city controlled and protected the fields of grain, orchards, and land for livestock, which, in turn, provided enough food to support the cities' growing populations.

With the city-states constantly at war with one another, their leaders began to think in terms of conquering others to create large empires. In c. 2350 B.C.E., Sargon, king of the city of Akkad, conquered the Sumerian cities one by one, allowing the Semitic-speaking Akkadians to overshadow the Sumerians. Calling himself the "king of Sumer and Akkad," Sargon was the first to unite the city-states under a single, powerful ruler. After some 200 years under Akkadian rule, the Mesopotamian city-states regained their independence under the third dynasty of Ur (2112–2004 B.C.E.), but they resumed their inter-urban warfare, which weakened them. Eventually, Hammurabi (1792–1750 B.C.E.), king of "Old Babylonia," launched a series of aggressive military campaigns. He extended his control over much of Mesopotamia, including Sumer and Akkad, and Sumerian influence

Stone tower and wall, Jericho, c. 8000 B.C.E. Before Sumer, a Neolithic community based at Jericho in the Jordan valley, Palestine, was the first to develop cereals of a fully domesticated type. In 8000 B.C.E. these farmers, keen to secure their settlement in the arid environment, constructed a stone perimeter wall 10 feet thick that was strengthened at one point by a circular stone tower more than 30 feet high. This wall is one of the earliest such defenses known.

How did the first cities in Mesopotamia differ from earlier villages?

Map of Nippur, 1500 B.C.E. This plan of Nippur, the ancient cultural center of Sumer, is the oldest known city map. Inscribed in a well-preserved clay tablet, 8¼ by 7 inches in size, the map is drawn accurately to scale and shows several of the city's key temples and buildings, its central park, its rivers and canals, and especially its walls and gates. The script is mostly Sumerian with a few words of Akkadian, the language of the Semitic people who eventually conquered the Sumerians. (Hilprecht Collection, Friedrich-Schiller University, Jena)

waned. The cities they had built died out, having fought one another to exhaustion. A series of foreign powers—Hittites, Assyrians, Babylonians again, Achaemenid Persians, and Greeks under Alexander the Great—variously conquered and controlled Mesopotamia. The Sumerian culture lived on, however, assimilated into their conquerors' literature, philosophy, religion, law, and patterns of urbanization.

View the **Map**: **The Ancient Near East** on **MyHistoryLab**

View the **Closer Look**: **A Board Game from Ancient Sumer** on **MyHistoryLab**

The Growth of the City-state

2.4   How did the first cities in Mesopotamia differ from earlier villages?

What were the characteristics of the urban revolution in Mesopotamia? How did its cities differ from the earlier villages? The most obvious feature was that the scale of the city-state—its physical size, population, and territorial control—was much greater than that of the village.

The Neolithic village housed a few dozen or a few hundred residents on a few acres. The largest Neolithic site in the Near East, Çatal Hüyük in Anatolia, grew by 5500 B.C.E. to occupy slightly more than 30 acres. It became a town. By comparison,

How did the
first cities in
Mesopotamia
differ from earlier
villages?

SUMER: KEY EVENTS AND PEOPLE

c. 3300 B.C.E.	Sumerians invent writing.
c. 3000	Sumerians become dominant power in southern Mesopotamia.
c. 2800–2340	Sumerian city-states: early dynastic period sees spread of Mesopotamian culture to the north.
c. 2350	Sargon captures Sumer and establishes Semitic dynasty at Akkad, the new capital.
c. 2112–2004	Third dynasty of Ur.
c. 1900	Ammorites at Babylon.
1792–1750	Reign of Hammurabi; Babylon is the new capital of Mesopotamia.
c. 1600	Invasion by Hittites and Kassites, destroying Hammurabi's dynasty.

the first cities of Mesopotamia were ten times larger, accommodating about 5,000 people.

Over time, the larger cities reached populations of 35,000–40,000 and covered more than 1,000 acres or 1½ square miles. The major cities were walled. The ramparts of Uruk (modern Warka, Biblical Erech), the city of the king-god-hero Gilgamesh, stretched to a circumference of 6 miles, engirdling a population of 50,000 by 2700 B.C.E. By 2500 B.C.E., the region of Sumer held 500,000 people, four-fifths of them in its cities and villages! Urbanism in Sumer became a way of life.

To support these growing urban populations, the range of control of the Sumerian cities over the surrounding countryside, and its agricultural and raw material resources, continued to expand. For example, the total sway of Lagash, one of the major cities, probably extended over 1,200 square miles. The king, priests, and private citizens controlled the fields of this area.

Networks of irrigation canals supported agriculture in this arid region and expanded Sumerian control over the land and its productivity. Irrigation permitted settlement to extend southward to central Mesopotamia, where cities would later emerge about 3300 B.C.E. The construction and maintenance of the canals required larger gangs of workers than the work teams that were based on family and clan alone. Loyalties that had been limited to blood relatives now extended beyond kinship to civic identity. Through the organizing of these public works projects, a sense of citizenship, based on a shared space rather than on blood kinship, was born. It was enshrined in legal principles that made geographical residence the basis of citizenship. These new loyalties and laws marked the beginning of city life.

Organizing the canal systems required more powerful leaders than villages had known. At first, this leadership appears to have been exercised by councils of respected elders, who worked closely with religious leaders. In times of crisis, especially during warfare with other cities, the council appointed a temporary single leader, but after about 2800 B.C.E., these men began to assume the position of hereditary kings and to rule in conjunction with temple priests. Political power and organization were both centralized and sanctified. Thus was the **state** born and consolidated.

Religion: The Priesthood and the City

Considerable power rested with the priests of the many deities of Sumer, because residents believed that survival in the harsh environment of ancient Mesopotamia depended partly on the will of the gods. In contrast to modern patterns, in which

KEY TERM

state Several definitions; here used for the total political organization of a group of people controlling their own territory.

How did the first cities in Mesopotamia differ from earlier villages?

the countryside is often considered more sacred and the city more secular, in ancient times the authority of the temple community vested enormous religious prestige and power in the city, and urban ritual practice was more fully elaborated than was its rural counterpart.

To consolidate their temporal and supernatural influences, the city priests built great temples, called **ziggurats**. Found throughout the region, ziggurats were a form of stepped temple built on a square or rectangular platform of small, locally produced sunbaked bricks. The baked bricks were covered by glazed bricks, which may have had religious significance. A small sanctuary rested atop the structure, which could reach as many as ten stories high. The ziggurat lacked internal chambers, and worshipers probably reached the sanctuary via external ramps. The walls themselves were more than seven feet thick to support the weight of the massive edifice. (Ziggurats are probably the model for the Bible's Tower of Babel, which was depicted as a challenge to the power of the God Jehovah.) The ziggurats dominated the fields that the priests controlled and farmed, rented out, or turned over to their servants and favorites. As their power increased, the priests built the ziggurats ever taller and more massive. From within these vast temple complexes, they controlled huge retinues, including artisans and administrators, and retained gangs of field workers to farm the temple's estates. Temples employed and fed multitudes. The chief temple in the city of Lagash in Mesopotamia, for example, provided daily food and drink (ale) to some 1,200 people by about 3000 B.C.E. The leading temples became virtual cities within cities.

Rituals, especially those of the priests and kings, suggest further the significance of religious thought in the minds of Sumerians. On New Year's Day, for example, the king of Ur in Sumer proceeded to the top of the city's major ziggurat, where he was symbolically married to the goddess of fertility, Inanna. The entire population witnessed this affirmation of his divinity.

Royal burials also asserted the divinity and authority of the king. Royal tombs were elegant. Their arches, vaults, and domes, suggesting new levels of architectural

KEY TERM

ziggurat A temple tower of ancient Mesopotamia, constructed of square or rectangular terraces of diminishing size, usually with a shrine on top built of blue enamel bricks, the color of the sky.

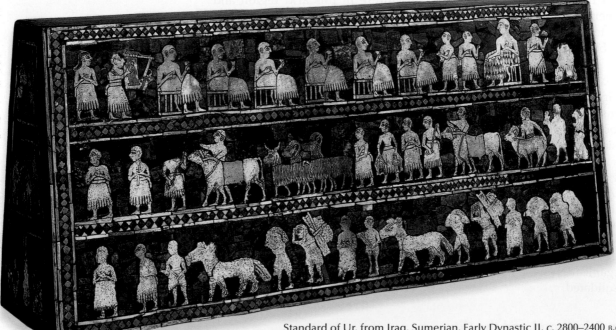

Standard of Ur, from Iraq. Sumerian, Early Dynastic II, *c.* 2800–2400 B.C.E. In Sumer the city-state was created as strong kings came to rule over walled cities and the surrounding countryside. This banqueting scene, found in a tomb in the royal cemetery at Ur, shows the court drinking the health of the king. The boxlike "standard" is thought to have rested on top of a long pole during festive processions. (British Museum, London)

skill, were built of brick and stone, and many of the funeral objects interred with the dead were of gold and silver. As in the other ancient civilizations we shall encounter in later chapters, some of the royal dead were accompanied by attendants who might have been sacrificed for the purpose and were buried nearby. They, too, were adorned with jewelry of gold and silver. The British archaeologist Sir Leonard Woolley (1880–1960) described the death pit adjacent to the royal burial place in Ur, which he excavated in the 1920s:

> Six men servants carrying knives or axes lay near the entrance lined up against the wall; in front of them stood a great copper basin, and by it were the bodies of four women harpists, one with her hands still on the strings of her instrument. Over the rest of the pit's area there lay in ordered rows the bodies of sixty-four ladies of the court. All of them wore some sort of ceremonial dress … Clearly these people were not wretched slaves killed as oxen might be killed, but persons held in honor, wearing their robes of office, and coming, one hopes, voluntarily to a rite which would in their belief be but a passing from one world to another, from the service of a god on earth to that of the same god in another place. (pp. 70–72)

In contrast to these elaborate royal burials, most common people were buried in small brick vaults in basement chambers of their own houses, and some were interred in cemeteries outside the city walls.

Occupational Specialization and Class Structure

The priests and the political-military rulers were only the most powerful of the new classes of specialists that emerged in the complex, large cities. Managers, surveyors,

Mesopotamian trade, c. 2000 B.C.E. The Sumerian trading network, revealed by the wide range of valuable and exotic materials used by Mesopotamian craftsmen, was both extensive and sophisticated, drawing on resources often well over 2,000 miles distant. Egyptian tomb paintings show Semitic merchants with donkey caravans, while some of the earliest writing is found on Sumerian clay tablets recording commercial transactions.

How did the
first cities in
Mesopotamia
differ from earlier
villages?

artisans, astronomers, brewers, warriors, traders, and scribes—all in addition to the farmers working their own fields and those of the temples and landowners—gave the cities a far more sophisticated hierarchical class structure than villages possessed.

Arts and Invention. Creativity flourished. Artisans crafted works of art in terra cotta, copper, clay, and colors surpassing village standards in their beauty and complexity. Cylinder seals (small cylinders of stone engraved with designs, for stamping clay tablets and sealing jars) became a common form of practical art in Sumer and spread as far as Anatolia and Greece. Astronomers established an accurate calendar based on lunar months that enabled them to predict the onset of seasons and to prepare properly for each year's planting and harvesting. Musicians created, designed, and played the lyre and composed and chanted songs, often dedicated to gods. Designers and architects, supervising armies of workers, built the canals of the countryside and the monuments of the cities.

Engraved cylinder seal (left) and impression (right). Seals were first used as signatures before the invention of writing. The cylinders produce continuous patterns that are repetitive, but the figures themselves are remarkably naturalistic.

Sumerians apparently invented the first wheels: the potter's wheel for ceramics and wagon wheels for transportation. They dramatically improved the plow, learning how to harness it to oxen. Metallurgists, smelting their new alloy of copper and tin, ushered in the Bronze Age. From the new metal they fashioned tips for the plow and an array of new tools: hoes, axes, chisels, knives, and saws. They turned their attention to weapons and produced lance points and arrowheads, swords, daggers, and harpoons. They made bronze vessels and containers, as well as smaller items such as nails, pins, rings, and mirrors.

Trade and Markets: Wheeled Cart and Sailboat. Trade was central to urban life. Sumerian traders carried merchandise by land, river, and sea, in the world's first wheeled carts and sailboats, as well as by donkey caravan. Rich in agricultural commodities and artisan production but poor in raw materials, Sumerians traded with the inhabitants of hilly areas to the north for wood, stone, and metal. They sailed into the Persian Gulf to find copper and tin, and continued along the Arabian Sea coast as far east as the Indus valley for ivory and ceramics. They traveled east overland through the passes of the Zagros Mountains to bring back carnelian beads from Elam. Shells from the Mediterranean coast that have been found in Sumer indicate trade westward, probably overland, as well.

How did the first cities in Mesopotamia differ from earlier villages?

Lady Pu-abi's headdress. The splendor of this gold ornament, discovered in the 1920s in the royal burial place of Ur, reflects the wealth of this Mesopotamian urban society, the skill of its craftsmen, the hierarchy of its people, and the anticipation of some form of future life. (University of Pennsylvania Museum)

In the city marketplace, merchants sold locally produced foodstuffs, including vegetables, onions, lentils and beans, more than fifty varieties of fish taken from the Tigris and Euphrates rivers, milk, cheese, butter, yogurt, dates, meat—mostly mutton—and ale. In vats in their homes, women, especially, brewed up to 40 percent of the barley and wheat harvest into ale for home use and for sale. For taste, effect, and storage purposes the Sumerians preferred ale to grain. (Hops had not yet been introduced to enable the processing of ale into beer.)

Thus, from king and priest through professionals, artisans, craftsmen, farmers, and laborers, specialization and division of labor and a hierarchical class structure marked the city's social and economic life as far more complex than that of the smaller, simpler village.

He-Goat and Flowering Tree. Offering stand for fertility god. Sumerian, from Ur, c. 2500 B.C.E. This offering stand was created with a magical as well as a functional purpose in mind, being intended to work as a fertility charm too. The goat, an ancient symbol of male sexuality, is shown rearing up against a flowering tree, emblem of nature's fecundity. (British Museum, London)

How did the first cities in Mesopotamia differ from earlier villages?

Monumental Architecture and Adornment

For the Sumerians, the size and elegance of their cities and monuments were a source of great pride. The earliest introduction to Gilgamesh, hero of the greatest surviving Sumerian epic, proclaims his excellence as city builder: "In Uruk he built walls, a great rampart, and the temple of blessed Eanna for the god of the firmament Anu, and for Ishtar the goddess of love. Look at it still today: the outer wall where the cornice runs, it shines with the brilliance of copper; and the inner wall, it has no equal."

Artwork adorned the city, especially the temple precincts. Sculptures, murals, mosaics, and especially stone bas-reliefs not only provided beauty and elegance, but also represented pictorially key scenes in the history of the cities and their rulers. The magnificence of this monumental architecture and art defined the image of the city, impressing residents and giving warning to enemies.

Writing

The Sumerians invented writing, thereby altering human history. Indeed historians so value writing as a means of communication and of recording events that they often call all the events prior to the invention of writing **prehistory**. For these historians, only when events are recorded in writing can they be called history, since without writing we cannot know directly what people thought and said.

The earliest Sumerian scribes first used writing, beginning about 3300 B.C.E., for business purposes, to note the contents of commercial packages, the names of their owners, and to catalog this information into lists. They employed styluses made of bone or of hollow reed stems to incise **pictograms**, picture representations of the objects of their writing, onto clay tablets. By 3000 B.C.E. they were representing the key features of the pictures in wedge-shaped signs that we call **cuneiform**. Some cuneiform signs represented whole words, but others represented individual phonetic sounds based on words.

KEY TERMS

prehistory Everything that occurred before the invention of writing.

pictogram (alternative: pictograph) A pictorial symbol or sign representing an object or concept.

cuneiform A writing system in use in the ancient Near East from around the end of the fourth millennium to the first century B.C.E. The earliest examples are in Sumerian. The name derives from the wedge-shaped marks (Latin: *cuneus*, a wedge) made by pressing the slanted edge of a stylus into soft clay.

THE EVOLUTION OF WRITING

Pictographic *c.* 3000 B.C.E.										
Early cuneiform representation *c.* 2400 B.C.E.										
Late Assyrian *c.* 650 B.C.E.										
Sumerian phonetic equivalent and meaning	k eat	mŭsen bird	sag head	gu ox	še barley	ud day	sŭ hand	ku fish	a water	b cow

The origins of writing. Writing was invented in west Asia in the fourth millennium B.C.E. and developed from the need to keep a record of business transactions. From the wedge-shaped marks formed by a hollow-shaped reed, or stylus, cuneiform script evolved gradually. In this pictographic script, stylized drawings are used to represent words: each pictograph stands for a syllable, and abstract concepts are conveyed by using concrete notions that are close in meaning (e.g. "open mouth" for "eat").

As the cuneiform became more sophisticated, so too did the subject matter, and by c. 2400 B.C.E. Sumerian writing began to take over the oral tradition, recording tales of heroes, proclaiming political and military victories, singing the poetry of lovers, praising the glories of gods, and lamenting the fall of cities. Written literature took form and flourished. Archaeologists have excavated tens of thousands of Sumerian clay tablets, containing literature as well as business notations, and transferred them to research institutions around the world.

Many later peoples in the region—Elamites, Babylonians, Assyrians, and Akkadians—adopted cuneiform to write their own languages. The conquests of Alexander the Great in the fourth century B.C.E., however, helped to introduce alphabetic writing—of the Aramaic language—and cuneiform died out. The last known cuneiform text was written in 75 C.E.

Although some of the earliest town dwellers in other parts of the world—the settlers of the Niger valley of West Africa, the Olmec and Teotihuacános of Mesoamerica, and the Chavin and Inca of the Andes Mountains of South America—achieved urban form and size without the use of any form of writing, most of the earliest cities did invent some system of recording. As in Sumer, these systems moved "from token to tablet"— that is, from a simple recording of business transactions and

Clay tablet with cuneiform, Jemdet Nasr, Iraq, 3000 B.C.E. This example of writing from Mesopotamia is among the earliest known anywhere in the world. (British Museum, London)

HOW DO WE KNOW?

Decoding Sumerian Writing

The Sumerians wrote no historical interpretive accounts of their accomplishments, but at least five kinds of written material help us to reconstruct their past. King lists give us not only the names and dates of many of the principal kings of the major cities, but also some chronology of their continuing warfare. Royal correspondence with officials illuminates relations with neighbors. Epics transmit Sumerian values and their sense of the heroic, and lamentations recount the continuing devastation wrought by their inter-city religious warfare. Finally, legal codes suggest the principles and hierarchies of their everyday life.

Despite Sumerian accomplishments, historians lost access to the Sumerians and their literature for at least 2,000 years. The locations of even the grandest of the historic sites passed from memory. Biblical scholars, however, kept alive an interest in the region, searching for locations mentioned in Scripture, and British officials arriving at the British East India Company's outpost in Baghdad revived this interest. They began to investigate the ruins of Babylon and its artifacts, and they dispatched their finds, including written tablets, back to London. Still, no one knew what the wedge-shaped symbols meant.

Then, in the 1830s and 1840s, at Behistun, near Kermanshah in Persia, a British army officer began to copy a huge inscription that had been incised into a 300-foot-high cliff to announce the military victories of the Persian king Darius I about 500 B.C.E. The officer, H.C. Rawlinson, had a scaffolding constructed so that he could reach the ancient writing, sometimes while suspended from a rope 300 feet above the surface of the earth. Rawlinson and other scholars found that the inscription actually included

three scripts that represented different but related languages: Old Persian, Babylonian, and Elamite. The Old Persian and Elamite were written in cuneiform scripts; the Babylonian in alphabetic script. The stone had probably been prepared to publicize Darius's triumphs in three of the major languages of his empire. The three inscriptions were translations of one another, enabling linguists who could already read the alphabetic script to crack the cuneiform—although it took several generations before scholars completed this task.

Later archaeological digs in Mesopotamia uncovered tens of thousands of tablets and fragments. One especially rich cache was the royal library of the Assyrian king Ashurbanipal (r. 668–627 B.C.E.) at Nineveh. Through texts and digs, scholars resurrected the Sumerian economy, belief systems, and culture. Most of the texts deal with practical, everyday business transactions and administration. One contains the first known recipe for the ale that Sumerians enjoyed so much. Others recorded the world's first written literature.

- Why do you think the ancient language and literature of Sumer, like those of Egypt, were lost for 2,000 years?
- How might the written records, once deciphered, complement the archaeological record known from excavations?
- How do the five kinds of record discovered in Sumerian writing differ from "historical interpretive accounts"? How do they contribute to an understanding of history even though they themselves may not be "historical interpretive accounts"?

2.1

2.2

2.3

2.4 How did the first cities in Mesopotamia differ from earlier villages?

The stela of vultures. This limestone tablet, or stela (sometimes spelt stele), depicts in **bas-relief** Lagash's victory over Umma, in about 2450 B.C.E. Some 3,600 of the enemy were slaughtered by King Eannatum of Lagash and his soldiers, who are seen here marching into battle. (Louvre, Paris)

KEY TERM

bas-relief In sculpture, relief is a term for any work in which the forms stand out from the background. In bas- (or low) relief, the design projects only slightly from the background and the outlines are not undercut.

ideogram (alternative: ideograph) A character or figure in a writing system in which the idea of a thing is represented rather than its name. Languages such as Chinese use ideograms.

registration of ownership through designated tokens, often marked with individual notations, through picture writing, to **ideograms**, and finally to phonetic, alphabetical writing.

Not all civilizations followed this sequence. In China, for example, the first writing seems to have been symbols inscribed on oracle bones. They seem to have been an attempt to divine the future. To this day Chinese writing is still ideographic and maintains a visible connection to its most ancient forms. The Chavin and Inca developed a form of recording transactions and chronology through knots made in strings, called *quipu*, but they did not develop an independent system of writing. Nor did the people of the Niger valley.

Writing facilitated communication, commerce, administration, religious ritual, and, later, the recording and transmission of literature. It enabled society to enlarge to a scale never seen before, and it encouraged a self-consciousness and historical analysis previously unknown. It created a "knowledge industry," transmitted through systems of formal education and headed by scribes. By 2500 B.C.E., Sumerians had apparently established a number of schools where students could master the skill of writing. In a sense, this textbook had its origins in Sumer some 5,000 years ago.

Achievements in Literature and Law

Much of what we know about the ancient Sumerian imagination and world vision comes from its literary works. *The Epic of Gilgamesh*, the most famous of the remaining literature, weaves together a series of tales about the hero Gilgamesh. Its most complete version comes from various shorter stories found in the library at Nineveh from about 750 B.C.E., but earlier fragments in the Sumerian excavations corroborate the antiquity of the core legends going back to the time when Gilgamesh ruled Uruk, about 2600 B.C.E.

2.1

2.2

2.3

2.4

How did the
first cities in
Mesopotamia
differ from earlier
villages?

SOURCE

The Epic of Gilgamesh

Like all epics, *Gilgamesh* recounts the deeds of a larger-than-life hero. The Sumerian epic introduces the first hero in written literature:

> I will proclaim to the world the deeds of Gilgamesh. This was the man to whom all things were known; this was the king who knew the countries of the world. He was wise, he saw mysteries and knew secret things. … When the gods created Gilgamesh they gave him a perfect body. Shamash the glorious sun endowed him with beauty, Adad the god of the storm endowed him with courage, the great gods made his beauty perfect, surpassing all others, terrifying like a great wild bull. Two-thirds they made him god and one-third man.

Aruru, the goddess of Uruk, who had also created Gilgamesh, created Enkidu, a forest dweller, who became Gilgamesh's friend and played a central role in the epic. *Gilgamesh* highlights the suggestive myth of Enkidu's seduction by an urban harlot who lures him from the wilderness to the pleasures of the city as well as to his wrestling match with Gilgamesh. The implication is that sexuality is experienced very differently in the city—more intensely and in more sophisticated fashion—than in the countryside. So, too, is friendship:

> The harlot and the trapper sat facing each other and waited for the game to come … on the third day the herds came; they came down to drink and Enkidu was with them … The trapper spoke to her: "There he is. Now, woman, make your breasts bare, have no shame, do not delay but welcome his love. Let him see you naked, let him possess your body. When he comes near uncover yourself and lie with him; teach him, the savage man, your woman's art, for when he murmurs love to you the wild beasts that shared his life in the hills will reject him." She was not afraid to take him, she made herself naked and welcomed his eagerness; as he lay on her murmuring love she taught him the woman's art.
>
> For six days and seven nights they lay together, for Enkidu had forgotten his home in the hills; but when he was satisfied he went back to the wild beasts. Then, when the gazelle saw him, they fled. Enkidu would have followed, but his body was bound as though with a cord, his knees gave way when he started to run, his swiftness was gone. And now the wild

creatures had all fled away; Enkidu was grown weak, for wisdom was in him, and the thoughts of a man were in his heart. So he returned and sat down at the woman's feet, and listened intently to what she said. "You are wise, Enkidu, and now you have become like a god. Why do you want to run wild with the beasts in the hills? Come with me. I will take you to the strong-walled Uruk, to the blessed temple of Ishtar and of Anu, of love and of heaven: there Gilgamesh lives, who is very strong, and like a wild bull he lords it over men." When she had spoken Enkidu was pleased; he longed for a comrade, for one who would understand his heart. "Come, woman, and take me to that holy temple, to the house of Anu and of Ishtar, and to the place where Gilgamesh lords it over the people. I will challenge him boldly."

With Enkidu's first encounter with Gilgamesh in the city, the epic also recounts the first example of male bonding, forged through a test of physical strength. When Gilgamesh and Enkidu first meet, they engage in a mighty wrestling match:

> They broke the doorposts and the walls shook, they snorted like bulls locked together. They shattered the doorposts and the walls shook. Gilgamesh bent his knee with his foot planted on the ground and with a turn Enkidu was thrown. Then immediately his fury died … So Enkidu and Gilgamesh embraced and their friendship was sealed.

The epic also unveils the hero's driving ambition for fame and glory, both for himself and for his city, as Gilgamesh courageously chooses to enter the strongholds of Humbaba, guardian of the forest, and, with Enkidu, to fight him.

> I will go to the country where the cedar is cut. I will set up my name where the names of famous men are written; and where no man's name is written I will raise a monument to the gods … I, Gilgamesh, go to see that creature of whom such things are spoken, the rumor of whose name fills the world. I will conquer him in his cedar wood and show the strength of the sons of Uruk; all the world shall know of it.

The importance of metallurgy and metals, especially for weapons, is highlighted:

(continued)

SOURCE (continued)

The Epic of Gilgamesh

[Gilgamesh] went to the forge and said, "I will give orders to the armorers: they shall cast us our weapons while we watch them." So they gave orders to the armorers and the craftsmen sat down in conference. They went into the groves of the plain and cut willow and box-wood; they cast for them axes of nine score pounds, and great swords they cast with blades of six score pounds each one, with pommels and hilts of thirty pounds. They cast for Gilgamesh the axe "Might of Heroes" and the bow of Anshan; and Gilgamesh was armed and Enkidu; and the weight of the arms they carried was thirty score pounds.

The victory of Gilgamesh and Enkidu over Humbaba parallels the massive assault by urbanites on the natural resources of the world, turning the products of nature into objects of trade and commerce, and using them to build cities.

Now the mountains were moved and all the hills, for the guardian of the forest was killed. They attacked the cedars, the seven splendors of Humbaba were extinguished. So they pressed on into the forest … and while Gilgamesh felled the first of the trees of the forest Enkidu cleared their roots as far as the banks of Euphrates.

Lower Mesopotamia has no stone, wood, or metal. To obtain these raw materials, Sumerians had to send parties over long distances to quarry, cut, and dig; to trade; and to conquer. The mixed responses of the gods to the murder of Humbaba suggest the deep ambivalence of the Sumerians to their own increasing power:

[Gilgamesh and Enkidu] set [the corpse of] Humbaba before the gods, before Enlil; they kissed the ground and dropped the shroud and set the head before him. When he saw the head of Humbaba, Enlil raged at them, "Why did you do this thing? From henceforth may the fire be on your faces, may it eat the bread that you eat, may it drink where you drink."

The Epic of Gilgamesh presents a world of many gods before whom humans are passive and frightened subjects. Gilgamesh, however, defers neither to human nor to god. Devastated by the death of his closest friend, Enkidu, he sets off to the underworld in search of eternal life. Along the way he encounters the Sumerian prototype of Noah. This man, Utnapishtim, tells him of a flood that destroyed all human life except his family. A god who counseled him to build a boat had saved them. In the bleak underworld of the dead, Gilgamesh obtains a plant that will give eternal youth, but on his return voyage a snake rises from the water and snatches it from him. Gilgamesh recognizes a fundamental truth: Misery and sorrow are unavoidable parts of human life. Resigned to his losses, Gilgamesh returns to Uruk. Finally, he dies at a ripe old age, honored and mourned by his fellow citizens.

A second form of written document that marks the evolution to a more complex society is the legal code. Archaeologists discovered at Ur fragments of a legal code that dates to the twenty-first century B.C.E., and legal systems must have existed even before this. Legal systems remained crucial for all Mesopotamian urban societies. The post-Sumerian code of the Babylonian King Hammurabi, formulated *c.* 1750 B.C.E. (but rediscovered only in 1901–02), seems to have been based on the earlier concepts.

The First Cities:
What Difference Do They Make?

We do know that early cities facilitated some of the accomplishments that people then and now considered vitally important: increases in human population (a questionable asset under today's conditions, but not then); economic growth; effective organization for common tasks; creative breakthroughs in technology, art, and, perhaps most significantly, in writing, record-keeping, and literature; the inauguration of a rule of law; and the formation of a non-kin-based community with a sense of purpose and humanity.

SOURCE

The Code of Hammurabi

As states grew larger, formal, written law codes replaced the customs and traditions of the farming villages. By the time of his death, around 1750 B.C.E., the Babylonian ruler Hammurabi had conquered Mesopotamia, uniting its warring city-states under his rule. To reinforce that unity he carried out many works of public service and set forth in the name of Shamash, the sun god, a code of laws that covered many aspects of daily life and business. The prologue set forth noble goals: "To make justice appear in the land, to destroy the evil and the wicked that the strong might not oppress the weak ... to give justice to the orphan and the widow."

The code provides a marvelous insight into the problems and nature of urban life at the time. It provides a detailed insight into property rights and urban crime, as well as social and gender divisions in the society. Finally, it gives students and scholars some idea of how justice was perceived in Hammurabi's world. The code is a list of 282 laws; only some of them are reproduced here. In the original list, they are not particularly organized; we have reorganized some of them here into three categories.

Property

Property laws incorporated laws of consumer protection for house buyers, boat renters, and contractors for services. In one case, a brutal punishment for faulty workmanship indicates that common people, too, were viewed as commodities. The sins of the fathers may be taken out on the children. The specific laws included:

- If [the collapse of a building] has caused the death of a son of the owner of the house, they shall put the son of that builder to death.
- If any one steal the property of a temple or of the court, he shall be put to death, and also the one who receives the stolen thing from him shall be put to death.

Urban Crime

Many laws provided for punishment for robbery and for personal injuries. Many

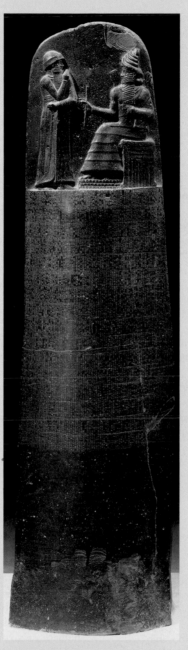

Stela of Hammurabi, from Susa, Iran, c. 1760 B.C.E. Hammurabi, the great king of Babylon, is the first known ruler to have created a detailed legal code; other societies with unknown rulers developed much earlier codes. On this commemorative stone slab, Hammurabi, standing, is receiving the Babylonian laws from the sun god Shamash. The laws themselves are inscribed below on the stela. (Louvre, Paris)

of the latter varied according to the social class of the person inflicting the injury as well as of the person suffering the injury:

- If anyone is committing a robbery and is caught, then he shall be put to death.
- If a gentleman has destroyed the eye of a member of the aristocracy, they shall destroy his eye.
- If he has broken another gentleman's bone, they shall break his bone.
- If he has destroyed the eye of a commoner or broken the bone of a commoner, he shall pay one mina of silver.
- If he has destroyed the eye of a gentleman's slave or broken the bone of a gentleman's slave, he shall pay one half his value.

Gender in Ancient Babylonia

Numerous laws governed marriage, bride-price, dowry, adultery, and incest. Although women did own the dowries given them, their rights of ownership were limited. Marriage is presented in large part as a commercial transaction, in which the groom's family pays a bride-price to the bride's father, while the bride's father gives her a dowry. Childlessness is grounds for divorce, but the husband must return his wife's dowry. Behavioral restraints in marriage are unequal: if the husband "has been going out and disparaging her greatly," the wife may leave, taking her dowry; if the wife is "a gadabout, thus neglecting her house [and] humiliating her husband," he may have her drowned.

- If a woman quarrels with her husband, and says: "You are not congenial to me," the reasons for her prejudice must be presented. If she is guiltless, and there is not fault on her part, but he leaves and neglects her, then no guilt attaches to this woman, she shall take her dowry and go back to her father's house.
- If she is not innocent, but leaves her husband, and ruins her house, neglecting her husband, this woman shall be cast into the water.

📖 **Read** the **Document**: "Hammurabi's Law Code" (1700s BCE) on **MyHistoryLab**

HOW DO WE KNOW?

Some Modern Critiques of Early Urbanization

Sumer's city-states had many accomplishments to their credit, but some historians have pointed out that their civilization came at the cost of increasing warfare, growing social inequality, and the oppression of women. These modern critiques reflect the importance of studying the past in order to understand the present more fully.

Politically, each of the major cities of Sumer was also a state, ruling over the contiguous agricultural areas and often in conflict with neighboring city-states. The artwork of the city-states often depicts royal armies, military expeditions, conquests, and a general appreciation, even an exaltation, of warfare. The fighting seems to have been frequent, and the main combatants were the largest of the city-states. Battles were fought hand-to-hand and also from donkey-drawn chariots.

The warfare was especially destructive because the kings and soldiers believed that they were upholding the honor of their gods. When cities are sacred, conflicts between them mean holy war, fights to the finish. The "Lamentation over the Destruction of Ur," which was addressed to Ningal, goddess of the Ekushnugal Temple, describes that city's utter destruction after the Elamites sacked it, exiled its ruler, and destroyed the temple c. 1950 B.C.E.:

> After your city had been destroyed, how now can you exist!
> After your house had been destroyed, how has your heart led you on!
> Your city has become a strange city; how now can you exist!
> Your house has become a house of tears, how has your heart led you on!
> Your city which has been made into ruins—you are no longer its mistress!
> Your righteous house which has been given over to the pickax—you no longer inhabit it,
> Your people have been led to slaughter—you are no longer their queen. (Kramer, p. 142)

Lewis Mumford, one of the most respected modern commentators on the history of cities, regarded this early union of power, religion, and continuous warfare as a permanent curse of urban life. "War," he wrote, "even when it is disguised by seemingly hardheaded economic demands, uniformly turns into a religious performance; nothing less than a wholesale ritual sacrifice." (p. 42)

The first Sumerian cities fostered division of labor into occupational categories. We have noted the roles of kings, priests, landowners, architects, scribes, long-distance traders, local merchants, artisans, cooks, farmers, soldiers, laborers—the whole panoply of occupational categories absent in villages but forming the backbone of a sophisticated urban economy and society. Priests and kings held great wealth and power and largely controlled the means of production, but it is not clear that they formed an exclusive category of "haves" versus "have nots." The spectrum seems to have been more varied, including a substantial group of middle classes. But there is, nevertheless, much evidence of the enormous power of the aristocracy.

At the bottom of the economic hierarchy were slaves. People entered slavery in four ways: some were captured in battle; some were sentenced to slavery as punishment for crimes; some sold themselves (or their family members) into slavery to cope with poverty and debt; and some were born into slavery. We have no record of the number or proportion of slaves in the general population of Sumer and its cities. The law codes' extensive regulations of slaves and slavery suggest, however, their widespread existence.

The socialist philosopher-historian Karl Marx argued In *The German Ideology* that the rise of cities brought about "the division of the population into two great classes." Marx's formulation was too stark, ignoring the broad range of classes in the city, but he does force us to think about the class structure in our own cities, including the relationship between rich and poor, and its implications for the health of society.

Finally, the transformation of society from a rural, egalitarian, kin base to an urban, hierarchical, territorial, class base may have provided the entering wedge for the subordination of women. Some women in Sumer had great power. Several seem to have held independent high administrative posts in major temples controlling large land holdings. The high status of Lady Pu-abi (c. 2500 B.C.E.) was revealed in her burial. She was adorned with gold (see illustration above) and buried with several other bodies, presumably those of servants, suggesting a woman of high rank, perhaps a queen. Shagshag, wife of King Uruinimgina (also known as Urukagina), c. 2300 B.C.E., held great power in the name of her husband.

Women in Sumer generally had certain basic rights, including the rights to hold property, engage in business, and serve as legal witness. Nevertheless, it is clear that women's legal rights were limited by their husbands. Even powerful women were often only pawns in the power struggles of men.

The feminist historian Gerda Lerner argues that before the evolution of city-states, with their warfare and hierarchical class structures, the status of women had been more equal to that of men. Kin groups had been the basic economic units of society, and women had had more power in these family groups than they did in the city-states that displaced them. Lerner claims that inequalities between men and women are not products of unchanging biological differences. Rather, the inequalities have been created by humans—and they can be altered by humans.

- What did Lewis Mumford learn about warfare from his study of ancient cities? How did this affect his view of modern warfare?
- What did Karl Marx learn about class relations from his study of ancient cities? How did this affect his view of class relationships in modern (nineteenth-century) cities?
- What did Gerda Lerner learn about gender relationships from studying ancient cities?

They did not always succeed, however. The city-states could not work out a system of government and regulation that would enable them to live in peace. At the same time powerful and vulnerable, oscillating between psalms of victory and lamentations of defeat, they seemed to fall into one of two painful alternatives: inter-state warfare or conquest by imperial rulers. Their shortcomings cost them dearly. As long as each political entity was a law unto itself—as were the city-states of Sumer, pre-Han China, classical Greece, medieval Europe, and India during much of its history—war was likely. This problem of warfare among competitive states persists to our own day, although the scale has escalated from the city-state to the nation-state.

The evolution of the large, complex city implies the evolution of a state capable of organizing and administering it. In aristocratic and monarchical Sumer, much depended on the disposition of the king. The legendary Gilgamesh ended his royal career devoted to, and honored by, his people, but it had begun differently. The epic tells us that in Gilgamesh's youth, "the men of Uruk muttered in their houses" about his faults:

> His arrogance has no bounds by day or night. No son is left with his father, for Gilgamesh takes them all, even the children … his lust leaves no virgin to her lover, neither the warrior's daughter nor the wife of the noble.

They realized that it should have been different—"The king should be a shepherd to his people"—but they apparently had to submit. The only recourse they saw was muttering in their houses and praying to their gods. They "tamed" the wild Enkidu and lured him to Uruk in hopes that he would befriend and "tame" Gilgamesh (see Source, above).

From the time of Sumer, the political questions, questions of how to organize and administer the city-state to achieve a good life, have been central to the process of urbanization. In modern times, scholars ask how well Sumer did, and many call attention to its shortcomings (see How Do We Know? box, opposite). They caution us to learn from the past so as not to repeat what they see as the mistakes of Sumer in our own cities: not to make warfare into a religious obligation; not to isolate the city from the countryside; not to establish oppressive class distinctions; not to institutionalize the patriarchal suppression of women.

Underlying these warnings, however, is yet another myth, the myth of the pre-urban agricultural village as an egalitarian, peaceful settlement well integrated into its natural surroundings. We do not know if this was so. Pre-urban villagers produced no written records, and their artifactual remains are thin, inconclusive, and subject to widely divergent interpretation. Scholars draw many of their conclusions concerning pre-urban life from observing isolated groups in today's world, such as the !Kung people (! implies a clicking sound) of the African Kalahari Desert of a generation ago. But here, too, interpretations vary, and are equally subject to debate.

THE EARLIEST URBAN SETTLEMENTS

3500 B.C.E.	Rise of Sumer, southern Mesopotamia.
3100	Emergence of Egyptian state; new capital at Memphis.
2500	Development of Mohenjo-Daro, urban civilization on the Indus plain.
1800	Urban growth after Shang dynasty established in northeast China.
1200	Formative period in Mesoamerica, marked by first shrine centers, especially the Olmec.
c. 400 B.C.E.	City-states in Mesoamerica and South America.
400 C.E.	Urbanization of Jenne-jeno, Mali, sub-Saharan Africa.

Sumer evolved in accord with the edicts of its kings and its priests. In the next two chapters, we shall examine the evolution of other primary cities and city-states around the world.

CHAPTER REVIEW

THE AGRICULTURAL VILLAGE

2.1 What was life like in the world's first agricultural villages?

The development of agriculture and the domestication of animals took place independently in different parts of the world, with the earliest agricultural villages forming in Mesopotamia's Fertile Crescent. There, people gathered wild grasses and eventually cultivated them. They domesticated animals, fashioned tools from stones, and began to make pottery and woven cloth. In other parts of the world, villages sometimes took on different forms.

THE FIRST CITIES

2.2 In what way were cities new creations, different from villages?

The first cities grew out of agricultural villages and developed in seven different regions of the world. The development of an agricultural surplus enabled the growth of urban centers with monumental architecture, social hierarchies, specialization of labor, trade, writing, and new organizational power that could be used in peace and war.

SUMER: THE BIRTH OF THE CITY

2.3 Who pioneered the world's first urban revolution and how did it change human life?

The Sumerian people gradually began to dominate Mesopotamia. They created dozens of warring city-states each with its own king, its own god(s), and its own powerful elites. Sargon, king of the Mesopotamian city of Akkad, first united these city-states under a single, powerful ruler, about 2350 B.C.E.

THE GROWTH OF THE CITY-STATE

2.4 How did the first cities in Mesopotamia differ from earlier villages?

Over time, the cities of the Fertile Crescent grew in size and population. Networks of irrigation canals supported agriculture and expanded productivity, requiring more workers and strong leadership. Powerful kings came to rule over walled cities and the surrounding countryside, and a sophisticated hierarchical class structure developed. Architecture and adornment, writing and literature grew, and a law code was introduced to give structure to this urbanizing world.

Suggested Readings

PRINCIPAL SOURCES

Adas, Michael, ed. *Agricultural and Pastoral Societies in Ancient and Classical History* (Philadelphia: Temple University Press, 2001). Excellent introductions to the history and historiography of this period. Especially useful are John A. Means, "Agricultural Origins in Global Perspective," pp. 36–70, and Sarah Shaver Hughes and Brady Hughes, "Women in Ancient Civilizations," pp. 116–50.

Diamond, Jared. *Guns, Germs, and Steel: The Fates of Human Societies* (New York: W.W. Norton, 1997). Now classic work on why some societies succeeded economically, while others did not. Fate seems determined by ecology; this argument is both a strength and a weakness of the book.

Fagan, Brian M. *People of the Earth: An Introduction to World Prehistory* (Upper Saddle River, NJ: Prentice Hall, 13th ed., 2010). Excellent general textbook introduction to prehistory.

Gilgamesh, The Epic of, trans. and ed. N.K. Sandars (Harmondsworth, Middlesex: Penguin Books, 1972). Very readable edition of the classic epic.

Kramer, Samuel Noah. *The Sumerians: Their History, Culture, and Character* (Chicago, IL: University of Chicago Press, 1963). A masterful, accessible summary by one of the greatest scholars in the field.

Kurlansky, Mark. *Salt: A World History* (New York: Random House, 2002). Lively history of salt as food, commodity, and object of struggle.

Lerner, Gerda. *The Creation of Patriarchy* (New York: Oxford University Press, 1986). Lerner brings a critical feminist perspective to studies of Sumer, although many scholars have criticized her scholarship here; her main field is American history.

Mithen, Steven. *After the Ice: A Global Human History, 20,000–5,000 B.C.* (Cambridge, MA: Harvard University Press, 2004). Travels the world, providing views of developments through the eyes of a mythical tourist, with clear analyses as provided by today's scholarship. Engaging and readable.

Ponting, Clive. *A New Green History of the Earth: The Environment and the Collapse of Great Civilizations* (New York: Penguin, 2007). An ecological history of the ancient world, arguing that most "improvements" in productivity actually harmed the ecology and ultimately backfired.

Pritchard, James B., ed. *Ancient Near Eastern Texts Relating to the Old Testament* (Princeton, NJ: Princeton University Press, 3rd ed. with supplement, 1969). Excellent compendium of primary source materials. Presentation is very scholarly and painstaking.

Reader, John. *Potato: A History of the Propitious Esculent* (New Haven, CT: Yale University Press, 2009). Scholarly and fascinating history of the potato and its global travels.

Roaf, Michael. *Cultural Atlas of Mesopotamia and the Ancient Near East* (New York: Facts on File, 1996). Another in the excellent Facts on File series, copiously supplied with maps and pictures as well as readable, scholarly, introductory text materials.

Trigger, Bruce. *Understanding Early Civilizations: A Comparative Study* (Cambridge: Cambridge University Press, 2003). Very scholarly. Stresses methods of comparative study, selection of parameters for study.

ADDITIONAL SOURCES

Aristotle. *Basic Works*, trans. and ed. Richard McKeon (New York: Random House, 1941). Aristotle's *Politics*, in particular, presents very early, very thoughtful concepts of urban governance.

Bairoch, Paul. *Cities and Economic Development: From the Dawn of History to the Present*, trans. Christopher Braider (Chicago, IL: University of Chicago Press, 1988). Comprehensive presentation of the importance of cities in economic history. Europe is the main focus.

Cohen, Mark. *The Food Crisis in Prehistory* (New Haven, CT: Yale University Press, 1977). Asks why people began to settle into farming and continue it.

Ehrenberg, Margaret. *Women in Prehistory* (Norman: University of Oklahoma Press, 1989). Fascinating mixture of data and speculation, from a feminist perspective.

Hudson, M., and B. Levine. *Privatization in the Ancient Near East and the Classical World* (Cambridge, MA: Peabody Museum of Archaeology and Ethnology, 1996). Papers from two conferences focusing on Hudson's view of the importance of private enterprise in the ancient world.

MacNeish, Richard. "The Origins of New World Civilization," *Scientific American*, (November 1964), pp. 29–37. Macneish looks at the agricultural origins. His analysis of the evolution of maize, under human guidance, is classic.

Marx, Karl. *Capital: A Critique of Political Economy*, trans. Ben Foulkes (New York: Vintage Books, 1977). Writing at the height of the Industrial Revolution in Western Europe, Marx explores the history of urbanization as part of his larger work.

Marx, Karl, and Friedrich Engels. *The German Ideology* (New York: International Publishers, 1939). Includes a critical examination of the capitalist city.

Mumford, Lewis. *The City in History* (New York: Harcourt, Brace and World, Inc., 1961). The master examines the history of all cities, urging his readers to see the importance of social life and community as the key to the good city.

Postgate, Nicholas. *The First Empires* (Oxford: Elsevier Phaidon, 1977). Comparative presentation of early city-states that preceded empires.

Sjoberg, Gideon. "The Origin and Evolution of Cities," *Scientific American* (September 1965), pp. 19–27. Sjoberg, a sociologist, stresses the differences in political life and technological sophistication between pre- and postindustrial cities in this general introduction.

Wheatley, Paul. *The Pivot of the Four Quarters* (Chicago, IL: Aldine Publishing Company, 1971). For this enormously learned geographer, early cities were primarily concerned with their relationship with the gods and the cosmos, as reflected in their structure and leadership.

Woolley, C. Leonard. *Excavations at Ur* (London: Ernest Benn, Ltd., 1954). One of the greatest of the excavators describes his expeditions and their results. Well illustrated and very accessible.

FILM

Guns, Germs, and Steel (2005; 1 hour). Jared Diamond's book represented in film. Excellent for classroom use in introducing early villages and agriculture. The presentation is in three parts of one hour each. The first one-hour part is excellent and germane to this chapter.

3 River Valley Civilizations

The Nile and the Indus

7000 B.C.E.–750 B.C.E.

The urban civilization of Mesopotamia was flanked by two other such civilizations: the Nile valley to the southwest and the Indus valley to the southeast. Scholarly opinion is divided as to whether these two cultures learned to build cities and states from the Mesopotamian example or invented them independently. Whatever the source of inspiration, the peoples of these three river valleys created separate and distinct patterns of urbanization and political life.

Mohenjo-Daro, present-day Pakistan, c. 2600–1800 B.C.E. When it flourished, Mohenjo-Daro held some 40,000 inhabitants in its carefully laid-out precincts, and it continued to exercise an attraction for thousands of years. The round stupa, or burial mound, that now crowns the settlement was built as part of a Buddhist monastery some 2,000 years after Mohenjo-Daro had ceased to be a city.

LEARNING OBJECTIVES

3.1 ((•

Describe the characteristics of Egypt's early cities, and how we know about them.

3.2 ((•

Tell what we know about the Indus valley civilization, and how we know.

((• Listen on **MyHistoryLab**

What were the
characteristics
of Egypt's early
cities? How do
we know?

3.1

3.2

In Mesopotamia's Tigris–Euphrates valley, development of the physical city and the institutional state went hand in hand. In the Nile valley, the creation of the Egyptian state had greater significance than the growth of individual cities. In the Indus valley, we have extensive archaeological information on the individual cities, but we know next to nothing about the formation of the state. Until scholars learn to decipher the script and language of the Indus civilization, our knowledge of its institutional development will remain limited.

Egypt: The Gift of the Nile

3.1 What were the characteristics of Egypt's early cities? How do we know?

Egypt has been called the "Gift of the Nile" because outside the valley of that great river the country is a desert. An immense, flowing ribbon of water, the Nile runs the length of the country from south to north, branching finally into an extraordinary delta as it approaches the Mediterranean. The river provides natural irrigation along its banks and invites further man-made irrigation to extend its waters into the desert to the east and west. Unlike the unpredictable floods of Mesopotamia, a more or less predictable flood of water poured through the Nile valley every July, August, and September, not only providing natural irrigation, but also carrying nutrient-rich silt that fertilized the land. (As we shall see, twentieth-century dam construction brought more control over the annual flood, and hydroelectric power, but also stopped the flow of silt.) Meanwhile, increased population filled in marshlands adjacent to the riverbed.

The vital significance of the Nile appears in this 4,000-year-old Egyptian poem:

Food bringer, rich with provisions,
   himself the author of all his good things,
Awe-striking master, yet sweet the aromas rising about him
   and, how he satisfies when he returns!—
Transforming the dust to pastures for cattle,
   bringing forth for each god his sacrifice.
He dwells in the underworld, yet heaven and earth
   are his to command, and the Two Lands he takes for his own,
Filling the storerooms, heaping the grainsheds,
   giving his gifts to the poor.   (Foster, p. 113)

The desert flanking the Nile valley protected Egypt from external invasion from the east and west; cataracts—precipitous, impassable waterfalls in the river—provided

AT A GLANCE: ANCIENT EGYPT			
DATE	**POLITICS**	**RELIGION AND CULTURE**	**SOCIAL DEVELOPMENT**
4000–3600 B.C.E.	• Nagada I		
3500 B.C.E.	• Early Dynasty (c. 3000–2700)	• Narmer Palette (c. 3200) • Hieroglyphics in use	• Villages in Nile valley
3000 B.C.E.	• Old Kingdom (c. 2700–2181)	• Ruler of Egypt becoming godlike	• First use of stone in building
2500 B.C.E.		• Step pyramid at Saqqara • Pyramids at Giza, including Great Pyramid (of Khufu)	• Irrigation programs along Nile
2000 B.C.E.	• First Intermediate Period (c. 2200–2040) • Middle Kingdom (c. 2030–1640) • Second Intermediate Period (c. 1640–1540)	• Golden age of art and craftwork (1991–1786)	• Social order upset; few monuments built (2181–1991) • Country divided into principalities (1786–1567)

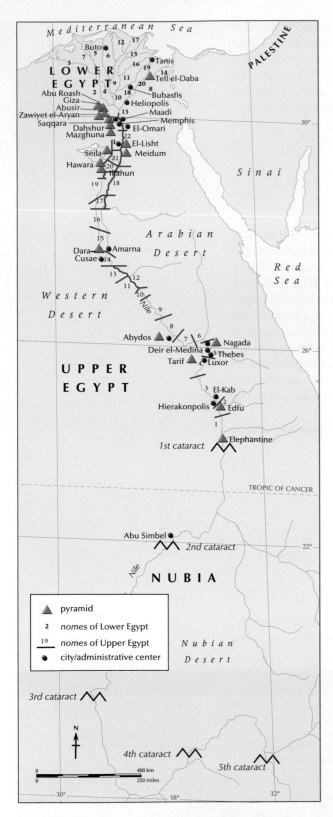

Land of the Nile. Stretching over 1,000 miles along the Nile River, ancient Egyptian civilization depended on a strong government. The kingdom was divided into Lower and Upper Egypt, and further subdivided into *nomes* (tax districts).

a buffer against Nubia to the south; and the Mediterranean provided a defensible northern border. As a result, for most of the first half of its 5,000 years of recorded history, Egypt was ruled by indigenous dynasties. The rule of the kings began about 3100 B.C.E. and continued with few exceptions for nearly 2,600 years, an unparalleled stretch of cultural and political continuity. These kings were later called pharaohs after the palaces they constructed, and gradually, pharaoh became the generic name for all Egyptian kings.

Monumental structures—such as the pyramids and Sphinx at Giza near modern Cairo in the north of Egypt, the temples at Karnak and Thebes in the south, and the pharaohs' tombs nearby in the Valley of the Kings—make clear the wealth, skill, and organizational capacity of ancient Egypt. However, we know less about the physical form of Egypt's ancient cities than about those of Mesopotamia. The Nile has washed away many ancient structures and eroded their foundations. On the other hand, we know much more about the Egyptian state than about almost any other. The written records of ancient Egypt, once they were deciphered, provided the institutional information.

Earliest Egypt: Before the Kings

In Egypt, as in Mesopotamia, agriculture provided the underlying sustenance for city life. By 12,000 B.C.E., residents of Nubia and Upper Egypt were using stones to grind local wild grasses into food, and by 8000 B.C.E. flour was being prepared from their seeds. (Upper or southern Egypt and Lower or northern Egypt derived their names from the flow of the Nile River, which originates south of Egypt and flows north to the Mediterranean Sea.) By 6000 B.C.E. the first traces appear of the cultivation of wheat and barley, grasses and cereals, and of the domestication of sheep and goats. To the west, the Sahara was becoming drier and some of its inhabitants may have moved to the Nile valley, bringing with them more advanced methods of cultivation.

By 3600 B.C.E. a string of villages lined the Nile, at intervals of 20 miles or so. The village economies were based on cereal agriculture. They were linked by trade along the river, although, since they mostly produced the same basic foodstuffs, trade was not central to their economy. The villages show little evidence of social stratification. These settlements characterized the "Nagada I" period (c. 3500 B.C.E.).

Gradually, population increased, as did the size of the villages, and by 3300 B.C.E. the first walled towns appeared in the upper Nile, at Nagada and Hierakonpolis. Tombs for rulers and the elite were built nearby, suggesting new levels of social stratification.

View the Map: The Spread of Agriculture on MyHistoryLab

The Written Record

Writing began early in Egypt, almost simultaneously with ancient Mesopotamia, about 3500–3000 B.C.E. Egyptians may have learned the concept of writing from Mesopotamia, but in place of cuneiform, they developed their own script based on tiny pictographs called **hieroglyphs,** a word based on the Greek for "sacred carvings." Some scholars believe that hieroglyphic writing in Egypt was completely independent of the Mesopotamian invention, and possibly preceded it.

Scribes, an important and highly regarded occupational group in ancient Egypt as in Mesopotamia, later invented two shorthand transcriptions of hieroglyphs: first, the more formal script, called hieratic; later, the more abbreviated, shorthand, demotic script. They wrote on stone tablets, on limestone flakes, on pottery, and on papyrus—a kind of paper—made by laying crossways strands of pith from the stalk of papyrus plants and pressing it until it formed sheets.

As in Mesopotamia, some of the earliest Egyptian writing is notation for business and administration. Over the millennia it grew into a rich literature, including chronological lists of kings, religious inscriptions, spells to protect the dead, biographies and autobiographies, stories, wisdom texts of moral instruction, love poems, hymns to gods, prayers, and mathematical, astronomical, and medical texts. From this literature, scholars have reconstructed a substantial picture of the history of Egypt.

For the earliest 500 to 1,000 years, until about 2400 B.C.E., the written records are thin. They do, however, provide a list of *nomes*, or administrative districts, suggesting the geographical organization of the Egyptian state as early as 2900 B.C.E. They also provide lists of the earliest kings of Egypt.

King lists written on stone about 2400 B.C.E., and on papyrus about 1200 B.C.E., combined with lists compiled in the third century B.C.E. by the Greek historian Manetho,

What were the characteristics of Egypt's early cities? How do we know?

3.1

3.2

KEY TERMS

hieroglyphs The characters in a writing system based on the use of pictograms or ideograms. In ancient Egypt, hieroglyphics were largely used for monumental inscriptions. The symbols depict people, animals, and objects, which represent words, syllables, or sounds.

nome An administrative district in ancient Egypt.

HOW DO WE KNOW?

Written Texts and Archaeological Excavations

Few modern Egyptian scholars had been interested in recovering the ancient past of their country, apparently because its pharaonic, polytheistic culture did not connect with their own monotheistic Islamic and Christian cultures. In Europe, however, scholars and researchers were attempting to understand the early history of the civilization. The interest in this scholarship was so great that when Napoleon Bonaparte led a French military invasion of Egypt in 1798, he brought along with his armies a contingent of scientists, literary scholars, and artists.

In 1799 one of Napoleon's officers working at a fort on the western, Rosetta branch of the Nile delta discovered a large, black basalt stone slab. This "Rosetta Stone" (see overleaf) carried an inscription from the year 196 B.C.E. issued by the Greek ruler of Egypt and written in three languages: the most ancient Egyptian script, hieroglyphs, at the top; demotic Egyptian, a simplified script based on the hieroglyphs, in the middle; and Greek at the bottom. The French dispatched copies of the inscription back to Europe, where scholars were working on deciphering the Egyptian hieroglyphs. Until this time, their efforts had not been successful because they mistakenly believed that all the hieroglyphs were ideographs, a kind of picture writing in which each symbol stood for a word or a concept. Now, however, a young French scholar of linguistics, Jean-François Champollion (1790–1832), using the Rosetta Stone to compare the ancient Egyptian forms with the Greek, which he knew, recognized that hieroglyphic writing combined several forms—ideographic, syllabic, and alphabetic. Once he made this discovery, he was prepared to crack the script. In 1822, after 14 years of research, which he had begun at age 18, he published the results of his work.

Champollion himself made only one trip to Egypt, in 1828–29. With an Italian student, he produced the first systematic survey of the history and geography of Egypt as revealed in its monuments and inscriptions. He earned the informal title "Father of Egyptology," and in 1831 a chair in Egyptian history and archaeology was created for him at the Collège de France.

Archaeological excavations, primarily in search of monumental objects, began in 1858, although tomb-robbing and the theft of ancient artifacts had been continuous from earliest times. The annual expeditions of the British Egyptologist W.M. Flinders Petrie (1853–1942), beginning in 1880, introduced more scientific archaeological studies of Egypt and of Nubia, immediately to the south. By about 1900, scholars had identified the basic outlines of Egypt's history from 3600 B.C.E. to their own time. Working with both text and artifacts, they could produce a doubly rich historical record.

- Why were modern Egyptian scholars no longer interested in the ancient past of their own country? Do you find this surprising? Why or why not?
- The earliest known alphabetic writing dates to about 1900 B.C.E. Its use in place of hieroglyphic writing has been described as revolutionary, "comparable to the invention of the printing press much later." Why?
- How do written accounts and monumental architecture complement each other in giving us a more complete understanding of ancient civilizations?

3.1
3.2

What were the characteristics of Egypt's early cities? How do we know?

The "Rosetta Stone," ancient Egyptian, 196 B.C.E. The inscription is transcribed in three different forms: hieroglyphics, a later Egyptian shorthand called "demotic," and Greek. By comparing the three, scholars were able to decipher the ancient hieroglyphs. (British Museum, London)

give the names of the entire sequence of Egypt's kings from about 3100 B.C.E, all the way through the Persian conquest in 525 B.C.E. and the victory of Alexander the Great in 332 B.C.E. After that event we have many sources for constructing the basic chronology of Egypt's political history.

📖 Read the Document: An Egyptian Folk Tale on MyHistoryLab

📖 Read the Document: Elders' Advice to Their Successors (2250, 2450 BCE) on MyHistoryLab

Unification and the Rule of the Kings

The king lists, records of the *nomes* of Upper Egypt, and inscriptions and designs on pottery suggest strongly that Egyptian national life and history began with the unification of the kingdom about the year 3100 B.C.E. This unity was forged from the diversity of peoples who came to inhabit Egypt. Semites from the desert to the east, Phoenicians from the sea coast, Blacks from Nubia and the heart of Africa, and Europeans from across the Mediterranean immigrated and amalgamated into a common national stock. They recognized one another and intermarried without apparent reference to race or ethnicity. Paintings of ancient Egyptians show them sometimes

What were the characteristics of Egypt's early cities? How do we know?

3.1

3.2

pale in color, sometimes black, very often red, perhaps reflecting their mixed ethnicity. Many historians believe that the colors may also be related to gender—women, mostly relegated to household chores, were usually depicted as pale; men, assumed to be outside the household, were often painted much darker.

Who first unified the upper and lower Nile into the single kingdom of Egypt? Most king lists mention Menes, but some cite Narmer. Some scholars believe that these were two different names for the same person. The event took place about 3100 B.C.E., but tombs of kings excavated at Abydos predate it by about 200 years. Perhaps these were kings of local regions, or perhaps unification was actually accomplished under a "predynastic" king before Menes, or unification may have been a long process and "Menes" simply symbolizes the whole process.

As Egypt became unified, the kings grew steadily more powerful, finally gaining a position as gods, who lived on earth and were responsible for maintaining *ma'at*, justice and order, throughout the kingdom. They were responsible for keeping the forces of nature balanced and for inviting the annual flooding of the Nile River that made Egyptian agriculture possible. An increase in monumental tombs and funerary objects suggests an increasing hierarchy and an uneven distribution of wealth, two common characteristics of state building. A more or less unified artistic style in both pottery and architecture after that time mirrors the unification of Egyptian politics. This era, called the Early Dynastic period, lasted about 400 years, from *c.* 3100 to *c.* 2686 B.C.E. By this time Egypt exhibited the cultural complexity associated with early civilizations, including a national religious ideology and the centralized control of political administration and even of artistic productivity.

📖 **Read** the **Document**: **Two Accounts of an Egyptian Famine** on **MyHistoryLab**

The Gods, the Unification of Egypt, and the Afterlife

Egyptian religious mythology gives great prominence to the political unification of the country. The triumph of Isis, Osiris, and their son Horus—three of Egypt's most important gods—over disorder and evil represents in mythic terms the significance of the unification of Egypt. Osiris represented order and virtue; his brother, Seth, disorder and evil. Seth tricked Osiris into lying down inside a box that was to be his coffin, sealed it, and set it floating down the Nile. Isis, Osiris' wife and sister, found the box and brought Osiris back home. Seth, however, recaptured the body and cut it into 14 separate pieces, which he scattered throughout Egypt and the eastern Mediterranean. Isis tracked down all the parts, brought them back to Egypt, reattached them, and briefly restored life to them. From the restored body, she conceived a son, Horus. Horus defeated Seth in battle and gave Osiris new life, this time as king and principal god of the underworld. In some representations Horus and Seth are seen in reconciliation, binding Egypt into a single state. Seth represents southern areas around Nagada and Thebes; Horus, less specifically, represents the north.

GODS OF THE EGYPTIANS	
Belief in one god (Aten, represented by the sun) was promoted during the reign of Akhenaten (r. 1353–1335), when the capital of Egypt was moved from Thebes to Amarna. At other times, the Egyptians worshiped a pantheon, whose main gods and goddesses are listed below.	
Amon-Re	The universal god, depicted as ram-headed
Anubis	The jackal-headed god of funerals, son of Nephthus and Osiris. He supervised the weighing of souls at judgment
Hathor	The goddess of love, represented either as a woman with a cow's horns or as a cow with a solar disk
Horus	The falcon-headed god of light
Isis	Goddess of magic and fertility; sister and wife of Osiris; as mother of Horus, she was mother goddess of all Egypt
Nephthus	Sister of Isis; a funerary goddess who befriended dead mortals at judgment
Osiris	Ruler of the underworld and chief judge of the dead; normally depicted mummified or as a bearded man wearing the crown of Upper Egypt and with a flail and crook in his hands
Ptah	Magician and patron of the arts and crafts; later became judge of the dead. Normally represented as a mummy or holding an *ankh* (looped cross)
Seth	The god of evil and the murderer of Osiris
Thoth	The supreme scribe, depicted either with the head of an ibis or as a dog-headed baboon

What were the
characteristics
of Egypt's early
cities? How do
we know?

Horus became the patron god of the Egyptian kings, the first Egyptian god to be worshiped nationally. In painting and sculpture he is often depicted in the form of a falcon, sometimes perched on the head or shoulder of the king, sometimes atop the double crown that symbolized the unity of Upper and Lower Egypt. The kings believed that if they lived proper, ordered lives they would be united with Osiris after they died.

This belief in the afterlife inspired the mummification of the dead—at least of those who could afford it—and the construction of Egypt's most spectacular monuments, the pyramids, as a final resting place for the dead kings until their soul and life force emerged for their journey through the afterworld. After passing through the ordeal of judgment in the next world, the souls might also revisit these elaborate tombs.

At first believed to be a preserve of the kings alone, later the afterworld was seen as a destination for important officials as well and, still later, for a larger proportion of the population. The belief in a utopian afterlife seems to have made optimists out of most Egyptians. Even those who may not have shared this belief were urged to enjoy life in this world to the full, as this 3,100-year-old song suggests:

> All who come into being as flesh
>   pass on, and have since God walked the earth;
>   and young blood mounts to their places.
> The busy fluttering souls and bright transfigured spirits
>   who people the world below
>   and those who shine in the stars with Orion,
> They built their mansions, they built their tombs—
>   And all men rest in the grave. …
> So, seize the day! Hold holiday!
>   Be unwearied, unceasing, alive,
>   you and your own true love;
> Let not your heart be troubled during your sojourn on earth,
>   but seize the day as it passes! …
> Grieve not your heart, whatever comes;
>   let sweet music play before you;
> Recall not the evil, loathsome to God,
>   but have joy, joy, joy, and pleasure!   (Foster, pp. 181–82)

Cities of the Dead

Burial sites, shrines, and sometimes towns were based on the need to provide final, collective resting places for the bodies of the most prominent Egyptians. As early as 3100 B.C.E., kings and members of the court were buried at Abydos, a 300-mile boat trip upriver, south of Memphis. Their tombs, called *mastabas*, were made of sun-baked mud bricks, with flat roof and sloping sides, designed to last forever. Inside the structure were the food, weapons, tools, and furniture that the king might need in the afterlife. His body was mummified and buried in an underground chamber. Abydos later became the center for the worship of Osiris.

Another group of high officials was buried in the north, close to Memphis, near Saqqara, in mud-brick tombs. Their funerary goods included copper objects and stone vessels. Over the centuries a series of burial sites grew up nearby, stretching some 45 miles along the Nile. At the beginning of the second dynasty, 2770 B.C.E., the royal necropolis, the city of tombs, was sited at Saqqara itself.

Women of elite families were usually buried in simple pyramid tombs, but in 1998 the more elaborate pyramid tomb of Ankhesenpepi II was uncovered at Saqqara and explored. She was the wife of two Egyptian kings of the sixth dynasty (c. 2345–c. 2181)—Pepi I followed by his nephew Merenre—and she was the mother

KEY TERM

mastaba A low, rectangular, benchlike structure that covered a grave. The architectural forerunner of the pyramid.

of a third king, Pepi II. Although her name means "she lives for Pepi," Ankhesenpepi II seems to have gained power also for herself. She is the first female known to have magical, biographical, hieroglyphic text—a format found frequently in the tombs of kings—inscribed in her tomb to facilitate her access to the afterworld.

Adjacent to the burial sites were the towns of the workers who built the increasingly elaborate tombs for the kings and aristocrats. Several of these workers' towns have been excavated, most notably Deir el-Medina, opposite Thebes in the south of Egypt, near the Valley of the Queens, although it dates to a later period. Mummification was also carried out in workshops in these towns.

The Growth of Cities

Unlike Mesopotamia, Egypt has almost no existing record of independent city-states. In Egypt, thousands of small, generally self-sufficient communities seem to have persisted under a national monarchy, but within a generally decentralized economy for the local production and consumption of food and basic commodities. Gradually, among the villages along the Nile, somewhat larger market towns must have grown up. Because administration, business, and transportation require some centralization, some of the villages began to house those functions. These selected villages, spaced strategically at larger intervals in the landscape, grew into larger settlements, and perhaps even into fully fledged cities.

In early dynastic Egypt, the siting of the administrative headquarters of the *nomes* would have given just such a boost to the towns in which they were located. Some settlements also hosted additional functions, including irrigation control and religious observance. The consolidation of villages into towns and towns into cities marks the beginning of "Nagada II" culture (*c.* 3300 B.C.E.), and the development of the site of Hierakonpolis along the Nile in Upper Egypt illustrates the process. Stretching for 3 miles along the banks of the river, Hierakonpolis ("Nekhen" in ancient Egyptian) did not have the form of a compact city, but it exercised many urban functions.

Archaeological excavations showed that the population of Hierakonpolis grew from a few hundred in 3800 B.C.E. to 10,500 by 3500 B.C.E. At least two cemeteries served the city: one for common people, another for the wealthier traders and more powerful administrators.

What precipitated the population growth, occupational specialization, and social hierarchy? One possibility is that local leaders introduced and implemented irrigation systems that saved agriculture and even enriched it during a period of severe drought. These changes enhanced the economy of the region and created subsequent growth and change. Indeed, Hierakonpolis seems to have been the capital from which King Menes, or Narmer, unified Egypt. The Narmer palette, a slate tablet illustrating this unification, was discovered there.

Political/administrative leaders continued to create irrigation systems along the Nile. These projects began in Old Kingdom Egypt, *c.* 2700–2200 B.C.E. They were expanded with the development of the Fayyum Lake region and the transfer of

Stela from the tomb of Djet (the "Serpent King"), Abydos, *c.* 3000 B.C.E. Horus, in the form of a falcon, is pictured above a serpent representing Djet, the "Serpent King," and the façade of a palace ("pharaoh" literally meant "great house" or "palace"). (Louvre, Paris)

What were the characteristics of Egypt's early cities? How do we know?

3.1

3.2

71

3.1

3.2

What were the
characteristics
of Egypt's early
cities? How do
we know?

population to it during the Middle Kingdom, *c.* 2030–1640 B.C.E. New technology arose during the New Kingdom, *c.* 1550–1050 B.C.E., with the beginning of *shaduf* irrigation, which used buckets attached to a huge, turning wheel to dip into the river, bringing up water that then poured into man-made irrigation channels. The general predictability of the Nile's constant flow and annual flood meant that Egypt had fewer problems with its water supply than did Mesopotamia, but even here control of water resources influenced the formation of cities and the state.

Egypt's cities, like those of other early civilizations, had a religious base as well as an administrative one. Hierakonpolis, for example, housed a temple and prominent tombs as well as a ruler's palace. Perhaps the city flourished because its temple community and worship became especially attractive to surrounding villages. The combination of irrigation, administration, and worship built the city.

Earlier archaeological reports seemed to suggest that after unification under a single king, Egyptian cities were not usually walled. The central government may have suppressed the kind of inter-city warfare that characterized Mesopotamia, rendering defensive walls unnecessary. Also, although invasions occurred from time to time and required defensive precautions, the desert to the east and west of the Nile valley usually provided an adequate natural shield.

More recent excavations, however, question this view of open cities. The walls of some cities have been uncovered, and archaeologists are beginning to suspect that walls of other cities may have been removed and the materials used for other purposes. Excavations at El-Kab, across the Nile from Hierakonpolis, revealed a city enclosed in a wall, 1,600 feet square, dating to 1788–1580 B.C.E. This wall, in turn, seems to have intersected a more primitive town, of circular or oval shape surrounded by a double wall.

Largest of all the Nile towns were the political capitals, first in the north at Memphis, later in the south at Thebes, and occasionally at other locations. Most of the spectacular temples and monuments at Thebes today, for example, date only to the eighteenth and nineteenth dynasties, 1550–1196 B.C.E. This was a period of substantial population growth in Egypt, rising from 1.5 million to between 2.5 and 5 million people. Archaeologists cannot excavate below these monuments to reach older urban levels, and the residential buildings of that older city are probably below the current water table. They are irrecoverable.

Other types of city completed the urban network. Trade cities, especially in the Nile delta, linked Egypt internally and to the outside world. As early as 3650 B.C.E., the city of Buto in the Nile delta near the Mediterranean served as the port of landing for shipping from the Levant (modern Syria, Lebanon, and Israel) and Mesopotamia. Further south but still in the delta, at El-Omari, many goods imported from the Mediterranean

The palette of King Narmer, *c.* 3200 B.C.E. This slate palette, used for ritual purposes, shows the power of King Narmer, who had just united Upper and Lower Egypt. In the top register, Narmer (left), wearing the double crown of authority over both Upper and Lower Egypt, inspects the bodies of dead enemies (right); at the bottom, the strength of the king is symbolized by the bull shown destroying the walls of a city. (Egyptian Museum, Cairo)

SOURCE

The Egyptian Book of the Dead and the "Negative Confession"

Many ancient Egyptian texts concern the attempt to secure eternal happiness after death.

A selection from these mortuary texts has been collected by modern scholars and titled *The Book of the Dead*. A segment of these texts presents the "negative confession" of a deceased person in the court of judgment of the dead, protesting his innocence of evil and crime:

I have not committed evil against men.
I have not mistreated cattle.
I have not committed sin in the place of truth.
I have not tried to learn that which is not meant for mortals.
I have not blasphemed a god.
I have not done violence to a poor man.
I have not done that which the gods abominate.
I have not defamed a slave to his superiors.
I have not made anyone sick.
I have not made anyone weep.
I have not killed.
I have given no order to a killer.
I have not caused anyone suffering.
I have not cut down on the food or income in the temples.
I have not damaged the bread of the gods.
I have not taken the loaves of the blessed dead.
I have not had sexual relations with a boy.
I have not defiled myself.
I have neither increased nor diminished the grain measure.

I have not diminished the measure of land.
I have not falsified the land records.
I have not added to the weight of the balance.
I have not weakened the plummet of the scales.
I have not taken milk from the mouths of children.
I have not driven cattle away from their pasturage.
I have not snared the birds of the gods.
I have not caught fish in their marshes.
I have not held up the water in its season.
I have not built a dam against running water.
I have not quenched a fire at its proper time.
I have not neglected the appointed times and their meat-offerings.
I have not driven away the cattle of the god's property.
I have not stopped a god on his procession.
I am pure: I am pure: I am pure: I am pure. …

Behold me—I have come to you without sin, without guilt, without evil, without a witness against me, without one against whom I have taken action. I live on truth, and I eat of truth.

I have done that which men said and that with which gods are content. I have satisfied a god with that which he desires. I have given bread to the hungry, water to the thirsty, clothing to the naked, and a ferry-boat to him who was marooned. I have provided divine offerings for the gods and mortuary offerings for the dead. So rescue me, you; protect me, you.

(Pritchard, pp. 34–36)

What were the characteristics of Egypt's early cities? How do we know?

3.1

3.2

Wooden model of a sailing boat from Meir, Egypt, *c.* 2000 B.C.E. The presence of a mummy on board this twelfth-dynasty model boat indicates that it was intended as a funerary artifact, used to symbolize the journey of the dead into the afterlife. We recognize important elements of early Egyptian vessels— from the large central sail to the figures on deck, representing the pilot, the owner, and sailors working the halyards. (British Museum, London)

What were the characteristics of Egypt's early cities? How do we know?

coast have also been found. In these ports, goods must have been offloaded for transshipment in smaller boats or by donkey caravans to Maadi, near Memphis. Maadi was the trade link between the delta and Upper Egypt.

👁 **Watch** the **Video**: **The Temple of Karnak** on **MyHistoryLab**

Monumental Architecture of the Old Kingdom: Pyramids and Fortresses

As in Mesopotamia, the increasing power of the Egyptian state inspired the construction of monumental architecture. In the third dynasty (2649–2575 B.C.E.), King Djoser's architect, Imhotep, elaborated the rather simple *mastaba* into a series of stepped stone slabs, one on top of the next, built to house the king's remains at death. This forerunner of the pyramids demonstrated an astonishing royal control over labor, finances, and architectural and building techniques. The administrative organization and economic productivity of government continued to increase, until,

The Sphinx and the Pyramid of Khefren, Giza. The greatest of all the pyramids, the burial tombs of the kings, are at Giza, near modern Cairo, and date to around 2600–2500 B.C.E. The face of the sphinx—a mythological creature with a lion's body and a human head—is thought to be a likeness of King Khefren, who ruled Egypt some time after 2600 B.C.E.

Step pyramid of King Djoser, Saqqara, Egypt, *c.* 2700 B.C.E. This step pyramid, forerunner to the ancient architectural masterpieces at Giza, developed from the *mastaba*, a low, rectangular, benchlike structure that covered a grave. The purpose of this early pyramid, effectively a 200-foot-high ziggurat without a temple on top, was to mark and protect the underground tomb chamber 90 feet below.

What were the characteristics of Egypt's early cities? How do we know?

3.1

3.2

by the end of this dynasty, Egypt had extended its control of the Nile valley as far south as the first cataract, its classical southern frontier. At the same time, Egypt's artistic genius continued to develop the sculpture of its tombs and the sophistication of its script. Old Kingdom rulers (*c.* 2686–*c.* 2160 B.C.E.) spent fortunes constructing pyramid tombs to preserve their mummified bodies for the afterlife.

Within a half-century, architects realized the beauty of filling in the steps of the multi-storied *mastaba* to create the simple, elegant, triangular form of the true pyramid. Kings of the fourth dynasty, 2575–2465 B.C.E., supervised the construction of the greatest pyramids in history. The 450-foot-high pyramids of Khufu (Cheops; r. 2551–2528 B.C.E.) and Khefren (r. 2520–2494 B.C.E.), and the smaller pyramid of Menkaure (r. 2490–2472 B.C.E.), all arranged in a cluster with the Sphinx, proclaim creative vision, organizational power, and aspirations to immortality. The sculpture, reliefs, paintings, and inscriptions in the pyramids and in the many tombs of court officials and other powerful men of the time express the highest artistic achievements of the era. Tombs of queens and officials are situated in proximity to the kings' pyramids in accordance with their inhabitants' power and rank. (Tomb-robbing was, however, so common that we have no idea how long any of them lay undisturbed in their tombs.) All these architectural, spiritual, political, and military accomplishments date to the millennium we now call the predynastic, early dynastic, and Old Kingdom.

Following Menkaure, however, whose pyramid was already smaller than those of Khufu and Khefren, the size and quality of these enormous monuments decreased, suggesting that Egyptian power generally was diminishing. At the height of the Old Kingdom, for example, Egyptian trading, raiding, and mining initiatives had extended southward into Nubia, above the first cataract of the Nile. These expeditions were protected and consolidated through the construction of the Buhen fortress at the second cataract, probably at about the time of the building of the great

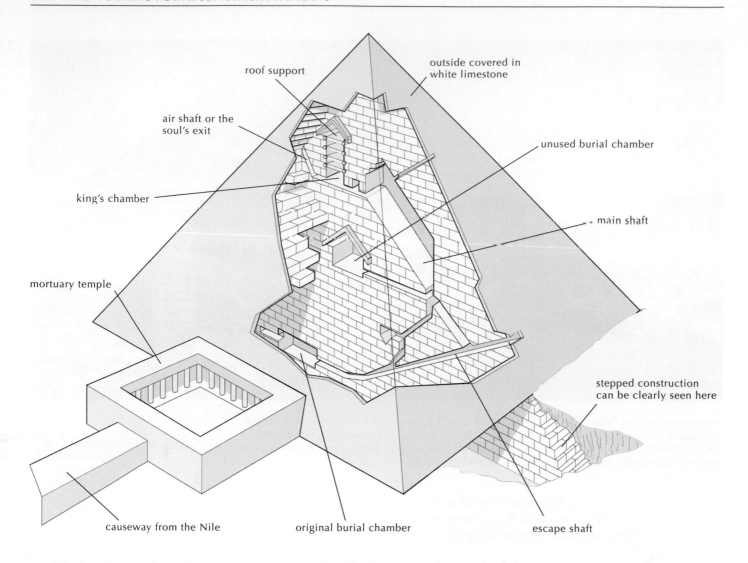

roof support

air shaft or the
soul's exit

outside covered in
white limestone

unused burial chamber

king's chamber

main shaft

mortuary temple

stepped construction
can be clearly seen here

causeway from the Nile

original burial chamber

escape shaft

Cutaway of Great Pyramid of Khufu, Giza. The rectangular plan and stepped form of Djoser's pyramid were gradually modified to become the colossal, smooth-faced monuments with which we are familiar. This pyramid is some 450 feet high on a square base occupying 13 acres, and was built using forced labor.

3.1
3.2

What were the characteristics of Egypt's early cities? How do we know?

pyramids. That fortress, however, also seems to have declined after about 2400 B.C.E., although trading and raiding expeditions continued.

The Disintegration of the Old Kingdom

Lists of the kings of ancient Egypt record a 3000-year chronology, beginning about 3200 B.C.E. The first dynasty, including King Narmer, succeeded in unifying upper and lower Egypt. The 32nd, and last, dynasty (330–305 B.C.E.) was imposed from outside by Alexander the Great after he conquered Egypt. (Some scholars refer to the rule of Ptolemaic, Greek, kings, 305–30 B.C.E., ending with Cleopatra, as a 33rd dynasty.) Within these three millennia, scholars today identify the three "Kingdoms," Old, Middle, and New, as unified, prosperous, and powerful eras in Egyptian history. In between them came periods of dissolution and instability.

For example, after the height of the era of pyramid building in the Old Kingdom, central authority began to weaken and provincial officials in each *nome*, called nomarchs, asserted their powers. They collected and kept the taxes for themselves, and their private armies ruled locally. Based on the size and records of cemeteries, the death rate seems to have increased at this time. Famine was prevalent. Apparently the Nile did not reach optimal flood heights for agriculture, and weak rulers could not create adequate irrigation works to compensate for the shortfall. Finally, in 2181 B.C.E. the Old Kingdom fell. At first, several nomarchs held independent local power. Then two separate centers began to stand out in the contest for power:

What were the characteristics of Egypt's early cities? How do we know?

3.1

3.2

Herakleopolis in the north and Thebes in the south. This period of disunity, the First Intermediate Period, lasted for almost a century and a half.

The Rise and Fall of the Middle Kingdom

In about 2040 B.C.E., King Mentuhotep of Thebes defeated his rivals in the north and reunited the kingdom, initiating the Middle Kingdom, c. 2030–1640 B.C.E. Trade revived, with two patterns achieving special prominence. One was the local caravan trade in spices, resins, and minerals across the northern Sinai desert, between the Nile delta and Palestine. The other—the long-distance trade carried by ship throughout the eastern Mediterranean—was commanded by royal families to bring in timber and resins, lapis lazuli, copper, and ivory for official construction and for adornment.

The fine arts and literature flourished. Among the finest literary gems of the Middle Kingdom was "The Autobiography of Si-nuhe," the narrative of a high-ranking court official who went into self-imposed exile until, in his old age, he was recalled to the capital and awarded great honors. The story reveals not only the intrigues of the court and the royal family, but also the sharp contrast between the life of the elite of the capital and the harsh rigor of the surrounding desert.

Most importantly, the Middle Kingdom saw the state develop more organization and power than ever before. Egypt was administered efficiently and spread its power aggressively into Nubia and the Middle East. Egypt became an empire, ruling over more distant, foreign peoples. From this time onward, Egypt's fate would be intertwined with that of its empire. The Middle Kingdom ended in part because

---

SOURCE

The Autobiography of Si-nuhe and the Glorification of Court and Capital

Si-nuhe, a high-ranking official and royal attendant, fled from the Egyptian court when a new king came to the throne. Apparently he feared that his loyalty to the new ruler was suspect and his safety endangered. A skilled warrior and administrator, even in self-imposed exile he earned high positions in several Asian kingdoms. In Si-nuhe's old age, however, the king of Egypt and his family invited him back to the court so that he could spend his last years "at home" in comfort and be buried with appropriate rites.

This personal tale of reconciliation is almost certainly based on reality. Its glorification of Egypt over other countries, of the city, and especially of the royal capital and the royal court over the countryside represented the beliefs of the Egyptian elite. This account of the career and moral personality of a court official, and of the excellence of the reigning king, is an outstanding example of the autobiographies inscribed in ancient Egyptian tombs. Si-nuhe's story became one of the most popular classics of Egyptian literature, and manuscripts that include it began to appear about 1800 B.C.E. and continued to about 1000 B.C.E. One modern scholar refers to it as "the crown jewel of Middle Egyptian literature." (Lichtheim, vol. I, p. 11)

Si-nuhe returned to the capital, then in the city of Lisht, near the Faiyum Lake.

So I went forth from the midst of the inner chambers, with the royal children giving me their hands. Thereafter we went to the Great Double Door. I was put into the house of a royal son, in which were splendid things. A cool room was in it, and images of the horizon. Costly things of the Treasury were in it. Clothing of royal linen, myrrh, and prime oil of the king and of the nobles whom he loves were in every room. Every butler was busy at his duties. Years were made to pass away from my body. I was plucked, and my hair was combed. A load of dirt was given to the desert, and my clothes to the Sand-Crossers. I was clad in fine linen and anointed with prime oil.

I slept on a bed. I gave up the sand to them who are in it, and wood oil to him who is anointed with it. I was given a house which had a garden, which had been in the possession of a courtier. Many craftsmen built it, and all its woodwork was newly restored. Meals were brought to me from the palace three or four times a day, apart from that which the royal children gave, without ceasing a moment.

There was constructed for me a pyramid-tomb of stone in the midst of the pyramid-tombs. The stone-masons who hew a pyramid-tomb took over its ground-area. The outline-draftsmen designed in it; the chief sculptors carved in it; and the overseers of works who are in the necropolis made it their concern. Its necessary materials were made from all the outfittings which are placed at a tomb-shaft. Mortuary priests were given to me. There was made for me a necropolis garden, with fields in it formerly extending as far as the town, like that which is done for a chief courtier. My statue was overlaid with gold, and its skirt was of fine gold. It was his majesty who had it made. There is no poor man for whom like has been done.

(Pritchard, pp. 18–22)

What do we
know about the
Indus valley
civilization? How
do we know?

the Nubians drove out their Egyptian conquerors, but more importantly because of the invasions of the Hyksos, or "princes of the foreign lands," who spoke a Semitic language and probably came from the north and east of the Sinai desert. The New Kingdom (*c.* 1550–1050 B.C.E.) would rise again as an empire by once more asserting its authority over Nubia and over large regions of Palestine and adjoining segments of Syria. These issues of empire and its significance for Egypt are discussed in the chapter entitled "Dawn of the Empires." One fascinating event from the New Kingdom period—the construction and destruction of the city of Akhetaten—belongs here, however, because it highlights the symbolic importance of capital cities.

Akhetaten, Capital City of King Akhenaten

Modern excavations at Amarna on the east bank of the Nile unearthed the ruins of an ancient Egyptian capital that owed its entire existence to the idiosyncratic vision of one ruler—King Amenhotep IV, better known as Akhenaten.

Within a few years of coming to the throne, Amenhotep IV (r. 1353–1335 B.C.E.) challenged the order of ancient Egypt by adopting a new monotheistic religion. Instead of worshiping a whole pantheon of gods, he offered his devotion to a single deity—Aten, god of the solar disk (or sun). Amenhotep appointed himself mediator between his people and the god. He abandoned his official dynastic name in favor of Akhenaten ("he who serves Aten"). The name of Amon, principal god of the old religion, was swiftly erased from inscriptions throughout Egypt, as were the words "all gods" in certain texts.

To bolster the new order and escape the power of the hostile priesthood, Akhenaten moved his capital 200 miles north from the established center, Thebes, to an untouched site in the desert. The city he built was named Akhetaten ("horizon of Aten"; present-day Amarna), and it was there that Akhenaten, the Great Royal Wife Queen Nefertiti, and their six daughters practiced the new religion.

The eccentricity of Akhetaten's ruler was reflected in the city's architecture, sculpture, and wall painting. Solid statements of eternity gave way to a freedom of expression that emphasized the here and now. Aten was worshiped in an open temple that ushered in the sun's rays, rather than in one of the dark, austere sanctuaries usually designated for worship. Residential buildings included spacious villas with large gardens and pools to house wealthy officials. In artistic expression, solemnity gave way to an unprecedented liveliness and invention. Artists showed the royal parents playing with their children or dandling them on their laps. Curious depictions of Akhenaten's drooping jaw and misshapen body capture his individuality, marking a departure from the highly stylized representations of previous pharaohs.

Akhenaten's isolated position, both geographically and intellectually, threatened the stability of Egypt's empire. When he died, Akhenaten's successors abandoned Akhetaten. The capital returned to Thebes, where the old religious and political order could resume. Subsequent pharaohs so hated Akhenaten's religion that they razed the city to the ground and used its building materials on other sites.

From this discussion of the varied cities of the Nile valley, with their abundance of archaeological and textual material, we move eastward about 2,500 miles to explore the earliest cities of the Indus valley with their very different structures and materials.

The Indus Valley Civilization and its Mysteries

What do we know about the Indus valley civilization? How do we know?

The civilizations of ancient Mesopotamia and Egypt never disappeared completely. Hebrew and Greek accounts and surviving artifacts, such as the spectacular pyramids, kept them alive in the popular imagination. Intermittent discoveries of tombs,

3.1

3.2

What do we
know about the
Indus valley
civilization? How
do we know?

and the thefts of their contents, added concrete evidence. Nevertheless, systematic excavating of sites and deciphering of texts did not occur in modern times until the mid-1800s.

The civilization of the Indus valley was lost almost entirely, so it is no surprise that its excavation did not begin until the 1920s and that its script is still not deciphered. The accidental discovery and systematic exploration of this long-lived and far-flung civilization is one of the great stories of mid- and late twentieth-century archaeology.

The Roots of the Indus Valley Civilization

In 1856, the British colonial rulers of India were supervising construction of a railway between Lahore and Karachi, along the Indus River valley. As they progressed, construction workers discovered hundreds of thousands of old fire-baked bricks in the semi-desert area and used them to lay the road bed. Scattered among the old bricks, workers discovered steatite stone seals marked with artistic designs. These seals and bricks were the first clue that the area had been home to an ancient and unknown civilization. Some were passed along to officers of the Archaeological Survey of India, and they took note of them, but formal systematic excavation began only in 1920 when John Marshall, Director General of the Archaeological Survey, commissioned his staff to survey a huge mound that rose above the desert floor where the seals had been found.

These excavations soon revealed a 4,500-year-old city. Archaeologists named the site Harappa, and they often used this name to designate the entire Indus valley civilization. Two years later, R.D. Banerji, an Indian officer of the Survey, recognized and began to excavate a twin site 200 miles to the southwest, later named Mohenjo-Daro, "Hill of the Dead." The two cities had many urban design and architectural features in common. Both were about 3 miles in circumference, large enough to hold populations of 40,000. With these two excavations, an urban civilization that had been lost for thousands of years was uncovered.

Before these excavations, scholars had believed that the civilization of India had begun in the Ganges valley with the arrival of Aryan immigrants from Persia or central Asia c. 1250 B.C.E. and the construction of their first cities c. 700 B.C.E. The discovery of the Harappan cities pushed the origin of Indian civilization back an additional 1,500 years and located it in an entirely different ecological zone.

As archaeologists explored more widely in the Indus valley, they found that civilization there began earlier, lasted longer, and spread farther than anyone had suspected. Some of its roots seem to lie in a settlement called Mehrgarh, in the foothills of the Bolan Pass, that has yielded early settlement artifacts going back to 7000 B.C.E. and, with ever-increasing sophistication, coming forward to 2500–2000 B.C.E. At its

AT A GLANCE: THE INDUS VALLEY

DATE	POLITICS	RELIGION AND CULTURE	SOCIAL DEVELOPMENT
7000 B.C.E.			• Traces of settlements; trade with Mesopotamia
3000 B.C.E.			• Cotton cultivated
2500 B.C.E.	• Height of Harappan civilization in northern India (2500–2000)		• Cities of Harappa and Mohenjo-Daro
2000 B.C.E.	• Collapse of Harappan civilization (2000–1900)	• Evidence of decline in standards of architecture	
1500 B.C.E.	• Immigration of Aryans into India (c. 1250)		
1000 B.C.E.	• Aryan immigrants reach west Ganges valley (c. 1000) and build first cities (c. 750)		• Iron tools used to clear Ganges valley for agriculture (c. 1000)

What do we
know about the
Indus valley
civilization? How
do we know?

height, it had major settlements as far west as the Makran Coast toward Iran, north
and east into Punjab and even the upper Ganges River valley, and south and east to
Dholavira in Kutch, and on to the banks of the Narmada River.

What was the relationship between this civilization and that of Mesopotamia?
At first, many scholars assumed that the Indus valley people learned the art of
city-building from the Sumerians and other peoples of Mesopotamia. But later scholars have argued that Harappa was not a derivative of Mesopotamia but grew up
independently. It is conceivable that the civilizations of both Mesopotamia and the
Indus had a common ancestor in the settlements of the hills and mountains between
them.

Written records, the key that reopened the civilizations of ancient Mesopotamia
and Egypt, are scarce in the Indus valley. The only written materials so far discovered
are seal inscriptions, which give only limited information. In addition, scholars have
not succeeded in their attempts to decipher the script; they differ substantially in
their interpretations. As a result, our understanding of Indus civilization is limited.
Artifactual remains give a good representation of the physical cities and settlements,
but not of their institutions. Moreover, while we can make educated guesses about
the function and meaning of the remaining artifacts and physical structures from our
own perspective, we do not have the words of the Harappans themselves to explain
their own understanding of their civilization.

The Design and Construction of Well-planned Cities

Archaeological evidence to date reveals an urban civilization with its roots as early
as 7000 B.C.E. in simple settlements, such as Mehrgarh in the hills. Over the millennia,
people moved down into the plains and river valley. At first, they may have practiced
transhumance, moving into the forested river valley only in the colder months, and

KEY TERM

transhumance The practice of
shifting residence and livestock
between mountains and valleys
according to the season of the
year.

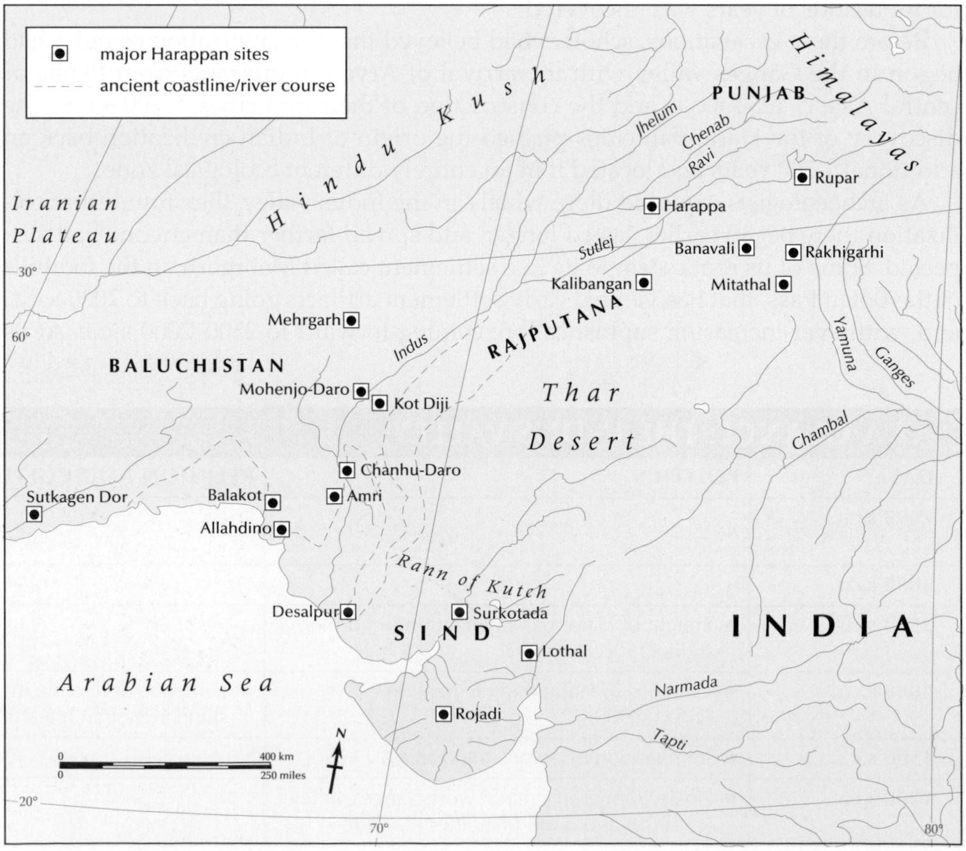

Cities of the Indus. Confined to the
north and west by mountains, and to the
east by desert, the Indus valley had, by
2500 B.C.E., developed a sophisticated
urban culture based on individual walled
cities sharing common patterns of urban
design. In terms of geographical extent
this civilization was the largest in the
world in its time.

3.1

3.2

What do we
know about the
Indus valley
civilization? How
do we know?

herding their flocks of sheep and cattle, including the humped zebu, back to the hills for the summer. Over time they may have decided to farm the river-watered alluvial lands of the valley and to settle permanently. They began to trade by boat along the Indus and even down the river into the Arabian Sea and, further, into the Persian Gulf and up the Tigris and Euphrates into Mesopotamia. Goods from the Indus valley have been found in Mesopotamia and vice versa.

Crafts and the Arts. Crafts of the Indus valley included pottery making, dyeing, metalworking in bronze, and bead making. Bead materials included jade from the Himalayas, lapis lazuli from Afghanistan, turquoise from Persia, amethyst from Mewar in India, and steatite, which was found locally. All these items suggest an active interregional trade. Small sculptures in stone, terra cotta, and bronze appear to represent priestly or governmental officials, dancing girls, and, perhaps, mother goddesses. Since there are no accompanying texts to explain exact identities, these can be only guesses. Dice and small sculptures of bullock carts were probably used as toys and games. The first known use of cotton as a fiber for weaving textiles occurred in the Indus valley, introducing one of India's, and the world's, most enduring and important crops and crafts.

Limestone dancing figure from Harappa, c. 2300–1750 B.C.E. This dancing figure displays a grasp of three-dimensional movement and vitality rare in the arts until much later periods. Human sculptures in contemporary Mesopotamia and Egypt are, by contrast, symbols of pure power, either immutable ideals of divinity or semidivine kingship. Indeed, this Harappan accomplishment is so extraordinary that some scholars have cast doubt on its early date. (National Museum of India, New Delhi)

Limestone bust from Mohenjo-Daro, c. 2300–1750 B.C.E. This half-figure with horizontal slits for eyes, flat, thick lips, and fringes of beard is thought to have represented a priest or shaman because of the way the robe is hung over its left shoulder. Despite its monumental appearance, the figure is only seven inches high. (National Museum of Pakistan, Karachi)

What do we
know about the
Indus valley
civilization? How
do we know?

Carefully Planned Cities. By about 2500 B.C.E., a thriving civilization encompassing 1,000 known sites reached its apex and maintained it for about 500 years. Each of the two largest settlements, Harappa and Mohenjo-Daro, had a core area of about 3 miles in circumference, and Mohenjo-Daro also had a suburb—residential or industrial— about a mile away. Each city accommodated about 40,000 people.

The two cities share similar features of design. To the northwest is a citadel, or raised area; to the south is a lower town. In Mohenjo-Daro, the citadel is built on an architectural platform about 45 feet above the plain, and it measures 1,400 by 450 feet. On the summit was a vast communal bath 8 feet deep and 23 by 29 feet in area. Numerous cubicles—perhaps small, individual baths—flanked it. Adjacent to the large bath was a huge open space, identified as a granary, where food was stored safe from possible flood. Other spaces may have been used for public meetings. Fortified walls mark the southeast corner, and it appears that the entire citadel was walled.

The lower city was laid out in a gridiron, with the main streets about 45 feet wide. Here were the private houses, almost every one with its own well, bathing space, and toilet, consisting of a brick seat over a drainage area. Brick-lined drains flushed by water carried liquid and solid waste to sumps, where it was collected and carted away, probably to fertilize the nearby fields. The town plan was orderly and regular. Even the prefabricated, fire-baked bricks were uniform in size and shape. A uniform system of weights and measures was also employed throughout.

Excavation of the two largest cities has now reached severe limits. The city of Harappa was vandalized for thousands of years before, as well as during, the railroad construction, and few artifacts remain to be discovered. Mohenjo-Daro sits on a high water table, and any deeper excavation threatens to flood the site. It is impossible to dig down to the foundation level of the city.

Further exploration of Mohenjo-Daro's surface, however, continues to yield fascinating results. A recent survey revealed an outlying segment about a mile away from the known city. Was it part of an industrial area or a residential suburb? It is impossible to determine. The discovery, however, identifies Mohenjo-Daro as a larger city than Harappa. Perhaps it was the capital city of the civilization. The regularity of plan and construction suggests a government with great organizational and bureaucratic capacity, but no truly monumental architecture clearly marks the presence of a palace or temple, and there is little sign of social stratification in the plan or buildings. Those burials that have been discovered are regular, with the heads pointing to the north, and with some grave goods, such as pots of food and water, small amounts of jewelry, simple mirrors, and some cosmetics. These were not the extravagant royal burials of Egypt or even Mesopotamia.

In more recent years, additional Indus valley cities have been discovered and excavated, giving a fuller idea of the immense geographical extent of this civilization. The new excavations generally confirm the urban design patterns of the earlier finds, but they add some new elements. The excavations at Dholavira, in Kutch, India, for example, begun in the late 1980s, revealed immense, ornamented gates at the principal entrances to the city, and playing fields in the area between the upper and lower cities. Dholavira was not located on a river, but in the elevated center of a small region that may have formed an island during the monsoon,

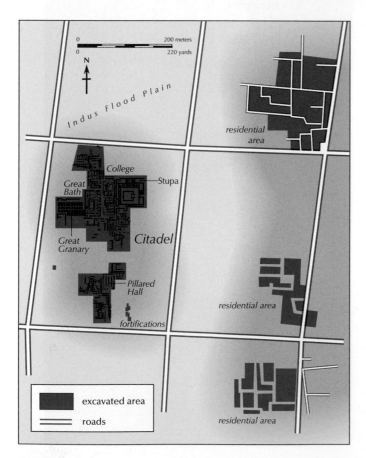

Planned cities. With an area of 150 acres and about 40,000 inhabitants, Mohenjo-Daro was a thriving Indus city. Excavations reveal a raised citadel area, containing ceremonial and administrative buildings, and a residential quarter centered on boulevards about 45 feet wide, with grid-patterned streets, an underground sewerage and drainage system, and a range of brick dwellings.

3.1

3.2

What do we
know about the
Indus valley
civilization? How
do we know?

EARLY SCIENCE AND TECHNOLOGY (7000–1000 B.C.E.)	
7000–6000	Pottery made in Middle East
c. 5500	Copper, gold, and silver worked in Mesopotamia and Egypt
c. 4000–3500	In Asia and Africa, potter's wheel and kiln invented; mud bricks used; spindle developed for spinning; basketmaking begins
c. 3500–3000	Plow and cart invented; bronze cast and cuneiform writing developed in Sumer
3100	Reed boats in Egypt and Assyria; appearance of hieroglyphs in Egypt
3000	Cotton cultivated in the Indus valley
c. 2500	Wooden boats used in Egypt; ink and papyrus writing material used
2050	First glass in Mesopotamia
1790	Mathematics and medicine practiced in Babylon
1740	War chariots introduced from Persia to Mesopotamia (and later Egypt)
1370	Alphabetic script used in western Syria
1000	Industrial use of iron in Egypt and Mesopotamia

when water levels around it were highest. Huge cisterns were cut into the rock of the upper city for collecting rainwater in this extremely arid area. Dholavira also demonstrates a stark contrast between the relatively spacious quarters of the upper city and the more modest accommodations of the lower. Among the 20,000 artifacts uncovered, however, the extraordinary extremes of wealth and poverty of Egypt and Mesopotamia do not appear.

Questions of Interpretation. Interpretations of Indus valley artifacts stress the apparent classlessness of the society, its equality, efficiency, and public conveniences. Some interpreters view these qualities negatively, equating them with oppressively rigid governments and drab lives. While some scholars emphasize that the Harappans apparently survived and prospered for centuries, others argue that the cities changed little over long periods of time and lacked the dynamism of the cities in Mesopotamia and Egypt. With no contemporary literature to guide us, interpretation of what is found is in the eyes, and the value system, of the beholder.

We also do not know if this uniform, planned civilization had a single capital city, or several regional capitals, or no centralized political system at all. We see careful planning in the urban forms, but we do not know if the Indus valley civilization developed urban institutions for governance, trade, religion, or worship, much less the quality of any such institutions. While Egypt had a state but, perhaps, few cities, the Indus valley had cities but no clearly delineated state. Indeed, some scholars argue that the Indus valley did not create state structures at all. Was it like Egypt before unification or after unification? Was it like Mesopotamia, with numerous city-states all participating in a single general culture? All three suggestions have been made.

Until the Harappan language is deciphered, its civilization will remain mysterious: How was it organized? Why did it disperse? How did it move eastward? In what ways did it enrich its successor, the Aryan civilization of the Ganges River valley?

Legacies of the Harappan Civilization

Waves of immigrants entered India from Persia and central Asia beginning around 1250 B.C.E. Our understanding of these immigrants, called Aryans in Sanskrit (a name related to Persians or Iranians), has changed with recent archaeological and linguistic scholarship. We used to believe that the Aryans came in one major military invasion,

3.1

3.2

What do we
know about the
Indus valley
civilization? How
do we know?

but we now think they came more peacefully, in waves of immigration over centuries. As they entered India through the mountain passes, and continued eastward toward the Ganges River basin, they encountered the already settled Harappans of the Indus valley. Interchange between the resident Harappans and the invading Aryans produced new, hybrid cultural forms that we know primarily from the Aryan records. Ironically, these records are almost entirely literary and artistic. Reversing the Harappan pattern, the early Aryans have left a treasure of literature, but virtually no architectural or design artifacts.

Four legacies of Harappa stand out. First, the Aryan invaders were a nomadic group, who must have adopted at least some of the arts of settlement and civilization from the already settled residents. Second, as newcomers to the ecological zones of India, the Aryans must also have learned methods of farming and animal husbandry from the Harappans. Later, however, as they migrated eastward into the Ganges valley, they confronted a new ecology based on rice cultivation and the use of iron. Here, Harappan skills were useless. Third, a three-headed figure frequently appearing in Harappan seals resembles later representations of the Aryan god Shiva. Perhaps an earlier Harappan god was adopted and adapted by the Aryans.

Finally, the Aryan caste system—which ranked people at birth according to family occupation, color, and ritual purity, and prescribed the people with whom they might enter into social intercourse and marry—may reflect the need of the Aryans to regulate relationships between themselves and the Harappans. To claim and maintain

HOW DO WE KNOW?

The Decline of Harappan Civilization

By about 2000 B.C.E. the architecture of the Indus civilization began to decline. New buildings and repairs to existing structures lacked attention to quality and detail. Residents began to leave the cities and towns along the Indus and to relocate northeastward into the Punjab to towns such as Kalibangan, and southeastward to towns such as Dholavira in Kutch and Lothal in Gujarat. Meanwhile, newcomers—squatters—seem to have moved into the old cities.

Archaeologists suggest a variety of reasons—most of them ecological—for the decline in the cities and the geographical redistribution of their populations: perhaps the river changed course or became erratic; perhaps the soil became too saline; perhaps the forests were cut down and the topsoil eroded. An older opinion—that the Indus civilization was destroyed by the invasion of Aryan peoples from somewhere northwest of India— is now less widely held. It rested on Harappan archaeological evidence and Aryan literature. Several sets of skeletal remains in Mohenjo-Daro indicate violent deaths, while Aryan religious texts suggest that the invaders burned and destroyed existing settlements. The *Rigveda*, one of the earliest and most important of these texts, tells of the destructive power of the god Indra:

> With all-outstripping chariot-wheel, O Indra, thou far-famed,
>   hast overthrown the twice ten kings of men
> With sixty thousand nine and ninety followers …
> Thou goest on from fight to fight intrepidly, destroying castle
>   after castle here with strength. (i, 53)
> … in kindled fire he burnt up all their weapons,
> And made him rich with kine and carts and horses. (ii, 15)

The Aryan god of fire, Agni, is still more fearsome:

> Through fear of you the dark people went away, not giving battle, leaving behind their possessions, when, O Vaisvanara, burning brightly for Puru, and destroying the cities, you did shine. (7.5.3)

Newer archaeological evidence, however, suggests that the decline, deurbanization, and dispersal of the Indus civilization seem to have preceded the Aryan invasion. Further evidence suggests that the Aryans may have swept into the region not in a single all-conquering expedition, but in a series of smaller waves of immigration. The arrival of the Aryans may have only completed the Harappan decay.

- Why does the formation of new cities such as Kalibangan and Lothal suggest the decline of the Indus valley civilization?
- Why did scholars once believe that Aryan invasions destroyed the Indus valley civilization? Why do they now question that belief?
- What is the range of alternative explanations that have been offered? Why are scholars uncertain about the accuracy of these explanations?

their own supremacy, the Aryans may have elaborated the social structures of an early caste system and relegated the native inhabitants to permanent low status within it.

The Aryan groups grew increasingly skilled and powerful as they moved east. The first known archaeological evidence of their urban structures dates to about 700 B.C.E. and is found in the Ganges valley. We will read more about it in the chapter entitled "Indian Empires."

The Cities of the Nile and Indus:
What Difference Do They Make?

To what extent do the river valley civilizations of the Indus and the Nile confirm or alter our views of the significance of cities? They do show us that cities come in very different forms and networks. In Mesopotamia they had appeared as warring city-states. Along the Nile they were parts of a single state that was first unified by about 3000 B.C.E. By 2000 B.C.E., following foreign conquests, they formed the core of an imperial state, and they continued to be unified through most of the next 2,500 years. In the Indus valley we do not know if the cities were independent city-states or parts of a unified state; it is apparent, however, from their design and cultural products that they comprised a single cultural unit. In all three areas, then, life in cities created the state and gave concrete form to its value system.

We also learn of the significance of archaeological and textual study in unearthing and recovering all these early civilizations. To greater or lesser degrees, all had been lost to history for thousands of years before being exhumed by scholars in the nineteenth and twentieth centuries. In the task of reconstruction, written records have been critical to understanding the social structures and value systems of these cities. In both Mesopotamia and the Nile valley, excavations and written records enable us to see clearly the presence of religious elements, alliances between rulers and priests,

The citadel of Mohenjo-Daro, *c.* 2300 B.C.E. and later. The citadel at Mohenjo-Daro, a massive, mud-filled embankment that rises 43 feet above the lower city, was discovered by the archaeologist Daya Ram Sahni while investigating the second-century C.E. Buddhist stupa (burial mound) that can be seen in the distance. The citadel's summit houses the remains of several impressive structures, of which the most prominent is the so-called Great Bath (foreground).

extensive temple complexes and, in Egypt, burial complexes as well, and, in both civilizations, extensive specialization of labor and social stratification. But before we take these characteristics as the normal ancestry of city life, we pause at the Indus valley excavations, for here we see no record of such intense occupation with the otherworldly or the afterlife. We see no record of such extensive specialization of labor nor of such extreme social stratification—although the more recent excavations at Dholavira exhibit significant differences between the richest and poorest residential areas. We also see little evidence of the levels of artistic accomplishment of Mesopotamia and Egypt. And, of course, without texts, we have no written record of religious, philosophical, legal, or administrative systems in the Indus valley.

To explore further the global legacy of city and state formation, we now turn to four other regions of indigenous, early city and state formation in places far from those we have studied and far from one another: the Yellow River valley of China, Mesoamerica, South America, and the Niger River valley of West Africa. We are in for some surprises.

CHAPTER REVIEW

EGYPT: THE GIFT OF THE NILE

3.1 What were the characteristics of Egypt's early cities? How do we know?

Egypt's early cities in the Nile River valley have left us a wealth of archeological and textual materials. Often dedicated to specific gods, these early cities had a religious base as well as an administrative one. The Egyptians introduced monumental architecture and extensive specialization in social, political, and economic life. Trade networks of goods and ideas flourished. With the invention of writing, bureaucrats, businessmen, and scholars had new means of recording transactions, biographies, and philosophical principles.

THE INDUS VALLEY CIVILIZATION AND ITS MYSTERIES

3.2 What do we know about the Indus valley civilization? How do we know?

Written records of the Indus valley are scarce and we have not been able to decipher them. Thanks to archaeology, however, we know that a reasonably consistent Indus valley civilization extended over an immense space, the most dispersed of any early civilization, over thousands of years. Cities were exceptionally well laid out on a grid pattern with channels for water and sewerage. They seem to have been less hierarchical than the cities of Egypt or Mesopotamia. The people of the Indus valley made the first known use of cotton fiber for textiles. Waves of immigrants later implanted some of their own practices in the valley even as they transplanted some Indus agricultural practices eastward.

Suggested Readings

PRINCIPAL SOURCES

Fagan, Brian. *People of the Earth: An Introduction to World Prehistory* (Upper Saddle River, NJ: Prentice Hall, 13th ed., 2010). The best available textbook introduction to prehistory.

Foster, John L., trans. and ed. *Ancient Egyptian Literature* (Austin, TX: University of Texas Press, 2001). A fine anthology of varied forms of literature, culled from the translator/editor of many previous collections, plus a few new pieces.

Hawass, Z. *Silent Images: Women in Pharaonic Egypt* (New York: Harry N. Abrams, 2000). A study of the female form in Egyptian art.

Kenoyer, Jonathan M. *Ancient Cities of the Indus Valley Civilization* (New York: Oxford University Press, 1998). Lavishly illustrated accompanying volume to museum exhibit.

Lesko, Barbara. "Women of Egypt and the Ancient Near East," in *Becoming Visible: Women in European History*, ed. Renata

Bridenthal, Claudia Koonz, and Susan Stuard (Boston, MA: Houghton Mifflin, 2nd ed., 1998). Interpretive survey of current issues and existing literature.

——, ed. *Women's Earliest Records: From Ancient Egypt and Western Asia* (Atlanta, GA: Scholar's Press, 1989). Primary sources.

Manley, Bill. *The Penguin Historical Atlas of Ancient Egypt* (New York: Penguin Books, 1996). Through maps and pictures, an excellent review of Egyptian history from predynastic times through Alexander's conquest. Special sections include coverage of foreign relations and warfare, urbanization, and women. Special emphasis on trade.

Nashat, Guity. "Women in the Ancient Middle East," in *Restoring Women to History* (Bloomington, IN: Indiana University Press, 1999). Interpretive survey of current issues and existing literature.

Possehl, Gregory L. *The Indus Civilization: A Contemporary Perspective* (Lanham, MD:

AltaMira Press, 2003). One of the final works of this great scholar before his death.

Spodek, Howard, and Doris Meth Srinivasan, eds. *Urban Form and Meaning in South Asia: The Shaping of Cities from Prehistoric to Precolonial Times* (Washington, DC: National Gallery of Art, 1993). The papers of an international conference by some of the leading archaeologists working in South Asian urbanization.

ADDITIONAL SOURCES

Hassan, Fekri A. "The Predynastic of Egypt," *Journal of World Prehistory* II, No. 2 (June 1988), pp. 135–85. Careful and comprehensive account of the research.

Lichtheim, Miriam. *Ancient Egyptian Literature: A Book of Readings* (Berkeley, CA: University of California Press, 3 vols., 1973). Wide-ranging, comprehensive account of 3,000 years of literature.

Mumford, Lewis. *The City in History* (New York: Harcourt Brace, and World, 1961). Mumford looks only at cities of the Western world, but he is thoughtful, opinionated, and persuasive on what makes a good city.

Noble Wilford, John. "Egypt Carvings Set Earlier Date for Alphabet," *The New York Times* (November 14, 1999), A–1, p. 16. Records the discovery of the earliest alphabetic writing yet found.

Pritchard, James B., ed. *Ancient Near Eastern Texts Relating to the Old Testament* (Princeton, NJ: Princeton University Press, 3rd ed., 1969). The most comprehensive and accessible anthology of texts. Presented with full scholarly annotation.

Shaw, Ian., ed. *The Oxford History of Ancient Egypt* (New York: Oxford University Press, 2004). Brings together experts on many aspects of ancient Egypt. Well illustrated and comprehensive.

Wheeler, Mortimer. *Civilizations of the Indus Valley and Beyond* (London: Thames and Hudson, 1966). Head of the Archaeological Survey of India presents a clear view of its early findings in layman's terms.

FILMS

Ancient Egypt, in particular, is the subject of a constant flow of documentaries of all types from sources, such as *National Geographic*, The History Channel, Time Life, the BBC, etc. These are often (over-) dramatized, but they usually include some scholarly comments and interesting perspectives. Many are easily available on YouTube. Search and choose. Among recent ones, see:

Ancient Egypt: Life and Death in the Valley of the Kings (2013; 59 minutes). Attempts to reveal daily life in ancient Egypt through texts and art found in Upper (southern) Egypt.

Sex in the Ancient World: Egyptian Erotica (2009; 45 minutes). Reveals erotica from ancient Egypt, especially the Turin Papyrus (*c.* 1150 B.C.E.) and various tomb paintings and graffiti. The filmmakers claim that the Turin Papyrus may have been a kind of men's magazine.

Ancient Egypt's Greatest Warrior (2005; 52 minutes). Calls Thutmosis III (r. 1479–1425 B.C.E.) "Egypt's Napoleon," and describes his battles to create an Egyptian empire from Syria to Nubia, and also his relationship to his stepmother, Hatshepsut.

The Egyptian Book of the Dead (2006; 1 hour 30 minutes). The ethical and moral principles expressed in *The Book of the Dead* show that while the Egyptians wrote of death, and prepared for it, they loved life.

Films on the Indus valley civilization are comparatively few, and they borrow footage from one another. Because the civilization's script is not deciphered, there is less to relate; also, the ancient civilization straddles the modern, hostile, border of India and Pakistan, so filming is difficult. Try:

Indus: The Unvoiced Civilization (2000; 1 hour). Produced by Japanese NHK, with others with whom it shares footage. Goes to both Pakistan and India, as well as the Gulf region. Good for visuals and some scholarly commentary. Not, however, a scholarly production.

4 A Polycentric World

Cities and States in East Asia, the Americas, and West Africa

1700 B.C.E.–1000 C.E.

This chapter completes the survey of the seven areas of primary urbanization. It covers the four areas that developed primary urbanization somewhat more recently: the Yellow River valley of China; two regions of the western hemisphere—Mesoamerica and the South American Pacific coastal plain with the adjacent Andes Mountains that tower above it; and the Niger River valley of West Africa. The first cities in these regions date from as early as 1700 B.C.E. in China to as late as 400 C.E. in the Niger valley. They include cities that were not in major river valleys as well as some that were. They all show at least some evidence of state formation, long-distance trade, and religious practices. But they include settlements that did not have written languages and records. In at least one of them—West Africa—the settlement pattern is so different from urbanization elsewhere that we are asked to stretch our definition of urbanization and challenge our value system in assessing its significance.

Warrior ear ornament, cleaned and reconstructed (tomb 1), Moche Royal Tombs, Sipán, Peru, first to sixth centuries C.E. The warrior armed for battle suggests a culture dominated by powerful warrior priests. (Bruning Archaeological Museum, Lambayeque, Peru)

LEARNING OBJECTIVES

4.1 🔊	4.2 🔊	4.3 🔊
Describe the characteristics of early Chinese cities.	Describe the differences between East Asian and American cities.	Explain the urban pattern of West African settlements.

🔊 Listen on MyHistoryLab

China: The Xia, Shang, and Zhou Dynasties

4.1   What were the characteristics of early Chinese cities?

What were the
characteristics
of early Chinese
cities?

4.1

4.2

4.3

The Earliest Villages

As early as the eighth millennium B.C.E., Neolithic pottery decorations marked the transition from hunting and gathering to the culture of farming and village life. This Yangshao culture, first excavated in 1921, was named for the location where it was discovered in China's western Henan province. Among other fascinating finds, in late 1999 archaeologists uncovered a set of tiny flutes carved some 9,000 years ago from the wing bones of a large bird. Three thousand years older than the next known musical instruments, from Sumer, one of them is still playable.

The Yangshao lasted to c. 2700 B.C.E. Farmers of this era grew millet, wheat, and rice, and domesticated pigs, dogs, goats, and perhaps horses. They lived mostly in river valleys, and the villages were often surrounded with earthen walls for defense. Ban Po is the best excavated village of the Yangshao culture. From archaeological evidence, it appears that individual nuclear families occupied these dwellings, while a larger building in the center of the village may have housed clan meetings.

Slightly later and slightly to the northeast, a more sophisticated Neolithic culture, the Longshan, grew up. The people of the Longshan made their pottery on wheels, whereas the Yangshao had coiled or molded their pots by hand. The Longshan people domesticated sheep and cattle, which were not seen in Yangshao sites. Longshan graves were dug under their own homes, while the Yangshao had buried their dead in graveyards far from their villages. Sometimes Longshan funeral urns were cemented into foundation walls, suggesting ancestor worship.

Several hundred miles to the east, somewhat further down the Yellow River in Shandong, and one or two centuries later, yet another branch of Longshan culture developed, with another distinct type of pottery, often characteristically reddish-brown and gray in color, quite different from the black pottery of the Longshan of Henan. Although the high points of Yangshao and the western and eastern Longshan cultures appeared at successively later times, they overlapped one another to a considerable extent.

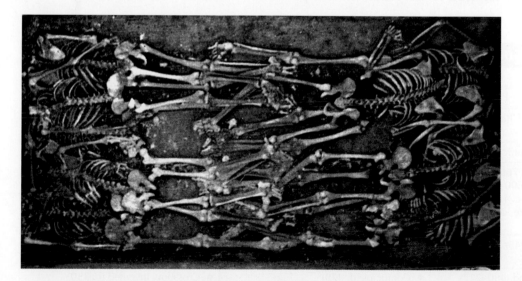

Headless skeletons of human sacrificial victims, tomb 1001, Anyang, China, c. 1495–1122 B.C.E. The royal tombs discovered at Anyang testify to the wealth and power of the Shang rulers. Numerous servants and prisoners-of-war gave their lives willingly or unwillingly to accompany their masters to the grave. The heads of the decapitated figures shown here were located elsewhere in the tomb.

The Henan Longshan culture seems to have been a harsh one. Excavations reveal the burials of victims of killing, some decapitated and showing signs of struggle, suggesting warfare between villages. The defensive walls of pounded earth that encircle some of the villages support this hypothesis, as does the presence of bronze knives.

The Beginnings of State Formation

Out of these struggles among villages, larger political units gradually emerged. Ancient Chinese historical texts tell of three early dynasties—the Xia, the Shang, and the Zhou—that ruled over large regions of China. In its time, each ruled over the most powerful single kingdom among the embattled states of northern China. All were based primarily around the Huang He (Yellow River) valley in northern China. State formation may have begun under the Xia, c. 2205–1766 B.C.E., although records are too sparse to recreate its cities and institutions. The archaeological record on urbanization under the Shang, c. 1600–1046 B.C.E., is far more revealing and reliable. The Zhou, c. 1046–256 B.C.E., consolidated both city and state, and left extensive archaeological remains and written records. None of the three dynasties succeeded in annexing all its enemies and building a single unified empire. That process would come later.

The traditional dating suggests that the states succeeded one another, but recent evidence indicates that there may, in fact, have been considerable overlap. For centuries, they may have coexisted in neighboring regions, with first one, then another, having comparatively greater power and prestige.

By the time of the Shang, if not already in the Xia dynasty, people had founded cities in northern China as centers of administration and ritual. State formation was well under way, and cities served as capitals and administrative centers. An urban network ruled the entire dynastic state. Capitals were frequently shifted, suggesting that new rulers wanted to make their mark through new construction, or that confrontation with neighboring, enemy states required strategic redeployments for improving offensive or defensive positions. Kings frequently entrusted the administration of regional cities to their blood relatives. It appears that rulers performed productive economic functions for their subjects, especially in the control of water. The ability to organize huge work gangs to construct irrigation channels and dikes for flood control confirmed their power and status. As a result, the lineages on top

AT A GLANCE: CHINA 800–100 B.C.E.

DATE	POLITICS	RELIGION AND CULTURE	SOCIAL DEVELOPMENT
8000 B.C.E.		• Neolithic decorated pottery	• Simple Neolithic society established
5000 B.C.E.	• Yangshao culture in China (5000–2700)	• Marks on Yangshao pottery possibly writing	• Penal code; defensive structures around villages
3500 B.C.E.	• Longshan late Neolithic culture	• Delicate Longshan ceramics	• Farming, with domesticated animals
2000 B.C.E.	• Xia dynasty (2205–1766) • Shang dynasty (c. 1600–c. 1046) • City of Zhengzhou (c. 1600) • Under Shang, bronze vases found in ceremonial burials	• Oracle bones • The "sage kings" in China known from legend; first known use of writing in this area	• Agricultural progress • Cities (by 1700) under control of Shang kings
1100 B.C.E.	• Zhou dynasty (c. 1045–256)	• Poetry extant from Zhou period	• Under Zhou, iron, money, and written laws in use
500 B.C.E.	• Warring States period (480–222) • Qin dynasty (221–206)	• Confucius (d. 479) • Great Wall of China begun (214) to keep out Xiongnu	• Crossbow invented (c. 350)
100 B.C.E.		• Sima Qian (d. 85)	

What were the
characteristics
of early Chinese
cities?

4.1

4.2

4.3

lived lives of considerable wealth while those on the lower levels had little, as sharp class differences emerged in the early dynastic states. The cemeteries of different classes were segregated into different neighborhoods within the city and its suburbs, and were of different quality.

In common with primary cities in other parts of the world, the Chinese cities were also religious centers, with the kings presiding over rituals as well as administration and warfare. Indeed, the warfare was necessary to supply the human and animal sacrifices that were central to the rituals.

Early Evidence of Writing. One of these early rituals has left us evidence of a crucial development in Chinese civilization: the invention of writing. Oracle bones—bones of birds, animals, and especially the shells of turtles—were inscribed with markings and writing for use in predicting the future. After they were marked, these bones were placed in a fire and tapped lightly with a rod until they began to crack. The cracks were then interpreted by specialists in predicting the future. A poem from the later Zhou dynasty noted the use of oracle bones in deciding the location of a new city:

> The plain of Chou was very fertile,
> Its celery and sowthistle sweet as rice-cakes.
> "Here we will make a start; here take counsel,
> Here notch our [turtle]."
> It says, "Stop," it says, "Halt.
> Build houses here."

(Chang, *Shang Civilization*, pp. 31–32)

Some of the oracle-bone inscriptions confirm the names and approximate dates of Xia and Shang rulers. Other bones suggest that their purpose was to communicate with the gods. The location of the bones and the content of their inscriptions encouraged archaeologists to search further in the north-central Chinese plains, near the point where the Yellow River flows out of the mountains, for evidence of China's early dynastic period.

Historical Evidence of the Xia Dynasty. Chinese legend long spoke of three ancient dynasties—the Xia, the Shang, and the Zhou. While many written records exist on the Zhou dynasty, historians were skeptical of the existence of the earlier dynasties until relatively recently. At Erlitou, east of Luoyang, in western Henan, archaeologists found a culture in precisely the areas described by ancient texts as the site of the legendary Xia dynasty. The pottery at Erlitou seemed intermediate in style and quality between the earlier Longshan and the later Shang. Although the link is not certain, many archaeologists took Erlitou to be representative of the Xia dynasty.

The Xia, like the later Shang and Zhou, seems to have been ruled by specific family clans, each with its own king. As in many cultures, kingship and kinship were linked. As head of both his biological clan and his geographical realm, the king performed rituals, divinations, and sacrifices; waged war; constructed irrigation and flood-control works; and administered his government. The king mediated between the world of the spirits and the world of humans. He was thought to be descended from the god of the spirits, who controlled human health, wealth, agriculture, and warfare. The king's assertion of his right to perform sacrifice in a particular place was, in effect, his assertion of his right to rule over that place. Rights over ritual implied rights over land and people.

Another critical task of the ruler was to tame the waters of the mighty, and hazardous, Yellow River. China's first settlements had avoided the immediate flood plain of the river, one of the most treacherous in the world. Its bed filled with the silt from the mountains, the Yellow River has jumped its course 26 times in recorded history, wreaking untold devastation. As early as the Longshan culture, people built great

HOW DO WE KNOW?

Ancient China

Three kinds of sources provide most of our direct information about early Chinese cities and dynasties: written texts, oracle bones, and artifacts uncovered archaeologically. (Scholars also sometimes take records, such as poetry, from later eras and infer that they may represent earlier conditions as well, as we shall see in the next pages.)

Texts

We have no literary texts from the Xia and Shang dynasties. Some scholars believe that the Zhou dynasty destroyed those that did exist. Much later texts ascribed to the Chinese teacher Confucius (551–479 B.C.E.) refer to the Xia and Shang dynasties, but give little detail. Later, Sima Qian (Ssu-ma Ch'ien; c. 145–85 B.C.E.), court historian of the Han dynasty, wrote the first of China's official historical annals. Sima, who had access to many texts that have not survived, devoted a chapter to the Shang royal house, beginning with its legendary founder, Xie, who moved his capital to a town called Shang, now believed to have been in eastern Henan. Successive rulers moved this capital eight times. Xie's fourteenth successor, Tang, established the hereditary dynasty of Shang. Sima's sources of information were limited, however, and his chapter mostly outlined the genealogy of the rulers, recounted moralistic tales of their rule, and briefly noted their capital cities.

Oracle Bones

A new source of information came to light in the 1890s and early 1900s. Numerous oracle bones—some apparently hidden away for many years, others recently uncovered—appeared in antiques markets in China. Over the decades more than 10,000 were discovered, mostly in the central plains of north China. These bones of birds and animals, and shells of turtles, were inscribed with symbolic notation, placed in a fire, and tapped with a rod until they began to crack. Specialists then "read" the cracks to predict the future. Some of the oracle-bone inscriptions confirmed Sima Qian's accounts of early Shang rulers. The location of the bones and the content of their inscriptions encouraged archaeologists to search further for additional oracle bones and other artifacts in the area around the ancient Shang capital of Anyang.

Archaeology

Archaeology was in fashion in China in the 1920s. Beijing Man had been discovered at Zhoukoudian, and in the process a new generation of Chinese archaeologists had received on-the-job training. Meanwhile, the new "doubting antiquity" school of Chinese historiography began to question the dating and to challenge the authenticity of many ancient Chinese historical events. In response, the newly established National Research Institute of History and Philology dispatched the young archaeologist Dong Zobin to explore the Anyang region. Dong recommended excavating for oracle bones. These excavations, mostly under the direction of Li Ji, uncovered not only bones but also sites from the Shang dynasty. These led to the discovery of artifacts from earlier eras as well. Scholars understood these to be evidence of the existence of the Xia dynasty. Ancient texts, bronzes, oracle bones, and excavations reinforced one another in recounting parts of ancient China's urbanization and state formation. Civil war in China, beginning in 1927, and war with Japan, beginning in 1937 (see "World War II"), interrupted excavations until 1950, but since then continuous archaeological research (except in 1966–74) has yielded new understanding.

- What historical evidence enabled the Xia dynasty to emerge from the realm of legend to its current status as the accepted first dynasty of ancient China?
- Politics and fashion as well as scholarly motives influence the kind of research that archaeologists can and do undertake. Discuss this assertion in terms of the excavation of the sites of early Chinese cities and dynasties.
- What kinds of skill do you think a "reader" of oracle bones must have had to be successful? What would have been considered success in this profession?

4.1
4.2
4.3

What were the characteristics of early Chinese cities?

levees and canals for flood control, drainage, and irrigation. Chinese legend credits the first success in taming the Yellow River to one of the cultural heroes of ancient history, Yu the Great of the twenty-third century B.C.E., legendary founder of the Xia dynasty. The legend reflects the idea of a royal house's gaining power through its ability to organize great gangs of laborers to construct a system of water control.

The Xia dynasty, according to mythology that is steadily being validated by archaeological finds, went further with human organization. It assembled armies, built cities, carved jade, cast and worked bronze into both weapons and ritual vessels, created the pictograms that would evolve into Chinese script, and may have designed China's first calendar.

Similarities Among the Three Dynasties. All three of these earliest dynasties, the Xia, Shang, and Zhou, built walled towns. Indeed, in written Chinese the same character, *cheng*, represents both city and city wall. At times these towns were loosely connected to one another, forming a network of rule and trade. At other times, when a single powerful king headed the dynasty, a single capital city predominated. Archaeologists see many similarities among the towns and the political structures of all three dynasties.

In the absence of earlier written records, scholars sometimes use literary evidence from later dynasties as evidence for patterns in the earlier dynasties. For example, in arguing for the supremacy of royal rule during the Shang dynasty, they find supporting proof from "Pei shan," a poem of the Zhou dynasty:

> Everywhere under Heaven
> Is no land that is not the king's.
> To the borders of all those lands
> None but is the king's slave.

(trans. Waley)

There is some evidence that women could wield power in the earliest of Chinese dynasties, but it is otherwise difficult to say much about gender relations in ancient China. By the time of the Shang dynasty, however, all evidence points to China as a patriarchal society wherein women had many fewer options than men.

City and State under the Shang and Zhou

By the time of the Shang dynasty, the ruler directly controlled a growing network of towns. The king ruled from his capital city. He apportioned regional cities to his designated representatives, who were usually blood relatives. These relatives received title to land, shares in the harvests, and rights to build and control the regional capital cities. In exchange, they represented and served the king and his interests in the provinces.

Territorially, the Shang dynasty was based in northern and central Henan and southwestern Shandong. At its most powerful it extended as far south as Wucheng, south of the Yangzi River; east to the Pacific, incorporating the Shandong Peninsula; north into Hebei and southern Manchuria; and west through Shanxi into the

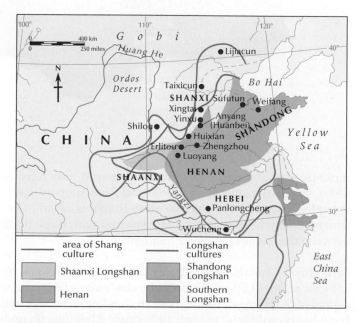

Shang China. Centered where the Huang He (Yellow River) enters its flood plain from the mountains of northeast China, the Longshan farming communities of about 2500 B.C.E. benefited from rich alluvial soils and extensive metal ore deposits. By 1800 B.C.E., a powerful, highly organized, urban metalworking culture, the Shang, had developed.

4.1 What were the
characteristics
of early Chinese
4.2 cities?

4.3

Inscribed oracle bone, China. Shang kings communicated with their ancestors through both sacrificial rituals and divination. Diviners would pose questions—about health, harvest, or politics—by applying a red-hot poker to animal bones or turtle shells and then analyzing the resulting heat-induced cracks. (Royal Ontario Museum, Toronto)

📖 Read the Document: Inscribed
Oracle Bone and Chinese Characters
on MyHistoryLab

mountains of Shaanxi. At its greatest extent it may have controlled 40,000 square miles. In addition, recent archaeological finds suggest that Shang cultural influence extended to regions and cities far away from this center of its political control. On the fringes, Shang territories were interspersed with those of other rulers, and warfare between them was apparently frequent.

Early Royal Capitals. Oracle bones identify a city named Yinxu, established about 1384 B.C.E., about 50 miles north of today's city of Anyang, as the seventh and final capital of the Shang dynasty. Some archaeologists believe that Luoyang was the first, but it has been difficult to excavate because it lies directly under a modern city. Today, most believe that Zhengzhou, about 100 miles southwest of Anyang, was the first dynastic capital, and it has been excavated extensively. Founded *c.* 1700 B.C.E., its core covered about 1¼ square miles and it was enclosed by a wall 4½ miles long and, in places, still surviving to a height of 30 feet.

Shang-dynasty bronze wine vessel, fourteenth to eleventh century B.C.E. The thousands of Shang bronze vessels that survive today continue to astonish us with their technical mastery and elegance. They testify to the elite's willingness to devote huge quantities of a precious resource to ritual purposes. During times of war, such bronzes were often melted down to produce weapons, but once peace resumed, they were recast into ritual objects. (British Museum, London)

Inside the walled area lived the royal family, the nobility, and their retainers. Outside this palace/ritual center was a network of residential areas; workshops making bone, pottery, and bronze artifacts; and cemeteries. The class divisions written into this spatial pattern were reinforced by the geography of the suburbs: to the north were the dwellings and graves of the wealthy and powerful, marked by ritual bronze vessels and sacrificial victims; to the south were the dwellings of the commoners and their burial places in trash pits. Occupations tended to be inherited within specific family units (compare the caste system of India discussed in the chapters entitled "Indian Empires" and "Hinduism and Buddhism," below). Many *zu*, or lineage groups, corresponded to occupational groups.

Capital of the Middle Period: Huanbei. In the intermediate years, between Zhengzhou and Yinxu, Huanbei (meaning 'north of the Huan River') seems to have served as a capital of the Shang dynasty, dating to about 1400 B.C.E. Discovered in excavations conducted by a joint team from the Chinese Academy of Social Sciences and the University of Minnesota, beginning in 1996, it stands within a two-square-mile enclosure surrounded by rammed-earth walls. In the center stood a palace/temple complex, the largest ever excavated from Shang times, and within the palace an enormous courtyard—the first ever discovered in China. Around the temple were 43 sacrificial pits, many containing human skulls, apparently the result of human sacrifices. Some were buried with pieces of jade, suggesting that they were people of some substance. An abundance of bronze objects have also been uncovered.

What were the
characteristics
of early Chinese
cities?

EARLY CHINESE CULTURE

5000 B.C.E.	Rice cultivation, basketry, weaving, use of wooden tools, primitive writing
3000	Domestication of sheep, cattle, water buffalo
2000	Human grave sacrifices
1900	Metalworking, class system, domestication of horse
1200	Chariots in warfare

Anyang: The Last Shang Capital. The final, most powerful, and most elaborate capital of the Shang dynasty was at Anyang itself. Shang texts report that the nineteenth king, Pan Gieng, moved his capital to Yin, and that the dynasty remained there until its fall 273 years later. Archaeologists identify that site as Anyang. This capital was the center of a network of sites stretching about 200 miles from northwest to southeast. The core area around Anyang is difficult to excavate fruitfully. The city burned to the ground, and farmers have been plowing the area, and robbers pillaging it, for 3,000 years. Remains of royal graves and of buildings that appear to be royal palaces hint at the greatness of the ancient city, but they do not yield many secrets. Nonetheless, scholars have found bronze treasures in royal graves.

The Shang excelled in crafting bronze. They produced bronze axes, knives, spears, and arrowheads as well as bronze utensils, ritual vessels, and sculptures. They also used horse-drawn chariots, which may have been derived from those of Indo-Europeans who migrated into China. The ability to use bronze in their weapons gave Chinese kings and warriors a decided advantage over their enemies, but it appears that most bronze was crafted for ritual use.

Cultural Outposts. The excavations in the Anyang region and the discoveries of the oracle bones gave evidence that the mythical Shang dynasty had been real, and that the area around Anyang had been its heartland. More recent excavations have shown that the cultural influence of the Shang reached far distant regions: massive bronzes discovered in the Yangzi River valley, more than 500 miles from Anyang; pits with hundreds of artifacts including elephant tusks, cowrie shells, and objects of jade, gold, and bronze at Sanxingdui, in Sichuan province, 700 miles to the west, dating to about 1200 B.C.E.; and at Jinsha, also in Sichuan, more bronzes cast in human forms. The objects were too different from those of Anyang for anyone to claim that all these regions formed a political unity, but they were similar enough to allow the claim of cultural unity.

The Zhou Dynasty. The Shang dynasty fell to the Zhou around 1122 B.C.E., but it did not disappear, just as the Xia had not disappeared when it had fallen to the Shang. Instead, in defeat, these kingdoms continued to exist, albeit with diminished territory and power. Until the Qin dynasty unified China in 221 B.C.E., the defeat of a dynasty did not mean that it completely disappeared. Rather, it became one of the many smaller kingdoms competing for power in continuous warfare in northern China.

The Zhou survived for more than 600 years, making it one of the longest-lasting Chinese dynasties. The Zhou made several important conceptual contributions to Chinese thinking about culture, politics, and military strategy. Moreover, with the advent of substantial written sources, we know much more about the Zhou than about the earlier Chinese dynasties.

One of the most important written sources for Zhou political thought is the *Book of Documents*, which describes the Zhou conquest of the Shang. As is often true, such a book is written from the perspective of the winners. In this case, the Zhou portrayed their victory as one of heroic soldiers over decadent forces led by a corrupt and

SOURCE

The Cosmo-magical City

In his classic and convincing *Pivot of the Four Quarters*, Paul Wheatley argues that ancient Chinese cities, like most ancient cities, began as ritual centers. He calls these cities "cosmo-magical." Archaeological and textual records support this interpretation for China. Consider, for example, this Zhou poem illustrating the siting of a royal capital. The process begins with reading the oracle shell of a tortoise to determine its location, and ends with sacrifices to mark the completion of construction:

> Of old Tan-fu the duke
> At coming of day galloped his horses,
> Going west along the river bank
> Till he came to the foot of Mount Ch'i.
> Where with the lady Chiang
> He came to look for a home.
>
> The plain of Chou was very fertile,
> Its celery and sowthistle sweet as rice-cakes.
> "Here we will make a start; here take counsel,
> Here notch our tortoise."
> It says, "Stop," it says, "Halt.
> Build houses here."
>
> So he halted, so he stopped,
> And left and right
> He drew the boundaries of big plots and little,
> He opened up the ground, he counted the acres
> From west to east;
> Everywhere he took his task in hand.
>
> Then he summoned his Master of Works,
> Then he summoned his Master of Lands
> And made them build houses.
> Dead straight was the plumb-line,
> The planks were lashed to hold the earth;
> They made the Hall of Ancestors, very venerable.
>
> They tilted in the earth with a rattling,
> They pounded it with a dull thud,

> They beat the walls with a loud clang,
> They pared and chiselled them with a faint *p'ing, p'ing;*
> The hundred cubits all rose;
> The drummers could not hold out.
>
> They raised the outer gate;
> The outer gate soared high.
> They raised the inner gate;
> The inner gate was very strong.
> They raised the great earth-mound,
> Whence excursions of war might start.

The rituals seem to have conferred worldly benefits. Potential enemies fled. The poem continues:

> And in the time that followed they did not abate their sacrifices,
> Did not let fall their high renown;
> The oak forests were laid low,
> Roads were opened up.
> The K'un tribes scampered away;
> Oh, how they panted!

Oracle records recognize more than 20 titles of officials grouped into three categories—ministers, generals, and archivists—"but the most important categories of officials insofar as our available data are concerned are the diviners … and the inquirers. … Jao Tsung-yi enumerated the activities of as many as 117 diviners and inquirers in the oracle records. Ch'en Meng-chia counted 120." (Chang, 1980, p. 192) Besides the diviners, a cadre of priests performed religious rituals, including human sacrifices.

Military force was needed to sustain these rituals, by providing the prisoners-of-war to be sacrificed when rituals demanded. Oracle records speak of Shang military campaigns of 3,000, 5,000, and even 13,000 troops. As many as 30,000 prisoners-of-war were claimed in one large battle, and 300 prisoners were sacrificed in a ritual of ancestor worship. Archaeological finds show that 600 humans were sacrificed at the completion of a single house; 164 for a single tomb.

---

debauched king. Nonetheless, they wanted to portray their strong connections and good relations with previous kings so that they would appear legitimate.

They also developed a heretofore unique explanation of why they should be considered the legitimate rulers of the region: the idea of the "**Mandate of Heaven**." The *Book of History* assumed a close relationship between Heaven and the king, but the king had the mandate to rule only if he acted in the interests of the people. If a king was weak, the theory argued that others had the right to remove him, with the "Mandate of Heaven." This doctrine would shape Chinese thinking on leadership for centuries.

While they were in power, the Zhou made several important contributions to Chinese culture. One of the most important was the *Book of Songs*, which includes a collection of China's earliest poetry, some of which appears to have been from earlier societies and transmitted orally until it was recorded. The poetry focuses on

KEY TERM

Mandate of Heaven A concept in China: the ruler had moral authority so long as the heavenly powers granted it to him on the basis of his good character. A well-functioning government was evidence that the ruler possessed the Mandate of Heaven. A poorly functioning government, especially when accompanied by such natural disasters as flood or drought, showed that the Mandate had passed away.

Burial pit, unearthed at Liulihe, Hebei province, Western Zhou period (1122–771 B.C.E.). Evidence for the centrality of ritual in ancient Chinese culture is found in this tomb, which contains the remains of horses and chariots. These important instruments of rule would have been regarded as valuable offerings to the gods and were thus buried along with their owner.

4.1

4.2 How did the first cities of the Americas differ from those of East Asia?

4.3

the exploits of kings and aristocrats, but also provides powerful insights into family life and gender relations in early China.

One poem, for example, describes the anxiety of a woman who became too old to marry. It makes clear that a man would pursue a woman in courtship and not the other way around, and that the woman would leave her family to join her husband's. Other poems speak of a deep distrust of women in politics and argue that men alone should be in the public sphere; women belonged at home. Challenging the notion of the Mandate of Heaven, at least one poem argues that women in politics, not Heaven, sowed disorder in dynasties. Still others deal with the give and take of seduction and love outside marriage.

The Zhou also transformed warfare, turning away from the chariots that seemed so useful earlier. They both developed cavalry, in which soldiers fought successfully with bows and arrows on horseback, and introduced infantry troops of draft foot soldiers who could effectively fight the cavalry with crossbows.

The Zhou expanded significantly, creating a much larger state than that ruled by the Shang. Recognizing the difficulty of ruling such a large state, the Zhou created a decentralized administration that left much power in local hands. In the end, this contributed to much instability, with the Zhou remaining in power at least nominally at the top, while facing competition from subordinates throughout China. Because of the chaos, by 480 B.C.E. a period subsequent scholars have named "the Warring States period" emerged, which lasted until the Qin dynasty unified the country in 221 B.C.E.

The Western Hemisphere: Mesoamerica and South America

4.2 How did the first cities of the Americas differ from those of East Asia?

The first cities of the Americas share several characteristics with those of East Asia. They began as religious shrine centers, linked by shamans, individuals who had special powers to communicate with the spiritual world on behalf of the community. They developed into city-states with important functions in politics and trade as well as in religion, and some even incorporated whole empires under their sway. Specific individual cities, most notably Teotihuacán, had enormous cultural influence over other settlements that were spread across great distances.

There were also great differences between the hemispheres. Geographically, the cities of the western hemisphere were built at the water's edge, usually near lakes or small rivers, but not on major river systems. Technologically, the people of the Americas did not use metals in their tools. In fact, they hardly used metal at all except for ornaments, jewelry, and artwork. They used neither wheels nor draft animals in transportation, perhaps because the Americas had no large, domesticable animals to use for pulling carts until horses and cattle were introduced by the Spaniards in the sixteenth century. Llamas served as pack animals for small loads in the Andes in South America, but otherwise goods were carried by hand, dragged, or shipped by canoe. Construction and transportation were therefore far more labor-intensive than

AT A GLANCE: THE EARLY AMERICAS

DATE	POLITICS	RELIGION AND CULTURE	SOCIAL DEVELOPMENT
6000 B.C.E.		● Stone tools in Mexico (6700 B.C.E.)	
5000 B.C.E.			● Plants (including maize) cultivated in Mesoamerica
3000 B.C.E.			● Villages established in Mesoamerica; gourds and beans grown
2500 B.C.E.	● Maya culture originated (2000)	● Pottery from Mesoamerica	
1500 B.C.E.	● Olmecs, Gulf of Mexico (c. 1500–400 B.C.E.) ● Zapotecs, southern Mexico (1400 B.C.E.–900 C.E.)	● Olmec center of San Lorenzo; pottery, mirrors, ceramics	
1000 B.C.E.	● Chavín, northern Peru (c. 900–200 B.C.E.)		
200 B.C.E.	● Moche, north coast of Peru (200 B.C.E.–600 C.E.)	● First Teotihuacán buildings, valley of Mexico	
100 B.C.E.	● Nazca, Peru (1–600)		
500 C.E.	● Tiwanaku, Bolivia (c. 200–1200) ● Maya culture (southern Mexico, Guatemala, Belize) at peak (325–900) ● Huari, Peru (c. 650–1200)	● Teotihuacán population 100,000 ● First fully developed towns in the Mississippi valley (c. 700) ● Teotihuacán culture at peak (500–650)	
1000 C.E.	● Toltecs (c. 950–1170) ● Chimú, northwest Peruvian coast (c. 1000–1470)		
1200 C.E.	● Aztecs (c. 1100–1521) ● Inca, Andean South America (c. 1200–1535)	● Aztec pictographs and hieroglyphs ● Aztec gold, jade, and turquoise jewels, textiles, and sculptures	● Aztec tribute empire over surrounding lands from capital of Cuzco

in most of Afro-Eurasia. Finally, except for the Maya, the Native Americans did not create writing systems. Some, such as the Zapotecs and Toltecs, used limited hieroglyphic symbols and calendar formats, but these did not develop into full, written languages. In Afro-Eurasia, only in the Niger River area did settlements grow into cities without developing writing systems.

In many respects, the cities of the western hemisphere still had one foot in the Stone Age. Urban society evolved much later in the Americas. Stone tools ground by hand first appeared in central Mexico about 6700 B.C.E.; the domestication of plants began about 5000 B.C.E.; villages were established about 3000 B.C.E.; pottery appeared about 2300 B.C.E.; and population suddenly increased about 500 B.C.E. These processes were much slower than in the river-valley civilizations of Eurasia, perhaps because humans arrived in the New World relatively recently. Also, the immigrants to the New World had longer journeys, from today's Alaska to the southern reaches of South America. Often, they seemed to found new towns and then abandon them for still newer ones, sometimes because they were defeated in battle; sometimes because the residents quarreled among themselves; and sometimes because they sought a better ecological niche. (See Source box, The Popul Vuh, below.)

Origins: Migration and Agriculture

Humans arrived in the western hemisphere across the Beringia land bridge (connecting Alaska and Siberia) about 15,000 years ago and then spread throughout both North and South America. By 5000 B.C.E., they were cultivating maize, at least in

4.1

4.2

4.3

How did the first cities of the Americas differ from those of East Asia?

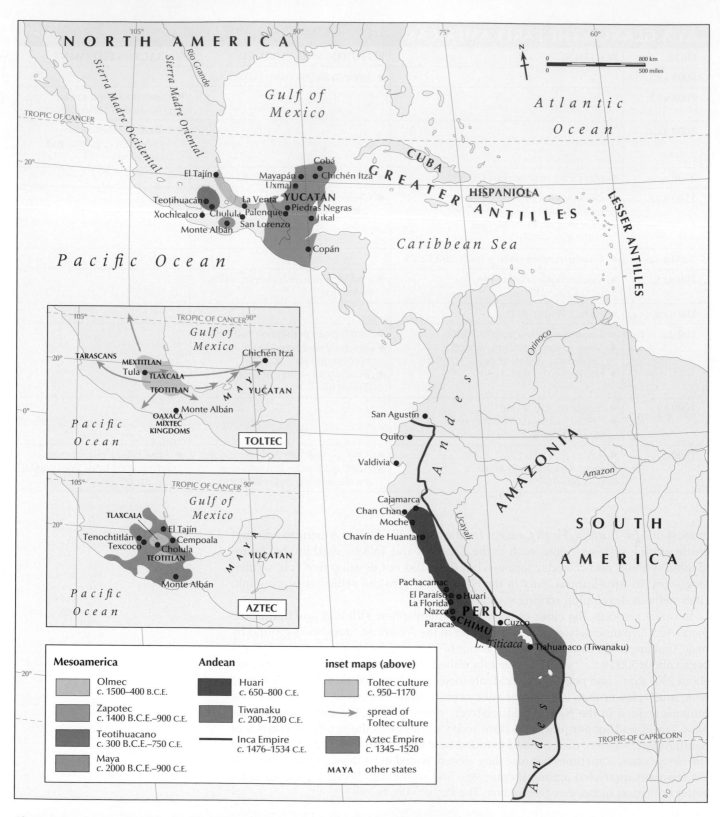

Classic cultures of the Americas. Sophisticated urban cultures developed in two tropical regions of the Americas: humid southern Mexico and the more temperate valleys of the central Andes. Both regions witnessed a succession of distinctive cultural and political centers. The Maya civilization of the Yucatán emerged, by 250 C.E., as the outstanding power in Mesoamerica, while the Huari empire of the Andes prefigured that of the Inca. In South America, urban civilizations appeared both near sea level along the Pacific coast and in the Andes Mountains, at altitudes from 6,500 to 12,000 feet.

4.1

4.2

4.3

How did the
first cities of the
Americas differ
from those of East
Asia?

small quantities, as well as gathering wild crops and hunting animals. By around 3000 B.C.E., they also grew beans and gourds.

Archaeologists and botanists have documented the beginnings of domestication of maize in the valley of Tehuacán, 200 miles southeast of Mexico City. Beginning with wild corn cobs about 5000 B.C.E., farmers slowly bred larger and more nutritious varieties, producing an early form of modern corn about 2,000 years ago. Later excavations in Peru showed that the cultivation of maize began there by 4000 B.C.E., perhaps introduced from Mesoamerica. In both regions, at about the same time, the other two staples of the American diet, beans and squashes, also appear. Further, in the Andes Mountains, potatoes and other root crops were also grown. The valley of Mexico and the high Andes of Peru thus became incubators of much of the civilization of the Americas from an early date. Agricultural innovation, urbanization, and the foundation of empires originated in these regions and spread outward.

Mesoamerican Urbanization: The First Stages

By 2000 B.C.E., the agricultural foundations for an urban civilization were in place in Mesoamerica. Farmers throughout present-day Mexico and Central America were cultivating maize, gourds, beans, and other food crops. In addition to farming dry fields, their methods included "slash-and-burn agriculture," which kept them moving from place to place in search of new land; "pot irrigation," dipping pots into wells and simply pouring the water onto the fields; canal irrigation; and, in low-lying swamplands, the creation of *chinampas*, raised fields or so-called hanging gardens. *Chinampas* were created by piling up the mud and the natural vegetation of the swamps into grids of raised land crisscrossed by natural irrigation channels. When the Spanish arrived in 1519, they estimated that the *chinampas* could feed an impressive four persons per acre; more recent archaeological estimates of their productivity suggest eight people.

Olmec Civilization along the Gulf Coast. On the basis of these agricultural systems, localized permanent settlements that centered on religious shrines and were led by local chiefs began to emerge. Trade and shared cultural and ceremonial practices gave a common character to specific regions within Mesoamerica. Along the Gulf coast of Mexico, the earliest of these civilizations, the Olmec, took shape from about 1500 B.C.E.

The Olmec built raised platforms, settlements, and shrines above the low-lying woodlands. The first that we know of was built at San Lorenzo about 1150 B.C.E. Labor brigades constructed *chinampas*, and the population of the settlement may have reached 2,500. Olmec artwork—representations of animals and mythological creatures in sculpture and bas-relief—suggests a shared religious basis for the society. The Olmec also developed rudimentary hieroglyphics, but no one has yet been able to

CIVILIZATIONS FLOURISHING IN CENTRAL AMERICA BEFORE COLUMBUS

Olmec	c. 1500–400 B.C.E. Gulf of Mexico. First complex society, or cluster of related societies, in region, with centralized authority. Known for carvings of giant stone heads and jade animals.
Maya	c. 2000 B.C.E.–900 C.E. S. Mexico, Guatemala, Belize. Most enduring of the Middle American civilizations, the Mayans had by 325 C.E. built many stepped pyramids and some astronomical observatories, smelted metal tools, and developed hieroglyphs.
Zapotec	c. 1400 B.C.E.–900 C.E. S. Mexico. Built ceremonial center of Monte Albán and peaked as a civilization around 200 C.E.

Colossal head from San Lorenzo, Veracruz, Mexico, before 400 B.C.E. Weighing around ten tons, this massive sculpted head is one of nine that were found at San Lorenzo. Made from basalt and carved with stone tools, the heads originally stood in rows on the site and are most probably portraits of Olmec rulers. All display the same full, resolute lips and broad, flat noses. Similar sculptures were found at La Venta. (Museo Regional de Veracruz, Jalapa, Mexico)

decipher them. About 900 B.C.E. the San Lorenzo site was destroyed, its artwork defaced. No one today knows why.

About a century later, some 100 miles to the northeast and closer to the Gulf of Mexico, Olmec peoples at La Venta built a small island in the middle of a swamp, and constructed on it an earth mound, half again as large as a football field and 100 feet high. Buildings atop the mound were probably used as temples. Monumental stone sculptures, including some of the giant stone heads typical of Olmec art, mark the space. Some of them probably served also as altars. The stone building materials were transported there from at least 60 miles away, the jade from much further. La Venta flourished for four centuries, until about 400 B.C.E. it, too, was destroyed and its monuments defaced. Again, no one today knows why.

Zapotec Civilization in the Oaxaca Valley. Olmec products—pottery, ritual objects, mirrors, and ceramics—appeared in the highlands around modern Oaxaca as early as 1150 B.C.E., along with natural products, such as obsidian and seashells from around the Gulf of Mexico. At first, therefore, scholars believed that the Zapotec culture of the Oaxaca valley was an offshoot of the Olmec. More recent finds in the village of San José Mogote, dating to 1400–1150 B.C.E., demonstrate, however, that the Zapotec settlements began as early as the Olmecs. The imported products reflected trading between the two groups.

Zapotec civilization peaked on the slopes of Monte Albán. By 400 B.C.E., ceremonial and public buildings dotted the summits of the hills. The settlement grew over the centuries, reaching its peak in the centuries after 200 C.E., when up to 50,000 people lived there. It was not entirely concentrated into a single city, but extended over 15 square miles, with some 2,000 terraces built into the hills, each with a house or two and its own water supply. Temples, pyramids, tombs, and an array of religious images suggest the importance of symbolism among the Zapotecs, too. Monte Albán peaked in population and creativity about 700 C.E. and then declined.

4.1
4.2
4.3

How did the first cities of the Americas differ from those of East Asia?

The Urban Explosion: Teotihuacán

Meanwhile, in the valley of Mexico, another civilization was coalescing, dominating the lands near it and finally creating a substantial empire. At its core, about 40 miles to the northeast of present-day Mexico City, stood Teotihuacán, one of the great cities of the ancient world. Teotihuacán represented a totally new kind of settlement in the Americas. It marked the beginning of a true urban revolution. At its peak, about 550 C.E., Teotihuacán accommodated about 100,000 inhabitants in some 8 square miles. Teotihuacán civilization had no system of writing, so, again, our knowledge is limited to the excavation and interpretation of physical artifacts.

The first buildings of Teotihuacán appeared about 200 B.C.E. One hundred years later, there were still only about 600 inhabitants. By 150 C.E., however, the population had grown to 20,000 and the area to 5 square miles. Then the population multiplied as the city exploded with religious, trade, artisanal, and administrative functions and personnel.

The city sat astride the major communication line between the valley of Mexico and the passes eastward to the Gulf of Mexico. Life in the city was a gift of the low-lying lake system of the valley of Mexico, especially of nearby Lake Texcoco. The lakes provided irrigation for the fields of the Teotihuacán valley, and salt, fish, and waterfowl. Basalt, limestone, and chert stone for building and clay for pottery were readily available in the valley, but other raw materials were imported, notably obsidian for tools and weapons from the surrounding mountains. Marine shells and copal (a tree resin used as incense) were imported from the Gulf region, and feathers of the quetzal bird came from the Maya regions of the southeast. Trading outposts of Teotihuacán appeared 700 miles south in Maya areas, and Teotihuacán ceramics have been found as far south as Tikal (see the discussion of Maya civilization, below). More than 400 workshops in the city produced pottery, obsidian manufactures, ornaments fashioned from seashells, and art and jewelry from jade and onyx.

A huge pyramid, the Pyramid of the Sun—at its base as broad as the great pyramid of Khufu in Egypt, though only half as high—dominated the Teotihuacán cityscape. The pyramid sits above a natural cave that early inhabitants enlarged into a clover-leaf-shaped chamber. The combination of natural cave and pyramid suggests that local people may have believed this cave to be the "navel of the universe." As Mircea Eliade (1907–86), the historian of religions, has demonstrated, the belief that all human life, or at least the lives of the local people, had emerged upward onto earth from a "navel," a single specific geographical point, was widely held in many civilizations of the ancient world. (The Garden of Eden story is a later variant of this belief.) Two additional massive shrines—the adjacent, smaller Pyramid of the Moon, and a central temple dedicated to the god Quetzalcoatl—enhance the religious dimensions of the city. Throughout its lifetime, and indeed even afterward until the Spanish conquest, Teotihuacán attracted multitudes of pilgrims from as far away as Guatemala.

The city was laid out on a monumental, geometric grid that centered on the 150-foot-wide Avenue of the Dead, the north–south axis of the city. More than 75 temples line this road, including the Pyramid of the Sun. The Pyramid of the Moon demarcated its northern terminal. The regularity of the city plan suggests a powerful government; indeed, a large administrative headquarters, the Ciudadela, dominates the southeastern terminus of the Avenue. The placement of the central Temple of Quetzalcoatl within the Ciudadela implies a close relationship between religion and administration.

At its peak, 500–650 C.E., Teotihuacán exercised a powerful imperial force over its immediate surrounding area and exerted spiritual, religious, cultural, economic, and military influence for hundreds of miles, especially to the south, into Maya areas. In 650, however, the city was deliberately burned down. Teotihuacán declined in significance. By 750 its power was broken, and its population scattered to smaller towns and rural areas. Several reasons have been suggested: the region may have become increasingly arid,

4.1
4.2
4.3

How did the first cities of the Americas differ from those of East Asia?

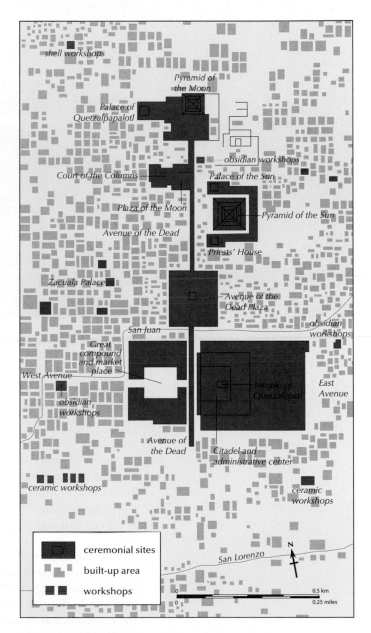

Teotihuacán. Between 400 and 750 C.E., high in the valley of Mexico, Teotihuacán was the dominant power in Mesoamerica. Covering around 8 square miles, with a population of 100,000, the city was laid out on a regular grid plan connecting the elements of a massive ceremonial complex. The residents thrived on agriculture, craftwork, and trade in ceramics and locally quarried obsidian.

View the Closer Look: Teotihuacán Ruins in Mexico on MyHistoryLab

4.1

4.2

4.3

How did the
first cities of the
Americas differ
from those of East
Asia?

Teotihuacán, Mexico, with the Pyramid of the Moon (foreground) linked to the Pyramid of the Sun
by the Avenue of the Dead. By 200 B.C.E. in the valley of Mexico, the combined effects of intensified
trading, growing religious activity, and huge surpluses of food led to the founding of this major city,
which for centuries enjoyed religious, political, and economic dominance in the region. Teotihuacán
reached an enormous size (8 square miles) and population (100,000) before eventually being
deliberately, and mysteriously, burned down in 650 C.E.

incapable of supporting so large a population; increasing density of population, augmented by government programs for moving rural populations into the city, might
have led to conflict and revolt from within; or neighboring city-states, pressured by
the increasing militarization in Teotihuacán, may have attacked the city. These are,
however, only educated guesses. In the absence of written records, no one knows
for sure.

Cities interact with one another in networks of exchange, so advances or declines
in one are usually echoed in the others. Teotihuacán and Monte Albán both declined
simultaneously about 750 C.E., but smaller, nonurban centers kept the political, cultural, and religious legacies of Teotihuacán alive in the region. (Compare this with
the experience of Western Europe after the decline of Rome, discussed in the chapter
entitled "Rome and the Barbarians.") Three subsequent civilizations—the Toltec, the
Aztec, and the Maya—absorbed and perpetuated its influence.

Successor States in the Valley of Mexico

When the Toltecs arrived in the valley of Mexico from the north and came to dominate the region from a new capital at Tula, about 900 C.E., they apparently ruled
on Teotihuacán foundations and built their chief ceremonial center in honor of

Quetzalcoatl. Their rule, however, was short-lived. About 1170 C.E., still newer immigrants destroyed the Toltec temples and government.

After Tula fell, the Aztecs entered the valley. They established settlements on the southeastern shores of Lake Texcoco and built Tenochtitlán as their capital, only 40 miles from the earlier site of Teotihuacán. As the Aztecs built their large, militaristic empire, the population of Tenochtitlán grew to 200,000. Militarism and the demand of their gods for human sacrifice led the Aztecs into a constant quest for captives to sacrifice and, therefore, into constant warfare with their neighbors. When the Spanish conquistadores arrived in 1519, the neighboring peoples helped them to overthrow the Aztecs and their empire. The Spanish then razed Tenochtitlán to the ground and established their own capital, Mexico City, atop its ruins.

4.1
4.2
4.3

How did the first cities of the Americas differ from those of East Asia?

The Rise and Fall of the Maya

Teotihuacán's third legacy was to the Maya. The Maya lived where their descendants still dwell today—in the Yucatán Peninsula of Mexico, in Guatemala, and in Belize. The Maya built on Olmec and Teotihuacáno foundations as well as on their own practices. They began to construct ceremonial centers in Yucatán and central America by 2000 B.C.E. Between 300 B.C.E. and 300 C.E., they expanded their centers to plazas surrounded by stone pyramids and crowned with temples and palaces. The classic phase, 300–600 C.E., followed with fully fledged cities and monumental architecture, temples, extensive sacrifices, and elaborate burials; and the Olmec and Teotihuacán cultural influences are evident. Maya culture flourished in the southern lowlands, and major construction took place at Palenque, Piedras Negras, Copán, Coba, and elsewhere.

The Great City of Tikal. Tikal, in today's Guatemala, is one of the largest, most elaborate, and most completely excavated of these cities. In its center, Tikal holds five temple pyramids, up to 230 feet high and built between 300 and 800 C.E. (One appeared so massive, powerful, and exotic that the filmmaker George Lucas used it as a setting for *Star Wars*.) As the first modern archaeologists hacked away the tropical rainforest and uncovered this temple core, they concluded that Tikal was a spiritual and religious center. Later, they uncovered housing and water cisterns that accommodated up to 50,000 people outside the temple precincts. This led them to change their assessment of Tikal. Instead of viewing it as a purely religious shrine, they began to see it as a large city of considerable regional political and economic significance as well. At the height of its powers, Tikal's authority covered almost 1,000 square miles containing 360,000 people. Most Maya states held only 30,000–50,000 subjects. The number of states ruled by kings grew from perhaps a dozen in the first century B.C.E. to as many as 60 at the height of the lowland civilization in the eighth century C.E.

The Maya also created an elaborate calendar that recorded three related chronologies: dates and events

A bloodletting rite, limestone lintel from Yaxchilán, Mexico (Maya), c. 725 C.E. The king, Lord Shield Jaguar, in his role as shaman, brandishes a flaming torch to illuminate the drama that is about to unfold. His principal wife, Lady Xoc, kneeling, pulls through her tongue a thorn-lined rope that falls into a woven basket holding blood-soaked strips of paper cloth. These will be burned and thereby transmitted to the gods. Few works of art made by the Maya capture so completely the link between their political and religious ideas in an appropriately sacramental style. (Having deciphered the hieroglyphics of the Mayan calendar, scholars know that this event took place on October 28, 709 C.E.) (British Museum, London)

HOW DO WE KNOW?

Great-Jaguar-Paw: Mayan King of Tikal

By deciphering, translating, and interpreting the stelae at Tikal, Linda Schele and David Freidel recreate an heroic moment of military victory in the life of the king Great-Jaguar-Paw and in the history of his kingdom. Their interpretation is based primarily on the stela illustrated below and on comparison with later stelae representing the same event:

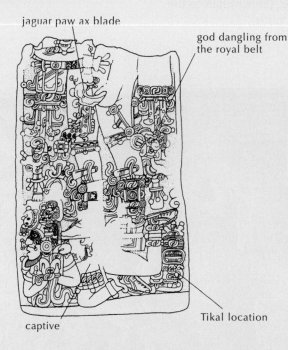

jaguar paw ax blade

god dangling from the royal belt

Tikal location

captive

Despite the fact that he was such an important king, we know relatively little about Great-Jaguar-Paw's life outside of the spectacular campaign he waged against Uaxactun. His reign must have been long, but the dates we have on him come only from his last three years. On one of these historical dates, October 21, A.D. 376, we see Great-Jaguar-Paw ending the seventeenth katun [a ritual cycle of twenty years] ... This fragmentary monument shows him only from the waist down, but he is dressed in the same regalia as his royal ancestors, with the god Chac-Xib-Chac dangling from his belt. His ankle cuffs display the sign of day on one leg and night on the other ... He holds an executioner's ax, its flint blade knapped into the image of a jaguar paw. In this guise of warrior and giver of sacrifices, he stands atop a captive he has taken in battle. The unfortunate victim, a bearded noble still wearing part of the

regalia that marks his noble station, struggles under the victor's feet, his wrists bound together in front of his chest. He will die to sanctify the katun ending at Tikal.

Warfare was not new to the Maya. Raiding for captives from one kingdom to another had been going on for centuries, for allusions to decapitation are present in even the earliest architectural decorations celebrating kingship. The hunt for sacrificial gifts to give to the gods and the testing of personal prowess in battle was part of the accepted social order and captive sacrifice was something expected of nobles and kings in the performance of their ritual duties. Just as the gods were sustained by the bloodletting ceremonies of the kings, so they were nourished as well by the blood of noble captives. Sacrificial victims like these had been buried as offerings in building terminations and dedications from late Preclassic times on, and possibly even earlier ...

The war waged by Great-Jaguar-Paw of Tikal against Uaxactun, however, was not the traditional hand-to-hand combat of proud nobles striving for personal glory and for captives to give to the gods. This was war on an entirely different scale, waged by rules never before heard of and for stakes far higher than the reputations or lives of individuals. In this new warfare of death and conquest, the winner would gain the kingdom of the loser. Tikal won the prize on January 16, A.D. 378 ...

The subjugation of Uaxactun by Great-Jaguar-Paw and Smoking Fog [his commander-in-chief], which precipitated this new kind of war and rituals, survives in the inscriptional record almost entirely in the retrospective histories carved by later rulers at Tikal. The fact that these rulers kept commemorating this event shows both its historical importance and its propaganda value for the descendants of these conquerors. (Schele and Freidel, pp. 144–48)

- What are all the symbols through which this stela represents the power and strength of Great-Jaguar-Paw?
- What does the war between Tikal and Uaxactun tell us about the increasing power of the state?
- What do you think Schele and Freidel mean by "the propaganda value" of commemorating the victory of Tikal over Uaxactun?

4.1
4.2
4.3

How did the first cities of the Americas differ from those of East Asia?

in cosmic time periods of thousands of years; historic events in the lives of specific rulers and their states; and the yearly cycle of agricultural activity. Maya rituals were permeated by the sense of living at once in the world of the here and now, and in a spiritual realm connected with other worlds and gods. Their kings were shamans, bridges between the two worlds.

Maya Civilization in Decline. By 900 C.E., the great classical period of the Maya people in the southern lowlands ended. No one knows why. The most frequent hypotheses

4.1

How did the
first cities of the
Americas differ
from those of East
Asia?

4.2

4.3

include: excessive population pressure on natural resources, especially agriculture; climatic changes beyond the ability of the Maya to adjust; and excessive warfare that wore out the people and destroyed their states. No one knows for sure.

No one knows, either, why at the time of the Maya decline in the lowlands, new Maya cities and states grew up in the northern highlands of the Yucatán peninsula, notably at Uxmal and Chichén Itzá. These cities, in turn, declined by 1200; and the last Maya capital, Mayapán, was constructed between 1263 and 1283. It adapted many of the cultural monuments of Chichén Itzá, but grew only to some 10,000–20,000 inhabitants. Mayapán seemed militaristic, beleaguered, and possessed of tough sensibilities

Temple I at Tikal, Guatemala (Maya), before 800 C.E. At its height, the city-state of Tikal covered almost 1,000 square miles and was home to 360,000 inhabitants. Its symbols of authority were centralized in its monumental shrines. This unusually steep stepped pyramid, about 154 feet high, would have been the backdrop for self-inflicted bloodletting and the sacrifice of prisoners-of-war as offerings to the gods.

SOURCE

The Popol Vuh ["Book of the People"]

The *Popol Vuh* is the most complete existing collection of creation myths and legends of early Maya history to survive the Spanish conquistadores. Originally written in Maya hieroglyphs, it was transcribed into Latin in the sixteenth century to confuse and escape the Church censors, who wanted to destroy the Maya culture. In the eighteenth century, a Dominican priest translated it into Spanish. The selection cited here captures the hunger for movement of the Quiché Maya, who repeatedly changed their location, building new towns and cities. It also speaks of the intense and lethal competition among various Maya groups leading to warfare and the subsequent human sacrifices of the defeated warriors to the gods of the victors.

Then they investigated the mountains near their citadel. They looked for a mountain on which to dwell, for they had become numerous. They who had received lordship in the East were now dead. They who had come to the peaks of each citadel had become aged grandfathers. But they were not content. They passed through numerous afflictions and misfortunes until at last they discovered the citadel of the grandfathers and the fathers.

This therefore was the name of the citadel that they came to:

THE FOUNDATION OF CHI IZMACHI

CHI IZMACHI, then, was the name of the mountain on which they dwelt as their citadel. There they settled and tested their glory. They ground their lime plaster and their whitewash in the fourth generation of lords. It is said that Co Nache and Beleheb Queh ruled then, along with the Lord Magistrate.

It was there at Chi Izmachi that Lord Co Tuha and Iztayul ruled as Ah Pop and Ah Pop of the Reception House. Under them it came to be a very fine citadel.

Only three great houses were built there at Chi Izmachi, not the twenty-four great houses of today. Yet there were three great houses:

Just one great house of the Cavecs;

Just one great house over the Nihaibs;

And just one of the Ahau Quichés.

There were only two swollen great houses, one each for the two lineage divisions at Chi Izmachi. Their hearts were united. There were no bad feelings or anger, only steadfast lordship. There was no contention or disturbance. There was only purity and a tranquil sense of community in their hearts. There was no envy or jealousy.

Yet their glory was still meager. They had not pulled together, nor had they become great. They attempted to strengthen their defenses there at Chi Izmachi. This act was surely a sign of their sovereignty. It was surely a sign of their glory, as well as their greatness.

However, this was seen by the Ilocab, who fomented war. They desired that Lord Co Tuha be murdered. They desired that there be but one lord over them. Thus the Ilocab wished to convince Lord Iztayul to murder him. But this plot against Lord Co Tuha did not succeed. Their envy merely fell on their own backs. This first attempt by the Ilocab to kill the lord failed. Yet it was the foundation of strife and the clamor for war.

Thus the Ilocab made a first attempt at invading the citadel, coming as killers. It was their desire that the Quichés be destroyed. They wished to exercise lordship in their own hearts. But when they came to seize it they were captured and despoiled, and few of them were ever set free again.

Then began the sacrifices. The Ilocab were sacrificed before the face of the god as payment for their offenses against Lord Co Tuha. Thus many were taken into captivity and enslaved. They became servants. They merely gave themselves up in defeat as a result of their clamor for war against the lord as well as his canyon-citadel. They had desired in their hearts to ruin and mock the lordship of the Quichés. But this was not accomplished. Thus they commenced to sacrifice these people before the face of the god.

Then they built their war defenses, and this was the beginning of the fortification of the citadel at Chi Izmachi. Thus they began to lay the foundation of their glory, because the sovereignty of the Quiché lord was surely great. Everywhere there were enchanted lords. None came to humiliate or mock them. They were but workers of greatness.

There they put down roots at Chi Izmachi, and there also their bloodletting god increased in greatness. And all the nations, the small and the great, became afraid. They witnessed the arrival of captive people to be sacrificed and killed by the glory and sovereignty of Lord Co Tuha and Lord Iztayul, in alliance with the Nihaib and Ahau Quichés. There were only three divisions of lineages there at the citadel named Chi Izmachi. …

These three lineages, and these three great houses, dwelt a long time there at Chi Izmachi. But then they looked for and found another citadel. And so they abandoned the peak of Chi Izmachi. (*Popol Vuh*, Christenson, pp. 249–50)

4.1

4.2   How did the
first cities of the
4.3   Americas differ
from those of East
Asia?

as evidenced by wholesale human sacrifice. The city was destroyed in civil wars in the mid-1400s.

By the time the Spanish conquistadores reached Mesoamerica in 1517, only a few small Maya towns remained. The period of Maya power and splendor had ended. The Toltecs, too, had fallen by then. The Aztecs had become the reigning power, and the Spaniards destroyed them.

📖 **Read** the **Document**: (Maya): Victory Over the Underworld on **MyHistoryLab**

HOW DO WE KNOW?

The Mysteries of Maya Writing

For centuries the connection between today's Maya—living an often impoverished existence—and the glories of their civilization in the third through the tenth centuries C.E. had been lost. Then, in 1839–41, a New York lawyer, John Lloyd Stephens, and a Scottish artist, Frederick Catherwood, discovered the remnants of the cities of Copán and Palenque in the rainforests of Mesoamerica, and the temples of Uxmal and Chichén Itzá in the Yucatán peninsula. Stephens and Catherwood wrote and painted what they saw and made rubbings of the designs they found on Maya stelae (stone marker tablets). Their research, published in 1841, opened the way for the modern academic study of the Maya at almost exactly the same time as H.C. Rawlinson and others were discovering the great archaeological sites of Mesopotamia and deciphering its language.

Stelae and other inscriptions demonstrated that the Maya had created a written language, but no one could read it. Even the Maya themselves, prevented by the Spanish from keeping their language alive, had forgotten the script. Scholars could read parts of the elaborate and sophisticated Maya calendar system, but they could not discern whether the events recorded were historical, mythical, or some combination of the two.

In the 1950s and 1960s, at Harvard University, Tatiana Proskouriakoff began to demonstrate that the Maya stelae recorded the reigns and victories of real kings who had ruled real states. Then the Russian scholar Yuri Knorozov demonstrated, against fierce opposition, that the Maya script included representations of phonetic sounds as well as of full words. By the 1970s a new generation of linguistic scholars began to decode the syntactical structure of the writing. They learned to distinguish the signs for nouns and those for verbs, and their place in the structure of the narrative. They were well on their way to discovering Maya history, and they were surprised by what they found.

The archaeologists Linda Schele and David Freidel finally mastered the hieroglyphs and scripts of the people of the city of Palenque. In contrast to previous beliefs that the Maya were peaceful and somewhat otherworldly in their concerns, as their massive temples seemed to indicate, Schele and Freidel found records of constant warfare among the local shaman kings and their profoundly religious local city-states. The Maya kingdoms fought in order to gain captives who would serve as slaves and human sacrifices to their demanding gods. The temples, it turned out, were the altars on which the sacrifices were performed. Schele and Freidel also discovered the exact lineage of the Palenque kings, and the picture of a tree used to symbolize the king, for the Maya represented their royal families as forests of trees and forests of kings.

- Why was it easier to decipher the cuneiform of Sumer and the hieroglyphs of Egypt than the symbols of Maya writing?
- Why had the Maya forgotten their own written language? Does the reason surprise you? Why or why not?
- In the How Do We Know box on Great Jaguar Paw, you can see an example of Maya writing. As you look at it, what seem to you to be the difficulties in deciphering the Maya written language?

Urbanization in South America

South America had few established trade links with Mesoamerica, but the two regions share many similarities. Both constructed religious shrine centers that seem to have dominated their general cultural foundations by about 1500 B.C.E. Both developed small city-states that defined local cultural variations from 300 to 200 B.C.E. Both created proto-empires throughout significant regions about 500–600 C.E.; and generated large, urban empires—the Aztecs in the valley of Mexico, the Inca in the Andes—and developed trading relationships between their coastal regions and their mountainous inland cores.

The contrast between coast and inland mountains is most dramatic in South America. The Pacific coast of Ecuador, Peru, and Chile is a desert in most places. The prevailing winds come not from the Pacific, but from the Amazon basin to the east. The Andes Mountains thus have little rainfall from the Pacific Ocean to trap on their western slopes, but they do intercept the precipitation from the Atlantic, making the eastern slopes fertile while leaving the west coast dry. The most spectacular urban civilizations of South America took root in the 10,000-foot-high plains and passes of the Andes rather than in the arid Pacific coast below. The contrast with the river-basin civilizations of Afro-Eurasia could not be more vivid.

Coastal Settlements and Networks

The Pacific coast is not, however, uninhabitable. It yields abundant quantities of fish, seaweed, and salt. Even today, these ocean products are traded to the mountain cities

4.1

4.2

How did the first cities of the Americas differ from those of East Asia?

4.3

How did the
first cities of the
Americas differ
from those of East
Asia?

CIVILIZATIONS OF SOUTH AMERICA

Chavín	c. 1200–200 B.C.E. Northern Peru. Farming society, comprising different regional groups, whose main town may have been a pilgrimage site.
Moche	200 B.C.E.–600 C.E. North coast of Peru. Modeled ceramics of animals in a realistic style. Religious and political life focused on the Huaca de la Luna (artificial platform) and Huaca del Sol (stepped pyramid).
Nazca	?1–600 C.E. Peru. Known principally for its series of water channels and causeways for irrigation. Seen from the air, their outlines, the "Nazca Lines," have appeared to be a mysterious symbol, perhaps a hummingbird 900 feet long.
Tiwanaku	c. 200–1200 C.E. Bolivia. Named for the ancient city, near Lake Titicaca, that was occupied by a series of five different cultures, then abandoned.
Huari	c. 650–1200 C.E. Peru. Empire whose style of architecture and artifacts, similar to Tiwanaku's, was dispersed throughout the region.
Chimú	c. 600–1470 C.E. Northwest coast of Peru. Large urban civilization (capital: Chan Chan) responsible for fine gold work, record-keeping, and aqueducts. Conquered by the Inca.
Inca	c. 1476–1534 C.E. Andean South America. Last and largest pre-Columbian civilization (capital: Cuzco) that was destroyed by Spanish conquistadores in the 1530s.

in exchange for their food crops. In some areas the cultivation of cotton is also possible, and coastal Peru rivals the Indus valley as the home of the first production of cotton textiles, about 4500 B.C.E. The quality of the textiles and the colorful designs dyed into the cotton show up most clearly in the burial cloths of semi-mummified bodies.

In addition, although climatically a desert, the coast does have some small mountain-fed rivers running through it. The same people who organized labor brigades to channel these rivers for irrigation also created ceremonial centers along the coast, beginning perhaps by 2000 B.C.E. The oldest of these shrine centers, and the one closest to the Pacific, is El Paraíso, near modern Lima, at the mouth of the Chillón River. Built in a typically U-shaped complex of buildings, El Paraíso appears to have been constructed by people from many separate villages and kin groups. Few lived at El Paraíso, but apparently the shrine served them all, and many used the location as a burial place.

The Moche. In the Moche valley of coastal northern Peru, settlements of up to 2,000 separate structures had grown up by 200 B.C.E. From about 200 B.C.E. to 600 C.E., in this and neighboring valleys, the Moche state established itself. The Moche created irrigation systems, spectacular monuments, and important tombs. In the late 1980s, at nearby Sipán, archaeologists discovered three royal tombs that demonstrate the social and political stratification of the society. Each tomb housed a lord, buried in shrouds, adorned with jewelry, some made of gold, and surrounded by servants and perhaps family members, and by animals—llamas, and at least one dog and one snake—that were buried with him. Paintings and ceramic designs within the tombs show priests engaged in warfare and performing human sacrifices of prisoners-of-war. The Moche built provincial centers in nearby river valleys from which they apparently ruled, traded, and introduced irrigation systems.

The Chimú. By about 600 C.E. the Moche had left the region, for reasons that are not entirely clear, and were succeeded by the Chimú kingdom which controlled twelve coastal river valleys. The Chimú built irrigation and water storage facilities, trade networks, and a powerful state that stretched some 1000 miles along the Peruvian coast. Their monumental capital, Chan Chan, built near the earlier Moche, was surrounded by a 35-foot-high mud wall, and it covered nearly 4 square miles, with palaces, temples, administrative offices, and housing for the common people. Chan Chan contained ten royal compounds. Apparently each king in turn built his own center, ruled from it during his life, and was buried in it after his death.

In each area they dominated, the Chimú built subsidiary administrative centers that formed a network reaching as far south as modern Lima. The Chimú empire reigned until it was conquered by the Inca in 1470. Ironically, thanks to the Inca transportation and communication network, Chimú artwork influenced western South America even more after the Inca conquest than it had before.

4.1

4.2

How did the first cities of the Americas differ from those of East Asia?

4.3

Urbanization in the Andes Mountains

Despite these coastal settlements and networks, most scholars believe that the core areas of South American urbanization were in the Andes, the 20,000-foot-high mountain chain that parallels the Pacific coast for the entire length of South America. From earliest times to today, there has been considerable "vertical trade," linking coastal lowlands with high mountain areas in an exchange of the various products of their different ecologies. With the trade came networks of cultural, religious, and political communication, and some archaeologists have argued that the civilization of the Andes Mountains was developed from a prior foundation along the sea coast far below.

The Chavín. The first known civilization of the Andes, the Chavín, flourished for about a millennium, 1200–200 B.C.E. The civilization is named for its best-known and largest ceremonial center at Chavín de Huantar, in central Peru, which flourished from about 900 to about 200 B.C.E. Chavín temples include a pantheon of gods preserved in paintings and carvings, including jaguar-like humans with serpents for hair, eagles, caymans, and many mixed figures, part-human, part-animal, reminiscent of similar figures in China. Like El Paraíso and the coastal shrines, Chavín seems to have been built by the joint efforts of many nearby kin and village groups. At its height, it held only 2,000 inhabitants, but its culture and its gods inspired common religious forms in the vicinity, and carried them throughout the high Andes.

View the **Closer Look**: **The Raimondi Stela at Chavín de Huantar** on **MyHistoryLab**

The Tiwanaku, Huari, and Nazca. Some 600 miles to the south, south of Lake Titicaca, on today's border between Peru and Bolivia, at an elevation of 12,000 feet, lay the largest open, flat plain available for agriculture in the Andes. By 200 C.E., Tiwanaku (Tihuanaco) at the southern end of the lake, near the modern city of La Paz, became the capital of the region. Its rulers irrigated their high plains (*altiplano*) region to support perhaps 20,000 people and to create a ritual center of monumental structures and religious and spiritual practices that suffused the Andes and the coast. The people of the *altiplano* traded their fruit, vegetables, llamas, and lake-caught fish in exchange for the seafood and perhaps seashells of the Pacific coast 12,000 feet below. When Tiwanaku collapsed, for reasons now lost to history, other states in the region, notably at Huari and Nazca, kept alive many of their administrative and religious practices. The Huari lands stretched for 1,000 miles along the Pacific and up into the mountains, centered on a capital city, Huari, and a line of about a dozen administrative centers along the spine of the Andes. The Nazca, in particular, built causeways and channels to control irrigation. The "Nazca lines" (see illustration, overleaf) were apparently part of this system, but were long (mis)understood as some kind of symbolic, ritual formation, visible only from far above.

The Inca. These five states—Chimú, Chavín, Tiwanaku, Huari, and Nazca—established foundations on which the Inca built their powerful but short-lived empire,

How did the
first cities of the
Americas differ
from those of East
Asia?

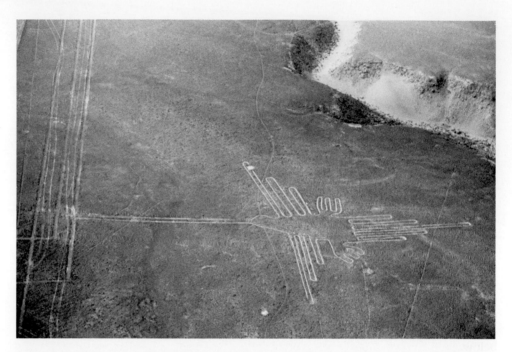

Nazca lines, San José pampa, Peru desert, c. 500 C.E. A successor state of Tiwanaku, the Nazca, created great patterns of lines drawn with pebbles on the desert surface. The overall designs, like this 900-foot-long figure that looks like a hummingbird, are comprehensible only from the air. For a long time they were viewed as indecipherable, mystical symbols. More recently they have been seen as outlines of irrigation channels and causeways.

which stretched for 2,000 miles from north to south and as far as 200 miles inland from the Pacific, and lasted from 1476 to 1534. The Inca adapted many of the gods and religious symbols, artwork, ceramics, and textiles of these earlier states. They built a new capital, Cuzco, at a height of 10,000 feet, and connected it to all the mountain and coastal regions of their empire by an astonishing 25,000-mile system of roads, with tunnels, causeways, suspension bridges, travel lodges, and storage places. The roads were sometimes broad and paved, but often narrow and unpaved, especially because the Inca had no wheeled vehicles. Enforced, *mit'a* labor was exacted from local populations for the construction.

In 1438, Cusi Yupanqui was crowned "Inca," or king-emperor, after he won a victory over a neighboring tribe, and forged his quarreling peoples into a conquering nation. Thereafter, the whole nation was called Inca. Cusi Yupanqui established a hereditary monarchy, and his descendants built a great empire from his early conquests. They employed the *mit'a* system, demanding unpaid labor for public construction for part of each year from all adults in the empire. The Inca did not develop writing, but they did create an abacus-like system of numerical records through the use of knots tied on string. These *quipu* held the administrative records of the empire. (See photograph of a *quipu* in the chapter "Establishing World Trade Routes".)

In each conquered region, the Inca established administrative centers, from which tax collectors gathered two-thirds of the crops and the manufactured products (such as beer and textiles), half for the state, and half for the gods and their priests. They established state workshops to produce official and consumer goods, and they seem to have encouraged significant standardization of production, for Inca arts and crafts show little variation over time and place. Inca religion apparently encouraged different gods and worship for different people. The sun god was the chief deity, and the emperor was considered his descendant; the nobility worshiped the military god Viracocha, while the common people continued to worship their own indigenous spirits, along with the newer sun god. The organization and the study of empire, however, take us to the Part entitled "From City-states to Empires."

4.1
4.2
4.3

How did urbanization in the Niger River valley differ from urbanization elsewhere?

Agricultural Towns in North America

Agricultural settlements took root in many locations in continental North America in the first few hundred years C.E. Several grew into small towns, reaching their maximum size about 1000–1400 C.E., and some scholars see in them the signs of early urbanization. Nevertheless, these towns are not included among the seven sites of primary urbanization because few of them reached a population size that might be considered urban; nor do they demonstrate clearly a nonagricultural base to their economies. They may also be derivative of earlier settlements to the south. For example, those in the southwestern United States, such as the Hohokam, Mogollon, and Anasazi peoples, show evidence in their artwork and building patterns of influences from Mexico and even South America.

The first fully developed towns in the Mississippi River valley appeared about 700 C.E. Their inhabitants built temple mounds and left evidence of elaborate ritual funerals, suggesting a hierarchical social and political organization. The largest of the temple-mound towns, Cahokia, occupied land along the Mississippi, across the river from and a few miles east of present-day Saint Louis. Cahokia held a population of 10,000 in the city and 38,000 in the region in the twelfth and thirteenth centuries. Such a large population probably included many craft specialists. Around the town were sited some 100 mounds, which served as burial tombs or as platforms for homes of the elite. The mounds resemble those of Mexican cities and suggest interchange between the two regions. Evidence indicates that a strong central authority controlled the town. For reasons that are not entirely clear, Cahokia, like almost all the towns of North America, was in decline or even deserted before the arrival of European invaders in the early 1500s. Archaeologists continue active research into the towns of North America, their cultures, and their links to one another and to other regions.

📖 Read the Document: **Nineteenth-century Description of Cahokia** on **MyHistoryLab**

West Africa: The Niger River Valley

4.3   How did urbanization in the Niger River valley differ from urbanization elsewhere?

Until the late 1970s, all the cities in sub-Saharan Africa that were known to archaeologists had developed along patterns introduced from outside the region. Meroe and Kush on the upper Nile had adapted urban patterns from Egypt. Axum in modern Ethiopia had followed examples of urbanization from both the Nile valley and the trading powers of the Indian Ocean. Port cities along the East African coast, such as Malindi, Kilwa, and Sofala, had been founded by traders from across the Indian Ocean. The walled stone enclosures, called **zimbabwes**, built in the region of modern Zimbabwe and Mozambique to house local royal rulers, had been initiated through contact with Swahili traders from the coast.

In West Africa, the first known cities, such as Timbuktu, Jenne, and Mopti along the Niger River, and Ife and Igbo Ukwu deeper south in the Yoruba lands near the tropical forests, had been built as centers of exchange. They were thought to be responses to the arrival of Muslim traders from North Africa who crossed the Sahara southward after the seventh century C.E. Archaeologists believed that Africans, like Europeans, had learned about city building from outsiders. This viewpoint has now been challenged.

📖 Read the Document: **Strabo on Africa (1st c. CE)** on **MyHistoryLab**

KEY TERM

zimbabwe (zim-bahb-way) Stone-walled enclosure or building built during the African Iron Age in the region of modern Zimbabwe and Mozambique. The structures were the courts of local rulers. They have been associated with foreign trade, integrated farming and animal husbandry, and gold production. The Great Zimbabwe is the ruins of the former capital of the Monomatapa Empire, situated in Zimbabwe and occupied from around the thirteenth to the sixteenth century C.E.

AT A GLANCE: EARLY AFRICA

DATE	POLITICS	RELIGION AND CULTURE	SOCIAL DEVELOPMENT
500 B.C.E.		• Nok terra-cotta sculptures • Bantu adopting settled agricultural lives	• Iron smelting
250 B.C.E.	• Jenne-jeno founded	• Copper and semi-precious stone ornaments from Niger	
500 C.E.	• Ancient Ghana		
1000 C.E.	• Foundation of Benin (c. 1000)		
1200 C.E.	• Ghana falls; Kingdom of Mali founded		• Cities in Niger valley (400 C.E.) recorded by Arab visitors

4.1

4.2

4.3 How did urbanization in the Niger River valley differ from urbanization elsewhere?

West Africa Before Urbanization

The most important developments of pre-urban West Africa were iron smelting, apparently initiated by contact with North Africa; the development of new artistic traditions, especially by the Nok peoples; and the spread of agricultural civilization by the Bantu people. Iron smelting entered the archaeological record in West Africa suddenly about 500 B.C.E. In most places the technology jumped directly from stone to iron, with only a few examples of copper-work in between. Most archaeologists interpret this technological jump to indicate that iron working was introduced from outside, probably from the Phoenician colonies along the North African coast, and they find evidence for this idea in the rock art of the Sahara Desert. Along the routes

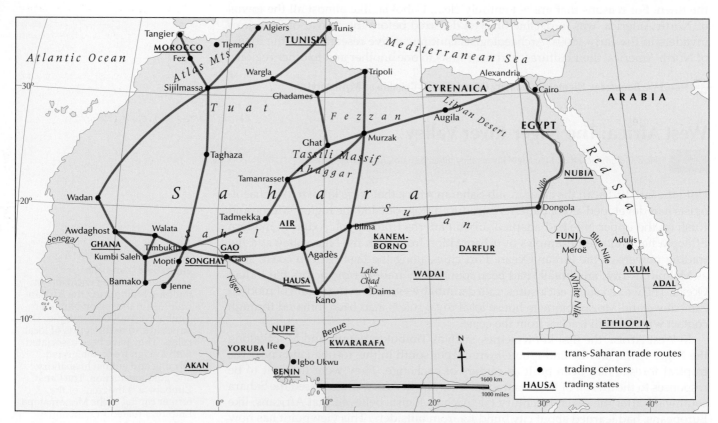

Trade across the Sahara, c. 500 C.E. Ivory, gold, hardwoods, and slaves were the magnets that drew trading caravans south across the arid Saharan wastes, often following routes established before the desert had formed. These routes linked the classical cultures of the Mediterranean and southwest Asia with an array of rich trading states strung along the Sahel/Sudan axis.

crossing the desert, rock engravings and paintings dating from between 1200 and 400 B.C.E. depict two-wheeled chariots that suggest trans-Saharan traffic.

In northern Nigeria, the Nok peoples were producing terra-cotta sculptures, especially of human heads, from about 500 B.C.E. Living in settlements along the Niger, near its confluence with the Benue in modern Nigeria, the Nok also built iron-smelting furnaces, dating to 500–450 B.C.E.

Meanwhile, also in the lower Niger, some Bantu peoples were giving up nomadic pastoralism for settled agriculture, although many remained nomadic for a long time. They began great, but gradual, migrations southward and eastward over thousands of miles, introducing their languages, their knowledge of iron production, and their experience with settled agriculture. In the thousand years between 500 B.C.E. and 500 C.E., the Bantu carried their languages, their new, settled way of life, and their metallurgical skills almost to the southern tip of Africa.

Jenne-jeno: A New Urban Pattern?

Neither the Nok nor the Bantu built cities. Other people of the Niger River, however, apparently did. In excavations that began in 1977 and continue today, archaeologists Susan and Roderick McIntosh uncovered Jenne-jeno, "Ancient Jenne," the first known indigenous city in sub-Saharan Africa. The Jenne-jeno settlement began about 250 B.C.E. as a small group of round mud huts. Its herding and fishing inhabitants were already using iron implements, and the village grew to urban size by 400 C.E., reaching its peak of settlement by about 900 C.E.

The physical form of the city was different from that of the other six centers we have studied. A central inhabited area of some 80 acres was surrounded by a city wall 10 feet wide and 13 feet high with a perimeter of 1¼ miles. Near this central area were some

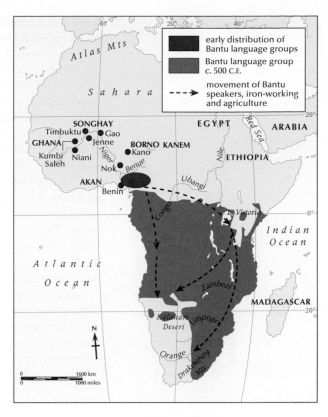

The spread of Bantu. About 1500 B.C.E. an extraordinary cultural migration began to transform sub-Saharan Africa. From their homeland near the Niger delta, groups of Bantu-speaking farmers began to move east and south, spreading cattle domestication, crop cultivation, and iron-working. By about 500 C.E., they reached southern Africa, the original hunter-gatherers having been marginalized to remote regions such as the Kalahari Desert.

View the **Map**: **Bantu Migration** on **MyHistoryLab**

4.1

4.2

4.3

How did urbanization in the Niger River valley differ from urbanization elsewhere?

Two men with an ibex, Tanzoumaitak, Tassili Mountains, Sahara, 7000–6000 B.C.E. Rock painting. Rock art of the Sahara at first represented such wild animals as buffalo, rhinoceros, hippopotamuses, giraffes, and elephants. By 6000 B.C.E. it was representing domesticated animals, such as ibex or goats, dogs, horses, and camels, suggesting a transition from hunting to pastoralism and settled agriculture.

4.1

4.2

4.3

How did urbanization in the Niger River valley differ from urbanization elsewhere?

forty smaller, but still substantial, additional settlements. They extended to a radius of 2½ miles. By the year 1000, the settled area may have contained 50,000 people.

Excavations through numerous levels have revealed that the people of Jenne-jeno ate fish from the river, rice from their fields, and beef from their herds. They probably drank the cows' milk as well. At least some wore jewelry and ornaments of imported copper and semi-precious stones. Dozens of burial urns, each up to 3 feet high, yielded human skeletons arranged in fetal position. The urns date from 300 to 1400 c.e., and their burial inside and adjacent to the houses suggests a reverence for ancestors. Statuettes in a kneeling position set into walls and under floors further suggest the probability of ancestor worship.

This part of the religious and cultural heritage of Jenne-jeno seems to have endured. Although not built primarily as a shrine center, Jenne-jeno included religious functions as an important part of its activities, as its modern counterpart does today. There are also similarities between the arrangement of the huts of Jenne-jeno 1,000 years ago and the grouping of family huts there today. In ancient times as in modern, it appears that the husband-father lived in one large central hut while his wives occupied the surrounding huts.

Jenne-jeno must have engaged in trade, because even in 250 B.C.E. its inhabitants were using iron and stone that had to be brought from at least 30 miles away. Sandstone for their grinding stones must have been imported from at least 60 miles away, while copper and salt came from hundreds of miles away. The McIntoshes have also discovered one gold earring, dating to about 750 c.e., in the region. The nearest site of gold mining was 500 miles away. Perhaps the people of Jenne-jeno traded the fish of the Niger and the rice of their fields for these imports. Some Jenne-jenoites may have become professional merchants.

Innovation in architectural concepts may also have come to Jenne-jeno from outside. By about 900 c.e., some rectangular houses began to appear among the circular ones, perhaps introduced through contact with northern peoples. Outside contact increased with the introduction of camel transportation across the Sahara about 300 c.e. and with the Muslim Arab conquest of North Africa about 700 c.e. Especially after 1200 c.e., Muslim traders crossing the Sahara linked the savanna and forest lands of the south to the cities of the Mediterranean coast. Most scholars have argued that these external contacts and trade possibilities encouraged the growing importance of such new cities as Timbuktu, Jenne-jeno, Niani, Gao, Kano, and, further south, Benin. The McIntoshes suggest an opposite perspective: that these cities predate the northern connections, and, indeed, their prosperity and control of the trade routes and the gold further to the south encouraged the northerners to dispatch their camel caravans across the Sahara. This debate remains unresolved.

By 1100, the settlements peripheral to Jenne-jeno began to lose population. Some of their inhabitants apparently moved to the central settlement. In another century the rural population also began to decline. By 1400, Jenne-jeno and its satellites were no more. Why? Perhaps warfare and slave-trading upset local stability. It is also possible that land rights and family structures shifted, reducing residents' interest in the region. Finally, it is possible that migration to other places along the Niger River simply allowed Jenne-jeno to decline slowly. We just do not know.

State Formation?

Could the settlements of the Middle Niger at Jenne-jeno be an example of early urbanism without a strong centralized government? Without a

Head from Jemaa, Nigeria, c. 400 B.C.E. The Nok were a nonliterate farming people who occupied the Jos Plateau in northern Nigeria during the first millennium B.C.E. Their distinctive sculptures—of elephants, snakes, monkeys, people, and even a giant tick—are all boldly modeled and skillfully fired in terra cotta. This powerful life-size head probably formed part of a full-length statue. (National Museum, Lagos, Nigeria)

state? It is possible. The population at Jenne-jeno lived in neighboring clusters that were functionally interdependent, rather than in a single urban center with a prominent core marked by large-scale, monumental architecture, as was found in most other centers of primary urbanization. This kind of development might be viewed as "a precocious, indigenous, and highly individual form of urbanism" (R. McIntosh, p. 203). In this case, it is possible that Jenne-jeno rose on the basis of trade and expanded into neighboring, interactive settlements, but without a hierarchical social structure or a strong, central authority. In contrast to primary urbanization in all the other regions of the world we have examined, Jenne-jeno may have experienced relative equality and cooperation among its citizens, rather than competition, dominance, and coercion.

On the other hand, a comparative assessment might suggest that Jenne had developed only to about the stage of the Olmec settlements and had not yet created the kind of centralized authority that emerged clearly and powerfully among the later Maya. Had Jenne-jeno persisted longer and grown larger, perhaps centralization and stratification would have developed. Indeed, the presence of a central settlement surrounded by smaller adjacent settlements suggests that some hierarchy was already emerging. Did Jenne-jeno represent an alternative kind of urbanization, or was it a settlement that was on its way to full-scale conventional urbanization? These are the kinds of questions of comparison that archaeologists—and historians—love to debate.

The First Cities:
What Difference Do They Make?

With the creation of cities, humanity entered into many new forms of living. The first of these cities, in the river valleys of Mesopotamia and the Nile almost 5,500 years ago, introduced not only new scale and density in human settlement patterns but also new technology in the metallurgy of copper, tin, and bronze; monumental scale in architecture; and specialization and hierarchy in social, political, and economic life. These cities flourished also as nodes in networks for the exchange of goods and ideas. The invention of writing in these cities not only gave new life to cultural creativity, but also provided new means of record-keeping for the bureaucrat, businessperson, and scholar. These new cities allowed and demanded complex and hierarchical government to keep them functioning. Although we sometimes see cities today as homes of secularism and heterogeneity, these early cities were also religious in the sense that they often existed to promote dedication to specific gods through their physical and ritual organization. Differences in climate and culture separate Egyptian from Mesopotamian urbanization, but they also shared many similarities. We know somewhat less about Egyptian urbanization because the Nile itself washed away many of its foundations, but more recent archaeology has uncovered Egyptian as well as Sumerian city walls and residential structures, suggesting that they also needed to protect their inhabitants from outsiders.

Sumer and Egypt provide what scholars sometimes refer to as a **"master narrative,"** a conventional, widely accepted view of historical transformation, suggesting that the historical process at other times and places will follow similar patterns. Each of our subsequent case studies has reinforced some dimensions of the "master narrative," while challenging others.

- Indus valley urbanization suggested that a generally consistent civilization could extend over an immense geographical space, over thousands of years. A few of its distinctive, planned cities stood out as capitals, but even after they were evacuated, other cities of the far-flung network kept the civilization alive.

Bronze kneeling figure, Jenne, Mali, c. 1100–1400. Archaeological activity since the 1970s has revealed Jenne-jeno, "Old Jenne," as a commercial center on the Niger River from about 250 B.C.E. Its traditions seem to have persisted through the centuries and into "new" Jenne, the city that now stands adjacent to the older excavation. Such statuettes as this one, produced in Jenne-jeno, may have been used in worship of and for ancestors. (Private collection)

KEY TERM

master narrative The conventional, widely accepted view of the historical record.

Moreover, Indus agricultural practices were adopted and adapted by invaders who transplanted some of them from the Indus valley to the Ganges valley.

- Early Chinese urbanization, represented in the historical record through oracle bones and through the geometrical design of city plans, placed added emphasis on the religious dimension of cities, although the rulers did not neglect to mobilize large and powerful armed forces.

- In the Americas, such cities as Teotihuacán and the later cities of the Maya demonstrated again the importance of monumental religious architecture, although each additional excavation reveals the extent of both long-distance trade and everyday, mundane activities. Urbanization in the Andes Mountains indicates that not all early cities needed riverbeds. Urban rulers could construct fabulous networks for trade, communication, and troop movement at forbidding altitudes. From their capital cities they could launch empires. They could also administer cities, and even empires, without having invented writing.

- In the Niger River valley of West Africa, the single primary urban settlement that has been excavated challenges the "master narrative," suggesting that cities may develop through the interrelationship of adjacent smaller settlements without the need for hierarchy, centralization, government structure, or written language. The data presented thus far may be, however, subject to different interpretations. Perhaps the central mound in Jenne-jeno does, in fact, represent some hierarchical structure. Or perhaps it is a collection of contiguous villages rather than an urban center. The interpretation depends in part on how far the definition of a city and its functions may be—and ought to be—stretched. Continuing excavation and interpretation will help to decide the degree to which the "master narrative" concerning early urbanization will hold up, and to what degree new, less rigid ideas of the role of urbanization in human history are yet be formulated.

CHAPTER REVIEW

CHINA: THE XIA, SHANG, AND ZHOU DYNASTIES

4.1 What were the characteristics of early Chinese cities?

The first cities in China were centers of administration and ritual, long-distance trade and religious practice. They were laid out according to priestly interpretations of oracle bone inscriptions. A king ruled from a capital and controlled a network of subordinate cities run by his representatives. He performed rituals, divinations, and sacrifices; waged war; saw to the construction of irrigation works; and administered the government. Cities contained bronze, pottery, and bone artifact workshops, and networks of residential areas. Archaeological evidence shows the class divisions in cities' spatial plans: the dwellings and decorated graves of the wealthy and powerful are in one area, and the dwellings of the commoners and their burial places are located in trash pits.

THE WESTERN HEMISPHERE: MESOAMERICA AND SOUTH AMERICA

4.2 How did the first cities of the Americas differ from those of East Asia?

Like the urban areas of East Asia, the first cities of the Americas began as religious shrine centers, then developed into city-states with functions in trade and politics as well as religion. They frequently made war with one another, and various groups succeeded one another as the most powerful.

Some cities wielded enormous influence over a wide area of settlements. The cities of the Americas were not built on major river systems as in East Asia. In Mesoamerica they emerged at water's edge, on lakes or small rivers; in South America they emerged on the shores of the Pacific below and in the Andes Mountains above. The Americans did not use metals for much of anything apart from jewelry and artwork. They did not invent the wheel nor use draft animals (except for llamas) for transportation. Only the Maya created writing systems.

WEST AFRICA: THE NIGER RIVER VALLEY

4.3 How did urbanization in the Niger River valley differ from urbanization elsewhere?

The first known cities in the Niger River valley of West Africa were built as centers of exchange. The people traded copper, sandstone, salt, and gold across the Sahara. It is possible that the people in Jenne-jeno, the only early city that has been found in this region so far, lived in clusters of interdependent communities, without a single core that included hierarchy, centralization, and government structure—the elements of urbanization found elsewhere. It may be that the people in the settlements of the Niger River valley experienced cooperation, rather than competition, equality rather than coercion.

Suggested Readings

PRINCIPAL SOURCES

Coe, Michael, Dean Snow, and Elizabeth Benson. *Atlas of Ancient America* (New York: Facts on File, 1986). One in the excellent series by this publisher, prepared by experts, with text, maps, pictures.

Fagan, Brian. *People of the Earth: An Introduction to World Prehistory* (Upper Saddle River, NJ: Prentice Hall, 13th ed., 2010). Outstanding anthropological textbook on prehistory.

Hessler, Peter. "The New Story of China's Ancient Past," *National Geographic* (July 2003), pp. 56–81. Journalist-scholar Hessler presents accessible, up-to-date information and illustrations of Shang urbanization, especially around Anyang, but also in southwest China, where it may not be Shang.

Loewe, Michael, and Edward L. Shaughnessy, eds. *The Cambridge History of Ancient China* (Cambridge: Cambridge University Press, 1999). The article by D.N. Keightley, "The Shang: China's First Historical Dynasty," pp. 232–91, is most relevant on the period and its archaeological finds, urban and other.

Mann, Charles C. *1491: New Revelations of the Americas Before Columbus* (New York: Vintage Books, 2006). Scholarly, accessible, a best seller. Summarizes much new scholarship; focuses more on the period just before Europeans arrived, but goes back even to before "Native Americans" arrived.

Mazurkewich, Karen. "Personal Journey: The Art of China; Unearthing a New History," *Asian Wall Street Journal*, May 14, 2004, p. 1. Report on the excavations at Huanbei, with discussion by the archaeologists.

McIntosh, Roderick James. *Ancient Middle Niger Urbanism and the Self-Organizing Landscape* (Cambridge: Cambridge University Press, 2005). The most recent book publication on Jenne-jeno by one of the two principal archaeologists involved in its excavation.

Murray, Jocelyn, ed. *Cultural Atlas of Africa* (New York: Facts on File, 1982). One in the excellent series by this publisher, prepared by an expert with text, maps, pictures, and time lines.

Schele, Linda, and David Freidel. *A Forest of Kings: The Untold Story of the Ancient Maya* (New York: William Morrow, 1990). Tells how the Mayan language was deciphered, by those who did it.

Smith, Michael E., and Marilyn Masson, eds. *The Ancient Civilizations of Mesoamerica: A Reader* (Oxford: Blackwell, 2000). Twenty-three outstanding scholars contribute. Several of the essays deal with urbanization. Classroom-tested by the editors.

Tang, Jigen, Zhichun Ding, and George Rapp. "The Largest Shang City Located in Anyang, China," *Antiquity* LXXIV:285 (September 20, 2000), p. 479. Brief account adding Huanbei Shang City, excavated since 1996, to the series of capitals established sequentially by the Shang dynasty.

The Times (London). *Past Worlds* (Maplewood, NJ: Hammond Inc., 1988). Excellent, comprehensive, scholarly introduction to archaeological prehistory, lavishly illustrated with maps and pictures.

ADDITIONAL SOURCES

Alva, Walter, and Christopher Donnan. *The Royal Tombs of Sipán* (Los Angeles, CA: Fowler Museum of Cultural History, University of California, 1993). Lavishly illustrated account of the excavation.

Chang, Kwang-chih. *The Archaeology of Ancient China* (New Haven, CT: Yale University Press, 3rd ed., 1977). The expert's account, somewhat dated, but still the standard.

——. *Shang Civilization* (New Haven, CT: Yale University Press, 1980). Comprehensive account by an archaeologist who participated in some of the most significant excavations.

Connah, Graham. *African Civilizations* (Cambridge: Cambridge University Press, 1987). Excellent, comprehensive textbook on prehistoric Africa. Covers the entire continent.

Curtin, Philip, Steven Feierman, Leonard Thompson, and Jan Vansina. *African History from Earliest Times to Independence* (New York: Longman, 2nd ed., 1995). A standard textbook by four distinguished experts.

de Bary, William Theodore, *et al.*, comp. *Sources of Chinese Tradition.*, Vol. 1. (New York: Columbia University Press, 1998). The best available anthology of classic writings. Good section on oracle bones.

Demarest, Arthur, and Geoffrey Conrad, eds. *Ideology and Pre-Columbian Civilizations* (Santa Fe, NM: School of American Research Press, 1992). Scholarly argument on the importance of ideas, both cosmo-magical and political, in the construction of pre-Columbian civilizations.

Ebrey, Patricia Buckley. *The Cambridge Illustrated History of China* (Cambridge: Cambridge University Press, 2nd ed., 2010). Only a short section on early urbanization, but places it in very accessible context, and the illustrations and maps are helpful.

Keightly, David N., ed. *The Origins of Chinese Civilization* (Berkeley, CA: University of California Press, 1983). An excellent account.

MacNeish, Richard S. "The Origins of New World Civilization," *Scientific American*, November 1964. Reprinted in *Scientific American, Cities: Their Origin, Growth, and Human Impact* (San Francisco, CA: W.H. Freeman and Company, 1973), pp. 63–71. Brief introduction, especially interesting on domestication of crops and animals.

McIntosh, Susan, and Roderick McIntosh. "Finding West Africa's Oldest City," *National Geographic* CLXII No. 3 (September 1982), pp. 396–418. Popular introduction based on early archaeological expeditions.

McIntosh, Susan Keech, ed. *Excavations at Jenné-Jeno, Hambarketolo, and Kaniana (Inland Niger Delta, Mali): The 1981 Season* (Berkeley, CA: University of California Press, 1995). Comprehensive, scholarly documentation on the excavations.

Millon, René. "Teotihuacán," *Scientific American*, June 1967. Reprinted in *Scientific American, Cities: Their Origin, Growth, and Human Impact*, pp. 82–91. Basic introduction to the early professional excavations of Mesoamerica's largest prehistoric metropolis.

Moseley, Michael E. *The Maritime Foundations of Andean Civilization* (Menlo Park, CA: Cummings, 1975). Argues that the Andean cities were founded on the basis of the Pacific coastal developments.

Popul Vuh: Sacred Book of the Quiché Maya People, translation and commentary by Allen J. Christenson (Norman: University of Oklahoma Press, 2007).

Scientific American, ed. *Cities: Their Origin, Growth, and Human Impact* (San Francisco, CA: W.H. Freeman and Company, 1973). Anthology of articles on urbanization culled from *Scientific American* articles. Still useful.

Waley, Arthur, trans. *The Book of Songs* (New York: Grove Press, 1996). Marvelous translation of poetry from the age of Confucius.

Wheatley, Paul. *The Pivot of the Four Quarters: A Preliminary Enquiry into the Origins and Character of the Ancient Chinese City* (Chicago, IL: Aldine, 1971).

FILMS

Legacy: The Origins of Civilization— China (1992; 1 hour). Michael Wood's idiosyncratic introduction to ancient China, with useful sections on the discovery of oracle bones and early cities. Good visuals.

Time-Life. *Lost Civilizations: China: Dynasties of Power* (2002; 1 hour). Also good visuals and interesting comments from experts explaining how the earliest cities functioned, and the role of regional rulers in establishing them.

National Geographic. *Megastructures: Machu Picchu* (2012; 46 minutes). Emphasizes the engineering and construction of this remote city in the Andes Mountains. Asks how the buildings functioned and how they were built.

Teotihuacán (2001; 27 minutes). Looks at the belief system that encouraged the Aztecs to build this huge and remarkable city, and at the engineering skill needed to build it.

West Africa (2009; 47 minutes). Includes a four-minute section on Jenne-jeno and its significance for later developments.

PART THREE

TURNING POINT: FROM CITY-STATES TO EMPIRES

2000 B.C.F.–1100 C.E.

What Are Empires and Why Are They Important?

From Gilgamesh onward, the rulers of city-states constructed city walls and mobilized armed forces. If situated at water's edge, they commanded ships and sailors as well. Their reputation rested on both military prowess and civilian administration. The literature from Mesopotamia, pre-imperial China, ancient Greece, and Mayan Mesoamerica abounds with tales of warfare among city-states. They fought incessantly.

Increasing military force transformed these city-states into empires. Sargon of Akkad (exact dates uncertain) set the example. His conquest of the quarreling city-states of Mesopotamia around 2250 B.C.E. created the first empire recorded in history.

After conquering the cities of the middle and upper Euphrates, Sargon marched into southern Anatolia. Then he turned eastward, capturing Susa, the capital city of the Elamites in western Iran. Sargon's empire lasted for only

A phalanx formation. The box-office success of the film *300* indicated the continuing power of Herodotus' history of the Persian Wars, and especially its story of the defensive strategy of Leonidas and his 300 men at Thermopylae. The film accurately shows the power of the phalanx, the company of soldiers protecting themselves and their fellows with the collective positioning of their shields.

about a century, but from his time onward Mesopotamia was usually ruled by a single empire, most frequently an invading force (like his own), but sometimes by an ambitious army arising from within. Sargon's rule ended the era of the Mesopotamian city-states and ushered in the era of empire.

The Meaning of Empire

New York proudly calls itself the Empire State. At least five states in the United States contain cities named "Imperial." California boasts an Imperial Valley and an Imperial County. Until recently, Britain maintained its "imperial gallon" as a measure of volume. Today, however, "empire" often carries negative connotations, and "imperialism" even more so. The demise within the past generation of many empires, most recently that of the Soviet Union, has met with general approval around the world. Why has the significance of "empire" changed so dramatically? What is an empire? How do empires rule?

The Assyrian army with its musicians, from the Palace of Ashurbanipal, Nineveh, seventh century B.C.E. Limestone relief. From earliest times armies included musicians whose horns and trumpets would encourage their own troops and frighten the enemies, and whose lyres, after battle, might bring some respite. (Louvre, Paris)

Empires grow from the conquest of one people by another. They have been as natural in human history as the desire of one people to exert control over other peoples and their resources, and they have arisen as frequently as rulers have been able to build military organizations capable of attaining those goals.

Scholars emphasize two forms of imperial rule: hegemony and dominance. The ruling powers themselves prefer hegemony, foreign rule that governs with the substantial consent of the governed people. Subjects in such an empire accept foreign rule willingly, if they can be persuaded that it is in their best interests. Subjects may benefit from the stability and peace imposed by imperial rule; the technological improvements it introduces; the more extensive networks it develops and opens for trade and profit; the cultural sophistication it exhibits and shares; and the opportunities for new kinds of advancement that membership in the empire may offer. If imperial membership is perceived to have such benefits, the subject peoples may welcome it peacefully, even eagerly. They may accept the ideology of the imperial power, its moral authority and its claim to legitimacy.

Should the imperial ideology not be acceptable, however, and should opposition arise, rulers will impose their government through dominance, the exercise of military force and sheer power. So the state expends vast sums on recruiting, training, and equipping its armies. It mobilizes its troops across the vast spaces of empire, dispatching them along the same roads that carry the imperial commerce. To subdue and overwhelm its enemies, the imperial government may deploy its power in acts of cruelty and arrogance.

Resistance to imperial rule is as normal as empires themselves. Sooner or later, the secrets of the imperial power spread among the conquered. Empires begin by using their superiority to rule, but eventually subject populations learn from the technology introduced by their conquerors: newer and more powerful weapons, materials, military formations, agricultural methods, administrative organizations, and techniques of production. They gain the capacity to challenge their rulers. Subject peoples, who may originally have felt some gratitude toward their imperial benefactors, may later grow resentful, restive, and finally rebellious.

The Dynamics of Empire

To inspire admiration and loyalty among allies, and caution among potential enemies, empires build monumental palaces for the emperor and the leadership cadre. They establish vast marketplaces stocked with exotic and luxurious goods, and they build highways and roads, ports and dockyards, to service them. Specific examples stand out, such as the grand canals linking the rich agricultural lands of southern China to the imperial capital in the north. Similarly, the phrase "All roads lead to Rome," the capital of an equally powerful empire, may have been an exaggeration, but its central idea was correct.

In order to function as a single political structure, empires create bureaucratic administrations with at least some uniformity in language, currency, weights, measures, and legal systems. Perhaps the most significant administrative task of all is the empire's collection of taxes from its subjects and tribute from the conquered. Such revenues provide the means to support armies and public works, and financial profits for the rulers.

Empires often encourage great creativity in the arts and in learning. They bring peoples of different languages, religions, ethnic origins, and cultural and technological levels under a single, centralized rule. Depending on the needs of the empire, some groups from among the subject populations are granted full citizenship; a few might even be invited to serve as local representatives of the distant imperial power. Those at the bottom, especially war captives, might be enslaved. A few—those who proved particularly dangerous or costly to the imperial rulers—might be executed as a warning to potential rebels.

Empires are not static: they rise and they fall. The causes of the decline and fall of empires include:

- Failure of leadership—the inability of the empire to produce or select rulers capable of maintaining the imperial structures;
- Overextension of the administration—the inability of the imperial rulers to sustain the costs of a far-flung empire while coping simultaneously with critical domestic problems;
- Collapse of the economy—the overextension of empire to territories so remote or so difficult to subdue and govern that costs outrun benefits;
- Doubts over the ideology—the end of belief in the justice or benefit of empire, which may occur either when cynical colonizers abandon the colonial enterprise, or when frustrated colonized peoples revolt, or both;
- Military defeat—external enemies and the colonized people combine in revolt.

The First Empires

Akkad provides the earliest example of empire-building, as we shall see in the chapter "Dawn of the Empires." Egypt provides the next example, and then we turn to the Persian Empire. In Persia's wars against the Greeks in the fifth

Battle of Til-Tuba between the Assyrian king Ashurbanipal and the king of Elam, from the palace of Ashurbanipal, 645 B.C.E. Stone relief. An Assyrian soldier holds the severed head of Teumann, king of Elam. (British Museum, London)

century B.C.E., we see a fundamental clash between monarchy and democracy, between a powerful consolidated empire and an alliance of independent city-states.

The great empires of the ancient world—Rome, China, and India—controlled vast areas, influenced tens of millions of lives, and have remained models even to our own time. They represent turning points in the history of most of humankind.

Rome, China, and India were so successful that their ideologies of empire—their explanations of why they should rule over others—prevailed for centuries. Indeed, the Roman Empire endured for almost a thousand years, from about 500 B.C.E. to almost 500 C.E.; if we include the Eastern Empire, based in Constantinople, Rome's duration is some 2,000 years. Moreover, Rome inspired an imperial image that was expressed throughout Europe centuries later in the so-called Holy Roman Empire. In the nineteenth and early twentieth centuries, many commentators compared the British Empire with Rome, and in the mid-twentieth century, many drew a similar comparison with the United States. The Chinese Empire, founded in 221 B.C.E., lasted more or less continuously until 1911 C.E., and some would argue that it persists even today in new, communist garb. The first emperor to rule almost all of the Indian subcontinent, Asoka (Ashok) Maurya (r. c. 265–238 B.C.E.), is still commemorated today on every rupee note printed in India. These three great empires, spanning almost all of Eurasia, maintained communication with one other and we include analysis of these links among them.

Turning Point Questions

1. How important are warfare and murder in the construction of empire?
2. What skills and powers, beyond the military, are necessary to consolidate and rule an empire?
3. What might be the tipping points that would turn a peaceful colony into a rebellious one?

Roman soldiers besieging a town, from *The History of the Nations*. Aquatint engraving by Antonio Nani. Rome's array of military devices—battering rams, equipment for scaling walls, catapults, and horses and chariots at the ready—facilitated its policy of the "new wisdom," namely, to defeat the enemy through patient, deliberate preparation, and the demonstration of overwhelming force. (Private collection)

5 Dawn of the Empires

Empire-building in North Africa, West Asia, and the Mediterranean

2000 B.C.E.–300 B.C.E.

O ur study of empires begins with the world's earliest known empires, in Mesopotamia and the Nile valley. We then discuss three warring empires that set new standards of empire-building, competition, and warfare: the Persian Empire consolidated its base of power in the Middle East and then attempted to conquer the independent Greek city-states of the Mediterranean. In response, the Greek city-states formed a successful coalition to fight off the Persians, but afterward, ironically, succumbed to the demands of Athens, which now proclaimed its own imperial power over its former allies. Throwing off Athenian domination, the Greek city-states squabbled and fought among themselves for a generation, until Alexander the Great swept down from his kingdom of Macedonia to the north, conquered them all, and turned eastward to defeat the mighty Persians. Alexander then established his own empire on foundations the Persians had built.

Abu Simbel. This temple (one of two) at Abu Simbel was built in the thirteenth century B.C.E. as a monument to Pharaoh Ramses II and his queen Nefertari. In 1968, to save them from being submerged when the Aswan High Dam was built on the Nile River, the two temples were removed and relocated at the edge of the newly formed Lake Nasser.

LEARNING OBJECTIVES

5.1 ((•
Describe the characteristics of early empires.

5.2 ((•
Discuss the long rule of Darius I.

5.3 ((•
Describe the political organization of the Greek city-state.

5.4 ((•
Explain how Greek culture spread throughout Alexander's empire.

((• Listen on MyHistoryLab

The Earliest Empires

| 5.1 | What were the characteristics of early empires? |

What were the
characteristics of
early empires?

5.1

5.2

5.3

5.4

The first empires were born in Mesopotamia and the Nile valley more than four thousand years ago, and we already see in them the characteristics of imperial rise and fall. Since many of the characteristics of imperial power expand upon a base in urban power, it is no surprise that the city-states of Mesopotamia provided fertile soil for the flowering of empires. Once established, the empire of Sargon inspired others to challenge and overthrow it, introducing a succession of empires in the region.

Egypt's empire began not in urban power but in state power. By 3000 B.C.E. Egyptian rulers had consolidated a single state unifying the Upper and Lower Nile. It took a thousand years before they successfully expanded their power over others, first over the Nubians to the south and later out of the Nile valley entirely, eastward into the Middle East and Mesopotamia. Egypt's imperial fates rose and fell with the shifting balance of strength between its own armies and administration, and those of its adversaries.

📖 **Read** the **Document**: **Suffering Explained (1800 BCE, 700 BCE)** on **MyHistoryLab**

Mesopotamia and the Fertile Crescent

Mesopotamia's independent city-states could not reach political accommodation among themselves. They fought one another constantly for land, irrigation rights, and prestige, and recorded their struggles in bas-relief artwork from third-millennium Sumer. This artwork and related cuneiform records enable archaeologists to reconstruct two main antagonists, the cities of Lagash and Umma, which, with their allied forces, dominated the Mesopotamian warfare of the time. Victory by any one of the city-states over any other, however, was frequently avenged in the next generation.

Sargon of Akkad. Geographically, the city-states of Mesopotamia were also vulnerable to immigrant groups crossing their territory and challenging their powers. About 2300 B.C.E., Sargon (r. c. 2334–2279 B.C.E.), leading an immigrant group of Semitic peoples from the Arabian peninsula, entered Sumer. The new arrivals settled in and around northern Sumer and called their land Akkad. Sargon led the Akkadians to victories over the leading cities of Sumer, over the Elamites to the east, over northern Mesopotamia, and over a swath of land connecting Mesopotamia to the Mediterranean. He founded his Akkadian capital at Agade, a city whose exact location is now unknown.

Historical records are skimpy, but those that do exist correspond to our assessment of the key characteristics of empire. First, the Akkadians conquered widely. Administrative tablets of the Akkad dynasty have been found as far away as Susa, several hundred miles to the east in Persia, suggesting a far-flung governmental administration. Second, after razing the walls of the major cities of Ur, Lagash, and Umma, Sargon displaced the traditional local civilian hierarchies with his own administrators, designated the "sons of Akkad." Third, the Akkadian language was used in administrative documents in Sumer. Fourth, measurements of length, area, dry and liquid quantities, and probably weight were standardized throughout the empire; indeed, people in the region used the Akkadian units of measure for more than a thousand years, far longer than the empire itself survived. Finally, Sargon imposed his own imagery and ideology of empire. Documents were dated from the founding of the Akkadian kingdom, legal oaths were taken in the name of the Akkadian king, and Sargon installed his own daughter as high-priestess of the moon god Nanna at Ur.

5.1
5.2
5.3
5.4

What were the
characteristics of
early empires?

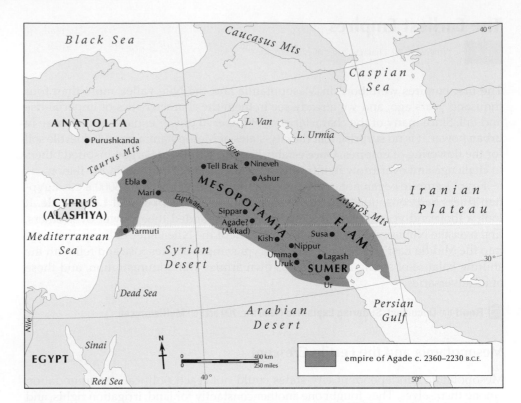

The empire of Sargon. During the third millennium B.C.E., Sargon established control over the city-states of southern Mesopotamia, creating the world's first empire. Building a capital at Agade, he founded the Akkadian dynasty, which for a century ruled the Fertile Crescent, from the Persian Gulf to the Mediterranean Sea.

Sargon's empire lasted for about a century and was followed by other outsiders, the Gutians, and then by a revival of internal Sumerian power under Ur-Nammu (r. c. 2112–c. 2095 B.C.E.). Culturally, Sumer was so advanced that it influenced even its conquerors, the Akkadians, the Gutians, and later arrivals. The Akkadian language, however, supplanted Sumerian by about 2000 B.C.E.

Waves of Invaders: The Babylonians and the Hittites. Throughout this time, waves of immigrants continuously entered the Fertile Crescent, attracted perhaps by empty land on its fringes, or perhaps by the presence in its heartland of already settled peoples on whom they could prey. Historians have not always been able to determine the specific origins of the immigrants, but two groups have stood out most clearly: Semites and Indo-Europeans. Each is designated by the family of languages that it spoke and (later) wrote; a common language probably indicates a degree of internal ethnic relationship as well.

Among the Semitic groups were the Amorites, who invaded and conquered Sumer about 1900 B.C.E. and founded their own new dynasty slightly to the north at Babylon. At first they employed Sumerian cultural and administrative forms, but over time they created new systems of their own. Their sixth ruler, Hammurabi (r. 1792–1750 B.C.E.), is most famous for his law codes, but he was also a skilled military leader who defeated the Sumerian city-states that had remained independent. He created the Babylonian Empire, imposing an administrative network that stretched from the Persian Gulf to Syria and endured for 250 years, until its defeat about 1500 B.C.E. by the Hittites, a new group of invaders.

While the Semitic Amorites had apparently immigrated from the south, the Hittites arrived as part of a vast movement of Indo-European peoples that originated in the north, apparently in the mountain regions of the Caucasus. This group of peoples spoke "Indo-European" languages, from which developed many of the principal languages of the lands to which they migrated and settled, from Britain in the northwest to Persia and India in the southeast.

In the course of their migrations, the Indo-Europeans also invented the decisive weapon of the age, the two-wheeled war chariot. Drawn by a horse, which bore part of the weight of the chariot, this new war machine had light wheels with a hub and spokes, and carried three warriors, at least one of whom could continuously shoot his wooden bow, reinforced with bone and sinew. Unlike the four-wheeled chariot, the Indo-Europeans' new design had great maneuverability.

The Hittites shared in this invention. When they settled in Anatolia, they also helped to usher in another innovation, iron-working technology that they developed in this iron-rich region. They established their capital in Hattushash, modern Bŏgazköy, Turkey, in the early second millennium B.C.E., extending their power over much of Anatolia and northern Syria. Much of what we know about them comes from some 25,000 cuneiform tablets that were discovered there. About 1590 B.C.E., they invaded and conquered Babylonia. About 1400–1200 B.C.E., during the New Kingdom of Egypt, the Hittites ruled as one of the most powerful nations of the Middle East. In c. 1274 B.C.E., in one of the greatest battles of the Middle East, they confronted the Egyptian armies at Qadesh, Syria. The two armies, each with about 20,000 men, and the Hittites with 2,500 two-wheeled chariots, fought to a draw. Within a few years these two great powers concluded treaties of peace and mutual defense, reaffirmed by royal marriages.

The Hittite Empire suddenly collapsed about 1193 B.C.E., perhaps under an onslaught from invaders, the "Sea Peoples," who arrived via the Mediterranean. City-state and regional outposts of Hittites survived until about 710 B.C.E., when they were defeated by the Assyrians and incorporated into their empire.

The Assyrians. Assyrians, descendants of the Akkadians, joined the other major participants in the continuous warfare in Mesopotamia. In the twentieth century B.C.E. they established an independent state and, through the trade of their private businessmen, achieved some prosperity. Then, after a period of subjugation by the Mitanni, they regained their independence in the thirteenth century only to lose it again to the Arameans c. 1000 B.C.E.

Around 900 B.C.E. a Neo-Assyrian (New Assyrian) kingdom began a series of conquests, sweeping westward to the Mediterranean coast, northward to Syria and Palestine, and southeastward into Babylon. Infantry provided their main force, while archers riding in chariots led the attacks, and battering rams and siege towers assaulted fixed positions.

More than most ancient empires, the Assyrians controlled conquered peoples through policies of terror and forced transfers of population. They tortured those they captured to instill fear. They also deported some peoples into exile from their homelands, including the "lost" ten of the tribes of Israel; that is, these tribes lost their sense of ethnic and religious identity and presumably assimilated to Assyrian culture, just as the conquerors had hoped. In other regions, the Assyrians imported their own people to settle among the defeated peoples and keep them under control.

Bronze head of an Akkadian ruler (?Sargon I), c. 2250 B.C.E. Exuding royal self-confidence, this near-life-size bronze head probably depicts Sargon I, founder of the Akkadian dynasty. For more than half a century, Sargon dominated one city-state after another until he had conquered most of Mesopotamia. After his death, his successors worshiped him as a god. (National Iraq Museum, Baghdad)

5.1
5.2
5.3
5.4

What were the
characteristics of
early empires?

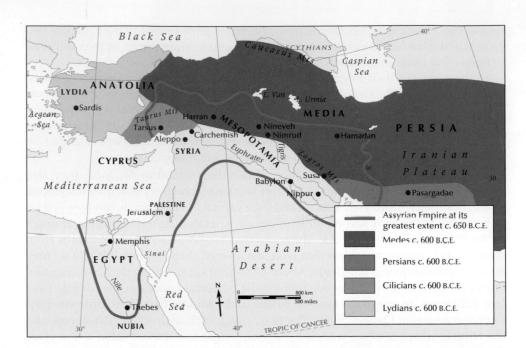

Assyria and its rivals. The shifting political map of southwest Asia was dominated between 850 and 650 B.C.E. by the powerful and martial Assyrians, who even occupied Egypt. Anatolia was fragmented into smaller states. To the north a powerful federation of Median tribes was a growing threat. In 614, in alliance with the Babylonians, they crushed Assyria.

King Esarhaddon (r. 680–669 B.C.E.) conquered Egypt in 671 B.C.E., making Assyria the greatest power of its day. His successors held the entire province, driving the Nubians from the southern regions and suppressing rebellions. Assyria finally withdrew from Egypt, defeated not primarily by the Egyptians but by internal dynastic struggles and by the combined forces of Babylonians, Arameans, the Medes of Iran, and Scythian invaders, who attacked Assyria's Mesopotamian heartland. The Assyrian capital, Nineveh, fell in 612 B.C.E.

Only the last of the Neo-Assyrian kings, Ashurbanipal (r. 668–627 B.C.E.), is known to have been literate, and he constructed a great library in his capital at Nineveh. Some 20,000 tablets are still preserved from that library, including the earliest complete version of *The Epic of Gilgamesh*.

The city-state political structures of Mesopotamia, and its geographical openness, had left the region very vulnerable. As the city-states fought destructively among themselves, they were repeatedly attacked by, and absorbed into, powerful foreign empires. The Mesopotamians had to expend their resources on warfare as their local units of government faced increasing challenges from ever-greater external powers.

Egypt and International Conquest

Egypt's empire was very different from Mesopotamia's. From early times Egypt was governed as a unified state. Geography had encouraged Egypt to become a single administrative unit, incorporating the entire Nile valley from the first cataract northward to the Mediterranean Sea. From 3000 B.C.E. to the present, Egypt has usually remained a single political unit, so we think of it as a kingdom with a single government ruling a single civilization rather than as an empire of one people ruling over others.

Egyptian forces did not always stay within their own borders. During the Middle Kingdom, c. 2030–1640 B.C.E., Egyptians conquered Nubia, the territory stretching southward some 900 miles from just above the first cataract in the Nile, at present-day Aswan in Egypt, to present-day Khartoum, capital of the Sudan. At first, this imperial conquest was only into lower Nubia, and Nubia's success in driving out the Egyptian conquerors was one of the factors that brought Egypt's Middle Kingdom to an end.

During the Second Intermediate Period (c. 1640–1540 B.C.E.), a time of disunity between periods of consolidation, immigrant Semitic groups, referred to in Egyptian texts as the Hyksos, ruled Lower Egypt. It is not clear if the Hyksos first came as traders or as nomadic immigrants, but as the Egyptian kingdom disintegrated they became rulers over large parts of the remains. Although later Egyptian rulers despised them, they are recognized as the legitimate 16th dynasty. A Semitic people, the Hyksos introduced bronze-making technology and horses and chariots to Egypt.

Under new leadership, Egypt became consolidated once again into the New Kingdom (c. 1550–c. 1050 B.C.E.), and the Hyksos were expelled. In pursuing the Hyksos into Palestine, the Egyptians began their active, direct involvement in Middle Eastern affairs. They remained an imperial presence in the region for several centuries. Thutmosis I (r. 1504–1492 B.C.E.) extended Egypt's control not only further south into Nubia than ever before (see "Middle and New Kingdom Egypt" map), but also northeast as far as the Euphrates River, creating Egypt's greatest historical empire. The small states of Syria and Palestine managed to remain self-governing, but Egypt stationed army units and administrative officials in the region and collected taxes. Egypt seemed more interested in access to these taxes, raw materials, and trading opportunities than in imperial governance.

The Art of Palace and Temple. The colonies of the New Kingdom enriched Egypt, helping to produce a period of great opulence and creativity. Because the pharaoh often traveled throughout the country, the Egyptians built a number of elegant palaces at various points along the Nile, from the delta all the way to the northern edge of Nubia. The state religion and the state administration were closely linked, so temple complexes dominated the towns that grew up around them. One of the greatest of these temples was constructed by Pharaoh Ramses II (r. c. 1279–1213 B.C.E.) at Abu Simbel, just north of the first cataract, and dedicated to the greatest gods of the New Kingdom and to Ramses II himself. (In the 1970s, the newly built Aswan dam threatened to flood the entire complex, including its grand sculptures, but the government saved them by relocating them.)

👁 **Watch** the **Video: Ramses II's Abu Simbel** on **MyHistoryLab**

In addition to Ramses II, another pharaoh calls for special note. One of the four female pharaohs, Hatshepsut (c. 1473–c. 1458 B.C.E.) was the widow of one pharaoh and served as regent to her stepson when he succeeded to the throne. For 15 years, however, until the boy grew up, Hatshepsut declared herself "king," since there was no official sanction for a female ruler. She encouraged artists to represent her as a man, wearing male clothing and with a king's beard. She built a temple at Deir

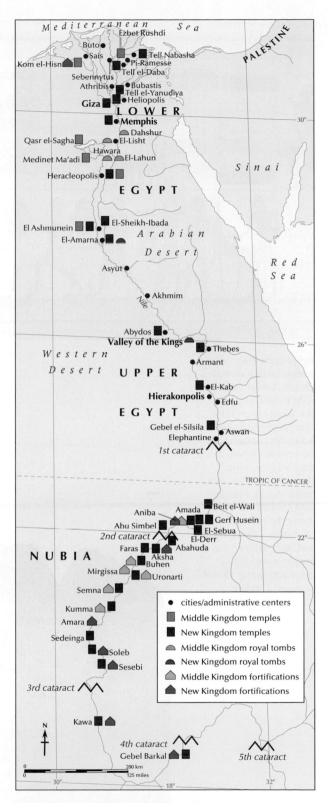

Middle and New Kingdom Egypt. By 2040 B.C.E. the unification of Egypt into a centralized, militaristic state was under way. Its hierarchic society focused on the priesthood and the dynastic succession of semi-god rulers, the pharaohs. The consolidation of power was reflected in the size and scale of royal building projects, including fortifications, new cities, temples, and grandiose tombs, and by conquests in Nubia.

129

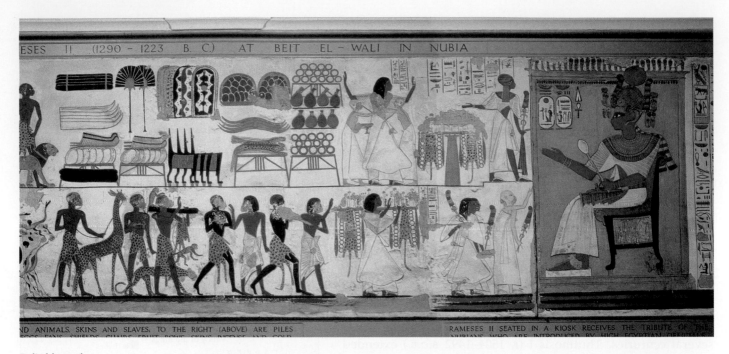

ESES II (1290 - 1223 B.C.) AT BEIT EL - WALI IN NUBIA

ND ANIMALS, SKINS AND SLAVES; TO THE RIGHT (ABOVE) ARE PILES

RAMESES II SEATED IN A KIOSK RECEIVES THE TRIBUTE OF

Relief from the temple of Beit el-Wali (detail), Lower Nubia, c. 2000–1850 B.C.E. The rich variety of produce here presented to Ramses II after his conquest of lower Nubia—bags of gold, incense, tusks, ebony logs, ostrich eggs, bows, shields, fans, and wild animals—seems to mirror the ethnic diversity on display. Pale-, brown-, and black-skinned peoples coexisted in Egypt and Nubia. (British Museum, London)

5.1

5.2

5.3

5.4

What were the characteristics of early empires?

Royal pyramids and adjacent iron slag heaps at Meroe, Sudan, c. 600 B.C.E. The rulers of Meroe and Egypt shared many artistic traditions, but often gave them a distinctive local interpretation, as can be seen in the forms of their pyramids and palaces.

el-Bahri near Thebes, which was devoted to the worship of the traditional god Amon, but which she also hoped would promote her as a deity after her death.

The End of Empire. Egypt's imperial control over remote and diverse peoples met resistance from local powers within the Fertile Crescent. The Hittites, the Babylonians, and, especially, the Mitanni mounted frequent revolts. (Egyptian pharaoh Ramses II reported the great, but indecisive, battle against the Hittites at Qadesh, noted above, as a brilliant victory, neither the first nor the last time that a government would claim military honors it had not won.) Egyptian control ended by about 1200 B.C.E., although its trading interests and political and economic influence in the region continued for centuries.

After suffering defeats in the Levant, Egypt was pushed back within its river domains, but by now these once again included Nubia. Early in the New Kingdom, Egypt had reconquered the heartland of central Nubia, the core of the sophisticated,

What were the characteristics of early empires?

5.1
5.2
5.3
5.4

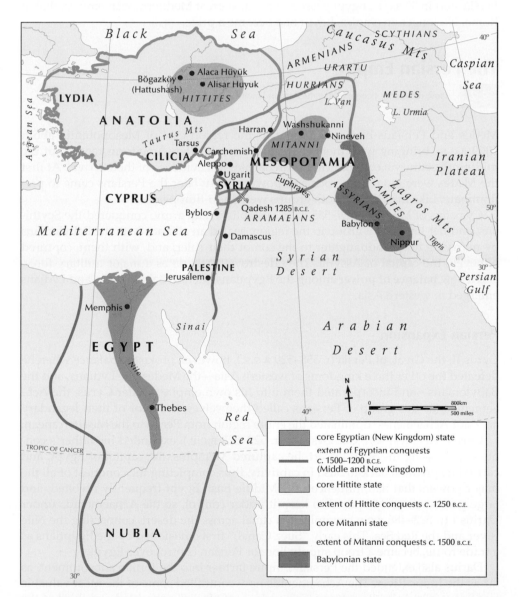

The empires of southwest Asia. Toward the end of the second millennium B.C.E., three empires fought for control of the Fertile Crescent. Egyptians, Mitanni of northern Mesopotamia, and Hittites of Anatolia came into direct conflict. Building on strong political control over their core regions, each dispatched powerful armies with the most up-to-date weapons to seize territory from the others.

5.1

5.2 How did Darius I
come to rule the
Persian Empire?

5.3

5.4

independent state and a source of gold, minerals, wood, and recruits for Egypt's army and police. It maintained its imperial power over this southern colony until c. 1050 B.C.E., when the colony broke free. The loss of empire, together with the loss of the gold, supplies, and slaves it had provided, helped to bring an end to the unified New Kingdom of the Egyptians and to usher in the Third Intermediate Period of divided rule (c. 1069–747 B.C.E.).

Three centuries later, Nubia marched northward to capture Egypt, reversing the relationship between colonizer and colonized. For half a century, 712–657 B.C.E., Nubia ruled over an empire of its own, which included all of Egypt. Thereafter Nubia remained strong, with its capital first at Napata and later at Meroe, while Egypt fell into decline.

In 671 B.C.E., while Nubians ruled southern Egypt, Assyrians conquered and occupied the north. Egypt could not regain its independence. The Persians conquered it in 525 B.C.E. Two centuries later, in 332 B.C.E., Alexander the Great captured Egypt from Persia, and in 30 B.C.E., Egypt passed to the next great Mediterranean empire, that of Rome. No longer an empire, Egypt had become a prize.

The Persian Empire

5.2   How did Darius I come to rule the Persian Empire?

Medes and Persians began to appear in the region east of Mesopotamia about 1300 B.C.E., bringing with them the use of iron. Written cuneiform records of the mid-ninth century B.C.E. confirm the archaeological evidence of their arrival. At first the Medes were more numerous and powerful, but later the Persians came to predominate. Like the Hittites, both groups were Indo-Europeans.

Cyaxares of Media (r. 625–585 B.C.E.) established an army; conquered the Scythians, another immigrant group in the region; sealed an alliance with the Babylonians by marrying his granddaughter to the son of their ruler; and, with them, captured Nineveh, the capital of Assyria. They destroyed Assyria as a major military force, and a new **balance of power** among the Egyptians, Medes, Babylonians, and Lydians emerged in western Asia.

Persian Expansion

Cyrus II, the Great, of Persia (r. 558–529 B.C.E.), however, broke the balance when he defeated the other three kingdoms of western Asia—the Medes, the Lydians, and the Babylonians—and incorporated them into his own empire. Under Cyrus, the Achaemenids (as this group of Persians called themselves, in honor of their legendary ancestor Achaemenes) dominated the entire region from Persia to the Mediterranean.

Cyrus II's eldest son, Cambyses II (r. 529–522 B.C.E.), expanded his father's conquests. Crossing the Sinai Desert, he captured Memphis, the capital of Egypt, and carried its pharaoh back to Susa in captivity, thus completing the conquest of all the major powers that had influenced the Middle East. Egypt frequently revolted, and large garrisons were required to keep it under control, so the Achaemenids under Darius I (r. 522–486 B.C.E.) completed a canal across the desert, connecting the Nile River and the Red Sea. This early "Suez Canal," first envisioned by the Egyptians as a trade route, became a troop supply line for Persian control over Egypt.

Darius also extended the Persian Empire farther into the Indian subcontinent, as far as the Indus River. The Achaemenids now controlled some of the most valuable trade routes in Asia; the **satrapy**, or province, of "India" submitted one-third of the annual cash receipts of the Achaemenids, and Indian troops served in the Achaemenid armies. From this time, Indian- and Persian-based powers would regularly confront one another across the borders of what are today Afghanistan and Pakistan.

KEY TERMS

balance of power In international relations, a policy that aims to secure peace by preventing any one state or alignment of states from becoming too dominant. Alliances are formed in order to build up a force equal or superior to that of the potential enemy.

satrapy A province or colony in the Achaemenid or Persian Empire ruled by a satrap or governor. Darius I completed the division of the Empire into provinces, and established 20 satrapies with their annual tributes. The term "satrapy" can also refer to the period of rule of a satrap.

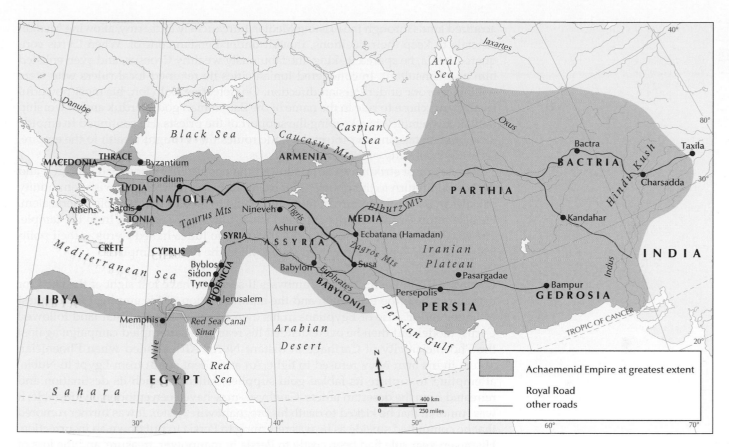

Achaemenid Persia. The Medes and the Persians were united under Cyrus the Great in 550 B.C.E. to form the Achaemenid or Persian Empire. Cyrus and his successors, notably Darius and Xerxes, extended the empire to the Indus in the east and to Egypt and Libya in the west, and twice invaded Greece.

Meanwhile, in the west, Darius expanded to the fringes of Europe, capturing Thrace and Macedonia, and bringing the Persian Empire to its greatest extent.

Attempts to advance further were stymied. The Scythians to the north and west fought a kind of guerrilla warfare that the massed forces of the Persians could not overcome. To the south and west, the Greeks defeated Persian armies of invasion. As we will see later in this chapter, a confederation of small, democratic Greek city-states managed to repulse the mighty Persian Empire.

📖 **Read the Document: Darius the Great: Ruler of Persia (522 BCE) on MyHistoryLab**

Imperial Policies

The Persian imperial form of rule and administration changed in the three generations from Cyrus II, its chief architect, through his son and successor, Cambyses II, to Darius I, its most powerful emperor. The differences among the three emperors became especially clear in their policies for achieving a balance between the power of the central government and the desire of local, conquered peoples for some degree of autonomy. Under Cyrus and Darius, Persia respected local customs and institutions even as the empire expanded, providing a good example of an **hegemonic** empire, ruling with substantial consent of the conquered. Cambyses was more dictatorial, and met an early end, leaving an apt example of an empire based on more ruthless military **dominance**.

Cyrus II. Cyrus respected the dignity of his opponents. When he conquered the Medes, he allowed their king to escape with his life. He administered his newly

5.1

5.2

How did Darius I come to rule the Persian Empire?

5.3

5.4

KEY TERMS

hegemony The predominance of one unit over the others in a group, for example, one state in a confederation. It can also apply to the rule of an empire over its subject peoples, when the foreign government is exercised with their substantial consent.

dominance The imposition of alien government through force, as opposed to hegemony.

133

acquired lands through the existing Median bureaucracy and army, allowing Median officials to keep their positions, though under Persian control. When Cyrus conquered Lydia, he spared its king, the fabulously wealthy Croesus, and even enlisted him as a consultant. In conquered Ionian cities he retained local rulers who were willing to work under Persian direction. On defeating Babylon, his most powerful rival, Cyrus chose to rule in the name of the Babylonian god Marduk and to worship daily in his temple, thus keeping the support of the priests. He continued to employ local bureaucrats and to protect the trade routes that brought wealth to the empire, securing the loyalty of the merchant classes.

Perhaps most strikingly, Cyrus allowed the peoples Babylonia had captured and deported to return to their homes. For example, he permitted the Jewish community of exiles in Babylon to return home to Judea and to rebuild their temple in Jerusalem. He also returned to them the gold and silver that had been taken from the temple. The 40,000 exiles who returned over 1,000 miles to Judea hailed Cyrus as their political savior and kept their renewed state loyal to the Persian Empire.

Cambyses II. Unlike his father, Cambyses II seems to have lost sight of the need for restraint in both the expansion and the administration of his empire. His conquest of Egypt and his use of Egyptians in his own administration of that land followed Cyrus' model, but then he overextended his reach. His attempted campaign against the Phoenician city of Carthage in distant North Africa failed when Phoenician sailors in his own navy refused to fight. An army sent south from Egypt to Nubia, attempting to capture its fabled gold supplies, failed to reach its destination and retreated from the desert in tatters. Cambyses may have been emotionally unstable; it was rumored that he kicked to death his pregnant wife/sister. It was further rumored that he committed suicide as he was returning to Persia to put down an insurrection. His seven-year rule had been costly to Persia in manpower, treasure, and the loss of support even among his own people.

Darius I. Darius, a general in the Persian army and prince of the Achaemenid dynasty, succeeded to the throne by murdering Bardiya (r. 522), who ruled briefly after Cambyses II. Darius ruled for 35 years. He was more deliberate, more balanced, and more capable as an administrator than Cambyses, and he became much richer as emperor than his predecessors. Like Cyrus, he used local administrators to staff local governments. He sought to create smaller, more efficient units of government by increasing the number of provincial administrative units, or satrapies, even faster than he expanded the empire. Some of the regional administrators, or satraps, were from the local elite; some were Persian. In each satrapy, loyalty to the empire was assured by the presence of Persian army units, which reported directly to the king, and by a secretary, who monitored the actions of the satrap and also reported back to Persia.

Darius commissioned the design of the first written Persian script. He established the tradition that royal inscriptions were to be posted in three languages—Old Persian, Babylonian, and Elamite. Among these trilingual inscriptions was a proclamation of Darius' ascent to power, inscribed on the "Behistun stone," a rock tablet that became the key to unlocking cuneiform writing 23 centuries later, when archaeologists discovered it in Behistun near Kermanshah, Iran. In the midst of the multitude of languages used across the empire, these three were to be the official written languages of administration. The most widely spoken public language was Aramaic, however, and this Semitic language of the common people throughout much of the eastern Mediterranean greatly influenced the development of formal Persian.

Legal codes varied among the satrapies to reflect local usage, and the Persian rulers frequently codified and recorded these laws. They rationalized tax codes. They evaluated, measured, and recorded the size and productivity of agricultural fields, and fixed the tax rate at about 20 percent. In each satrapy a Persian collector

5.1

5.2

5.3

5.4

How did Darius I
come to rule the
Persian Empire?

Homage rendered to Darius, bas-relief, Persepolis, Iran, 550–330 B.C.E. On New Year's Day,
ambassadors of each of Persia's 20 and more satrapies presented themselves to the emperor in his
audience hall at Persepolis. Darius, bejeweled and arrayed in royal robes of purple and gold, received
them.

gathered the various taxes—on industry, mining, ports, water, commerce, and sales.
The satraps remitted most of the revenues to Persia, but some were retained locally
for administrative and development expenses.

Darius built, maintained, and guarded an imperial system of roads, the most
famous of which was a 1,700-mile royal road stretching from his capital at Susa to
Sardis across Anatolia (but not quite reaching the Mediterranean). Along these roads
he established a series of inns for travelers and a royal courier service with stations
about every 15 miles. He completed the construction of the Nile–Red Sea canal,
which the Egyptians themselves had abandoned.

To increase agricultural production, Darius renewed the irrigation systems of Mesopotamia, and encouraged the introduction of new crops from one part of the empire
to another. He standardized the empire's gold coinage, and permitted only his own
imperial mints to strike the official coinage, the gold daric, in his name. Agriculture
and commerce flourished, and not only for the benefit of the wealthy. Craftsmen
produced goods for everyday use—leather sandals, cheap cloth, iron implements
and utensils, and pottery—in increasing quantities.

Substantial sums of the enormous wealth of the flourishing empire went to the
construction of four capital cities. The most sumptuous and lavish of them, and the
one most Persian in style, was built by Darius and named "Parsa," Persia. The Greeks
later called it "Persepolis," the city of the Persians.

Symbols of Power

Although the records of ancient Persia speak of painting as one of its arts, little has
been found. Our greatest knowledge of Persian art comes from imperial architecture
and design, most especially at Persepolis. The outstanding architectural monument

Apadana, principal audience hall, Persepolis, Iran, 521–486 B.C.E. Persepolis was destroyed by Alexander the Great. Still visible today are columns from the Apadana of Darius I.

5.1

5.2   How did Darius I
come to rule the
5.3   Persian Empire?

5.4

in this capital was a fortified citadel that held ceremonial and administrative buildings. Immediately below it was a large complex of residential palaces, probably the homes of the court.

Alexander and subsequent conquerors looted and burned the city, as we shall see, and the dominant remains today are forests of 60-foot-high columns, which have survived to indicate the grandeur of the city at its height. The largest and highest of all the remaining structures in the palace is the audience hall of Darius. Its façade is covered by creatures—lions, bulls, and griffins—asserting the power of the emperor and intimidating visitors. These visitors—many of them representatives from Persia's subject lands come to pay their respects in a procession before the emperor—are immortalized in bas-reliefs on the façades of the building and its stairways. The array of reliefs suggests the imperial power of Persia over its empire, and yet a place of honor seems to have been found for each of the delegates.

In accordance with the political theory that had evolved in imperial Persia, the emperor legally possessed all the property of the realm as well as the power of life and death over his subjects. Darius did not, however, choose to become a god. He

5.1

5.2

What was the
nature of the
Greek city-
state political
organization?

5.3

5.4

was probably a follower of the religion of the teacher Zarathustra, or Zoroaster as the Greeks called him. Zoroastrian scriptures date him to about 600 B.C.E., although modern scholarship places him as much as 1,000 years earlier. In a series of hymns, called *Gathas*, Zoroaster described a conflict between Ahuramazda, the god of goodness and light, and Ahriman, who embodied the forces of evil and darkness. Individuals had to choose between them, and they would be rewarded or punished for their choice on a final day of judgment. The *Avesta*, a later, fuller book of Zoroastrian scripture, further elaborated on the concept of an afterlife and the resurrection of the dead. Although, like Cyrus, Darius did not impose his own religious beliefs on the peoples he conquered, Zoroastrianism, with its roots in Persia, did spread rapidly under his rule. Darius also tried to soften the imposition of imperial administration and tax collection by maintaining local traditions and by enlisting members of the local elite to serve in his administration. Like Cyrus II, Darius managed to balance imperial majesty with local autonomy. At the western end of his empire, however, his neighbors and rivals, the Greeks, fought back against his attempts to rule over them.

The Greek City-states

5.3 What was the nature of the Greek city-state political organization?

The Greek historian Herodotus (d. *c.* 420 B.C.E.) has represented the warfare between Persians and Greeks as one of the great turning points in world history: a war between civilizations, between Asia and Europe, between empire and city-state, between tyranny and democracy. So, in the midst of our discussion of empire, we insert this flashback to consider the nature of Greek city-state democracy, its strengths and weaknesses in its warfare against the Persian Empire. At the end of our account, we will share in Thucydides' melancholy realization that, after their brilliant victory over the Persians, the freedom-loving Greeks fell victim to a new, home-grown imperialism imposed on them by Athens, their leader in the war against the Persians.

The Greek city-states had deep historic roots of their own. Long before the Persian Empire, civilizations had risen and fallen on the Greek peninsula, its neighboring islands, and the island of Crete in the eastern Mediterranean Sea. Archaeological excavations show that for some five hundred years in Greece and for a thousand in Crete, local, brilliant, urban civilizations had flourished.

View the **Closer Look**: **The Trireme** on **MyHistoryLab**

Early City-states of the Aegean

The Minoans. Immigrants began to settle on Crete about 6000 B.C.E. Scholars call these people Minoans after the legendary King Minos of ancient Crete. By 3000 B.C.E. they had built villages, and by 2000 B.C.E. they erected the first and largest of at least four major palace complexes on the island, at Knossos. The palaces combined three functions: they were elaborately furnished royal residences, centers for religion and ritual, and headquarters for administering the Cretan economy. The craftspeople of Crete produced bronze tools, gems, and extraordinarily fine pottery in the form of eggshell-thin vessels, which they exported throughout the eastern Mediterranean. As an island kingdom located at the crossroads of multiple trade routes, Crete excelled in commerce. Pictographic writing existed from at least 2000 B.C.E., and syllabic writing was introduced *c.* 1700 B.C.E. Known as Linear A, this script has not yet been deciphered.

About 1450 B.C.E., some, now unknown, disaster led to the destruction of three of the major palaces. (For a time scholars believed that eruptions of the volcano Thera might have caused the destruction, but deep-sea excavations show that the eruption

AT A GLANCE: ANCIENT GREEKS, PERSIANS, AND THEIR NEIGHBORS

DATE	POLITICS	RELIGION AND CULTURE	SOCIAL DEVELOPMENT
600 B.C.E.	• Cyaxares of Media (r. 625–585) • Age of Greek tyrants (657–570)	• Zoroaster (630–553)	• City-states in Greece
550 B.C.E.	• Cyrus II (r. 558–529); defeat of Medes, Lydia, Babylon • Peisistratus (d. 527) controlled Athens • Cambyses II (r. 529–522) conquered Egypt	• Pasargadae and Susa developed	• Nile–Red Sea canal
500 B.C.E.	• Darius I (r. 522–486); Persian Empire extended to Indus River; war against Greek city-states • Ionian revolt (499) • Battle of Marathon (490) • Xerxes I (r. 486–465) • War between Athens and Sparta: First Peloponnesian War (461–451)	• Pythagoras (d. c. 500) • Piraeus established as port of Athens • Persepolis built	• Athens at the height of its power. Acropolis built (c. 460); architecture, city-state democracy, political philosophy flourished
450 B.C.E.	• Pericles (c. 495–429) and Delian League • Second Peloponnesian War (431–404) and end of Athenian power	• Persian script written down • "Golden Age" of Athens • Aeschylus (525–456) • Herodotus (d. c. 420) • Sophocles (c. 496–406) • Euripides (480–406) • Thucydides (d. c. 401)	• Persian Empire: regional laws codified; roads built; centralized administration; irrigation systems extended
400 B.C.E.		• Socrates (c. 470–399)	
350 B.C.E.	• Philip II (r. 359–336) and Alexander the Great (r. 336–323) extended Macedonian Empire • Athens and Thebes defeated (338), ending Greek independence • Alexander conquered Asia Minor (334) and Egypt (332), and reached Indus (326)	• Aristophanes (c. 450–385) • Plato (c. 428–348) • Aristotle (384–322) • Demosthenes (384–322) • Alexandria (Egypt) founded (331) • Persepolis burned (331)	• Spread of Hellenistic culture
300 B.C.E.	• Ptolemies in Egypt • Seleucids in Asia		

5.1

5.2

5.3 What was the nature of the Greek city-state political organization?

5.4

was too early, c. 1625 B.C.E., and too distant to have caused such devastation.) Crete seems to have become more deeply enmeshed in the affairs of the Greek mainland at this time. A new script, known as Linear B, was created for transcribing Greek, suggesting that this had now become the language of Crete. In 1370 B.C.E. the palace at Knossos was also destroyed, and Crete came under the sway of Mycenae, the leading city-state of mainland Greece. The glories of Knossos were lost, preserved for thousands of years only in legend.

The Mycenaeans. The Greek poet Homer (c. 800–c. 750 B.C.E.), author of the *Iliad* and *Odyssey*, portrays the Mycenaeans as brave and heroic warriors as well as active sailors and traders. They carried on extensive trade and cultural exchange with Crete, including sharing the use of Linear B script. After 1450, when several of Crete's important towns were destroyed, Mycenae came to dominate the relationship.

Mycenae was home to several small kingdoms, each with its own palace or citadel and accompanying cemetery of beehive-shaped tombs. The greatest of the cities was Mycenae itself, capital of Homer's legendary king Agamemnon. This administrative center of the entire region was surrounded by a colossal wall up to 25 feet thick. Its massive entrance gate was adorned with huge stone lions looking down on all who entered and left. The site is rich in the evidence of warfare: weapons, armor, paintings of warriors, and, at the seashore a few miles distant, ships of war. Some of the kings, at least, were quite wealthy: one was buried with 11 pounds of gold, and the funeral "mask of Agamemnon" was a work of consummate craftsmanship in gold. Scholars have been unable to discover the reason for the fall of Mycenaean civilization; perhaps it was invaded, perhaps it imploded in internal warfare. By the end of the twelfth century B.C.E., all the palaces and towns of Mycenae had been destroyed or abandoned.

Their fall ushered in the Greek "Dark Ages," a period of general upheaval throughout much of the eastern Mediterranean. The Greeks even lost their knowledge of how to write. Apparently, additional waves of nomadic immigrants entered Greece from the north. By about 850 B.C.E. the peoples of Greece began to emerge from an age of darkness and once again to settle, to build towns, to trade overseas, to receive new waves of immigrants that increased their population, and to restore their written culture.

The Greek Polis: Image and Reality

The Greeks developed a very different form of political organization from that of the Persian imperial structure. The Greek city-state, or polis, was an intentionally small, locally organized government based on a single central city with enough surrounding land to support its agricultural needs. Most of the city-states had populations of a few thousand, with only the very largest of them exceeding 40,000 people.

Death mask ("Mask of Agamemnon"), gold, sixteenth century B.C.E. When archaeologists in the late nineteenth century discovered this brilliant death mask at Mycenae, the leading city-state of ancient Greece, they naturally claimed that it represented Mycenae's King Agamemnon himself, leader of the Greek forces in their war against Troy. Later judgments differed, because the date of the mask was too early. (National Archaeological Museum, Athens)

Geography and topography played a large part in limiting the size of the Greek city-state. In and around the Greek peninsula, mountains, rivers, and seas had kept the units of settlement rather small and isolated. (To the north, where farmland was more expansive, as it was in Macedonia, geographically larger states developed within such centralized city capitals.) When a region could no longer support an expanding population, it hived off colonies to new locations. Most of the Greek city-states in Anatolia, for example, seem to have originated as colonial settlements of older cities on the Greek mainland, part of an array of Greek city-states that spread along the Mediterranean coast, extending as far west as present-day Marseilles in France and Catalonia in Spain. Although separate and usually independent politically, the city-states were united culturally by the use of the Greek language, a myth-history centered on Homer's *Iliad* and *Odyssey*, and such festivals as the Olympic Games, held every four years after 776 B.C.E.

Each polis developed its own form of government. Councils of nobles governed some cities, while others fell under the rule of a single powerful individual. Here we recount the fate of the city of Athens, in particular, for three reasons: it was a leader among the Greek city-states; it gave birth to the modern concept of political democracy; and it has left us the most historical records. Of all the major cities of Greece—for example, Sparta, Corinth, Thebes, and Syracuse—Athens seems to have moved farthest from rule by kings and oligarchies in the direction of rule by the people, democracy.

About 600 B.C.E., Solon (c. 630–c. 560 B.C.E.), who had risen to high office as a general and a poet, ended the monopoly over public office held by the Athenian hereditary aristocracy. Because the only surviving accounts of his administration date to at least 500 years after his death, Solon's accomplishments are not entirely clear,

5.1

5.2

5.3

5.4

What was the nature of the Greek city-state political organization?

139

SOURCE

Homer and the Value System of Early Greece

Historical folk tales survived from the era of Mycenae through the Dark Ages. From these tales, which had probably circulated orally since the twelfth century B.C.E., the poet Homer (c. 800–c. 750 B.C.E.) wove his two great epic poems, the *Iliad* and the *Odyssey*. The *Iliad* tells of the Trojan War, which, Homer writes, a coalition of Greek city-states launched against the Trojans in retaliation for the seduction of Helen, the wife of the king of Sparta, by Paris, the son of the king of Troy. Just as the war begins in a personal vendetta, so, too, individual feuds during the war break out among the Greeks themselves, for personal more than for political reasons. The bitter personal quarrel between Agamemnon, brother of the king of Sparta and himself king of Mycenae, and Achilles, the mightiest of the Greek warriors, cripples the effectiveness of the Greek coalition and dominates the storyline of the *Iliad*. The *Odyssey* tells the still more personal postwar story of the ten-year struggle of Odysseus, king of Ithaca, to return to his home and of his ultimate reunion with his wife, Penelope, and son, Telemachus.

Although some literary critics believe that "Homer" was really more than one author, most today believe that just one person wrote, or dictated, the epics. The stories on which Homer bases his poetic accounts were probably well known among the Greeks of his time. Homer's lasting reputation and fame rest on his skill in crafting these stories into coherent narratives told in poetry of great power. Further, by focusing on personal stories within the national epics, Homer created images of human excellence (*arete* in ancient Greek) at levels of heroism that inspire readers to this day. He writes with equal power of excellence in war and in love.

Bravery in warfare is a cardinal virtue, and, in the *Iliad*, Homer portrays Hektor, the mightiest of the Trojans, praying that his son might inherit his own strength in battle, and even surpass it. The child's mother would apparently share this vision of her son as warrior:

Zeus, and you other immortals, grant that this boy, who is my
  son,
may be as I am, preeminent among the Trojans,
great in strength, as am I, and rule strongly over Ilion;
and some day let them say of him: "He is better by far than his
  father,"
as he comes in from the fighting; and let him kill his enemy
and bring home the blooded spoils, and delight the heart of his
  mother.

(*Iliad*, VI: 476–81)

Praising excellence in warfare and combat, Homer portrays Odysseus, Telemachus, and their allies as fierce raptors swooping down upon the men who had spent years harassing Penelope and attempting to seduce her while Odysseus fought in Troy and struggled to return home:

After them the attackers wheeled, as terrible as falcons
from eyries in the mountains veering over and diving down

with talons wide unsheathed on flights of birds,
who cower down the sky in chutes and bursts along the
  valley—
but the pouncing falcons grip their prey, no frantic wing avails,
and farmers love to watch those beaked hunters.
So these now fell upon the suitors in that hall,
turning, turning to strike and strike again,
while torn men moaned at death, and blood ran smoking
over the whole floor.

(*Odyssey*, XXII: 310–19)

Homer sang equally vividly, and far more sweetly and poignantly, of excellence in love. As the *Odyssey* moves toward its conclusion, the hero and heroine, Odysseus and Penelope, are reunited after a wartime separation of 20 years:

Now from his breast into his eyes the ache
of longing mounted, and he wept at last,
his dear wife, clear and faithful, in his arms,
longed for as the sunwarmed earth is longed for by a swimmer
spent in rough water where his ship went down
under Poseidon's blows, gale winds and tons of sea.
Few men can keep alive through a big surf
to crawl, clotted with brine, on kindly beaches
in joy, in joy, knowing the abyss behind:

and so she too rejoiced, her gaze upon her husband,
her white arms round him pressed as though forever.

(*Odyssey*, XXIII: 234–44)

So they came
into that bed so steadfast, loved of old,
opening glad arms to one another,
Telemachus by now had hushed the dancing,
hushed the women. In the darkened hall
he and the cowherd and the swineherd slept.
The royal pair mingled in love again
and afterward lay reveling in stories:
hers of the siege her beauty stood at home
from arrogant suitors, crowding on her sight,
and how they fed their courtship on his cattle,
oxen and fat sheep, and drank up rivers
of wine out of the vats.
  Odysseus told
of what hard blows he had dealt out to others
and of what blows he had taken—all that story.
she could not close her eyes till all was told.

(*Odyssey*, XXIII: 298–313)

War and love, the bloody heroism of the battlefield and the warm intimacy of family life—Homer addressed both in imagery that has inspired readers, and listeners, to this day.

5.1

5.2

5.3

5.4

What was the nature of the Greek city-state political organization?

but he is always presented as having moved Athens towards democracy. It appears that Solon gave to all free men the right to participe and vote in the decision-making public assembly, although only those meeting certain income levels could be elected to high public office. The Council of Four Hundred, which he also created, represented the interests of the wealthy and noble factions, while the assembly balanced them with the voices of more common men. Perhaps more importantly, Solon canceled all public and private debts, and abolished the practice of enslaving people to pay off their debts.

Solon's reforms came under attack when he left office, leading to a decade or so of struggle between rich and poor and between men of different hereditary clans. About 550 B.C.E., Peisistratus seized control of the government as a "**tyrant**," the Greek term for a single autocratic ruler. Peisistratus fostered economic growth through loans to small farmers; export promotion programs; road construction; and public works, including major building programs for the beautification of Athens. On his death in 527 B.C.E., the city-state again fell into disarray and even civil war. In 510 B.C.E., at the invitation of a faction of Athenian noblemen, the king of Sparta, already Athens' greatest rival, invaded the city and deposed the descendants of Peisistratus.

Nevertheless, the ideals of Solon survived. A new ruler, Cleisthenes (*c.* 570–*c.* 508 B.C.E.), came to power as a tyrant and dramatically reorganized the city and its surrounding countryside. He did away with the aristocratic family centers of power by registering each Athenian as a citizen according to his geographical residence, or **deme**, in the city. Similarly, he reorganized the electoral districts of Attica, the region around Athens, into ten electoral units, creating new political identities and allegiances. The assembly resumed meeting about every ten days, and all male citizens were expected to participate; 6,000 were necessary for a quorum. Above the assembly, and setting its agenda, was a Council of Five Hundred, even more open than Solon's Council of Four Hundred had been, since members were selected from each deme for one-year terms by lottery, and members were not allowed to serve for more than two terms. In organizing themselves by deme, Athenians based their political identity on geographical residence in the city, not on heredity and kinship, nor on class and wealth.

A red-figure cup by the sculptor Douris, fifth century B.C.E. The figures depict scenes from the education of a young man: learning to play the flute, and learning to read and write, all under the watchful eye of a pedagogue. (Staatliche Museen zu Berlin)

KEY TERMS

tyrant A ruler with absolute power, sometimes granted through election in times of crisis, sometimes seized through force of arms.

deme A rural district or village in ancient Greece, or its members or inhabitants. The demes were a constituent part of the polis but had their own corporations with police powers, and their own cults, officials, and property.

5.1
5.2
5.3
5.4

What was the nature of the Greek city-state political organization?

This new concept of civic identity allowed the city to welcome new residents and the ideas they brought with them, regardless of their place of origin. It allowed people of different ethnic origins, even of enemy ethnic stock, to enter the city, although they were not eligible for full citizenship, which was restricted to free men born in the deme. The human interaction in the small Greek city-state nurtured the intellect of its citizens. Life in the polis meant constant participation in a kind of ongoing public seminar. As Socrates (c. 470–399 B.C.E.), the leading philosopher of fifth-century Athens, said: "I'm a lover of learning, and trees and open country won't teach me anything, whereas men in the town do."

When Darius I's Persian Empire challenged the Greek city-states, Athens took the lead in forming a coalition against it. The contrast between the combatants was stark: city-state versus empire; local administration versus imperial power; evolving, decentralized democracy versus established, centralized imperial control. Persia was a huge, centrally governed empire; each Greek city-state was independent, although many had joined into regional confederations and leagues for mutual assistance and trade. A single emperor who set policies for the entire empire headed Persia; an assembly of all its adult, free, male citizens, for the most part, governed each individual Greek city-state. These assemblies passed laws, judged criminal and civil cases, carried out administration and implementation of legislation, and arranged for military defense as the need arose. The Greek city-states were moving toward democracy; they understood their legal systems to be their own creation and responsibility, neither ordained by the gods nor imposed by a powerful external emperor.

War with Persia

Some of the Greek city-states in Anatolia had earlier fallen under Darius' empire. Although they were permitted to retain their own form of local government as long as they paid their taxes to Persia, some of them revolted and called on the Greek cities of the peninsula for help. Athens tried, half-heartedly and unsuccessfully, to assist its overseas relatives with ships and soldiers. According to the historian Herodotus (see below), Darius was furious at this interference. He ordered one of his servants to remind him, every day at dinnertime, "Master, remember the Athenians." In 490 B.C.E., Darius I dispatched a naval expedition directly across the Aegean to punish Athens for its part in the revolt in Anatolia.

War with the Persians tested the Greeks' fundamental mode of political organization. How could the tiny Greek city-states hold off Darius' imperial armies and keep their incipient democracies alive? First, they had the enormous advantage of being close to home, with a good knowledge of local geography and conditions. Second, the largest among them, especially Athens and Sparta, chose to cooperate in defense against a common enemy.

When the Persian fleet of 600 ships landed 48,000 soldiers at Marathon in 490 B.C.E., a force of some 10,000 Greek **hoplite** soldiers, joined by about 1,000 soldiers from Plataea and another 1,000 slaves, confronted them. The hoplite forces were deployed in solid phalanxes, columns of soldiers arrayed in tight lines, the left arm and shield of one man pressed against the right shoulder of the other, row on row. If a soldier in the front row fell, one from the next line took his place. (In these hoplite formations, each individual soldier is crucial to the welfare of all. Many analysts have seen in this egalitarian military formation the rationale for Athenian political democracy.)

The discipline of the Athenians defeated their enemy at Marathon: Persia lost 6,400 men, Athens 192. The Athenian general sent his fastest runner, Pheidippides, racing back to Athens to tell of the victory, to strengthen the resolve of the Athenians at home, and to hasten their preparations for battle against the surviving Persian forces. Pheidippides delivered the message, and died of exhaustion on the spot. (Today's marathon race is named for his 26-mile run.)

KEY TERM

hoplite A heavily armed foot soldier of ancient Greece, whose function was to fight in close formation, usually in ranks of eight men. Each soldier carried a heavy bronze shield, a short iron sword, and a long spear for thrusting.

Xerxes I (r. 486–465 B.C.E.), Darius' son, succeeded him and mounted a renewed attack on the Greek mainland by land and sea in 480 B.C.E. Courageous resistance by the Spartan general Leonidas and his troops at Thermopylae cost the lives of all the defenders, but won time for the Athenians to evacuate their city and regroup their forces. Xerxes continued to push onward to Athens, capturing, burning, and plundering the city and its Acropolis (its "city on high," as the religious citadel in an ancient Greek city was called), but the Athenian warriors had withdrawn to the nearby port of Piraeus and the Bay of Salamis. At Salamis, a force of some 1,000 Persian ships confronted a much smaller fleet of some 300 Greek triremes, a ship named for the three levels in which its approximately 170 rowers were arranged. One of Xerxes' most trusted naval advisers, Artemisia, a widowed queen among the people of Halicarnassus and a captain of one of the ships, counseled waiting and watching. Xerxes, however, followed the majority and sailed into battle. The Athenians maneuvered the Persians into a bottleneck in the Salamis Channel and destroyed 200 of their ships while losing only 40 of their own. Xerxes sailed for home, and Persia never again attacked Greece by sea.

The Persians did, however, continue to fight by land. In 479 B.C.E., in alliance with their subjects in Macedonia and some northern Greeks, they prepared an army of some 100,000 men on the edge of the plains opening southward to Athens and the Peloponnese. Sparta and Athens formed an alliance with other city-states to field an opposing army of about 40,000. Despite initial confusion in the ranks, the allied Spartan and Athenian forces destroyed the Persian armies and their camp, annihilated the elite guard, and killed the leading Persian general. At about the same time, the Greek fleet defeated the surviving Persian fleet at Mycale, on the Ionian coast of Anatolia.

In the face of these losses, and with weaker leadership at home, Persia left Europe, never to return in such force. The small Greek city-states, led by arch-rivals Athens and Sparta, had shown an ability to combine in the face of a common enemy. They had demonstrated the virtues of small-scale, local units of society and the resilience of popular, democratic forms of government. Conversely, the Persians had exhibited one of the great flaws of empire: the tendency to overextend its powers.

The Golden Age of Athenian Culture

Under the military and civic leadership of Pericles (c. 495–429 B.C.E.), Athenians took immense pride in their city-state, its democratic philosophy and artistic creativity. During the war years, the Persians had destroyed and burned much of Athens. When victory was secure, the Athenians began to rebuild.

Athens rose from a plain, and with each level upward its functions and architecture became more exalted. At the bottom were the houses of commoners, built simply from local materials of stone and mud, with little concern for architectural merit. Further up the hill was the **agora**, or civic and market center, with clusters of buildings for trade in goods, ideas, and political decision-making. These public buildings were more elegant, designed for greater comfort and show. In the splendor of the agora Athenians demonstrated the value placed on public life and on physical

What was the nature of the Greek city-state political organization?

KEY TERM

agora A central feature of ancient Greek town planning. Its chief function was as a town market, but it also became the main social and political meeting-place. Together with the acropolis, it normally housed the most important buildings of the town. Later, the Roman forum fulfilled this function.

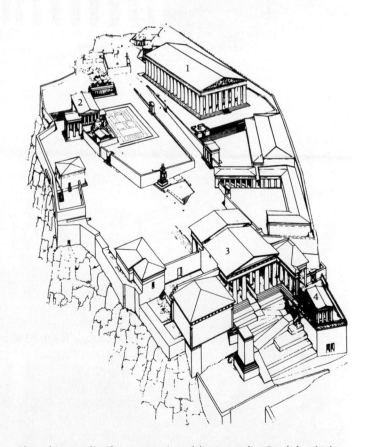

Plan of Acropolis. The construction of the Acropolis (Greek for "high city"), beginning in c. 460 B.C.E. under the leadership of Pericles, signified the start of a Golden Age for Athens. The plan above indicates some of its most celebrated buildings—the Parthenon (1), the Erechtheum (2), the Propylaea (3), and the Temple of Athena Nike (4).

View the **Closer Look**: **The Erechtheum: Porch of the Maidens** on **MyHistoryLab**

Parthenon, Athens, 447–432 B.C.E. The Parthenon on the Athenian Acropolis was a temple dedicated to the goddess Athena, the city's patron-deity. It was built at the initiative of Pericles as a symbol of Athens' growing importance, and represents, in architectural terms, the summit of classical Greek achievement.

SOURCE

Pericles' Funeral Oration

As political and military leader of Athens, 460–429 B.C.E., Pericles delivered this eulogy at a mass funeral of troops who had died in battle in the early years of the Peloponnesian War. As reported by Thucydides, it is one of the great proclamations of the civic, aesthetic, moral, and personal virtues of the Athenian city-state:

Our system of government does not copy the institutions of our neighbors. It is more the case of our being a model to others, than of our imitating anyone else. Our constitution is called a democracy because power is in the hands not of a minority but of the whole people. When it is a question of settling private disputes, everyone is equal before the law; when it is a question of putting one person before another in positions of public responsibility, what counts is not membership of a particular class, but the actual ability which the man possesses. No one, so long as he has it in him to be of service to the state, is kept in political obscurity because of poverty …

We [obey] those whom we put in positions of authority, and we obey the laws themselves, especially those which are for the protection of the oppressed, and those unwritten laws which it is an acknowledged shame to break …

When our work is over, we are in a position to enjoy all kinds of recreation for our spirits … all the good things from all over the world flow in to us, so that to us it seems just as natural to enjoy foreign goods as our own local products …

Our love of what is beautiful does not lead to extravagance; our love of the things of the mind does not make us soft. We regard wealth as something to be properly used, rather than as something to boast about. As for poverty, no one need be ashamed to admit it: the real shame is in not taking practical measures to escape from it. Here each individual is interested not only in his own affairs but in the affairs of the state as well: even those who are mostly occupied with their own business are extremely well informed on general politics—this is a peculiarity of ours: we do not say that a man who takes no interest in politics is a man who minds his own business; we say that he has no business here at all. We Athenians, in our own persons, take our decisions on policy or submit them to proper discussions: for we do not think that there is an incompatibility between words and deeds; the worst thing is to rush into action before the consequences have been properly debated …

I declare that our city is an education to Greece, and I declare that in my opinion each single one of our citizens, in all the manifold aspects of life, is able to show himself the rightful lord and owner of his own person, and do this, moreover, with exceptional grace and exceptional versatility.

(Thucydides, *History of the Peloponnesian War*, Book II:37–41; pp. 145–48)

prowess and discipline. Nearby were gymnasia for exercise and competition. An amphitheater where plays were regularly performed was carved out of the hillside. At the top of the hill, on the Acropolis, surrounded by a wall, were the chief temples of the city. Pericles hired the architects and urban designers Ictinus and Callicrates to rebuild the Acropolis (plundered by the Persians) and build the Parthenon, the temple dedicated to Athena, the city's patron goddess. The sculptor Phidias carved the friezes on the Parthenon and created a 40-foot-high statue of Athena to reside within it.

As the architectural projects flourished, Pericles founded a colony in southern Italy and took a fleet into the Black Sea. More importantly, he encouraged naval battles against Sparta and Corinth, as well as Persia, in order to promote his radical egalitarian democracy at home. Rowers typically were poorer than hoplites, but benefited from regular salaries and the spoils of war and empire. Eventually, Pericles realized his strategy was flawed, concluding that his imperial ambitions threatened the very Athenian democracy he cherished.

Historians. The city's historians began to reflect on its origins and accomplishments, and the challenges it had faced. Indeed, the modern profession of history as a systematic attempt to understand the influence of past experience on the present began in Athens. Two of the most outstanding historians of the fifth century B.C.E. have given us the history of the city and its relationships with its neighbors. Herodotus wrote *The Persian Wars*, and in the narrative recaptured a general, if anecdotal, history of the whole eastern Mediterranean and eastward as far as Persia and India from a Greek perspective. Thucydides (d. *c.* 401 B.C.E.), far more systematically and carefully, recounted the subsequent *History of the Peloponnesian War*, the war between Athens and Sparta that lasted from 431 B.C.E. until 404 B.C.E.

5.1

5.2

5.3

5.4

What was the nature of the Greek city-state political organization?

SOURCE

Socrates on the Rights of the State over the Individual

Condemned to death on trumped-up charges of corrupting the political morals of youth and blaspheming against the gods of Athens, Socrates is offered the opportunity to escape and live out his life in another city-state. He refuses. He notes that the state has acted through formal legal process and has the right to execute him. He, in turn, has the obligation to accept the sentence.

Are you too wise to see that your country is worthier, more to be revered, more sacred, and held in higher honor both by the gods and by all men of understanding, than your father and your mother and all your other ancestors; and that you ought to reverence it, and to submit to it, and to approach it more

humbly when it is angry with you than you would approach your father; and either to do whatever it tells you to do or to persuade it to excuse you; and to obey in silence if it orders you to endure flogging or imprisonment, or if it sends you to battle to be wounded or to die? That is just. You must not give way, nor retreat, nor desert your station. In war, and in the court of justice, and everywhere, you must do whatever your state and your country tell you to do, or you must persuade them that their commands are unjust. But it is impious to use violence against your father or your mother; and much more impious to use violence against your country. (Plato, *Crito*, XII:51:b)

📖 **Read** the **Document: Thucydides on Athens (5th c. BCE)** on **MyHistoryLab**

Philosophers. Philosophers such as Socrates and his student Plato introduced questions, methods of analysis and of teaching, and examinations of the purpose of life that continue to command attention for their range and depth. Plato's prize student, Aristotle, later wrote that man is a "political animal," a creature of the polis, or city-state, and many of the key works in Greek history, drama, and philosophy explored the working of the city-state itself and the relationship of the individual to it.

For the philosopher Socrates, the Athenian state was father and mother; he derived his sense of self and purpose from the education the state gave him and from his continual debates with fellow citizens both in public and in private. Socrates argued for the supremacy of the city-state over the individual. The citizen had obligations to the state for all the benefits he received from it, but had no rights to claim against the power of the state.

Socrates took philosophy personally and seriously. He opposed and satirized the **sophist** philosophers of his day who earned their salaries by training future statesmen to argue any side of any question without necessarily staking any personal commitment. Through his incessant questions, he taught his students to be thoughtful but critical about the truths of others and about their own truths, and, after having reached their own conclusions, to live their own truths fully even if it meant their death, as it did for Socrates himself (see Source box "Socrates on the Rights of the State over the Individual," above).

Plato (*c.* 428–348 B.C.E.) was Socrates' leading pupil and the founder of the Academy, which endured for centuries as Athens' leading school of philosophy. His philosophical works dealt with many topics, including love, justice, courage, and the nature of the state. Plato conceived of ideal situations, whether realistic or not. The ideal state, according to Plato, would be administered by a philosopher-king, who by virtue of innate good character and intensive training would know and do what was best for all citizens in the state. Similarly, Plato saw love beginning with emotional and sexual passion between individuals and subsequently transforming into the contemplation of universal ideals.

Aristotle (384–322 B.C.E.) addressed an astonishing array of subjects—logic, physics, astronomy, metaphysics, religion, rhetoric, literary criticism, and natural science—but he, too, devoted some of his most important writing to ethics and politics. His analysis of the principal forms of constitutional government in his *Politics*

5.1
5.2
5.3
5.4

What was the nature of the Greek city-state political organization?

KEY TERM

sophist An itinerant professor of higher education in ancient Greece, who gave instruction for a fee. The subjects taught, which included oratory, grammar, ethics, mathematics, and literature, had the practical aim of equipping pupils for successful careers. The sophist professor taught his students to argue all sides of every question, regardless of their merit. **Sophistry** is this kind of clever argumentation, regardless of merit.

What was the
nature of the
Greek city-
state political
organization?

remains a useful introduction to the field even today. Aristotle later tutored Alexander the Great, although that world-conqueror seems to have thoroughly rejected his teacher's argument for small units of government like the city-state. Aristotle argued:

> If the citizens of a state are to judge and to distribute offices according to merit, then they must know each other's characters; where they do not possess this knowledge, both the election to offices and the decision of lawsuits will go wrong. When the population is very large they are manifestly settled at haphazard, which clearly ought not to be. (*Politics* VII:4, p. 326)

Alexander, clearly, was not persuaded.

Dramatists. Drama developed and flourished in the theaters of Athens. The pursuit of justice, morality, and equity was a core theme. Athenian playwrights invented the dramatic forms of tragedy and comedy, and their most important plays all include themes related to the evolution of their city and its institutions.

The *Oresteia* trilogy by Aeschylus (525–456 B.C.E.) follows three generations of murders within the royal family of Atreus, as one act of revenge provokes the next. Finally, in a trial at Athens, Athena, patron goddess of the city, acquits Orestes, suggesting that divinely ordained vengeance will be replaced by human justice and the cycle of murder will be ended.

Oedipus Rex by Sophocles (*c.* 496–406 B.C.E.), perhaps the most famous single play of ancient Athens, centers on the family tragedy of Oedipus' unknowing murder of his own father, the king of Thebes, and his subsequent marriage to his own mother. The play opens with the people of Thebes gathered around King Oedipus—before his tragedy is revealed—crying out for his help in arresting a plague that is afflicting the city. Oedipus' own moral corruption has brought the plague on the city, although that is revealed only later. Sophocles' *Antigone* confronts the conflict between loyalty to family and loyalty to the city-state, as Antigone chooses to bury her brother Polynices, despite the royal decree to leave his corpse unattended as an enemy of the state.

Euripides (480–406 B.C.E.) saw more clearly Athens' move toward imperialism, and criticized it in *The Trojan Women*. The hilarious, sexually explicit comedy *Lysistrata* by Aristophanes (*c.* 450–385 B.C.E.) portrays the women of Athens and Sparta agreeing to go on strike sexually until their men stop fighting the Peloponnesian Wars. As long as the men make war, the women will not make love! The best of the Athenian dramatists addressed directly the political and social issues that confronted their city.

📖 Read the **Document**: **Greek Poetry (800–400 BCE)** on **MyHistoryLab**

The Limits of City-state Democracy

Socrates' justification of the state demonstrates that even in the most democratic Greek city-state, government could exact respect and service from the citizen, but the citizen had few rights vis-à-vis the state. The citizen had the right, and indeed the obligation, to participate in the activities of the state and to serve the state, but not to have the state serve him.

For women, even the right of participation was absent. Women born of two Athenian parents were regarded as citizens, enjoyed some legal protection, and had responsibilities for performing certain religious rituals of great importance for the state. But, like slaves, they were excluded from attending the meetings of the assembly, holding annual public offices, serving as jurors, initiating legal cases on their own, or owning property in their own names. They had to have a man speak for them before judges and juries. Women's segregation from public life in ancient Greece perpetuated long-standing beliefs that there is a public sphere and

A second-century C.E. copy in marble of the statue of Athena Parthenos, dedicated in 438 B.C.E. Phidias' 40-foot Athena, the divine guardian of the city, dominated the central chamber of the Parthenon on the Acropolis. This miniature Roman copy of the destroyed statue hardly suggests the glittering magnificence of the enormous gold-and-ivory original, a powerful symbol of the might of the goddess and her city, Athens. (Acropolis Museum, Athens)

a private sphere, and that women should be confined to the latter. Pericles captured this belief in his famous funeral oration, when he delivered this advice to the widows of fallen warriors: "Great will be your glory in not falling short of your natural character; and greatest will be hers who is least talked of among the men, whether for good or for bad."

Since many Greeks believed that true friendship was possible only among equals, many Greek men sought relationships, including sexual relationships, with other men outside their households, even when they held their marriages in high esteem. Greek vases, especially those used in male drinking parties, often carried paintings that glorified the phallus. Given this evidence, some historians have concluded that this culture was misogynistic—hating women—and that the exaltation of masculinity could have been at the root of the constant warfare and militarism of ancient Greek society. (see How Do We Know? box, below).

Plato recognized the prejudice against women in his society. When he suggested in his visionary *Republic* that women should be treated equally with men in their access to the highest professional and civic responsibilities, and in the education needed to achieve them, he knew his ideas were revolutionary for Athens in his time and that they would be greeted with derision. Plato himself believed that men were generally more talented than women, but he argued that both should be offered equal access to political opportunity. On the subject of gender equality, he seemed to remain consistent with his general philosophy: the state should encourage each citizen to reach his or her educational potential, and should direct the most talented into governmental affairs. Plato wrote:

> There is no occupation concerned with the management of social affairs which belongs either to women or to men, as such. Natural gifts are to be found here and there in both creatures alike; and every occupation is open to both, so far as their natures are concerned, though woman is for all purposes the weaker ... Now, for the purpose of producing a woman fit to be a Guardian, we shall not have one education for men and another for women ... If we are to set women to the same tasks as men, we must teach them the same things. They must have the same two branches of training for mind and body and also be taught the art of war, and they must receive the same treatment.

Aristotle confirmed Plato's apprehensions, but not his optimism nor his sense of potential equality. Aristotle wrote of women: "The temperance of a man and of a woman, or the courage and justice of a man and of a woman, are not, as Socrates maintained, the same; the courage of a man is shown in commanding, of a woman in obeying." He quotes with approval the general view that "Silence is a woman's glory." In practice, Athens followed Aristotelian rather than Platonic views on the role of women in public life.

Even among males, only the sons of native-born Athenian mothers and fathers were eligible for citizenship. Slaves captured in war, and even allies, could not gain citizenship. When classical Athens reached its maximum population of 250,000, only about one adult Athenian in six qualified for citizenship. These limits on Athenian democracy increased domestic social strains.

From City-state to Small Empire. Ironically, the city-state of Athens, having led the Greek city-states in the struggle against the Persian Empire, subsequently set out to construct an empire of its own. Following major victories in the Persian wars, Athens assembled its principal allies into the Delian League, with its council and treasury situated in Delos. At first, membership was voluntary, but soon Athens forbade withdrawal. Some cities left the League, usually because they could not pay the tribute Athens demanded. Many found it difficult to supply triremes, because they lacked the shipyards of their larger ally. In response, Athens might declare war against them. As a result, "the Athenians as rulers," in the words of Thucydides, "were no longer popular as they used to be."

By 461 B.C.E., many of the Greek city-states turned to Sparta to help them to resist Athenian coercion. Although the two city-states had been allies in the war against the Persians, they had chosen very different political forms: Athens was ruled through a limited democracy, Sparta through a military elite; Athens proposed the

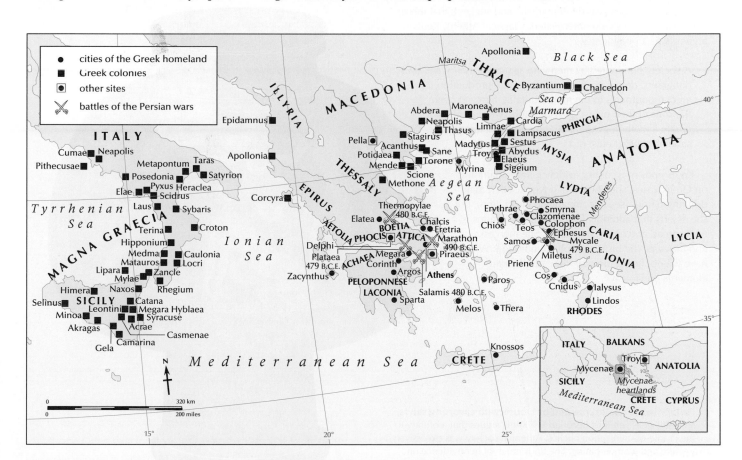

Classical Greece, *c.* 500 B.C.E. The hilly terrain and sea-boundaries of Greece discouraged the growth of large settlements, and Greek philosophers also stressed the importance of local community. When population grew too great, the citizens encouraged their younger cohort to establish new city-states of their own. The resulting spread of settlements established Greek influence all the way from Sicily to Anatolia.

HOW DO WE KNOW?

Gender Relations in Ancient Greece: Voices from the Vases

Understanding and representing the quality of gender relations has become a central task of historians.

For ancient Greece, historians have reached consensus that women were second-class citizens. Indeed, legally they were not citizens at all. In ancient Athens, in most respects the most democratic of all Greek polities,

> They had no role in the political sphere. Women could not speak or vote in the Assembly, could not sit on juries in the law courts. Women's private lives were also relatively circumscribed, for example, in the choice of a marriage partner or the age at which to marry, which for Athenian girls was generally as soon as they were ready to bear children, at fourteen or fifteen. (Kaltsas and Shapiro, p. 13)

Within these general restrictions on women, however, scholars have staked out differing interpretations. Most fascinating, some of these scholars have used the paintings on Greek vases as their evidence. In *The Reign of the Phallus: Sexual Politics in Ancient Athens*, art historian Eva Keuls rages against Athens as both cruelly misogynist and aggressively militaristic, and suggests that these two characteristics were interrelated. Classical Athens, Keuls argues, was a phallocracy,

> A society dominated by men who sequester their wives and daughters, denigrate the female role in reproduction, erect monuments to the male genitalia, have sex with the sons of their peers, sponsor public whorehouses, create a mythology of rape, and engage in rampant saber-rattling. (Keuls, p. 1)

Keuls finds most of her evidence in the paintings on Greek vases, specifically of a type used in male drinking parties (see accompanying illustration), but she asserts that additional support for her claims is widespread and easily accessible. She then asks, and answers, the historiographical question: Why have we not heard more of these phallocratic elements previously?

The story of phallic rule at the root of Western civilization has been suppressed as a result of the near-monopoly that men have held in the field of Classics, by neglect of rich pictorial evidence, by prudery and censorship, and by a misguided desire to protect an idealized image of Athens. (p. 1)

This contrary view, of women enjoying their domestic and religious roles, permeated an art exhibition at the Onassis Cultural Center in New York in 2008–09, titled *Worshiping Women: Ritual and Reality in Classical Athens*, and in the accompanying catalogue of the same name. The curators of the exhibition argue that

> the focus on the exclusion of women from political life has obscured the important roles that women played in the religious life of the polis, often in very public and visible ways. Unlike modern Western societies, religious observance permeated every aspect of life in the ancient Greek city and was inseparable from "secular" affairs, which meant that

Psykter (wine cooler) painted by Douris with cavorting satyrs, 500–490 B.C.E. Feminist historian Eva Keuls argues that, contrary to the cradle-of-civilization clichés, Athenian society was excessively warlike and women-hating. She finds much of her evidence on Greek vases of the type used at male drinking parties. (British Museum, London)

women's activities in cults, rituals, and festivals marked a major contribution to the civic life of Athens.

The accompanying vase-illustration of a newly wed bride receiving gifts from her female relatives, probably in the female quarters of her new home, represents that perspective. Just in front of the bride's left hand, Eros, the god of love, presents his gift, a necklace. In this setting women reign supreme, although the exhibition catalogue reminds us that through marriage the bride passes "from the possession of her father to that of her husband" (Kaltsas and Shapiro, p. 318).

Another vase in the exhibition presents a third perspective: males and females cavorting freely in sport and play, without any indication of superiority or inferiority, of domination or suppression. Although these creatures are mythical male satyrs and female maenads, rather than humans, the message of equality between the genders seems clear.

Vase painting, no less than drama, poetry, philosophy, and formal historical studies, can provide insights into gender relations—and the insights are complex, varied, and subject to interpretation.

- Does the drinking vase support Keuls' overall viewpoint? Why or why not?
- What elements, if any, in the *Worshiping Women* exhibition might support Keuls' viewpoint? Who are the sponsors of the exhibit and catalogue?
- Do you believe that young men and women of Athens could have identified with the activities of the maenads and satyrs of the vase? Why or why not?

Attic red-figure nuptial lebes with lid, clay, 410 B.C.E. This vase depicts the day after the marriage ceremony, when gifts are presented to the bride. Eros himself, the god of physical love, personifying happiness and beauty, presents a necklace. The scene apparently takes place in the women's quarters of the house, and includes the mothers of the bride and of the groom. (National Archaeological Museum, Athens)

How did
Greek culture
spread from the
Mediterranean
to India,
Afghanistan,
Russia, and
Egypt?

cultural development of all its citizens, Sparta stressed universal military service for its able-bodied male citizens; Athens prided itself on its cosmopolitan sea-borne trade and openness to outside influences, Sparta was an armed camp. For ten years, from 461 to 451, Athens and its allies confronted Sparta and its allies in intermittent warfare. During these wars, contradicting its own democratic traditions, Athens exploited its allies. In 454 B.C.E. Pericles moved the treasury of the Delian League to Athens and appropriated its funds in order to create at Athens a spectacular center of power and authority, particularly by building the Parthenon and expanding the fleet. A democracy at home, Athens was fast becoming an imperial power holding sway over its neighbor.

The Peloponnesian War

Relationships between Athens and its neighbors also deteriorated. Pericles' imperialistic policies encroached on its own allies as well as on those of Sparta. Fearful that the Athenians would use their navy to destroy Spartan control over its own alliance system, the Peloponnesian League, Sparta determined to destroy Athens' power. In 432 B.C.E. Sparta attacked Athens, and the Peloponnesian War began in earnest. The struggle was for power, not for higher ideals.

Thucydides, historian of the conflict, portrays Athens setting forth its claims increasingly bluntly. He reports the arrogant Athenian ultimatum ordering the people of the island of Melos to submit to Athenian authority:

> Our opinion of the gods and our knowledge of men lead us to conclude that it is a general and necessary law of nature to rule whatever one can. (V:105; p. 404)

Much weaker than Athens, Melos nevertheless chose to resist. When the Athenians finally conquered the Melians in 415 B.C.E., they killed all the men of military age whom they captured, and sold the women and children into slavery. Throughout Greece, admiration for Athens turned to loathing.

By 404 B.C.E. Sparta, supported by Persian funding, defeated Athens and captured the city. The Spartans may have benefited especially from the warlike spirit of their women. Although the Spartan women did not go into battle themselves, legend had it that they commanded their husbands and sons who were departing for battle to return either carrying their shields—victorious—or carried on their shields—dead.

The Peloponnesian War between Athens and Sparta and their allies had dragged on for a full generation. Both sides were exhausted. Nevertheless, warfare soon resumed among the Greeks, with Thebes and Corinth now entering the lists as major contenders. Each major city-state sought advantage over the others, and the stronger continued to force the weaker into subordinate alliances as intermittent warfare sputtered on.

📖 Read the Document: Plutarch on Life in Sparta (1st c. BCE) on MyHistoryLab

The Empire of Alexander the Great

5.4   How did Greek culture spread from the Mediterranean to India, Afghanistan, Russia, and Egypt?

To the north of the squabbling Greek city-states lay the rougher, less urbanized Macedonia, a borderland between Greece and the Slavic regions to the north and east. The principal language and culture of Macedonia were Greek, but other languages and cultures were also present. While the Greeks looked upon the Macedonians as semi-barbaric, the Macedonian kings, first Philip II (r. 359–336 B.C.E.) and then his son Alexander (the Great) (r. 336–323 B.C.E.), came to view the Greeks as undisciplined and ripe for conquest. The Macedonian conquest of Greece turned out to be only the beginning of one of the greatest, but very short-lived, of the empires that spanned Europe and Asia.

5.1

5.2

5.3

5.4

How did Greek culture spread from the Mediterranean to India, Afghanistan, Russia, and Egypt?

The Conquests of Philip

In 359 B.C.E., in the Macedonian capital of Pella, Philip II persuaded the Macedonian army to declare him king, in succession to his brother, who had died in warfare. After consolidating his power in Macedonia, Philip declared two goals. The first of these was to unify and bring peace to Greece; the second was to liberate the Greek city-states in Asia Minor from Persian control. Skillful as a diplomat and careful to introduce economic improvements in the lands he conquered, Philip nevertheless realized that his army was the real key to achieving his goals. He built up its phalanxes, armed the soldiers with spears up to 15 feet long, and augmented the foot soldiers with powerful and swift cavalry. Philip led the troops himself, suffering numerous, serious wounds in battle.

Between 354 and 339 B.C.E. Philip conquered the Balkans from the Danube to the Aegean coast and from the Adriatic to the Black Sea. To pacify and administer the area, he established new towns, which were populated by both Macedonians and local peoples. Similarly, he employed many local people in his administration. Within Greece proper, his accomplishments were more mixed. He won some allies, such as Thessaly; defeated the armies of several city-states; and mediated the end of a war between two coalitions of Greek city-states. He was honored with election as president of the Pythian Games at Delphi in 346 B.C.E., but Athens and Thebes bitterly opposed his overtures for greater power in Greece.

The orator Demosthenes (384–322 B.C.E.) delivered three "Philippics," public addresses calling Athens to battle against the Macedonian king and predicting the end of Athenian democracy if Philip defeated the city-state. In the face of this opposition, Philip met Athens and its allies in battle, defeating them at Chaeronea in 338 B.C.E. Philip now sought to create a self-governing league of Greek city-states, to accomplish his first goal, and to forge an alliance between Macedonia and the league to fight Persia, his second goal. But he was assassinated in 336 B.C.E. His 20-year-old son, Alexander, continued his father's mission.

The Reign of Alexander the Great

No stranger to warfare, Alexander had fought by his father's side just two years beforehand as he defeated Athens at the Battle of Chaeronea. Applauded by the army, Alexander succeeded to the throne without opposition and continued his father's career of conquest. Over the next 12 years, his disciplined army traversed some 22,000 miles, conquering lands that stretched from Egypt in the west to the Indus River in the east. Alexander's empire became the largest known up to his time, and in 324 B.C.E. he declared himself a god.

Like his father, Philip, and the Persian emperors Cyrus II and Darius I, Alexander followed a policy of benevolent despotism much of the time. But, also like them, he implemented this policy only after his power had been amply demonstrated. Unfortunate Thebes provided an early site for this demonstration. Soon after assuming the throne, Alexander had marched north to the Danube River to suppress revolts in Thrace. Mistakenly informed that Alexander had been killed in battle, Thebes revolted against his local forces. Alexander quickly marched his troops back to Thebes, captured and sacked the rebel city, killed 6,000 of its inhabitants, and sold into slavery 20,000 of those who survived.

In 334 B.C.E. Alexander was ready to cross into Asia, where his first major victory came at Granicus. From there he continued southward, forcing the Persians out of the Greek cities that lined the Ionian coast. To make sure that the Persians would not return, Alexander marched eastward through Anatolia with 35,000 Greek troops,

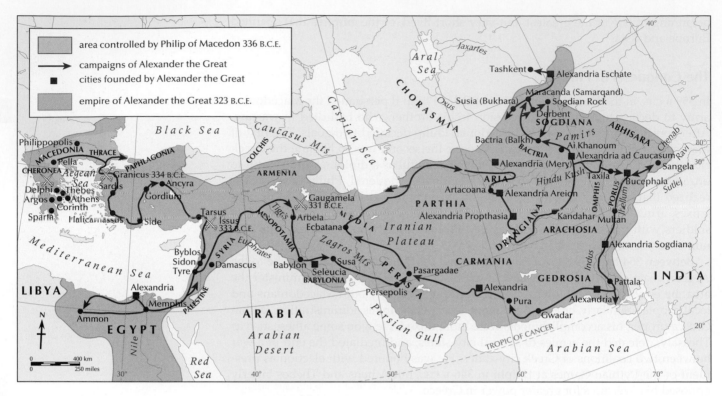

The empire of Alexander. In 338 B.C.E. the Greek city-states were defeated by Philip of Macedon. His son, Alexander, extended the imprint of Greek culture far beyond its Mediterranean homeland. In a series of whirlwind campaigns between 334 and 323 B.C.E., Alexander gained control of Syria and Egypt and then destroyed the might of Persia. He took his armies east to the Indus and north to central Asia, but died at age 33 in Babylon.

5.1

5.2

5.3

5.4 How did Greek culture spread from the Mediterranean to India, Afghanistan, Russia, and Egypt?

routing the 300,000-man army of the Persian emperor Darius III at Issus in 333 B.C.E. and forcing Darius himself into flight.

Alexander continued southward down the coast of the eastern Mediterranean. At Tyre, which held out in siege against him for seven months, he again demonstrated power and brutality, killing 7,000 men and selling 30,000 captives, mostly women and children, into slavery. Elsewhere, however, Alexander showed the velvet glove, respecting local religions, ruling through local hierarchies, and maintaining local tax rates. To drive Persia from the Mediterranean basin and to establish his own control, Alexander continued south and then west, conquering Egypt. He was welcomed as Egypt's liberator from Persian rule and treated as a god by the Egyptian priests of the god Amon, whose shrine he visited. At the western end of the Nile delta, Alexander laid the foundation of what would be for several centuries the most attractive and cultured city of the Mediterranean coast, Alexandria.

His appetite whetted (a common experience with empire-builders once they begin their careers), Alexander moved onward to conquests previously unplanned. He set out to conquer the Persian Empire and make it his own. He marched northeastward across the Fertile Crescent and through Mesopotamia. At Gaugamela in 331 B.C.E. he again faced the Persian emperor, Darius III, and again routed him. The historical capital cities of Babylon, Susa, Persepolis, and Pasargadae lay open to Alexander. He destroyed Persepolis, Darius' own capital, almost totally. Then, having captured the heartland of the Persian Empire, he set off to conquer the eastern half as well, finally reaching and capturing the Indus River valley in the east, and Sogdiana, across the Oxus River, in the northeast.

Although Alexander wanted to continue into India as far as the Ganges, his troops mutinied. They would go no farther. As he was returning from his new frontiers,

The "Alexander Mosaic," first-century B.C.E. mosaic copy from Pompeii of a painting by Philoxenos, c. 300 B.C.E. This mosaic portrays the Battle of Issus (333 B.C.E.) in terms of a personal duel between Alexander the Great and Darius III, emperor of Persia. Darius (right) is shown about to turn and flee in his chariot as the youthful Alexander (left), wild-haired and helmetless, charges toward him. (Museo Archeologico Nazionale, Naples)

View the **Image**: **Mosaic of Alexander the Great** on **MyHistoryLab**

5.1

5.2

5.3

5.4

How did Greek culture spread from the Mediterranean to India, Afghanistan, Russia, and Egypt?

Alexander contracted a fever. Weakened both by the hardships of war and by heavy drinking, he died in Babylon in 323 B.C.E., only 33 years old. Several accounts report that he was poisoned; some said the instigator was his own former teacher Aristotle. On his deathbed Alexander reputedly declared, "Let the job go to the strongest." In the battle for succession among his generals, Alexander's wife, Roxane, and their 13-year-old son were murdered.

The empire Alexander created did not survive two generations. In the east, local rulers regained power in India and Afghanistan. In the west, the Greeks returned to their internal warfare, finally breaking up once more into individual city-states, kingdoms, and leagues. Macedonia remained a separate kingdom and continued to meddle in Greek affairs.

Two major kingdoms emerged from the dissolution of Alexander's empire: Egypt under the dynasty of Ptolemy, which ruled through a Greek and Macedonian elite until the Roman conquest; and the empire established by Seleucus I Nicator (d. 281 B.C.E.), who was governor of Babylon when the empire split apart, and who added to his own domain Iran, Afghanistan, and Anatolia. But the Seleucid Empire, too, fragmented. Parthians reclaimed Persia in the east, and Anatolia divided into numerous local governments. By 200 B.C.E. the Seleucid Empire was limited primarily to the area around Syria.

The Legacies of Alexander

What were the legacies of the empire Alexander built? He made the language and culture of Greece dominant among the ruling intellectual and commercial elites from the Mediterranean east to India, Afghanistan, and the borders of Russia, and south as far as Egypt. A common dialect of Greek, known as Koine, spread as the language of educated people throughout the ancient western world.

Waves of Greek administrators, businessmen, and soldiers followed Alexander's conquests and helped to transmit Greek culture. At the same time, local customs, especially the imperial ceremonial forms of Persia, endured and transformed the simplicity of the earlier **Hellenic** culture into the more complex, elaborate, and cosmopolitan Hellenistic culture that flourished from the time of Alexander until the death of the last Macedonian queen of Egypt, Cleopatra, in 30 B.C.E. One striking example of the mixture of **Hellenistic** and local cultures—this time from India—can be seen in some of the first representations of the Buddha in sculpture from the area of India/ Pakistan after it was conquered by Alexander. These sculptures represent the Buddha wearing a toga (illustrated in the chapter entitled "Indian Empires," below).

To facilitate travel and commerce, as well as conquest and administration, Alexander built roads, canals, and whole new cities, including at least 16 Alexandrias across the length and breadth of his conquests, using the gold and silver captured

KEY TERMS

Hellenic Having to do with Greek culture before the time of Alexander the Great.

Hellenistic Having to do with Greek culture after the time of Alexander, when Hellenic culture was influenced by Persian culture, with its greater emphasis on political empire, government power and centralization, and more ornate artwork.

HOW DO WE KNOW?

Evaluating Alexander the Great

Alexander remains a controversial figure. He was reputed to have murdered hundreds of thousands to achieve his power, yet his admirers see in him a creative genius who aimed at forging a unified Greco-Persian culture that extended into central Asia. By some he was called Alexander the Great; by others Iskander the Accursed. Subsequent historians and other scholars are unsure whether he was an innocent multiculturalist or an imperial monster. There seems to be no question that he believed in his own divinity, but much about this young man remains unknown.

By the end of his life, however, few sorrowed over Alexander's death. The historian Peter Green, who has written an historiographical sketch of Alexander's reputation through the ages, found that the conqueror's image has changed dramatically over time.

The earliest remaining accounts of Alexander's life date from the first century B.C.E., at least 200 years after his death, while the most reliable and fullest of the earliest biographies still extant, that written by Arrian Flavius Arrianus, dates to the second century C.E. For the most part, all historians work from these same basic records, but their assessments reflect the issues and conditions of their own day.

Arrian, who lived at the height of the Roman Empire, and approved of it, praises Alexander for his conquests. Alexander was the prototype of Rome's own Caesars. Closer to our own times, in the late eighteenth and nineteenth centuries, during the democratic era of the American and French revolutions, and of the Greek War for Independence (see the chapter entitled "Migration"), historical opinion turned against Alexander. George Grote's *History of Greece* (1888) represented both Philip and Alexander as "brutalized adventurers simply out for power, wealth, and territorial expansion, both of them inflamed by the pure lust for conquest" (Green, 1991, p. 482).

On the other hand, Johann Gustav Droysen, an ardent advocate of a reunified, powerful Germany (see the chapter entitled "The Industrial Revolution"), saw Alexander as a model. Droysen's scholarly biography *Alexander der Grosse* (1833)

praised Alexander for introducing Greek culture into large parts of Asia.

As the British Empire expanded in the nineteenth and early twentieth centuries, many British scholars also adopted a favorable view of Alexander. William Tarn's two-volume biography saw his conquests as instrumental in spreading a social philosophy of the Brotherhood of Man, bringing together Greeks and Persians, the conquerors with the conquered. Even in our post-imperial day, Cambridge University scholar N.G.L. Hammond agrees, citing the essay by the biographer Plutarch (c. 46–126 C.E.):

> He harnessed all resources to one and the same end, mixing as it were in a loving-cup the lives, manners, marriages and customs of men. He ordered them all to regard the inhabited earth as their fatherland and his armed forces as their stronghold and defense.

Nonetheless, Green remains critical, arguing that his own assessment is closest to that at the time of Alexander's death:

> His all-absorbing obsession through a short but crowded life, was war and conquest. It is idle to palliate this central truth, to pretend that he dreamed … of wading through rivers of blood and violence to achieve the Brotherhood of Man by raping an entire continent. He spent his whole life, with legendary success, in the pursuit of personal glory, Achillean *kleos*; and until very recent times this was regarded as a wholly laudable aim. The empire he built collapsed the moment he was gone; he came as a conqueror and the work he wrought was destruction. (Green, 1991, p. 488)

- What seems to be the basis for Green's interpretation of Alexander's career?
- Would you consider Alexander a hero or a villain?
- In light of America's increasing use of power overseas, how do you think scholarly interpretation of Alexander might change?

from Persia to finance much of the construction. The most famous and illustrious Alexandria was the metropolis in Egypt, which became the leading Mediterranean city of its day. Egyptian Alexandria housed palaces, administrative centers, theaters, stadia, the greatest library of Greek knowledge, containing 700,000 manuscripts, and the final resting place of Alexander himself.

At the eastern end of the empire, on the Oxus River in today's Uzbekistan, the Greeks constructed, on Persian foundations, Ai Khanoum, a small, well-defended city centered on a palace. Ai Khanoum was rediscovered and excavated only in the 1960s, and archaeologists believe it may prove to be Alexandria Oxiana, a lost city from the age of Alexander the Great.

Between Alexandria in Egypt and Ai Khanoum in central Asia were dozens of cities and small towns, which served as seeds of Greek culture throughout the empire. The Alexandrian Empire and its successors built a Hellenistic **ecumene**—that is, a unified urban culture, encompassing vast lands and diverse peoples. Some of its cities, which had long, independent Greek heritages, retained strong elements of their pre-Alexandrian culture and even their autonomy. These were the cities of the Greek heartland, such as Athens, Sparta, Thebes, Corinth, and Delphi. Others were cities of empire, built later by Alexander and his successors either from the ground up or on existing but relatively minor urban bases. These cities served as new regional capitals, to administer the new empire, extend its economy, and broadcast its culture.

Alexander and his successors also administered their empire through the existing indigenous urban framework, but added to it the principal institutions and monuments of Hellenistic culture: temples to Greek gods, frequently set on a walled acropolis; theaters; an agora; civic buildings, such as a council chamber and town hall; gymnasia; and stadia. Examples of this style of urban Hellenization in newly conquered lands included Susa, Damascus, Tyre, Kandahar, and Merv. Residents of these varied cities might feel themselves to be both citizens of the locality and participants in a semi-universal ecumene. A sharp division intensified between the cities with their high culture, now very much Hellenized throughout the empire, and the rural areas, which continued their traditional patterns of life without much change.

The empire encouraged the flow of trade and culture in many directions. Greek ships have been found as far west as the British Isles and as far east as the Indian Ocean. European, African, and Asian trade routes intersected at Taxila, Ai Khanoum, Begram, and Merv. The Persians had begun to create an Asian–African–European *ecumene*; Alexander carried the process further and deeper. Rome, already beginning to rise by the time of Alexander, would later extend a similar imperial mission throughout much of Europe to the west and north, although Rome would not control the east, as we shall see in "Rome and the Barbarians."

Empire-building:
What Difference Does It Make?

Mesopotamians, Egyptians, Persians, Greeks, and Macedonians launched their imperial ambitions from very different backgrounds. Mesopotamians and Greeks began as city-states; Egyptians and Persians as consolidated nations. Sargon conquered Mesopotamia, creating the first empire. Out of the fractious chaos of the Greek city-states Macedon built its small state to imperial dimensions under a father and son who ruled as ambitious and skillful kings. Although our coverage was necessarily sketchy, we have seen that each empire erected a central capital from which it could control the provinces; provided a uniform language, coinage, and legal system across the empire; constructed a road and communications network; articulated an ideology of empire that won the loyalty of many of its citizens and subjects; and created art and architecture to impress on friend and foe alike the power of the empire. Each assembled military forces to apply coercion where necessary.

KEY TERM

ecumene A word of Greek origin referring to the inhabited world and designating a distinct cultural-historical community.

A time finally came for each empire to rein in its ambitions and limit further expansion. Sometimes it reached the limit of its capacity to conquer and administer profitably; sometimes it was defeated in war; often it encountered a combination of both these humbling experiences.

The imperial armies of Alexander the Great refused to proceed to newer, more distant conquests beyond the Indus River. So he turned back toward home. Ironically, Alexander's school tutor had been the philosopher Aristotle, who had written: "To the size of states there is a limit." Aristotle's ideal political unit was the Greek city-state because it promoted the maximum personal participation in democratic government through intense social and political interaction among the citizens.

In choosing to build an empire, Alexander was neither the first nor the last student to disregard his teacher's advice. (Alexander wanted the city-states of Greece to be self-governing, but he did not want other areas to have such powers.) Nor was Aristotle the first or last to weigh the relative merits of small, local democratic government units against those of large, centralized bureaucracies. Similar debates still go on in our own day. Debates over the usefulness, limits, and legitimacy of empire were also central to the political thought of ancient Rome, China, and India, the three huge empires that are the focus of the chapters entitled "Rome and the Barbarians," "China," and "Indian Empires."

CHAPTER REVIEW

THE EARLIEST EMPIRES

5.1 What were the characteristics of early empires?

The world's first empires, like the first cities, arose in Mesopotamia and the Nile River valley. The emperor Sargon established control over Mesopotamia's far-flung independent city-states. He standardized measurements and the use of the Akkadian language in the empire's documents, and he replaced local leaderships with his own administrators. Mesopotamia's city-state structure and its geographical openness left the region vulnerable. After Sargon, outside empires continually attacked and absorbed the region's city-states.

The Egyptian empire, in contrast, began as a single unified state, which then slowly expanded its power over others. By about 2000 B.C.E. it conquered Nubia in the southern Nile valley; by about 1500 B.C.E. it conquered parts of Mesopotamia. (At other times, Egypt was conquered by the Nubians and by peoples of Mesopotamia.) The empire constructed enormous royal building projects, including new cities, elegant palaces, temple complexes, tombs, and fortifications. Egypt's hierarchical society was focused on the dynastic succession of its semi-god rulers, the pharaohs.

THE PERSIAN EMPIRE

5.2 How did Darius I come to rule the Persian Empire?

Darius I took over the Persian Empire that Cyrus II had established and ruled it for 35 years. He softened the imposition of imperial administration and tax collection by maintaining local traditions and bringing local elites into his administration. He created more efficient units of government by increasing the number of local governments. At the same time, he created an imperial system of roads, with a series of inns for travelers and a royal courier service along the roads. He built a new capital city, later called Persepolis. He renewed the region's irrigation systems, encouraged the introduction of new crops, and standardized the empire's coinage, called the daric after himself.

THE GREEK CITY-STATES

5.3 What was the nature of the Greek city-state political organization?

The Greeks developed a very different form of political organization from that of the Persians. The Greek city-state, or polis, was an intentionally small, locally organized government based on a single central city. With enough surrounding land to provide for its agricultural needs, each city-state had its own form of government and was individually independent. Athens, in particular, took pride in its government by all of its free, adult, male citizens (but not by its women or its slaves or newcomers to the city). These assemblies passed laws, judged criminal and civil cases, implemented legislation, and arranged for military defense as needed. The Greek city-states understood their legal systems to be their own creation and responsibility: not imposed by an emperor or decreed by the gods. Athens was proud of its ability to unify the Greek city-states in successful warfare against the Persian empire, and of the "golden age" of culture that followed. Its former allies, however, especially Sparta, accused it of imperial ambitions. The Peloponnesian War among the rival Greek city-states followed.

THE EMPIRE OF ALEXANDER THE GREAT

5.4 How did Greek culture spread from the Mediterranean to India, Afghanistan, Russia, and Egypt?

Alexander, who came from Macedonia, Greece's northern neighbor, made the language and culture of Greece dominant among the ruling elites all across his enormous empire. The waves of Greek administrators, soldiers, and businessmen who followed Alexander's conquests helped transmit Greek culture, although they permitted many local customs, and prior Persian practices, to remain. Alexander built roads, canals, and cities across the empire, at least 16 of them named Alexandria, and in the cities he and his successors built stadia, theaters, gymnasia, and temples, all in the Hellenistic style.

Suggested Readings

PRINCIPAL SOURCES

Baines, John, and Jaromir Malek. *Atlas of Ancient Egypt* (New York: Facts on File, 1980). Two noted experts continue the excellent books in this series with fine text, maps, pictures, time lines, and breadth of coverage.

Green, Peter. *Alexander of Macedon* (Berkeley, CA: University of California Press, 1991). An excellent, thoughtful biography with good historiographical coverage as well.

——. *The Greco-Persian Wars* (Berkeley, CA: University of California Press, 1996). A revision of a classic on the wars.

Hanson, Victor Davis. *The Wars of the Ancient Greeks* (London: Cassell & Co, 1999). A readable volume that incorporates recent scholarship on Greek warfare.

Kagan, Donald. *The Peloponnesian War* (New York: Viking, 2003). Distills the great scholarship, and increases the readability, of his earlier four-volume work. Based largely on Thucydides, but includes considerable additional scholarship and new perspectives.

Levi, Peter. *Atlas of the Greek World* (New York: Facts on File, 1982). The series continues its excellent, broad coverage with outstanding text, maps, pictures, and time lines.

Past Worlds: The (London) Times Atlas of Archaeology (Maplewood, NJ: Hammond, Inc., 1988). Beautifully produced, superbly researched atlas with fine text and excellent pictures as well.

Postgate, J.N. *Early Mesopotamia* (London: Routledge, 1992). Scholarly analysis and clear presentation.

Thucydides. *History of the Peloponnesian War*, trans. Rex Warner (Harmondsworth, Middlesex: Penguin Books, 1972). The definitive primary source, cynically philosophical about political motives, the product of bitter and cynical events.

Wycherley, R.E. *How the Greeks Built Cities* (Garden City, NY: Anchor Books, 1969). Excellent introduction to the urban plans of the Greek cities, with good attention to the significance of the buildings and designs, and to the variety of city-states.

ADDITIONAL SOURCES

Aristotle. *Basic Works*, ed. and trans. Richard McKeon (New York: Random House, 1941). Direct introduction to the work of the philosopher, whose works continued authoritative for at least 2,000 years.

Bernal, Martin. *Black Athena: The Afroasiatic Roots of Classical Civilization* (New Brunswick, NJ: Rutgers University Press, 1987). Bernal demonstrates the influence of Egyptian culture on ancient Greece. Because of the title the book became involved in racial debates, but the text does not concentrate on race.

Hamilton, J.R. *Alexander the Great* (London: Hutchison University Library, 1973). A standard biography.

Hammond, Mason. *The City in the Ancient World* (Cambridge, MA: Harvard University Press, 1972). A history of the ancient Western world through an analysis of its cities.

Hammond, N.G.L. *The Genius of Alexander the Great* (Chapel Hill, NC: University of North Carolina Press, 1997). A standard biography.

Herodotus. *The Persian Wars*, trans. George Rawlinson (New York: Modern Library, 1942). Some consider this the first secular book of history. Mixes myth with history in recreating the great clash of civilizations between the Greeks and the Persians.

Homer. *Iliad*, trans. Robert Fagles (New York: Penguin Books, 1998). The story that inspired the ancient Greeks in warfare, and gave us insight into their world.

——. *Odyssey*, trans. Robert Fagles (New York: Penguin Books, 1999). The great story of the journey of Odysseus through one trial after another from the Trojan war back to his home in Greece.

Hornblower, Simon. *The Greek World 479–323 B.C.* (London: Methuen, 1983). A standard historical survey.

Kaltsas, Nikolaos, ed. *Athens–Sparta* (New York: Alexander S. Onassis Public Benefit Foundation, 2006). Catalog of a 2006–07 museum exhibition comparing the two city-states, primarily through their art.

Kaltsas, Nikolaos, and Alan Shapiro, eds. *Worshiping Women: Ritual and Reality in Classical Athens* (New York: Alexander S. Onassis Public Benefit Foundation [USA] in collaboration with the National Archaeological Museum, Athens, 2008). Catalog of a 2008–09 museum exhibition of the same name.

Keuls, Eva C. *The Reign of the Phallus: Sexual Politics in Ancient Athens* (New York: Harper and Row, 1985). Opinionated, belligerent, engaging feminist critique of ancient Athens; evidence taken from painting on drinking vessels.

Mumford, Lewis. *The City in History* (New York: Harcourt, Brace and World, 1961). Classic history with a strong argument for small, manageable cities with a strong sense of community.

O'Brien, John Maxwell. *Alexander the Great: The Invisible Enemy* (London: Routledge, 1992). Critical biography.

Plato. *The Collected Dialogues of Plato*, ed. Edith Hamilton and Huntington Cairns (New York: Bollingen Foundation [distributed by Pantheon Books], 1961). The complete works of the classic philosopher of ideal types.

Plutarch. *The Lives of the Noble Grecians and Romans*, trans. John Dryden, revised by Arthur Hugh Clough (New York: Modern Library, n.d.). Writing from the height of the Roman Empire, this Greek historian preserves many materials that have otherwise been lost as he assesses the accomplishments of many of the Greek and Roman greats.

Robinson, Eric W., ed. *Ancient Greek Democracy: Readings and Sources* (Malden, MA: Blackwell, 2004). Very useful selection of primary documents on the function and limits of ancient Greek democracy.

Saggs, H.W.F. *The Might that Was Assyria* (London: Sidgwick & Jackson, 1984). Fine general survey.

Sophocles. *Oedipus Rex* and *Oedipus at Colonus*, trans. Robert Fitzgerald in *The Oedipus Cycle* (San Diego: Harcourt Brace Jovanovich, 1969). Two of the most famous plays from ancient Greece.

Tacitus. *The Annals of Imperial Rome*, trans. Michael Grant (Baltimore, MD: Penguin Books, 1959). Primary source by this government official and historian of Rome, often very critical of the growth of empire.

Tarn, W.W. *Alexander the Great* (Cambridge: Cambridge University Press, 2 vols., 1948). Laudatory biography.

FILMS

PBS Home Video. *Athens. The Dawn of Democracy* (2007; 2 hours). Superb analysis of the rhetoric, reality, and historic evolution of Athenian democracy. Excellent visuals; outstanding scholars. Recent research. Narrated by Bettany Hughes.

BBC Horrible Histories: *Wife Swap: Spartans and Athenians*, YouTube (2009; 4½ minutes). Hilarious parody of the family styles of the two city-states. Makes some telling points.

300 (2007; 1 hour and 57 minutes). Film based on the historical story of Leonidas, as related through the 1999 graphic novel of the same name, leading 300 Spartan warriors to their doom in a defense against Persian invaders which nevertheless inspired Sparta and other Greek city-states to unite and keep the Persians out. Testosterone-fueled violence. Single-dimensional characters. Huge box-office success. For the information and the fun of it, read the variety of perspectives on the film presented in Wikipedia.

6 Rome and the Barbarians

The Rise and Dismemberment of Empire

753 B.C.E.–1453 C.E.

All roads, by land and sea, led to Rome, the capital of one of the longest-lasting and most influential of empires. Situated on the Tiber River, not far from the sea, Rome served as the center of communication and trade for the entire Italian peninsula. To the surrounding sea the Romans gave the name "Mediterranean," the middle of the earth, for it is itself surrounded by the three continents that they knew: southern Europe, northern Africa, and western Asia. Later, as Roman armies conquered and ruled an empire that encompassed all these lands and many territories still more distant, they began to call the Mediterranean *Mare Nostrum* ("Our Sea").

Battle line formed with shields by the Romans against the Dacians, from Trajan's Column, Rome, *c.* 113 C.E. Plaster cast of marble original. The Romans adapted the Greek phalanx into a more maneuverable, but tightly configured, array of foot soldiers with shields, spears, and daggers. Victory memorials, such as Trajan's Column celebrated the resulting successes in battle. Compare with the Greek phalanx in the chapter opener entitled "From City-state to Empire". (Museo della Civiltà, Rome)

LEARNING OBJECTIVES

6.1	6.2	6.3	6.4	6.5	6.6	6.7
Describe the formation of the early Roman republic.	Understand the Roman republic as a military society.	Understand how the Romans won support from conquered peoples.	Trace the generals' power struggles and the end of the Republic.	Describe the achievements of Augustus and the Roman Principate.	Understand why the Roman Empire declined.	Discuss how the eastern empire survived after the end of the Roman Empire.

🔈 Listen on MyHistoryLab

At its greatest extent, in the second century C.E., the Roman Empire ruled between 70 and 100 million people of vastly diverse ethnic, racial, religious, and cultural roots. Geographically, it sprawled over 2,700 miles east to west and 2,500 miles north to south, extending from Scotland to the Persian Gulf. At its most powerful, between 27 B.C.E. and 180 C.E., Rome enforced the *Pax Romana*, the Roman peace, a reign of stability and relative tranquility throughout all these vast regions.

From the first, this empire evoked both praise and condemnation. The Latin poet Virgil (70–19 B.C.E.) led one of the greatest choruses of praise, describing Rome as a gift of the gods, and praising its citizens for successfully carrying out their mandate: "Remember Romans/ To rule the people under law, to establish/ The way of peace." Virgil praised the sheer size of the empire, its roads, its cities, its trade, and its monuments. Most of all, however, he cited the *Pax Romana*, the peace and prosperity established through Rome's rule of law, enforced by Rome's armies.

The historian Tacitus (*c.* 56–*c.* 120 C.E.) mocked this praise of peace and prosperity: "Robbery, butchery, and rapine they call 'Empire.' They create a desert and call it 'Peace.'" Writing a century after Virgil, and viewing the empire through the eyes of a defeated Celtic chieftain, Tacitus characterized the *Pax Romana* as a policy of brute military conquest and destruction. This chapter will explore the conditions underlying both of these contradictory points of view.

6.1
6.2
6.3
6.4
6.5
6.6
6.7

How did the early Republic take shape?

From Hill Town to Republic, 753–133 B.C.E.

6.1 How did the early Republic take shape?

The legendary date for the founding of the city of Rome is April 21, 753 B.C.E., and although this is probably not exact, it is approximately correct. (Romans today still celebrate April 21 as the birthday of their city, with free concerts and public festivities.) According to this legend, beloved by the Romans, Romulus and Remus—twin sons of Mars, the god of war—founded the city at the site where they were rescued from the Tiber River and suckled by a nurturing she-wolf. (See the Etruscan statue illustration, below.)

KEY TERM

Pax Romana The "Roman peace," that is, the state of comparative concord prevailing within the boundaries of the Roman Empire from the reign of Augustus (r. 27 B.C.E.–14 C.E.) to that of Marcus Aurelius (r. 161–180 C.E.), enforced by Roman political and military control.

Capitoline wolf, *c.* 500 B.C.E. According to legend, Rome was founded by Romulus and Remus, twin sons of Mars, at the spot where they were rescued from the Tiber River and suckled by a she-wolf. The group of she-wolf with twins was adopted as the symbol of Rome, although the children in this particular statue were added almost 2,000 years later, during the Renaissance. (Museo Capitolino, Rome)

6.1 How did the early Republic take shape?

6.2

6.3

6.4

6.5

6.6

6.7

For two and a half centuries, the kings of neighboring Etruria, the land to the north of Rome, ruled the city. The Romans learned much from the Etruscans about city-building, art, religion, mythology, and even language. As Rome entered the Mediterranean trade networks of the Etruscans, merchants and craftworkers immigrated to the city. The Etruscan king Servius Tullius (578–534 B.C.E.) reformed the military, creating the *comitia centuriata*, a deliberative ruling council organized by hundreds (*centuriae*), representing the soldiers of Rome. This assembly of Roman citizens persisted for centuries after Etruscan rule had ended, reinforcing the connection between the armies of Rome and its government.

Patricians and Plebeians in the Early Republic

About 509 B.C.E., the wealthy, powerful citizens of Rome drove out the Etruscan kings. They declared Rome a **republic**, a government in which power resides in its citizens, who elect officials to represent them in decision-making. However, the new government perpetuated the class conflict that was already a staple of Rome's Etruscan history. Full citizenship under the early Republic included only seven to ten percent of the population: the wealthy, the powerful, and those with hereditary residential ties to Rome. These were the **patricians** (from the Latin *pater*, "father"). Patricians were also called "free men," to distinguish them from the overwhelming majority, the **plebeians**. Plebeians lacked long-standing hereditary ties to the state and usually lacked property as well, so they could not serve as officers in the military and were excluded from government, as were slaves (usually, men captured in war) and women.

The two classes, patricians and plebeians, had already become polarized under Etruscan rule. The patricians forbade intermarriage with the plebeians and monopolized for themselves not only membership in the Senate, but also the religious offices of the state. The plebeians had looked to the Etruscan king as their protector, and the fall of the monarchy further reduced their status.

The Struggle of the Orders. The first conflict between patricians and plebeians, the Struggle of the Orders, broke out 15 years after the fall of the monarchy and persisted through more than a half-century (494–440 B.C.E.) of the early Republic. The plebeians relied on their ultimate strengths: their bodies and their numbers. They were the foot soldiers of Rome, and their periodic boycotts of military service threatened the city of Rome itself. In 451 B.C.E., in an attempt to resolve the conflict, a commission of ten patricians codified Rome's existing customary practices into the Law of the Twelve Tables, so named because they were inscribed on 12 tables of ivory (or, perhaps, bronze).

The patricians, with their legal skills, outfoxed the plebeians, who were horrified when they recognized the severity of the laws that were imposed upon them. The laws were often written without explicit distinction between plebeian and patrician, but they were especially hard on the weak and the impoverished, and hardest of all on slaves. All these people were most likely to be plebeians. For example, after a 30-day grace period, debtors could be arrested and brought to court, held in chains or stocks, and, after 60 days, sold into slavery or even killed. The punishment for pasturing animals on someone else's land or for cutting crops from someone else's field secretly by night was death by hanging. Slaves had the fewest rights, and the lowest human value, of all. The financial punishment for bruising or breaking the bone of a free man was twice that for similar injuries to a slave. The punishment for theft by a free man was flogging and arranging some form of repayment; for theft by a slave it was flogging and execution by being thrown from the Tarpeian Rock on the Capitoline Hill in Rome (Lewis and Reinhold, I:109–13).

Slowly, under pressure, however, the patricians yielded power. For example, a series of laws that relieved debts were enacted, which helped plebeians especially,

KEY TERMS

republic A state that is ruled not by a hereditary leader (as in a monarchy) but by a person or persons appointed under the constitution.

patrician Born to a family with long-standing residence and prominence in Rome, a patrician was an aristocrat. About seven to ten percent of Rome's population were patricians.

plebeian A citizen of ancient Rome who was not a member of the privileged patrician class. Beginning in the later Republican period, the term "plebeian" implied low social class.

tribune In ancient Rome, a plebeian officer elected by the plebeians and charged to protect their lives and properties, with a right of veto against legislative proposals of the Senate.

magistrate An official elected by the Senate of Rome to administer the Republic under the supervision of the Senate. There were many different ranks of magistrate, serving different functions. At the end of their term of office they became senators themselves.

consul Under the Roman Republic, one of the two magistrates holding supreme civil and military authority.

although indebtedness continued to be a problem throughout Roman history. Plebeians gained representation along with patricians in Rome's Senate, and they gained the right to elect two **tribunes**, officers charged with defending their legal rights.

The Senate of Rome

The Roman Senate was the legislative and consultative body of the government. The Senate elected a variety of **magistrates** to carry out the administration of the Republic, sometimes under the control of the Senate, at other times with greater independence. As magistrates ended their one-year (renewable) term of office, they automatically became senators themselves. The Senate and the magistrates were part of the Etruscan heritage. The Etruscans had had a senate, composed of the elders of the society, which elected and advised the king. Similarly, the Roman Senate, in the days of the Republic, decided policy, especially concerning peace and war, and appointed and advised the magistrates. At the highest executive level, two **consuls** held power that extended over all the lands Rome ruled. Nominated by the Senate and elected by citizens in the *comitia centuriata* (the popular assembly of leaders of Rome's soldiers, another holdover from Etruscan rule), the consuls held office for one year. At first only patricians could serve as consuls, but in 360 B.C.E. the first plebeian consul was elected. In later years of the Republic the consuls usurped the power of the Senate and gained the power to appoint the senators.

How did the early Republic take shape?	6.1
	6.2
	6.3
	6.4
	6.5
	6.6
	6.7

AT A GLANCE: THE ROMAN EMPIRE 500–50 B.C.E.

DATE	POLITICS	RELIGION AND CULTURE	SOCIAL DEVELOPMENT
500 B.C.E.	• Rome independent of Etruscan rule (509); Republic founded		
450 B.C.E.	• Rome sacked by Gauls (390)		• Laws of Twelve Tables promulgated
350 B.C.E.	• Roman expansion into Italy south of Po (327–304)		
300 B.C.E.	• First Punic War (264–241)		• Earliest Roman coinage (280–275)
250 B.C.E.	• Second Punic War (219) • Hannibal invaded Italy • Roman conquest of Cisalpine Gaul (202–191)	• Stoicism—Zeno	
200 B.C.E.	• Rome annexed Spain (197) • Conquest of Macedon (167)	• Polybius (200–118)	
150 B.C.E.	• Third Punic War (149–146) • T. Gracchus tribune (133) • G. Gracchus tribune (123 and 122) • Gallia Narbonensis a Roman province	• Carthage destroyed • Corinth destroyed	• *Pax Romana* led to widespread trade throughout Empire; roads built
100 B.C.E.	• Sulla conquers Greece • Civil war in Rome (83–82) • Conquest of Syria (66) • First Triumvirate (60)		• Spartacus slave revolt (73–71)
50 B.C.E.	• Civil war (49) • Julius Caesar dictator (47–44) • Second Triumvirate (43) • Annexation of Egypt (31) • Augustus Caesar (63 B.C.E.–14 C.E.)	• Cicero (106–43) • Virgil (70–19) • Jesus (c. 4 B.C.E.–c. 30 C.E.) • Augustus deified on his death • Forum in Rome • Livy (59 B.C.E.–17 C.E.)	

AT A GLANCE: THE ROMAN EMPIRE 1–550 C.E.

DATE	POLITICS	RELIGION AND CULTURE	SOCIAL DEVELOPMENT
1 C.E.	• Christianity reaches Rome • Invasion of Britain (43)		
50 C.E.	• Trajan (r. 98–117)	• Seneca (c. 4–65) • Destruction of Temple in Jerusalem (70) • Pompeii and Herculaneum buried by eruption of Vesuvius (79)	• Jewish revolt (66–73) • Roman women gain new rights
100 C.E.	• Dacia conquered by Trajan • Hadrian (r. 117–138)	• Tacitus (c. 56–c. 120) • Trajan's column and forum (112–113) • Pantheon in Rome • Hadrian's Wall	
150 C.E.	• Marcus Aurelius (r. 161–180)		
200 C.E.	• Caracalla (r. 212–17) • Decius (r. 249–51)	• Baths of Caracalla	• Roman citizenship for all males
250 C.E.	• Gallienus (r. 253–68)	• Persecution of Christians	
300 C.E.	• Constantine (r. 306–37)	• Edict of Milan (313) • Constantinople inaugurated (330)	
350 C.E.		• St. Augustine (354–430) • End of state support for paganism (394)	
400 C.E.	• Sack of Rome (410)		
450 C.E.	• End of Roman Empire in West (476)		
550 C.E.			• Justinian codifies Roman law; with Theodora, beautifies Constantinople

6.1

6.2

6.3

6.4

6.5

6.6

6.7

How did the early Republic take shape?

The early empire ruled by armed force, and all Rome's senators were veterans of military service. They could be either patricians or plebeians. However, because soldiers provided their own arms, only men with some wealth and property could command and rise in the ranks. They in turn were ordered by class, according to the quality and cost of the weapons they provided, and then divided into military units called **centuries**, or groups of approximately 100, as they had been under the Etruscans. The *centurions*, leaders of the centuries, met in assembly to elect the senators and the magistrates, including the consuls.

At each level of administration, the officials were paired, so that they would have to consult with each other and neither could seize excessive power. The power of the former Etruscan kings, for example, was now shared between the two consuls in this new system of checks and balances; each consul had the power of veto over the other. (In extraordinary emergencies, the Senate could appoint a **dictator**, a leader with absolute emergency powers, elected for the limited term of six months.)

Roman Military Power

From its beginning, Rome was a military state. Rome's armies were central to its life, and they excelled in organization and technology. When necessary, they adopted creative innovations. Although at first they copied the Greek hoplite phalanxes (see the chapter entitled "Dawn of the Empires") in their military deployment, later Roman armies were reorganized. Small, flexible units, armed with swords and throwing javelins in place of the older spears, lined up with less experienced, younger troops in front, more tested troops behind them, and then, as the final resort, veterans of courage and proven valor. If the front ranks could not hold and fell back into the rear lines, the advancing, overconfident enemy was suddenly confronted by a compact mass of soldiers of the greatest numbers and skill.

KEY TERMS

centuries The smallest units of the Roman army, each composed of some 100 foot soldiers and commanded by a *centurion*. A legion was made up of 60 centuries. Centuries also formed political divisions of Roman citizens.

dictator A leader elected at a time of crisis by the Senate of Rome for a short term, usually six months, and vested with extraordinary powers to deal with the situation.

Although it had never previously possessed a navy, Rome built one that conquered Carthage, the greatest seapower of the day. The Romans learned to build sophisticated warships by capturing one from Carthage and copying it. Confronting great walled towns in the east, Rome developed unprecedented machinery to besiege the walls, catapult firepower into them, and batter them down. The Roman preference for massing overwhelming strength and their willingness to let time work on their side through siege warfare brought many victories with minimal losses of their own.

The Expansion of the Republic

6.2 How did Rome build its empire on military expansion?

The Roman Republic established alliances with other nearby city-states in west-central Italy, and began to challenge the Etruscans. In 396 B.C.E., after a siege of six years, the Romans captured Veii, a principal Etruscan city only 12 miles from Rome. Celtic invaders sacked Rome itself in 390 B.C.E., but the setback was brief, and Rome's expansion continued. By 264 B.C.E., Roman armies controlled all of Italy south of the Po valley.

6.1
6.2
How did Rome build its empire on military expansion?
6.3
6.4
6.5
6.6
6.7

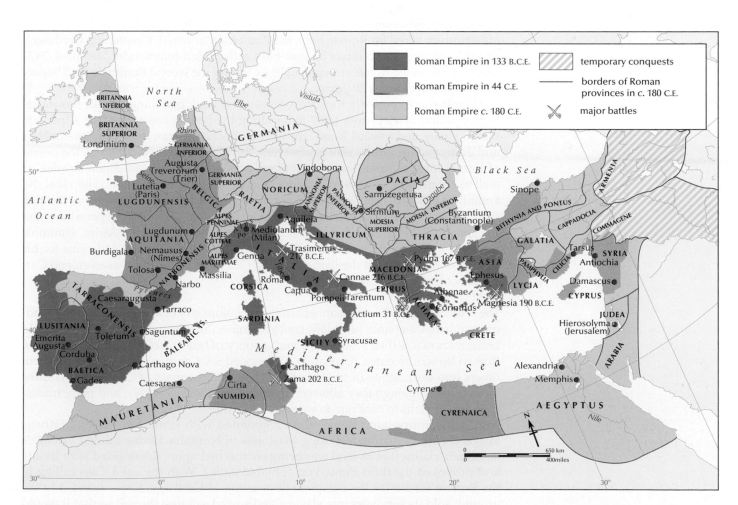

The Roman Empire. Rome built its empire on military expansion, first within Italy by overthrowing its neighbors, then across the Mediterranean by defeating the Carthaginians, then northwest to Gaul and Britain and north to the Danube. Rome offered many benefits to the peoples it conquered, but finally its power rested in its armies.

6.1

6.2   How did Rome
      build its empire
6.3   on military
      expansion?
6.4

6.5

6.6

6.7

Rome became a society geared for war. Roman armies, and its new navy, continued to expand Roman rule. For the next 140 years its troops were almost constantly on the move. The most bitter and decisive of their battles were the three Punic Wars against Carthage.

The Punic Wars

Carthage, only 130 miles across the narrow waist of the Mediterranean from Italy, had developed as a major trade outpost of Phoenician seafarers. Just as Rome dominated Italy, the Carthaginians controlled the north-central coast of Africa and the western Mediterranean. One of their trade networks focused on the mineral wealth of Spain, especially its silver mines. To protect that route, Carthage developed ports and cities in Sicily and Sardinia. It even controlled trade outposts on the Italian mainland in Etruria. Carthage and Rome were set on a collision course.

The three wars that broke out are known as the Punic Wars after the Roman term for Phoenicians, *Punici*. The fighting opened in Sicily in 264 B.C.E. By 241 B.C.E., when the first Punic War ended, Rome was victorious both on land and at sea. It took control of Sicily and imposed taxes on the island. Four years later, Rome took advantage of a mutiny among Carthaginian troops in Sardinia to occupy Sardinia and Corsica. In 227 B.C.E., it annexed the islands. For the first time, Rome had provinces outside the Italian peninsula.

Carthage, however, rebuilt its forces, especially in Spain. When the Spanish city of Saguntum asked for Roman help, the Romans intervened, threatening Carthage's Spanish colonies. The brilliant 27-year-old Carthaginian commander Hannibal (247–183 B.C.E.) defeated Rome's troops in 219 B.C.E., and the second Punic War had begun. It continued for almost 20 years.

Hannibal unexpectedly took the offensive by land, marching tens of thousands of troops and 37 elephants 1,000 miles along the French coast, over the Alps, into the Po valley, and toward Rome. In two months he overran most of northern Italy and destroyed the armies sent against him. But Hannibal could not break the power of Rome. Most of Rome's allies remained loyal, and Rome raised new armies, as well as recapturing cities that had previously gone over to Hannibal. Hannibal did annihilate a Roman army at Cannae in southern Italy, but ultimately he was isolated there. Meanwhile, Rome won victories in Spain in 211–206 B.C.E., especially under the general Publius Cornelius Scipio. In 204 B.C.E. Scipio invaded Africa. Hannibal returned to defend his homeland, but Scipio, later named Scipio Africanus for his victory, defeated him at the Battle of Zama (202 B.C.E.). The war was over, and Carthage became a dependency of Rome.

The "New Wisdom." In its treatment of the rebellious city of Capua and its surrounding region of Campania, just to the south of Rome, the Romans exhibited what would become known as their "New Wisdom," a policy of brute force toward their enemies. Roman leaders executed 70 senators, imprisoned 300 Campanian aristocrats, and put others into the custody of trusted allies. They sold the mass of Campanian citizens into slavery, although they allowed resident aliens, former slaves, and petty tradesmen and artisans to continue to work.

A half-century later, Rome again responded with brute force after Carthage attacked Rome's African ally, King Masinissa of Numidia. Disregarding Carthage's legitimate claims that its land was being encroached upon, Rome sided with its ally and provoked the third Punic War (149–146 B.C.E.). With the aged Cato calling in the Roman Senate for the complete destruction of Carthage, Rome razed it to the ground, sold its survivors into slavery, and sowed salt into the soil so that it would never again flourish. The Romans annexed all of Carthage into the Roman province of Africa. Rome had become mistress of the Mediterranean.

SOURCE

Artifactual Records

Rome has bequeathed rich material artifacts. Much of the infrastructure of the empire—its roads, aqueducts, stadia, public baths, forums, temples, triumphal arches—as well as substantial parts of many of the military camps and cities it constructed still stand. Roman coinage and statuary are everywhere.

The cities of Pompeii and Herculaneum, comprising a total population of about 20,000, were buried in dust and cinders in the volcanic eruption of Mount Vesuvius in 79 C.E. Archaeologists uncovered these remains, forgotten for almost two millennia, in the late eighteenth century, providing an unparalleled view of the structure and furnishings of these provincial towns. Preserved like time capsules, they reveal their urban design, buildings, furniture, and household objects.

Pompeii was a walled town, with seven gates, a forum, a council chamber, offices of magistrates, temples dedicated to Apollo and Jupiter, market buildings, a stock exchange, a law court, a theater, auditoriums, an amphitheater for gladiatorial contests and wild beast hunts, three Turkish-style baths, workshops, shops, brothels, and homes. Carbonized food, preserved and sealed in hot volcanic mud, suggests that at least some of the inhabitants ate well. Walls, surviving to their full height, have preserved vivid murals from the residences and businesses. At least some Pompeians had cultivated aesthetic sensibilities. Some of the art in the seven brothels indicates also a cultivated taste for pornography.

In the countryside, archaeologists have also been able to reconstruct *latifundia*, rural estates that were controlled by rich owners who bought up family farms and ran them as plantations. Offshore searches have uncovered sunken ships in the Italian Mediterranean that shed light on Roman trade missions and their cargoes.

Archaeological digs have also uncovered the history of the many Gothic, Celtic, and other groups of migrating peoples who lived on the fringes of the empire, later settled within its territories, and finally established their own states on those lands as the empire disintegrated. Their settlements, burial grounds, tools, and artwork yield significant information about their lives, even though they had no writing systems until they learned from the Romans.

With such extensive artifacts complementing the rich documentary record, scholars can reconstruct the rise and fall of the Roman Empire and its relationships with neighboring peoples. Relatively abundant materials provide the sources also to explore new topics, such as the extent of slavery, the treatment of women, and patterns of health and disease in ancient Rome.

The young Hercules wrestling with a snake, fresco, House of the Vettii, Pompeii.

The body of a man petrified by ash from the eruption of Mount Vesuvius, Pompeii, 79 C.E.

6.1

6.2 How did Rome
build its empire
6.3 on military
expansion?

6.4

6.5

6.6

6.7

Rome's brutal use of military power served as a warning to potential foes. Roman generals were not pressed to win quick, brilliant victories, but to defeat the enemy through patient, deliberate preparation and decisive force. Ideally, the enemy would be so awed by Roman forces that it would never dare oppose them. Rome might prefer to rule by hegemony, with the consent of the people it conquered, but ultimately it did not flinch from the brute force of domination.

Further Expansion

After Rome had eliminated the Carthaginian threat with the end of the second Punic War, it turned to the conquest of the Gauls in northern Italy and annexed their territory, 202–191 B.C.E. It annexed Spain in 197 B.C.E. but treated that province so harshly that constant revolts simmered until Rome finally crushed them in 133 B.C.E. Rome then turned its power toward Gaul (modern France). In southern Gaul, Rome's ally Massilia (Marseilles) asked for help against Gallic tribes, and by 121 B.C.E. Rome had annexed most of the region.

The Eastern Mediterranean. The Romans were opportunists, seizing land wherever they saw weakness. Even as they conquered territory in the west, they expanded in the east as well. In the eastern Mediterranean, the Romans encountered Macedonians and Greeks, the proud heirs of Alexander the Great, who still ruled the lands that he had conquered and Hellenized. Rome's first battle on Greek soil came in 200 B.C.E., and it was the start of the complete restructuring of political power in the eastern Mediterranean.

At the death of Alexander the Great in 323 B.C.E., his empire had divided into three regional kingdoms. In 203–202 B.C.E. two of these kingdoms, Macedonia and Syria, where the Seleucid dynasty ruled, combined to threaten the third, Egypt, where the Ptolemaic family ruled. Neighboring Greek city-states encouraged Rome to use these divisions to establish its own balance of power in the region. Rome accepted the invitation. It warned Macedonia not to interfere in Greek affairs. When Philip V of Macedon (r. 211–179 B.C.E.) rejected this warning, the Romans attacked and defeated him. In victory, the Romans declared the Greek city-states of the eastern Mediterranean "free," granting them nominal independence, but, in fact, placing them under Roman control.

Rome had similarly warned Antiochus III, the Great, of Syria (r. 223–187 B.C.E.) to stay out of Europe and Egypt. When Antiochus ignored the warning, Roman forces crushed him, pushed him back to Syria, and forced him to pay a huge indemnity.

In the next generation, Rome decisively defeated Philip V's son Perseus in 168 B.C.E., ending the Macedonian monarchy. In the same year, Rome again protected Egypt from the Seleucids, asserting its own control of the eastern Mediterranean.

Here, too, Rome applied the brutal tactics of the "New Wisdom." In 148 B.C.E., when the Greek city-state of Corinth and its allies flouted Roman wishes, and even attacked Roman envoys, Rome razed Corinth to the ground, sold all its surviving inhabitants into slavery, and carried its artistic works to Rome. Recognizing Rome's power, the king of Pergamum, in Asia Minor, bequeathed his lands to Rome at his death in 133 B.C.E. Throughout the Mediterranean, Rome was now the dominant power.

In the east, the general Gnaeus Pompeius Magnus (Pompey the Great) (106–48 B.C.E.) added Syria and most of Asia Minor to the empire. In 63 B.C.E. he captured Jerusalem, the capital of Judea, allowing a Jewish king to rule as a client-monarch. Pompey favored such indirect rule through local potentates throughout the east, where sophisticated governmental structures had existed for centuries. He also founded some 40 cities as centers of Roman political influence.

View the **Closer Look**: Spoils from Jerusalem on the Arch of Titus in Rome on **MyHistoryLab**

The Politics of Imperial Rule

6.3 How did the Romans win support from the people they conquered?

Empires are ultimately sustained by military force, but successful empires must also win at least some degree of support from among the conquered peoples. Beginning with its early conquests, Rome had often won such support through its political, cultural, economic, and ideological policies, but most importantly through the granting of citizenship. As it expanded, Rome frequently offered its opponents a choice between alliance and conquest. Subsequently it bestowed various levels of Roman citizenship throughout Italy to induce its residents to support Rome and join its armies.

6.1

6.2

6.3

6.4

6.5

6.6

6.7

How did the Romans win support from the people they conquered?

Citizens of Rome

All free men from Rome were automatically citizens of Rome; the rest of the men of Italy, however, were not. In 381 B.C.E. the town of Tusculum, some 15 miles from Rome and surrounded by Roman territory, seemed poised to oppose Rome. The Romans won over the Tusculuns by offering incorporation into Rome and full citizenship, including voting rights, legal rights over property, legal enforcement of contracts, the right to marry Roman citizens, freedom from property taxes, and protection against arbitrary arrest and punishment. In 338 B.C.E. full citizenship was bestowed on four additional Latin cities, in the vicinity of Rome, while some other cities were granted partial citizenship.

In 91 B.C.E. Marcus Livius Drusus the Younger was elected tribune. Drusus proposed extending citizenship and the vote to all Rome's Italian allies, but the Senate rejected the proposal. Drusus was later assassinated, leaving the Italians frustrated and furious. So began the "Social War" or "War of the Allies." After two years, however, Rome did offer full citizenship to all Italians who had remained loyal, and even to those who agreed to put down their arms. It extended full citizenship north as far as the Po River, and partial citizenship up to the Alps. So, grudgingly, citizenship was offered as an inducement to loyalty. In newly annexed lands, the aristocrats, the group to whom Rome usually granted these rights and obligations, regarded even partial citizenship as attractive.

The Politics of Private Life

Asymmetrical power relationships characterized all of Roman life—private as well as public—under the Republic. The earliest enduring social structure in Rome was the **patron–client relationship**. Strong men acted as protectors of the weak; the weak, in turn, provided obedience and services for the strong, as requested.

In civilian life, patrons, usually patricians, would provide legal protection and representation for their clients, usually plebeians. In exchange, the client was expected to help to pay fines and public charges levied against his patron and to help to provide dowries for his patron's daughters at marriage. To mark the symbolism of the relationship, the client was to present himself periodically at the residence or office of the patron, and the patron was to give him a small gift at that time. The patron–client relationship was also protected by law, and a patron who defrauded a client was subject to execution, later commuted to exile and confiscation of property.

The relationship of ex-masters to ex-slaves was of patron to client, and it was frequently characterized by warm feelings, especially if freedom was granted by gift of manumission rather than by the slave's purchase. These relationships often endured through several generations. Similar patron–client relationships between strong and weak later characterized Rome's imperial control over conquered provinces.

KEY TERM

patron–client relationship In a patron–client relationship, the patron offers protection and, often, employment, while the client offers obedience, labor, and services in exchange. Sometimes these relationships are formalized under law. More frequently they exist in place of law, in situations where legal structures are weak or nonexistent. Patron–client relationships are common throughout world history.

HOW DO WE KNOW?

Contemporary Historians Evaluate the History of Rome

During the later Republic historians began consciously to write the history of the city. Their accounts were often ambivalent, revealing a mixture of pride in the conquests and achievements of their empire with skepticism and even hostility toward the abandonment of the earlier republican ideals.

The most famous of the early historians was Polybius (c. 200–c. 118 B.C.E.), a Greek taken to Rome as a political captive. Polybius marveled at the overwhelming event of his own time, Rome's conquest of an empire through its victories over Carthage, Macedonia, and Spain:

> There can surely be no one so petty or so apathetic in his outlook that he has no desire to discover by what means and under what system of government the Romans succeeded in less than fifty-three years [220–167 B.C.E.] in bringing under their rule almost the whole of the inhabited world, an achievement which is without parallel in human history.
>
> (*The Histories* I:1, cited in Finley, p. 443)

Livy (59 B.C.E.–17 C.E.) praised the glories of Rome's imperial expansion, but he decried the resulting class conflict between Rome's aristocrats and its common people, which was currently ripping apart Rome's self-governing, elected, republican form of government.

Tacitus (c. 56–c. 120 C.E.) continued the story to the height of imperial power. He praised the heroism of the Roman conquerors, but he also understood the anguish and bitterness of the conquered peoples. In *Agricola*, Tacitus attributes to the Celtic chieftain Calgacus one of the most devastating critiques of imperialism ever articulated. In Tacitus' account, Calgacus condemns the Romans, whose tyranny cannot be escaped by any act of reasonable submission.

> These brigands of the world have exhausted the land by their rapacity, so they now ransack the sea. When their enemy is rich, they lust after wealth; when the enemy is poor, they lust after power. Neither East nor West has satisfied their hunger. They are unique among humanity insofar as they equally covet the rich and the poor. Robbery, butchery, and rapine they call "Empire." They create a desert and call it "Peace."
>
> (I:129)

As the empire began to decay, mainstream historians added more critical perspectives. Dio Cassius (c. 150–235 C.E.) nostalgically recalled the rule of Augustus as Rome's golden age and lamented the empire's subsequent decline "from a monarchy of gold to one of iron and rust." Like Tacitus, he cited and sympathized with the frustration and rage of those like Boudicca, the warrior-queen of the Celts, who led her armies in revolt against the Romans in 61 C.E.:

> We have been despised and trampled underfoot by men who know nothing else than how to secure gain.
>
> (Lewis and Reinhold, II:334)

Other historians illuminated the empire from its fringes rather than from its center, and they, too, were often critical of the effects of empire on its subjects. For Jewish historians, such as Philo of Alexandria (c. 13 B.C.E.–c. 45 C.E.) and Josephus (c. 37–c. 100 C.E.), and Christian theologians, such as Tertullian (c. 155–c. 225 C.E.) and St. Augustine, bishop of Hippo in North Africa (354–430 C.E.), the Roman Empire was not the central concern, but it was an inescapable presence. These historians, philosophers, and theologians had to take account of Rome's power in their own teaching, writing, and actions. From their marginal positions, they usually counseled realistic accommodation to Rome's power.

In addition to these formal histories, leading men of the empire left important documents that shed light on their times. The great orator and political leader Cicero (106–43 B.C.E.) left dozens of letters, 57 public speeches, and extensive writings on public affairs. Julius Caesar's account of the Gallic Wars describes his military organization and strategy, the Roman virtues that characterized his troops, and the lands and peoples against which he fought. It is the only account of a Roman war written by a participant that has endured to today. In part, Caesar was writing a propaganda piece, preparing the path for his later assertion of personal power in Rome.

Caesar's accounts are filled with great slaughter. For example, in 58 B.C.E., he reported that his armies slaughtered 226,000 Helvetii, with only some 110,000 surviving. In the same year he reports killing almost an entire German army of 120,000 men and, the next year, almost every soldier in a Belgic army of 60,000 men. He captured the region around Namur in northern France and sold all 53,000 inhabitants into slavery. In 56 B.C.E., he massacred two German peoples, killing as many as 460,000 people, including women and children. By the end of nine years of war in Gaul, Caesar reports a total of 1,192,000 enemy killed and another million captured.

- Which Roman authors and historians saw the expansion of the Roman Empire as unfortunate for the people of Rome? Why? Do you agree? Why or why not?
- Name Jews and Christians whose writings shed light on the Roman Empire. What topics did they address that are useful in understanding empires?
- If you could join archaeologists at a Roman site, which site would you like to explore? Why?

The Roman Family

Patron–client relationships also marked the structure of the family. The father of the family, the *paterfamilias*, had the right of life and death over his children as long as he lived. In reality, most fathers were not tyrants, and in exercising the right to choose their children's occupations and spouses, and to control their economic possessions, they would normally try to consider their children's needs and desires. Nevertheless, fathers had the legal power to act as they wished: they continued to have control over their daughters' economic lives even after their marriages, for this did not pass to the husbands. These rights were enshrined in the law of *patria potestas*, the right of the head of the household.

According to Roman custom and practice, a woman's role was subordinate to a man's. A woman was legally subject to her father as long as he lived. After his death, she was required to obey the advice of her husband or a legally appointed guardian in any kind of legal or business transaction. Actual practice was, however, more liberal. If a woman had reached adulthood, she usually gained her independence at the death of her father, as did her brothers. Also, at least as early as the fifth century B.C.E., a wife could block the legal powers of her husband by absenting herself from his home for three nights in a row each year.

The families of the bride and groom arranged their marriages. Motherhood was considered the most significant rite of passage for a woman. Freeborn women were exempted from the legal control of their father, husband, or guardian after giving birth to three children; women who had been freed from slavery were exempted after the birth of four.

Romans respected women if they lived chastely and more or less contentedly within these guidelines of family, motherhood, and domesticity. The feminine ideal was the faithful and loyal *univira*, the "one-man woman." A woman caught in adultery was banished from her home and might well be executed; men apprehended in adultery were not punished. Women found drinking wine could also be punished; men could not. These principles of behavior were, of course, fully applicable only to the upper classes. The masses of lower-class free women entered the working world outside the home, and slaves had little control over their lives. The prevalence of prostitution and brothels further indicate the limited applicability of the Roman female ideal.

Class Conflict: Urban Splendor and Squalor

Imperial expansion exacerbated class conflicts within Rome. The benefits of the conquests went mostly to the rich, while the independent small farmers who served as the troops were often bankrupted by the wars. After serving in the army for years, they would return home to find that in their absence their wives and children had not been able to maintain the family farms and might even have sold them to owners of large estates, called *latifundia*, and left for the city, impoverished.

Class divisions were most glaring in the capital. The city of Rome itself grew seemingly without limit and without adequate planning. As Rome came to control Italy and then the Mediterranean, the city's population multiplied, reaching one million by about the first century C.E.

Some of the newcomers were wealthy and powerful, and they adorned the city by adding new examples of Greek architecture and urban design to the earlier Etruscan forms. They replaced wood, mud, and local volcanic rock with concrete and finer

6.1
6.2
6.3
6.4
6.5
6.6
6.7

How did the Romans win support from the people they conquered?

KEY TERM

paterfamilias The head of a family or household in Roman law—always a male—and the only member to have full legal rights. The *paterfamilias* had absolute power over his family, extending to life and death.

Mosaic of Neptune and Amphitrite (detail), Herculaneum, before 79 C.E. Art sometimes seems to contradict the legal evidence concerning gender relationships in the Roman Empire. The artist responsible for this mosaic of the sea god Neptune and his wife, Amphitrite, has accorded the couple apparent equality.

6.1
6.2
6.3
6.4
6.5
6.6
6.7

How did the Romans win support from the people they conquered?

stone. Augustus himself would later boast that he had found Rome a city of brick and left it one of marble (see below). A modern urban historian has described the private homes of the wealthy patricians as models of comfort:

> The houses of the patricians, spacious, airy, sanitary, equipped with bathrooms and water closets, heated in winter by hypocausts, which carried hot air through chambers in the floors, were perhaps the most commodious and comfortable houses built for a temperate climate anywhere until the twentieth century; a triumph of domestic architecture. (Mumford, p. 220)

The poor also came streaming into the city, but from bankrupt family farms. For them, Rome was a nightmare. The contrast was shocking.

> Not only were these buildings unheated, unprovided with waste pipes or water closets, unadapted to cooking; not merely did they contain an undue number of airless rooms, indecently overcrowded: though poor in all the facilities that make for decent daily living, they were in addition so badly built and so high that they offered no means of safe exit from the frequent fires that occurred. And if their tenants escaped typhoid, typhus, fire, they might easily meet their death in the collapse of the whole structure. Such accidents were all too frequent …
>
> The main population of the city that boasted its world conquests lived in cramped, noisy, airless, foul-smelling, infected quarters, paying extortionate rents to merciless landlords, undergoing daily indignities and terrors that coarsened and brutalized them, and in turn demanded compensatory outlets. (Mumford, pp. 220–21)

Canopus, Hadrian's Villa, Tivoli, c. 135 C.E. Rome's wealthy and powerful elites commanded private luxuries beyond the imagination of the average Roman. The Villa of the emperor Hadrian comprised a series of buildings, gardens, and pools—this one representing a well-known Egyptian canal—laid out on the side of a hill in Tivoli. The complex was designed to bring the more sophisticated pleasures of city life to the country.

Attempts at Reform

The most exemplary of the leaders who tried to achieve equity for Rome's poorer citizens were the reforming Gracchi brothers, Tiberius Sempronius Gracchus (163–133 B.C.E.) and Gaius Sempronius Gracchus (153–121 B.C.E.). In 133 B.C.E., while serving as tribune of the people, the office established to protect the interest of the plebeians, Tiberius proposed distributing some public lands among the poor, especially among poor soldiers. Opposed to this liberal proposal, and fearing that Tiberius was attempting to gain too much political power for himself, a number of senators, supported by their clients, clubbed him and 300 of his supporters to death. This was the first political murder over a public policy issue in Rome in nearly 400 years; class conflict boiled over into violence within the Senate itself. Despite the murder, the redistribution of public land did take place.

In 123 B.C.E., Gaius Gracchus was elected tribune. He extended his brother's plan for land redistribution by establishing new colonies for the resettlement of some of the poor people of Rome in the regions conquered in the Punic Wars, including Carthage itself. He also introduced subsidized grain sales—later extended into a dole of free bread—to Rome's poor people. Gaius argued that citizenship should be granted to all Latins and to the local civic officials in all other communities.

He was not equally sensitive to the problems of non-Italians, however, for his legislation exploited the provinces by enabling Roman knights, the second tier of the military elite, to serve as "**publicans**," or **tax farmers**. These tax farmers struck an agreement with the state to turn over a fixed amount of net taxes from their region while retaining the right to collect as much as they were able and to keep the balance for themselves. Tax farming enabled the state to collect taxes without monitoring the process; it enabled the tax farmers to become wealthy; and it exploited the people who were being taxed, leaving them without protection. Gaius auctioned off the collection of taxes in Asia. While this profited the elite and helped to secure their loyalty to him personally, it impoverished the residents of the Roman province of Asia. Many senators became increasingly hostile to Gaius Gracchus, and in 121 B.C.E. he too was assassinated, along with his fellow tribune, Flaccus. Some 3,000 of his supporters were executed.

The reforms of the Gracchi brothers seemed blocked, but in fact they laid the foundations for the events that led to the end of the Republic a century later. They

KEY TERM

publicans or **tax farmers**
Collected taxes on behalf of the government, paying in an agreed sum but keeping for themselves any surplus they could extort. The system was extremely oppressive to those who were taxed.

Column of Trajan, Rome, dedicated 113 C.E. The Romans built tall commemorative columns in order to celebrate the power and military might of the empire. The Column of Trajan is covered with a continuous strip of carving that tells the story of the emperor Trajan's victories over the barbarian tribes along the Danube.

6.1
6.2
6.3
6.4
6.5
6.6
6.7

How did the
Romans win
support from
the people they
conquered?

challenged the power of the Senate and exposed the problems of the poor and the
war veterans, while their enemies employed violence, murder, and thuggery as tools
for fashioning and implementing public policy.

"Bread and Circuses." A new method of coping with class conflict developed: **"bread
and circuses."** Rome bribed the poor, many of them former soldiers from its conquering armies, with a dole of free bread. Up to 200,000 people were served each day.
The dole encouraged them to while away their time in public religious festivities,
races, the theater, and gladiatorial contests of great cruelty, which pitted man against
man and man against beast in spectacles witnessed by tens of thousands. The public
arenas of Rome, including Rome's largest race-track and stadia, could accommodate
about half of Rome's adult population. On days of gladiatorial contests of strength,
endurance, and cunning, hundreds of men and as many as 5,000 animals, including
elephants and water buffalo, might be slaughtered in a single day. This combination
of free food and gory spectacle was offered to keep the unemployed urban masses
compliant.

Later, emperors continued these policies without actually solving the problems of
unemployment and lack of dignity. Until its final collapse, the empire was threatened
by unrest and revolt, and one of the reasons for the later popularity of Christianity in
Rome was its message of compassion and salvation for the poor and downtrodden
(see the chapter entitled "Judaism and Christianity").

Slavery in Roman Life

As wealthy Romans assembled vast estates and Roman armies captured valuable
underground mineral resources, they needed labor for farming and mining. Increasingly, they turned to the acquisition of slaves. Through military conquest, piracy,
and raids in foreign regions, Rome accumulated slaves numbering perhaps in the
millions. Short wars yielded thousands, longer conflicts hundreds of thousands. In
his nine years in Gaul (see below), Julius Caesar may have captured nearly half a
million slaves. As much as a quarter of Rome's agricultural labor force was slave
labor. Among the one million residents of the city of Rome, as many as 400,000 were
slaves.

"Every slave we own is an enemy we harbor," was a sardonic Roman proverb
by the time of **Caesar Augustus** (Lewis and Reinhold, I:245). That emperor proclaimed in his epitaph that in successful campaigns against pirates, "I turned over to
their masters for punishment nearly 30,000 fugitive slaves who had taken up arms
against the state" (Lewis and Reinhold, I:569). Three great slave revolts grew into
wars. During the Great Slave War in Sicily (134–131 B.C.E.), 70,000 slaves resorted to
armed resistance. In 104–100 B.C.E., a second revolt broke out in Sicily when it seemed
that Germanic tribes would invade Italy and keep the imperial troops occupied in
the north. Finally, Spartacus, a runaway slave who had been forced into training as
a gladiator, led a revolt among his fellow gladiators that continued for two years,
73–71 B.C.E. In the end, after suffering many defeats, the Romans crushed the Spartacus revolt mercilessly. Some 100,000 slaves were killed in the fighting, and 6,000
captured slaves were crucified along the roads leading into Rome, their torture and
death serving as a brutal warning to any other potential rebels.

Slaves continued throughout the imperial centuries as a threat within the Roman
Empire. When foreign armies later invaded Rome successfully, slaves often revolted
and joined them. For example, when an army of Goths invaded in 410 C.E., "day by
day almost all the slaves who were in Rome poured out of the city to join the barbarians, who now numbered about forty thousand" (Zosimus, *New History*, cited in
Lewis and Reinhold, II:626).

📖 **Read** the **Document**: **Slaves in Roman Law (2d c., 5th c. CE)** on **MyHistoryLab**

KEY TERMS

bread and circuses Provision by
the government of free food and
entertainment, designed to divert
the masses, and especially the
poor masses, from engaging in
political action.

Caesar Augustus "Caesar" and
"Augustus" are both titles of the
emperor Octavian. Caesar means
ruler or emperor, and the word
comes down to the present in
the title czar or tsar. Augustus
means dignified, even majestic.
It was sometimes used in place
of Octavian's given name. The
words could also be reversed as
Augustus Caesar.

The End of the Republic

6.4 How did the generals' power struggles lead to the end of the Republic?

In the militaristic empire that was Rome, generals gained power. At first Rome's military leaders were constrained by the aristocratic Senate and the general assembly of Rome, but later they themselves began giving the orders. Eventually their struggles for power would lead to civil war and the end of the Republic.

Generals in Politics

General Gaius Marius campaigned to have himself elected consul in 107 B.C.E. He broke with the normal practice of recruiting only troops who owned property, and accepted soldiers who were indebted to him personally for their maintenance. Elected consul six times between 107 and 100 B.C.E., Marius restructured the armies

Arch of Trajan, Benevento, 114–117 C.E. Triumphal arches are another peculiarly Roman means of celebrating the power of the ruler and his empire. This particular arch, dedicated to Trajan, stands at the point where the road to Brindisi, a port on the east coast of Italy, branches off the Appian Way, the first major road in the Romans' strategic network.

6.1
6.2
6.3
6.4
How did the generals' power struggles lead to the end of the Republic?
6.5
6.6
6.7

6.1
6.2
6.3
6.4 How did the generals' power struggles lead to the end of the Republic?
6.5
6.6
6.7

to increase their efficiency. He arranged large allotments of land for veteran soldiers in North Africa, Gaul, Sicily, Greece, and Macedonia, a move that solved temporarily one of the great problems of Rome: how to accommodate soldiers returning home after long tours of duty. The armies now depended for their welfare on Marius rather than on the state.

The generals began to compete among themselves for power. At the highest level, the struggle between the generals Lucius Sulla and Gaius Marius precipitated civil war in Rome. To fight against Mithridates VI, king of Pontus (r. 120–63 B.C.E.), the Senate called Sulla. Marius, however, arranged to have the command transferred to himself. In response, Sulla rallied soldiers loyal to him and invaded Rome, initiating the first civil war (83–82 B.C.E.). He declared Marius an outlaw and left with his troops for Greece, where he defeated Mithridates. Meanwhile Marius, joined by another general, Lucius Cornelius Cinna, seized Rome and banned Sulla. Sulla returned with his army, invaded Italy and Rome, had himself declared dictator, a position he held for two years, and then abdicated.

Twenty years later, in 60 B.C.E., two great generals, Julius Caesar and Pompey, and Marcus Licinius Crassus, a wealthy businessman who became a military commander, formed a **triumvirate**, a ruling alliance of three men. The three competed among themselves, however, until Caesar defeated the others.

The Dictatorship of Julius Caesar

Born in Rome of an aristocratic patrician family about 100 B.C.E., Caesar felt the hand of the military dictator Sulla as a young man when Sulla ordered him to divorce his wife, Cornelia, daughter of Cinna, Sulla's great rival. Caesar refused. Biographers are not sure whether this was because of Caesar's love for Cornelia, exceptional personal pride, an assessment that the alliance with Cinna's faction would, in the long run, prove advantageous, or some combination of calculations. In any case, Caesar's refusal was unusual in a world where aristocratic marriages—and divorces—were usually contracted for political purposes. (Caesar, for example, later married his 17-year-old daughter to the 47-year-old Pompey.) No one else, not even Pompey the Great, refused Sulla's commands. It was also out of character for Caesar himself, a man who had already begun to earn a growing reputation for marital infidelity, including rumors of some homosexual activity (Grant, *Julius Caesar*, pp. 23–24, 33–39).

To escape Sulla's grasp, Caesar fled into exile in the Greek islands where he studied philosophy and oratory until he was pardoned and returned to Rome. He was elected magistrate in 65 B.C.E., with responsibilities for producing public games. Pouring his own money as well as public and borrowed funds into the task, he won widespread acclaim. His prominence increased when he was elected chief priest, *pontifex maximus*, of the Roman state in 63 B.C.E., a position of greater prestige and patronage than religious significance. Reaching toward the pinnacle of political power, Caesar was elected to the judicial office of **praetor** in 60 B.C.E. and to the highest executive office of consul in 59 B.C.E. A military man, he sometimes used strong-arm methods to intimidate the Senate, on one occasion having his fellow consul attacked and beaten.

In Rome, military prowess counted most, and Caesar was Rome's most successful general. In 58 B.C.E. he led his armies on a mission to dominate Gaul and protect it from invaders. (This move also got him out of Rome at the end of his term as consul, thus escaping legal prosecution for his abuse of power in office.) Nine years of military campaigns brought all of Gaul under Rome. Caesar also briefly crossed the Rhine River, to demonstrate that Rome had the capacity to invade the Germanic territories if it wished, and he twice invaded Britain, also briefly.

The triumvirate broke down when Crassus was killed as he sought to extend Rome's empire in the east. Pompey now saw Caesar as his direct rival, and Rome again dissolved into civil war. Pompey was defeated in a series of battles and was finally killed while seeking refuge in Egypt. Caesar ruled Rome alone, but only briefly.

KEY TERMS

triumvirate Literally, an association of three strong men. An unofficial coalition of Julius Caesar, Pompey, and Crassus formed in 60 B.C.E. After Caesar's murder in 44 B.C.E., a triumvirate including his heir Octavian (later Augustus), Mark Antony, and Marcus Lepidus was appointed to maintain public order.

praetor In ancient Rome, the term was originally applied to the consul as leader of an army. In 366 B.C.E. a further praetor was elected with special responsibility for the administration of justice in Rome, with the right of military command. Further praetors were subsequently appointed to administer the increasing number of provinces.

Jealous of, and frightened by, his extraordinary powers, Roman senators stabbed Caesar to death on the Ides of March (March 15), 44 B.C.E.

In his three years as dictator, Caesar revised the Roman calendar, creating the Julian calendar, which lasted for 1,500 years (and is still used by some churches); reorganized Rome's city government; extended citizenship to the peoples of many conquered provinces; continued the policy of free bread and circuses; and appointed many of his opponents to public office in an attempt at reconciliation. He resolved one of the most intractable problems of Rome's citizens: the debts that had piled up during the years of civil war. He forced creditors to accept payment in land and property valued at prewar prices, and he canceled all interest due since the wars began. Caesar selected his sister Julia's grandson, Gaius Octavius (63 B.C.E.–14 C.E.), later called Octavian, as his heir. Following Caesar's assassination, this adopted son avenged his death by murdering 300 senators and 2,000 knights; triumphed over Lepidus and Mark Antony, the two rivals who had been his colleagues in a second triumvirate; and became the unchallenged ruler of Rome for more than half a century.

To avert civil war, Octavian used his sister Octavia as a diplomatic and political tool, marrying her to his rival, Antony (83–30 B.C.E.), in 40 B.C.E. In 36 B.C.E., Antony openly married the alluring and seductive queen of Egypt, Cleopatra (r. 51–30 B.C.E.), even though he was already married to Octavia, and established his headquarters in Egypt, the richest state in the east. By sharing local rule with Cleopatra, Antony betrayed Rome's imperial policies. Eventually, Antony discarded and divorced Octavia, humiliating Octavian personally as well as infuriating him politically. The warfare between the two men became especially bitter. Octavian finally defeated Antony and Cleopatra in the decisive naval battle at Actium (31 B.C.E.), formally annexed Egypt, and seized the Egyptian treasury for himself. Octavian now controlled more wealth than the Roman state.

Augustus of Prima Porta, early first century C.E. With the gratitude of the Senate of Rome, which was weary of civil warfare among its generals, Augustus transformed Rome into an imperial monarchy under his control. (Musei Vaticani, Rome)

The Roman Principate, 30 B.C.E.–330 C.E.

6.5   What were the achievements of Augustus and the Principate?

By 30 B.C.E., following 14 years of civil war, Octavian had become master of a reunified Roman world. A grateful Senate, weary of seemingly endless civil wars, heaped him with honors, including, in 27 B.C.E., the title *Augustus*, meaning "sacred" or "venerable." His achievements were immense, and after his death the Romans designated him a god.

6.1
6.2
6.3
6.4
6.5
6.6
6.7

What were the achievements of Augustus and the Principate?

6.1

6.2

6.3

6.4

6.5

6.6

6.7

What were the achievements of Augustus and the Principate?

With Augustus, Rome became an imperial monarchy, a territorial, political, and economic empire ruled by a single military commander, the *imperator* (from which the term "emperor" is derived), and his armies. For years generals had wanted this centralized power. Now, in gratitude for his ending the civil wars, the Senate was willing to turn it over to Augustus. Augustus rejected the title of monarch, preferring to be called *princeps*, or first citizen. This gesture of humility fooled no one. With Augustus' reign, even though the Senate and the consuls and other magistrates survived, the imperial form of government began. From Augustus on, all real power in the Roman state lay in the hands of the emperor.

Augustus ruled Rome for 56 years until his death in 14 C.E. He fought wars that stabilized the borders of the empire while ensuring peace and facilitating trade, commerce, and economic growth throughout the Mediterranean. He restructured imperial administration into a form that lasted for almost two centuries. He inaugurated public projects that beautified Rome and kept its workers employed. He pacified the Roman masses and won over the aristocracy. He patronized the arts and literature, which flourished in a "Golden Age." He built new roads and cities throughout the length and breadth of the empire.

Family Life in the Age of Augustus

Augustus instituted conservative policies concerning family life. The growth of urban life, especially in Rome itself in the first century B.C.E., offered new opportunities to a few upper-class Roman women to gain education and even to participate in public life, although usually behind the scenes. New marriage laws enabled them to live as equals of their husbands and gave them the right to divorce and to act without

SOURCE

The Legacy and Epitaph of Augustus Caesar

Primary sources on Augustus' life are limited, and almost all his autobiography has been lost. Therefore, the *Res Gestae Divi Augusti* ("Account of the Accomplishments of Augustus") has become a crucial text. Written for the people of Rome by Augustus himself shortly before he died, and inscribed on several temples throughout the empire, it is his own statement of how he wanted to be remembered. Its 35 paragraphs cover the honors bestowed on him; his personal donations for public purposes; and his accomplishments in war and peace:

1. At the age of nineteen, on my own initiative and at my own expense, I raised an army by means of which I liberated the Republic ... the people elected me consul and a triumvir for the settlement of the commonwealth ...

3. I waged many wars throughout the whole world by land and by sea ... and when victorious I spared all citizens who sought pardon ... About 500,000 Roman citizens were under military oath to me.

15. To the Roman plebs I paid 300 sesterces apiece in accordance with the will of my father [Julius Caesar]; and in my fifth consulship [29 B.C.E.] I gave each 400 sesterces in my own name out of the spoil of war, reaching never less than 250,000 persons ... And in my fifth consulship [29 B.C.E.] I gave out of the spoils of war 1000 sesterces apiece to my soldiers settled in colonies ... received by about 120,000 persons ... In my thirteenth consulship [2 B.C.E.] I gave 60 denarii apiece to those of the plebs who at that time were receiving public grain ... a little more than 200,000 persons.

19. I built ... the senate house and ... the temple of Apollo ...

22. I gave a gladiatorial show three times in my own name, and five times in the names of my sons or grandsons; at these shows about 10,000 fought ... Twenty-six times I provided for the people ... hunting spectacles of African wild beasts in the circus or in the Forum or in the amphitheaters ...

23. I turned over to their masters for punishment nearly 30,000 slaves who had run away from their owners and taken up arms against the state.

28. I established colonies of soldiers in Africa, Sicily, Macedonia, in both Spanish provinces, in Achaea, Asia, Syria, Narbonese Gaul, and Pisidia. Italy, moreover, has 28 colonies established by me which grew large and prosperous in my lifetime ...

31. Royal embassies from India, never seen before any Roman general, were often sent to me. (Lewis and Reinhold, I:561–72)

reference to a legal guardian. They could own and control wealth in their own name. Women did not have access to the professions or to public political office, but several exercised great influence over their husbands, brothers, and sons.

Augustus sought to restore the earlier family order. He made adultery a criminal offense, punishable by exile, confiscation of property, and even execution. Indeed, he exiled his own daughter and only child, Julia, a charming and intelligent woman who offended him with her frequent and publicly known affairs. He encouraged marriage and childbearing, and punished celibacy. These laws were widely opposed and disobeyed, but they reveal the link in Augustus' mind between a well-ordered family and a well-ordered empire, a link that was repeated in the official policies of many empires throughout history. (Compare China and India, Britain, Japan, and Germany.)

6.1
6.2
6.3
6.4
6.5 What were the achievements of Augustus and the Principate?
6.6
6.7

The Military under Augustus

Within Italy, captured city-states were required to supply not gold and taxes but men for the armies. At the time of Julius Caesar, the average Italian male served seven years in the army. Under Augustus, soldiering became more professional: men enlisted for between 16 and 25 years and were paid regular wages. Conquered peoples outside Italy also contributed troops to Rome's armies, while invaders were often encouraged to settle in Roman territories and to enlist in Roman armies. An outward spiral of imperial expansion resulted. As Rome expanded, so did its armed forces; it then expanded further, in part to capture the wealth needed to pay its larger armies; this expansion, in turn, enlarged its armies once more.

In the field, the soldiers built their own support systems: military camps; administrative towns; strings of fortress watchtowers along the borders; roads; and aqueducts. Many of the walled military camps were kernels from which sprouted later towns and cities, one of Rome's most distinctive contributions. (See illustration of Timgad, below.) These urban outposts established Rome's military and administrative rule in the midst of remote rural regions. In the reign of Augustus, these nodes were linked by 50,000 miles of first-class roads and 200,000 miles of lesser roads. The roads facilitated commerce and communication, but their original and fundamental purpose was to enable the swift movement of troops throughout the empire.

The Roman Empire Expands

As the empire continued to expand through military conquest, Rome's generals demanded, and were granted, increasing powers until, with Augustus, they supplanted republican, civilian government with an administration headed by the military commander-in-chief. Before we analyze the significance of this political transformation, however, let us complete our account of the continuing geographical expansion of the empire.

Augustus annexed modern Switzerland and Noricum (modern Austria and Bavaria) in 16–15 B.C.E., and established Rome's historical frontier in central Europe at the Danube River. After an attempt to conquer central Germany failed in 9 C.E., the Rhine became the normal border in the northeast.

In the 40s C.E. the Romans conquered modern England and Wales, which became the Roman province of Britain. Some 2,000 miles to the east, the emperor Trajan (r. 98–117 C.E.) conquered Dacia (modern Romania), and briefly annexed Armenia and Parthia (Mesopotamia).

Trajan's successor, Hadrian (r. 117–138 C.E.), consolidated Roman gains. He permanently withdrew the Roman forces from Mesopotamia back to the Euphrates and built a wall, west to east, across the narrow neck of the northern part of Britain. Twenty-five years later, his successor, Antoninus Pius (r. 138–161 C.E.), built another wall some 50 miles further north. The limits of the Roman Empire had been reached.

6.1
6.2
6.3
6.4
6.5
6.6
6.7

What were the
achievements of
Augustus and the
Principate?

The policy of granting citizenship to consolidate empire continued on a limited basis as Rome expanded. In 14 C.E. Augustus Caesar announced that there were 4,937,000 citizens in the empire, about two million of them in the provinces. At that time, the total population of the empire was between 70 and 100 million. In 212 C.E., the emperor Caracalla (r. 212–17) officially proclaimed citizenship for all free males in the empire, although ambiguous legal restrictions limited the effect. Provincials could occupy the highest offices in the empire: senator, consul, and even emperor. The emperor Trajan was from Spain; Septimius Severus (r. 193–211) was from North Africa; Diocletian (r. 284–305) was from Dalmatia (modern Croatia).

The development of international law, the *jus gentium,* the law of nations, also helped to unite and pacify the empire. After its victory in the first Punic War in 241 B.C.E., Rome interacted more than ever with foreigners and with subjects of Rome who did not have citizenship. To deal with legal cases between Romans and others, a new official, the foreign magistrate, was appointed. The *jus gentium* evolved from his judgments. Over time, this law was codified, first by Hadrian, and later, in the east, by the emperor Justinian (see box below).

Economic and Trade Policies

Imperial rule and the opening of imperial markets brought opportunities for economic development and profit in the conquered provinces, although most of these opportunities went to the local wealthy elite who possessed the capital and skills to take advantage of them. In general, Roman rulers were solicitous of the upper classes in the provinces, both because of a shared class position and because they believed that the loyalty of this elite was crucial to maintaining Roman hegemony.

The cost of this imperial role, however, could be heavy, and it eventually became oppressive. The Romans levied tribute, taxes, and rents, and recruited soldiers from

HOW DO WE KNOW?

Roman Law: Theory and Practice

Modern historians have generally praised Rome's incipient international legal system as:

one of the most potent and effective ideas that the Romans ever originated … It demonstrated that a body of law could be established upon a foundation acceptable to the members of different peoples and races at any and every phase of social, economic, and political evolution; and so it brought the laws of the Romans nearer to universal applicability than any others that have ever been devised. (Grant, pp. 104–05)

Legal theory and practice, however, did not always coincide in ancient Rome (as they do not always coincide today). The poor did not receive the same protection and benefits as the rich; soldiers abused their authority; laws were not applied consistently. The satirist Juvenal (c. 55–c. 127 C.E.) ridiculed the inability of Rome's legal system to curb the violence of Roman soldiers:

Your teeth are shattered? Face hectically inflamed, with great black welts? You know the doctor wasn't too optimistic about the eye that was left. But it's not a bit of good your running to the courts about it. If you've been beaten up by a soldier, better keep it to yourself. (cited in Boardman, *et al.*, p. 575)

In practice, the law was also not as universal as it claimed, and those challenging the empire might not reap its benefits. Jewish nationalist writers, for example, compared the hypocrisy of Rome's laws to the ambiguous associations of the unclean pig:

Just as a pig lies down and sticks out its trotters as though to say "I am clean" [because they are cloven], so the evil empire robs and oppresses while pretending to execute justice. (cited in Boardman, *et al.*, p. 582)

Beginning about the second century C.E., preferential treatment for the wealthy and the powerful entered explicitly into the law, deepening class antagonisms and weakening the empire.

- On what basis do historians differ when evaluating the quality of the Roman legal system?
- The modern historian Michael Grant writes about Rome's system of international law while the satirist Juvenal lived in ancient Rome and wrote about its local criminal law. How is each author's perspective affected by his time and expertise?
- What do you think is the effect on society of a legal system that gives preferential treatment to one group over another?

6.1

6.2

6.3

6.4

What were the
achievements
of Augustus and the
Principate?

6.5

6.6

6.7

the peoples they conquered. They settled their own soldiers in captured lands, turning those lands into Roman estates and enslaving millions of people to work on them. They exploited their political power for the economic advantage of their own traders and military and administrative elite. As the size and wealth of the empire grew, many Romans felt that they had conquered the world but lost their souls. They spoke not of victory, but of loss. The historian Livy, writing at the height of the age of Augustus, lamented the end of innocence:

> With the gradual relaxation of discipline, morals first gave way, as it were, then sank lower and lower, and finally began the downward plunge which has brought us to the present time, when we can endure neither our vices nor the cure. (cited in Lewis and Reinhold, I:8)

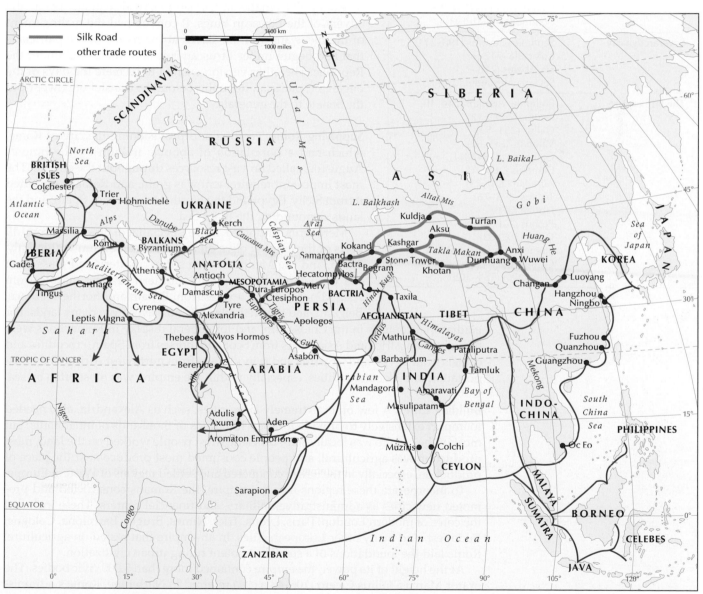

Eurasian trade. The commercial links that bound the ancient world were both extensive and sophisticated. Self-sustaining individual networks—the Saharan caravans, the Arab dhows plying the Indian Ocean, the fleets of Chinese junks coasting East Asia, and, most famously, the silk routes traversing central Asia—linked at key entrepôts such as Alexandria and Oc Eo by sea, and Ctesiphon and Kashgar by land, to form a truly intercontinental trading system.

ROMAN EMPERORS

	Augustus (27 B.C.E.–14 C.E.)
Julio-Claudian dynasty	Tiberius (14–37)
	Caligula (37–41)
	Claudius (41–54)
	Nero (54–68)
Flavian dynasty	Vespasian (69–79)
	Titus (79–81)
	Domitian (81–96)
Age of the Antonines	Nerva (96–98)
	Trajan (98–117)
	Hadrian (117–138)
	Antoninus Pius (138–161)
	Marcus Aurelius (161–180)
	Commodus (180–193)
Severan dynasty	Septimius Severus (193–211)
	Caracalla (212–17)
	Elagabalus (218–22)
	Severus Alexander (222–35)
The late empire	Philip the Arabian (244–49)
	Decius (249–51)
	Gallus (251–53)
	Valerian (253–60)
	Gallienus (253–68)
	Claudius (268–70)
	Aurelian (270–75)
	Tacitus (275–76)
	Florian (276)
	Probus (276–82)
	Carus (282–83)
	Numerianus (283–84) and
	Carinus (283–85)
	Diocletian (284–305)

6.1

6.2

6.3

6.4

6.5   What were the achievements of Augustus and the Principate?

6.6

6.7

Livy proclaimed the widely held myth of an older, golden age of simplicity, and lamented its loss:

> No state was ever greater, none more righteous or richer in good examples, nor ever was where avarice and luxury came into the social order so late, or where humble means and thrift were so highly esteemed and so long held in honor. For true it is that the less men's wealth was, the less was their greed. Of late, riches have brought in avarice, and excessive pleasures the longing to carry wantonness and license to the point of personal ruin and universal destruction. (cited in Lewis and Reinhold, I:8)

This nostalgia had two related but different versions. One drew on examples from the days of simple, rustic equality before the advent of the Etruscan kings. It condemned the maltreatment of the plebeians and the slaves at the hands of the patricians that had begun under Etruscan rule and intensified under the Republic. The other version wished to recreate the days of the oligarchic, patrician Republic, before the transfer of power from the Senate to the generals.

Supplying Rome. Feeding and provisioning the city of Rome, which had a population of about a million by the time of Augustus, called on vast resources throughout the empire. The most important requirement was grain, and Romans imported it from Sicily, Egypt and the North African coast, Spain, and the lands surrounding the Black Sea.

Merchants imported more specialized products from all parts of the empire: olive oil and wine came from within Italy, Spain, and the Mediterranean shores; pottery and glass from the Rhineland; leather from southern France; marble from Asia Minor; woolen textiles from Britain and northern France, Belgium, and the Netherlands; and slaves from many lands. For gladiatorial contests in the Colosseum, and for general display in Rome, lions were brought from Africa and Asia, bears from Scotland, horses from Spain, crocodiles and camels from Egypt, and leopards and rhinoceroses from northwest Africa. The transportation of bulk commodities, especially within the empire, was most often by sea.

Building Cities. A few other extremely large cities, such as Alexandria, also needed to import extensively to provide for their hundreds of thousands of inhabitants, but most of the empire was locally self-sufficient. Most people worked on the land, most production was agricultural, and people consumed most produce near the place of production, especially in the newly conquered and settled regions of Western Europe.

To incorporate these regions into the empire, the Romans constructed and promoted new cities as administrative, military, and financial centers. These included the cores of modern London, Paris, Lyons, Trier, Nîmes, Bruges, Barcelona, Cologne, Budapest, and many other European cities. In an empire that rested on agriculture, Rome laid the foundations of a small but potent ruling urban civilization.

At the height of its power, the empire contained more than 5,000 civic bodies. The orator Marcus Tullius Cicero (106–43 B.C.E.) referred to Narbonne, Rome's administrative capital in southern Gaul from about 118 B.C.E., as "a colony of Roman citizens, a watchtower of the Roman people, a bulwark against the wild tribes of Gaul" (cited in Mumford, p. 209). Roman rule especially attracted and benefited the urban upper classes in the conquered regions, and helped to urbanize some leaders of the newly arriving German settlers.

Engineering Triumphs. Cities are physical places as well as institutions, as we have argued earlier. Not only did the Romans build the institutional cores of their new and renovated administrative cities, but also they built their infrastructure: administrative and defensive fortresses, public buildings, temples, stadia, baths, markets, roads, and aqueducts. Rome itself was the greatest challenge. To build, garrison, and sustain the imperial capital required engineering skills beyond any known before. Several illustrations throughout this chapter, depicting examples of Roman architecture of stone and marble that still stand to this day, testify to its beauty, utility, and endurance. The architectural and engineering skills mastered in Rome were then applied throughout the empire. On the other hand, the Romans paid little attention to the needs of the poor, whose wooden and mud structures vanished long ago.

Luxury Trades. People of wealth and power could command specialty goods. Supplying their demands generated small but significant streams of intercontinental, long-distance, luxury trade. For this commerce to flourish, trade routes had to be protected and kept safe. The *Pax Romana* secured the Red Sea routes, which allowed the importation of frankincense, myrrh, and other spices from the Arabian peninsula and the Horn of Africa and spices and textiles from India, some of them transshipped from vessels coming from China. By the first century C.E., sailors had discovered that by sailing with the summer monsoon winds they could reach India from Egypt in about four months. They could then return with the winter monsoon, completing the round trip within a year.

Rome's repayment in this exchange was mostly precious metals. Hoards of gold coins from Rome have been discovered in southern India, with smaller treasuries in China, Southeast Asia, and East Africa. The historian Pliny the Elder (23–79 C.E.) complained that the trade drained Italy's precious metals, but the profits to be made back home were extraordinary: "In no year does India absorb less than 50,000,000 sesterces of our Empire's wealth, sending back merchandise to be sold with us at a hundred times its original cost" (cited in Lewis and Reinhold, II:120).

Overland routes were also vital. The need for safety and protection was most evident in the silk trade, which prospered when Augustan Rome, Parthian Mesopotamia and Iran, Kushan India, and Han China—the four empires that spanned the silk routes—were at their peak. Goods from Luoyang and Xian in China crossed the mountains of central Asia, connecting finally at one of the great trading emporia of Begram, Bactra, or Merv. From there, they continued onward into the Mediterranean.

Silk, light and valuable, was the principal export westward, but the caravans also carried lacquerware, bronzes, and other treasures. A storehouse discovered in 1938 in Begram, which stood at the crossroads of China, India, Persia, and the

The Roman aqueduct at Segovia, Spain, early first or second century C.E. Unlike the Greeks, the Romans are remembered less for their art than for their great engineering feats. The need to improve the water supply to Roman settlements increased with urban population growth, and the popularity of the public bathing houses heightened the demand even more. The Romans developed a massive network of aqueducts to channel water into cities across uneven terrain.

6.1

6.2

6.3

6.4

What were the achievements of Augustus and the Principate?

6.5

6.6

6.7

The Colosseum, Rome, c. 72–80 C.E. Built to house spectacular entertainments, such as mock sea-battles and gladiatorial combats, for audiences of up to 50,000 people, the Colosseum combined Greek decorative traditions with Roman engineering ingenuity, epitomized in the advanced use of concrete as a building material.

6.1

6.2

6.3

6.4

6.5   What were the achievements of Augustus and the Principate?

6.6

6.7

Mediterranean, revealed some of the principal luxury goods of this intercontinental trade: lacquerwork from China; ivory statues and carvings from India; alabaster, bronze, and glass works from the Mediterranean. Astonishingly, many of the carriers of these treasures seem to have been the steppe nomads of central Asia, the Huns and other peoples, who at other times attacked and plundered the empires across which they now traded.

Officially, the Roman upper classes scorned trade as beneath their status. Unofficially, they often entered into contracts with freed men, their own ex-slaves, to front for their commercial enterprises. Trade was lucrative, and the aristocrats did not wish to lose the profits. The preferred methods of earning a livelihood were from land ownership, tax collecting for the state, or military conquest, but even generals, such as Julius Caesar, profited from the sale of slaves captured in war.

Roman traders could be very exploitative. Especially when working in Rome's provinces, they often inspired great hatred. When Mithridates VI, king of Pontus in

6.1
6.2
6.3
6.4
6.5
6.6
6.7

What were the achievements of Augustus and the Principate?

northern Anatolia, invaded the Roman province of Asia in 88 B.C.E., he encouraged Asian debtors to kill their Roman creditors. Eighty thousand Italian and Italian–Greek businessmen were reported murdered (Grant, p. 184).

In the late second century C.E., internal revolts and external attacks by Germanic peoples brought an end to the *Pax Romana* and introduced major obstacles to this trade. Roads and markets were no longer secure, and only items that could be consumed locally were worth producing. For example, manufacturers cut back sharply the production of glass, metals, and textiles in northern Europe. Provisioning Rome and other cities became more difficult. The population of cities fell and the protection they could offer declined, as did their levels of consumption. They provided less opportunity for making a profit and less incentive to producers. Trade and productivity faltered. As the *Pax Romana* began to break down politically and militarily, trade declined and became more localized.

The Golden Age of Greco-Roman Culture

Roman cultural achievements had lagged far behind those of Greece, but as Rome conquered the Greek city-states, it began to absorb their culture. The Roman aristocratic classes adopted Greek language and literature as well as the architectural, sculptural, and painting traditions of the Greeks. The Romans now borrowed from the Greeks as they had earlier borrowed from the Etruscans.

Rome carried this polyglot culture outward in its conquests in Europe and Asia. Its schools in the provinces spread Greek as well as Latin among the tribal Goths and Gauls. Greek was the language of high culture. Latin, however, became the language of administration. Roman troops constructed amphitheaters, stadia, and baths wherever they went, the Roman invention of concrete making such construction feasible. In these settings Roman rulers provided theaters and spectacles modeled on those in Rome.

Rome's sense of its own superiority doubtless encouraged its conquest of other peoples, whom it deemed inferior, and was encouraged, in turn, by the success of those conquests. Rome's greatest epic poem, the *Aeneid*, written by Virgil during the reign of Augustus, sings the emperor's praises and celebrates Rome's superiority.

> … Behold the Romans,
> Your very own. These are Iulus' children,
> The race to come. One promise you have heard
> Over and over: here is its fulfillment,
> The son of a god, Augustus Caesar, founder
> Of a new age of gold, in lands where Saturn
> Ruled long ago; he will extend his empire
> Beyond the Indies, beyond the normal measure
> Of years and constellations, where high Atlas
> Turns on his shoulders the star-studded world.

At the same time, Virgil upholds the concept of *noblesse oblige*, the duty of the superior to help the inferior:

> … remember Romans,
> To rule the people under law, to establish
> The way of peace, to battle down the haughty,
> To spare the meek. Our fine arts, these, forever.
> (*Aeneid*, VI:822–31, 893–96; trans. Rolphe Humphries)

In the *Aeneid*, Virgil incorporates many of the forms of the earlier Greek epics, especially Homer's *Odyssey*, but he adds his own notes of an intensely imperialistic triumphalism.

Timgad, North Africa. Timgad, in Algeria, was founded as a military and administrative fortress around 100 C.E. and designed as a perfect square with a grid plan for the streets. The Romans tended to adhere to standard templates of town construction, despite variations in local topography, and Timgad is one of the clearest surviving models of what a provincial headquarters looked like.

Stoicism. Romans borrowed philosophical as well as literary ideas from the Greeks. Many thoughtful Romans were attracted to Stoicism, a philosophy founded by the Greek Zeno about 300 B.C.E. Stoicism took its name from the *stoa*, the covered walkway, in Athens where he taught. Zeno began with a cosmic theory of the world as a rational, well-ordered, and coherent system. Therefore humans should accept, without joy or grief, free from passion, everything that takes place in this world. Lucius Annaeus Seneca (*c.* 4 B.C.E.–65 C.E.), a Roman Stoic living three centuries later, elaborated:

> What is the principal thing? A heart … which can go forth to face ill or good daunt-less and unembarrassed, paralyzed neither by the tumult of the one nor the glam-our of the other. (Seneca, *Natural Questions*, cited in Lewis and Reinhold, II:165–66)

A corollary of Zeno's moral philosophy stated that people should treat one another with decency because we are all brothers and sisters. Cicero, one of Rome's most important orators, commentators, and statesmen, and much influenced by Stoic beliefs, wrote:

> The private individual ought first, in private relations, to live on fair and equal terms with his fellow citizens, with a spirit neither servile and groveling nor yet domineering. (Cicero, *On Duties*, cited in Lewis and Reinhold, I:273)

6.1

6.2

6.3

6.4

6.5   What were the
        achievements of
6.6   Augustus and the
        Principate?
6.7

6.1
6.2
6.3
6.4
6.5
6.6
6.7

What were the
achievements of
Augustus and the
Principate?

How, then, did Stoics address the conditions of slavery in Rome? Although Stoics did not advocate the end of slavery, they did propose more humane treatment. Writing on the treatment of slaves, Seneca proposed a kind of Golden Rule:

Treat those below you as you would be treated by those above you. (Seneca, *Moral Epistles*, cited in Lewis and Reinhold, II:180)

At this, however, Tacitus accused Seneca, one of Rome's richest citizens, of hypocrisy:

"By what wisdom, by what principles of philosophy had he acquired 300,000,000 sesterces within four years of [receiving Emperor Nero's] royal favor? At Rome the childless and their wills are snared in his nets, as it were; Italy and the provinces are drained by his enormous usury" (*Annals* XIII:xlii, cited in Lewis and Reinhold, II:165–6, n. 58).

Stoicism reached the height of its influence in Rome with the selection of Marcus Aurelius Antoninus as emperor (r. 161–180 C.E.). He ruled through two decades of almost continuous warfare, economic upheaval, internal revolts, and plague. Through it all, Marcus Aurelius remained courageous and Stoic. He recorded his thoughts in his *Meditations*, one of the most philosophically reflective works ever written by a man in a position of such power:

Keep thyself then simple, good, pure, serious, free from affectation, a friend of justice, a worshipper of the gods, and help men. Short is life. The universe is either a confusion, and a mutual involution of things, and a dispersion; or it is unity and order and providence … If the [latter], I venerate, and I am firm, and I trust in him who governs. (VI:30, 10)

📖 **Read** the **Document: Marcus Aurelius, The Meditations, Book Two (167 CE) on MyHistoryLab**

Religion in Imperial Rome

Officially, Rome celebrated a religion centered on the person of the emperor-god. Augustus, in particular, had rebuilt temples and encouraged the worship of ancestral gods. After the deification of Augustus at his death, the official priesthood offered animal sacrifices to him and later to his successors, adding these to the traditional sacrifices to the major pagan gods, especially Jupiter, Juno, and Minerva. People celebrated the birthdays and death anniversaries of the emperors as holidays.

Beyond these rituals, however, Roman religious policies allowed a great deal of flexibility. For the most part, as long as people venerated the emperor and did not question the legitimacy of the state, Roman emperors allowed diverse religious practices to flourish.

GREEK AND ROMAN GODS

In the second century B.C.E., Greece was absorbed by the Roman Empire. In the process the Romans adopted and adapted many Greek myths, linking their own gallery of gods to Greek legends and deities.

Greek	Roman	
Aphrodite	Venus	Goddess of love and beauty
Apollo, Phoebus	Apollo, Phoebus	Greek god of sun, god of music, poetry, and prophecy
Ares	Mars	God of war
Artemis	Diana	Virgin huntress, goddess of the moon
Asclepius	Aesculapius	God of medicine
Athena (Pallas)	Minerva	Goddess of wisdom and art
Cronus	Saturn	Father of the supreme god: Zeus or Jupiter
Demeter	Ceres	Goddess of the harvest
Dionysus	Bacchus	God of wine and fertility
Eros	Cupid	God of love
Hades	Pluto, Dis	God of the underworld
Hephaestus	Vulcan	God of fire
Hera	Juno	Queen of heaven, wife of Zeus/Jupiter, goddess of women and marriage
Hermes	Mercury	Messenger of the gods, god of roads, cunning, commerce, wealth, and luck
Hestia	Vesta	Goddess of the hearth
Hymen	Hymen	God of marriage
Irene	Pax	Goddess of peace
Pan	Faunus	God of flocks and shepherds
Persephone	Proserpina	Goddess of corn and the spring, goddess of the dead
Poseidon	Neptune	God of the sea
Zeus	Jupiter, Jove	Supreme ruler of gods and men, king of heaven, and overseer of justice and destiny

6.1
6.2
6.3
6.4
6.5 What were the achievements of Augustus and the Principate?
6.6
6.7

Mystery Religions. Mithraism, a religion that worshiped the Persian sun god Mithra as mediator between god and man, emphasized discipline and loyalty. It was especially popular within the military, particularly among the Germanic and eastern troops who were attracted to its message of fighting vigorously against both internal passions and external military opponents. Two religions that were popular in early imperial Rome centered on goddesses, and were especially attractive to women. Like Mithraism, both were mystery religions—that is, they had rituals of initiation that defied rational understanding and that were unknown to outsiders. These could include orgies and baptisms. One such faith worshiped Cybele, the venerated earth-mother of Asia Minor. Another worshiped the Egyptian goddess Isis, with her annual promise of rebirth and a variety of dramatic rituals to be observed throughout the year.

Rome and the Jews. Rome did not, however, tolerate sects that challenged the authority of the empire or the emperor. The government cracked down on worship of the god Bacchus, for example, in 186 B.C.E., fearing that lower-class members of this cult might turn against the state. The same antagonism toward potential revolt put Rome on a collision course with the Jews of Judea, in the eastern Mediterranean.

After conquering the eastern Mediterranean from the Seleucid inheritors of Alexander the Great, the Romans turned their attention to Judea. For at least a century the region had been fragmented, and often in the throes of open warfare, among contending factions and people of a wide variety of beliefs and political commitments: Seleucids; pagans, who believed in many gods; and Jews. In the chapter entitled "Judaism and Christianity" we shall see how the Jews, from their roots in the seventeenth century B.C.E., developed a religion based on monotheism (the worship of one god) and a fierce sense of ethnic nationalism. Here, we note only that both of these qualities evoked strong opposition among the Roman rulers. The zealous monotheism of most of the Jews left no room for worship of the Roman emperor as a god, and the ethnic nationalism meant that a spirit of revolt against Roman authority was always simmering. From the time that Rome conquered Judea and turned it into a subject state, in 63 B.C.E., fighting broke out frequently, not only between Jews and Romans, but also among Jewish political and religious factions that differed on the proper behavior toward the Roman conquerors and toward one another. In response to three major revolts by the Jews, the Romans destroyed Jerusalem and its principal Jewish Temple, established the Roman colony of Aelia Capitolina on its site, destroyed Judea as a Jewish state, and exiled the Jews from this land, with repercussions that would last for centuries.

Rome and the Early Christians. One of the religious factions that grew up among the Jews in Judea venerated the preacher, exorcist, and miracle worker Jesus of Nazareth (c. 4 B.C.E–c. 30 C.E.). Many of Jesus' followers believed him to be divine and later called him Christ, or the Messiah (the anointed one of God). The discussion of his ministry and its emergence from Jewish roots will also wait for the chapter entitled "Judaism and Christianity" in the unit on religion. Here, suffice it to say that the Roman government clashed with the early Christians, followers of Jesus, much as it did with Judaism, on the grounds of its monotheism, resistance to emperor worship, and potential as a force for political revolution.

For the first three centuries of its existence, many Romans viewed Christianity as atheistic because it rejected the divinity of the emperor. Some Romans saw the new Christian religion as treasonable because it spoke of a kingdom of heaven that was distinct from the Roman earthly empire. Finally, the Roman governor of Judea, Pontius Pilate, tried and crucified Jesus, partly because he was a threat to the religious and political stability of the imperial colony. By the time of Marcus Aurelius, however, despite continued persecution, Christianity was making serious inroads into Roman thought. The Stoic philosophy was not far removed from the Christian

6.1

6.2

6.3

6.4

6.5

6.6

6.7

Why did the
Roman Empire
decline and fall?

concept of an orderly world and concern for social welfare. To these beliefs, Christianity added faith in a god actively intervening in human affairs, and, specifically, the doctrines of the birth, life, miracles, and resurrection of Jesus. At first it attracted the poor, who were moved by Jesus' concern for the downtrodden, but later, more powerful classes also joined, attracted by both the organization and the message of Christianity. The new religion promoted greater freedom for women, and it began to incorporate some of the sophistication of Greek philosophy, attracting a new intellectual leadership. By 313, when the joint emperors Constantine (272–337) and Licinius (263–325) issued the Edict of Milan, proclaiming equal toleration for Christians and non-Christians, estimates suggested that one in ten inhabitants of the Roman Empire was a Christian (Lewis and Reinhold, II: 553).

When Constantine ruled alone, after 324, he favored Christianity as a religion that had brought miraculous benefits to himself personally and to his empire, and he granted it official recognition and legal status. Christianity spread freely throughout the conquered lands and peoples of northwestern Europe. The network of roads and towns created to facilitate administration also served to transmit the Christian message, and members of the clergy frequently served as a bridge between the religious practices of Christian Rome and those of others. After emerging as the official state religion in 380, Christianity succeeded in having government support for polytheistic cults terminated in 394. Even the most widespread of these cults, Mithraism, with its message of loyalty to the emperor, died out. Christianity emerged triumphant. (For a fuller discussion of early Christianity and its relationship to the Roman Empire, see the chapter entitled "Judaism and Christianity.")

The Dismemberment of the Roman Empire

6.6   Why did the Roman Empire decline and fall?

Rome labeled many of its neighbors on its far-flung borders "barbarians," including the Celts of central Europe, the various Germanic groups of northern and eastern Europe, and the steppe nomads of central Asia. These "barbarians" spoke unknown foreign languages. They did not have cities, written languages, formal government structures, established geographical boundaries, codified laws, or labor specialization. Some, like the Celts and Germans, lived in villages and carried on settled farming. Nomadic steppe peoples spent their lives riding, herding, and often fighting among themselves in far-off central Asia. Such peoples, the Romans must have thought, could benefit from the civilizing influences of the empire. Perhaps Virgil had this in mind when he was writing the *Aeneid*.

Invaders at the Gates

The Celts had arrived in central Europe as early as 2000 B.C.E. Burial sites indicate their respect for horse-riding warriors and the slow development among them of iron technology in weapons and tools. The Hallstatt cemetery in Austria reveals a greater use of iron by the eighth century B.C.E. and includes items of Greek manufacture. A cemetery at La Tène in what is now Switzerland shows continuing Greek and then Roman influences from the fifth century B.C.E. to the first century C.E.

By 400 B.C.E., the Celts were expanding their territory. In 390 B.C.E. they managed to sack the city of Rome. By 200 B.C.E. Celtic groups had covered central Europe and were pushing out toward Spain, the British Isles, the Balkans, and Anatolia. Learning from Greek and Roman examples, they built fortified towns throughout their territories. The largest of these covered more than half a square mile. Celtic women enjoyed more freedom than did Roman women, which evoked the scorn of some Roman writers. Tacitus, who seemed to appreciate Calgacus' revolt in 83–84 C.E., was

6.1
6.2
6.3
6.4
6.5
6.6
6.7

Why did the
Roman Empire
decline and fall?

far more critical of the failed Celtic revolt of 61 C.E. in Britain led by the female army leader Boudicca. Ultimately, Rome conquered the Celtic peoples. They were killed, or assimilated, or fled to Ireland, Scotland, and Wales, where, to some degree, they continue today to preserve the Celtic language and culture.

The Goths—an array of Germanic peoples (primarily Visigoths and Ostrogoths), distinguished in part by their use of Germanic languages, in part through their residence in lands that later became Germany—settled at first in northern Europe outside the Celtic and Roman strongholds. Indeed, much of what we know of this early period comes from burials in the bogs of modern-day northern Germany and Denmark. By 600 B.C.E. these Germanic peoples had established small villages, and by about 500 B.C.E. they had begun working with iron. With the discovery of richer iron deposits and contact with Greek and Roman technology, the Goths developed more sophisticated tools and weapons.

Romans and Germans had faced each other along the Rhine since Julius Caesar had conquered Gaul, and along the Danube from the time Augustus had secured that border. They had skirmished, traded, and at times penetrated each other's territories. Recent archaeological excavations show that leaders of the Germans adopted for themselves many of the tools, weapons, and luxury goods of the conquering Romans. Roman goods, and some values, spread through imitation as well as by force.

In 370 C.E., steppe nomads began to invade across the thousands of miles from central Asia, bringing pressure to bear on the whole of Europe. In response to this pressure, the Goths began to migrate westward, pushing more vigorously into Roman territory. These massive Germanic invasions upset the rough balance of power that existed between Rome and the Goths, and threatened the stability of the empire. Ultimately, the Goths formed their own states within the imperial territories. A second Germanic emigration occurred about 500 C.E. as a response to floods in the areas of north Germany and Denmark. Among the emigrant Germanic groups, the Saxons sailed across the North Sea and the English Channel to Britain, where they came to form a substantial part of the population.

The Romans called all the steppe peoples who invaded Europe from central Asia in 370 C.E. "Huns." In fact, however, the Huns were only one of the many groups of warrior-nomads who inhabited the flat grasslands from European Russia to Manchuria. They virtually lived on their horses, herding cattle, sheep, and horses as well as hunting. They slept in tents and used wagons to transport their goods as they moved from place to place, especially in their annual shift between summer and winter locations.

Although they lived in tent encampments, the Huns' living arrangements and political structures were by no means haphazard. Many groups had chiefs and even governments, and their leaders lived in the most elaborate of the tents. When the Huns invaded Europe, Romans observed emissaries of various peoples enter the tent of Attila, their leader, to conduct political negotiations.

At the time Augustus ruled Rome, groups of steppe nomads engaged in battles that would ultimately help to topple the Han dynasty in China. They also launched the attacks on India that would make two of the groups the rulers of northern India: the Kushanas, 150–300 C.E., and the Hunas, 500–550 C.E. The Huns arrived in Europe in 370 C.E., defeating and displacing the Alans, Ostrogoths, and Visigoths, and pushing them in the direction of Rome. The "domino effect" that would ultimately destroy the empire had begun.

Decline and Dismemberment

Rome proved vulnerable to the invaders, especially after a plague that wiped out up to a quarter of the population of some areas in 165–180 C.E. Historians debate the exact severity and impact of this plague, but it diminished the numbers and

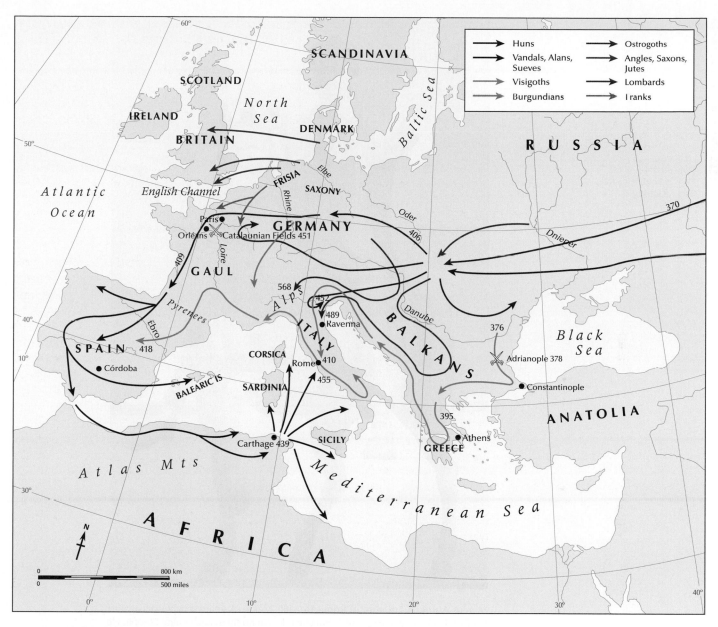

The coming of the barbarians. Rome's control of northern and Western Europe declined in the fourth century C.E. as successive waves of Germanic peoples began to migrate and colonize the outer reaches of the empire. When the Huns began to advance westward from central Asia they pushed before them additional Gothic peoples who increased the pressure on Rome. Other Huns were meanwhile pushing south into India and east into China.

undermined the self-confidence of the empire's population. During the reign of Marcus Aurelius (r. 161–180 C.E.), the Marcomanni, a Germanic tribe from Bohemia, began to invade the Danube basin. Some penetrated into Greece and across the Alps and into Italy. "Barbarian" invasions continued for hundreds of years, ultimately leading to the break-up of the Roman Empire.

For seven years, 168–175, Marcus Aurelius fought the invaders, but he also recognized that they could be assimilated into the empire for mutual benefit. The Marcomanni wanted to establish settlements, so he offered them land within the borders of the empire that they could farm; they were soldiers, so he also offered them positions in Rome's armies.

6.1
6.2
6.3
6.4
6.5
6.6 Why did the Roman Empire decline and fall?
6.7

6.1
6.2
6.3
6.4
6.5
6.6 Why did the Roman Empire decline and fall?
6.7

Marcus Aurelius, Emperor of Rome 161–180. Marcus Aurelius fought wars against the Parthian Empire in Asia and Germanic tribes in northern and central Europe. He is equally famous as the philosopher/author of the *Meditations*, a classic Stoic text on duty and service, which remains influential today. His magnificent bronze statue, now housed in the Capitoline Museum at the center of modern Rome, is the only complete bronze equestrian statue to survive from antiquity.

Some of the Gothic groups also accepted assimilation into the empire. Some wished simply to plunder and withdraw; others wished to seize portions of the empire for themselves and settle.

The Crisis of the Third Century. Invaders repeatedly penetrated the borders represented by the Danube and the Rhine. In 248 the emperor Decius (r. 249–51) defeated an invasion of Goths in the Balkans but was himself killed by another Gothic group. The Goths continued into the Balkans and beyond into Asia Minor. They took to ships and attacked Black Sea commerce, in the process cutting off large parts of Rome's grain supplies. Meanwhile, further west, Franks and Vandals swept across the Rhine into Gaul and Spain, and as far south as North Africa.

HOW DO WE KNOW?

The "Barbarians"

Roman and Chinese Sources

The steppe peoples had no written language, and their nomadic lifestyle left few archaeological remains. We know about them in part from burials, especially those of the Scythians, a group living in southern Russia and in the Altai Mountains of Mongolia. Mostly we know of them from the accounts of the peoples whose lands they invaded: Romans, Greeks, Chinese, and Indians. All these accounts report them as fierce, mobile, swift, and terrifying warriors on horseback, armed with powerful bows, swords, and lances. In more peaceful times, the Huns carried the goods of the overland silk routes through central Asia.

Latin histories did not mention the Huns until Ammianus Marcellinus (c. 330–95 C.E.) described them:

> They are without fixed abode, without hearth, or law, or settled mode of life, and they keep roaming from place to place, like fugitives, accompanied by the wagons in which they live; in wagons their wives weave for them their hideous garments, in wagons they cohabit with their husbands, bear children, and rear them to the age of puberty …
>
> This race of untamed men, without encumbrances, aflame with an inhuman desire for plundering others' property, made their violent way amid the rapine and slaughter of the neighboring peoples as far as the Halani [the Alans, on the river Don]. (cited in Lewis and Reinhold, II:623)

Five hundred years earlier, the Chinese historian Sima Qian had depicted them as coarse warriors:

During the Ch'ien-yuan reign [140–134 B.C.E.] … the Son of Heaven made inquiries among those of the Hsiung-na [Xiongnu; Huns] who had surrendered and been made prisoners, and they all reported that the Hsiung-na had overcome the king of the Yueh-chih and made a drinking vessel out of his skull. The Yueh-chih had decamped and were hiding somewhere, constantly scheming how to revenge themselves on the Hsiung-na. (Sima Qian, p. 274)

Further elaboration by Sima delineates several groups of steppe nomads who frequently fought among themselves and sometimes invaded China itself. Both his description and that of Ammianus Marcellinus reflect the similar fear with which settled, imperial powers viewed their powerful, nomadic adversaries.

- What examples of barbarism does Ammianus Marcellinus cite from Rome? How do they compare with those cited by Sima Qian from China?
- What advantages did horse-mounted warriors with bows, swords, and lances have against the might of the empires of Rome and China?
- If we had records from the "barbarians" about the "civilized" peoples whose land they were invading, how do you think they would describe them?

The empire struck back. The emperor Gallienus (r. 253–68) created a mobile cavalry and moved the imperial military headquarters from Rome to Milan in the north, better to confront invaders into Italy. In a series of battles Roman armies preserved Italy for the empire. Aurelian (r. 270–75), an even more brilliant and energetic general, succeeded Gallienus as emperor after the latter died in a plague. In a series of battles, Aurelian protected Rome's western and northern borders, although he abandoned Dacia and pulled back to the Danube.

In the east, too, Rome defeated revolts. The greatest challenge came as the new, expansive Sassanid dynasty in Persia confronted Rome in Armenia and Syria. In 260 the Roman emperor Valerian (r. 253–60) was captured and held prisoner for the rest of his life in humiliating conditions. (Legend told that after his death he was stuffed and preserved in a Persian temple.) Nevertheless, Rome recaptured its eastern areas, partly because the Sassanians treated the inhabitants of these lands so badly that they revolted. In another revolt against Rome, Zenobia, the widow of the leader of semi-independent Palmyra, declared the independence of Syria and Mesopotamia, and annexed Egypt. Her revolt lasted only a few years, and in 273 Aurelian defeated her, took her back to Rome in chains, and put her on public display, fully bedecked in jewels.

The Fragmentation of Authority. Continuing warfare forced the decentralization of Rome's power from the capital to distant provincial battlefields, and from civilian control by the Senate in Rome to generals in the field. Soldiers in Gaul, Britain, and Spain declared their general Postumus (r. 259–68) the independent emperor of those

6.1
6.2
6.3
6.4
6.5
6.6
6.7

Why did the
Roman Empire
decline and fall?

6.1

6.2

6.3

6.4

6.5

6.6 Why did the
Roman Empire
decline and fall?

6.7

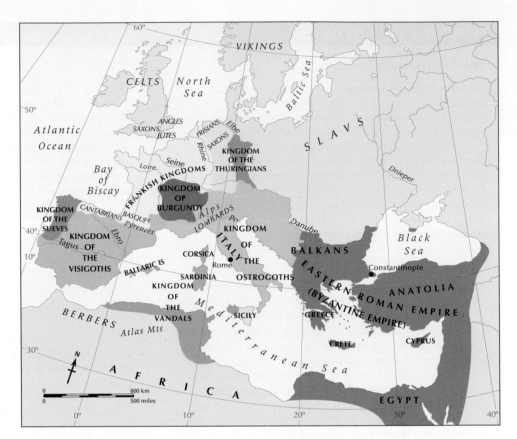

Rome's successors. Following the sack of Rome by the Ostrogoths in 455 C.E., a new map of Europe emerged. The Roman power base had shifted east to Constantinople, forming the Byzantine Empire. The steppe invaders, keen to emulate the Romans, had created new kingdoms in Italy, Africa, and Iberia, while Germanic peoples were struggling to create a new power balance in the north.

regions, but Aurelian defeated their mutiny in 274. Militarily, the empire staged an extraordinary comeback.

In the belief that an aura of pomp and majesty would be helpful in asserting central control, the emperor Diocletian (r. 284–305) claimed for himself a sanctity and splendor never before seen in Rome. The expense of his battles and the extravagance of his court bankrupted the empire and brought misery to its inhabitants. To cope with the attacks on distant borders, emperors established regional capitals. In 330 Constantine established Constantinople as a secondary capital for ruling the entire eastern region. After 395, one emperor in Rome and another in Constantinople formally divided the Roman Empire, west and east.

"Barbarian" tribes continued to breach the imperial borders and defenses. Valentinian I (r. 364–75) was the last emperor capable of driving them back effectively. From this time on, impelled by the invasion of the Huns, the Germans pushed against Roman defenses in increasing numbers. In 378 Valentinian's brother, the eastern Emperor Valens (r. 364–78), lost two-thirds of the eastern armies—and his life—in battle against the Visigoths at Adrianople. Valens' successor, Theodosius I (r. 379–95), who ruled from Constantinople, settled Visigoths within the empire, requiring them to provide soldiers and farmers for the imperial armies and lands. This "federate" status for Goths and other "barbarians" became a common pattern, with Goths, Franks, Alans, and Vandals settling within the imperial borders in increasing numbers. The empire was Roman in name, but was a mixed enterprise in terms of population, armies, and leadership. Increasingly, emperors avoided Rome and preferred to reside in such cities as Milan and Trier.

Alaric the Visigoth (*c.* 370–410) invaded Italy in 401 and, in response, the emperor Honorius (r. 395–423) removed the capital from Milan to Ravenna, a more defensible city on the east coast of Italy. Alaric invaded Italy again in 407, and in 410 he sacked Rome. At the end of 406, combined armies of Goths, Vandals, Suevi, Alans, and Burgundians crossed the Rhine into Gaul and moved into Spain. At first they sacked, looted, and burned, but within a few years they established their own settlements and local kingdoms, displacing or merging with Roman landlords. The Vandal King Geiseric (r. 428–77) crossed into North Africa, seizing Carthage and its agriculturally rich hinterlands. Gaining control of a fleet, he challenged Roman control of the Mediterranean. The Romans could not defeat him.

Why did the Roman Empire decline and fall?

The Huns were building up their own imperial confederacy in central Europe. Their most powerful leader, Attila (*c.* 406–53), commanded them from 434 to 453. His territory stretched from the Baltic to the Danube. He invaded Italy in 451, threatening Rome and withdrawing only on the intervention of Pope Leo I. After Attila's death, his armies dissolved and never again regained their power. In 476, the German general Odoacer deposed the last Roman emperor in the west. Odoacer became the first barbarian king of Italy (r. 476–93), and thus the five-centuries-old Roman Empire came to an end.

In the west, the Roman imperial system continued to function for at least two more centuries, but its leadership and its legions were in the hands of Germans and other invading groups. The groups carved up the empire into several distinct regions. There was no central government. Rome was no longer capital of an empire.

📖 **Read** the **Document: Huns & Goths** on **MyHistoryLab**

Causes of the Decline and Fall

Structural problems had been visible in the Roman Empire even at the height of its power. Internally, the conflict between the elite and the masses continued, under different names, throughout the history of the Republic and the empire. The cost of sustaining the empire by military force overtaxed the imperial economy, impoverishing the middle classes and the remaining agricultural classes. The small, independent farmers, the class that had first built up the Roman Republic, were ruined. Although the rich continued to live off their estates in Italy and elsewhere and the senatorial classes continued to do well, popular support for the imperial ideal had disappeared. In earlier times, an ever-expanding frontier had brought new economic resources to support the empire, but expansion had come to an end in the second century. The empire was overextended.

In addition, the quality of the empire depended on the quality of its emperors, but Rome had no viable system of succession. In the century between Marcus Aurelius and Diocletian, more than 80 men assumed command as emperor, and many of these were assassinated. In the third century C.E., as fighting in the border regions decentralized the empire, competing armies fought to have their generals selected as emperor. The results were devastating to the economy, administration, and morale of the empire.

Rome could no longer win its frontier battles against invaders, but neither could it continue to assimilate Goths and others into its armies and settlements as subordinates. The Roman armies and vast territories of the empire had become heavily Germanic, and when whole tribes of Goths began to serve together in single units under Gothic commanders, questions arose concerning the army's loyalty to the empire. Romans and Germans saw each other as "other," alien, and the Romans even forbade intermarriage. As Germanic peoples began to take over leading positions, the empire effectively ceased to be Roman.

The rise of Christianity as the principal religion and philosophy of the empire also suggested that the Roman desire for earthly political power was evaporating.

6.1
6.2
6.3
6.4
6.5
6.6
6.7

6.1
6.2
6.3
6.4
6.5
6.6
6.7   What allowed
the eastern
empire to survive
after the end
of the Roman
Empire?

At first, Christianity was accepted by the poor, who used it as a means of expressing their disaffection toward the power of the Caesars. Later, when Constantine declared Christianity a legitimate state religion in 313, and the favored state religion in 324, more mainstream Romans also converted. Christianity offered an alternative focus for human energy. The eighteenth-century English historian Edward Gibbon argued, in his classic *History of the Decline and Fall of the Roman Empire*, that Christianity turned people against this-worldly attractions and power. Later historians regard this as an overstatement. They point to growing numbers of imperial administrators who converted to Christianity as evidence that the new religion and the Roman Empire were compatible. Christianity did, however, preach that eternal salvation was more important than fighting for the empire, and it siphoned energy toward more spiritual and humanitarian goals, and toward competition with other religious groups.

More recently, scholars have suggested that climate change reduced agricultural productivity and hurt the economy. Still others have noted that epidemics killed up to a quarter of the population in some imperial centers between 165 and 180 C.E. and again between 251 and 266 C.E. These diseases sapped the empire of manpower and left it more open to attack. Such biological and ecological arguments complement the more traditional explanations of Rome's fall: overextension; financial and military exhaustion; a failure of leadership; the rise of new, alternative value systems; and the infiltration of Germanic peoples, which fragmented the empire into new, separate, independent states that no longer wished to be subordinated to Rome.

The Eastern Empire, 330–1453 C.E.

6.7   What allowed the eastern empire to survive after the end of the Roman Empire?

On May 11, 330, Emperor Constantine inaugurated the "New Rome which is Constantinople," to share with Rome, as co-capital, the administration of his huge empire. From its inception three complementary elements characterized the new city: Greek language and culture; Roman law and administration; and Christian faith and organization. While the western half of the empire survived for only another century and a half, the eastern empire continued on its own until 1453. It became an empire in its own right, later called Byzantium after the name of the Greek city around which Constantinople was built.

Resurgence under Justinian

Like the west, the east had to withstand military attack. Germanic tribes crossed the Danube, but found Constantinople impregnable, defended behind huge walls built by the emperor Theodosius II (r. 408–50). Using German mercenaries, the eastern emperor Justinian I (r. 527–65) recaptured many of the western regions, including North Africa, southern Spain, Sicily, Italy, and even Rome itself, but the costs in wealth and manpower crippled his empire. After his death most of these western conquests were lost, while the Persians constantly warred with the remnants of the Roman Empire in the east.

Justinian's legal, administrative, and architectural initiatives produced more lasting results. He codified the system of law that had been developing in Rome over the centuries in four great works, known collectively as the Justinian Code, thus helping to perpetuate an administration of great competence. In time, the Code became the basis for much of modern European law. He adorned Constantinople with numerous new buildings, crowned by the Church of Hagia Sophia, the Church of Holy Wisdom. He had churches, forts, and public works constructed throughout the empire.

6.1
6.2
6.3
6.4
6.5
6.6
6.7

What allowed the eastern empire to survive after the end of the Roman Empire?

Justinian and Theodora. Emperor Justinian (top) expanded the eastern empire, codified the precedent-setting Justinian Code of law, and built lasting architectural monuments throughout the empire. His wife, the Empress Theodora (bottom), disagreed with him on religious issues, but inspired him to fight against his enemies, and argued for laws favorable to women in the Justinian Code. Here they are enshrined in the astonishing mosaics (c. 547 C.E.) of the St. Vitale Church, Ravenna, Italy.

Theology was closely intertwined with politics in the eastern empire. Disputes that appeared to concern only theology frequently had political consequences, and here Justinian seemed to overreach. When many Syrian and Egyptian Christians declared themselves Monophysites, believers that Jesus' nature was only divine, not human, Justinian oppressed them in the name of theological conformity and imperial authority. In his religious zeal, he created antagonisms that smoldered for centuries and contributed to the loss of these provinces to the Muslims in the seventh century. Theodora, the emperor's wife, was among the Monophysites; her father was a priest in the sect, and she often advocated for them even in the face of her husband's opposition.

6.1
6.2
6.3
6.4
6.5
6.6
6.7

What allowed the eastern empire to survive after the end of the Roman Empire?

Justinian had reason to allow this opposition. First, he must have loved her deeply. Theodora grew up, like her mother, as an actress and dancer, and some accounts say a prostitute (as these professions usually elided into one another). As heir to the throne, Justinian was not legally permitted to marry a woman of such a background; his uncle, the emperor Justin I, repealed the law for his nephew's sake. Moreover, in 532, when urban warfare broke out between factions in Constantinople, and Justinian was prepared to flee the city, Theodora persuaded him to remain and fight. He—and later historians—credited this decision with saving his throne. She is also considered responsible for introducing court practices that emphasized the supremacy of the royal couple over everyone else at court and in the military. Theodora and Justinian were both active sponsors of Christianity, although they promoted different, competitive, and often clashing sects. Theodora was Justinian's partner in beautifying Constantinople architecturally, and she contributed also to the legal system, which he was codifying. She was most concerned with laws affecting women, giving them greater rights in divorce settlements, including property ownership and guardianship rights over children. She advocated for the death penalty for rape, called for revoking the law sentencing adulterous women to death, and wanted an end to exposing unwanted children to their deaths. She is credited with enduring contributions to raising the status of women.

📖 Read the Document: The Reign of Justinian from Secret History (558) Procopius on MyHistoryLab

Religious Struggles

Troops burst out of Arabia after 632, inspired with the religious zeal of Islam. Emperor Heraclius (r. 610–41) had defeated the Persian Empire, but he and his successors could not hold back these new invaders. The Arabs captured much of the land of the eastern empire, including Syria and Egypt, with their disaffected Monophysites.

By this time, so much had changed in the relationship between Rome and Constantinople that the eastern empire had taken on an identity of its own as the Byzantine Empire. For centuries, the Christian Byzantine Empire based in the Balkans and Asia Minor would confront Islam militarily and religiously. The Byzantine Empire organized its armies into **themes**, administrative districts and army units, in which peasants were given farms in payment for their military service. These themes and the impregnable fortifications of Constantinople were the empire's bulwark in confronting Arab armies.

The iconoclastic controversy, the bitter battle over the use of images, or icons, in Christian worship, began in 726, in large part as a response to the Arab invasions. Islam rigorously excluded religious imagery, and its armies were hugely successful. Some eastern clergy thought these two facts might be linked. They became **iconoclasts**, arguing that Christianity should enforce the Biblical commandment against the worship of idols by also banning icons. They campaigned to break and discard religious images, and the reigning Byzantine emperors supported them. For more than a century, until it was rescinded, this decision split what became known as the Eastern Orthodox hierarchy and positioned its mainstream in opposition to the western Church. It added to the strain in the political–religious relationship between the western Church and the Byzantine Empire.

The great leaders of the Byzantine Empire were known for their combination of military prowess and religious leadership. Basil I (r. 867–86), for example, kept control of the Balkans and crushed the Bulgar invaders; initiated a dynasty that reconquered Crete, Syria, southern Italy, and much of Palestine from the Arabs; and also healed the religious rift with Rome for a time.

Ultimately, however, beginning in the late eleventh century, a combination of religious and political antagonisms contributed to the decline of the Byzantine Empire. Battered from the north by invading Normans and Slavs, the Byzantine rulers turned

KEY TERMS

theme A theme was originally a military unit stationed in one of the provinces of the Byzantine Empire, but it later applied to the large military districts that formed buffer zones in the areas most vulnerable to Muslim invasion.

iconoclast An "image-breaker," or a person who rejects the veneration of icons, on the grounds that the practice is idolatrous.

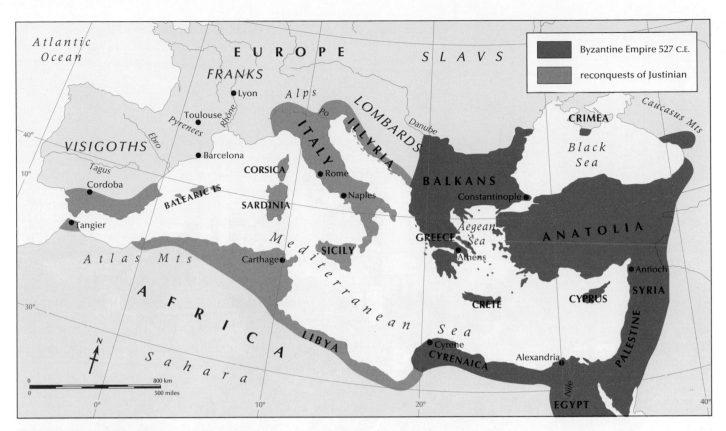

The Byzantine Empire. Despite the erosion of Roman power in Western Europe by 457 C.E., the East Roman or Byzantine Empire survived with varying fortunes for another 1,000 years—Greek-speaking and Orthodox Christian—until 1453. Centered on Constantinople, its heartland straddled the crossroads between Europe and Asia. Only briefly, under Justinian (r. 527–65), did it recover control of the western Mediterranean.

to the pope in Rome for help against the Islamic Seljuk Turks who had overrun Asia Minor from the east. In response, the pope called for crusades, military campaigns to recapture Jerusalem and the Holy Land from the Muslims. But, in 1204, crusaders en route to Palestine defied the pope's explicit orders. They conquered and sacked Constantinople, poisoning the relationship between the eastern and western churches for centuries. The Byzantines recovered the city in 1261, but their empire was irreparably weakened. In 1453 it finally succumbed to the Turks.

A Millennium of Byzantine Strength

How did the Byzantine Empire manage to survive for 1,000 years after Rome had fallen? The administrative system of the Byzantines deserves much of the credit, as a modern historian has explained:

> Consisting of a group of highly educated officials trained primarily at the university or, rather, "higher school" of Constantinople, the civil service was organized into a hierarchical system of considerable complexity even by today's standards. Taxes were collected regularly, justice was administered, armies were raised and put into the field, and the functions of the state in general were very adequately carried out. It may be said that in its period of greatest power (330–c. 1050) the Byzantine government, despite all its faults (excessive love of pomp and protocol, bureaucratic tendencies, and frequent venality), functioned more effectively, and for a longer period, than virtually any other political organism in history. (Geanakoplos, p. 3)

6.1
6.2
6.3
6.4
6.5
6.6
6.7

What allowed the eastern empire to survive after the end of the Roman Empire?

Hagia Sophia, Constantinople, 532–37 C.E. The Hagia Sophia (Church of the Holy Wisdom), built under the Emperor Justinian, is an imposing visual symbol of the power of the eastern empire. The dome, unusual in churches, represented the canopy of heaven. Later, Islamic mosques would often employ this form. The minarets, or pointed towers, at the four corners, were added in the fifteenth century when the Ottomans captured Constantinople and the church was converted into a mosque.

◉ **View** the **Image**: **The Interior of Hagia Sophia** on **MyHistoryLab**

6.1
6.2
6.3
6.4
6.5
6.6
6.7

What allowed the eastern empire to survive after the end of the Roman Empire?

The ruling classes were never as isolated and alienated from the common people as in the west. The eastern empire was also less geographically overextended. Even when it lost its more distant territories, it could defend its heartland. Its sources of wealth and military manpower were in Thrace and Anatolia, geographically close to its center of political power in Constantinople, which remained an impregnable fortress for almost 1,000 years. In these settled lands, the Byzantine Empire had an older and stronger urban tradition than the west, and its cities remained viable centers of commerce long after most cities in the west had all but disappeared. The fiercest of the invading Germanic tribes turned away from these more settled regions and marched westward, toward the more open agricultural lands of the Roman Empire. In all these ways, the east was different from the west and was able to survive as an imperial state for another 1,000 years.

The Legacy of the Roman Empire:
What Difference Does It Make?

The Roman Empire laid foundations that have lasted until today in language, law, urban and regional development, and religious organization. Rome's language, Latin, was the official language of the empire, and it persisted as one of the two languages (with Greek) known by all educated Europeans until the seventeenth century. It survived until the mid-twentieth century as the language of ritual prayer for the Roman Catholic Church. It formed the base of the Romance languages (Italian, Spanish, Catalan, Portuguese, French, and Romanian) and contributed substantially to English.

Roman law, which developed and was codified over several centuries, inspired the transition to modern, codified law in much of Europe. It was the ancestor of the Napoleonic Codes that the French general and emperor institutionalized wherever he ruled in early nineteenth-century Europe.

The hundreds of towns that Rome founded and developed as administrative and military centers throughout the empire provided the nuclei around which the urban structure of much of modern Europe and northern Africa developed. The 50,000 miles of well-paved roads that connected the cities of the empire laid the foundation for much of modern Europe's land transportation patterns.

Even after its decline and fall, about 476, the Roman Empire continued to shape the vision and the administration of hundreds of millions of people. In 330 the emperor Constantine inaugurated Constantinople as an eastern, sister capital of the Roman Empire, and that city dominated much of the eastern Mediterranean until 1453.

Meanwhile in Western Europe, the Roman Catholic Church adapted the Roman imperial administrative organization for its own uses. This basic organization persists to the present. When the Emperor Constantine gave Christianity legal status throughout the empire and chose it as his own religion, he opened the gates for its unprecedented growth. What later became known as the Holy Roman Empire, which ruled much of central Europe for some 900 years from 800, also styled itself a successor to Rome, although the comparison was somewhat far-fetched.

Images of the Roman Empire remain powerful even to our own times. The British Empire, which girdled the globe from the eighteenth to the mid-twentieth century, proudly described itself as recreating and extending the imperial military power, administration, legal system, and technological superiority that had characterized Rome. They spoke of administering a "Pax Britannica." More recently, many political analysts have referred to the exercise of American political and military power around the globe as a "Pax Americana."

CHAPTER REVIEW

FROM HILL TOWN TO REPUBLIC, 753–133 B.C.E.

6.1 How did the early Republic take shape?

After driving out the ruling Etruscan kings, Rome's wealthy, powerful citizens declared Rome a republic, with power residing in a body of citizens and the representatives they elected. However, the early Republic was led by the small percentage of the population that was wealthy, powerful, and had hereditary residential ties to Rome: the patricians. The vast majority of people were in the plebeian class; they had no hereditary ties to the state and usually no property, which meant they were excluded from government. These two orders struggled for years in the early Republic, including armed struggles and political assassinations. Slowly, the patricians yielded power, and the plebeians gained representation in the Senate.

THE EXPANSION OF THE REPUBLIC

6.2 How did Rome build its empire on military expansion?

Rome was a military state from its beginning, and as it expanded across Italy, it became a society geared for war. Roman armies excelled in organization. They developed armies of small, flexible units, armed with swords and javelins, and went to battle with the least experienced soldiers in the front, the veterans reinforcing them from the rear. Rome also developed sophisticated siege warfare, and catapults to besiege walls and batter them down. As the Romans expanded their possessions steadily outward, by land and sea, their policy of brute force, called their "New Wisdom," served as a warning to all potential foes. In addition, many captives were forced into slavery.

CHAPTER REVIEW (continued)

THE POLITICS OF IMPERIAL RULE

6.3 How did the Romans win support from the people they conquered?

Rome was a republic at home, but an empire outside its borders. Rome often won support even from the people it conquered through political, cultural, economic, and ideological policies that often appeared beneficial, and especially through the granting of citizenship. Full Roman citizenship included voting rights, legal rights over property, legal enforcement of contracts, the right to marry Roman citizens, freedom from property taxes, and protection against arbitrary arrest and imprisonment. The further away from Rome, the fewer the conquered people who were granted citizenship; but they were the elites and they helped Rome to govern.

THE END OF THE REPUBLIC

6.4 How did the generals' power struggles lead to the end of the Republic?

Generals were naturally powerful in a militaristic empire such as Rome. They raised and funded their own armies, so the soldiers were dependent on them, rather than on the state. Sometimes generals fought one another in civil war, as did Lucius Sulla and Gaius Marius, 83–82 B.C.E. Ultimately, Sulla won and had himself declared "dictator." Later Julius Caeser also took power mostly on the basis of his military prowess and organization.

THE ROMAN PRINCIPATE, 30 B.C.E.–333 C.E.

6.5 What were the achievements of Augustus and the Principate?

With Augustus, and for two centuries after his death, Rome became an imperial monarchy, a territorial, political, and economic empire ruled by a single military commander. Augustus stabilized the borders of the empire, ensuring peace and facilitating trade, commerce, and economic growth. He established the *Pax Romana*, an era of peace in an empire under Roman rule, although some critics saw this as simply as suppression of any revolt. Similarly, some critics saw the domestic policies of the empire as overly patriarchal. The public projects Augustus inaugurated beautified Rome and kept its workers employed. Continuing the policy of "bread and circuses," he kept the masses pacified. He built roads and cities, stadiums and baths and aqueducts, throughout the empire. A new "golden age" of arts and literature flourished under his patronage.

THE DISMEMBERMENT OF THE ROMAN EMPIRE

6.6 Why did the Roman Empire decline and fall?

Continual warfare drained the treasury and led to the fragmentation of authority, as power shifted from civilian control by the Roman Senate to rival generals in the battlefields. German troops were inducted into Roman armies; some ultimately declared their independence from Rome. Invasions originated from Asia and pushed against the peoples bordering the empire, who, in turn, invaded Rome. They fragmented the empire into independent states that refused to live under Rome's rule. The new ethic of Christianity, sympathetic to the poor and the suppressed, may have undermined the desire of some Romans to devote themselves to further conquest. Recent scholars have suggested that climate change reduced the agricultural productivity of the Roman Empire, others that epidemic diseases left it more vulnerable to attack, still others that lead in the pipes carrying water reduced intellectual capacity.

THE EASTERN EMPIRE, 330–1453 C.E.

6.7 What allowed the eastern empire to survive after the end of the Roman Empire?

To govern the Roman Empire more efficiently, the Emperor Constantine established a new, second capital in the east. After Rome was sacked, the eastern segment of the empire survived for almost a thousand years as the Byzantine Empire. It was less overextended geographically than the Roman Empire. Its sources of wealth and military manpower were located near the center of political power, which allowed the empire to defend its heartland. The government was very well organized, with a hierarchical civil service, regular tax collection, and a well-ordered military. The western system of law was codified in the Byzantine Empire in the Justinian Code, which helped the government function and eventually became the basis of much of modern European law.

Suggested Readings

PRINCIPAL SOURCES

Boardman, John, Jasper Griffin, and Oswyn Murray, eds. *The Oxford History of the Classical World* (New York: Oxford University Press, 1993). Very useful array of expert articles on Greece and the Roman Empire.

Cornell, Tim, and John Matthews. *Atlas of the Roman World* (New York: Facts on File, 1983). The series of atlases in the Facts on File series are encyclopedic in their coverage, and extremely accessible as well.

Goldsworthy, Adrian. *How Rome Fell: Death of a Superpower* (New Haven, CT: Yale University Press, 2010). Looks at both weakening from within and the challenge of outsiders who ultimately dismembered the empire.

Grafton, Anthony, Glenn W. Most, and Salvatore Settis, eds. *The Classical Tradition* (Cambridge, MA: Harvard University Press, 2012). A reference work of 500 articles in more than 1000 pages. Remarkably comprehensive and useful.

Herrin, Judith. *Byzantium: The Surprising Life of a Medieval Empire* (Princeton, NJ: Princeton University Press, 2007). A consummate scholar presents a readable overview of 11 centuries of history.

Lewis, Naphtali, and Meyer Reinhold, eds. *Roman Civilization: Selected Readings:* Vol I *The Republic and the Augustan Age;* Vol II *The Empire* (New York: Columbia University Press, 1990). This documentary collection is indispensable.

MacCulloch, Diarmaid. *Christianity: The First Three Thousand Years* (New York: Penguin, 2009). Clear and readable on all the aspects of early Christianity in the Roman Empire—and much more.

MacMullen, Ramsay. *Romanization in the Time of Augustus* (New Haven, CT: Yale University Press, 2000). Argues that Roman ways of life were eagerly sought by conquered peoples, especially their leaders, and spread through imitation more than by force. Several of MacMullen's other very readable books illuminate class and religious relationships in imperial and post-imperial Rome. See especially *Roman Social Relations, 50 B.C. to A.D. 284* (New Haven, CT: Yale University Press, 1981).

Time-Life Books. *Time Frame 400 B.C.–200 A.D.: Empires Ascendant* (Alexandria, VA: Time-Life Books, 1988) and *Time Frame A.D. 200–600: Empires Besieged* (Alexandria, VA: Time-Life Books, 1988). These books are more at the advanced high-school level than college, but all volumes in this series are backed by excellent scholarship, clear and effective prose, and lavish, superb illustrations. These two volumes contain important chapters on Rome.

Woolf, Greg ed. *The Cambridge Illustrated History of the Roman World* (New York: Cambridge University Press, 2003). Excellent and lavishly illustrated collection of essays by outstanding scholars.

Woolf, Greg. *Rome: An Empire's Story* (New York: Oxford University Press, 2012). Lucid history of the empire, plus an evaluation of its influence on imperial thinking in the western world to the present.

ADDITIONAL SOURCES

Antoninus, Marcus Aurelius. *Meditations*, trans. H.G. Long, in Whitney J. Oates, ed., *The Stoic and Epicurean Philosophers* (New York: Modern Library, 1940). The classic statement of Stoicism by an emperor of Rome known also for his ruthless military conquests.

Aries, Philippe, and Georges Duby, eds. *A History of Private Life*: Vol. I *From Pagan Rome to Byzantium* (Cambridge, MA: Harvard University Press, 1987). Life cycle, marriage, family, slavery, the household, architecture, the private attitudes of public officials, work and leisure, wealth, public opinion, pleasure, religion, and community are the subjects of three of the fascinating, lengthy essays in this book.

Bradley, K.R. *Slavery and Society at Rome* (Cambridge: Cambridge University Press, 1994). A comprehensive, accessible review.

Brown, Peter. *The World of Late Antiquity, A.D. 150–750* (New York: Harcourt Brace Jovanovich, 1971) and *The Rise of Western Christendom* (Malden, MA: Blackwell, 1996). Brown's scholarship and clarity of presentation on the world of the late Roman Empire and the rise of Christianity make these excellent introductions.

Clark, Gillian. *Women in Late Antiquity: Pagan and Christian Life Styles* (Oxford: Oxford University Press, 1993). Looks at daily life, legal status, family relations, and identity at a time when Christianity and Pagan viewpoints are both prevalent.

Fantham, Elaine, *et al. Women in the Classical World* (New York: Oxford University Press, 1994). A collection of essays on gender relations through texts and artwork.

Finley, M.I., ed. *The Portable Greek Historians* (New York: Viking Press, 1959). An
excellent anthology, with perceptive comments.

Frank, Andre Gunder, and Barry K. Gillis, eds. *The World System: Five Hundred Years or Five Thousand* (New York: Routledge, 1993). Many new explorations of trade in the ancient world, and new ways of understanding trade as the context of political as well as economic system-building, make this a fascinating interpretive study.

Garland, Lynda. *Byzantine Empresses: Women and Power in Byzantium, AD 527–1204* (London: Routledge, 1999). Accounts of Theodora—among many others—are useful in assessing her much-debated position as feminist, religious partisan, and savior of Justinian's throne.

Geanakoplos, Deno John. *Byzantium: Church, Society, and Civilization Seen Through Contemporary Eyes* (Chicago, IL: University of Chicago Press, 1984). An excellent analysis of the strengths of the Byzantine Empire, stressing its bureaucratic organization.

Gibbon, Edward. *The History of the Decline and Fall of the Roman Empire*, 3 vols. (New York: Modern Library, 1932). Available in several abridgements. This classic, two-centuries-old study includes important analyses of the Germanic nations, the Huns, the confrontation with early Islam, and the origins of early modern Europe as well as the fall of Rome. Fascinating for its perspective from the age of the European Enlightenment.

Goldsworthy, Adrian. *Caesar: Life of a Colossus* (New Haven: Yale University Press, 2006). Fast-paced, engaging biography, first from a military point of view, by a military historian, but comprehensive on private as well as public life.

Grant, Michael. *Julius Caesar* (New York: McGraw-Hill, 1969). Older biography, but still valuable for its attempt to present the man in terms of the development of Rome into an empire. Attempts to reconstruct the thinking of the politician/general.

Johns, Catherine. *Sex or Symbol? Erotic Images of Greece and Rome* (London: British Museum Press, 1989). An outstanding presentation of selections from the special collections of the British Museum on Greece and Rome, introducing an analysis of the function of sexual art in religious rituals, drama, and erotic titillation.

Jones, A.H.M. *Augustus* (New York: W.W. Norton & Co., 1970). The basic introduction to this pivotal emperor and his accomplishments. Jones is another classical master scholar-writer. Among his many other books, note *The Later Roman Empire, 284–602: A Social, Economic, and Administrative Survey*, 2 vols. (Oxford: Basil Blackwell, 1990).

Luttwak, Edward N. *The Grand Strategy of the Roman Empire* (Baltimore, MD: Johns Hopkins University Press, 1976). A fascinating analysis of Rome's military strategy, stressing "The New Wisdom" of application of overwhelming strength.

Mumford, Lewis. *The City in History* (New York: Harcourt, Brace, and World, 1961).
Mumford's classic, moralistic analysis of historic urbanization sees Rome, both city and empire, as a catastrophe of the exploitation of the poor and vulnerable by the rich and powerful.

Procopius. *Secret History*, trans. Richard Atwater (Chicago, IL: P. Covici, 1927; New York: Covici Friede, 1927; reprinted Ann Arbor, MI: University of Michigan Press, 1961). Available online: http://www.fordham.edu/halsall/basis/procop-anec.asp. The most comprehensive ancient source on Justinian and Theodora. A controversial account.

Runciman, Steven. *Byzantine Civilization* (Cleveland, OH: World Publishing Co., 1933). Even after 75 years, this is still a fascinating and readable introduction.

Virgil. *Aeneid*, trans. Rolphe Humphries (New York: Charles Scribner's Sons, 1951). Writing in the age of Augustus, Virgil gives the classic, idealized statement of Rome's mission.

Wells, Peter. *The Barbarians Speak: How the Conquered Peoples Shaped Roman Europe* (Princeton, NJ: Princeton University Press, 1999). Reviews and extends studies of the relationships between Romans and "Barbarians" based on recent archaeological findings.

FILMS

Spartacus (1960; 3 hours and 17 minutes). This Hollywood blockbuster celebrates the slave revolt of Spartacus in 73–71 B.C.E. Directed by Stanley Kubrick and written by Dalton Trumbo, based on a novel by Howard Fast, this film sees the life and politics of Rome from the viewpoint of the slave.

Roman City (2000; 1 hour). Traces the evolution of Rome and cities throughout the Roman Empire. Based on the book *City* by David Macaulay, and narrated by him. Combines narration and animation in a fascinating presentation.

Time-Life. *Lost Civilizations: Rome: The Ultimate Empire* (2002; 50 minutes). Emphasizes the violence underlying the creation and perpetuation of empire, and the violence of the gladiatorial contests in the Colosseum. Includes comments by major scholars along with vivid images and quotations.

When Rome Ruled: Ancient Superpower (2010–11:8 hours). A National Geographic Special with all the strengths – visual beauty; interesting, up-to-date expert commentary – and some of the drawbacks – over-dramatization – of the genre. Originally 8 hours on TV, later available commercially in 6 parts on 3 DVDs.

Crash Course in World History: Rome (2012; 12 minutes). One in a series of 42 frenetic introductions to major subjects in world history. Pitched more at the high-school level. Fun. Informational. Take a look.

7 China

Fracture and Unification: The Qin, Han, Sui, and Tang Dynasties

221 B.C.E.–900 C.E.

B y the fifth century B.C.E. the Zhou (Chou) dynasty (1100–256 B.C.E.) was in decline. As the dynasty began to weaken, the powerful, independent states of the region fought among themselves so constantly that China's historians have named the years between about 481 and 221 B.C.E. the Warring States period. After hundreds of years of warfare, in 221 B.C.E. the Qin (Ch'in) dynasty defeated the others, unifying north China and creating the first unified Chinese Empire.

The Great Wall of China. Begun 214 B.C.E., rebuilt repeatedly. "The seven wonders of the world are not comparable to this work," wrote one awestruck seventeenth-century European observer of this most imposing relic of China's past. Faced with brick and stone and averaging 25 feet high and wide, the 1,500-mile-long wall is studded with towers that serve as signaling stations, warning of the approach of mobile enemies.

LEARNING OBJECTIVES

7.1 ((
Describe the philosophies of rule in the Chinese empire.

7.2 ((
Understand the influence of Confucianism on the Chinese bureaucracy.

7.3 ((
Explain the elements of China's underlying unity.

7.4 ((
Define "empire" in relation to China.

((Listen on MyHistoryLab

What were the
philosophies
of rule in the
Chinese empire?

7.1

7.2

7.3

7.4

This chapter will consider the Chinese Empire during its first 1,100 years, from 221 B.C.E. to 907 C.E. During this time China created political and cultural forms that would last for another 1,000 years, and perhaps even to the present.

We examine the key accomplishments under China's imperial rulers—the conquest, consolidation, and confirmation of the empire—and the expansion of China to include "outer China," the distant, conquered provinces inhabited by people not ethnically Chinese. In addition, we outline relationships with peoples to the south and southwest, who were ultimately incorporated into China, and with Korea and Japan, whose cultures were profoundly influenced by China. We close by comparing and contrasting the Chinese Empire with that of Rome.

The Qin Dynasty

7.1 What were the philosophies of rule in the Chinese empire?

The Qin dynasty expanded from a geopolitical base around the confluence of the Yellow and Wei rivers to control the whole of north China and a segment of the south. The Qin conquest ended centuries of fighting among the dynasties of north China that began with the decline of the Zhou dynasty and lasted through the period of the Warring States. The Qin defeated other regional states over the course of perhaps a century, until by 221 B.C.E. it could rightfully claim to have established a unified empire, the first in China's history. Although the dynasty itself lasted only a few years after it succeeded in establishing the empire, the empire persisted with few interruptions to the present.

Military Power and Mobilization

Armed force was fundamental in the Qin's conquest. The *Book of Songs*, dating from the early years of the Zhou dynasty, suggests the constant nature of warfare in early China:

Which plant is not yellow?
Which day don't we march?
Which man does not go
To bring peace to the four quarters?

Which plant is not brown?
Which man is not sad?
Have pity on us soldiers,
Treated as though we were not men!

… We are neither rhinos nor tigers
Yet are led through the wilds,
Have pity on us soldiers,
Never resting morn or night.   (trans. Waley)

The Qin not only conquered north China but also defeated the Xiongnu (Hsiung-na), border tribes (probably related to the groups that the Romans called the Huns) to the north and west of China proper. They gained authority over northern Korea, and defeated some of the Yue tribes in the south. The first Qin ruler to govern a unified China was Qin Shi Huangdi (r. 221–210 B.C.E.), "the first august emperor of the Qin," not unlike the title "Caesar Augustus of Rome" that Octavian bestowed upon himself.

In addition to their military efforts, the Qin also mobilized tens of thousands of men for enormous public works projects. After conquering the other states of northern China, they fortified and linked the defensive walls that had been

Terra-cotta army from the tomb of Qin Shi Huangdi, Qin dynasty, 210 B.C.E. The vastness of the terra-cotta army—it comprised thousands of soldiers, still being uncovered—buried near the tomb of the First Emperor of Qin, and the care with which each life-size figure was molded, suggest at once the enormous power of the Qin army and the emperor's concern with the afterlife.

7.1 What were the philosophies of rule in the Chinese empire?

7.2

7.3

7.4

KEY TERM

barbarians The Greeks first used the term "barbarous" to designate foreign and uncivilized peoples, those whose languages sounded to Greek ears like the sound *barbar*, rather than like Greek. Today, "barbarian" continues to refer to persons who are considered foreign and uncivilized, and may, in the extreme, also refer to people who are violent, uncontrolled, and, perhaps, uncontrollable.

constructed by local rulers into the 1,500-mile Great Wall of China over a seven-year period with a workforce of one million laborers. This wall was to keep the northern Xiongnu "**barbarians**" out of China proper and, with its 40-foot-high watchtowers constructed every few hundred yards, to serve as a first warning in case of attempted invasion.

The first emperor also conscripted 700,000 laborers to construct his palace, a complex large enough to hold 40,000 people. But perhaps even more impressive was Qin Shi Huangdi's tomb. In 1974 archaeologists digging near his mausoleum discovered a ceramic army of some 7,000 life-size soldiers and horses, arranged in military formation and armed with bronze weapons, spears, longbows, and crossbows (a Chinese invention). In 1976, a second excavation uncovered an additional 1,400 chariots and cavalrymen in four military units. The next year archaeologists discovered a much smaller pit, holding what appeared to be a terra-cotta officer corps. These thousands of figures were not mass-produced. Craftsmen modeled and painted each figure separately, even down to its elaborate hairstyle, which symbolized its specific military office. The figures apparently represented the elite of the imperial troops and were fashioned to accompany the emperor to his tomb and afterlife.

EARLY ADVANCES IN WEAPONRY

3000 (B.C.E.)	War chariot invented. In Mesopotamia and southeastern Europe first metal swords and shields made (bronze).
2000	First armor made, from bronze scales, in Mesopotamia.
c. 700	The Phoenicians and Egyptians invent galleys—warships powered by oars.
500	Giant crossbows and catapults used by the Greeks and Carthaginians.
200	Hand-held crossbow now being used in China.
300 (C.E.)	Stirrups used in China.
950	Gunpowder used by Chinese for signaling devices and fireworks.
1250–1300	Bronze and iron cannon probably used by the Chinese; in Europe, first recorded use of cannon is 1326.

Economic Power

The Qin undertook enormous public works projects to increase the economic productivity of the empire. During the centuries of their rise to power, they built canals and river transport systems in both the Wei River system in the north and the Min River system in Sichuan in west-central China. In Sichuan they irrigated the region around Chengdu, turning it into a granary for the nation. The transportation and irrigation systems they built in the northern state of Shanxi transformed it into an area so rich in agricultural productivity and the means of transporting it that they could control all of north China from this base. As ironworking became increasingly important in Chinese military and economic development, the Qin also captured the richest sources of iron ore and two of China's best ironworking facilities, crucial resources for fashioning both tools and weapons.

Administrative Power

Administratively, Qin Shi Huangdi ruled through a bureaucracy. He did away with the system of personal allegiance by which officials were appointed on the basis of their personal, often family, ties to the court and therefore owed allegiance to the emperor himself rather than to the empire as an institution. Instead, the emperor chose people for office on the basis of ability; their tasks were fixed and governed by systematic, formalized, written rules, and their work was rewarded or punished according to the degree of their efficiency and fidelity. The Qin divided the empire into some 40 administrative units called "commanderies." Each commandery was staffed with three leading officials: a civil authority, a military authority, and an inspector representing the emperor. The three officials served as checks and balances on one another: no one individual could assert too much power and threaten the control of the emperor at the center.

The Qin standardized as they centralized. They fixed weights and measures, values of coinage, and the size of cart axles and of the roads they traveled. They standardized the legal code. Perhaps most significant of all, the Qin standardized the written form of the Chinese language, possibly the most important single act of political and cultural unification in China's history. To this day, despite great variation in the local forms of spoken Chinese, written Chinese is uniform throughout the country, just as the Qin established it.

Competing Ideologies of Empire

In their public proclamations, Chinese emperors stressed the importance of their philosophy to the actual process of building, sustaining, and guiding their empire. In

AT A GLANCE: CHINA 500 B.C.E.–900 C.E.

DATE	POLITICS	RELIGION AND CULTURE	SOCIAL DEVELOPMENT
500 B.C.E.	• Warring States period (481–221)	• Confucius (551–479)	
250 B.C.E.	• Zhou dynasty ends (256) • Qin Shi Huangdi initiates Qin dynasty (221–206) • Revolts against Qin (207)	• Han Fei Tzu (d. 233) • Daoism • Legalism • Great Wall	
200 B.C.E.	• Liu Bang (206–195) first emperor of Han dynasty		
150 B.C.E.	• Han Wu (141–87)	• Confucian Academy established (124)	• Travels of Zhang Qian
100 B.C.E.	• Reign of usurper Wang Mang (9–23 C.E.)	• Sima Qian (145–85) • Invention of paper	
50 C.E.		• First mention of Buddhism in China	
200 C.E.	• Han dynasty ends (220) • Age of Disunity (221–331) • Three Kingdoms (220–80)		
300 C.E.	• Jin dynasty (265–316) • Northern Wei dynasty (386–534)	• Buddhism expands • Gu Kaizhi (334–406)	
600 C.E.	• Sui dynasty (581–618) • Tang dynasty (618–907)	• Invention of block printing • Grand Canal completed (610) • Buddhist cave art	• Boundaries of empire extended to Mongolia, Turkestan, Afghanistan, Pakistan, and Iran • Tang briefly held northern Korea and Vietnam
650 C.E.	• Empress Wu (625–705)		• First pharmacopoeia
700 C.E.	• Battle of Talas River (751) • An Lushan rebellion (755–63)	• Wang Wei (701–62) • Li Bai (701–61) • Du Fu (712–70) • Porcelain produced	
800 C.E.		• Repression of Buddhism	
900 C.E.	• Collapse of Tang, leading to disunity (907–60) • Song dynasty (960–1279)		

7.1

7.2

7.3

7.4

What were the philosophies of rule in the Chinese empire?

addition, the official historians who compiled China's records were an elite trained in philosophy. As a result, China's history includes a profound concern with the conflicts over the philosophy and ideology of empire. These philosophies and ideologies emerged during the late Zhou dynasty and the period of the Warring States (c. 481–221 B.C.E.). The chaos of the times induced some individuals to engage actively in a search for solutions to Chinese political and social problems; others to disengage and find tranquility apart from society and politics. The three schools of thought that emerged in this period—Confucianism, Daoism (Taoism), and Legalism—deeply influenced every dynasty that ruled China after the Qin.

Confucianism. Kong Fuzi (551–479 B.C.E.), known in Latin as Confucius, a philosopher and political adviser from the small state of Lu in modern Shandong, sought to reform China by redefining Chinese political and ethical thought. Confucius began his career as a scholar. He mastered the six arts of ritual, music, archery, chariot driving, calligraphy, and arithmetic, and then began his career as a teacher. At a time when China was divided into many states, often in conflict, he formulated principles that he thought would bring peace, contentment, dignity, and personal cultural development at least to the elite of his time. Although Confucius was unsuccessful in finding employment as an adviser in any single state, his disciples kept his vision alive, and it has permeated Chinese thought and, often, government policy.

Confucius felt that good government depended on good officials, men of *jen*, or humanity, benevolence, virtue, and culture. Although he was not much concerned with the supernatural, he did believe that a moral order pervaded the universe and that it could be understood. In contrast to the tumult of his own day, Confucius believed that the early days of the Zhou dynasty had been a golden age of peace and order, wisdom and virtue. In those days, political leaders had understood the importance of social hierarchy, ritual, music, and art. The neglect of these elements of humanism and rationalism, and the absence of schools that taught them to new leaders, had reduced China to chaos.

Confucius and his disciples canonized five of China's earliest historical texts as especially fine examples of the philosopher's own thought and his concern for history, music, the arts, and rituals:

- the *Book of Documents*, a collection of various statements of early kings and their ministers;
- the *Book of Changes*, the *I Ching*, which details methods of predicting the future through casting sticks;
- the *Book of Songs*, which contains 305 poems, about half of which relate to the everyday lives of ordinary people, half to issues of court politics and rituals;
- the *Spring and Autumn Annals*, which contains brief chronologies from Lu, Confucius' home state;
- *Rites and Rituals* (three texts, grouped as one), which combines both philosophies and rituals of the court.

In addition, Confucius' disciples recorded his own teachings in *The Analects* (see box overleaf). A large body of interpretation and commentary grew up around each of these texts.

Confucius believed in the essential goodness and educability of each individual, and believed that the virtues of the past could be regained. He believed in the centrality of the "gentleman" (*junzi*), the moral leader who had the vision to move the society toward peace and virtue. Such a gentleman would and should be concerned about political leadership and the proper ordering of the state. For Confucius, however, gentlemen were not born but made, fashioned through proper education. Believing that character, not birth, was important, he taught whoever would come to him, but Confucius' own era was too violent for his teachings to find immediate acceptance.

The Qin dynasty did not welcome his teachings either, but the next dynasty, the Han, did. Under the Han, Confucius' ethical and political values came to dominate the culture and thought of China's scholars and intellectuals, and they continued powerful for most of the following 2,000 years, also influencing the political thought of Korea, Japan, and Southeast Asia.

Moreover, because Confucius expressed his ideas in such general terms, subsequent disciples could adapt them to particular problems. Thus, Confucianism evolved and often transformed into new forms that sometimes maintained its core values and sometimes changed them. For example, Mencius (Mengzi) (*c.* 371–*c.* 289 B.C.E.) had an optimistic view of human nature and believed that education would function to bring out the best in people. He encouraged government leaders to rule in the best interests of the people and society by encouraging harmony according to Confucian principles. Another disciple, Xunzi (Hsün-Tzu) (312–235 B.C.E.), took a more negative view of human nature. Having many years of experience in government, he emphasized different aspects of Confucian thought. Most important, he believed that human nature was inherently selfish and that only through education and participation in rituals would people learn to put the needs of society ahead of their own. Unlike Mencius, Xunzi proposed an education that would emphasize restraints on human behavior.

What were the philosophies of rule in the Chinese empire?

7.1
7.2
7.3
7.4

SOURCE

Confucius and *The Analects*

We have no record that Confucius wrote down his own teachings. *The Analects*, a collection of thoughtful perceptions attributed to him, was apparently recorded and compiled by disciples of his disciples. Because these aphorisms—497 verses in 20 chapters—are brief, unelaborated, unorganized, and written in ideographic form, their exact meaning is not always clear, but these same qualities promote the reader's engagement with and interpretation of the text. *The Analects* have been part of the education of every Chinese school student for centuries, at least until the communist revolution in 1949. The selections here represent typical subjects for Confucius: the importance of formal, humanistic education in forming proper character; teaching and learning by example; focus on the present; and respect for others, especially parents and elders.

> A young man is to be filial within his family and respectful outside it. He is to be earnest and faithful, overflowing in his love for living beings and intimate with those who are humane. If after such practice he has strength to spare, he may use it in the study of culture.
>
> Lead them by means of regulations and keep order among them through punishments, and the people will evade them and will lack any sense of shame.
>
> Lead them through moral force (*de*) and keep order among them through rites (*li*), and they will have a sense of shame and will also correct themselves.
>
> In education there should be no class distinctions.
>
> Shall I teach you what knowledge is? When you know something, to know that you know it. When you do not know, to know that you do not know it. That is knowledge.
>
> The noble person is concerned with rightness; the small person is concerned with profit.
>
> I am not one who was born with knowledge; I am one who loves the past and is diligent in seeking it.
>
> The Three Armies can be deprived of their commander, but even a common person cannot be deprived of his will.
>
> The wise have no doubts; the humane have no sorrows; the courageous have no fears.

> Before you have learned to serve human beings, how can you serve spirits …?
>
> When you do not yet know life, how can you know about death?
>
> Look at nothing contrary to ritual; listen to nothing contrary to ritual; say nothing contrary to ritual; do nothing contrary to ritual.
>
> What you would not want for yourself, do not do to others.
>
> Zigong asked about government. The Master said, "Sufficient food, sufficient military force, the confidence of the people." Zigong said, "If one had, unavoidably, to dispense with one of these three, which of them should go first?" The Master said, "Get rid of the military." Zigong said, "If one had, unavoidably, to dispense with one of the remaining two, which should go first?" The Master said, "Dispense with the food. Since ancient times there has always been death, but without confidence a people cannot stand." (de Bary and Bloom, pp. 45–60)

Throughout Chinese history, some groups rebelled against Confucius' ethical principles. Peasant rebels, a frequent presence throughout the centuries, condemned Confucius' emphasis on order and harmony. In the late nineteenth and twentieth centuries, as China saw itself fall behind the technological and military achievements of the Western world, Confucian traditions were challenged with renewed vigor (see the chapters entitled "Nationalism, Imperialism, and Resistance," and "Cold War, New Nations, and Revolt against Authority"). Critics argued that Confucianism was incompatible with equality, scientific education, rebellious youth movements, dignity of physical labor, peasant equity, and equal rights for women. The communist government that has ruled China since 1949 attacked Confucius especially bitterly in 1973 and 1974 during the Cultural Revolution, asserting that in his own day Confucius had served as a representative of the slave-owning aristocracy. As communism has more recently been transformed in contemporary China, the study of Confucianism is returning to China's schools.

KEY TERM

Legalism A school of Chinese philosophy that came into prominence during the Period of the Warring States and had great influence on the policies of the Qin dynasty. Legalists took a pessimistic view of human nature and believed that social harmony could be attained only through strong government control and the imposition of strict laws, enforced absolutely.

Legalism. Rejecting Confucianism, the Qin favored a philosophy of government known as **Legalism**, which was characterized by strict laws and strict enforcement, with rewards for those who observed the laws and swift and appropriate punishment for those who broke them. During his reign, Qin Shi Huangdi set up inscriptions on stone in various parts of his empire proclaiming his values and policies. For example, after he put down a rebellion in the far northeast, he inscribed on the city walls:

> Then he mobilized armies, and punished the unprincipled, and those who perpetrated rebellion were wiped out.
>
> Armed force exterminates the violent and rebellious, but civil power relieves the guiltless of their labors, and the masses all submit in their hearts.

What were the
philosophies
of rule in the
Chinese empire?

7.1

7.2

7.3

7.4

Achievements and toil are generously assessed, and the rewards even extend to cattle and horses, and his bounty enriches the land.

The August Emperor gave a vigorous display of his authority, and his virtue brought together all the states, and for the first time brought unity and supreme peace.

City walls were demolished [suggesting that peace had been established so that walls were no longer necessary for defense], waterways were opened up, and obstacles were flattened.

When the physical features of the land had been determined, there was no conscript labor for the masses, and all under heaven was pacified.

Men take pleasure in their farmland, and women cultivate their tasks, and all matters have their proper arrangement.

His kindness protects all production, and for long they have been coming together in the fields, and everyone is content with his place. (Sima Qian, trans. Dawson p. 74)

In another inscription he wrote:

When the sage of Qin took charge of his state, he first determined punishments and names, and clearly set forth the ancient regulations.

He was the first to standardize the system of laws, examine and demarcate duties and responsibilities, so as to establish unchanging practices. (p. 82)

He proclaimed a code of sexual conduct:

If a man commits adultery, to kill him is no crime, so men hang on to the standards of righteousness.

If a wife elopes to remarry, then the son will not have a mother, and so everyone is converted into chastity and purity. (p. 83)

In his rulings, Qin Shi Huangdi followed many of the policies of the political philosopher Han Fei Tzu (d. 233 B.C.E.), a student of the Confucian scholar Xunzi. Han Fei Tzu called himself a Legalist because he believed that strict laws, strictly enforced, were the best assurance of good and stable government. Han Fei Tzu summed up the power of the law:

To govern the state by law is to praise the right and blame the wrong ... To correct the faults of the high, to rebuke the vices of the low, to suppress disorders, to decide against mistakes, to subdue the arrogant, to straighten the crooked, and to unify the folkways of the masses, nothing could match the law.

The means whereby the intelligent ruler controls his ministers are two handles only. The two handles are chastisement and commendation. (Han Fei Tzu, I:45–7)

Read the **Document: Legalism: The Way of the State (475–221 BCE)** on **MyHistoryLab**

Daoism. Daoism (Taoism) was a philosophy of spontaneity in the face of nature and the cosmos. It was a mystical philosophy, not usually directly applicable to government, but often a solace to public men in their private lives, especially after retirement. Daoism is often seen as an inspiration to artists, and, because it advocates a high regard for nature, it is often seen as an inspiration to natural scientists as well.

The legendary founder of Daoism and the author of its key text, the *Daodejing* ("The Way and its Power") is Laozi (*c.* 604–*c.* 517 B.C.E.), but the school and the book more likely date to the third or fourth centuries B.C.E. Laozi's teachings are cloaked in paradox and mystery:

The Way that can be spoken of is not the constant Way;
The name that can be named is not the constant name.

7.1 What were the philosophies of rule in the Chinese empire?

7.2

7.3

7.4

Rejecting the emphasis on sophisticated learning and education that characterized Confucian thought, Daoists believed that untutored simplicity was powerful:

Do away with sageliness, discard knowledge,
And the people will benefit a hundredfold.
Do away with humaneness, discard righteousness,
And the people will once more be filial and loving,
Dispense with cleverness, discard profit,
And there will be no more bandits and thieves.
These three, to be regarded as ornaments, are insufficient.
Therefore let the people have something to cling to:
Manifest plainness,
Embrace uncarved wood,
Diminish selfishness,
Reduce desires.

What is softest in the world
Overcomes what is hardest in the world.
No-thing penetrates where there is no space.
Thus I know that in doing nothing there is advantage.
The wordless teaching and the advantage of doing nothing—there are few in the
world who understand them.

Those who followed Daoism believed in a natural order or path (Dao). They taught that government should leave people alone:

The more prohibitions there are in the world,
The poorer are the people.
The more sharp weapons people have,
The more disorder is fomented in the family and the state.
The more adroit and clever men are,
The more deceptive things are brought forth.
The more laws and ordnances are promulgated,
The more thieves and robbers there are.
Therefore the sage says:
I do nothing (*wuwei*),
And the people are transformed by themselves.

(de Bary and Bloom, pp. 79–90)

This Daoist view of simplicity diminishes the need for government: "Let the state be small and the people be few" (de Bary and Bloom, p. 94). Nor is there need to travel. Beauty, peace, and joy are to be found at home:

Though neighboring states are within sight of one another,
And the sound of cocks and dogs is audible from one to the other,
People will reach old age and yet not visit one another. (p. 94)

Daoism can be viewed as a rejection of Confucian principles, but over time many Chinese embraced both Confucianism and Daoism, allowing the former to shape their public lives, while gaining solace from the latter in their private lives. Because Daoism allowed the individual to find his or her own path, over time it began to embrace a variety of popular beliefs, alchemy, mysticism, and magic, all reinforced through a variety of rituals. Finally, Daoism may have facilitated the acceptance of Mahayana Buddhism (see the chapter entitled "Hinduism and Buddhism") in China, since both stressed the idea of transcending the material world.

📖 Read the Document: **Daoism: The Classic of the Way and Virtue (500s–400s BCE)**
on **MyHistoryLab**

The Struggle between Legalism and Confucianism. The philosophies of Legalism and Confucianism collided during the Qin dynasty. In direct contrast to the Confucianists' reverence for the past, the prime minister Li Si (Li Ssu) (*c.* 280–208 B.C.E.) argued that the administration of the Qin was far superior to the government of any earlier time. The Qin success was the result of its decision to replace personal, *ad hoc* administration with an orderly system of laws and appointment to office on the basis of efficiency in accordance with Legalist principles.

Li Si recommended that the Confucian classics be collected and burned so that the past could no longer be held up as an alternative to present policies. In 213 B.C.E. the Qin burned the books. Subsequently, as Confucian scholars continued to oppose Qin Shi Huangdi, the emperor had 460 scholars buried alive. Sima Qian, the official, Confucian historian of the Han government, recorded these acts of anti-intellectualism

<table>
<tr><td>What were the philosophies of rule in the Chinese empire?</td><td>7.1</td></tr>
<tr><td></td><td>7.2</td></tr>
<tr><td></td><td>7.3</td></tr>
<tr><td></td><td>7.4</td></tr>
</table>

HOW DO WE KNOW?

The Grand Historians

The Chinese valued recording the past both for itself and for the moral principles it was believed to teach. China therefore prepared and transmitted the most fully and continuously documented history of any ancient empire. Building on this legacy of historical literature, the Han emperor Wu (r. 141–87 B.C.E.) created a new official position, Grand Historian of the Han court, with the responsibility of preparing a comprehensive history of the entire Chinese past.

The first person to hold the post was Sima Tan (d. 110 B.C.E.). He was succeeded by his son Sima Qian (145–85 B.C.E.), one of the greatest of all historians. Father and son transformed their task from one of writing dynastic chronologies to one of evaluating the quality of governments and rulers. They created the art of Chinese history as a commentary on politics and ethics.

At the very end of his great work *Shi Qi*, 130 chapters recounting the history of China from mythological times almost to his own, Sima Qian includes an autobiographical sketch:

> Qian was born at Longmen. He ploughed and kept flocks on the sunny slopes of the mountains near the Yellow River. By the age of ten he was reading aloud the ancient writings. At twenty he journeyed south to the Yangtze and Huai rivers, ascended Kuaiji to search for the cave of Yu, espied Jiuyi, went by water down to Yun and Xiang, journeyed north and crossed the Wen and Si to investigate the traditions in the cities of Qi and Lu, and observed the customs handed down by Master Kong [Confucius], and took part in the archery competition held at Mount Yi in Cou. He suffered distress in Po, Xie, and Pengcheng, and returned home via Liang and Chu. Afterwards Qian served as a palace gentleman, and received orders to be sent on the western expedition to the south of Ba and Shu. Having gone south and captured Qiong, Ze, and Kunming, they returned and made their report on the mission. (trans. Dawson, p. xix)

So Sima Qian's training included farming, literature, travel, adventure, anthropological research, archery, court service, and warfare. If historians improve with their own experience of life, since it enables them to understand more fully the lives of the people they study, then Sima Qian was off to a good start.

The highlight of Sima Qian's historical writing is its emphasis on biography, a traditional Chinese literary form that he developed into a vehicle for commenting on the political and ethical policies of the state not only in the past but also in his own time. His judgments could be fierce, and they sometimes got him into trouble. His support for his friend General Li Ling at a time when the general was in great disfavor in court led to Sima Qian's castration. Later, the Han emperor Wu was so angered by Sima Qian's account of his father, Emperor Jingdi, that he had that chapter removed. Eventually, however, imperial feelings mellowed, and Sima Qian won his reputation as the greatest master of the early Chinese historical tradition.

Sima Qian completed his accounts up to about 100 B.C.E. A later historian, Ban Biao (3–54 C.E.), added tens of chapters of "Supplementary Chronicles," and his son Ban Gu (32–92 C.E.) wrote the *Han Shu* ("History of the Han Dynasty") to 22 C.E. Ban Gu established the tradition of compiling a history of each dynasty, a form that continued in the *Hou-Han Shu* ("History of the Later Han") and endured into the twentieth century.

Because the official histories carry their own Confucian, conservative biases, and focus almost entirely on the central government and its court, unofficial material from the provinces is especially useful in giving additional viewpoints. Grave sites and tombs yield documents, inscriptions, and engravings, and these often include relief sculptures of the activities of the deceased during his or her life. The burial goods represent in miniature the deceased's house, tools, carriages, boats, farms, and equipment. They often included terra-cotta figures or painted frescoes of entertainers, musicians, servants, and maids, who had enriched the life of the deceased.

- What were the reasons for recording an official court history of each dynasty?
- What were the reasons for the rise, fall, and return to prominence of Sima Qian?
- How would you evaluate the training of Sima Qian as an historian?

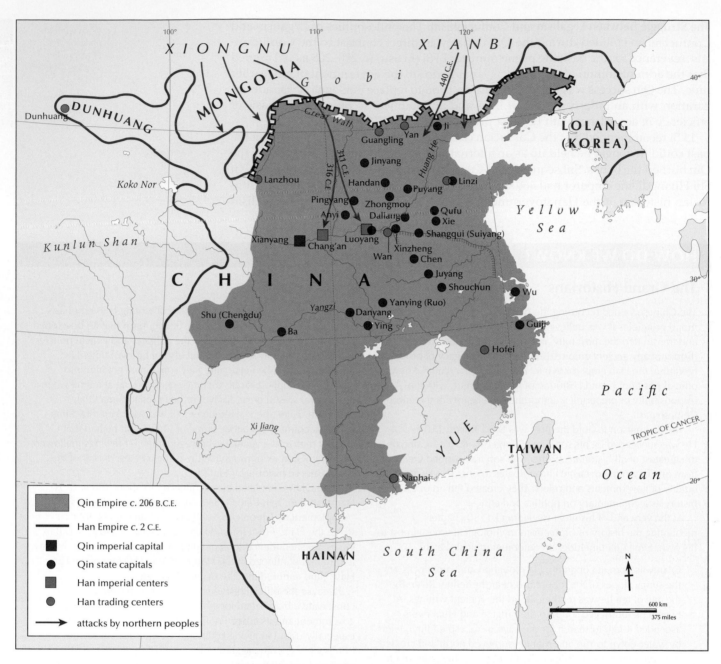

Classical China. In 221 B.C.E., two centuries of internecine rivalry—the "Warring States" period—ended with the rise to centralized power of the Qin dynasty, but internal revolt and external pressure on the borders precipitated further civil war. The Han dynasty emerged as the new rulers in 202 B.C.E. They refortified the northern walls and extended imperial control far to the south and west. In the northwest, they penetrated the Gansu corridor as far as Dunhuang and the central Asian silk routes.

7.1 What were the philosophies of rule in the Chinese empire?

7.2

7.3

7.4

and brutality, which leave the Legalist Qin with a dismal reputation. The cruel intrigues and struggles for succession that helped to end the Qin dynasty confirm that view.

The Mandate of Heaven. One of the enduring philosophical concepts of Chinese imperial politics was the Mandate of Heaven (see the chapter entitled "A Polycentric World"). Heaven—not a personal god but the cosmic forces of the universe—underpinned rulers of high moral stature and undercut those who lacked it. An omnipotent heaven conferred its mandate, or authority to rule, on the moral and revoked it from

CHAPTER SEVEN: CHINA 221 B.C.E.–900 C.E.

7.1
7.2
7.3
7.4

How did
Confucianism
influence
the Chinese
bureaucracy?

the immoral. Dynasties were thus held accountable for their actions, and they could not expect to rule forever. Their loss of cosmic connection would be made manifest, not only in the usual political and economic strife of a weak administration, but also through nature itself going awry in the form of floods, droughts, or other natural disasters. Throughout Chinese history, rebels against an emperor would claim evidence of his having lost the "Mandate," while those supporting new rulers would proclaim their possession of it.

The Fall of the Qin Dynasty

Qin Shi Huangdi died in 210 B.C.E. and was buried in the enormous mausoleum he had created, accompanied by the vast ceramic army he had ordered. Within four years his apparently powerful, centralized, productive, well-organized dynasty had collapsed. Despite the apparent strengths, the Qin had oppressed to their breaking point the nation and its peasantry, the 90 percent of the population who paid the taxes, served in the armies, built the public works projects, and the women who supported all these projects through their work at home. The final crisis began when the emperor sent several hundred thousands of these peasants to fight the Xiongnu in the far north and northwest on both sides of the Great Wall. As the *Han History* later reported,

> For more than ten years they were exposed to the rigors of military life, and countless numbers died ... Although the men toiled at farming, there was not enough grain for rations; and the women could not spin enough yarn for the tents. The common people were ruined. (cited in Elvin, p. 27)

In addition to these systemic problems, the fight over the succession to Qin Shi Huangdi's throne destroyed the dynasty. A contest for power broke out among the late emperor's son, the minister Li Si, and another court official, the eunuch Zhao Gao. (Eunuchs were men who had been castrated so that they could be trusted around the women of the court; without families of their own, they could usually be relied upon for their loyalty to the emperor.) In the struggle, the emperor's son murdered many of his father's supporters on the advice of his minister. Fear and disloyalty flourished. Each contestant seemed concerned only for his own survival and aggrandizement. Qin Shi Huangdi had instituted bureaucracy in place of personal rule throughout the empire, but personal politics still dominated the imperial court. Finally, Zhao forced the emperor's son to commit suicide, but then he himself was assassinated. While the court was convulsed in these internal struggles, rebels broke into the capital at Xianyang and captured power. Warfare continued until, in 206 B.C.E., the rebel leader Liu Bang emerged victorious and established the Han dynasty.

Han historians proclaimed their belief that the Qin dynasty had lost the Mandate of Heaven. Nevertheless, the Qin had brought China to a new stage of political development: the empire had been founded; an effective bureaucratic administration had been established; and careers had been opened to new men of talent. All these innovations were to last, in changing measure, for 2,000 years.

The Han Dynasty

7.2   How did Confucianism influence the Chinese bureaucracy?

When Liu Bang (r. 206–195 B.C.E.) prevailed in the warfare that ended the Qin dynasty, the empire remained intact. One ruling family fell and another took its place and asserted its own control, but the empire itself continued united under a single emperor. The principal Legalist ministers who had guided the Qin were replaced, but the administrative bureaucracy continued to function.

How did
Confucianism
influence
the Chinese
bureaucracy?

A Confucian Bureaucracy

Change came in the leadership style of the new dynasty. Liu Bang was himself a commoner and a soldier, perhaps illiterate, with many years of warfare still ahead of him—he died in battle in 195 B.C.E.—but as his ministers he chose educated men with Confucian principles. Slowly, a new social and political hierarchy emerged, with scholars at the top, followed by farmers, artisans, and merchants. Legalism still influenced the administrative systems, and Daoism's emphasis on nature and emotion continued to be attractive, but Confucius' ethical teachings captured the imagination of the court.

The influence of Confucianism appeared in four other areas. First, history became more important than ever. The appointment of Sima Tan and then his son Sima Qian as court historians established the tradition of imperial record-keeping (see box above). The Confucian notion of the importance of tradition and continuity prevailed over the Legalist idea of discounting the past.

Second, in 124 B.C.E. the most powerful and longest-lived of the Han rulers, Wudi or Emperor Wu (r. 141–87 B.C.E.), the Martial Emperor, established an elite imperial academy to teach specially selected scholar-bureaucrats the wisdom of Confucius and its applicability to problems of governance. The emperor also declared that knowledge of the Confucian classics would be a basis for promotion in the imperial civil service. Although the academy could at first educate only 50 men, it multiplied in size until, in the later Han period, it could accommodate 30,000 men. In Han times, the landed aristocracy still gained most of the places in the bureaucracy, but the principle of appointment and promotion based not on birth but on success in an examination in the Confucian classics was finally established during the Tang dynasty (618–907 C.E.).

Third, an imperial conference of Confucian legal scholars was convened in the imperial palace in 51 B.C.E. to codify the principles for applying case law. This established and consolidated the Chinese legal system for centuries to come.

Finally, Confucian scholars, both male and female, began to establish principles of conduct for women. Confucius had spoken of the importance of five relationships in human society: ruler–subject; father–son; husband–wife; older brother–younger brother; and friend–friend. The first four were hierarchical relationships of superior–inferior. Little, however, had been written about the role of women. During the Han dynasty several Confucian scholars addressed the topic. They urged women to be self-sacrificing, serving others, especially the males in their lives: father, brother(s), husband, and son(s). The Source box (opposite) includes examples of such advice by Ban Zhao, sister of one of the Han court historians, and Liu Xiang, who wrote *Biographies of Heroic Women*.

📖 **Read** the **Document**: **Sima Qian on Qin Shihuang (145–86 BCE)** on **MyHistoryLab**

Jade burial suit of Princess Tou Wan, Western Han dynasty, late second century B.C.E. As a very hard stone, jade was believed to be an effective preservative. When Princess Tou Wan, daughter-in-law of Emperor Jingdi, died, a burial suit was created for her using 2,160 pieces of jade tied together with gold wire. (National Museum of China, Beijing)

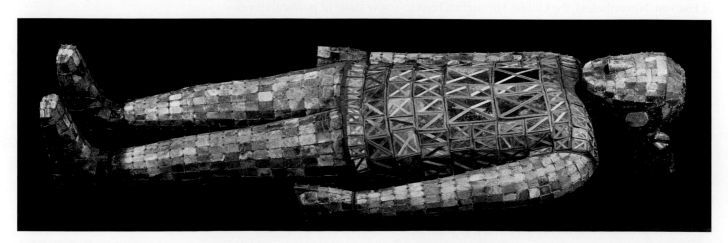

SOURCE

Treatises about Women in Han Society

During the Han dynasty, several authors decided to address the subject of women's role in society. Unfortunately, we have far more records on aristocratic women than we do on the peasantry. Ban Zhao (45–116 C.E.), sister of the famous court historian Ban Gu, wrote *Admonitions for Women*, a text of advice on the virtues appropriate for aristocratic women, divided into seven sections on humility, resignation, subservience, self-abasement, obedience, cleanliness, and industry. Ban Zhao explained:

In ancient times, on the third day after a girl was born, people placed her at the base of the bed, gave her a pot shard to play with, and made a sacrifice to announce her birth. She was put below the bed to show that she was lowly and weak and should concentrate on humbling herself before others. Playing with a shard showed that she should get accustomed to hard work and concentrate on being diligent. Announcing her birth to the ancestors showed that she should focus on continuing the sacrifices. These three customs convey the unchanging path for women and the ritual traditions.

Humility means yielding and acting respectful, putting others first and oneself last, never mentioning one's own good deeds or denying one's own faults, enduring insults and bearing with mistreatment, all with due trepidation.

Industriousness means going to bed late, getting up early, never shirking work morning or night, never refusing to take on domestic work, and completing everything that needs to be done neatly and carefully. Continuing the sacrifices means serving one's husband-master with appropriate demeanor, keeping oneself clean and pure, never joking or laughing, and preparing pure wine and food to offer to the ancestors. (Ebrey, p. 75)

Placing a similar stress on the virtues of self-sacrificing service, Liu Xiang (79–8 B.C.E.) wrote the *Biographies of Heroic Women*, which recounted the virtues of 125 women. He especially praised the mother of the philosopher Mencius, the greatest of the Confucian scholars. Liu Xiang quotes Mencius' mother telling her son of her concept of women's obligations:

A woman's duties are to cook the five grains, heat the wine, look after her parents-in-law, make clothes, and that is all! Therefore she cultivates the skills required in the women's quarters and has no ambition to manage affairs outside the house. The *Book of Changes* says, "In her central place, she attends to the preparation of the food." The *Book of Songs* says, "It will be theirs neither to do wrong nor to do good,/ Only about the spirits and the food will they have to think." This means that a woman's duty is not to control or to take charge. Instead she must follow the "three submissions." When she is young, she must submit to her parents. After her marriage, she must submit to her husband. When she is widowed, she must submit to her son. These are the rules of propriety.

The pervasive Confucian stress on hierarchy and deference permeates these prescriptions for women's conduct. However, throughout Han times—but not after—women could inherit property, divorce, and remarry after divorce or widowhood. And even the most highly placed women sometimes rebelled against Confucian ideals.

The greatest exception to the general rule of subordination of women, at least in public, came during the Tang Dynasty, when Wu Zetian clawed her way to power to rule as "Emperor", 690–705 C.E. She had already held effective power for decades through her control over previous emperors who were her husbands, consorts, and sons. Condemned by later Confucian historians for her extraordinary treachery and violence in eliminating rivals and opponents, she was nevertheless also praised for her effective administration of the civil service, her patronage of literature and the arts, her support of Buddhist temples and monks, and her military successes, including the conquest of Korea to the east and large parts of central Asia to the west. A colorful and commanding presence, Wu Zetian has been the subject not only of historians' evaluations but also of numerous works of historical fiction, films, and television productions.

Military Power and Diplomacy

The Han emperors were no less militaristic than the Qin. Confucian principles of moral rectitude held sway among the educated elite, but the government did not dispense with formal legal systems, nor did it forsake offensive or defensive warfare. The standing army numbered between 300,000 and one million, and all able-bodied men between the ages of about 20 and 56 were conscripted, serving for one year of training and one year of duty in the capital or in battle on the frontiers. They could be recalled in case of warfare.

Throughout the Han dynasty, China was engaged in incessant battles with the Xiongnu and other tribes around the Great Wall. Indeed, as we shall see shortly, the Han forced open a corridor through Gansu in the direction of Xinjiang (Turkestan). One reason for this expansion was to open markets for silk in the west. Parthian

7.1

7.2

How did
Confucianism
influence
the Chinese
bureaucracy?

7.3

7.4

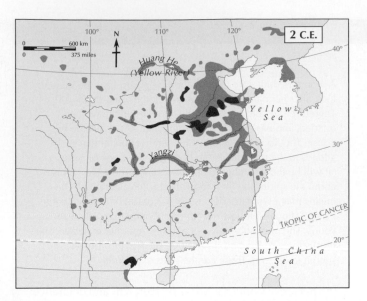
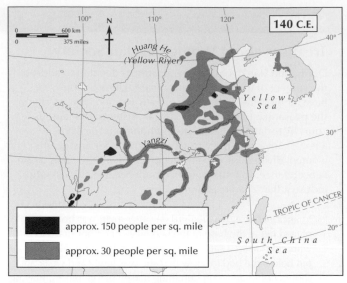

approx. 150 people per sq. mile

approx. 30 people per sq. mile

7.1

7.2 How did
Confucianism
7.3 influence
the Chinese
7.4 bureaucracy?

Chinese expansion. A substantial shift in Chinese population distribution began during the first two centuries C.E., a fact that can be traced from Han census records. As land-hunger and pressure from the Xiongnu and the Tibetans on the northern border forced migration from the densely populated northeast, and as techniques for rice cultivation in the humid basin of the Yangzi improved, the lands to the south were mastered, and population clusters developed along the river valleys. Nevertheless, because of warfare and extreme flooding, the total population actually declined from 58 million to about 48 million.

traders carried goods on this trade route as far as Rome. China also wanted to secure a supply of horses from distant Bactria for the military. As the Chinese Empire expanded, emperors sought new ways of regulating foreign affairs with neighboring peoples, including nomadic groups, such as the Xiongnu. They created a "tributary system," in which the neighboring tributary group would acknowledge Chinese dominance and offer gifts (tribute) to the emperor. In exchange the emperor would send gifts to the ruler of the tributary group. On the northern and western borders, where Chinese, Mongol, Tibetan, and barbarian forces fought, each learned the strengths and weaknesses of the others. A Chinese strength was the crossbow. An important Mongol and Tibetan strength was cavalry, mounted on strong, fast horses. To achieve military parity, the Han emperors sought and found a supply of equivalent horses in central Asia. The Gansu corridor served as an access route, and Emperor Wu garrisoned it with 700,000 soldiers. Administrative records written on wooden strips have survived to tell of the lives of these immigrant soldier-colonizers in some detail.

Population and Migration

In both the south and the northern border regions, the Han established military–agricultural colonies to provide defense and economic development. The Chinese attempted to win the local populations over to Chinese culture. Often they succeeded, but not always. On the borders and in the southeast they met opposition, and rebellions against the Chinese settlers erupted in 86, 83, and 28–25 B.C.E.

During the later Han dynasty the population of northern China declined dramatically, even as the population of the south was expanding, perhaps from immigration from the north as well as from natural growth. The earliest preserved census in the world, taken in China in the year 2 C.E., shows the Chinese heartland clearly to be in the north; the southern population was sparse, mostly settled along the rivers. The second preserved census, taken 138 years later in 140 C.E., showed a sharp overall

7.1

How did
Confucianism
influence
the Chinese
bureaucracy?

7.2

7.3

7.4

decline of 10 million people, from about 58 million to about 48 million. The regional distribution had shifted from 76 percent in the north and 24 percent in the south, to 54 and 46 percent respectively. In absolute terms the population of the south actually went up by more than 50 percent, from 14 million to 22 million, while the entire north declined from 44 million to 26 million.

Xiongnu and Tibetan massacres along the northern and western borders contributed to population losses, as did the floods caused when the Yellow River broke its banks and twice changed course, in about 4 C.E. and again in 11 C.E. The military and natural turbulence also impoverished China's civilian population. Meanwhile, the imperial government allocated more and more resources to support the army, expansionism, and the court in the capital city, Chang'an.

In the south, in general, there was little indigenous population and little hostility or resistance to the increase in Han Chinese. The regional Yue or Viet tribes were more often involved in fighting one another, although in 40 C.E. there was a revolt, and violence broke out on at least seven occasions between 100 and 184 C.E. Perhaps the increased resistance in the later years was evoked by the vast increase in the flow of population from the north to the south.

View the Image: **Han Chinese House** on **MyHistoryLab**

Economic Power

Han rulers also encouraged the expansion of China's iron industry. They developed the technique of liquefying iron and pouring it into molds to produce cast iron and later steel. In spite of the demographic decline in the north, the economy of Han China grew with the exploitation of new sources of wealth from along the Yangzi River, Sichuan, and the south. New inventions in mining (including salt mining), paper production, the compass, the breast-strap harness for horses, a redesigned plowshare, hydraulic engineering, and the tapping of natural gas increased wealth and productivity.

The road through the Gansu corridor to Xinjiang brought increased knowledge of distant lands and new trade possibilities. In 138 B.C.E. Emperor Wu dispatched Zhang Qian to inner Asia to seek enemies of the Xiongnu who might serve as allies of the Chinese. Zhang returned 12 years later without new alliances but with precious new information on lands as far west as Bactria, in modern northern Afghanistan. New trade possibilities opened in the import of horses and the export of silk. Parthian traders served as intermediaries between the Chinese and Roman empires. By 57 B.C.E., Chinese silk had reached Rome. The first silk route had been opened. Geography and cartography flourished, and gazetteers began to be published.

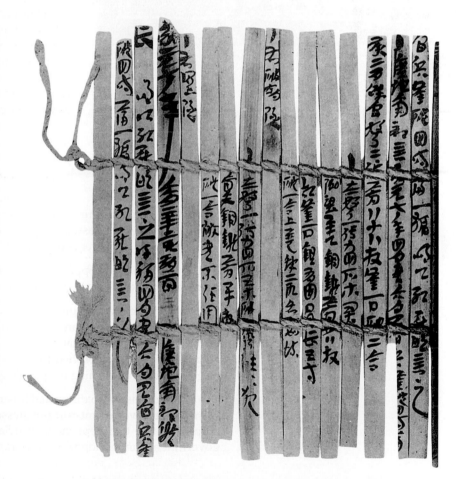

Inventory written on bamboo, 95 B.C.E. Government bureaucracy expanded with military and economic power under the Han dynasty, producing an enormous number of documents on wooden and bamboo strips. This inventory lists the equipment of two infantry units. (British Library, London)

Stone relief of harnessed cattle found at Mizhi, Shaanxi province, c. 25–220 C.E. Technological advancements, such as the development of the animal-drawn plow, went hand in hand with the increase in the area of cultivated land under the Han dynasty.

7.1

7.2

How did Confucianism influence the Chinese bureaucracy?

7.3

7.4

The cost of military expeditions and garrisons and the expenses of the self-aggrandizing court ate up the gains, however. Having dramatically lowered the land revenues when they first took office, the Han emperors began to raise them again. They also began to nationalize private enterprise by bringing it under state control, not in order to promote efficiency or honesty but to gain the profits for the state. Although commerce and business were theoretically held in low regard by Confucianists, businessmen flourished under the Han, and Sima Qian praised their enterprise:

> A family with a thousand catties of gold may stand side by side with the lord of a city; the man with a hundred million cash may enjoy the pleasures of a king. Rich men such as these deserve to be called the "untitled nobility," do they not? (Sima Qian, trans. Watson, p. 356)

Emperor Wu sought to expropriate some of this wealth to pay for his military ventures and his imperial court. He altered coinage, confiscated the land of the nobility, sold offices and titles, and increased taxes. He established government monopolies in the production of iron, salt, and liquor, and he took over part of the grain trade, arguing that this was a means of stabilizing prices, but actually intending to secure profits for his government and its border wars. On his death, his successor, Emperor Zhao, arranged a debate between his chief minister, who advocated continuing the state monopolies on salt and iron, and a number of Confucian scholars, who opposed them. The minister defended and explained the emperor's policy:

> He established the salt, iron, and liquor monopolies and the system of equitable marketing in order to raise more funds for expenditures at the borders. … [O]ur critics … would have the men who are defending our passes and patrolling our walls suffer hunger and cold. … Abolition of these measures is not expedient! (de Bary and Bloom, p. 361)

The Confucianists opposed the policy of costly military expansion and the government plan to take over businesses in order to finance it:

> Never should material profit appear as a motive of government. Only then can moral instruction succeed and the customs of the people be reformed. But now in the provinces the salt, iron, and liquor monopolies, and the system of equitable marketing, have been established to compete with the people for profit, dispelling rustic generosity and teaching the people greed. (pp. 360–61)

The Confucianists also distrusted businessmen as self-serving and corrupt, and they feared that government-run businesses would increase that corruption. The new emperor came to accept the Confucian argument and relinquished at least some government-run monopolies temporarily.

Fluctuations in Administrative Power

The bureaucracy of the early Han seemed to run well, and the adoption of Confucian principles tempered some of the harshness of the Legalist codes. In addition, the wars that the Qin had pursued to establish China's borders made fighting somewhat

How did Confucianism influence the Chinese bureaucracy?

less necessary for the Han. For 200 years even the problems of succession, problems that had ultimately helped to destroy the Qin dynasty, were negotiated effectively, if sometimes quite cruelly. Nevertheless, the absence of clear principles of imperial succession continued, and in 9 C.E. the Han temporarily fell from power because there was no clear successor.

An Interregnum. In 1 B.C.E., the eight-year-old Emperor Ping inherited the throne. A regent, Wang Mang, was appointed to run the government during the boy's minority, and when Ping died in 9 C.E., Wang Mang became the *de facto* ruler, declaring himself founder of a new dynasty. His policies, however, alienated virtually everyone. These policies—fighting against the Xiongnu, breaking up large estates, reinstating the prohibition on the sale of land, fixing the prices of commodities, terminating the status of the Han nobility and reducing them to commoners, cutting bureaucratic salaries, confiscating villagers' gold in exchange for bronze—inflamed rich and poor, nobility and commoners, and urban and rural folk.

To add to his problems, just at the beginning of Wang Mang's regency, the shallow, silt-laden Yellow River again broke its banks and changed course twice in five years, wreaking immense devastation to property, and loss of life. In 23 C.E., a combination of Xiongnu invasions in the north, the rebellion of Han nobles near the capital, and the revolt of the Red Turbans—a mass movement beginning in 18 C.E. centered in the Shandong peninsula, which had been most devastated by the Yellow River's flooding—brought down Wang Mang and led to the reinstatement of the Han dynasty.

A Weakened Han Dynasty. The later Han dynasty, 23–220 C.E., did not have the same strength as the former Han. To cope with continuing incursions, the later Han made alliances with the barbarians, inviting them to settle within the Great Wall, to provide soldiers for Chinese armies, and even to intermarry with the Chinese, policies that were similar to Rome's actions in its border regions. Although this pattern demonstrated the weakness of the Chinese central government, it also contributed to the **sinicization** of the tribal barbarians, who learned the language, culture, and administrative patterns of the Chinese. Reversing the pattern of tribute of the years of strong government, the later Han gave silk cloth to the border tribes so that they would not invade. Later Han emperors also moved the capital from Chang'an eastward to the less exposed city of Luoyang.

The movement of population to the south increased the wealth of the empire generally, but the increase went largely to merchants and landlords. Peasants continued to be exploited and oppressed by the exactions of both their landlords and the imperial government. As government taxes increased, peasants sold off their private holdings and went to live and farm under the jurisdiction of local landlords, where they sought to evade government taxes and military conscription.

The landlords themselves faced a dilemma. As members of the governing elite, they were obliged to collect and remit taxes to the central government and to turn over their tenants for conscription, but as landlords and local potentates, it was to their advantage to retain the taxes and the tenants' labor for themselves. Strong central governments

KEY TERM

sinicization The adoption and absorption by foreign peoples of Chinese language, customs, and culture.

Two concubines in front of a mirror, *Admonitions …*, Gu Kaizhi, fourth century C.E. As the Han dynasty collapsed, artists lamented the neglect of the Confucian codes of behavior. Here the court painter Gu Kaizhi (334–406 C.E.) illustrates the text of the poet Zhang Hua (c. 232–300 C.E.): "Men and women know how to adorn their faces, but there is none who knows how to adorn his character …" (British Museum, London)

7.1

7.2

7.3   What were
       the elements
7.4   of China's
       underlying unity?

were capable of demanding loyalty and collection; the later Han, however, frequently failed. Peasants absconded, the government's tax and labor bases diminished, and provincial notables developed independent power bases. Peasant revolts, which would become endemic in most of China, broke out with increasing frequency.

Peasant Revolt and the Fall of the Han. The beginning of the end of the Han is usually dated to 184 C.E., when a revolt of hundreds of thousands of peasants broke out. Zhang Jue, a Daoist healer who proclaimed that a new era would begin with the fall of the Han, launched the rebellion, called the Yellow Turban revolt for the headgear worn by the rebels. It broke out simultaneously in 16 commanderies throughout the south, east, and northeast of China. Although this specific revolt was suppressed, it triggered a continuous string of additional outbreaks.

At least four factions struggled for power within the palace: the emperor, who, after the death of Emperor Ling in 189, was a child; the bureaucrats, advisers, palace guards, and regent to the young emperor; the approximately 2,000 eunuchs in the court; and the women of the court and their families. Since each emperor had several wives and consorts, competition among them was fierce, both for their own recognition and for recognition of their sons at court, especially in the selection of the heir to the emperor. After the death of an emperor, his widows and his mother often remained embroiled in court politics to defend their own positions and those of their family.

In the last decades of Han rule, 189–220 C.E., the court was buffeted from the outside and divided on the inside. For example, on September 25, 189 C.E., generals in the court murdered hundreds of eunuchs to remove their influence. By the year 220, when the last Han emperor, Xian, abdicated, the court had no center and the lands of the empire had already been divided among numerous competing warlords.

Disintegration and Reunification

What were the elements of China's underlying unity?

The fall of the Han brought the disintegration of China into three separate states, but the ideal of a united Chinese empire was not lost. The empire was restored for 50 years, 265–316 C.E., then divided again for 273 years until 589 C.E., when a new dynasty introduced a unification that would last for more than three centuries. Even during periods of disintegration, elements of an underlying unity endured, for China has deep and pervasive common cultural traditions, just as, during periods of powerful imperial rule, elements of divisive regionalism persisted, since China is a huge and diverse country.

Ecology and Culture

On the fall of the Han dynasty, China divided into three states: the Wei in the north, ruling over some 29 million people; the Wu in the south, ruling over 11 million; and the Shu in the west, ruling over 7 million. From 265 to 316 C.E. a single dynasty, the Jin (Chin), reunited China briefly. Then, from 316–589 C.E., China was divided north from south, more or less by the Huai River basin, halfway between the Yellow River to the north and the Yangzi River to the south.

This division was characterized by a number of geographical features. To the north, the top soil is a fine yellow dust, called loess. Borne by winds from the west, it is 250 feet deep to the north of Chang'an, a region with little irrigation. The agriculture in this region has been dry-field farming not dependent on massive irrigation projects and mostly carried on by owner-operators. Its principal crops are wheat, millet, beans, and turnips. The region is intensely cold in winter. The south,

7.1

7.2

7.3

7.4

What were
the elements
of China's
underlying unity?

by contrast, has many waterways, which are useful for both irrigation and navigation. The warmer weather, even subtropical in the far south, makes it possible to grow rice and tea, which were introduced from Southeast Asia probably toward the end of the Han dynasty. The area is typically organized into landlord–tenant estates.

During the centuries of imperial division, six successive dynasties governed the south, while a series of non-Chinese barbarian dynasties ruled the north. Warfare and ecological disaster in the north steadily reduced the population, while people moved south, shifting the balance of population to a southern majority. It appeared that the Chinese Empire, like that of Rome, had lost control of its original homeland and divided forever.

While China was divided politically, however, its culture and ethical ideology persisted, keeping alive its traditions of unity. In the south, especially, the arts, painting, calligraphy, and poetry flourished, frequently with the themes of spiritual survival amid political disarray. The Chinese language, too, continued to unite all literate Chinese as their means of communication.

In the north, China was more open to new social and ethnic syntheses. The Chinese absorbed the barbarians into their continuing cultural life, and, through intermarriage, into China's genetic pool as well. When scholars today note the homogeneity of China's population as "95 percent Han," they are referring to cultural rather than ethnic homogeneity and recognizing the openness of China toward accepting and assimilating neighboring peoples who accept the culture of the "Han." The Chinese themselves echo the importance of this common culture, referring to all who have accepted it as "people of the Han." The nomadic peoples living on the northern borders and settling within the Great Wall at the invitation of the later Han emperors had already begun to absorb Chinese culture. When they became powerful enough to conquer north China, they found that they needed to enlist Chinese bureaucrats to administer their gains. In many regions, the administrators appointed by the new rulers were descended from families whom the Han had employed. Thus, below the surface of foreign rule, a powerful stratum of Chinese elites remained in place.

The most powerful and longest ruling of the nomadic conquerors became the most assimilated. This was the Northern Wei dynasty (r. 386–534 C.E.), also named the Toba Wei after the tribal group that founded it. The longer it ruled, the more assimilated its people became. In 493–94 C.E. they moved their capital from the far west to one of the former Han capitals, Luoyang, in order to consolidate their control of the northeast. But in Luoyang they wore Chinese dress and adopted Chinese names, and many intermarried. The Toba also made their own contributions to China's administrative practices, instituting a new pattern of urban organization by wards in Luoyang. Subsequent dynasties used this system when laying out the restored capital at Chang'an. Still later, Japanese imperial planners copied it in Nara. Similarly, in their attempts to keep agricultural populations from fleeing from northern China, the Toba took over all land ownership for the state and continued to redistribute it in "equal fields" as each generation of cultivators died and new ones inherited the land. According to the "equal fields" system, all families received some land in return for paying a tribute in goods or labor.

The developing, new aristocracy of mixed Chinese–Toba blood alienated the unassimilated Toba troops who

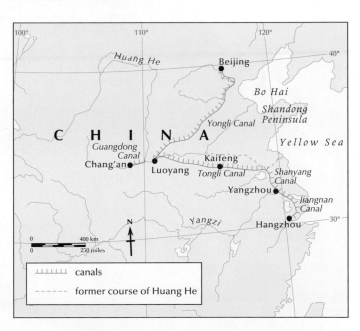

Chinese technology. Classical Chinese cultures were administratively and technologically sophisticated. They mastered diplomacy, bureaucracy, navigation, architecture, chemistry, mechanics, astronomy, printing, and, most dramatically, hydrology. Terraced farming, intensive irrigation systems, and the construction of thousands of miles of navigable canals harnessed the often unpredictable rivers of eastern China, and opened up the inland cities to commerce.

garrisoned the frontiers. They finally revolted and defeated the Northern Wei government in 534 C.E., opening the way for the Sui dynasty, a family of mixed Chinese and foreign parentage, which reunited China.

Buddhism Reaches China

While China was beset by this dynastic turmoil, a new religion was spreading through the country. During the Han dynasty, Buddhism had entered China from its birthplace in India. It is first noted in Chinese historical records in the first century C.E.

Siddhartha Gautama, the Buddha, "the enlightened one" (c. 563–483 B.C.E.), introduced a religion of compassion in the face of a world of pain. Buddhism is discussed at length in the chapter entitled "Hinduism and Buddhism." Here, however, we ask why and how this religion, which later died out in its own native soil in India, was able to take root in far-off China, even in the face of early opposition by Confucian scholars and bureaucrats and an institutionalized Daoist establishment.

Over time, Buddhism's very foreignness may have contributed to its success. The nomadic conquerors who succeeded the Han may have felt comfortable accepting, and even sponsoring, a religion that, like themselves, came from outside China.

Second, Buddhism arose in India, to a large degree, as an antipriestly religion favored by the merchant classes. These merchants sponsored Buddhist monasteries, convents, and cave temples along the silk routes between India and China, some of

Hill of the Thousand Buddhas, Jinan, Tang dynasty. The increased power of the Buddhist religious establishment in Tang times is reflected in the growth of cave paintings and sculptures. The merchants and missionaries who brought Buddhism to China along the silk route also brought ideas about the iconography of temples and the depiction of the Buddha.

which remain impressive even today. When Buddhism arrived in China with the silk-route merchants, Chinese merchants were already familiar with it, and the new religion appeared cosmopolitan rather than exclusively Indian.

Buddhism persevered in China, securing patronage in several regional courts, capturing the hearts of millions of followers, and ultimately becoming one of the unifying elements in Chinese culture. Eventually it mixed with Confucianism and Daoism, bringing popular new spiritual, intellectual, cultural, and ritual innovations.

Reunification under the Sui and Tang Dynasties

Despite almost 400 years of imperial fragmentation, many elements of Chinese unity were potentially at hand: language, ideology, culture, administration at the local level, aristocratic families with deep roots, and sufficient imperial prestige

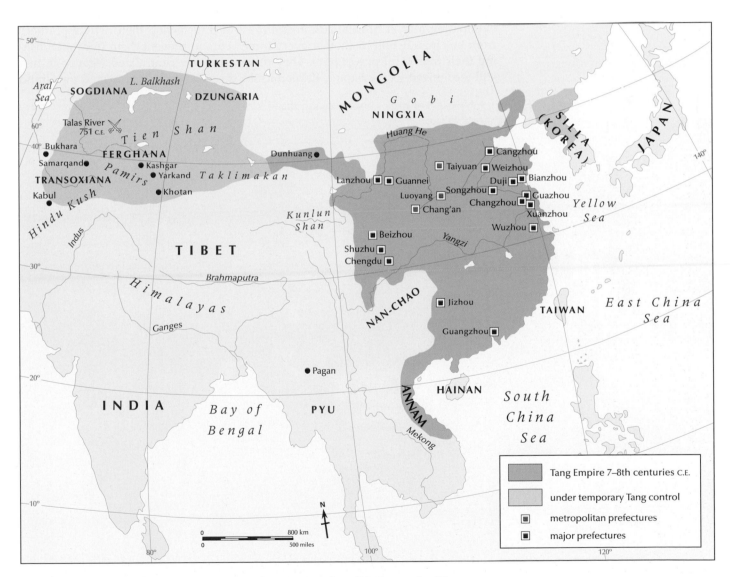

The Tang revival. The Sui dynasty (581–618 C.E.) and its successor, the politically organized Tang, restored the Chinese imperial impulse four centuries after the decline of the Han, extending control along the silk route as far as the Tien Shan mountain range and the arid Ferghana basin. Trade flourished. China finally reached its western limits when its forces were defeated by the imperial armies of the Muslim Abbasid empire at the Talas River in 751 C.E.

7.1

7.2

7.3   What were
       the elements
7.4   of China's
       underlying unity?

and administrative expertise that even China's conquerors were assimilated to it. To reunite the empire required the restoration of military power, economic productivity, and administrative integration. The Sui dynasty (581–618 C.E.) provided all three.

The Short-lived Sui Dynasty. The Sui dynasty was founded by the emperor Wen (Yang Chien) (r. 581–604 C.E.), a general from one of the northern Chinese states, who usurped power in his own state and then succeeded in conquering and unifying all of inner China. Militarily, Wen raised the status of his militia, settled them on their own lands, and gave them property rights. He thus created an effective, committed, and loyal standing army of peasant-farmers. A powerful crossbow, protective body armor, and constant drills to achieve precision in maneuvers and battle made these troops a formidable fighting force.

Ideologically, the first Sui emperor and his son Yang (Yang Kuang) (r. 604–15), who succeeded him, employed a combination of Confucian, Daoist, and Buddhist symbolism and practice to win popular loyalty. Administratively, they centralized authority, eliminating a layer of local administrators and transferring their own appointees from one jurisdiction to another every three years to prevent them from establishing their own local power base. They drew up a new centralized legal code that still recognized local customs. Economically, the Sui dynasty completed the Grand

Canal at Suzhou. From about the fifth century B.C.E., the Chinese built canals, partly to tame their rivers, mostly to facilitate trade. The Sui dynasty (581–618 C.E.) connected the major sections of the existing north–south canals to the Grand Canal of China, the longest canal in the world, stretching from Hangzhou in the south to Beijing in the north. As the Grand Canal passed through cities, such as Suzhou, it also connected to canals within the city for local trade.

7.1

7.2

7.3

7.4

What were
the elements
of China's
underlying unity?

Canal from Hangzhou in the south to Luoyang in the center. The canal linked the Yangzi and Yellow river systems, and extensions connected it to the rebuilt capital in Chang'an and, later, to Beijing. The canal allowed the transportation of the agricultural produce of the rapidly developing south to the political-military centers of the north.

The expense of mobilizing and dispatching imperial troops and administrators on their far-flung missions depleted the treasury of the Sui dynasty. The Grand Canal produced many economic benefits, but it cost dearly in manpower. Built in seven years, the canal required the labor of 5.5 million people, and to complete some sections, all commoners between the ages of 15 and 55 were pressed into service. As many as 50,000 police supervised the construction, flogging and chaining those who could not or would not work, and ordering every fifth family to provide one person to supply and prepare food. In addition to these public works, three costly and disastrous military campaigns in Korea and central Asia wasted lives and treasure and sapped the loyalty of the troops. Finally, the leading general of the Sui seized control of the state and, under the imperial name Gaozu, established the new Tang dynasty in 618.

When the Sui fell, after overextending itself militarily and economically, the Tang dynasty (618–907) continued and even strengthened these attributes of empire. Moreover, the Sui and Tang extended China's reign to truly imperial dimensions—that is, beyond China proper to "outer China," Mongolia, Turkestan, and central Asia, as far as the frontiers of modern Afghanistan, Pakistan, and Iran. China also held strong cultural sway over Tibet, although without achieving direct political control. These lands were larger than all of "inner China" in area, although they held perhaps only 5 percent of its population. In addition, Tang China held northern Vietnam and, briefly, northern Korea. China's cultural influence at this time was extremely strong in Japan as well (see below).

Arts and Technology under the Tang Dynasty. Tang policies built on those of the Sui, consolidating and improving them where possible. The Tang dynasty relied more than ever on the imperial examination system to provide its administrators, and in 754 the emperor founded a new Imperial Academy, the Han-Lin Yuan (the Forest of Pens).

The arts and technology, often reinforcing each other, flourished under the Tang as never before. The world's first block printing was invented, partly in response to the needs of Buddhists to disseminate their doctrines, for under the Tang the Buddhist religious establishment became increasingly powerful. Buddhist religious art found expression also in further cave sculptures and paintings. New ceramic manufacturing methods led to the production of the first true porcelain, a product of great beauty and durability. For centuries, China alone knew the secret of its manufacture. Millers developed machinery and gears for converting linear and

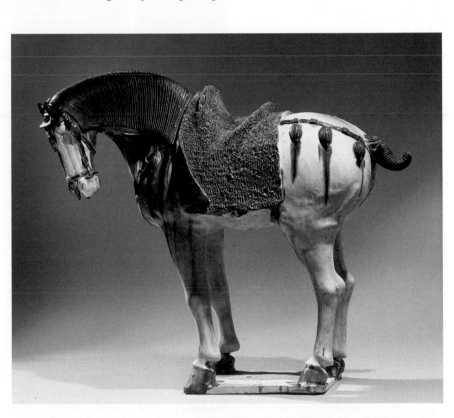

Pottery figure of a Ferghana horse, excavated from a tomb, Tang dynasty (618–907 C.E.). The Tang dynasty opened the Grand Canal, stimulated growth in trade, and expanded the boundaries of the empire. For much of this they were dependent on the mobility of the army, which in turn was dependent for covering great distances on the famed Ferghana horses, immortalized in literature as "the horses that sweated blood." (Idemitsu Museum of Arts, Tokyo)

7.1

7.2

7.3   What were
       the elements
7.4   of China's
       underlying unity?

Ceramic model of a group of musicians seated on a camel, Tang dynasty (618–907 C.E.), excavated from a tomb in a suburb of Xi'an. The beards, facial features, and costumes of some of the musicians in this group suggest that they are from central Asia. Such models, commonly found in the tombs of the Tang elite, are evidence of a taste for the goods that came along the silk route from the west, and for the central Asian music that accompanied them.

rotary motion, encouraging further development of both water- and windmills. In 659, China produced the world's first pharmacopoeia, which listed the contents and uses of all known medicines.

Finally, Tang-era poetry of meditation, nature, politics, fate, suffering, and individual identity transmitted its living legacy even to today's readers in China and beyond. Each of the three most famous Tang poets has been seen as linked to a different cultural tradition: Wang Wei (701–62) to Buddhism; Li Bai (Li Bo) (701–61) to Daoism; and Du Fu (Tu Fu) (712–70) to Confucianism, although each was influenced by all three traditions. Du Fu's "Autumn Meditation" expresses the tension between the high-stakes hustle-bustle of the imperial court under stress and his own desire for a life of peace within nature:

> I've heard them say Chang'an's like a chessboard;
> sad beyond bearing, the happenings of these hundred years!
> Mansions of peers and princes, all with new owners now;
> in civil or martial cap and garb, not the same as before.
> Over mountain passes, due north, gongs and drums resound;
> wagons and horses pressing west speed the feather-decked dispatches.
> Fish and dragons sunk in sleep, autumn rivers cold;
> old homeland, those peaceful times, forever in my thoughts!

(trans. Watson, p. 134)

The three centuries of Sui and Tang rule consolidated the theory and practice of Chinese imperial rule even to the present (although today there is no emperor). Since 581, China has been divided into two administrations only once, in 1127–75, and fragmented into several regions only twice, in 907–59 and 1916–49. Apart from these three periods, totalling 133 years, China has stood united for a continuous period of more than 14 centuries.

7.1
7.2
7.3
7.4

What were
the elements
of China's
underlying unity?

Caravanserai, **Kirghizstan, Tang dynasty (618–907 C.E.).** The silk route led traders through hundreds of miles of inhospitable terrain, such as this barren and mountainous region of Kirghizstan in central Asia. This Tang dynasty-era *caravanserai*, the oldest complete example in existence, would have protected traders from the elements and from preying bandits.

What is the
meaning of
"empire" in
relation to China?

Imperial China

7.4   What is the meaning of "empire" in relation to China?

We opened this unit on empires by noting that the word "empire" signifies rule by one people over another. Let us examine this definition in relation to China. First, within the borders of China, empire frequently meant the **assimilation** of others. In the north, many of the tribal groups against which China fought and against which its rulers constructed the Great Wall nevertheless came to enlist in China's armies, settle its land, assimilate its culture, adopt its language and calligraphy, and intermarry with its peoples.

The ethnic Chinese and the "barbarians" regarded this process as mutually beneficial. Both also understood the dangers: the barbarians might lose their culture and even find themselves in civil war with others of their ethnic group who rejected assimilation; the Chinese might be conquered by their new allies. Indeed, both of these results did occur frequently, and the interchanges transformed the cultures of both the barbarians and the Chinese.

The West and Northwest

The most geographically far-reaching of China's expansions beyond the borders of inner China were to the northwest and west. Emperor Wu's expansion into Gansu and beyond did not survive the early Han dynasty; similarly, the expansion of the Sui and Tang even deeper into central Asia did not survive the Battle of the Talas River and the An Lushan revolt. Nevertheless, China's cultural and symbolic influence over these regions persisted, even after its political, military, and direct economic power was gone. (In the seventeenth century, under the Qing dynasty, China returned to dominate these areas, and it rules them today.)

The South and Southwest

Processes of assimilation also took place in southern China, but they have made much less of a mark in the records. China as an ethnic, cultural, and political entity developed first in the north, around the Yellow River, but as Chinese peoples moved south of the Yangzi they met people of other ethnic groups. As the Chinese encroached, some southern peoples retreated still further south to preserve and develop their own separate national identities. The Vietnamese are the clearest example of this pattern. Other groups of southerners remained as distinct, separate tribal groups, usually in remote areas somewhat difficult to access. Occasionally, these peoples revolted against the Chinese invasion and takeover of their land. The Miao gave the clearest example of this response. Most of the rest assimilated, including some Vietnamese and Miao, without making a lasting impression on the historical records.

Vietnam

For a thousand years China held Annam (northern Vietnam) as a colony. The Han dynasty conquered Annam and incorporated the area as a province of China in 111 B.C.E. It remained part of China until 939 C.E., when, not long after the collapse of the Tang, the Vietnamese rebel Ngo Quyen declared himself king of the independent state of Dai Viet.

During and after Chinese colonization, the Vietnamese were locked in a love–hate relationship with Chinese culture and politics. Chinese scholars and officials, many of them fleeing imperial policies in China, brought to Vietnam their own ideographic script, Confucian ethical principles, and the Confucian literary classics. The Vietnamese adopted them all.

KEY TERM

assimilation The process by which different ethnic groups lose their distinctive cultural identity through contact with the dominant culture of a society, and gradually become absorbed and integrated into it.

What is the meaning of "empire" in relation to China?

Buddhism also arrived in Vietnam by way of China. The rest of Southeast Asia absorbed Buddhism in its Theravada form from India; Vietnam adopted Mahayana Buddhism as it had developed in China, after about the fifth century C.E. These cultural innovations appealed primarily to the Vietnamese aristocracy. At the level of practical technology, the Chinese also introduced a number of valuable agricultural innovations: the construction of a huge network of dams and waterworks that protect against monsoon flooding every year; the use of human excrement as fertilizer; market gardening; and intensive pig farming.

Although they adopted many Chinese customs, the Vietnamese resented foreign hegemony by the colossus to its north. For example, the two Trung sisters led a military revolt in 39 C.E., succeeded in evicting the Chinese, ruled jointly over Vietnam for

HOW DO WE KNOW?

Poetry as a Source for History

Du Fu's "Ballad of the Army Carts" repeats the heartbreaking pain of war as the troops describe the seemingly endless fighting and dying:

Carts rattle and squeak,
Horses snort and neigh—
Bows and arrows at their waists, the conscripts march away.
Fathers, mothers, children, wives run to say goodbye.
The Xianyang Bridge in clouds of dust is hidden from the eye.
They tug at them and stamp their feet, weep, and obstruct their
  way.
The weeping rises to the sky.
Along a road a passer-by
Questions the conscripts. They reply:
They mobilize us constantly. Sent northwards at fifteen
To guard the River, we were forced once more to volunteer,
Though we are forty now, to man the western front this year.
The headman tied our headcloths for us when we first left here.
We came back white-haired—to be sent again to the frontier.
Those frontier posts could fill the sea with the blood of those
  who've died,
But still the Martial Emperor's aims remain unsatisfied.
In county after county to the east, Sir, don't you know,
In village after village only thorns and brambles grow,
Even if there's a sturdy wife to wield the plough and hoe,
The borders of the fields have merged, you can't tell east from
  west.
It's worse still for the men from Qin, as fighters they're the
  best—
And so, like chickens or like dogs, they're driven to and fro.
Though you are kind enough to ask,
Dare we complain about our task?
Take, Sir, this winter. In Guanxi
The troops have not yet been set free.
The district officers come to press
The land tax from us nonetheless.
But, Sir, how can we possibly pay?
Having a son's a curse today.
Far better to have daughters, get them married—
A son will lie lost in the grass, unburied.
Why, Sir, on distant Qinhhai shore

The bleached ungathered bones lie year on year.
New ghosts complain, and those who died before
Weep in the wet grey sky and haunt the ear.

(Seth, pp. 48–49)

Du Fu probably wrote this poem of exhaustion and discontent after two decisive and disastrous military operations. In the first, the Battle of the Talas River, on one of the most distant of China's western frontiers, 2,000 miles from Chang'an, Arab armies defeated China in 751. China lost control of its central Asian holdings, and the silk route was opened to the cultural influence of Islam, which displaced Buddhism and Confucianism. Four years later, An Lushan, one of China's frontier generals of Turkish extraction, revolted. Although the Chinese put down the revolt in 763, the cost of the warfare, and the vulnerability it revealed, weakened the Tang dynasty for the entire century and a half leading up to its fall.

The Tang dynasty had extended China's border farther than any other except the Qing (Manchu), which ruled 1,000 years later (1644–1912). Tang holdings in central Asia had flanked and protected the silk route and brought new opportunities for wealth. Ultimately, however, these lands cost more than they brought in economically and militarily. The border groups—Turks, Uighurs, Khitans, and other ethnic groups—no longer accepted Chinese domination, but continually probed the Tang border fortifications. Finally, China ceded control of central Asia to them. In China proper, agricultural and commercial wealth continued to grow, but the central, imperial government could no longer control it. Regional rulers grew in authority and power. In 907 the Tang dynasty finally disappeared, as China splintered into ten separate states. Yet the imperial idea and pattern held. In 960 the Song dynasty arose, ruling all of China until 1127, and the south until 1279.

- What elements of the poem might suggest that Du Fu was influenced by Confucianism?
- Who is the poem's main speaker? What are his feelings about the war?
- How does the poem help us to understand the feelings of the Chinese after the battle's defeat and subsequent developments?

7.1
7.2
7.3
7.4 What is the meaning of "empire" in relation to China?

two years, but committed suicide when their revolt was crushed. They are revered in Vietnam to this day. Leaders of numerous less dramatic revolts against China are also viewed as national heroes, yet, paradoxically, the most profound adoption of Chinese administrative reforms occurred in the fifteenth century, when Vietnam was independent. As a result of Chinese direct rule in the earlier period and Chinese power and proximity during later periods of Vietnamese independence, the country became a Confucian state, with an examination system, an intellectually elitist administration somewhat aloof from the masses, and an intense desire for independence from China.

Korea

Korea came under direct Chinese rule only briefly, but Chinese cultural hegemony profoundly influenced the peninsula. The Han Emperor Wu first conquered north ern Korea in 109–108 B.C.E., along with Manchuria. Military garrisons established Chinese control and influence.

Korea, like Vietnam, had borrowed heavily from prehistoric China, including much of Shang technology and, later, iron technology, paper production, printing, lacquerwork, porcelain (although Korean double-fired, pale-green celadon ware had a distinct beauty all its own), wheat and rice agriculture, and the ideographs of written language. In 1446 C.E., at the initiative of their king, Koreans created a written system called *han'gul*, based on phonetics, which they proudly describe as the most scientifically formulated of all the world's scripts. Until after World War II, however, Korean elites suppressed the use of the simple *han'gul*, preferring the more prestigious, more elitist, and more difficult Chinese ideographs.

After the collapse of the Han in 220 C.E., Korea broke free of direct control, although it remained a **vassal** of the Chinese. Some of China's colonies remained in place, but without military capacity. The Sui dynasty sent three expeditions to conquer Korea, but all ended in disaster. The expansive Tang dynasty also tried to retake Korea in the seventh century and succeeded in occupying much of the peninsula in 668–76 C.E. Ultimately, however, Korea regained and maintained its independence, although it was often forced to accept **tributary status**, acknowledging China's regional dominance.

China's power over Korea can be seen far more in terms of cultural hegemony than in terms of political-military rule. Confucianism, law codes, bureaucratic administration, literature, art, and Mahayana Buddhism entered Korean life from China, independent of government pressure. In 935 C.E., after the fall of the Tang, Korea's Silla dynasty also fell. The Koryo dynasty, which took its place, built a new capital at Kaesong, just north of today's South Korean capital, Seoul, and modeled it on Chang'an, the Tang capital in China. Both China and Korea spoke of a "younger brother/older brother" relationship between the two countries.

Japan

China never conquered Japan, but Japan did accept China's cultural hegemony. Indeed, through the seventh and eighth centuries C.E. Japan actively and enthusiastically attempted to model its state, religion, technology, art, and language on those of China. As the Korean peninsula stands between the Chinese mainland and the four major islands of Japan, much of the importation of Chinese forms came to Japan through Korea.

Immigration and Cultural Influences. Although archaeological records show that Japan was populated by the Jomon people of the coastal regions at least as early as 10,000 B.C.E., rice agriculture seems to have begun only about 300 B.C.E., when it was introduced from southern China. Bronze tools and weapons arrived about the first century B.C.E., and the technology for making iron tools about 200 years later.

KEY TERMS

vassal A low-ranking political ruler or state that is subordinate and pays homage to a more powerful one.

tributary status The relationship of a low-ranking state to a more powerful one, recognized formally by the regular payment of tribute.

Waves of immigrants from Korea and China arrived in Japan between about 200 B.C.E. and about 500 C.E. By 500 C.E., approximately one-third of Japan's nobility claimed Korean or Chinese descent, and many artisans and metalworkers in Japan had come from Korea. All was not peaceful between Japan and Korea, however, and invasions and raids were launched from both sides. In this period, the Chinese represented the Japanese by an ideograph that signifies "dwarf," presumably suggesting an inferior status.

In 405 C.E., a Korean scribe named Wani traveled to Japan to teach the Chinese script. This became Japan's earliest written language, and Japan's recorded history begins only in the eighth century C.E. Most of our knowledge of these earlier years comes either from archaeological records or from references in the literature of China and Korea. These archaeological and literary materials tell of the formation of an embryonic Japanese state about the third century C.E., when a clan of people worshiping the sun goddess established their rule over the Yamato Plain in central Honshu Island. Ultimately, the imperial line of Japan claimed descent from this group. They used Chinese written characters and accepted elements of both Confucianism and Buddhism to enrich the polytheistic practices of the indigenous religion, Shinto, and its deification of the Japanese emperor.

After China succeeded in reestablishing its own powerful empire under the Sui and Tang dynasties, Japanese rulers dispatched numerous delegations of hundreds of members each to China to learn and adopt Chinese models. The Chinese calendar and many methods of government were introduced. In 604 C.E. a new 17-point "constitution" was introduced, a guide that was modeled on Chinese practice. The document included reverence for Confucianism and Buddhism, and for the sovereign of Japan, and, on a more mundane level, asserted the government's monopoly over the collection of taxes.

Officially, the Japanese elite recognized the emperor as the head of Japan, but, in fact, he was little more than a figurehead; real power belonged to those behind the throne. Bloody struggles for control of the court in Japan brought Nakatomi no Kamatari to power in 645 C.E. He took the surname Fujiwara, and under this name his family dominated the politics of Japan for centuries to come. (One descendant, Prince Konoe Fumimaro, served as prime minister in 1937–39 and again in 1940–41.) Fujiwara adopted Chinese culture, religion, and government as the way to centralize and unify Japan and to assert his own control. He proclaimed the Taika ("great change") reforms in 646 C.E., consolidating provincial administration and constructing an extensive road system. The reforms also abolished private ownership of land and redistributed it at each generational change.

In 710 C.E. two acts further consolidated centralized rule. First, a new capital, modeled on Chang'an, was built at Nara. Second, the Japanese ruler now claimed to rule through divine mandate, although, unlike the Chinese Mandate of Heaven, it could never be revoked. (To this day, the same family occupies the imperial throne, although after World War II, its divinity

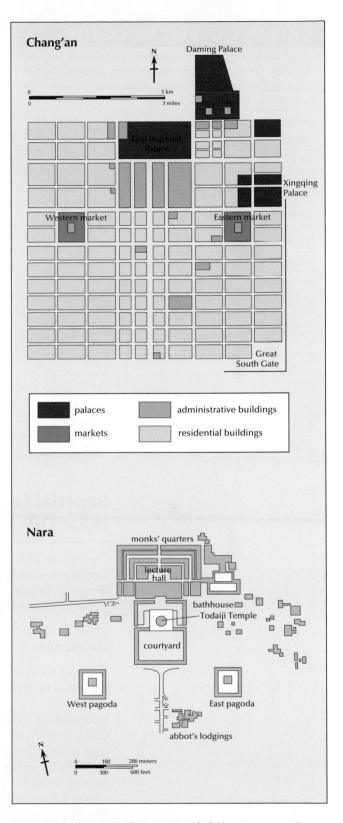

Asian imperial capitals. The Tang capital of Chang'an was grid-planned as a massive rectangle more than five miles square, focusing on the imperial quarters and housing about a million people within its walls. The newly centralized Japanese Yamato state built Nara in imitation of Chang'an: a grid plan incorporated the Todaiji Temple complexes.

233

CHINA'S IMPERIAL DYNASTIES

Listed below are all the imperial dynasties, starting with the Qin, and the two major preimperial ruling houses. Gaps in the date sequences mark those periods when the country was divided between two or more rulers.

Shang	c. 1600–1100 B.C.E.
Zhou	c. 1100–256
Qin	221–206
Han	202 B.C.E.–220 C.E.
Three Kingdoms: Kingdom of Shu Han, Kingdom of Wei, Kingdom of Wu	220–65
Northern and Southern Dynasties	265–589
Western Jin	265–317
Eastern Jin	317–419
Northern Wei	386–534
Sui	581–618
Tang	618–907
Song	960–1279
Yuan (Mongol)	1279–1368
Ming	1368–1644
Manchu (Qing)	1644–1912

was officially repudiated.) At about the same time, again following Chinese models, the Japanese began to record their history for the first time, in the *Nihongi* (in Chinese), and their legends in the *Kojiki*, which was written in a mixture of Chinese and Japanese forms.

The emperor served as the chief priest of Japan's Shinto faith, but as Shinto is a religion that worships the gods of nature—streams, trees, rocks—it can be practiced anywhere. Buddhism, by contrast, provides a more centralized form of organization, through monasteries and temples. Many new Buddhist temples were, therefore, constructed in Chinese form at Nara to centralize worship in Japan. From that time onward Buddhism and Shinto have coexisted in Japan, with millions of Japanese declaring themselves devotees of both faiths.

As centuries passed and Japan became more secure in its own political organization and cultural identity, the reliance on Chinese models declined. But in the centuries when its basic cultural and political identity was formed, Japan had followed carefully and devotedly the hegemonic examples of China, without compulsion or force of any sort.

📖 **Read** the **Document: Selection from Nihongi, "The Age of the Gods"** on **MyHistoryLab**

Imperial Legacies for the Future:
What Difference Do They Make?

The Roman and Chinese empires are among the greatest in history in terms of longevity, population, geographical extent, and lasting influence. A comparison between them will help to clarify the characteristics and significance of each and to establish guidelines for thinking about other empires of other times, and our own.

Differences

Not surprisingly, there are important differences between these two huge empires, separated by such great distances.

Geopolitical. China's heartland was far larger and more cohesive, geographically and culturally, than Rome's. Rome had as its heartland only central Italy, and even after conquering Italy, it held just that single peninsula bounded by the Alps and the Mediterranean Sea. In the time of Augustus in Rome and the Han dynasty in China, the Roman and Chinese empires each held about 60 million people, but in Rome only a few of those millions lived in Italy. In China virtually all inhabited "inner China." Ninety percent of them were in the north China plain.

Ideological. Although Confucian China spoke of a mythological golden age of equality among people living in harmony with one another and with nature, realistically the Confucianists believed that the best possible government was a well-ordered empire. Many philosophers and writers in imperial Rome, on the other hand, believed in an actual, historical republican past (albeit an idealized past), and always looked back to it as a golden age. Roman imperial expansion and stratification were often regarded as violations of the earlier republican ideals.

Longevity and Persistence. Rome's empire rose, fell, and disappeared, although it lived on as a concept. China's empire has lasted for the past 2,000 years. Dynasties have come and gone, sometimes the empire has broken into fragments, and sometimes it has been ruled by conquering "barbarians," but finally the empire endured as a single political entity. Today, although there is no emperor, China's geopolitical unity continues.

Policy and Powers of Assimilation. As China moved both north and south, it assimilated a great number of the peoples it invaded and conquered. Nonethnic Chinese were absorbed culturally and biologically. Many of the 95 percent of today's Chinese population who are called "Han" are descended from ancestors who were not. Confucian and Buddhist ideology held the empire together, supported by the power of the emperor and his armies. Rome's empire was held together by law and backed by military power. Selected non-Romans could gain citizenship under law, but ethnically and culturally the conquered peoples remained "other." Intermarriage with noncitizens was usually forbidden. Romans maintained the cultural distinctions between themselves and those they conquered far more than did the Chinese.

Language Policy. The Chinese language unified the Chinese Empire across space and through time—even today—far more than Latin did the Roman Empire. Chinese was never subordinated to another language and culture, as Latin was to Greek for many years and in many regions. Nor did Chinese compete with regional languages as Latin ultimately did. Indeed, Chinese helped to bring even neighboring countries—Vietnam, Korea, and Japan—together into a single general cultural unit.

Ideology and Cultural Cohesion. China's Confucian bureaucracy provided a core cultural identity throughout the empire and beyond. Even the alternative political-cultural philosophies of China—such as Daoism, Legalism, and, later, Buddhism—usually (but not always) served to broaden and augment the attraction of Confucianism. Rome's emperor worship did reinforce its cohesion, but its principal philosophies of polytheism, Stoicism, and, later, Christianity did not significantly buttress or augment its imperial rule. The last two may even have diminished popular loyalty to the empire, except in its later continuation in the east as the Byzantine Empire.

Influence on Neighbors. The Roman Empire influenced the lands it conquered, but had less influence on those outside its boundaries. China exercised lasting hegemonic influence even on neighbors it did not conquer, such as Japan, or conquered only briefly, such as Korea. A considerable part of this legacy was religious and cultural as well as political, economic, and administrative.

Similarities

The many points of similarity between China and Rome reveal some basic truths about the nature of empire.

Relations with Barbarians. Both empires faced nomadic groups from central Asia who threatened and penetrated their boundaries. Indeed, the Huns, who invaded Europe, and the Xiongnu, who invaded China, may have belonged to the same ethnic group. Both empires settled the "barbarians" near their borders and enlisted them in their imperial armies. In both cases, the barbarians came to hold great power. Ultimately, however, they dismembered the Roman Empire, while they were absorbed by the Chinese.

Religious Policies. Both empires incubated foreign religions, especially in times of imperial disorder. In China, Buddhism was absorbed into Confucianism and Daoism and helped to sustain the national culture in times of political trouble. In Rome, however, Christianity did not save the empire. In fact, by challenging the significance of earthly power it may even have contributed to the empire's weakness. On the other hand, the political organization of the Roman Empire provided a model for the Roman Catholic Church.

The Role of the Emperor. Both empires ascribed divine attributes to the emperor, and both frequently had difficulty in establishing rules for imperial succession. The Romans often attempted to choose their best general, while the Chinese selected a man who could control the imperial family and court. Neither empire believed that a single imperial family should rule forever. The Chinese believed that eventually the Mandate of Heaven would pass from one dynasty to another.

Gender Relationships and the Family. The family was extremely important for both empires, and both empires subordinated women to men at all stages of life. Both drew analogies between hierarchy and loyalty in a well-run family and those in a well-run empire. Both empires used marriage as a means of confirming political alliances with foreign powers. Both periodically felt that excessive concern with sexual

The Nandaimon, or "Great South Gate," of the Todaiji Buddhist temple, 745–52 C.E. The first Japanese Buddhist temples—modeled on the Buddhist temples of China—are among the oldest surviving timber buildings in the world. So faithful and enduring are they that they have become our best examples of Chinese architecture for the period.

relationships distracted energy from the demands of sustaining the empire, and both proclaimed strict codes of sexual morality.

The Significance of Imperial Armies. In both empires the army was crucial in creating and sustaining the political structure in the face of domestic and foreign enemies. The Roman Empire was established and ruled by generals, as were the Qin, Han, Sui, and Tang dynasties in China. Both empires were periodically threatened and usurped by rebel generals asserting their own authority. The cost of the armies, especially on distant, unprofitable expeditions, often drained the finances of the government and encouraged its subjects to evade taxes and military service and even to rise in revolt. Both empires established colonies of soldier-colonizers to garrison and develop remote areas while simultaneously providing compensation and retirement benefits for the troops.

Overextension. Both empires suffered their greatest challenges in confronting simultaneously the strains of overexpansion and the subsequent internal revolts that were triggered by the costs incurred. In Rome these dual problems, along with the barbarian invasions, finally precipitated the end of the empire in the west. In China they led to the loss of the Mandate of Heaven and the downfall of dynasties. The external battles against Qin-Jurchen border tribes, for example, combined with the revolt of the Yellow Turbans, brought down the later Han; the loss of the distant Battle of the Talas River, combined with the internal revolt of An Lushan, sapped Tang power.

Public Works Projects. Throughout their empire the Romans built roads, aqueducts, public monumental structures, administrative/military towns, and the great capital cities of Rome and Constantinople. The Chinese built the Great Wall, the Grand Canal, systems of transportation by road and water, public monumental structures, administrative/military towns throughout the empire, and several successive capitals, notably Chang'an and Luoyang.

The Concentration of Wealth. In both empires, the benefits of imperial wealth tended to flow toward the center and to the elite in the capital cities. The capitals grew to unprecedented size. Both Chang'an and Rome housed more than one million people.

Policies for and against Individual Mobility. To maintain power and stability in the face of demands for change, both empires periodically bound their peasantry to the soil and demanded that the sons of soldiers follow their fathers' occupation. Both found these policies difficult to enforce. Both offered some individual mobility through service in their armies. In addition, the Chinese examination system allowed advancement within the imperial bureaucracy.

Revolts. Both empires experienced frequent revolts against the emperor and his policies. In Rome, which housed a much larger slave population, slaves led some of the revolts. In China they were more typically initiated by peasants. Rome attempted to forestall mass revolts in the capital and other large cities through the provision of "bread and circuses." Both empires faced constant challenges from those living on their peripheries.

Peasant Flight. In both empires during times of upheaval, peasants sought to evade taxes and conscription by finding refuge as tenants on large, landed estates. Whenever imperial government was weak, the largest of these estates challenged the power of the central government.

The influence of the early Chinese Empire continues today, not only in China itself, but also in East Asia, Southeast Asia, and central Asia. Consistent patterns in language, culture, geopolitical organization, and international relations are there to be discovered through the ages. The same is true of Rome throughout the areas it ruled directly in Western and southern Europe, the Mediterranean, and North Africa. To a lesser degree, its influence extends to eastern Europe and to the European settler colonies in the Americas, Australia, and New Zealand. The imperial ideals of China and Rome have entranced many who have studied them, and repelled many as well. As we turn to study the empires of ancient India, these models help to guide our thinking.

CHAPTER REVIEW

THE QIN DYNASTY

7.1   What were the philosophies of rule in the Chinese empire?

Confucianism, Daoism, and Legalism emerged as the leading philosophies of government and of life in China. The Qin dynasty favored Legalism, implementing strict laws and strict enforcement, with rewards for people who followed the laws and swift punishment for those who broke them. Confucianism, adopted by the Han, and generally dominant thereafter, held that good government depended on good officials, moral men of humanity and virtue, wisdom and order. Confucius thought such men could be fashioned through proper education. The Qin burned the books of the Confucianists and apparently killed many Confucian scholars; the Han, Confucian scholars in turn, vilified the Legalists. Daoism was a mystical philosophy, not directly applicable to government. It believed in simplicity and the power of a natural order or path (Dao). Alongside all of these philosophies, Chinese imperial authorities also recognized the importance of a large, powerful imperial army to carry out its will, and it recognized the importance of a productive, accommodative peasantry.

THE HAN DYNASTY

7.2   How did Confucianism influence the Chinese bureaucracy?

Following Confucian principles, a social and political hierarchy emerged in Han China, with scholars at the top, followed by farmers, artisans, and merchants. The Confucian value of the importance of tradition and continuity prevailed, and an elite academy was established to teach scholar-bureaucrats Confucianism's applicability to governing. The Chinese legal system was codified according to Confucian principles. The emperor declared that knowledge of the Confucian classics should be a basis for promotion in the imperial civil service, a principle that was finally established in the examination system of the Tang dynasty.

DISINTEGRATION AND REUNIFICATION

7.3   What were the elements of China's underlying unity?

Even during periods of disintegration, between imperial dynasties, an underlying unity has endured in China. Its cultural and ethical ideologies kept its traditions of unity alive: the arts, painting, calligraphy, poetry; its language, ideology, administration, and theory and practice of imperial rule. China's Confucian bureaucracy provided a core cultural identity throughout space and time.

IMPERIAL CHINA

7.4   What is the meaning of "empire" in relation to China?

The extension of the Chinese empire frequently meant the assimilation of others. Most of the tribal peoples that China conquered gradually came to enlist in China's armies, assimilate its culture, adopt its language and calligraphy, and marry its people. The ethnic Chinese, too, considered this process mutually beneficial. China also exercised lasting hegemonic influence on people it did not conquer, such as the Japanese, who, unforced, adopted many Chinese patterns of life and culture, architecture and politics as they formed their own identity.

Suggested Readings

PRINCIPAL SOURCES

Blunden, Caroline, and Mark Elvin. *Cultural Atlas of China* (New York: Facts on File, 1983). Excellent introductory coverage to history and culture, lavishly illustrated with maps and pictures. Excellent as both narrative and reference.

de Bary, William Theodore, ed., *Sources of East Asian Tradition*, Vol. 1: *Premodern Asia* (New York: Columbia University Press, 2008). Selections from Columbia's outstanding series on China, Japan, and Korea.

de Bary, William Theodore, and Irene Bloom, eds. *Sources of Chinese Tradition*, Vol. I: *From Earliest Times to 1600* (New York: Columbia University Press, 2nd ed., 1999). The premier primary source reference to the thought of the elite of ancient China.

Ebrey, Patricia Buckley, ed. *Chinese Civilization: A Sourcebook* (New York: The Free Press, 2nd ed., 1993). This primary sourcebook covers social and economic materials of everyday life of common people.

Ebrey, Patricia Buckley, Anne Walthall, and James Palais. *East Asia: A Cultural, Social, and Political History*, Vol. 1: *To 1800* (Florence, KY: Wadsworth Publishing Co., 3rd ed., 2013).

Elvin, Mark. *The Pattern of the Chinese Past* (Stanford, CA: Stanford University Press, 1973). Most Chinese history has been written dynasty by dynasty. Elvin seeks to identify deeper patterns of change in the economy and social life. Introduces new approaches.

Twitchett, Denis, ed. *The Cambridge History of China*, Vol. III: *Sui and T'ang China, 589–906*, Part I (Cambridge: Cambridge University Press, 1979). Comprehensive, standard compendium of analysis and narrative.

Twitchett, Denis, and Michael Lowe, eds. *The Cambridge History of China*, Vol. I: *The Ch'in and Han Empires, 221 B.C.–A.D. 220* (Cambridge: Cambridge University Press, 1986). Comprehensive, standard compendium of analysis and narrative.

Waley, Arthur, trans. *The Book of Songs* (New York: Grove Press, 1996). Classic text from a master translator.

Watson, Burton, trans. *The Selected Poems of Du Fu* (New York: Columbia University Press, 2002). An excellent selection and translation.

ADDITIONAL SOURCES

Andrea, Alfred, and James H. Overfield, eds. *The Human Record*, Vol. I (Florence, KY: Wadsworth Publishing Co., 7th ed., 2011). Excellent array of primary sources, arranged and cross-referenced to provide its comprehensive course of study.

Creel, H.G. *Confucius: The Man and the Myth* (Westport, CT: Greenwood Press, reprinted 1972 from 1949 ed.). Little is known about Confucius the man. This classic study tells us what is known and how it has been represented and interpreted.

Friedman, Edward. "Reconstructing China's National Identity: A Southern Alternative to Mao-Era Anti-Imperialist Nationalism," *Journal of Asian Studies* LIII, No. 1 (February 1994), pp. 67–91. An analysis of continuing differences between China's southern, coastal, commercial regions, and its more bureaucratic and politically oriented interior and north.

Han Fei Tzu. *The Complete Works of Han Fei Tzu*, 2 vols., trans. W.K. Liao (London: Arthur Probsthain, 1959). The basis of the Legalist tradition.

Hughes, Sarah Shaver, and Brady Hughes, eds. *Women in World History*, Vol. I (Armonk, NY: M.E. Sharpe, 1995). A reader with materials drawn from all over the world.

Lattimore, Owen. *Inner Asian Frontiers of China* (London: Oxford University Press, 1940). Classic statement of the relationship between China proper and the areas north and west of the Great Wall.

Lockard, Craig A. "Integrating Southeast Asia into the Framework of World History: The Period Before 1500," *The History Teacher* XXIX, No. 1 (November 1995), pp. 7–35. Establishes a point of view for understanding Southeast Asia as a part of the world. Designed for teaching, but widely useful for its range of subjects and their context.

Murphey, Rhoads. *East Asia: A New History* (Boston, MA: Addison-Wesley, 2nd ed., 2000). Standard textbook history.

Needham, Joseph. *The Shorter Science and Civilization in China*, Vol. I, abridged by Colin A. Ronan (Cambridge: Cambridge University Press, 1978). First volume in Needham's monumental work opening up the empire's scientific accomplishments to an English-reading audience.

Past Worlds: The (London) Times Atlas of Archaeology (Maplewood, NJ: Hammond, 1988). Excellent introduction to the entire subject, including archaeology of ancient China. Lavishly illustrated with maps, pictures, and charts.

SarDesai, D.R. *Southeast Asia: Past and Present* (Boulder, CO: Westview Press, 7th ed., 2012). Standard introductory text.

——. *Southeast Asian History: Essential Readings* (Boulder, CO: Westview Press, 2006). Primary documents.

Schirokauer, Conrad, *et al. A Brief History of Chinese and Japanese Civilizations* (Florence, KY: Wadsworth Publishing Co., 4th ed., 2012). A standard text, now updated.

Schwartz, Benjamin I. *The World of Thought in Ancient China* (Cambridge, MA: Harvard University Press, 1985). Fine analysis of philosophies and policies in ancient Chinese thought and politics.

Seth, Vikram. *Three Chinese Poets: Translations of Poems by Wang Wei, Li Bai, and Du Fu* (New York: HarperCollins, 1993). Translations of classical poetry of classical poets. The insistence on rhyme is sometimes monotonous.

Sima Qian. *Historical Records*, trans. Raymond Dawson (New York: Oxford University Press, 1994). Translation from the works of China's preeminent dynastic historian. Clear and readable, with introduction to and evaluation of the historian's life and work.

——. *Records of the Historian: Chapters from the Shih Chi of Ssu-ma Ch'ien*, trans. Burton Watson (New York: Columbia University Press, 1969). Translation from the works of China's preeminent dynastic historian. Places the work in the context of Chinese history and literature.

Sullivan, Michael. *The Arts of China* (Berkeley, CA: University of California Press, 4th rev. ed., 2000). Well-illustrated introduction to classical Chinese painting, sculpture, and fine arts.

Sun Tzu [Sunzi]. *The Art of War*, trans. Thomas Cleary (Boston, MA: Shambhala, 1988). Accessible translation of the classic treatise on fighting a war, often through not fighting. A Zen approach. Consulted by Chinese strategists, including Mao.

Waley, Arthur, trans. *Chinese Poems* (New York: Dover, 2000). Marvelous collection.

FILMS

Hero [Yingxiong] (2002: 99 minutes) Set at the beginning of the Qin dynasty, depicts the battles and assassinations required to establish the new emperor. A blockbuster in China, directed by award-winning Zhang Yimou. Many reviewers saw it as a justification for China's dictatorial Communist government.

Red Cliff [Chi Bi] (2009: 148 minutes) As the Han dynasty declines, four generals connive and fight it out for the succession. Based on a classical story, frequently retold. This version compresses an original two-film sequence, emphasizing the battles, but the political intrigue remains.

Legacy: The Origins of Civilization—China (1992; 1 hour). Michael Wood takes us on a journey into China's past, showing highlights visually, including oracle bones. Beautifully produced. Brief interviews with a few experts. More idiosyncratic than the Time-Life documentary.

Time-Life. *Lost Civilizations: China: Dynasties of Power* (2002; 1 hour). Beautiful visual representation. Brief interviews with a few experts. More of an overview than Wood's reflections.

8 Indian Empires

Cultural Cohesion in a Divided Subcontinent

1500 B.C.E.–1100 C.E.

What do we mean by "India"? In this chapter we include the entire subcontinent of south Asia, which includes not only the present-day country of India, but also its neighbors: Pakistan, Bangladesh, Nepal, and Bhutan. Geographers call the entire region a subcontinent because it is so large and so clearly bounded by powerful natural borders. Along its entire southern perimeter it is a peninsula surrounded by oceanic waters: the Arabian Sea to the west and the Bay of Bengal to the east. To the north, the Himalaya Mountains, the highest in the world, form an almost impenetrable barrier. At the eastern and western ends of the Himalayas, rugged spurs of the great range complete the ring of demarcation, but these mountains are lower and more negotiable. Passes, such as the Khyber Pass, make entrance accessible through the northwest mountains, as does a route through the desert along the western Makran coast.

LEARNING OBJECTIVES

8.1	8.2	8.3	8.4
Describe the important literature of the Aryan immigrants.	Understand the philosophy of the Maurya and Gupta empires.	Describe the consequences of the Hunas' invasion of India.	Compare India's empires with those of China and Rome.

((Listen on MyHistoryLab

Prince Gautama, Ajanta Cave 1, Maharashtra, India, c. 450–500 C.E. The rock-cut sanctuaries of Ajanta in the northwest Deccan were abandoned for centuries until they were rediscovered in 1817 by British soldiers hunting tigers. The 29 cave temples contain some of the earliest surviving Indian painting and mark the last true flowering of Buddhist art in the subcontinent prior to the ascendancy of Hinduism. Here Prince Gautama, an earlier incarnation of the Buddha, is seated in an ornamental pavilion. Servants are pouring holy water over him.

The peoples who came to India before 3000 B.C.E., for whom we have no historical record, seem to have arrived from a variety of approaches, probably including some by sea from Africa, Southeast Asia, and the islands of the Pacific. Since 3000 B.C.E., all the major immigrations have come from the northwest. In modern times British traders and rulers also came by sea. They had an important impact on the subcontinent, but they did not stay.

The geographical area of the subcontinent is equal to about one-fourth the size of Europe. The entire region has been unified into a single empire only once, under British rule in the nineteenth and early twentieth centuries. Asoka Maurya (r. *c.* 265–238 B.C.E.) was the first person to come close to achieving that goal, but he never captured the far south. Usually, as today, a number of rulers controlled different regions of the subcontinent. It is not surprising, then, that Indian empires did not last more than a few hundred years. Yet, unlike Rome, and much more like China, India has maintained a persistent cultural unity over several thousand years. In this chapter we will begin to consider why India dissolved politically into many separate states; in the chapter entitled "Hinduism and Buddhism" we will consider the religious and cultural institutions that nevertheless served to bring a loose unity to the subcontinent. We will consider India as an empire based as much on cultural cohesion as on political and military unity.

What was the most important literature of the Aryan immigrants?

8.1

8.2

8.3

8.4

New Arrivals in South Asia

8.1 What was the most important literature of the Aryan immigrants?

The first cities in south Asia appeared in the Indus valley about 2500 B.C.E. That civilization—the Harappan—began to fade about 1500 B.C.E. for reasons that are not fully understood. Perhaps simultaneously, perhaps somewhat later, new waves of "Aryan" immigrants arrived. These new arrivals are named not for their race, but for Sanskrit and the other related **Indo–Aryan** languages they spoke. Archaeologists

KEY TERM

Indo–Aryan A subgroup of the Indo-Iranian branch of the Indo-European group of languages, also called Indic, and spoken in India, Sri Lanka, Bangladesh, and Pakistan. The Indo–Aryan languages are descended from Sanskrit, the sacred language of Hinduism.

HOW DO WE KNOW?

Pottery and Philology

Archaeology can tell us comparatively little about the Aryan way of life in the Ganges River valley. The valley is a humid, subtropical region, where heavy monsoon rains have washed away ancient settlements. It is also densely inhabited, making archaeological excavation difficult if not impossible. As a result, we know less about the Aryan settlements along the Ganges than we do about the earlier Indus valley, where the sparsely populated desert sites allowed relatively easy excavation.

Nevertheless, the distribution of pottery—painted grayware dating primarily from before 500 B.C.E., and northern black polished ware from after that date—helps us to identify and follow the waves of Aryan immigration into the Ganges valley. The more recently discovered ocher-colored pottery in the western Ganges valley and the presence of black and red ware further east suggest that by the time the Aryans arrived indigenous peoples had already settled on the land. Since the late 1970s, archaeological digs have uncovered small settlement sites dating from 1000–600 B.C.E. throughout the Ganges valley. However, it is difficult to trace in any detail the spread and nature of early Aryan civilization without additional excavations of many other cities and small towns.

Philology, the study of the origin and evolution of language as an indication of general cultural evolution, helps to establish the dispersion of Indo–Aryan peoples by tracking the spread of their languages. The first known surviving specimens of writing in the Ganges valley are Asoka's rock and pillar inscriptions in Brahmi script, which date to the third century B.C.E. To track the oral transmission patterns of earlier centuries, anthropologists study texts that recorded them in written form at a much later time, and compare them with the distribution and evolution of today's spoken languages.

• Why is there more archaeological evidence about the Indus valley than about the Ganges valley?
• What is the evidence that indigenous peoples preceded the Aryans in the Ganges valley?
• How do the study of pottery and philology complement each other in an analysis of early settlements in the Ganges valley?

8.1

What was the
most important
literature of
the Aryan
immigrants?

8.2

8.3

8.4

are not certain of the geographical origins of the new arrivals; some claim they came from central Asia, others from the Iranian plateau, while a few suggest Europe. In successive waves of immigration, the nomadic and pastoral Aryans, riding the horses of central Asia and light, spoke-wheeled chariots, mixed with indigenous peoples, migrated slowly eastward, and reached the Ganges valley about the year 1000 B.C.E.

Chronicles of the Aryan Immigrants

The greatest sources of information for the Aryan immigrations, settlements, and empires are written materials that preserve earlier oral traditions. Bards and chroniclers collected and composed these materials, although they did not attempt to establish a chronological, interpretive record of the sort found in Greece or Rome or China.

The Vedas. The earliest existing source is one of the four Vedas, the *Rigveda*, 1,028 hymns composed in Sanskrit, about 1500–1200 B.C.E., at the time the Aryans were moving into the subcontinent. The Vedas are religious reflections rather than historical records, but to the extent that they refer to the life of the Aryan peoples who wrote them, their accounts are probably reliable. They do refer to conquests made by the Aryans in the course of their migrations southward and eastward. Three other Vedas, the *Samaveda*, *Yajurveda*, and *Atharva Veda*, were composed some centuries later. Other religious literature of the Vedic millennium (1500–500 B.C.E.) include the *Brahmanas*, which give instructions on rituals and sacrifices, and the *Upanishads*, which are mystical speculations. These were composed about 700 B.C.E. and afterward.

The *Puranas*, or legends and folk tales from earliest times, were finally collected and written down between about 500 B.C.E. and 500 C.E. They contain genealogical lists of rulers from before the first humans were born until historic times, mixing fact and fable, human and divine, and making no attempt to distinguish between them. The tales of the *Puranas* bring the gods of the Aryans into the popular imagination.

The *Mahabharata* and the *Ramayana*. India's two great epics, the Mahabharata and the Ramayana, recount events that took place between 1000 and 700 B.C.E., although the texts themselves place the action in earlier mythic times. Neither is a historical account, but both provide valuable information on the social structures, the ways of life, and the values of the time in which they were written.

Some ten times longer than the Bible, the *Mahabharata* is the longest single poem in the world. Its central story is of a great civil war fought between two branches of the same family. Into its tales, subplots, and asides are woven myth, speculation, folklore, moral teaching, and political reflection, which are central to India's living culture. The intermingling of the great themes of life, death, family, warfare, duty, and power give the *Mahabharata* continuing universal appeal. The most famous single segment of the *Mahabharata* is the profound religious meditation and instruction called the *Bhagavad-Gita*, or "Song of God." The *Gita* takes the form of advice given to a warrior facing battle, but it expands into divine advice on life, death, and rebirth.

The *Ramayana*, which is much shorter, refers to somewhat later times, and there are many versions. The first known written version in Sanskrit was composed by Valmiki about 700 B.C.E. Its core story tells of the victory of the mythical god-king Rama over Ravana, the demon ruler of Sri Lanka, who had kidnapped Rama's wife, Sita. The diverse versions of the *Ramayana* indicate its great popularity and the variety of its uses. Some focus on the battles between north and south, perhaps a reference to the first Aryan invasions of the south about 800 B.C.E. Some southern versions, however, tend to justify Ravana as defending the south against Rama's invasions from the north. The role of Sita is also told in different ways. Men more frequently praise Sita for her adoration of Rama and her willingness to renounce even her life so that his reputation might remain intact. Women, however, are often critical of Rama for inadequately defending Sita in the first place, then for doubting her fidelity to him

Scenes from the *Ramayana*, Indian School, 1713 C.E. After Ravana, the many-headed king of Lanka, abducts his wife, Sita, the god-king Rama sets off to retrieve her with his brother Laxman (with bow and arrow) and an army of monkeys. This rich gouache illustration presents several chapters from the story. (British Library, London)

📖 **Read** the **Document**: Excerpt from the *Ramayana* on **MyHistoryLab**

What was the most important literature of the Aryan immigrants?

8.1

8.2

8.3

8.4

during her captivity in Sri Lanka, and, finally, for bowing to public skepticism of her loyalty by exiling her from his royal court.

Indian sailors, merchants, and priests carried their culture to Southeast Asia, and the *Ramayana* has become a national epic in several of the countries of that region, especially Thailand and Indonesia, where it is often dramatized by live actors and through puppetry. In India, the story is retold each year on the holiday of Dussehra, which celebrates the victory of good over evil with great color and pageantry. Broadcast on Indian national television in serialized form for about a year each in the mid-1980s, the *Mahabharata* and the *Ramayana* drew audiences of hundreds of millions for each weekly episode. Ever popular, these programs are rebroadcast frequently. In the 1980s, the British theater producer Peter Brook staged nine-hour versions of the *Mahabharata*—one in English and one in French—and then restructured the English version as a five-hour film and DVD.

Despite these literary sources and their implicit evidence of major political and social change, there are no purely historical written records for these crucial centuries in Indian history. Gradually, however, other records do begin to appear and to cast light on the changes that were taking place. Codes of law and statecraft, such as the *Artha-sastra* from around 300 B.C.E. and Asoka's rock inscriptions about half a century later, illuminate politics and imperial ideology. Many more such codes appeared in later times, together with Buddhist and Jain texts that usually include chronologies and some interpretation.

AT A GLANCE: INDIA 600–100 B.C.E.

DATE	POLITICS	RELIGION AND CULTURE	SOCIAL DEVELOPMENT
600 B.C.E.	• *Janapadas* established		
500 B.C.E.	• Gandhara and Sind held by Persian Empire (*c.* 518) • *Maha-janapadas* established (500–400)	• Buddha, Siddhartha Gautama (*c.* 563–483) • Puranas written (*c.* 500 B.C.E.–500 C.E.) • Vedic period ends (1500–500)	
400 B.C.E.	• Nanda dynasty in Magadha (*c.* 364–324)		
300 B.C.E.	• Alexander the Great in south Asia (327–325) • Chandragupta Maurya (r. *c.* 321–*c.* 297) founds Mauryan dynasty (324–185) in Magadha • Kautilya writes *Artha-sastra* (*c.* 300)	• *Mahabharata* and *Ramayana* (*c.* 300 B.C.E.–300 C.E.)	
250 B.C.E.	• Bindusara Maurya (r. *c.* 297–*c.* 272) • Asoka Maurya (r. *c.* 265–238)	• Rock inscriptions of Asoka • Asoka enhances spread of Buddhism • Asokan lion column	• Mauryan empire extended from Afghanistan to Bay of Bengal to Deccan
200 B.C.E.	• Sunga dynasty (185–173) • Mauryan Empire fractures, along with unity of India (185)	• Jain influence increases	
150 B.C.E.	• Menander (Milanda) king of Indo-Greek Empire (*fl.* 160–135)	• Sanchi stupa	• Trade contacts with Southeast Asia
100 B.C.E.	• First Shaka king in western India (*c.* 94)	• Sangam poetry from Tamil culture	

8.1

8.2

8.3

8.4

What was the most important literature of the Aryan immigrants?

Visitors from outside have also given periodic "snapshot" accounts of India. These include the observations by Megasthenes (*c.* 350–*c.* 290 B.C.E.), a Greek ambassador and historian sent to the court of Chandragupta Maurya about 300 B.C.E., and Menander (Milinda; *fl.* 160–135 B.C.E.), a Greek king of northwest India who became a Buddhist. Later, about 400–700 C.E., Faxian (Fa-hsien; *fl.* 399–414 C.E.) and Xuanzang (Hsuan-tsang; 602–64 C.E.), Buddhist pilgrims from China, recorded further observations. The travelers' reflections echo their own positions and interests, but in general depict a prosperous country. The earliest of the four visitors, Megasthenes describes India's geography and history, combining many myths with the actual campaigns of Alexander the Great and Indian military forces. He was also fascinated with India's caste system, which he believed to have included seven castes. Like all the travelers, he was impressed by government's respect for foreigners. Faxian, who came much later, traveled as a pilgrim to places associated with the Buddha's life. He described India as a country of rich and prosperous cities, where peace and order prevailed and the wealthy provided for the poor and the disadvantaged.

📖 **Read** the **Document**: **Excerpt from *Mahabharata* on MyHistoryLab**

The Establishment of States

Both archaeological and written sources reveal that, as they settled in India, the Aryans began to build a new urban civilization and to form new states. By 700–600 B.C.E., numerous political groupings, called *janapadas* (populated territories), began to emerge. Leadership of the territories was centered in specific family lineage groups, and as these lineages grew larger and cleared more forest land to expand their territorial control, the *janapadas* began to take on the political form of states with urban capitals and political administrations. Some constituted themselves as republics, others as monarchies. By 500–400 B.C.E., about the time the Persian armies of Darius reached the Indus, 16 large *maha-janapadas* had emerged in northern India.

KEY TERM

janapada A large political district in India, beginning about 700 B.C.E.

AT A GLANCE: INDIA 50–1100 C.E.

DATE	POLITICS	RELIGION AND CULTURE	SOCIAL DEVELOPMENT
50 C.E.	• Height of Kushana power under Emperor Kanishka (r. c. 78–c. 103)	• *Bhagavad-Gita*	
100 C.E.		• Gandhara Buddha • Rise of Mahayana Buddhism	• Trade flourishes between India and the central Asian trade routes
200 C.E.		• Increasing Hindu–Buddhist influence on Southeast Asia	
300 C.E.	• Gupta Empire (c. 320–540) established by Chandra Gupta I (r. 320–c. 330)	• Sanskrit used for official business • Hindu ascendancy over Buddhism	• Indian trade contacts with Oc Eo, Funan (300–600)
350 C.E.	• Samudra Gupta (r. c. 330–c. 380) expands dynasty throughout north and into south		
400 C.E.	• Chandra Gupta II (r. c. 380–c. 415) expands empire to maximum • Kumara Gupta (r. c. 415–55)	• Cultural "golden age" • Panini, Sanskrit grammarian (fl. c. 400) • Faxian, Buddhist pilgrim (fl. 399–414) • Ajanta caves (c. fifth to eighth century)	
450 C.E.	• Skanda Gupta (r. 455–67) repulses Huna invasion from central Asia (c. 460) • Budha Gupta (r. 467–97)	• Kalidasa composes "Meghaduta" and *Shakuntala*	• Sanskrit in Southeast Asia; Indian gods; Buddhism
500 C.E.	• Hunas gain control of north	• Classical urban culture declines	
600 C.E.	• Pallavas rise to power at Kanchipuram, south India, under Mahendravarman I (r. c. 600–c. 611) • Harsha-vardhana (r. 606–47) rules north India from Kanauj • Chalukyas rule central India under Pulakeshin II at Badami (608–42)	• Xuanzang, Buddhist pilgrim (602–64)	
700 C.E.	• Arabs conquer Sind (712)	• Ellora temple complex (757–90) (see chapter "Hinduism and Buddhism") • Borobudur, Java (778–824) • Khajuraho temple complex (1025–50) (see chapter "Hinduism and Buddhism") • Vedantic philosophy flourishes • Angkor Wat, Cambodia	
1100 C.E.	• Cholas defeat Srivijaya Empire, Sumatra		

By about 300 B.C.E. four of these large states dominated the rest, and one, Magadha, was beginning to emerge as an imperial power over all. As we saw in the chapter entitled "Dawn of the Empires," Alexander had reached the Indus in 326 B.C.E. and had wanted to continue his sweep all the way across the subcontinent to the ocean that he believed to be at the end of the world. His troops, however, mutinied, refused to proceed further, and forced Alexander to withdraw. Soon thereafter Chandragupta Maurya, the ruler of Magadha, marched his troops into northwest India to fill the power vacuum. With this triumph the Maurya dynasty began to carve out India's first empire.

The Empires of India

8.2 What were the philosophies of the Maurya and Gupta empires?

For the following 15 centuries, comparatively brief but influential empires alternated with long periods of decentralized and often weak rule. India nevertheless retained a strong sense of cultural unity, based in large part on its familial, social, economic, and

8.1

What were the philosophies of the Maurya and Gupta empires?

8.2

8.3

8.4

8.1

8.2

8.3

8.4

What were the
philosophies of
the Maurya and
Gupta empires?

religious institutions, along with its widely shared heritage of literary epics. In the following pages, therefore, we analyze not only the two major imperial dynasties of ancient India, the Mauryas and the Guptas, but also the more permanent institutions that mediated between the individual and the state. The religious philosophies and social practices of Hinduism that inspire much of the statecraft of these dynasties are discussed briefly here, and are treated much more fully in the chapter "Hinduism and Buddhism." Hinduism, as we shall see, is not a specific set of dogmas and rituals, but rather the variety of religious beliefs and practices of the peoples of India—excluding only those who explicitly reject them in favor of a different religion. This separation in the discussion of political and religious practices is somewhat artificial, but it allows us to recognize the importance of each system separately and to see them interacting in support of each other.

The Maurya Empire

The Maurya family dynasty succeeded to the throne of Magadha in 324 B.C.E. Its founder, Chandragupta Maurya (r. *c.* 321–*c.* 297 B.C.E.), may have first imagined an India-wide empire from a possible meeting with Alexander the Great, and he conquered much of northern India between 321 and 297 B.C.E. His son Bindusara (r. *c.* 297–*c.* 272 B.C.E.) expanded still further the empire that his father had created, and Bindusara's son Asoka brought the empire of the Mauryas to its greatest extent, ruling from modern Afghanistan in the northwest to the Bay of Bengal in the east and well into the Deccan peninsula in the south. By this time India may have held as many as 100 million people.

Government under the Maurya Dynasty. The Maurya dynasty created an imperial government that ruled over or displaced earlier political structures based only on family lineage. Hereditary family lineage did not cease to be important—after all, the imperial ruling dynasty was itself a lineage—but a new state apparatus stood above it in authority and power. The Mahabharata told of a large family of cousins disintegrating into two hostile armies fighting over the inheritance of power. By the time of the Mauryas, however, this kind of civil war was over. The state stood above such individual families and lineages.

The new empire expressed its theory of politics in the *Artha-sastra*, or manual of politics and economics, which has been attributed to Kautilya, a minister of Chandragupta Maurya. (The date of composition is not certain, and the text may actually have been written down later, but its ideas were current under the Mauryas. The *Artha-sastra* text was lost to historians and was rediscovered only in 1909.) The text spoke of *danda niti*, translated into English alternatively and provocatively as the "policy of the scepter" or the "policy of the big stick." It had a cutthroat view of interstate competition. Even in the earlier age of the *janapadas*, Indian political thought had already expressed itself in terms of the "justice of the fish"—that is, larger states swallowed smaller ones. The *Artha-sastra* postulated that every state must be on constant guard against its neighbors, for all were potential enemies. It counseled that strong states be hedged in through mutual treaties among their neighbors, providing a balance of power, while weak states

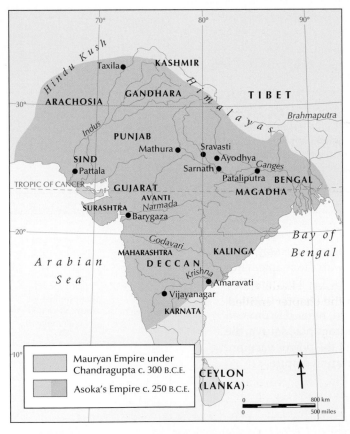

Mauryan India. A younger contemporary of Alexander the Great, Chandragupta Maurya seized control of the kingdom of Magadha and annexed lands to the west, eventually controlling by 300 B.C.E. the strategic trade routes of the Ganges and Indus basins. His grandson Asoka extended the empire west into Seleucid Persia, and south via the wealthy kingdom of Kalinga to gain control of the Deccan by 250.

8.1

8.2

8.3

8.4

What were the
philosophies of
the Maurya and
Gupta empires?

Indo-Greek coins (obverse and reverse), central Asia. The Indian subcontinent was linked to the silk route by trade routes that passed through Afghanistan and the Kushan Empire and continued westward. These economic connections account for the large quantity of Indo-Greek coinage, such as this example showing the Macedonian king Demetrius I (c. 337–283 B.C.E.). (British Museum, London)

should be attacked and conquered. The *Artha-sastra* regarded the immediate circle of neighbors as potential enemies but the next circle beyond them as potential allies, in keeping with the doctrine that "the enemy of my enemy is my friend." Kautilya's advice included suggestions for collecting taxes and encouraging trade. He was also obsessed with using spies. In this competitive world of constant warfare, the state had come into its own.

Regulating Domestic Life. The state had many internal regulatory functions, as well. First among these was the requirement to provide a stable setting in which people had the opportunity to seek the four major goals of life in accordance with Hindu philosophy: *artha* (wealth), *kama* (sensual pleasure), *dharma* (the fulfillment of social and religious duties), and *moksha* (the release from earthly existence and union with the infinite power of the universe, achieved, if at all, at the time of death).

The state helped to enforce rules of behavior between males and females. As in most parts of the world, this relationship charged men with power over women and the responsibility for protecting them, while women were expected to run the household in accordance with the wishes of men and to be available for the pleasure of men. As the *Kama Sutra* explained, "By a girl, by a young woman, or even by an aged one, nothing must be done independently, even in her own house." Women's property rights were always very limited, and in some periods they had none. On the other hand, some professions, notably weaving, were open to women. Hindu views of women's proper role and behavior are discussed briefly in the chapter entitled "Hinduism and Buddhism."

The state also regulated the behavior of its subjects in terms of the rules of caste. In Hindu belief, each person has a social, economic, and ritual position, which is inherited at birth directly from his or her parents. Although this status may, in practice, be changed with difficulty, in theory it remains for life and influences one's status in reincarnation. Caste not only governs private behavior, but also gives people different, unequal status under law. (The origins, rationale, and functions of the caste system as part of Hindu religious belief are discussed in detail below.) It was the task of the state to enforce these caste distinctions, especially their differential rankings, liabilities, and rights in legal proceedings.

Read the **Document**: **Cast(e)aways? Women in Classical India** (200 CE, 6th c. CE)
on **MyHistoryLab**

Regulating Institutional Life. The state also regulated religious establishments. The larger Hindu temples and Buddhist monasteries developed considerable economic and political power based on the land and resources donated to them by devout followers, especially wealthy landlords, businessmen, and kings. The religious institutions exercised influence over a wide range of public and private decisions made by their devotees; meanwhile, the state attempted to regulate their wealth and power.

The state also enforced rules developed by India's **guilds**, associations of businessmen and producers. Closely associated with the *jati*, or subcastes, these mostly urban groups convened to set work rules, prices, and weights and measures, and to enforce quality control. Independent of the state, the guilds could nevertheless call on it to enforce the regulations on which they had agreed.

Some students of Indian social structures have asked why the business guilds seem never to have attempted to gain direct control of the government in India, as they did in medieval Europe. The answer is not entirely clear, but caste distinctions designated some people for government and military careers, and others for business. Caste regulations separated those who were permitted to take up the bow and the sword and use force to gain control of government from those who could wield influence only through wealth. In Europe, businessmen armed themselves and hired troops; in India, it seems, they did neither. They sought to use their wealth to influence the warrior classes, but not by taking up arms against them.

Recognizing their responsibilities for regulating the interests of conflicting groups internally and the need to remain constantly vigilant against powerful neighbors, Chandragupta Maurya and his son Bindusara attempted to build a highly centralized administration. They appointed well-paid central ministers and bureaucrats, recruited a powerful military, and deployed an efficient system of spies dispersed throughout the empire.

KEY TERM

guild A sworn association of people who gather for some common purpose, usually economic. Guilds of craftsmen or merchants were formed in order to protect and further the members' professional interests and for mutual aid. Compare guilds in Europe, in the chapter entitled "The Opening of the Atlantic and the Pacific."

"The Bimaran reliquary," Gandhara, first century C.E. The central figure of the Buddha is flanked by the Hindu gods Indra and Brahma. This mixed grouping reflects the crossroads nature of the Gandhara region, the border between today's Pakistan and Afghanistan. (British Museum, London)

Asoka, India's Buddhist Emperor. At first Asoka followed the policies of his father and grandfather, and he was especially effective at enlarging the empire through military force. Nine years into his administration, however, he abruptly changed course. In 260 B.C.E. Asoka defeated Kalinga (today's Odisha, formerly Orissa), incorporating this eastern kingdom into his empire. Recoiling from the mass killing required for the military conquest, he determined to become a different person and a different ruler. He converted to Buddhism, a religion firmly committed to nonviolence, and dispatched missionaries throughout his realm and beyond, to parts of south India, Syria, Greece, Egypt, and, probably, Southeast Asia. He sent his own son on a mission to Sri Lanka, and as a result the island kingdom permanently converted to Buddhism.

For 30 years after the Battle of Kalinga, Asoka's reign brought general peace to India. The accompanying, universalistic ethic of Buddhism appealed to a people who were increasingly settling down from nomadism into stable agricultural and urban life. In diminishing the importance of the priestly *brahmin* castes, Buddhism proved especially attractive to merchant castes and guilds, groups that supported Asoka's rule.

Successor States Divide the Empire. Following Asoka's death in 238 B.C.E., no emperor was strong enough to maintain centralized power, and the Mauryan Empire went into a half-century of decline. The Mauryan dynasty came to

SOURCE

Asoka, India's Buddhist Emperor

Until just over 100 years ago, little was known about Asoka, the Mauryan emperor who held sway over the bulk of the Indian subcontinent from 265 to 238 B.C.E. In the nineteenth century, however, edicts that Asoka had inscribed on pillars and rocks to spread his name and ideals were deciphered, and for the first time in modern history Asoka's identity and teachings were understood.

Asoka had constructed at least seven pillar edicts and had inscribed at least 14 major and numerous minor rock edicts that have been discovered and excavated in many regions of India. Most are written in Brahmi script and are the oldest existing writing in India. The script, although an early variant of Sanskrit, had been lost for centuries until a British official, James Prinsep, redeciphered it in 1837. Prinsep analyzed the collective significance of the rock and pillar edicts discovered up to his time along with materials on Asoka found in early chronicles in Sri Lanka.

Asoka's famed conversion to Buddhism, a dramatic turning-point in his life, is described in the Thirteenth Major Rock Edict. The carnage he had created in his military victory at Kalinga and the suffering of his victims had left Asoka with a terrible sense of remorse. As reparation for his actions, he proclaimed his renunciation of violence and acceptance of *Dhamma*, the teachings of the Buddha that promote compassion, tolerance, and honesty.

> A hundred and fifty thousand people were deported, a hundred thousand were killed and many times that number perished. Afterwards, now that Kalinga was annexed, the Beloved of the Gods [Asoka] very earnestly practiced *Dhamma*, desired *Dhamma*, and taught *Dhamma*. (Thapar, *Asoka*, p. 255)

He did not, however, renounce the conquest and annexation of Kalinga, and while he disavowed violence as a general principle, he seemed to retain it as an option of state policy, especially in dealing with the tribal people of the forests:

> The Beloved of the Gods conciliates the forest tribes of his empire, but he warns them that he has power even in his remorse, and he asks them to repent, lest they be killed. (p. 256)

To spread his message and promote a universal faith, Asoka dispatched missionaries throughout his empire and beyond. He also made his own journeys to practice *Dhamma* and help to alleviate suffering, especially in rural areas. The Sixth Major Rock Edict proclaims Asoka's dedication to public welfare:

> I consider that I must promote the welfare of the whole world, and hard work and the dispatch of business are the means of doing so. Indeed there is no better work than promoting the welfare of the whole world. And whatever may be my great deeds, I have done them in order to discharge my debt to all beings. (p. 253)

Asoka's projects for improving the welfare of his people included the founding of hospitals, the planting of medicinal plants and trees, and the building of some 84,000 stupas (Buddhist burial mounds) and monasteries. In his bid to create a more tolerant, compassionate society, Asoka granted religious groups outside Buddhism the freedom to worship, but at the same time encouraged them to respect the beliefs and practices of other sects. He banned animal sacrifice.

Asoka's active contribution to the spread of Buddhism had a lasting impact. His inscriptions offer us tangible evidence of the great influence Buddhism had not only on his own life but also on Indian life and thought as a whole.

📖 **Read** the **Document**: Emperor Asoka, from *The Edicts of Asoka* on **MyHistoryLab**

Lion capital of the pillar erected by Asoka at Sarnath, Mauryan, c. 250 B.C.E. The polished sandstone columns erected by the emperor Asoka at places associated with events in the Buddha's life, or marking pilgrim routes to holy places, are of special interest for their 7-foot-high capitals. These provide us with the best remaining examples of Mauryan imperial art and are rich in symbolism. For instance, the Buddha was spoken of as a "lion" among spiritual preachers, whose sermon penetrated to all four corners of the world, just as the lion's roar established his authority in the forest.

Buddha of the "great wonders." Gandhara, third to fourth century C.E. The Hellenistic draping style of the Buddha's clothing illustrates another example of the crossroads nature of the Gandhara region. The Buddha's right hand is raised in the *abhaya mudra*, or hand position expressing reassurance. His palm is marked with the Wheel of the Buddha's Doctrine of Enlightenment. (Musée Guimet, Paris)

an end, and with it the unity of India, when a military commander assassinated the last Maurya king in 185 B.C.E. India dissolved again into a variety of contesting states.

The Sunga dynasty (185–173 B.C.E.) came to rule the core region that remained from Magadha. Indo-Greeks, the inheritors of Alexander's empire stationed in Afghanistan and Bactria, invaded in 182 B.C.E. and captured the northwest all the way through to the coastal cities of Gujarat. They produced a hybrid culture with the Indians they conquered. King Menander, an Indo-Greek, carried on a profound conversation with the Buddhist monk Nagasena, who introduced the king to his religion. Their dialogue is still studied today as the *Questions of King Milindu*. Gandharan art, synthesizing Greek and Indian contributions, flourished in this period, as did the city of Taxila, the great center of trade, culture, and education in the northwest. Finally, large caches of Indo-Greek coinage reflect the importance of trade routes running through the northwest and linking India to the great silk routes of central Asia.

New invaders conquered and displaced the old. In the chapter on China we read of tribal wars in East Asia, on the borders of China, which pushed Mongol groups westward to Rome. One of these tribal groups, the Shakas, invaded and ruled parts of northwest and western India for about a century, from about 94 B.C.E. to about 20 C.E. They, in turn, were displaced by yet another, larger nomadic tribal group from East Asia, known in India as the Kushanas. The geographical extent of Kushana rule is not entirely known, but it seems to have included today's Afghanistan, Pakistan, Kashmir, and India as far south as Gujarat and its ports. The legendary Kushana king, Kanishka (r. *c.* 78–*c.* 103 C.E.), seems also to have promoted Buddhism, and may have adopted it himself. With a single government controlling all these lands, trade between the subcontinent and the central Asian silk routes flourished.

The Gupta Empire

In 320 C.E. a new dynasty began its rise to power in the Ganges valley, apparently through a fortunate marriage. The founder came from a dynasty of no historical fame, but he married a princess of the powerful Licchavi lineage. Reflecting a deep sense of history and a desire to gain legitimacy, he deliberately named himself after the founder of the Mauryan Empire and became Chandra Gupta I (r. 320–*c.* 330 C.E.). His son Samudra Gupta (r. *c.* 330–*c.* 380 C.E.) earned a reputation as one of India's greatest military conquerors. The record of his battles, inscribed on an existing Asoka pillar at Allahabad, touches all regions of India: the far south, the east to Bengal and even Assam, the north to Nepal, and the mountain kingdoms of central India, which had often remained independent because of their inaccessibility.

8.1

8.2   What were the philosophies of

8.3   the Maurya and Gupta empires?

8.4

Samudra's son and successor, Chandra Gupta II (r. *c.* 380–*c.* 415 C.E.), conquered the remaining Shakas and annexed western India, including prosperous Gujarat and its ports on the Arabian Sea, for the first time in three centuries. By marrying his daughter to the head of the Vakataka lineage, he cemented an alliance with the Vataka kingdom in central India. Other Gupta alliances were established through marriages with other powerful lineages in the Deccan. The fourth Gupta emperor, Kumara Gupta (r. *c.* 415–55 C.E.), presided over a great empire now at peace.

Gupta rule was often indirect. Following many of their distant military victories, the Gupta emperors abdicated the tasks of administration and withdrew, demanding only tribute payments. Nor did their alliances with other kingdoms and lineages call for direct rule. In the Ganges valley heartland of the empire, the Gupta emperor himself appointed governors at the provincial level, and sometimes even at the district level. At the most local level of the village and the city, however, the Guptas allowed considerable independence to local administrators. The area they administered directly was much smaller than the Mauryan Empire; the two centuries of Gupta rule and influence are considered India's "golden age" more for their cultural brilliance than for their political power.

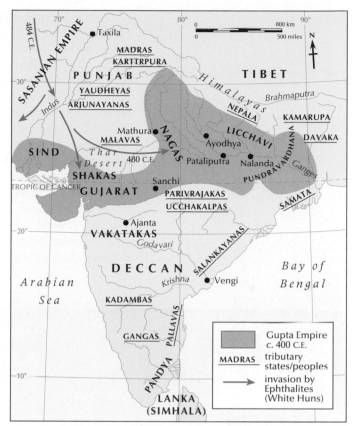

Gupta India. In the fourth century C.E. the indigenous Gupta dynasty gained control of the middle Ganges and rapidly built an empire straddling the subcontinent from Sind to the Ganges delta, augmented by a web of treaty and tributary arrangements with neighboring powers. This classical age of Indian empires was destroyed by invasions of central Asian peoples in the late fifth century C.E.

Plaque of musician with lyre, central India, fifth century C.E. During the Gupta period, terra-cotta plaques, such as this cross-legged lyre player, were used to adorn the exterior of temples. This one comes from one of the few surviving examples of free-standing brick temples decorated in this way at Bhitargaon in the Gupta heartland. (British Museum, London)

8.1

What were the philosophies of the Maurya and Gupta empires?

8.2

8.3

8.4

251

8.1

8.2

8.3

8.4

What were the
philosophies of
the Maurya and
Gupta empires?

A Golden Age of Learning. The Guptas presided over a resurgence of Sanskrit literature and Hindu philosophy. The great playwright Kalidasa (fifth century C.E.) composed two epic poems: a lyrical poem, "Meghaduta," and the great drama Shakuntala, the first Sanskrit drama translated into a Western language in modern times. Much of the important literature that had been transmitted orally was now transcribed into writing, including the Purana stories of legend and myth. Further emendations were made to the great epics, the *Mahabharata* and *Ramayana*.

The Gupta Empire began to use formal, standardized Sanskrit for its official correspondence. Panini (*fl. c.* 400 B.C.E.) had fixed the essentials of Sanskrit grammar in his *Astadhyayi* (perhaps the most systematic grammar ever produced in any language), but the Mauryas and most other earlier rulers had used Prakrit, a variant of Sanskrit that was closer to the common language of the people. Now Sanskrit law codes, such as the *Laws of Manu*, and manuals of statecraft, such as Kautilya's *Artha-sastra*, were studied, revised, and further codified. Many locally powerful officials patronized scholars, humanists, and artists. Important academic centers for Buddhist learning flourished at Taxila in the northwest and Nalanda in the Ganges valley. Chinese

Wall-painting illustrating the *Vishvantara Jataka*, Cave 17, Ajanta. Gupta period, fifth century C.E. Prince Vishvantara, was, in Buddhist legend, a prior incarnation of the Buddha. The prince was so generous that people jealous of him had him and his family exiled from his father's kingdom. Here the prince informs his wife of the edict.

Buddhist scholars visited and described these academies; by contrast, their descriptions of Hindu academies have not been preserved to the present.

The Resurgence of Hinduism. The Guptas, however, were more dedicated to promoting Hindu religious authority and learning. Major systems of Hindu philosophy returned to favor. The most influential, *Vedanta* (the culmination, or end, of the Vedas), expanded on the teachings of the Upanishads. Vedanta philosophy posed a powerful, attractive, alternative vision to Buddhism, and Hinduism began to regain ascendancy over Buddhism in India.

The caste system was elaborated and enforced in more detail. Rulers, high-level administrators, and wealthy landlords gave patronage to *brahmins* in the form of land grants and court positions. *Brahmin* priests also asserted their role in ritual performance. Buddhism, which had flourished through the patronage of earlier empires and the support of business classes, ceded the performance of many of its own rituals to *brahmin* priests, and began to decline.

Despite its military and cultural achievements, the Gupta dynasty's power began to wane in the late fifth century C.E. The subcontinent was once again politically divided and subject to one wave of invader-rulers after another. These internal divisions and conquests by outsiders—notably the Mughals in the sixteenth century and British in the eighteenth—continued until the modern independence of India and Pakistan in 1947 and of Bangladesh in 1971.

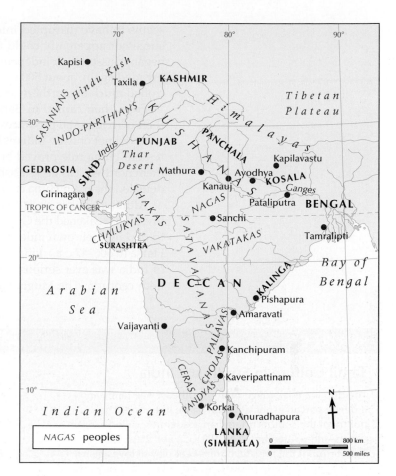

Classical south Asia. After the decline of the Gupta empire, India had no centralized empire for almost 1,000 years. Local powers grew up, often based on different languages and ethnicities. More powerful groups occupied the richest lands, while the weaker were forced into the hills. The roots of today's separate states of India lie in some of these early ethnic kingdoms.

Huna Invasions End the Age of Empires

8.3 What were the consequences of the Hunas' invasion of India?

In the fifth century, new conquerors came through the passes of the northwest, overthrowing the Gupta Empire and establishing their own headquarters in Bamiyan, Afghanistan. These invaders were the Hunas, a branch of the Xiongnu, the nomadic Mongol tribes that roamed the regions north of the Great Wall of China and sometimes invaded. In previous expansions, they had driven other groups west, even into the Roman Empire, as we saw in the chapter "Rome and the Barbarians." Domino-fashion, these groups pushed one another westward. The Shakas had invaded India as a result of this sequence in about 94 B.C.E. The Kushanas followed about a century later. Now the Hunas themselves arrived in force. These same ethnic peoples were called Huns in the Roman Empire, which they invaded under Attila in 454 C.E.

View the **Image: Elephanta Water Cave, India** on **MyHistoryLab**

The Hunas and their Legacy

Skanda Gupta (r. 455–67 C.E.) repulsed the first Huna invasions, which occurred about 460 C.E. But the continuing Huna presence across India's northwest border

8.1

8.2

8.3

What were the
consequences
of the Hunas'
invasion of India?

8.4

What were the
consequences
of the Hunas'
invasion of India?

seems to have disrupted international trade and reduced Gupta wealth. Skanda's successor apparently could not hold the empire together, and regional strongmen began to assert their independence. With central control thus weakened, Huna armies invaded again, about 500 C.E., and for the next half-century they fought in, and controlled much of, northern and central India.

From their capital in Bamiyan, Afghanistan, the Hunas ruled parts of India as their own imperial provinces. As in Rome, they earned a reputation for great cruelty, reported not only by Indians but also by Chinese and Greek travelers who visited the region. Huna rule proved brief, however. In 528 C.E. Indian regional princes drove them northwest as far as Kashmir. About a generation later, Turkic and Persian armies defeated the main Huna concentrations in Bactria, removing them as a force in India.

Although it was short-lived, the Hunas' impact on India was considerable. Their invasion weakened the Gupta Empire, enabling regional powers to dismember it and to declare their own independence. Except for a brief reign by Harsha-vardhana or Harsa (r. 606–47 C.E.), king of the north Indian region of Kanauj, no further unification of India was ever seriously attempted from inside the subcontinent until the twentieth century. (The Mughal and British Empires, discussed in the chapters entitled

SOURCE

Tamil Culture in Southeast India

The dominant language of the southeast was Tamil, and it developed an especially expressive literature. The poetry of the southern Tamilian academies, called *sangam* poetry and written between 100 B.C.E. and 250 C.E., set in counterpoint the private, bittersweet play of love against a public atmosphere of warfare and strife. This poetry was lost until scholars rediscovered it in the later decades of the nineteenth century. It has been brought to the attention of the English-speaking world especially through the efforts of the late A.K. Ramanujan.

A King's Double Nature
His armies love massacre,
he loves war,

yet gifts
flow from him ceaselessly.

Come, dear singers,
let's go and see him in Naravu

where, on trees
no axe can fell,
fruits ripen, unharmed
by swarms of bees,
egg-shaped, ready
for the weary traveller
in the fields of steady, unfailing harvests;
where warriors with bows
that never tire of arrows
shiver
but stand austere
in the sea winds
mixed with the lit cloud
and the spray of seafoam.

There he is,
in the town of Naravu,
tender among tender women.

Harvest of War
Great king,

you shield your men from ruin,
so your victories, your greatness
are bywords.

Loose chariot wheels
lie about the battleground
with the long white tusks
of bull-elephants.

Flocks of male eagles
eat carrion
with their mates.

Headless bodies
dance about
before they fall
to the ground.

Blood glows,
like the sky before nightfall,
in the red center
of the battlefield.

Demons dance there.
And your kingdom
is an unfailing harvest
of victorious wars.

(trans. Ramanujan, pp. 131, 115)

What were the
consequences
of the Hunas'
invasion of India?

Bronze figure of Nataraja, Tamil Nadu, southern India, Chola Dynasty, c. 1100 C.E. For their mastery on conveying grace in motion through the solidity of bronze, Chola sculptures are considered among the finest artistic works of ancient India. (British Museum, London)

"The Unification of World Trade" and "Nationalism, Imperialism, and Resistance," were created by invasions from outside, although the Mughals later settled within the subcontinent.)

The urban culture of north India dimmed. The Buddhist monasteries, which the Hunas attacked with especial force, never recovered. On the other hand, by opening up their invasion routes the Hunas indirectly enriched India's population pool. Gurjaras and Rajputs entered western India more or less along with the Hunas, and settled permanently. The modern Indian states of Gujarat and Rajasthan are named for them and their descendants.

The legacies of the Hunas in India—the destruction and dismemberment of the Gupta Empire, the reduction in interregional trade, the decline of culture, and the introduction of new nomadic groups into already settled imperial lands—quite closely mirror those of their Hun brothers in the Roman Empire. Even the timings were similar, products of the same emigration from central Asia. Of the great empires of the ancient world, only China was capable of defeating or assimilating these invaders without losing its own coherence and identity.

What were the
consequences
of the Hunas'
invasion of India?

Earthenware sculpture, Nilgiri Hills, south India, early centuries C.E. *Adivasis*, or tribals, produced distinctive artwork. A buffalo cult among the Todas, the largest of the Nilgiri Hills tribal groups, led to the creation of this characterful figurine, made to decorate the lid of an urn containing ashes. (British Museum, London)

Regional Diversity and Power

The history of the Indian subcontinent tends to be written from the perspective of the Ganges valley as the center of political power and influence. (The settlements of the central Indus valley discussed in the chapter entitled "River Valley Civilizations" did not endure, and the region is now a desert.) The Aryans established their centers in the Ganges region; the Mauryas continued the pattern; so did the Guptas; the later Mughals established their capitals there; the British ultimately followed Mughal patterns by also placing their capital at Delhi; and today's government of independent India has followed suit. But other regions of India have always been important, too. Even at times when India has been unified, regional powers have regularly challenged the supremacy of the Ganges heartland. In periods such as the millennium from 500 to 1500 C.E., when India had no central empire, the outlying regions asserted their status as independent states.

The major regions of India speak different languages from one another, although imperial rulers have usually introduced a unifying link language for interregional communication: Prakrit under Asoka; Sanskrit under the Guptas; Persian under the Mughals; and English under the British. Today, India uses two official languages, Hindi and English. Pakistan uses Urdu and English, and Bangladesh uses Bengali.

The peoples of different regions have immigrated into the subcontinent from different places and at different times, some preceding the Aryans, others following them. In regions dominated by Aryans, many of these non-Aryans (people who spoke other languages) found a place within the social system of the Aryans. The highly stratified Aryan society—marked by caste and *jati*—could make room for the absorption of various groups by creating new categories for them within the existing hierarchies. When not consolidated into larger empires, these diverse groups have created their own political-cultural administrations. The peoples of Gujarat in the west and Bengal and Orissa in the east have all seen themselves as distinct ethnic

What were the consequences of the Hunas' invasion of India?

groups, even when they were ruled from the north, and as independent when that rule was broken. Regional dynasties came and went.

The indigenous tribal peoples—referred to today as *adivasis* ("original inhabitants"), because their immigration predates any historical records—generally inhabit less accessible areas, frequently hilly tracts that are not easy to farm. They have attempted to protect their independence from outside exploitation by maintaining their inaccessibility.

The most distinct and separate region was the far south. Here, several lineage and ethnic groups fought to maintain their independence: the Pandyas in the extreme southeast; the Pallavas just north of them along the coast; and then the Cholas and the Chalukyas. Along the southwest coast, the Perumal and Cera lineages dominated. The place of their origin and the time of their immigration are not clearly known, but their languages form a linguistic family called Dravidian, not related to the Sanskritic family of languages of the north. In the Source box above, two poems provide a taste of the literary richness of Tamil, one of the four principal Dravidian languages.

Sea Trade and Cultural Influence: From Rome to Southeast Asia

Imperial governments based inland in the Ganges valley and the northwest based their economic power on their control of land and overland trade through the mountain passes connecting to the silk routes. Many of the regional, coastal powers, on the other hand, profited more from trade by sea. They maintained wide-ranging external connections, from the Roman Empire in the west to Southeast Asia in the east.

Under the Roman emperor Caesar Augustus (r. 27 B.C.E.–14 C.E.), Rome annexed Egypt, thereby opening up a trade route to the east by way of the Red Sea. Rome's great wealth generated a powerful economic demand for goods from Asia. Roman traders learned from the Arabs to sail with the southwest monsoon winds from the Red Sea to the west coast of India. About six months later they could sail back with the northeast monsoon, completing the round trip within a year.

KEY TERM

Adivasis "Original inhabitants." The aboriginal peoples of the Indian subcontinent, who are outside the caste system and live somewhat separately from the rest of society, generally in remote places. Previously referred to as "tribals," they are today sometimes referred to as *vanvasis*, or forest dwellers.

HOW DO WE KNOW?

Coins and Excavations

In his great compendium of trade in the Indian Ocean, *The Periplus of the Erythrean Sea* (c. 50 C.E.), a Greek merchant wrote of the Roman trade with Malabar, the southwest coast of India,

> They send large ships to the market-towns on account of the great quantity and bulk of pepper and [cinnamon]. There are imported here, in the first place, a great quantity of coin; topaz, thin clothing, not much; figured linens, antimony, coral, crude glass, copper, tin, lead, wine, not much, but as much as at Barygaza [the flourishing port of Gujarat, further north] … There is exported pepper, which is produced in quantity in only one region near these markets … Besides this there are exported great quantities of fine pearls, ivory, silk cloth, spikenard from the Ganges, [cinnamon] from the places in the interior, transparent stones of all kinds, diamonds and sapphires, and tortoise shell. (cited in Kulke and Rothermund, p. 106)

Numerous hoards of Roman gold coins throughout south India provide archaeological evidence of trade between Rome and India. In 1945, the British archaeologist Sir Mortimer Wheeler discovered the remnants of a Roman trading post at Arikamedu, a fishing village adjacent to Chennai (formerly Madras). He excavated the brick foundations of large halls and terraces, cisterns, fortifications, and ceramics that had been produced in Italy between 30 B.C.E. and 35 C.E. This outpost suggests that the traders actually carrying the goods across the Arabian Sea were foreign rather than Indian: Arabs, Jews, and Romans. The Roman historian Pliny complained that Rome was sending around 50 million sesterces a year to India to buy its luxuries, although he also noted that they sold in Rome for 100 times that amount.

- What seems to have been the main item exported from Europe to pay for Indian goods?
- Why was this pattern of exports disturbing to the Roman Pliny?
- Is it surprising to you that India's import–export trade with Rome was apparently not carried by Indians, but by Arabs, Jews, and Romans? Why or why not?

What were the
consequences
of the Hunas'
invasion of India?

Southeast Asia: "Greater India"

Some of the luxury goods shipped to Rome originated in Southeast Asia and were transshipped via India. Indian sailors traveled to all the coastal countries of modern Southeast Asia: Myanmar (formerly Burma), Thailand, Cambodia, Vietnam, Malaysia, and Indonesia. To anchor this trade, they established settlements in port cities such as Oc Eo in Funan, in the southernmost part of modern Vietnam. When they arrived, the sailors and settlers found *brahmin* priests and Buddhist monks already there. Long before any of these trade ventures, in the third century B.C.E., King Asoka had dispatched missionaries to Sri Lanka and to Myanmar to begin the process of converting these lands to Buddhism. Local mythology and Chinese historical records tell (quite different) stories of the arrival of a *brahmin* priest named Kaundinya. As a result of his activities, Funan adopted Sanskrit as the language of the court and encouraged Hinduism.

Funan remained an independent state, not an Indian province. Indeed, in the third century C.E. Funan extended its own rule to southern Vietnam, Cambodia, central Thailand, northern Malaya, and southern Myanmar from its capital at Vyadhapura, near present-day Phnom Penh. Wherever Funan expanded, it encouraged the adoption of Indian culture.

Ironically, Funan later infused Indian culture even among those who conquered it. When Champa expanded southward into Funan lands, the kings of Champa began

Borobudur, Java, late eighth century C.E. This monument, the supreme example of Buddhist art in Southeast Asia and Indonesia, is a fantastic microcosm, reproducing the universe as it was imagined in the Mahayana school of Buddhist theology. The relief sculptures, of which there are some 10 miles, represent the doctrine of *karma*, the cycle of birth and rebirth, of striving, and release from the Wheel of Life.

Angkor Wat, Angkor, Cambodia, early twelfth century C.E. Dedicated to the Hindu god Vishnu, this huge jungle-bound temple complex once served as the centerpiece of the Khmer Empire, originally founded in 880 C.E. Decorated with extensive relief sculpture, the temples of Angkor Wat were intended to emulate mountains in dressed stone.

8.1

8.2

What were the consequences of the Hunas' invasion of India?

8.3

8.4

to adopt the cultural, linguistic, and architectural styles of the Pallavas of south India that were then current in Funan. Bhadravarman, a Champa king, built the first Champa temple to the Hindu god Shiva.

Two additional areas under Funan hegemony later established independent states with strong Hindu and Buddhist cultural elements: Java and the kingdom of Srivijaya in Sumatra. In Java, the ruling Sailendra dynasty built an extraordinary Buddhist temple at Borobudur in 778–824 C.E. When the Sailendras attacked the Khmer peoples of present-day Cambodia, the Khmers unified their defenses under King Jayavarman II (r. 790–850 C.E.). He established a new capital and introduced Hindu temples and philosophies into the whole region around it at Angkor, which later became the location of one of Hinduism's greatest temples, constructed by Jayavarman VII (r. 1181–1219 C.E.).

8.1

8.2

8.3

8.4

How do India's
empires compare
with those of
China and Rome?

The diffusion of Indian religious and cultural forms continued for centuries throughout Southeast Asia. It proceeded almost entirely peacefully, spread by priests and traders. A few exceptions, however, stand out. Two south Indian kings did send military expeditions to Southeast Asia. The Pallava king Nandivarman III (r. c. 844–66 C.E.) supported a military camp on the Isthmus of Siam to protect a group of southern Indian merchants who were living and working there. The Chola king Rajendra I (r. 1014–47 C.E.) dispatched a fleet to Sumatra and Malaya and defeated the Srivijaya Empire. It appears that his goal was to keep the trade routes open and to support India's sailors on the competitive sea lanes; he claimed no territory. In 1068–69 C.E., the Cholas apparently intervened in a dispute among rival claimants to rule in Malaya, conquered a large part of the region, but then turned it over to their local client.

India, China, and Rome: Empires and Intermediate Institutions

8.4 How do India's empires compare with those of China and Rome?

A comparison of the long-lived Roman, Indian, and Chinese empires alerts us to the need to analyze empires not only from the top-down perspective of the central administration but also from the bottom up—from their foundations in local regions and institutions.

Comparing India, China, and Rome is not straightforward. To begin with, India lacks the detailed political, military, economic, administrative, and personal records that would facilitate comparison in any detail. Rome and China compiled official histories, and a wide variety of personal accounts have also survived to the present. For India, on the other hand, we must often rely on the observations of foreign visitors for our best accounts. Even the life, writings, and policies of Asoka, now regarded as ancient India's greatest emperor, were lost from historical conscious-ness for centuries until his rock and pillar edicts were deciphered in the nineteenth century.

Administration

Both Rome and China built institutionalized bureaucracies and systems of admin-istration, lasting for centuries in Rome and millennia in China. By contrast, India's states and empires generally seemed to be extensions of family lineages. Even the most powerful of ancient India's empires, the Mauryan and Gupta, were family holdings. Despite the administrative rigor suggested by Kautilya's *Artha-sastra*, even Chandragupta Maurya's dynasty began to weaken after the death of his grandson Asoka. In India, power remained more personal than institutional.

International Relations

The *Artha-sastra* characterized interstate relations by the law of the fish, the large swallow the small: "When one king is weaker than the other, he should make peace with him. When he is stronger than the other, he should make war with him." Despite Asoka's renunciation of the excessive use of force, the constant rise and fall of king-doms and small empires throughout India suggest that Kautilya's view generally prevailed. We do not have records of internal revolts against states and empires in India. Instead, dissidents would abscond to a neighboring state where they felt they could live more freely and where they might join the official military to fight against their former ruler.

Invasion of the Hunas

Indian empires did not expand politically or militarily beyond the borders of the subcontinent. Later trade missions in Southeast Asia exported cultural and religious innovations along with their material cargo, but they made little attempt to establish political rule there. On the other hand, outsiders frequently invaded the subcontinent.

Remarkably, the one political experience that the empires of India, Rome, and China shared was invasion and at least partial conquest by the Hunas (Huns, Xiongnu) and by the peoples they displaced. Indeed, the Hunas/Huns play an important role in world history, especially from the third through the sixth centuries C.E. History records not only the builders and sustainers of sedentary empire, but also their nomadic challengers.

Local Institutions and the State

In Rome and China, government touched much of the population directly, through taxes, military conscription, imperial service, and aggressive bureaucracy. The state was fundamental to all areas of life. In India, on the other hand, the state seemed to preside over a set of social institutions that were already deeply rooted and were more persistent through time. These institutions included family lineages, aware and proud of their histories; caste groups, each presiding over its own occupational, ritual, and ethnic niche; guild associations, overseeing the conditions of economic production and distribution; local councils, providing government at the village and town level; and religious sects, which gave their members a sense of belonging, identity, and purpose. The state was important in overseeing the activities of all these groups, but it existed only in the context of their existence. States and empires came and went, but these varied, pervasive institutions carried on in their own rhythms. In India political authority was intimately connected, and sometimes subordinated, to familial, cultural, and religious power.

Indian Empires:
What Difference Do They Make?

Ancient Indian empires shed light both on the later history of India and on the structure of empires generally. Modern India is a direct descendant of its ancient empires and shares their diversity, their many languages and ethnic groups incorporated into the whole, their "unity in diversity." The ancient texts—philosophical, political, and epic—continue to provide a common cultural imagery to the majority of Indians today, and their influence extends to large parts of Southeast Asia. Questions concerning the ethics of rule—answered quite differently by such practitioners of politics as Emperor Asoka and such political advisers as Kautilya, author of the *Artha-sastra*—continue to be debated. Most of all, the power of the subdivisions of empire—regions, castes, guilds, village organizations—retain their importance in modern India and in its south Asian neighbors as well.

The tension between center and periphery, between centralized bureaucracy and regional interest groups, which marks all empires to some degree was—and is—especially prominent in India. While China and Rome draw most attention for their ability to build the central institutions of empire and impose them on their subjects, Indian imperial structures integrated and balanced existing local forms of organization. This is a matter more of degree than of complete difference in philosophy of government: Asoka was willing to use brute force to conquer and subdue enemies of his empire even after his adoption of Buddhism; Rome and China were willing to accommodate local interests if they did not threaten imperial control. Nevertheless, more than Rome or China, India gives us an example of empire built up by integrating its constituent parts rather than by defeating or completely assimilating them.

Because these patterns continue to reappear in empires throughout history and around the globe, these early explorations of Rome, China, and India give us some of the tools we need to analyze the successes—and the failures—of imperial structures down to our own times.

CHAPTER REVIEW

NEW ARRIVALS IN SOUTH ASIA

8.1 What was the most important literature of the Aryan immigrants?

India's two great epics, the *Mahabharata* and the *Ramayana*, recount events from 1000 and 700 B.C.E. Although neither is a historical account, both have given us valuable information on the social structures, ways of life, and values of the time in which they were written. The *Mahabharata* is the longest single poem in the world – ten times longer than the Bible. It includes the *Bhagavad-Gita*, or "Song of God," a profound religious meditation and instruction. There are many versions of the *Ramayana*. Its core story tells of the mythical god-king Rama's victory over the demon-king Ravana, who had kidnapped his wife, Sita. Some versions of the story focus on the battles between north and south; some versions tell the story of Sita in different ways.

Even before these epics, the Aryans brought with them religious literature that formed the basis of Hinduism: the four *Vedas*, the sacrificial rituals of the *Brahmanas*, and the mystical philosophy of the *Upanishads*.

THE EMPIRES OF INDIA

8.2 What were the philosophies of the Maurya and Gupta empires?

The Mauryas and the Guptas were the two major imperial dynasties of ancient India, several centuries apart. They contributed the permanent governing institutions that mediated between the individual and the state. Much of the statecraft of each empire was inspired by religious philosophies and social practices: the Mauryas, after Asoka, by Buddhism; the Guptas by Hinduism. Hinduism is not a specific set of dogmas and rituals, but rather encompasses the variety of religious beliefs and practices of the peoples of India. As new ethnic groups were absorbed by Hinduism, their gods were added to the Hindu pantheon.

HUNA INVASIONS END THE AGE OF EMPIRES

8.3 What were the consequences of the Hunas' invasion of India?

The Hunas (the same ethnic peoples called Huns in the Roman Empire) came through the mountain passes of northwest India in the fifth century C.E. Their legacies include the destruction and dismemberment of the Gupta Empire, a reduction in interregional trade, the decline of culture, and the introduction of new nomadic groups. These consequences closely mirror those of the Huns in the Roman Empire of about the same time period.

INDIA, CHINA, AND ROME: EMPIRES AND INTERMEDIATE INSTITUTIONS

8.4 How do India's empires compare with those of China and Rome?

Comparing India, China, and Rome is not an easy task. Rome and China compiled extensive histories and personal accounts, which have survived to the present day. India does not have the detailed military, economic, administrative, and so on, records that would allow straightforward comparisons. Rome expanded its empire mostly through military conquest, while both China and India also absorbed many of their neighbors through more peaceful cultural assimilation. The political empires of Rome and China persisted far longer than those of India, although the cultural legacies of all of them persisted in various forms till today.

Suggested Readings

PRINCIPAL SOURCES

Embree, Ainslee, ed. and rev. *Sources of Indian Tradition*, Vol. I: *From the Beginning to 1800* (New York: Columbia University Press, 2nd ed., 1988). The principal source for materials on ancient India, especially on high culture, philosophy, and politics.

Kulke, Hersmann, and Dietmar Rothermund. *A History of India* (New York: Routledge, 5th ed., 2010). Brief, accessible, excellent introductory history. Kulke brings his considerable expertise on ancient India to the section on empires.

Thapar, Romila. *Ancient Indian Social History* (New Delhi: Orient Longman, 1978). Principal introduction to the institutions of ancient India.

——. *Asoka and the Decline of the Mauryas* (Delhi: Oxford University Press, 1998). Principal introduction to the empire of the Mauryas.

——. *Early India: From the Origins to A.D. 1300* (Berkeley, CA: University of California Press, 2003). Updates Thapar's classic *History of India* (1966). Definitive, if lengthy, introduction.

——. *Interpreting Early India* (New York: Oxford University Press, 1992). Philosophy of studying ancient India, opposing the use of history to advance political programs.

ADDITIONAL SOURCES

Allchin, F.R., *et al. The Archaeology of Early Historic South Asia: The Emergence of Cities and States* (Cambridge: Cambridge University Press, 1995). Somewhat dated, but very accessible, wide-ranging introduction for a nonspecialist.

Bryant, Edwin. *The Quest for the Origins of Vedic Culture: The Indo–Aryan Migration Debate* (New York: Oxford University Press, 2001). A painstakingly scholarly assessment of claims that the Aryans may have originated within the same regions and peoples as Mohenjo-Daro. Evidence for this interpretation is scanty, however.

Craven, Roy C. *Indian Art* (London: Thames and Hudson, 1997). Concise but lavishly illustrated and well-explained introduction.

Green, Peter. *Alexander of Macedon, 356–323 B.C.* (Berkeley, CA: University of California Press, 1991). For Alexander at the threshold of India.

Hammond Atlas of World History (Maplewood, NJ: Hammond, 5th ed., 1999). Indispensable atlas of world history.

Hughes, Sarah Shaver, and Brady Hughes, eds. *Women in World History*, Vol. I: *Readings from Prehistory to 1500* (Armonk, NY: M.E. Sharpe, 1995). Good readings on India.

Huntington, Susan, and John Huntington. *Art of Ancient India* (Boston, MA: Weatherhill, 1985). Introduction to Indian art. Black-and-white illustrations, perceptive discussion.

Lockhard, Craig A. "Integrating Southeast Asia into the Framework of World History: The Period Before 1500," *The History Teacher* XXIX, No. 1 (November 1995), pp. 7–35. Designed for preparing syllabi, with good conceptual scheme for understanding Southeast Asia.

Past Worlds: The (London) Times Atlas of Archaeology (Maplewood, NJ: Hammond, 1988). Fascinating introduction to history through archaeological finds. Lavishly illustrated with maps, pictures, and charts.

Ramanujan, A.K., ed. and trans. *Poems of Love and War: From the Eight Anthologies and the Ten Long Poems of Classical Tamil* (New York: Columbia University Press, 1985). An outstanding poet and scholar translating classical Tamil poetry.

Richman, Paula, ed. *Many Ramayanas: The Diversity of a Narrative Tradition in South Asia* (Berkeley, CA: University of California Press, 1991). The *Ramayana* has many interpretations and uses. Richman provides an astonishing, scholarly array of them.

Rowland, Benjamin. *The Art and Architecture of India: Buddhist/Hindu/Jain* (New York: Penguin Books, 1977). Still a useful introduction.

SarDesai, D.R. *Southeast Asia: Past and Present* (Boulder, CO: Westview Press, 7th ed., 2012). Standard introductory text.

Schwartzberg, Joseph E., ed. *A Historical Atlas of South Asia* (Chicago, IL: University of Chicago Press, 1978). Scholarly, encyclopedic coverage of history through geography. A superb research tool.

Spodek, Howard, and Doris Srinivasan, eds. *Urban Form and Meaning in South Asia: The Shaping of Cities from Prehistoric to Precolonial Times* (Washington, DC: National Gallery of Art, 1993). Papers from an outstanding international scholarly seminar.

Thapar, Romila. *Cultural Pasts: Essays in Early Indian History* (New Delhi: Oxford University Press, 2000). Principal introduction to the institutions of ancient India.

Tharu, Susie, and K. Lalita, eds. *Women Writing in India 600 B.C. to the Present*, Vol. I (New York: The Feminist Press, 1991). Beginning of the movement to include women's materials in the history of ancient India. Wide-ranging subjects.

Trautmann, Thomas, ed. *The Aryan Debate* (New York: Oxford University Press, 2008). Many perspectives on the view that the Aryans were indigenous to northwest India, and perhaps related to the people of Mohenjo-Daro.

FILMS

Legacy: The Origins of Civilization: India (1992; 58 minutes). Written and presented by Michael Wood. Especially strong on the religious life of India (weaker on other aspects).

Peter Brook's Mahabharata (1990; 5 hours and 25 minutes). A modern, highly acclaimed representation of the classical work, based on his nine-hour stage production, with an international cast.

Mahabharata (1988–1990; 94 episodes, 45 minutes each). Produced and directed by B.R. Chopra and Ravi Chopra. Most popular weekly serial broadcast on Indian TV. Work stopped each Sunday morning as much of the country paused to watch.

Ramayana: The Complete Series (1987–1988; 78 episodes, 45 minutes each). Indian TV blockbuster serial based on the classic story and directed by Ramanand Sagar. Credited with increasing devotion to Hindu mythology in north India. Inspired the production of Chopra and Chopra's *Mahabharata*.

PART FOUR

TURNING POINT: CREATING WORLD RELIGIONS

2500 B.C.E.–1500 C.E.

Religion: Ancient Roots

From earliest times people have felt the need to establish relationships with powers that they believed could protect and support them in life, provide a sense of meaning and purpose, and promise some form of existence after death. (Eliade, *Ordeal by Labyrinth*, p. 154.) Some people have imagined these forces as abstract and remote; others have regarded them as having personalities, as gods, sometimes even in human form. (Some people, of course, do not believe in such powers at all, or are skeptical.)

Early burial rituals reveal evidence of religious beliefs. Archaeologists discovered Neanderthal burials with flint tools, food, and cooked meat at Teshik-Tash in Siberia; the burial of a Neanderthal male with a crippled right arm at the Shanidar cave in the Zagros Mountains of Iraq; and graves covered with red ocher powder, including some group burials, in France and central Europe. As modern humans evolved, they introduced far more elaborate burials. Perhaps the most extraordinary yet uncovered are at Sungir about 100 miles east of Moscow, in Russia. Dating back 32,000 years, the five skeletons uncovered there include one—apparently an adolescent boy—buried with about 5,000 beads, 250 canine teeth of foxes, and carved ivory statues and pendants, and another—apparently an adolescent girl—with 5,274 beads in addition to other objects. These burial rituals suggest that the earliest humans believed life might continue in some form, even after death.

We have already seen that many early cities and states were dedicated to particular gods or goddesses, and

Stonehenge, Wiltshire, England. A ring of massive stone pillars, some with lintels across them, is set in a field of numerous graves and was apparently a shrine for worship. Construction began about 3000 B.C.E. Various theories of its early uses cannot be verified since there are no written records. It remains one of the most popular, and mysterious, sites in England, mostly for tourism, but some also come to worship.

sometimes even carried their names. Gilgamesh, builder of the city of Uruk in Mesopotamia, was two-thirds a god and sought eternal life. In Babylon, Hammurabi transmitted his legal code in the name of the god Shamash. Egyptian hymns proclaimed the divinity of the pharaohs. Chinese of the Shang dynasty used oracle bones to augur the will of transcendent powers. Athens was named for the goddess Athena. When city-states went to war in the names of their gods, the fighting was especially bloody.

The empires we discussed in Part Three sought the validation provided by religious leaders and, in exchange, gave financial and political backing to their religious institutions. These links between political and religious powers were deep and abiding. The caste system of Hinduism established a reciprocal relationship between priests and rulers that provided India with a sense of unity and continuity through the millennia. The emperor Asoka promoted Buddhism. In several states of South and Southeast Asia, Buddhist priests were called upon to validate the

authority of rulers. (Confucianism, one of the pillars of the Chinese imperial system, presents a profound theory of ethical human relationships, but, unlike the religions just mentioned, Confucianism has little otherworldly focus.) In the western world, rabbis interpreted Jewish law; Roman emperors doubled as high priests; Constantine, emperor of Rome, safeguarded early Christianity; the prophet Muhammed served as political as well as religious head of the Muslim community.

Part Four focuses in greater depth on the role of religion throughout human history, but especially from about 300 C.E. to about 1200 C.E. In this period Hinduism became more fully defined and systematized throughout India; Buddhism rose to great importance in China, Japan, and Southeast Asia; Judaism, exiled from its original home in Israel, spread with the exiles throughout much of western Asia, the Mediterranean basin, and northern Europe; Christianity grew into the great cultural system of Europe; and Islam radiated outward from Arabia, across North Africa westward to the Atlantic and to the far corners of the eastern hemisphere, as far as Indonesia. These five religions often confronted one another, sometimes leading to syncretism, the borrowing and adaptation of ideas and practices; sometimes to competition; and sometimes to direct conflict.

Miracles, Manifestations, and the Historian

Organized religious groups usually build on the religious experiences reported by their founders and early teachers. All five of the religions we study in this part grew from such experiences, and many of these experiences were called miraculous—that is, they are contrary to everyday experience, and they can be neither proved nor disproved. For example, most Hindus believe that gods have regularly intervened in human life, as Krishna is said to have done at the Battle of Kurukshetra. They also believe in the reincarnation of all living creatures, including gods. Buddhists believe in the revelation of the Four Noble Truths and the Eightfold Path to Siddhartha Gautama (the Buddha) under the bo tree at Bodh Gaya in northern India; most also believe that Siddhartha was a reborn soul of an earlier Buddha and would himself be born again. Most Jews have believed in special divine intervention in the lives of Abraham and his descendants, a special divine covenant with the Jewish people, and a revelation of divine law at Mount Sinai. Most Christians have believed in the miracle of Jesus' incarnation as the Son of God and his resurrection after death. Most Muslims believe that God revealed his teachings to Muhammad through the angel Gabriel.

Historians, however, cannot study miracles or judge their authenticity. Historical study seeks proof of events, and such proof is not usually available for miracles. Almost

Moses, Tomb of Pope Julius II, Michelangelo Buonarroti, Rome, 1513. Marble. Moses carries the tablets of the law under his right arm. The statue references the Biblical account of Moses receiving the tablets directly from God. Compare the image of Moses in the mosaic in San Vitale, Ravenna, in the chapter "Judaism and Christianity." (San Pietro in Vincoli, Rome)

265

identity combined with political power, group boundaries became even more important, marking in-group from outside-group, separating "us" from "them," sometimes even leading to violent conflict. Historians study these manifestations and effects of religious beliefs:

- **The sanctification of time.** Each religion creates its own sacred calendar, commemorating each year the key dates in the history of the religion and in the life of its community. It marks dates for the performance of special rituals, celebrations, fasts, and community assemblies. In addition to the community calendar, members of religious organizations create their own individual and family calendars to mark the rites of passage—the great life-cycle events of birth, puberty, marriage, maturity, and death. Religions especially formulate rules of marriage in an attempt to channel the raw, powerful, mysterious, and often indiscriminate forces of youthful sexuality into conformity with the norms of the group.

Krishna instructs Arjuna, India, tenth century c.e. One of the most beloved of the gods of Hinduism, Krishna is often painted in dark blue or black, suggesting his origins as a god of one of India's pre-Hindu tribal groups. He is most famous as the spiritual guide and the chariot driver of Arjuna in the *Bhagavad Gita* religious treatise, and, separately as a great lover, sporting with the milkmaids who often surround him as he plays his seductive flute.

MAJOR RELIGIONS OF THE WORLD, 2011

Religion	Number of followers	Percentage of world population
Christians	2,298,093,000	32.8
Roman Catholics	1,184,358 000	16.9
Protestants	426,065,000	6.0
Orthodox	275,808,000	3.9
Anglicans	87,925,000	1.2
Independents	348,511,000	5.0
Unaffiliated Christians	116,082,000	1.7
Muslims	1,560,391,300	22.3
Hindus	959,941,000	13.7
Nonreligious/agnostics	665,069,410	9.9
Chinese folk religionists	568,451,000	8.0
Buddhists	467,546,000	6.7
Ethnic religionists	269,252,000	4.0
Atheists	136,991,000	2.0
New-religionists	63,201,000	0.9
Sikhs	24,285,000	0.4
Jews	14,875,000	0.2
Baha'is	7,417,000	0.1
Confucianists	6,470,490	0.1
Jains	5,383,400	0.1
Shintoists	2,763,900	0.0
Zoroastrians	198,500	0.0

(Numerical data from *Encyclopedia Britannica Book of the Year 2012*)

by definition, a belief in miracles is a matter of faith, not of proof. Moreover, history is the study of the regular processes of change over time, while miracles, again by definition, are one-time-only events, which stand outside and defy the normal processes of change.

What can be studied are the manifestations and effects of religious beliefs on people's behavior. Sincere believers in religious miracles restructure their lives accordingly, creating and joining religious organizations to spread the word about these miracles and about their own experiences with them. These new organizations formulate rules of membership, and they infuse their beliefs into everyday life by establishing sacred time, sacred space, sacred liturgy, and sacred literature and culture. Historically, when religious

- **The sanctification of space.** Each religion creates its own sacred geography by establishing shrines where miraculous acts are said to have occurred; where saints were born, flourished, or met their deaths; and where relics from the lives of holy people are preserved and venerated. The most sacred of these sites become centers of pilgrimage. Whole cities, and especially their sacred quarters, have been dedicated to gods and goddesses, and thought to be under their special protection.
- **The sanctification of language and literature.** Each religion shapes its own use of language, literature, and artistic imagery. The Sanskrit Vedas and epics, the Pali Buddhist Tripitaka, the Hebrew Bible, the Greek New Testament, and the Arabic Quran have provided linguistic and literary canons across the millennia. Subsequent chapters of this book quote religious scriptures extensively because of their centrality to the world's languages, literatures, and imagery.
- **The sanctification of artistic and cultural creativity.** Religious sensibilities often inspire specific creative efforts, and religious groups often encourage the creation of art, music, and drama to express and enhance their message.
- **The sanctification of family and ancestors.** Many religions link living generations to those that have gone before. Through prayers and periodic ritual performances such as visits to graves and shrines, current generations are informed that even ancestors who are no longer living still deserve, and require, respect and reverence. Ancestor remembrance and worship situate current life in a deeper historical context, and may promote a more conservative outlook on life.
- **The creation of religious organization.** If a powerful leadership emerges, individual religious experience may find expression in institutional structure and more complex organization. At one extreme this may be a hierarchical structure with a single leader at the apex and an array of administrative and spiritual orders down to the most local level, the form of the Roman Catholic Church. At another extreme there may be no formal overall organization, and no formal set of rules and regulations, but instead a loose association of local communities related to one another through common beliefs and social structures, the usual form of Hinduism.

Turning Point Questions

1. How do religions convey ethical messages?
2. In what ways do religions contribute to the arts and the humanities?
3. How have religions affected political and economic institutions?

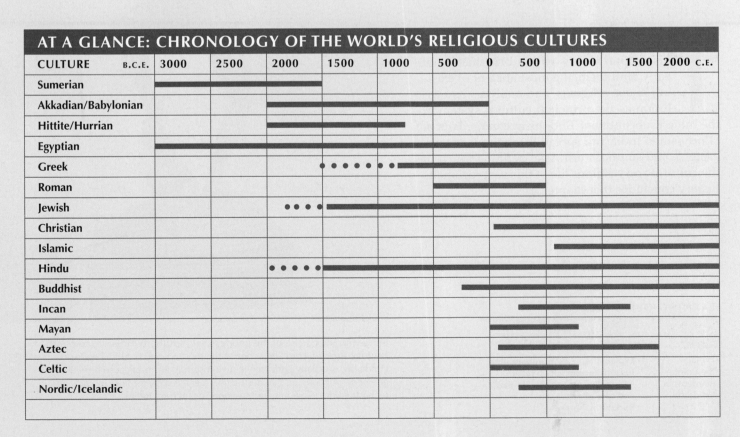

AT A GLANCE: CHRONOLOGY OF THE WORLD'S RELIGIOUS CULTURES

CULTURE	B.C.E. 3000	2500	2000	1500	1000	500	0	500	1000	1500	2000 C.E.
Sumerian	████	████	████	████							
Akkadian/Babylonian			████	████	████	████					
Hittite/Hurrian			████	████	████						
Egyptian	████	████	████	████	████	████					
Greek				• • • • •	████	████	████				
Roman						████	████	████			
Jewish			• • •	████	████	████	████	████	████	████	████
Christian							████	████	████	████	████
Islamic									████	████	████
Hindu			• • • •	████	████	████	████	████	████	████	████
Buddhist						████	████	████	████	████	████
Incan								████	████	████	
Mayan						████	████	████	████		
Aztec							████	████	████		
Celtic						████	████	████			
Nordic/Icelandic								████	████	████	

267

9 Hinduism and Buddhism

The Sacred Subcontinent: The Spread of Religion in India and Beyond

1500 B.C.E.–1200 C.E.

This chapter begins with a brief history of early Hinduism, the most ancient of existing major religions, and analyzes its evolution as the principal cultural system of the Indian subcontinent. Buddhism emerged out of Hinduism in India and spread throughout central, eastern, and southeastern Asia, defining much of the cultural and religious life of this vast region. Its history concludes this chapter.

Shiva with the corpse of the goddess Sati, southern India, seventeenth century. Bronze. Lord Shiva, one of the most revered of all the gods of Hinduism, is usually portrayed in awe-inspiring forms because he is the god of destruction, but that destruction sets the stage for later rebirth and reconstruction. (Government Museum, Trivandrum, India)

LEARNING OBJECTIVES

9.1 ((	9.2 ((	9.3 ((
Explain the unique elements in Hinduism.	Explain the reasons for the emergence and spread of Buddhism.	Compare the two religions of the Indian subcontinent.

((Listen on MyHistoryLab

AT A GLANCE: HINDUISM AND BUDDHISM

DATE	POLITICAL/SOCIAL EVENTS	LITERARY/PHILOSOPHICAL EVENTS
1500 B.C.E.	• Caste system	• *Rigveda* (1500–1200)
900 B.C.E.		• *Brahmanas* (900–500)
800 B.C.E.		• *Upanishads* (800–500)
500 B.C.E.	• Siddhartha Gautama (Buddha) (c. 563–483) • Mahavir (b. 540), Jain teacher	• Buddha delivers sermon on the Four Noble Truths and the Noble Eightfold Path
300 B.C.E.		• *Mahabharata* (c. 300 B.C.E.–300 C.E.) • *Ramayana* (c. 300 B.C.E.–300 C.E.)
200 B.C.E.	• Buddhism more widespread than Hinduism in India (until 200 C.E.); spreading in Sri Lanka • Mahayana Buddhism growing in popularity	
10 C.E.	• Fourth general council of Buddhism codified Theravada doctrines • Buddhist missionaries in China (65 C.E.)	• Nagarjuna (*fl. c.* 50–150 C.E.), philosopher of Mahayana Buddhism
300 C.E.	• Spread of Hinduism to Southeast Asia	
400 C.E.	• Hindu pantheon established • Buddhism declining in India	• Puranas written (400–1000) • Faxian's pilgrimage to India • Sanskrit; Hindu gods, temples, and priests in Southeast Asia; Buddhism in Southeast Asia
500 C.E.	• Bhakti begun in south India • Buddhist monks to Japan	
600 C.E.	• Buddhist monks to Southeast Asia • Buddhism flourishes under Tang dynasty (618–907)	• Xuanzang's pilgrimage to India
700 C.E.	• Hindu temples and shrines begin to appear in India • Buddhism begins to decline in China • Buddhism becoming established in Japan	• Hindu philosopher Shankaracharya (788–820) • Saicho (767–822), Japanese Buddhist priest • Kukai (774–835), Japanese Buddhist priest
800 C.E.	• Hindu priests in Southeast Asia • Emperor Wuzong attacks Buddhism in China	• Earliest printed book, *The Diamond Sutra* (868) • Hindu philosopher Ramanuja (c. 1017–1137)
1000 C.E.	• Muslim invasion of India (1000–1200) • Buddhist institutions close in India	

Hinduism

9.1   What is unique in the history of Hinduism?

Hinduism began before recorded time. The other major religions of the world claim the inspiration of a specific person or event—Abraham's covenant; the Buddha's enlightenment; Jesus' birth; Muhammad's revelation—but Hinduism emerged through the weaving together of many diverse, ancient religious traditions of India, some of which precede written records. Hinduism evolved from the experience of the peoples of India.

🔍 **View** the **Image**: **Nine Hindu Planets** on **MyHistoryLab**

The Origins of Hinduism

Because Hinduism preserves a rich body of religious literature written in Sanskrit, the language of the Aryan immigrants of 1700–1200 B.C.E., scholars believed until recently that Hinduism was a product of that migration. Even the excavations at Mohenjo-Daro and Harappa, which uncovered a pre-Aryan civilization, did not at first alter these beliefs. But as excavation and analysis have continued, many scholars

What is unique in the history of Hinduism?

9.1
9.2
9.3

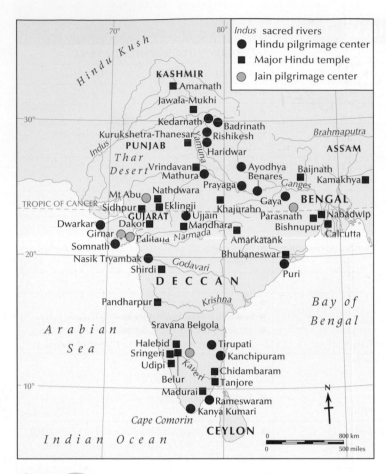

Hindu south Asia. Hinduism is the oldest of the world's leading religions, although its geographic range has been mostly confined to the peoples of south Asia, where its impact has been profound, exemplified by the sacred geography of the subcontinent. Rivers, mountains, and regions associated with divine mythology are important, and networks of pilgrimage centers and temples provide cultural unity.

have come to believe that the Indus valley civilization may have contributed many of Hinduism's principal gods and ceremonies. Excavated statues seem to represent the god Shiva, the sacred bull Nandi on which he rides, a man practicing yogic meditation, a sacred tree, and a mother goddess. Archaeologists increasingly argue that the Aryans absorbed religious beliefs and practices, along with secular culture, from the Indus valley and from other groups already living in India when they arrived.

Contemporary anthropological accounts support this idea that Hinduism is an amalgam of beliefs and practices. These accounts emphasize Hinduism's remarkable ability to absorb and assimilate tribal peoples and their gods. Today, 100 million people, about ten percent of India's population, are officially regarded as *adivasis*, original inhabitants (previously referred to as "tribals"). These peoples were living in India before the arrival of the Aryans, and they have largely attempted to escape Aryan domination by retreating into remote hilly and forested regions, where they could preserve their own social systems. Hindus have, however, pursued them and their lands, building temples in and around tribal areas. These temples recognize tribal gods and incorporate them with the mainstream deities in an attempt to persuade the *adivasis* to accept Hindu religious patterns. Indeed, one of Hinduism's most important gods, Krishna, the blue/black god, was apparently a tribal god who gained national recognition.

As India's peoples have been diverse, so its evolving religious system is diverse. The concept of "Hinduism" as a unified religion comes from outsiders. Greeks and Persians first encountering India spoke of India's belief systems and practices collectively as "Hinduism," that is, the ways of the peoples on the far side of the Indus River. When Muslims began to arrive in India, beginning in the eighth century C.E., they adopted the same terminology.

Sacred Geography and Pilgrimage

Hinduism is closely associated with a specific territory, India. Almost all Hindus live in India or are of Indian descent. Within India itself a sacred geography has developed. Places visited by gods and by saints, as well as places of great natural sanctity, have become shrines and pilgrim destinations. Pilgrims traveling these routes have created a geography of religious/national integration, and modern transportation in the form of trains, buses, and airplanes has increased the pilgrim traffic throughout India. Some of the most important shrines are at the far corners of India, such as Dwarka on the far west coast, Badrinath in the far north, Puri on the east coast, and Rameshwaram near the southern tip. Travel to all these shrines would thus provide the pilgrim with a "Bharat Darshan," a view of the entire geography of India. Such pilgrimage routes have helped to unify both Hinduism and India.

Each locality in city and village is also knit together by religious shrines, ranging from the simple prayer niche, containing pictures and statues of the gods of the

9.1 What is unique in the history of Hinduism?

9.2

9.3

Modern *puja* shrine, India. In this contemporary, crowded, one-room urban apartment the *puja* corner, with its images and pictures of various gods, and its oil lamps, finds its place alongside a television set and the cooking utensils of the household.

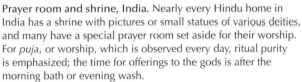

What is unique in the history of Hinduism?

9.1

9.2

9.3

Prayer room and shrine, India. Nearly every Hindu home in India has a shrine with pictures or small statues of various deities, and many have a special prayer room set aside for their worship. For *puja*, or worship, which is observed every day, ritual purity is emphasized; the time for offerings to the gods is after the morning bath or evening wash.

kind found in even the most humble home; through neighborhood shrines, nestled perhaps in the trunk of an especially sacred tree; to local and regional temples.

The Central Beliefs of Hinduism

Hinduism has none of the fixed dogmas of most otherworldly religions, and great flexibility and variety of beliefs exist under the general term "Hindu." Nevertheless, sacred texts do provide a set of beliefs and orientations toward life that are very widely shared. Over time, the introduction of new texts to the Hindu legacy marked the evolution of Hinduism as a living, changing system of beliefs and practices.

The *Rigveda*. Between about 1500 and 1200 B.C.E. *brahmin* priests of the nomadic pastoralist Aryan peoples entering India composed the *Rigveda*, a collection of 1028 verses of Sanskrit poetry, the oldest and most venerated of the four books called, collectively, Vedas. These verses invoke many early gods, including Agni, the god of various kinds of fire; Indra, a phallic god of rain and fertility; Surya, god of the sun; and Varuna, the sovereign of the world who assures that the cosmic law is maintained. They include references to music, dance, and acting as modes of worship.

9.1

9.2

9.3

What is unique
in the history of
Hinduism?

Vedic worship also takes the form of animal sacrifice offered on sacred altars. The *Rigveda* speculates on the creation of the world and on the significance of life in this world, but it does not pretend to offer conclusive answers:

> Who really knows? Who shall here proclaim it? whence things came to be, whence this creation. … This creation, whence it came to be, whether it was made or not— he who is its overseer in the highest heaven, he surely knows. Or if he does not know …? (X:129; Embree, p. 21)

Caste. The Rigveda also introduces the mythic origin and rationale of the caste system, one of the most distinctive features of Hindu life. Caste began, the Rigveda suggests, in a primeval sacrifice of a mythical creature, Purusha. He was carved into four sections, each symbolizing one of the principal divisions of the caste system:

> When they divided Purusha, in how many different portions did they arrange him? What became of his mouth, what of his two arms? What were his two thighs and his two feet called? His mouth became the *brahman* [priest]; his two arms were made into the *rajanya* [or *kshatriya*, warrior]; his two thighs the *vaishyas* [business people and farmers/landlords]; from his two feet the *shudra* [person of the lower working class] was born. (X:90; Embree, pp. 18–19)

Apparently, the Aryans were even then thinking of a social system that separated people by occupation and sanctioned that separation through religion. The caste system that developed in India was probably the most rigidly unequal and hierarchical of any in the world. Caste status was hereditary, passing from parent to child at birth. Each caste was subject to different local legal rules, with upper castes being rewarded more generously and punished less severely than lower. Only upper castes were permitted to receive formal education, and the separate castes were not to intermarry nor even to dine with one another. Their vital fluids were distinct and different, and the blood and semen of one group were not to mingle with those of another. The food fit for one group was not necessarily appropriate for others: *brahmin* priests were to be vegetarians, but *kshatriya* warriors were to eat meat.

Commentators throughout the centuries have searched for additional roots of the caste system, more grounded in social, economic, and political rationales. Many have seen India's caste system as a means of ordering relationships among the multitude of immigrant groups in India's multiethnic population, consolidating some at the top and relegating others to the bottom. Others have seen caste as the result of a frozen economic system, with parents doing all they could to make sure that their children maintained at least the family's current occupational status. They sacrificed the possibility of upward mobility in exchange for the security that they would not fall lower on the social scale.

Many suggested that the system was imposed on the rest of the population by an extremely powerful coalition of *brahmin* priests and *kshatriya* warrior-rulers. Such dominant coalitions are common in world history, and the Indian situation was simply more entrenched than most.

Historians employ the insights of anthropologists as they attempt to understand the historical origins and basis of the caste system. Anthropological observation shows that the four generalized castes of the Vedas are not the actual groupings that function in practice today. Instead, India has tens of thousands of localized castes, called *jatis*—indeed, there are thousands of different *brahmin* groups alone. In practice, caste is lived in accordance with the accepted practices of these local groupings, in the 750,000 villages, towns, and cities of India. From customary law to dining patterns to marriage arrangements, caste relationships are determined locally, and there is no national overarching religious system to formulate and enforce rules. Residents of any given village, for example, may represent some 20 to 30 castes, including all the various craftworkers and artisans. There may be more than one caste claiming

Gouache illustration from Bhanudatta's *Rasamanjari*, 1685. Krishna, the eighth *avatar* (incarnation) of Vishnu, is always depicted with blue or black skin, perhaps because he was originally a god of tribal groups, later assimilated into mainstream Hinduism, along with the peoples who worshiped him. He is renowned for his prowess as a warrior and a lover. In this scene from one of his amorous adventures, a woman stops a forester from felling the tree under which she has arranged to meet Krishna for a romantic tryst.

What is unique
in the history of
Hinduism?

9.1

9.2

9.3

brahmin status, or *kshatriya*, *vaishya*, or *shudra* status. Anthropologists therefore differentiate between the mythological four *varna* groups of the Vedic caste system and the thousands of *jati* groups through which caste is actually lived in India. Both historians and anthropologists are convinced that the same multitude of castes that they find "on the ground" today existed also in the past. Eventually "outcastes," or "untouchables," emerged, people who were outside the caste system because of the "polluting" work they performed, which might include dealing with dead animals or handling those who died.

Throughout Indian history there have been revolts against the hierarchy of the caste system. In the twentieth century and into the present century the government of India has acted assertively to eliminate the historic discrimination of the caste system, as we shall see in the chapter entitled "China and India." Nevertheless, through the millennia, caste has usually been more important than government in determining the conditions of life of most people. Personal identity and group loyalty were formed far more by caste locally than by government, which tended to be remote.

The *Brahmanas* and *Upanishads*. A second collection of Sanskrit religious literature, dating from about 900–500 B.C.E., sets out rules for *brahmins*, including procedures for sacrifice and worship. These scriptures, the *Brahmanas*, include discussions of the origins of various rituals and myths of the immortal gods.

The *Upanishads*, composed 800–500 B.C.E., are devoted primarily to mystical speculation and proclaim the oneness of the individual and the universe. The universal

273

9.1

9.2

9.3

What is unique
in the history of
Hinduism?

KEY TERMS

atman The soul of each
individual person, identical in
its substance to *Brahman*, the
universal power. Thus each
individual soul is part of the great
soul of the universe.

samsara The process and cycle of
living, dying, and being reborn.

maya Illusion. The manifest
world in which we appear to live
is only illusion; there is a reality
beyond what we experience here
on earth.

dharma The duty of each person,
determined in large part by his or
her caste.

karma The doctrine that actions
have their own appropriate
consequences. A person's actions
carry their own rewards (or
punishments) because they set the
directions of his or her life.

spirit, *Brahman*, and the soul of each individual, *atman*, are ultimately the same substance, just as individual sparks are the same substance as a large fire. In time, each *atman* will be united with the universal *Brahman*. To reach this unity, each soul will experience reincarnation (*samsara*) in a series of bodies, until it is purged of its attachments to the physical world—which in any case is *maya*, or illusion—and achieves pure spirituality. Then, at the death of this final body, the *atman* is released to its union with the *Brahman*.

The *Upanishads* introduce several concepts fundamental to almost all strands of Hinduism. **Dharma** is the set of religious and ethical duties to which each living creature in the universe is subject. These duties are not the same, however, for each creature; they differ according to ritual status. **Karma** is the set of activities of each creature and the effects that these activities have on its *atman*. Each action has an effect on the *atman*; activities in accord with one's *dharma* purity the *atman*; activities in opposition to one's *dharma* pollute it. "Good *karma*," the good effects brought about by actions in accord with *dharma*, will finally enable the *atman* to win its release from *maya*, the illusions of life on earth; escape *samsara*, or reincarnation; and reach *moksha*, the ultimate union with the *Brahman*. Thus Hinduism sees reward and punishment in the universe as a natural consequence. Good, *dharmic* actions carry their own reward for the *atman*; activities opposed to *dharma* carry their own negative consequences. Activities in this life earn good or bad *karma*.

The *Upanishads* also introduce the concept of the life cycle, with its different duties at each stage. The first stage, *brahmacharya*, is the youthful time of studies and celibacy; the second, *gruhasta*, the householder stage, is for raising a family; the third, *vanaprastha*, literally forest-wandering, is for reflection outside the demands of everyday life; and the last, *sannyasin*, is for immersion in meditation in preparation for death and, ideally, for *moksha*.

MAJOR HINDU GODS AND GODDESSES

A shrine with images of one or more of the thousands of gods in the pantheon can be found in every devout Hindu home. The most widely worshiped gods are probably Shiva with his consort Parvati, and Vishnu with his consorts Lakshmi and Saraswati. But most Hindus offer at least some form of devotion to more than one god.

Brahma	The creator god, whose four heads and arms represent the four Vedas (scriptures), castes, and *yugas* (ages of the world).
Ganesh	The elephant-headed god, bringer of good luck.
Kali	Shiva's fierce consort—the goddess of death—is shown as a fearsome, blood-drinking, four-armed black woman.
Krishna	The eighth *avatar* (incarnation) of Vishnu, depicted with blue or black skin. He is honored for his skills as a lover and a warrior; with his consort Radha.
Rama	The personification of virtue, reason, and chivalry; with his consort Sita, revered for her loyalty.
Shiva	God of destruction, whose dancing in a circle of fire symbolizes the eternal cycle of creation and destruction.
Sitala	Mothers traditionally pray to this goddess to protect their children from disease, especially smallpox.
Vishnu	The preserver, a kindly god, who protects those who worship him, banishes bad luck, and restores good health; with his consorts Lakshmi, the goddess of wealth, and Saraswati, the goddess of wisdom and the arts.

 View the **Image: Hindu Gods** on **MyHistoryLab**

These early scriptures established a set of principles that constitute the core of Hindu belief: caste, *dharma*, *karma*, life stages, *samsara*, and, ultimately, *moksha*, the union of the individual *atman* with the universal *Brahman*. They represent a rational system of order in the universe and in individual life. They teach the importance of *dharmic* activities in this world in order to reach *moksha* in the deeper reality beyond. They are transmitted from *guru*, or teacher, to *shishya*, or student. The codification of many of these specific behavioral norms for each caste in *The Law of Manu* attempted to institutionalize the position of the priests and to elaborate on core Hindu beliefs. Written in the first or second century B.C.E., the treatise almost certainly reflected earlier practices, spelling out the appropriate relationships between social classes and between men and women.

Although it reveres the *brahmin* priest (not to be confused with the *Brahman* spirit of the universe), Hinduism is ultimately accessible to each individual, even to those of low caste. Despite the hierarchy of the caste system, Hinduism allows enormous spiritual scope to each individual. It has no core dogma that each must affirm. Each individual Hindu may claim his or her own unique sense of spirituality. This universal accessibility of Hinduism is most clear in three later forms of literature that have become a kind of folk treasury (in contrast to the Vedas, *Brahmanas*, and *Upanishads*, which are the province of the *brahmin* priests).

The Great Epics. In the chapter entitled "Indian Empires" we discussed India's two great epic poems, the *Ramayana* and the *Mahabharata*. The latter's central story revolves around the civil war between two branches of the family of the Bharatas (from whom India derives its current Hindi name, Bharat). The *Mahabharata* presents moral conflicts, the dilemma of taking sides, and the necessity of acting decisively. At its center stands the *Bhagavad-Gita* ("Song of God"), a philosophical discourse on the duties and the meaning of life and death.

The *Bhagavad-Gita* opens on the field of Kurukshetra before the final battle between the two branches of the Bharata family. Arjuna, leader of one branch, despairs of his options: if he fights, he kills his cousins; if he does not fight, he dies. He turns to his chariot driver, the Lord Krishna, for advice. Krishna's reply incorporates many fundamental principles of Hindu thought. First, Krishna speaks of the duty of Arjuna, a *kshatriya* by caste, to fight: "For a *kshatriya* there does not exist another greater good than war enjoined by *dharma*" (II:31). Each person has a unique *dharma*, largely determined by caste. In this philosophy, changing one's vocational duty is no virtue:

> Better is one's own *dharma* that one may be able to fulfill but imperfectly, than the *dharma* of others that is more easily accomplished. Better is death in the fulfillment of one's own *dharma*. To adopt the *dharma* of others is perilous. (III:35)

The *Bhagavad-Gita* summarizes many of the key doctrines of Hinduism. Lord Krishna promises to help people who do their duty, and points the way toward spiritual fulfillment. The text demonstrates considerable assimilation within Hinduism, for the lord Krishna is dark-skinned, usually represented as blue or black in color. He appears to be originally a non-Vedic, non-Aryan tribal god, perhaps from the south. His centrality in this most revered Sanskrit text suggests the continuing accommodation between the Aryans and the indigenous peoples of India. The *Gita* provided the basis for the continuing emphasis in Hinduism on **bhakti**, mystical devotion to god. "No one devoted to me is lost … Keep me in your mind and devotion, sacrifice to me, bow to me, discipline your self toward me, and you will reach me" (IX:31,34) is one of many statements in the *Gita* that called for this devotion. *Bhakti* was a revolt within Hinduism against formality in religion, against hierarchy, and against the power of the *brahmin* priesthood. *Bhakti* continues today in the hymns and poetry of the common people and in the multitudes of devotional prayer meetings in every corner of India.

The two epics generally also reflect greater prestige for women than did earlier Sanskrit texts. In the *Ramayana*, Sita appears as a traditionally subordinate wife to Rama, but her commitment to honor and duty surpasses even his; she defends Rama's honor even when he fails to defend hers. She is more heroic than he, although her heroism is defined by her role as dutiful wife. Rama is implicitly criticized for his inability to defend her both from Ravana and from the gossip of his own subjects. In some versions, the criticism is made explicit. In the *Mahabharata* Draupadi is the

Burning the effigy of the evil Ravana. Each year, at the time of the festival of Dusshera, acting troupes throughout India retell the story of the *Ramayana*, climaxing with the victory of Rama over Ravana, the evil king who abducted Rama's wife, Sita. In Ahmedabad, huge effigies of Ravana and his allies are burned, to the delight of the crowds who come to witness this celebration of the triumph of good over evil.

What is unique in the history of Hinduism?

9.1

9.2

9.3

KEY TERM

Bhakti Devotion to god; a personal dedication to and worship of god, often through meditation, music, chanting, dance—different from more formal rituals.

SACRED WRITINGS OF HINDUISM

Vedas	The most sacred of the Hindu scriptures, meaning "divine knowledge." They consist of collections of writings compiled by the Aryans: *Rigveda* (hymns and praises), *Yajurveda* (prayers and sacrificial formulas), *Samaveda* (tunes and chants), and *Atharva-Veda* (Veda of the Atharvans, the priests who officiate at sacrifices).
Upanishads	Philosophical treatises, centering on the doctrine of Brahma.
Brahmanas	Instructions on ritual and sacrifice.
Ramayana	An epic poem, telling how Rama (an incarnation of the god Vishnu) and his devotee Hanuman, the monkey god, recover Rama's wife, Sita, who has been abducted by the demon king Ravana.
Mahabharata	"Great Poem of the Bharatas." Includes the *Bhagavad-Gita* ("Song of God") and consists of 18 books and 90,000 stanzas. The central narrative of civil war, and the innumerable sidebars, emphasize the struggle to do one's duty faithfully.

9.1

9.2

9.3

What is unique in the history of Hinduism?

wife of five noble brothers, and she protects, defends, and inspires them in their struggles, going far beyond the subservient role that women play in the majority of Aryan literature. In the epics, the female force, *shakti*, has gained recognition.

The *Puranas*. The most popular of the gods of Hinduism, Vishnu and Shiva, appear in the *Puranas*, a collection of ancient stories. Here, too, female goddesses appear, often as consorts of the principal gods, such as the goddesses Lakshmi and Saraswati with the lord Vishnu; and the goddesses Parvati, Durga, and Kali with the lord Shiva. These goddesses also help to balance the rather suppressed position of females evident in the earlier Aryan literature.

Temples and Shrines

By the seventh century C.E., fundamental changes had taken place in the form of Hindu worship. Personal prayer, often addressed to representations of the gods in statues and pictures, displaced sacrifice. Hindus built temples of great beauty. The caves at Ellora in western India were fashioned into temples in the eighth century, reflecting the early importance of caves in Hindu worship. Within the cave-temples, sculpture and painting demonstrate the artistic development in religious worship.

SOURCE

The *Bhagavad-Gita* from the *Mahabharata*

Lord Krishna counsels Arjuna to do his duty in leading the fighting of a civil war, even though the warrior has no desire to shed the blood of his relatives. Krishna continues with additional advice—on the importance of proper action for its own sake regardless of praise or condemnation, on reincarnation, and on Lord Krishna's grace upon those who seek him—much of which has been accepted by many Hindus then and now as key principles of life.

Krishna advises Arjuna to act. He notes three kinds of yoga, or discipline, which bring people to spiritual liberation: the yoga of knowledge; the yoga of devotion; and the yoga of action. (The yoga of physical discipline and meditation, known widely today in the West, is yet another form.) In this case, Krishna tells Arjuna, the yoga of action is required:

Do your allotted work, for action is superior to nonaction. Even the normal functioning of your body cannot be accomplished through actionlessness. (III:8)

The key, however, is performing the action because it is right, without concern for its results or rewards.

Action alone is your concern, never at all its fruits. Let not the fruits of action be your motive, nor let yourself be attached to inaction … Seek refuge in the right mental attitude. Wretched are those who are motivated by the fruits of action. (II:49)

Nonattachment is the ideal:

He who feels no attachment toward anything; who, having encountered the various good or evil things, neither rejoices nor loathes—his wisdom is steadfast. (II:59)

… He who behaves alike to foe and friend; who likewise is even-poised in honor or dishonor; who is even-tempered in cold and heat, happiness and sorrow; who is free from attachment; who regards praise and censure with equanimity; who is silent, content with anything whatever; who has no fixed abode, who is steadfast in mind, who is full of devotion—that man is dear to me. (XII:18–19)

In reply to Arjuna's specific anxiety about killing his cousins, Krishna reminds him of the doctrine of reincarnation:

As a man discards worn-out clothes to put on new and different ones, so the disembodied self discards its worn-out bodies to take on other new ones.

… Death is certain for anyone born, and birth is certain for the dead; since the cycle is inevitable, you have no cause to grieve! (II:22, 27)

Krishna also assures Arjuna of his abiding concern for him, and of the god's power to help him: "If I am in your thought, by my grace you will transcend all dangers" (XVIII:58). Arjuna does fight, and wins, and in the end all the warriors who die are reborn.

What is unique
in the history of
Hinduism?

9.1

9.2

9.3

Kandariya Mahadeo Temple at Khajuraho, Chandela, c. 1025–50 C.E. The 20 surviving temples
at Khajuraho, although ravaged by time, are still among the greatest examples of medieval Hindu
architecture and sculpture in north India. Beneath the soaring towers, layered bands of sculptures writhe
in a pulsating tableau of human and divine activity. The depictions of athletic lovemaking, which so
scandalized nineteenth-century European travelers, can be linked to *tantric* sects of Hinduism, then
prevalent in the Chandela region.

The bas-reliefs and artwork in the temples at Kanchi and Mahabalipuram in the
south, also built in the eighth century, continue to dazzle viewers today. Magnificent
temples flourished everywhere in India, but especially in the south of the subcontinent. Sexual passion and the union of male and female entered into forms of worship,
symbolically representing passion for, and union with, god, as the temple sculptures
at Khajuraho in north India about 1000 C.E. illustrate.

9.1   What is unique
       in the history of
9.2   Hinduism?

9.3

Religion and Rule

Wealthy landowners and rulers, who sought validation of their power and rule through the prestige of *brahmin* priests, often patronized temples. As in many religions, rulers supported priests, while priests affirmed the authority of the rulers. This was especially true in the south. At least as early as the eighth century, new rulers who seized lands occupied by indigenous tribal peoples often imported *brahmin* priests to overawe the *adivasis* with their learning, piety, and rituals, and to persuade them of the proper authority of the king. To pacify the *adivasis*, their gods might be incorporated into the array of gods worshiped in the temple by the priests, just as the *adivasis* would begin to worship the major gods of Hinduism. Anthropologists describe this process as an interplay between the "great" national tradition and the "little" local tradition. As new lands were opened, and *adivasis* were persuaded to accept the new ruling coalition, the temples grew larger and more wealthy.

In exchange for their support, kings rewarded priests with land grants, court subsidies, and temple bequests. *Brahmin* priests and Tamil rulers in southern India prospered together as temples took on important economic functions in banking and money-lending for the villages in their region. Hindu colleges, rest-houses for pilgrims, centers of administration, and even cities grew up around some of these temples.

Bronze sculpture of Vishnu, early Chola period, first half of tenth century C.E. Vishnu is beloved as the tender, merciful deity—the Preserver—and, as the second member of the Hindu trinity, he complements Brahma the Creator and Shiva the Destroyer. He is said to come to earth periodically as an *avatar*, an incarnation in various forms, to help humankind in times of crisis. (Government Museum and National Art Gallery, Madras)

Kailasanatha Temple at Ellora, Rashtrakuta, *c.* 757–90 C.E. Carved into an escarpment of volcanic stone, the 33 shrines of Ellora have for centuries been a pilgrimage center for Hindus, Buddhists, and Jains. The monolithic stone shaft in the foreground, 60 feet high, would have originally supported a trident symbol of Shiva, to whom this temple is dedicated.

HOW DO WE KNOW?

Hinduism in Southeast Asia

Evidence for the influence of Hinduism in Southeast Asia comes from a variety of sources. Even today, the historical stamp of Hinduism endures in Southeast Asia in the names of cities, including Ayuthia in Thailand, derived from Ayodhya in northern India; in the influence of Sanskrit on several Southeast Asian languages; in the popularity of the *Ramayana* and other Hindu literature in the folklore and theater of the region. Moreover, Hindu temples still stand, most spectacularly the Angkor Wat temple complex in Cambodia (see the chapter "Indian Empires,").

Evidence of Hindu influence in Southeast Asia appears also in early reports of Chinese visitors, archaeological remains, and epigraphy (inscriptions on metal and rock). These records are, nevertheless, sparse. *Brahmin* priests appear in the Southeast Asian records only after 800 C.E. It is, therefore, difficult to answer the question "What brought Indian power and prestige into Southeast Asia from about the third century to about the fourteenth century?"

Three theories explaining the appearance of Indian influence in Southeast Asia have been suggested. One argued that Indians initiated contact and attempted to introduce their religion and culture into Southeast Asia. This theory, which stressed the use of military might, is no longer accepted. As noted in the chapter "Indian Empires," there is very little record of Indian military action in the area, and none suggesting a desire for conquest. A second theory—that Indian traders brought their culture with them—has wider acceptance, but it also encounters serious opposition. Trade connections between India and Southeast Asia were numerous, long-standing, and intense. Some cultural and religious influence must have accompanied them, but these contacts were by sea, while much of the Hindu influence was found inland.

A third theory argued that local rulers invited *brahmin* priests to come from India to southeast Asia to build temples, to promote agricultural development on land specially granted to them, to invoke the Hindu gods to validate their authority, and to convince the local population of this divine validation. In the words of one historian, these priests were to serve as "development planners." They brought with them from India principles of government, religious law, administration, art, and architecture. In promoting these religious/political practices through the priests, Southeast Asian rulers were emulating the policies of the Pallava and Chola kings of southern India. But Hinduism did not survive in Southeast Asia. It was superseded by Buddhism and, later, by Islam.

Local kings and Southeast Asian rulers also invited Buddhist monks as well as Hindu priests to Southeast Asia to help to establish and consolidate their power, and they found the Buddhist monks to be as useful as the Hindu *brahmins*, for they served similar political and administrative functions, but in the name of Buddhism. For example, the ruler of the Srivijaya Empire in the East Indies welcomed 1,000 Buddhist monks to his kingdom in the late seventh century C.E. Jayavarman VII, the Buddhist ruler of the Khmer kingdom at the end of the twelfth century, added Buddhist images to the great temple of Angkor Wat, which had been built earlier in the century to honor the Hindu god Vishnu.

By about the fourteenth century, Hinduism had died out in Southeast Asia, while Buddhism continued to thrive. In fact, Buddhism became an enormously successful proselytizing religion throughout Asia. In India, on the other hand, Buddhism withered away, while Hinduism flourished.

- Of the theories explaining the spread of Hinduism in Southeast Asia, why does the theory of the priest as "development planner" seem the most convincing?
- What is the evidence for the coexistence of Hinduism and Buddhism, for a time, in Southeast Asia?
- What was the functional relationship between priests and rulers in Southeast Asia?

Hinduism in Southeast Asia

What is unique in the history of Hinduism? 9.1 9.2 9.3

Hinduism did not generally attract, nor did it seek, converts outside India, but Southeast Asia was an exception. Here, the initiative for conversion grew out of politics, as it had in southern India. The powers of the Hindu temple and the *brahmin* priesthood were imported to validate royal authority in Southeast Asia from as early as the third century C.E. to as late as the fourteenth century.

Trade contacts between India and Southeast Asia date back to at least 150 B.C.E. Indian sailors carried cargoes to and from Burma (Myanmar), the Straits of Malacca, the Kingdom of Funan in modern Cambodia and Vietnam, and Java in modern Indonesia. By the third century C.E., Funan had accepted many elements of Indian culture, religion, and political practice. Chinese envoys reported a prosperous state with walled cities, palaces, and houses. Sanskrit was in use, as was some Indian technology for irrigation and farming. By the fifth century it appears that Sanskrit had spread, Indian calendars marked the dates, and Indian gods, including Shiva and Vishnu, were worshiped, as were representations of the Buddha (see below). Hindu temples began to appear with *brahmin* priests to staff them.

Buddhism

9.2   How did Buddhism emerge and spread?

Buddhism was born in India, within the culture of Hinduism, and then charted its own path. Like Hinduism, it questioned the reality of the earthly world and speculated on the existence of other worlds. Unlike Hinduism, however, Buddhism had a founder, a set of originating scriptures, and an order of monks. In opposition to Hinduism, it renounced hereditary caste organization and the supremacy of the *brahmin* priests. Buddhism spread to Southeast Asia, gaining acceptance as the principal religion of Myanmar, Thailand, Cambodia, Laos, and Vietnam until today. It won multitudes of adherents throughout the rest of Asia as well, in Sri Lanka, Tibet, China, Korea, and Japan. Yet in India itself, Buddhism lost out in competition with Hinduism and its priesthood, virtually vanishing from the subcontinent by about the twelfth century C.E.

The Origins of Buddhism

All we know of the Buddha's life and teaching comes from much later accounts, embellished by his followers. While there is much doubt about almost every aspect of the Buddha's life and teachings, the accounts that exist tell the following story.

The Life of the Buddha. Siddhartha Gautama was born about 563 B.C.E. in the foothills of the Himalaya Mountains of what is now Nepal. His father, a warrior chief of the *kshatriya* caste, received a prophecy that Siddhartha would become either a great emperor or a great religious teacher. Hoping that his son would follow the former vocation, the chief sheltered him as best he could so that he would experience neither pain nor disillusionment.

When he was 29 years old, Siddhartha started to grow curious about what lay beyond the confines of his father's palace. Leaving his wife, Yasadhara, and their son, Rahula, he instructed his charioteer to take him to the city, where he came across a frail, elderly man. Never having encountered old age, Siddhartha was confused. His companion explained that aging was an inevitable and painful part of human experience. As Siddhartha took further excursions outside the palace, he soon came

---

SOURCE

The "Address to Sigala": Buddhism in Everyday Life

Much of the Buddha's moral and ethical instruction is directed to the monks of the Sangha. In the "Address to Sigala," however, the Buddha speaks to laypeople about their relationships and responsibilities toward one another. The address includes practical advice to husbands and wives, friends, employers, and employees. The lengthy address is translated and summarized here by A.L. Basham.

Husbands should respect their wives, and comply as far as possible with their requests. They should not commit adultery. They should give their wives full charge of the home, and supply them with fine clothes and jewelry as far as their means permit. Wives should be thorough in their duties, gentle and kind to the whole household, chaste, and careful in housekeeping, and should carry out their work with skill and enthusiasm.

A man should be generous to his friends, speak kindly of them, act in their interest in every way possible, treat them as his equals, and keep his word to them. They in turn should watch over his interests and property, take care of him when he is "off his guard" [i.e. intoxicated, infatuated, or otherwise liable to commit rash and careless actions], stand by him and help him in time of trouble, and respect other members of his family.

Employers should treat their servants and workpeople decently. They should not be given tasks beyond their strength. They should receive adequate food and wages, be cared for in time of sickness and infirmity, and be given regular holidays and bonuses in times of prosperity. They should rise early and go to bed late in the service of their master, be content with their just wages, work thoroughly, and maintain their master's reputation. (*Digha Nikaya*, iii:161; cited in Basham, p. 286)

to see that pain was an integral part of life, experienced in illness, aging, death, and birth. The search for a remedy for this pervasive sorrow became his quest.

On his fourth and final trip he met a wandering holy man who had shunned the trappings of wealth and material gain. Siddhartha decided to do likewise. Bidding farewell to his family for the last time, he set out on horseback in search of an antidote to sorrow and a means of teaching it to others.

For six years Siddhartha wandered as an ascetic. Nearing starvation, however, he gave up the path of asceticism. Determined to achieve enlightenment, he began to meditate, sitting under a tree at Bodh Gaya near modern Patna, in India. Mara, the spirit of this world, who tempted him to give up his meditation with threats of punishment and promises of rewards, tested his concentration and fortitude. Touching the ground with his hand in a gesture, or *mudra*, repeated often in sculptures of the Buddha, Siddhartha revealed these temptations to be illusions. On the forty-ninth day of meditation he reached enlightenment, becoming the Buddha, "He Who Has Awakened." He had found an antidote to pain and suffering. He proceeded to the Deer Park at Sarnath, near Banaras, where he delivered his first sermon, beginning by setting forth the Four Noble Truths of suffering. The source of suffering, he taught, was personal desire and passion:

> This is the [first] Noble Truth of Sorrow. Birth is sorrow, age is sorrow, disease is sorrow, death is sorrow, contact with the unpleasant is sorrow, separation from the pleasant is sorrow, every wish unfulfilled is sorrow—in short all the five components of individuality are sorrow. This is the [second] Noble Truth of the Arising of Sorrow. [It arises from] thirst, which leads to rebirth, which brings delight and passion, and seeks pleasure now here, now there—the thirst for sensual pleasure, the thirst for continued life, the thirst for power. (Basham, p. 269)

Its antidote followed from this analysis:

> This is the [third] Noble Truth of the Stopping of Sorrow. It is the complete stopping of that thirst, so that no passion remains, leaving it, being emancipated from it, being released from it, giving no place to it. And this is the [fourth] Noble Truth of the Way which Leads to the Stopping of Sorrow. It is the Noble Eightfold Path—Right Views, Right Resolve, Right Speech, Right Conduct, Right Livelihood, Right Effort, Right Recollection and Right Meditation. (p. 269)

A new consciousness could be achieved by a combination of disciplining the mind and observing ethical precepts in human relationships. In the face of continuing rebirths into the pain of life, the Buddha taught that right living could bring release from the cycle of mortality and pain, and entry into *nirvana*, a kind of blissful nothingness. On the metaphysical plane, the Buddha taught that everything in the universe is transient; there is no "being." There exists neither an immortal soul nor a god, neither *atman* nor *Brahman*. The Buddha's teachings about the illusion of life and about rebirth and release were consistent with Hindu concepts of *maya*, *samsara*, and *moksha*, but the Buddha's denial of god put him on the fringes of Hindu thought. His rejection of caste as an organizing hierarchy and of the Hindu priests as connoisseurs of religious truth won him powerful allies—and powerful opponents.

Although much of the Hindu priesthood opposed the Buddha's teachings, the kings of Magadha and Koshala, whose territories included most of the lower Gangetic plain, befriended and supported him and the small band of followers gathered around him. The Buddha taught peacefully and calmly until about 483 B.C.E., when, at the age of 80, he died, surrounded by a cadre of dedicated monks and believers, the original Buddhist *Sangha* (order of monks). See the illustrations from Dunhuang China and from Japan later in this chapter. The threefold motto of all devout Buddhists became "I seek refuge in the Buddha; I seek refuge in the Doctrine; I seek refuge in the *Sangha*."

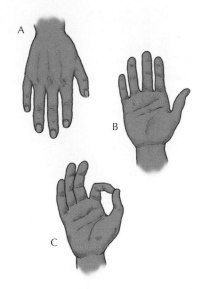

Mudras. Indian classical sculpture and dance use gestures of the hand and fingers—*mudras*—to convey moods and meanings. The Buddha's *mudras* typically show him in meditation with the right hand straight down pointing towards the earth (A); in protection of others, and counseling a lack of fear with the right hand at shoulder height, facing outward (B); in knowing, with the tips of the thumb and the index together, forming a circle, and the hand held with the palm inward toward the heart (C). Keep these *mudras* in mind as you observe classical Indian forms in this textbook.

9.1

How did Buddhism emerge and spread?

9.2

9.3

KEY TERM

mudra A hand gesture with specific meaning or significance in Indian classical sculpture and dance. One specific *mudra*, for example, indicates teaching, another fearlessness, another revelation, etc. (for example, see illustration of statue of Buddha, below).

The _Sangha_. The _Sangha_ was open to all men regardless of caste, and thus drew the antagonism of _brahmins_, although some did join. For a time, women were permitted to form their own convents, but only under special restrictions. Today, Buddhist nuns exist only in Tibet.

The monks wore saffron robes and shaved their heads. They practiced celibacy and renounced alcohol, but did not have to take a vow of obedience to the order and were intellectually and spiritually free. Decisions were made through group discussion, perpetuating the pattern of the early republics of the north Indian hills. Monks studied, disciplined their spirits, meditated, and did the physical work of their monasteries. At first they wandered, begging for their living, except during the rainy months of the monsoon. But as monasteries became richer, through donations of money and land, the monks tended to settle down. They also tended to give up begging, which diminished their contact with the common people.

👁 **Watch** the **Video**: **Siddhartha Gautama** on **MyHistoryLab**

🔎 **View** the **Closer Look**: **The Buddha's Footprints** on **MyHistoryLab**

The Emergence of Mahayana Buddhism

A series of general councils began to codify the principles, doctrines, and texts of the emerging community. The first council, convened shortly after the Buddha's death, began the continuing process of collecting his teachings. The second, about a century later, began to dispute the essential meaning of Buddhism. The third, convened at Pataliputra, Asoka's capital, revealed more of the differences that would soon lead to a split over the question of whether the Buddha was a human or a god.

By this time an array of Buddhist _caityas_, or shrines, was growing. In addition to monasteries, great stupas, or monuments filled with Buddhist relics, were built at Barhut, Sanchi, and Amaravati (see map, below). Between 200 B.C.E. and 200 C.E. there were more Buddhist than Hindu shrines in India. Theological discussion flourished, with a heavy emphasis on _metta_, or benevolence; nonviolence; _dharma_, or proper behavior (although not related to caste, since Buddhism rejected hereditary caste); and tolerance for all religions.

The fourth general council, convened in the first century C.E. in Kashmir, codified the key doctrines of Buddhism as they had developed from earliest times. These were the principles of the Theravada ("Doctrine of the Elders") branch of Buddhism, which we have been examining and which is today the prevailing form in Sri Lanka and Southeast Asia, except for Vietnam.

By now, however, a newer school of Mahayana Buddhism had been growing for perhaps two centuries and had become a serious challenge to Theravada. _Mahayana_ means "the Greater Vehicle," and its advocates claimed that their practices could carry more Buddhists to **nirvana** because they had **bodhisattvas** to help. A _bodhisattva_ was a "being of wisdom" on the verge of achieving _nirvana_ but so concerned about the welfare of fellow humans that he postponed his entrance into _nirvana_ to remain on earth, or to be reborn, in order to help others.

In addition, Mahayana Buddhism taught that religious merit, achieved through performing good deeds, could be transferred from one person to another. It embellished the concept of _nirvana_ with the vision of a Mahayana heaven, presided over by Amitabha Buddha, a Buddha who had lived on earth and had now become a kind of father in heaven. Subsequently, Mahayanists developed the concept of numerous heavens with numerous forms of the Buddha presiding over them. They also developed the concept of the Maitreya Buddha, a suffering servant who will come to redeem humanity.

Some theologians note the similarity of the concept of this Maitreya Buddha to the Christian Messiah, and some suggest that the Buddhists may have borrowed it. They also suggest that Christians may have borrowed the narratives of the virgin birth of

KEY TERMS

nirvana In Theravada Buddhism, the blissful nothingness into which a soul that had lived properly entered after death, and from which there would be no further rebirth. (Compare _nirvana_ among Jains, below.) In Mahayana Buddhism, _nirvana_ became an abode of more active bliss, a kind of heaven, filled with heavenly activities.

bodhisattva A "being of wisdom" worthy of entering _nirvana_, but who chooses to stay on earth, or be reborn, in order to help others. In Mahayana Buddhism, the Buddha himself is considered also to be one of the _bodhisattvas_.

Great Stupa, Sanchi, third century B.C.E. to first century C.E. With its four gloriously carved gates and majestic central hemisphere, the Great Stupa of Sanchi is the most remarkable surviving example of the 84,000 such Buddhist shrines reputedly erected by the emperor Asoka during the Mauryan Empire. This "world mountain," oriented to the four corners of the universe, contained a holy relic, the object of pilgrims' devotion, and is topped by a three-tiered umbrella representing the Three Jewels of Buddhism: the Buddha, the Law, and the community of monks.

9.1

9.2

How did Buddhism emerge and spread?

9.3

the Buddha and of his temptation in his search for enlightenment, and applied them to Jesus. There are significant similarities in the stories of these two men/gods and their biographies. Further, Mahayanists spoke of three aspects of the Buddha: Amitabha, the Buddha in heaven; Gautama, the historical Buddha on earth; and the most revered of all the *bodhisattvas*, the freely moving Avalokiteshvara. Theologians ask: To what degree do these three Buddhist forms correspond to the Father, Son, and Holy Spirit of Christianity as it was developing at the same time? How much borrowing took place between India and the Mediterranean coast, and in which direction?

Within India, Mahayana Buddhism began to challenge Hinduism more boldly than Theravada had. Wishing to compete for upper-caste and upper-class audiences, Mahayanists began to record their theology in Sanskrit, the language of the elite, rather than the more colloquial Pali language, which Theravada had preferred. Mahayana theologians, most notably Nagarjuna (*fl. c.* 50–150 C.E.), elaborated Buddhist philosophy and debated directly with *brahmin* priests. Buddhist monasteries established major educational programs, especially at Nalanda in Bihar, where the Buddha had spent much of his life, and at Taxila, on the international trade routes in the northern Punjab.

Buddha in Prayer Hall of Drepung Monastery 2, near Lhasa, Tibet. This statue reflects the importance of Indian traditions, but the facial features are more central Asian and even Chinese, while the elaborate headdress, frame, and gilt surfaces suggest an appreciation of wealth that was not part of earlier, Theravada Buddhism. Drepung Monastery, established in 1416, was closely associated with the Dalai Lama and his branch of Buddhism. It became the largest and one of the richest in Tibet.

The Decline of Buddhism in India

From its beginnings in India, Buddhism's strongest appeal had been to *kshatriya* rulers and *vaishya* businessmen, who felt that *brahmin* priests did not respect them. The Buddha himself came from a *kshatriya* family, and his early friendship with the *kshatriya* kings of Magadha and Koshala had ensured their support for his movement. Later kings and merchants also donated huge sums of money to support Buddhist monks, temples, and monasteries. Many people of the lower castes, who felt the weight and the arrogance of all the other castes pressing down on them, also joined the newly forming religion. They were especially attracted by the use of the vernacular Pali and Magadhi languages in place of Sanskrit, and the absence of the financial demands of the *brahmins*.

However, Buddhism began to lose strength in India around the time of the decline of the Gupta Empire (*c.* 320–550 C.E.). Regional rulers began to choose Hinduism over Buddhism, and alliances with priests rather than with monks. At the popular level, lower castes—who had found the anticaste philosophy of Buddhism attractive—apparently also began to shift their allegiance back toward more orthodox Hinduism as an anchor in a time of political change. Also, without imperial assistance, merchants' incomes may have decreased within India, reducing their contributions to Buddhist temples. By the fifth century C.E., the Chinese Buddhist pilgrim Faxian noted weaknesses in Indian Buddhism.

Mahayana Buddhism, with its many godlike Buddhas and *bodhisattvas* inhabiting a multitude of heavens, seemed so close to Hinduism that many Buddhists must have seen little purpose in maintaining a distinction. Finally, Buddhists throughout their history in India had relied on Hindu *brahmin* priests to officiate at their life-cycle ceremonies of birth, marriage, and death, so Hindu priests could argue that they always had a significant claim on Buddhist allegiance.

Readers who are accustomed to the monotheistic pattern of religions claiming the undivided loyalty of

9.1

9.2

9.3

How did Buddhism emerge and spread?

SACRED WRITINGS OF BUDDHISM	
Tripitaka	"The Three Baskets": *Vinaya*, on the proper conduct of Buddhist monks and nuns; *Sutta*, discourses attributed to the Buddha; and *Abhidhamma*, supplementary doctrines. Written in Pali.
The *Mahayanas*	(*Mahayana* is Sanskrit for "Greater Vehicle.") The body of writings associated with the school of Buddhism dominant in Tibet, Mongolia, China, Korea, and Japan. Includes the famous allegory the Lotus Sutra, the Buddhist "Parable of the Prodigal Son."
Milindapanha	Dialogue between the Greek king Milinda and the Buddhist monk Nagasena on the philosophy of Buddhism.
Buddha's Four Noble Truths	Suffering is always present in life; desire is the cause of suffering; freedom from suffering can be achieved by overcoming desires; the Eightfold Path provides the means to accomplish this.

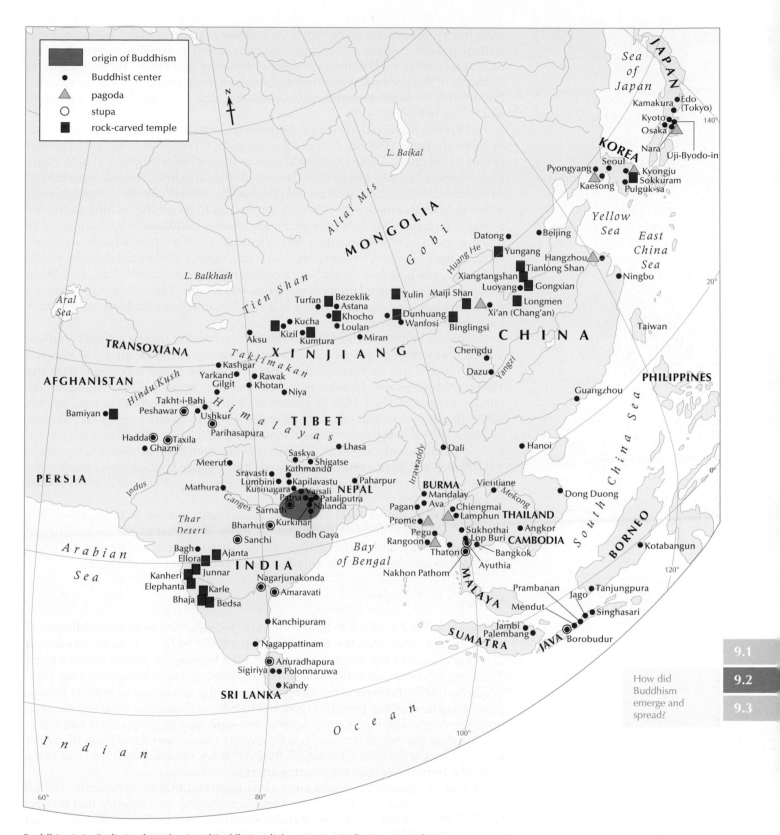

origin of Buddhism

• Buddhist center

▲ pagoda

○ stupa

■ rock-carved temple

N

Sea of Japan

Edo (Tokyo)

Kamakura

140°

Kyoto

Osaka

Nara

KOREA

Uji-Byodo-in

L. Baikal

Yellow Sea

East China Sea

Pyongyang

Seoul

Kyongju

Kaesong

Sokkuram

Pulguk-sa

MONGOLIA

Gobi

Datong

Beijing

20°

L. Balkhash

Yungang

Hangzhou

Huang He

Tianlong Shan

Xiangtangshan

Luoyang

Gongxian

Ningbo

Aral Sea

Tien Shan

Turfan

Bezeklik

Yulin

Maiji Shan

Xi'an (Chang'an)

Longmen

Astana

Kucha

Khocho

Dunhuang

CHINA

Kizil

Loulan

Wanfosi

Taiwan

Aksu

Kumtura

Miran

Binglingsi

TRANSOXIANA

Taklimakan

XINJIANG

Chengdu

Kashgar

Dazu

Yangzi

AFGHANISTAN

Hindu Kush

Yarkand

Rawak

PHILIPPINES

Gilgit

Khotan

Niya

Takht-i-Bahi

Guangzhou

Bamiyan

Peshawar

Himalayas

TIBET

Ushkur

Parihasapura

Hadda

Taxila

Lhasa

Hanoi

Ghazni

Saskya

Dali

South China Sea

PERSIA

Meerut

Shigatse

Kathmandu

Indus

Sravasti

Paharpur

BORNEO

Mathura

Lumbini

Kapilavastu

BURMA

Vientiane

Dong Duong

Ganges

Kusinagara

Vaisali

NEPAL

Mandalay

Irrawaddy

Patna

Pataliputra

Pagan

Ava

Sarnath

Nalanda

Chiengmai

Mekong

Thar Desert

Bharhut

Kurkihar

Prome

Lamphun

THAILAND

Bodh Gaya

Sanchi

Pegu

Sukhothai

Angkor

Kotabangun

Bay of Bengal

Rangoon

Lop Buri

CAMBODIA

Arabian Sea

Bagh

Ellora

Ajanta

Thaton

Bangkok

Kanheri

Junnar

INDIA

Nagarjunakonda

Ayuthia

Elephanta

Karle

Nakhon Pathom

120°

Bhaja

Bedsa

Amaravati

MALAYA

Prambanan

Tanjungpura

Kanchipuram

Jago

Mendut

Singhasari

Nagappattinam

Jambi

JAVA

Palembang

Borobudur

SUMATRA

Anuradhapura

Sigiriya

Polonnaruwa

Kandy

SRI LANKA

Ocean

0°

100°

60°

80°

Buddhist Asia. Radiating from the site of Buddha's enlightenment at Bodh Gaya in northeast India, Buddhism spread through Asia in three directions following established trade routes: north across the Hindu Kush and along the silk route to Xinjiang, China, and Korea, eventually reaching Japan; south to Sri Lanka; and east through Burma (then Myanmar) to the kingdoms and islands of Southeast Asia.

9.1

9.2

9.3

How did Buddhism emerge and spread?

9.1

9.2

9.3

How did
Buddhism
emerge and
spread?

their followers will recognize here a very different pattern. Many religions, especially polytheistic religions, expect that individuals will incorporate diverse elements of different religions into their personal philosophy and ritual. We will see more examples of this personal **syncretism** and loyalty to multiple religions as we examine Buddhism's relationship with Confucianism in China and with both Confucianism and Shinto in Japan.

As Hinduism evolved, it became more attractive to Buddhists. Theologians such as Shankaracharya (788–820 C.E.) and Ramanuja (c. 1017–1137 C.E.) advanced philosophies based on the Vedic literature known to the common people, and built many temples and schools to spread their thought. At the same time, Hinduism, following its tradition of syncretism, incorporated the Buddha himself into its own polytheistic universe as an incarnation of Vishnu. A devotee could revere the Buddha within the overarching framework of Hinduism. Finally, neither Buddhism nor Hinduism gave much scope to women within their official institutions of temples, schools, and monasteries. For Hinduism, however, the home was much more central than the public institution, and here women did have a central role in worship and ritual. Buddhism was much more centered on its monasteries and monks. The comparative lack of a role for women, and the comparative lack of interest in domestic life generally, may have impeded its spread.

Buddhism in India declined still further when Muslim traders gained control of the silk routes through central Asia. The final blow came with the arrival of Muslims during the first two centuries of their major invasions of India, between 1000 and 1200 C.E. Muslims saw Buddhism as a competitive, proselytizing religion, unlike Hinduism, and did not wish to coexist with it. Because Buddhism was, by this time, relatively weak and relatively centralized within its monasteries and schools, Muslims were able to destroy the remnants of the religion by attacking these institutions. Buddhist monks were killed or forced to flee from India to centers in Southeast Asia, Nepal, and Tibet. Hinduism survived the challenge because it was much more broadly based as the religion of home and community and far more deeply rooted in Indian culture.

In the 1950s, almost 1,000 years after Buddhism's demise in India, about five million "outcastes" revived Buddhism in India in protest at the inequalities of the caste system, and declared their allegiance to the old/new religion. These "neo-Buddhists" are almost the only Buddhists to be found in India today.

Jainism

Jainism is another religion of India, with many similarities to early Buddhism. At about the time of the Buddha, the teacher Mahavir (b. 540 B.C.E.), the twenty-fourth in a long lineage of Jain religious leaders, guided the religion into its modern form. The religion takes its name from Mahavir's designation *jina*, or conqueror. Like Theravada Buddhists, Jains reject the caste system and the supremacy of *brahmin* priests, postulating instead that there is no god, but that humans do have souls that they can purify by careful attention to their actions, and especially by practicing nonviolence. If they follow the eternal law of ethical treatment of others and devotion to the rather austere rituals of the faith, Jains believe they will reach *nirvana*, which is an end to the cycle of rebirth rather than a rewarding afterlife.

Jainism's emphasis on nonviolence is so powerful that Jains typically do not become farmers lest they kill living creatures in the soil. In a country that is overwhelmingly agricultural, Jains are usually urban and often businessmen. Jainism did not spread outside India, and its four million adherents today live almost entirely in India. Because Jains, like earlier Buddhists, employ *brahmin* priests to officiate at their life-cycle events, and because they intermarry freely with several Hindu *vaishya* (business) subcastes, some consider them a branch of Hinduism, although they do not usually regard themselves as Hindus. One of the regions of Jain strength in India

KEY TERM

syncretism refers to the merging of different traditions from different origins into a single unified practice.

How did Buddhism emerge and spread?

Jain nuns on their way to worship. Although most Jains are laypersons, important monasteries house priests and nuns. These nuns wear mouth-cloths to prevent injury to insects that might otherwise be inhaled.

is western Gujarat, the region where Mahatma Gandhi grew up (see the chapter "China and India"). The Mahatma attributed his adherence to nonviolence in large part to the influence of Jainism.

Buddhism in China

Because of its decentralization and vast geographical diffusion, Buddhism has taken on different forms from place to place, time to time, and state to state. It arrived in new locations in foreign form, but over time each regional culture put its own stamp on Buddhism. We must, therefore, examine the faith and practice of Buddhism in each region separately, by studying the works of the monks, missionaries, poets, architects, and sculptors who spread the faith.

Arrival in China: The Silk Route. The long, thin line of communication over which pilgrims and missionaries carried the message of the Buddha from India to China and beyond was the silk route, the same route that carried luxury products between China and India and then on to the west. The first Buddhist missionaries are mentioned in Chinese records about 65 C.E. They established their first monastery at Luoyang. Over the centuries, many more were built within China and along the silk route.

Chinese pilgrims traveled the silk route in the opposite direction to visit and study in the land of the Buddha, and some, most notably Faxian, who visited in 399–414 C.E., left lasting records of their observations. Thousands came to study at Taxila and Nalanda.

Several of the pilgrims who traveled these routes, especially Faxian, in the early years of the fifth century C.E., and Xuanzang, in the early years of the seventh, brought back both Buddhist texts and important firsthand information from India and the lands along the silk routes. Turning north from India through Kashgar, and then east to Khotan, Turfan, Dunhuang, and on to Chang'an in the heart of China, Buddhist pilgrims provisioned these trade routes with rest-houses, temples, and monasteries, some of them built into caves.

Relations with Daoism and Confucianism. Although Buddhism first appeared in China in the first century C.E., at the height of the Han dynasty, it took firmer root after the dynasty eventually fell. Confucianism, China's dominant philosophy, was

SOURCE

The Transience of Life: A Woman's Perspective from the Tang Dynasty

This anonymous poem of the Tang dynasty, discovered in the Dunhuang cave and translated by Patricia Ebrey and Lily Hwa, illuminates the Buddhist sense of the transience of life as experienced by a woman of high status.

A Woman's Hundred Years

At ten, like a flowering branch in the rain,
She is slender, delicate, and full of grace.
Her parents are themselves as young as the rising moon
And do not allow her past the red curtain without a reason

At twenty, receiving the hairpin, she is a spring bud.
Her parents arrange her betrothal; the matter's well done.
A fragrant carriage comes at evening to carry her to her lord.
Like Xioshi and his wife, at dawn they depart with the clouds.

At thirty, perfect as a pearl, full of the beauty of youth,
At her window, by the gauze curtain, she makes up in front of
  the mirror.
With her singing companions, in the waterlily season,
She rows a boat and plucks the blue flowers.

At forty, she is mistress of a prosperous house and makes plans.
Three sons and five daughters give her some trouble.
With her lute not far away, she toils always at her loom.
Her only fear that the sun will set too soon.

At fifty, afraid of her husband's dislike,
She strains to please him with every charm.
Trying to remember the many tricks she had learned since the
  age of sixteen.
No longer is she afraid of mothers- and sisters-in-law.

At sixty, face wrinkled and hair like silk thread,
She walks unsteadily and speaks little.
Distressed that her sons can find no brides,
Grieved that her daughters have departed for their husbands'
  homes.

At seventy, frail and thin, but not knowing what to do about it,
She is no longer able to learn the Buddhist Law even if she
  tries.
In the morning a light breeze
Makes her joints crack like clanging gongs.

At eighty, eyes blinded and ears half deaf,
When she goes out she cannot tell north from east.
Dreaming always of departed loves,
Who persuade her to chase the dying breeze.

At ninety, the glow fades like spent lightning.
Human affairs are no longer her concern.
Lying on a pillow, solitary on her high bed,
She resembles the dying leaves that fall in autumn.

At a hundred, like a cliff crumbling in the wind,
For her body it is the moment to become dust.
Children and grandchildren will perform sacrifices to her spirit.
And clear moonlight will forever illumine her patch of earth.

(Ebrey, p. 104)

9.1

9.2

9.3

How did
Buddhism
emerge and
spread?

intimately tied to the fate of the imperial government, and only after this central political structure collapsed could Mahayana Buddhism find a place. The mystical character of Mahayana Buddhism especially attracted Daoists. To some degree, the two beliefs competed, but some of the competition eventually led to each validating the other. For example, some Daoists claimed that the Buddha was actually Laozi as he appeared in his travels in India. Many Buddhists, in turn, accorded to Laozi and Confucius the status of *bodhisattva*. In this way, competition sometimes turned into mutual recognition.

As a foreign religion, Buddhism also had special appeal for some of the rulers of northern China in the third through the sixth centuries C.E., since they, too, were outsiders. The Toba rulers of the Northern Wei dynasty (386–534 C.E.) occasionally persecuted Buddhists as a threat to the state, but mostly they felt some kinship to this religion of outsiders. They patronized Buddhist shrines and monks, but they also regulated them.

In the south, with its abundance of émigrés from the northern court, Confucianism was crippled by the severance of its connection with the government. In contrast, newly arriving Buddhists won followers by proposing an organized, aesthetic philosophy for coping with the hazards of life in semi-exile. In southern China, Buddhist arts of poetry, painting, and calligraphy flourished, and monasteries in the south offered refuge to the men who might have been part of the governing Confucian aristocracy in other times. In the southern state of Liang, the emperor Wu (r. 502–49

9.1

9.2

9.3

How did
Buddhism
emerge and
spread?

C.E.) declared Buddhism the official state religion, built temples, sponsored Buddhist assemblies, and wrote Buddhist commentaries.

Doctrinally, Buddhism had important differences from Confucianism, but the two world perspectives seem to have reached some mutual accommodation. For example, Confucianism encouraged family cohesion and the veneration of ancestors, while Buddhist monks followed lives of celibacy; but Buddhist laypeople also valued family, and the monks themselves venerated the Buddha and *bodhisattvas* as their spiritual ancestors. Nevertheless, tension between the two belief systems and organizations never completely dissipated. Confucians thought in terms of government order and control, while Buddhists tended toward decentralized congregational worship within a loose doctrinal framework. In many areas of China, as Buddhist monasteries became wealthy from the donations of local magnates and landlords, Confucian governments moved to regulate their power.

Buddhism's network of pilgrims and monks crisscrossed China, helping to integrate the nation. Through almost four centuries of division in China, from the fall of the Han (220 C.E.) to the rise of the Sui (581), Buddhism continued to grow in both north and south. Indeed, the founder of the Sui dynasty, a Buddhist himself, also patronized Confucianism and Daoism, seeing all these belief systems as vital to earning legitimacy for his government. The Tang dynasty extended this veneration.

Buddhism under the Tang Dynasty. For most of the Tang dynasty (618–907), the intellectual, spiritual, and artistic life of Buddhism flourished. Eight major sects developed, each with a different interpretation of the original message of the Buddha, the importance of rules and regulations, rituals, meditation, scholarship, disciplinary exercises, and devotion. Among the larger and more significant schools was the Pure Land Sect. Its devotees believed that anyone could reach the Pure Land of paradise after death through faith in the Buddha Amitabha, the presiding authority in that realm. Members of the sect demonstrated their faith by continuously repeating the name Amitabha. Devotees also meditated on Guanyin, the *bodhisattva* of mercy (see How Do We Know box, below).

Another sect, Chan Buddhism, taught the importance of meditation. Some followers believed in lengthy disciplines of meditation, which would gradually lead to enlightenment; others in spontaneous flashes of insight, which would lead to the same goal. Both Pure Land and Chan were adopted in Japan as well, where the meditative exercises of Chan became known as Zen.

Buddhists are credited with inventing woodblock printing as a means of reproducing their sacred texts. The earliest woodblock print known is an illustrated copy of the *Diamond Sutra* from 868 C.E., discovered in the Dunhuang Caves. Most of the Buddhist art and architecture of Tang China was destroyed in later persecution, confiscation, and warfare. Its leading representations are now seen in Japan, which, at just about this time, adopted much of Chinese Buddhism as its own and then modified it (see below).

The only woman ever to rule China in her own name, "Emperor" Wu (r. 690–705 C.E.) was a great patron of Buddhism. First ruling indirectly through Emperor Gaozong (d. 683), whose concubine she was, and then, after his death, through two of their sons, in 690 she proclaimed herself the emperor of a new dynasty, which she named the Zhou (not to be confused with the earlier Zhou dynasty discussed early in the chapter entitled "A Polycentric World"). She patronized Buddhism as a means of legitimizing her rule, declaring herself a reincarnation of Maitreya, the Buddha of future salvation. The empress built temples in every province of China. Before she was deposed in 705, she had overseen the warfare that expanded the Tang to its greatest geographical extent, including Xinjiang and Tibet.

Buddhism's Decline in China. Political and military defeats started Buddhism on its decline during the late Tang period in China. In far-off central Asia, Muslim forces

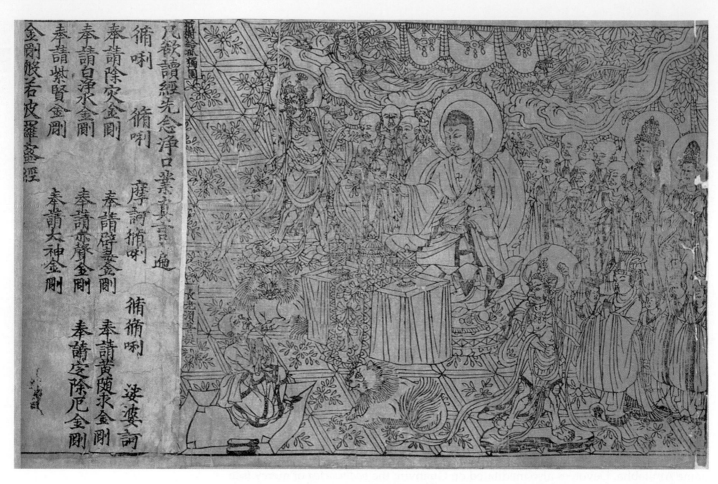

Diamond Sutra, 868 C.E. This superb frontispiece, showing the Buddha preaching to an elderly disciple, comes from the *Diamond Sutra*, a Sanskrit tale transmitted along the silk routes and translated into Chinese in the fifth century. Produced by woodblock to a high standard of technical and artistic achievement, the 17-foot-long sutra is the world's earliest printed book. (British Library, London)

9.1

9.2

9.3

How did
Buddhism
emerge and
spread?

defeated Chinese forces in the decisive Battle of the Talas River in 751. Four years later, the revolt of General An Lushan in northeast China occupied the imperial armies for eight years. China's power in central Asia was broken, and with it the power of Buddhism in these regions. Islam would become the world religion of most of central Asia. Only in Tibet did Buddhism remain powerful, supported by state power. It was carried there from eastern India about the eighth century in a newly emerging form called *vajrayana* Buddhism, "the vehicle of the thunderbolt," or tantric Buddhism, for its *tantras*, or scriptures advocating magic rituals. Tantric Buddhism venerated not only buddhas, *bodhisattvas*, and other divinities, but also their wives or feminine counterparts, new additions to the growing array of sacred personalities. Tantric rituals were secret, esoteric, sometimes sexual, and only for the initiated.

Almost a century later, the Tang emperor Wuzong (r. 840–46) attacked Buddhism and its monasteries. Wuzong was a Daoist, personally opposed to Buddhism. He feared the power of the Buddhist establishment, and the wealth and influence of its various monasteries, especially when the Tang had been weakened by external defeats and internal revolts. Wuzong confiscated the lands and wealth of the Buddhist monasteries. He forced monks and nuns to leave the monasteries, claiming that he personally had defrocked 260,500 monks and nuns. He destroyed sacred texts, statues, and shrines, leaving only 49 monasteries and 800 monks in all of China. Later rulers alternated between reversing and reimposing Wuzong's policies. Although

9.1

9.2

9.3

How did
Buddhism
emerge and
spread?

Dying Buddha, Cave 428, Dunhuang, China, early sixth century C.E. The monastery at Dunhuang was one of the most important of those along the silk route, and the paintings in its 460 caves are spectacular. Here, *bodhisattvas* attend the Buddha at his death, appearing rather ascetic, abstract, and enchanted. Compare the scene from Japan, illustrated in How Do We Know box, below.

Buddhism has remained a presence in China, even to today, it has never recovered its numbers, vitality, or influence.

Buddhism in Japan

Shintoism. Long before Buddhism arrived in Japan, the people of Japan followed "The Way of the Kami," later called Shinto. *Kami* were the powers and spirits inherent in nature. Found everywhere, they could be called upon to help in time of human need. Shrines to the *kami* were built throughout the land, always including a mirror in tribute to the sun goddess, a sword, and a jewel.

Accounts of the *kami* appear in the earliest Japanese records, the *Kojiki* (712 C.E.) and *Nihon shoki* (720 C.E.). These semi-mythological records give a basic history of early Japan, but they—and all accounts of Buddhist saints—must be read with some caution, because they blend myth with factual record. According to the *Kojiki* and *Nihon shoki*, the highest of the *kami* were Amaterasu, the sun goddess, and her obstreperous brother Susa-no-o. Amaterasu's grandson Niniqi descended to earth and set out to conquer Japan. He established himself as Japan's first emperor in 660 B.C.E., and all subsequent emperors trace their lineage directly back to this mythological founder.

With the later arrival of Buddhism, the *kami* continued to have a distinguished and venerated position, often as minor buddhas or *bodhisattvas*. Conversely, the buddhas and *bodhisattvas* were accepted as especially powerful and exalted *kami*, capable of helping those in need. The royal family in Japan knew that the emperor Asoka in India had adopted Buddhism, and they emulated his decision.

Buddhism's Arrival in Japan. Buddhism first came to Japan from China in 552 C.E., via the Paekche kingdom of southwest Korea. The *Nihon shoki* tells of the Paekche

KEY TERM

kami In Japanese thought, the powers and spirits inherent in nature.

How did
Buddhism
emerge and
spread?

king sending Buddhist texts and statues and asking for help in a war against another Korean kingdom, the Silla.

From the beginning, Buddhism had political as well as religious implications. Clans close to the Japanese emperor were divided in their reception of the foreign religion. Those who accepted it regarded Buddhism as a force for performing miracles, especially healing the sick, and many Buddhist monks were especially skilled in medicine. A minority of the clans, however, thought the new religion ought to be banned.

Buddhism found acceptance at a political level in Japan a half-century later under Prince Shotoku Taishi (573–621). The prince effectively ruled the country as the regent to the ruler of the Yamato Plain, the western region of Japan. An enthusiastic Buddhist, Shotoku built many temples, including the Horyuji Temple in the capital city of Nara. A scholar of Buddhist theology, he invited Buddhist clergy from Korea, and he dispatched four Japanese missions to Sui China to learn more about Buddhism,

Horyuji Temple, Nara, Japan, 670 C.E. Through the seventh and eighth centuries the Japanese court enthusiastically welcomed Chinese political and artistic forms (see the chapter "China"). This is Japan's earliest surviving example of Buddhist architecture, which was adopted along with Chinese writing, painting, and sculpture. It became a central shrine for all of Japan.

9.1

How did
Buddhism
emerge and
spread?

9.2

9.3

both as a religious system and as a model for centralizing his political rule. At this time China was the premier state of eastern Asia, and Buddhism was seen as one of the principal constituents of its power. In 604, Prince Shotoku introduced a kind of constitution to centralize and strengthen the Japanese government. Among its 17 articles, the first promoted Confucian principles of social organization and the second declared that the Japanese people should "sincerely reverence the three treasures ... the Buddha, the Law, and the Monastic orders" (Embree, p. 50).

Buddhism's Role in Unifying Japan. A century later, in 710, the ruling clans of Japan moved their capital to Nara, then called Heijo. Continuing to regard China as the model state of their day, the Japanese rulers copied much of the Chinese structure of authority and administration. They used Chinese ideographs as their written language and adopted Chinese patterns of bureaucracy, taxation, architecture, and land reforms. They modeled their new capital on the city plan of Chang'an, building a smaller version of that Chinese capital at Nara.

Within Nara, Japan's rulers built numerous Buddhist temples, including several of national significance. They encouraged the creation of a system of monasteries and convents throughout the provinces, with the Todaiji monastery, built by the emperor Shomu (r. 715–49), at the apex. That great temple contains one of the world's great repositories of art, holding several thousand treasures from the eighth century, including painting, sculpture, calligraphy, textiles, ceramics, jade, metal- and lacquer-work, masks for drama, and musical instruments.

Buddhism became a pillar in the structure of Japanese national unity and administration. It did not replace Shinto, the indigenous worship of spirits, especially spirits of nature. Rather, it complemented the indigenous system. The emperor performed the official rituals of both Shinto and Buddhist worship.

Buddhism introduced a measure of centralization. Shinto, a less formal system of belief and worship, had spread throughout Japan with no need of a central shrine for its worship of nature. By contrast, the Horyuji Temple near Nara became a central shrine for the nation. In 741 the emperor ordered that a Buddhist temple and pagoda be established in each province. Buddhism and Shinto coexisted in Japan in a pattern that continues today.

As in China, the power and wealth of Buddhist monasteries and temples in Japan, and especially in Nara, alarmed some members of the court. To reduce the power of the Buddhist clergy and to increase the power of his own lineage, Emperor Kammu (r. 781–806) moved the capital again, from Nara to Heian (modern Kyoto) in 794. This move initiated the Heian period in Japanese history and coincided with the decline of the Tang Empire in China. The Japanese government dispatched its last official mission to China in 838. With Japan on the ascendant and China in decline, Japan's Buddhism developed along its own paths, helped by substantial imperial patronage. The emperor himself patronized two young Japanese monks who founded the Tendai and Shingon schools of Buddhism, the two most powerful and enduring Buddhist movements in Japan.

Japanese Buddhism Develops New Forms. The Buddhist priesthood itself became increasingly Japanese, no longer reliant on priests from the Chinese mainland. It also entered more profoundly into politics. The priest Saicho (767–822) studied Tiantai (Tendai in Japanese) Buddhism in China and introduced it into Japan. Based on the Lotus Sutra, Tendai taught that each person could achieve enlightenment through sincere religious devotion. On Mount Hiei, northeast of Kyoto, Saicho built the Enryakuji monastery, which grew rapidly and steadily into one of the most important temple communities in Japan.

Saicho had intended his monastery to remain aloof from politics, and he therefore built it far from the national capital in Nara. Ironically, however, when the capital was moved to Kyoto, the monastery again found itself geographically close to the

HOW DO WE KNOW?

The Buddha Imagined in Art

As Buddhism spread through India, and then by land across the silk routes to China and on to Korea and Japan, and by sea to Sri Lanka, Southeast Asia, and Indonesia, the image of the Buddha was transformed. Even his message was transformed, most notably from the simple, ascetic Theravada Buddhism of the early centuries in India to the more complex and colorful Mahayana Buddhism of China and East Asia. Naturally enough, each era and each region had its own context for understanding the Buddha and his message. Each created its own form of worship and evolved its own forms of temple architecture to house that form. We can gain a clearer understanding of the art from a knowledge of the philosophy. Similarly, we can gain a clearer understanding of the philosophy from the art.

All the illustrations in this chapter and the previous one concerning the evolution of Buddhism should be examined

Teaching Buddha, from Sarnath, India, Gupta dynasty, fifth century C.E. Siddhartha Gautama sought to understand the causes of and the remedy for human suffering. After many trials, he finally found his answer on the forty-ninth day of intense meditation. As the Buddha, the Enlightened One, he began to teach his new message. The *mudra*, the hand gesture, here represents the Buddha teaching. (Archaeological Musem, Sarnath)

Guanyin, Buddhist deity, Northern Song dynasty, China, *c.* 1200 C.E. Guanyin, a *bodhisattva*, or enlightened being who remains in this world to relieve human suffering, was a very popular subject in Chinese art: this example in painted wood is particularly sensuous and refined. Buddhist deities are considered to have the spiritual qualities of both genders, and by this date the feminine qualities were accentuated. (Nelson-Atkins Museum of Art, Kansas City, Missouri)

carefully for what they reveal about the changing manifestations of Buddhism. For example, compare an early (fifth-century) representation of the Buddha from Sarnath, north India, with a representation of a *bodhisattva* from northern China, some seven centuries later, and a seventeenth/eighteenth-century Japanese illustration of the Buddha's death.

The first illustration, far left, suggests the simplicity of the early Theravada form, presenting the Buddha as teacher, with a number of disciples attending to his discourse. The Buddha found enlightenment through meditation, and the cross-legged lotus position of this sculpture recalls that moment. The Buddha's facial features are characteristic of the people around Sarnath, the place, not far from the Buddha's home, where he reached enlightenment, and where the sculpture was created. The hand gestures, or *mudras*, of Buddhist and Hindu iconography are symbolic. The hand gesture here represents the act of teaching.

The second illustration, center, presents one of the most famous *bodhisattvas* ("enlightened beings"), from China, about 1200. This *bodhisattva* appears androgynous (both male and female) and also Chinese, adapted to Buddhism's new geographic setting. Often, even representations of the Buddha himself take on the appearance of the people who revere him. *Bodhisattvas*, since they can appear anywhere, always take on the form of the local people from among whom they emerge. Note the sensuousness of this representation, quite different from the asceticism of Siddhartha Gautama.

The final representation, on this page, has brought the entire cosmos into the picture. As the Buddha lies dying, he is surrounded by family, followers, and even a wide array of animals. His mother looks down from heaven. The Buddhist universe has expanded a long way in time and space from the early Buddhist image of a single man meditating alone under a bo tree until he reached enlightenment.

Dying Buddha, Japanese scroll, seventeenth to eighteenth century C.E. Here the dying Buddha is attended by human disciples, *bodhisattvas*, grieving animals, and representatives of other worlds. From across the river, another disciple leads the Buddha's mother and her retinue down from heaven to attend his last teaching. Compare the scene as represented at Dunhuang, China, above. (University of Pennsylvania Museum)

Hoodo (Phoenix Hall), Byodoin Temple, Uji, Japan, eleventh century C.E. The Phoenix Hall of the Byodoin Temple, with its jauntily uplifted roof-corners, indicates how over time the Buddhist style took on a distinctively Japanese flavor and shed its Chinese influence. Contrast with the Horyuji Temple, illustrated above.

9.1

9.2 How did Buddhism emerge and spread?

9.3

KEY TERMS

mantra A formula of words and sounds that are believed to possess spiritual power, a practice of both Hinduism and Buddhism.

mandala A symbolic circular diagram of complex geometric design used as an instrument of meditation or in the performance of sacred rites in Hinduism and Buddhism.

national political center. Saicho encouraged the monks to add teaching, administration, and social work in the service of the nation to their religious duties, merging Confucian and Buddhist value systems. His monastery grew to house tens of thousands of monks in some 3,000 buildings. By the eleventh century, an era of deep and violent political fissures in Japanese political life, many Shinto and Buddhist temples supported standing armies to protect themselves and their extensive land holdings and branch temples. Troops from the Mount Hiei monastery began to enter the capital, demanding additional lands and thus completely reversing Saicho's original wishes. The Buddhist clergy thereafter became increasingly intertwined with Japanese politics.

Kukai (774–835), another Japanese Buddhist priest who had studied in China, also returned home to preach a new form of Buddhism. He became abbot of the monastery of the great Toji temple at Kyoto, where he introduced Shingon ("True Word") Buddhism. This emphasizes the repetition of mystic incantations or *mantras*; meditation on colorful, sometimes stunning, geometrically ordered religious paintings, called *mandalas*, of buddhas and *bodhisattvas* in their heavens; complicated rituals; music; and ecstatic dancing. Because the transmission of these forms was closely guarded among believers, Shingon Buddhism was also called Esoteric Buddhism. Creating more accessible forms as well, Kukai introduced rituals, such as the austere and beautiful tea ceremony, in which a formal ritual surrounding the serving and drinking of tea invites deep meditation. Kukai is also credited with inventing the

How do the
two religions
of the Indian
subcontinent
compare?

kana **syllabary**, a Japanese script in phonetic letters rather than **ideograms**. These innovations, in addition to mysterious, secret rituals, use of herbal medicines, and the elegant pageantry of Shingon, gave Kukai's monastery great popularity and power.

Another Chinese form of Buddhism that deeply influenced Japan was dedicated to Amida or, in Sanskrit, Amitabha, the Buddha of the Infinite Light. In the tenth century, two priests, Kuya (903–72) and Genshin (942–1017), popularized this sect, which taught the importance of chanting the *mantra nembutsu*, "Praise to Amida Buddha." Amidism grew in subsequent generations through the organizational abilities of a series of monks, including Ryonin (1072–1132), who taught the counting of rosary beads to accompany the repetition of the *nembutsu*, a practice that spread to most sects of Japanese Buddhism. By the late twelfth century, Amidism established its independence from other Buddhist sects. Its message of uncomplicated, universal access to salvation had great appeal to the masses.

Chan Buddhism (Zen in Japanese) appeared in Japan during the seventh century, but began to flourish only after the twelfth century. Much of Zen's popularity was a result of the teachings of Eisai, a Buddhist monk who believed that in addition to meditation, Zen should defend the state. Its emphasis on martial arts made Zen Buddhism particularly attractive to the increasingly powerful warrior class. Since then it has deeply influenced Japanese culture, and it remains important in Japan today.

Lasting Buddhist Elements in Japanese Society. Three other elements gave Buddhism a prominence and significance in Japanese life that have continued till today. First, Japanese Buddhism cultivated an especially pure aesthetic dimension, which we have seen here in the representations of the Buddha and *bodhisattvas* and of the architecture and art of the Japanese Buddhist temples. This appreciation of artistic creativity is apparent throughout Japan in formal gardens, in painting and calligraphy, and in the art of presentation of everything from self, to gifts, to tea, to food. Second, Buddhism's emphasis on the transience of all life has inspired much of the greatest Japanese literature, from the *Tale of Genji*, written by Lady Murasaki (c. 978–c. 1015) at the Japanese court 1,000 years ago, to the novels of Mishima Yukio (1925–70), who committed *seppuku*, ritual suicide, immediately after completing his last novel. Third, Buddhism has coexisted and even merged to some degree with indigenous Shinto worship and belief.

📖 **Read** the **Document: Excerpt from Lady Murasaki Shibuku's Diary (11th c.) on MyHistoryLab**

By the twelfth century Japan had entered its Buddhist Age. Despite occasionally being attacked as a foreign religion and as an excessively wealthy and powerful organization, Buddhism has remained one of the two national religions of Japan. Most Japanese continue to mingle Buddhism and Shinto in their aesthetic and spiritual lives as well as in their ritual practices.

Comparing Hinduism and Buddhism

9.3 How do the two religions of the Indian subcontinent compare?

Hinduism and Buddhism have undergone enormous transformation through their thousands of years of history. Geographically, Hinduism spread across the Indian subcontinent from its roots in the encounter between Aryan immigrants and the indigenous peoples of the Indus valley and northern India. It extended briefly even to Southeast Asia (where a single Hindu outpost still remains on the Indonesian island of Bali). Buddhism spread from the Buddha's home region in the Himalayan foothills throughout India, where it subsequently died out, and most of East and

KEY TERMS

syllabary A writing system in which each symbol represents the syllable of a word, in contrast to **ideogram**.

ideogram (alternative: ideograph) A character or figure in a writing system in which the idea of a thing is represented rather than its name. Languages such as Chinese use ideograms.

Southeast Asia, where it flourishes. Buddhism's array of monasteries and temples, and its veneration of the homeland of the Buddha himself, mark its sacred geography.

Both religions established their own sacred calendars and their control over life-cycle events. In this, Hindu priests took a commanding position since even Buddhists (and Jains) employed them to officiate. Within India this continuing role of the *brahmin* priests ultimately helped Hinduism to absorb Buddhism. Outside India, where no other major religion was already in place, Buddhist priests performed their own rituals and came to predominate.

Both groups developed sacred languages. Buddhists felt that Sanskrit was narrowly limited to Hindu priests and so used Pali, a language closer to the vernacular. Over time, as the common people expressed their own religious feelings in their own languages, the leaders of both religions responded by also using the vernacular. Both religions inspired extensive literature, including philosophy, mystical poetry, drama, and folk tales. Both generated their own artistic traditions in painting, sculpture, and temple architecture.

Organizationally, Buddhism, especially in its early Theravada form, was seen as a religion of its monks. Many common people found comfort and meaning in their philosophy and supported them, but ultimately they turned to *brahmin* priests for their ritual needs. Within Hinduism the caste system structured all classes and occupations into a single framework of relationships, with *brahmins*, *kshatriyas*, and sometimes *vaishyas* predominating. Buddhism's later Mahayana form, with its multitudes of gods, *bodhisattvas*, and heavens, reached out to more people ritually as well as emotionally.

The evolution of Hinduism and Buddhism demonstrates the flexibility of great world religions. A small sect may define itself narrowly, proclaiming a core set of principles and practices and adhering to them rigidly. For its small membership, these restrictions may be the very attraction of the sect. But for a religion to grow in numbers, it must be open organizationally, doctrinally, and ritually to the varied spiritual, psychological, and social needs of diverse peoples. Like the empires we studied earlier, a world religion must be able to accommodate, satisfy, and absorb people of various languages, regions, classes, and previous spiritual beliefs and practices. World religions expand their theologies and practices to incorporate ever more members, until they reach the limits of their flexibility.

Finally, religions and governments have been historically interdependent. Buddhism flourished thanks to the early support of the Buddha's royal allies and later through the backing of the emperor Asoka. It spread to Southeast Asia and to Japan as kings offered their support in exchange for Buddhist legitimation. In China, Buddhism found its opening after Confucian dynasties fell and people searched for new belief systems and new leaders. Hinduism flourished as kings in India struck their own agreements with *brahmin* priests. Conversely, when governments turned against particular religious groups, they could devastate them. And when sizable religious groups shifted their support away from a ruler, they undermined his authority. We shall find more examples of this mutual antagonism in later chapters.

Hinduism and Buddhism: *What Difference Do They Make?*

Hinduism keeps alive a major religion of active polytheism. Although many Hindus would argue that behind all the gods a single reality pervades the world, others would argue, more literally, that there are indeed many different gods with influence over the world and its creatures. These advocates of polytheism find a consistency between the diversity of life forms and experiences and the multitude of gods of existence.

Hinduism has given a general cultural unity and depth to much of south Asia, in its arts and literature, its complex and sophisticated philosophical systems, and its hierarchical social, economic, and political order, which is based on caste forms. Today, the government and people of India cope with these legacies in a world that generally proclaims publicly the equality of all people. As a result, contemporary India confronts many conflicts between the historic claims of caste hierarchy and the contemporary demands for equality. Political and religious leaders clash over the most appropriate direction for future development.

Buddhism also continues as the basis of the culture and religion of hundreds of millions of people, most of them in East and Southeast Asia. The religion takes many different forms, from the relative austerity of the Theravada Buddhism of Sri Lanka, to the more elaborated and otherworldly Mahayana forms of Southeast Asia, and the more mystical and isolated forms of Tibetan tantric Buddhism. In many lands Buddhism is practiced freely, often in conjunction with other religions, as in Japan. In China, however, especially in Tibet, Buddhism struggles for survival against a hostile government. To understand religions in history, we must see them in the context of the political, social, and economic systems in which they are embedded.

We turn in the next chapters to three religions—Judaism, Christianity, and Islam—that have been militantly monotheistic. Although Judaism has remained relatively limited in its numbers, Christianity and Islam have been aggressive in their desire to win converts and are now the largest of the world's religions, with over two billion and 1.5 billion followers respectively. Their relationships with the governments alongside which they exist have been checkered. Their impact on spiritual, cultural, social, and aesthetic life has been immense.

CHAPTER REVIEW

HINDUISM

9.1   What is unique in the history of Hinduism?

The roots of Hinduism (like those of Judaism) are the most ancient of the existing major religions. Unlike the world's other major religions, which claim the inspiration of a specific person or event, Hinduism emerged out of the many diverse, ancient traditions of India, including those of immigrants, like the Aryans, who contributed their writings, philosophies, and social system based on family, caste, and locality. Hinduism evolved as the principal cultural system of the Indian subcontinent.

BUDDHISM

9.2   How did Buddhism emerge and spread?

Buddhism emerged out of Hinduism in India and spread throughout central, eastern, and southeastern Asia. Like Hinduism, it questioned the reality of the earthly world and speculated on the existence of other worlds. But Buddhism had a founder—Siddhartha Gautama, the Buddha (the Enlightened One)—a set of scriptures, and an order of priests. Buddhists believed that life was filled with suffering, but the ascetic teachings of the Buddha provided a means of coping. Buddhism was carried by missionaries throughout Sri Lanka, East and Southeast Asia and came to define much of the cultural and religious life of the region, although it virtually died out in India. Later forms of Buddhism were less ascetic, more mystical, and frequently supported by political rulers.

COMPARING HINDUISM AND BUDDHISM

9.3   How do the two religions of the Indian subcontinent compare?

Hinduism and Buddhism differ in key areas, including their principal beliefs and their ideas about the role of the clergy, the role of the home, social hierarchy, and relationship to the government. Buddhism did not accept the caste system, which made it more acceptable to people contesting the power of Brahmans, but, in India, Brahman power ultimately won out. In most other locations, however, Buddhism endured while Hinduism did not.

Suggested Readings

PRINCIPAL SOURCES

Basham, A.L. *The Wonder that Was India* (New York: Grove Press, 1954). Graceful, comprehensive, standard introduction to early Indian history. Dated on the Indus valley, but still valid on imperial India.

Bhagavad Gita, trans. Barbara Stoler Miller (New York: Bantam Books, 1986). A fine, readable, clear translation of one of the greatest classics of Hinduism.

de Bary, William Theodore, *et al.*, comps. *Sources of Japanese Tradition*, Vol. I: *From Earliest Times to 1600* (New York: Columbia University Press, 2nd ed., 2002). Best available repository of primary sources from the literature.

deBary, William Theodore, and Irene Bloom, eds. *Sources of Chinese Tradition*, Vol. I: *From Earliest Times to 1600* (New York: Columbia University Press, 2nd ed., 1999). Best available repository of primary sources from the literature.

Doniger, Wendy. *The Hindus: An Alternative History* (New York: Penguin, 2009). A brilliant work emphasizing changes throughout the history of Hinduism, and the contributions of marginalized groups: women, *adivasis*, outcastes.

Ebrey, Patricia Buckley, ed. *Chinese Civilization: A Sourcebook* (New York: The Free Press, 2nd ed., 1993). An excellent sourcebook, drawn much more from the lives of common people.

Embree, Ainslee, ed. and rev. *Sources of Indian Tradition*, Vol. I: *From the Beginning to 1800* (New York: Columbia University Press, 2nd ed., 1988). Best available repository of primary sources from the literature.

ADDITIONAL SOURCES

Allchin, F.R., *et al. The Archaeology of Early Historic South Asia: The Emergence of Cities and States* (Cambridge: Cambridge University Press, 1995). Accessible, wide-ranging introduction, for nonspecialists.

Andrea, Alfred, and James Overfield, eds. *The Human Record*, Vol. 1 (Florence, KY: Wadsworth Publishing Co., 7th ed., 2012). Excellent collection of primary sources on world history.

Appadurai, Arjun. *Worship and Conflict under Colonial Rule* (Cambridge: Cambridge University Press, 1981). Demonstrates the interweaving of the major temples with the politics, economics, and social structures of their region.

Berger, Peter L. *The Sacred Canopy* (New York: Anchor Books, 1967). A classic introduction to the importance of religion and religious organizations in society.

Blunden, Caroline, and Mark Elvin. *Cultural Atlas of China* (New York: Facts on File, 1983). Superb introduction to China, with fine interpretive essays, maps, and pictures. Especially strong on geography and its implications.

Bodde, Derk. *Essays on Chinese Civilization*, ed. Charles Le Blanc and Dorothy Borei (Princeton, NJ: Princeton University Press, 1981). A classic set of essays on the significance of Chinese civilization.

Conze, Edward. *Buddhist Scriptures* (New York: Penguin Books, 1959). Basic source readings.

Craven, Roy C. *Indian Art* (London: Thames and Hudson, 1997). Excellent introduction to Indian art, especially of the classical period.

The Dhammapada, trans. Juan Mascaro (New York: Penguin Books, 1973). Fine translation and introduction to this Buddhist literary and religious classic.

Dimmitt, Cornelia, and J.A.B. van Buitenen, ed. and trans. *Classical Hindu Mythology* (Philadelphia, PA: Temple University Press, 1978). An exposition of Indian mythology and texts by masters in the field.

Eberhard, Wolfram. *China's Minorities: Yesterday and Today* (Belmont, CA: Wadsworth Publishing, 1982). Fills in the picture for non-Han Chinese, a subject often overlooked.

Eliade, Mircea. *Ordeal by Labyrinth* (Chicago, IL: University of Chicago Press, 1982). Elegant exposition of the role of religion in society.

——. *The Sacred and the Profane* (New York: Harper Torchbooks, 1959). Thought-provoking introduction to the way in which religion moves people and encourages them to create institutions.

——. *Yoga: Immortality and Freedom* (Princeton, NJ: Princeton University Press, 1969). The philosophy of yoga presented clearly and profoundly.

Elvin, Mark. *The Pattern of the Chinese Past* (Stanford, CA: Stanford University Press, 1973). Elvin explores especially the economy of China, its highs and lows.

Elwin, Verrier. *The Aboriginals* (New York: Oxford University Press, 1944). Brief pamphlet introducing *adivasis* and their problems in twentieth-century India.

Hall, Kenneth R. *Maritime Trade and State Development in Early Southeast Asia* (Honolulu, HI: University of Hawaii, 1985). Especially good on the relationships between India and Southeast Asia in trade and in political evolution.

Hall, Kenneth R., and John K. Whitmore, eds. *Explorations in Early Southeast Asian History: The Origins of Southeast Asian Statecraft* (Ann Arbor, MI: Center for South and Southeast Asian Studies, University of Michigan, 1976). Set of outstanding seminar papers.

Hammond Atlas of World History (Maplewood, NJ: Hammond, 5th ed., 1999). Indispensable world-history atlas.

Hughes, Sarah Shaver, and Brady Hughes, eds. *Women in World History*, Vol. I: *Readings from Prehistory to 1500* (Armonk, NY: M.E. Sharpe, 1995). Includes short but interesting sections on husbands and wives, Sita and Rama, and Buddhist nuns.

Kulke, Hermann, and Dietmar Rothermund. *A History of India* (New York: Routledge, 5th ed., 2010). Brief, accessible, excellent introductory history.

Lewis-Williams, David. *The Mind in the Cave: Consciousness in the Origins of Art* (London: Thames and Hudson, 2002). Exploration of meaning in earliest art; includes religious speculations.

Lockard, Craig A. "Integrating Southeast Asia into the Framework of World History: The Period Before 1500," *The History Teacher* XXIX, No. 1 (November 1995), pp. 7–35. Concern with pedagogy leads also to a good conceptual scheme for understanding Southeast Asia.

Martin, Rafe. *The Hungry Tigress: Buddhist Legends and Jataka Tales* (Berkeley, CA: Parallax Press, 1990). Classic legends and tales as a means of transmitting the essential moral lessons of Buddhism.

Murphey, Rhoads. *History of Asia* (Upper Saddle River, NJ: Pearson, 6th ed., 2008). Useful especially for its crossregional explorations.

Needham, Joseph. *The Shorter Science and Civilization in China*, Vol. I, abridged by Colin A. Ronan (Cambridge: Cambridge University Press, 1978). The classic study of Chinese science, demonstrating its methods, findings, and significance.

Nelson, Lynn, and Patrick Peebles, eds. *Classics of Eastern Thought* (San Diego, CA: Harcourt Brace Jovanovich, 1991). Fine collection of basic texts.

Ramanujan, A.K., ed. and trans. *Poems of Love and War: From the Eight Anthologies and the Ten Long Poems of Classical Tamil* (New York: Columbia University Press, 1985). An outstanding modern poet and scholar translating classical Tamil poetry.

——, trans. *Speaking of Śiva* (Harmondsworth, Middlesex: Penguin Books, 1973). Further translations specifically on the Lord Shiva in the imagination of India.

Richman, Paula, ed. *Many Ramayanas: The Diversity of a Narrative Tradition in South Asia* (Berkeley, CA: University of California Press, 1991). The *Ramayana* has many interpretations and uses. Richman provides an astonishing, scholarly array of them.

Rowland, Benjamin. *The Art and Architecture of India: Buddhist/Hindu/Jain* (New York: Penguin Books, 1977). Indian religion can be understood only with reference to its art and architecture. A fine introduction.

SarDesai, D.R. *Southeast Asia: Past and Present* (Boulder, CO: Westview Press, 7th ed., 2013). Good on the context of the spread of Buddhism.

Schwartzberg, Joseph E., ed. *A Historical Atlas of South Asia* (Chicago, IL: University of Chicago Press, 1978). Scholarly, encyclopedic coverage of history through geography. A superb research tool.

Smart, Ninian. *The World's Religions* (Cambridge: Cambridge University Press, 1989). Fine, comprehensive introduction to the major religions.

Thapar, Romila. *Ancient Indian Social History* (New Delhi: Orient Longman, 1978). Thapar's works offer the most accessible, clear, comprehensive introduction to ancient India, its politics, institutions, leaders, economy, social groups, and religions.

——. *Asoka and the Decline of the Mauryas* (New Delhi: Oxford University Press, 1998). Principal introduction to the empire of the Mauryas.

——. *Early India: From the Origins to AD 300* (Berkeley, CA: University of California Press, 2003). Updates her classic *History of India* of 1966. Definitive, if lengthy, introduction.

——. *Interpreting Early India* (New York: Oxford University Press, 1992). Philosophy of studying ancient India, opposing the use of history to advance political programs.

Tharu, Susie, and K. Lalita, eds. *Women Writing in India 600 B.C. to the Present*, Vol. I (New York. The Feminist Press, 1991).

Includes writings from various regions of India, and puts them into context.

Twitchett, Denis, ed. *The Cambridge History of China*, Vol. III: *Sui and T'ang China, 589–906*, Part 1 (Cambridge: Cambridge University Press, 1979). Comprehensive, scholarly, follows Buddhism through its flourishing in China.

Twitchett, Denis, and Michael Lowe, eds. *The Cambridge History of China*, Vol. I: *The Ch'in and Han Empires, 221 B.C.–A.D. 220* (Cambridge: Cambridge University Press, 1986). Comprehensive, scholarly, helps to understand early Buddhism in China.

Zimmer, Heinrich. *Philosophies of India* (New York: Meridian Books, 1956). Classic introduction to the texts and concepts.

FILMS

Legacy: The Origins of Civilization. Disc 1: *India* (1992; 52 minutes). Presented by Michael Wood. (Over)emphasizes the religious nature of Indian civilization. Beautiful images.

An Indian Pilgrimage: Ramdevra (1974; 30 minutes). Follows several contemporary Hindu pilgrims as they travel from their homes to a pilgrim shrine in Rajasthan. Worship is only part of the lengthy, colorful process. New York: Ambrose Video Pub., c2002, c1992.

The Buddha—PBS Documentary – Part 1 (2012) (56 minutes) The man, his message, its spread around the world, and many comments by people today who value and follow his teachings.

10 Judaism and Christianity

Peoples of the Bible: God's Evolution in West Asia and Europe

1700 B.C.E.–1000 C.E.

Into a world that believed in many gods who often fought with one another and interfered capriciously in human life, the Hebrews introduced and perpetuated the concept of a single god whose rule was both orderly and just. In contrast with the many gods of polytheism, each with his or her own temperament and judgment, the new monotheism provided a more definitive statement of right and wrong. At the same time, it demanded much greater conformity in both faith and action, calling for adherence to a strict code of ethics within a community governed by laws proclaimed by a single god. The Hebrews' belief in one god was not simply a reduction in the number of gods from many to one. Their god represented a new religious category of a god above nature and free from compulsion and fate. Their belief in only one god, however, also confronted them with a fundamental theological dilemma, a dilemma for all monotheistic religions: If there is only one god, and if that god is both all-powerful and caring, then why does human life on earth often appear so difficult and unjust?

The four evangelists, from the Gospel Book of Charlemagne, early ninth century. With the exception of the cross, the best-known symbols in early Christianity were associated with the four gospels. Based on a text in the Book of Revelation (4:7), Matthew was represented by a man, Mark by a lion, Luke by a winged ox, and John by an eagle. (Cathedral Treasury, Aachen, Germany)

LEARNING OBJECTIVES

10.1 ((	10.2 ((	10.3 ((
Tell the story of Judaism, its rise and its evolving beliefs.	Trace the evolution of Christianity.	Understand the role of Christianity in the Roman Empire.

((**Listen** on MyHistoryLab

The Hebrews' early home was in the Middle East, and other peoples in that region sometimes expressed similar ideas. In Egypt, for example, Akhenaten also proclaimed a belief in one god. His declaration of faith, however, came several centuries after that of the Hebrews. More importantly, his new faith did not survive his death and had no lasting effects on his country. Later pharaohs rejected Akhenaten's beliefs and his style of worship. In Mesopotamia, Hammurabi of Babylon issued a law code in the name of his god Shamash, by the year 1750 B.C.E., some 500 years before Hebrew sacred texts record a similar gift of a legal system from their god YHWH, through their leader Moses. Over time, however, the code of Hammurabi was forgotten in Mesopotamia while the Hebrew people kept their legal codes alive as they evolved into the Jewish people.

In their early years the "Hebrews" were known as the people whose legendary founder, Abraham, came from *eber*, meaning "the other side" of the Euphrates River. Later they took on the name of Jews, in honor of one of their tribes, Judah, and of the new territory that they claimed in Judea, in the modern land of Israel and Palestine.

Today there are only about 15 million Jews worldwide, but their role in history has been disproportionate to their numbers. Many of their core beliefs were incorporated into Christianity and Islam, the two great monotheistic faiths that have come to include half the world's population today. Meanwhile Judaism itself adapted to changing conditions over time and space, maintaining its own core beliefs, traditions, and identity as an independent religious community. We begin this chapter with a study of Judaism and then proceed to Christianity, which emerged from it, and challenged it. In the next chapter we explore Islam and the interactions among all three of these closely related, but often bitterly antagonistic, monotheistic religions.

Judaism

10.1 How did Judaism arise and what are its evolving beliefs?

The story of Judaism, as recorded in Hebrew scriptures, begins some 3,800 years ago with one man's vision of a single, unique God of all creation. They tell us that God and Abraham sealed a covenant stating that Abraham's descendants would forever revere and worship that God, and God, in return, would forever watch over and protect them. From then until now Judaism has remained a relatively small, family-based religion, with branches throughout the world, but focused in part in Israel, the land that Jews believe God promised to Abraham.

The Sacred Scriptures

Our knowledge of early Jewish history comes from the scriptures known collectively as the **TaNaKh**: Torah (the Five Books of Moses), Nevi'im (the Books of the Prophets), and Ketuvim (additional historical, poetic, and philosophic writings). Christians have incorporated the entire TaNaKh into their Bible, referring to these scriptures collectively as the "Old Testament." Because the New Testament is written in Greek and the Old Testament in Hebrew, the TaNaKh is often referred to as the "Hebrew Bible."

The narratives of the five books of the Torah abound with miracles, as God intervenes continuously in the history of the Jews. The Torah begins with God's creating the world and contracting his covenant with Abraham. Over the next several generations, the Torah continues, famine struck Israel (then called Canaan), the land God promised to Abraham. Abraham's grandson and his family traveled to the Nile valley of Egypt in search of food. At first invited by the pharaoh to remain as permanent residents, they were later enslaved. About 1200 B.C.E., after 400 years of slavery, the Jews won their freedom and escaped from Egypt under the leadership of Moses through

KEY TERM

TaNaKh A Hebrew term for the books of the Bible that are written in Hebrew. The word is composed of the initial letters of the words Torah (first five books of the Bible, traditionally attributed to Moses), Nevi'im (the books of the Prophets), and Ketuvim (additional historical, poetic, and philosophic writings). These are the three sections of the Hebrew Bible.

AT A GLANCE: JUDAISM AND CHRISTIANITY 1700 B.C.E.–900 C.E.

DATE	POLITICAL/SOCIAL EVENTS	LITERARY/PHILOSOPHICAL EVENTS
1700 B.C.E.	● Abraham travels from Mesopotamia to Israel (c. 1750)	
1600 B.C.E.	● Hebrew slavery in Egypt	
1200 B.C.E.	● Moses (?1300–?1200) ● Exodus from Egypt; legal codes formulated; return to Palestine; tribal government under Judges	
1000 B.C.E.	● Period of Kings begins with Saul, David, and Solomon ● First temple in Jerusalem	
900 B.C.E.	● Jewish kingdom divides into Israel and Judea	
800 B.C.E.	● Prophets exhort Jewish nation (800–500) ● Assyrians conquer Israel and exile Jews (721)	● Numbers (850–650) ● Genesis (mid-fifth to eighth century) ● Prophets Isaiah, Amos, Micah
700 B.C.E.		● Josiah begins to write down Torah (640) ● Deuteronomy (mid-seventh century) ● Leviticus (mid-seventh century) ● Jeremiah
600 B.C.E.	● Babylonians conquer Judea, exile the people, and destroy the first temple (586) ● Jews permitted to return to Judea and rebuild the temple (538)	● Book of Job (600)
300 B.C.E.		● Books of TaNaKh (the Jewish Bible) edited and canonized
100 B.C.E.	● Birth and death of Jesus (c. 4 B.C.E.–c. 30 C.E.)	
10 C.E.	● Rome captures Jerusalem (63) ● Christianity emerges from Judaism ● St. Paul, Saul of Tarsus, organizes early Christianity (d. c. 67) ● Rome destroys second temple (70)	● Gospels (70–100) ● Acts (70–80) ● Epistles of Paul (50–67)
100 C.E.	● Rome exiles Jews from Judea; Jewish diaspora throughout Mediterranean basin and west Asia (135) ● Rabbinical tradition developed (first to fourth century)	
200 C.E.	● Christians persecuted under Severus, Decius, and Diocletian	● Babylonian and Jerusalem Talmuds edited and published (200–500)
300 C.E.	● Christianity legalized (313); declared the official religion of the Roman Empire (392) ● Council of Nicaea (325) ● Georgia and Armenia convert to Christianity (c. 330)	
400 C.E.	● Council of Chalcedon (451)	● Augustine's The City of God and Confessions
500 C.E.	● Monasticism in Europe ● Clovis converted to Christianity ● St. Benedict founds monastery of Monte Cassino	
600 C.E.	● England converted to Christianity	● Venerable Bede, Ecclesiastical History of the English People
700 C.E.	● Iconoclastic controversy	
800 C.E.	● Coronation of Charlemagne (800) ● St. Cyril and St. Methodius convert Russia, translate the Bible, and create the Cyrillic alphabet	● Einhard, Life of Charlemagne
900 C.E.	● Missionaries proliferate among the Vikings	

the miraculous intervention of God. During their journey back to Israel through the wilderness of the Sinai Desert, the contentious group of ex-slaves was forged into a small but militant nation. The Torah records a dramatic miracle at Mount Sinai in which God revealed a set of religious and civil laws for them to follow.

DATE	POLITICAL/SOCIAL EVENTS	LITERARY/PHILOSOPHICAL EVENTS
1000 c.e.	• Christians capture Toledo from Muslim control and begin *reconquista* (1085) • Split of Western and Eastern Christianity (1054) • First Crusade (1095–99)	
1100 c.e.	• Second Crusade (1147–49) • Third Crusade (1189–92)	• Rabbi Benjamin of Tudela (d. 1173) travels widely in Europe and the Middle East
1200 c.e.	• Fourth Crusade (1202–04) • Children's Crusade (1212) • Crusaders capture Constantinople (1204–61) • Fifth to Eighth Crusades (1218–91)	
1300 c.e.	• Monastic orders	
1400 c.e.	• Christians capture Granada, Spain, complete the *reconquista* (1492), expel Jews and Muslims	

AT A GLANCE: JUDAISM AND CHRISTIANITY 1000 C.E.–1400 C.E.

For centuries, Jews and Christians believed that these earliest books of the Bible, which describe the creation of the world and the earliest history of the Jewish people, were the literal word of God. During the past two centuries, scholarship has given us a new sense of the historical place of these books. Today historians ask: When and where were the books of the Hebrew Bible composed and how valid are they as historical documents?

Modern scholarly analysis of the TaNaKh texts became a prominent academic enterprise in Germany during the early nineteenth century. The founders of "Biblical criticism" noted certain inconsistencies in the Biblical texts. For example, the first chapter of Genesis reports that God created man and woman simultaneously, "male and female he created them," while the second chapter reports that God first created man and then removed one of his ribs and created woman from it. The critics noted also that different names are used for God in the Hebrew text—most notably YHWH and Elohim—and they suggested that the different names represent the stylistic preferences of different authors. They noted similarities between the stories and laws of the Bible and those in the literature of other peoples of the region, and they suggested that some of the external stories had found their way into the Biblical accounts. Through rigorous analysis, the Biblical scholars argued persuasively that Josiah (r. 640–609 B.C.E.), the king of the Jewish state of Judea, first made the decision to begin to edit and write down the definitive edition of oral texts that had been passed from generation to generation.

The story of Josiah's reign is told in the Biblical book of 2 Kings, chapters 20–21. Struggling to survive in the face of the powerful Assyrian Empire, Josiah was anxious to promote allegiance to the state and its religion. He centralized Jewish worship in the national

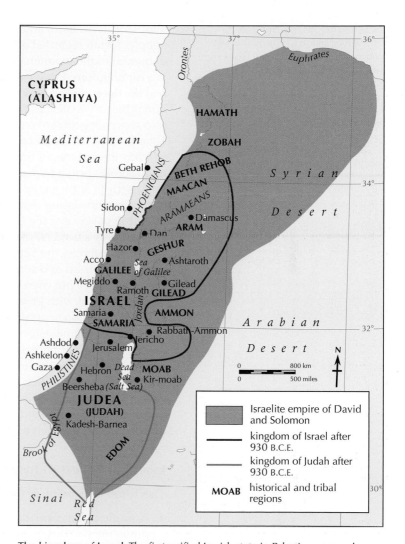

The kingdom of Israel. The first unified Jewish state in Palestine emerged around 980 B.C.E. under King David. He united the tribes of Israel during a period of decline among their more powerful neighbors—Egypt and the Hittites. After the death of his son Solomon (926 B.C.E.), tribal rivalries divided the empire into the kingdoms of Judah and Israel, but the sense of cultural unity survived.

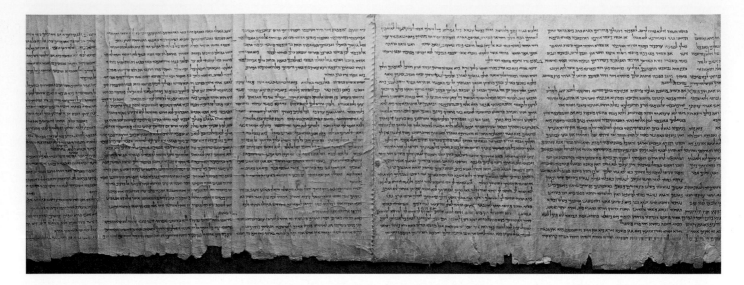

Dead Sea Scrolls, Isaiah scroll 1Q Is. 9 verses 58.6–63.4. The 500 or so documents that make up the Dead Sea Scrolls—which date between about 250 B.C.E. and 70 C.E., and were rediscovered in 1947—appear at one time to have formed the library of a Jewish community. As well as providing evidence of the accuracy of Hebrew biblical texts, they give information about the life of the community itself. (Israel Museum, Jerusalem)

10.1

How did Judaism arise and what are its evolving beliefs?

10.2

10.3

temple in Jerusalem, and collected and transcribed the most important texts of his people. Josiah regarded adherence to the laws laid down in these scriptures as fundamental to the maintenance of the Jewish religion, the Jewish people, and his own Jewish kingdom. From existing literary fragments, folk wisdom, and oral history he had the Book of Deuteronomy, the fifth book of the TaNaKh, written down. Soon, additional literary materials from at least three other major interpretive traditions were also woven together to create the books of Genesis, Exodus, Leviticus, and Numbers. Together with Deuteronomy, these books formed the Torah, or "Five Books of Moses."

With the ravages of time, older copies of the Torah, written in Hebrew on parchment scrolls, began to perish and new ones were copied. The oldest existing Hebrew manuscripts of the entire Torah date only to the ninth to the eleventh centuries C.E., but fragments dating to as early as the second century B.C.E. have been discovered. Stored in caves near the Dead Sea in Israel, these Dead Sea Scrolls have been rediscovered only since 1947. Another very early edition of the Torah is a Greek translation from the Hebrew, the Septuagint. It was prepared for the Greek-speaking Jews of Egypt in the third and second centuries B.C.E. It still exists and is consistent with the Hebrew texts of our own time. In short, the written text of the Torah appears to have been preserved with great fidelity for about 2,600 years, although the oral texts on which the written scriptures were based date back much farther.

The Torah remains one of the greatest examples of myth-history. Although its stories should not necessarily be read as literal, historical records, their version of events gave birth to the Jewish people's concept of itself and helped to define its character and principal beliefs. The stories of the Torah tell us what the Jewish people, and especially their literate leadership, have thought important about their own origins and mission. They also define images of God that have profoundly influenced the imagination and action of Jews, Christians, and Muslims for millennia.

Essential Beliefs of Judaism in Early Scriptures

The Torah fixes many of the essential beliefs and principles of Judaism:

- A single caring God, demanding obedience, who administers rewards and punishments fairly and in accordance with his fixed laws:

  Hear, O Israel, the Lord is our God, the Lord alone. You shall love the Lord your God with all your heart, and with all your soul, and with all your might. (Deuteronomy 6:4–5)

  Know therefore that the Lord your God is God, the faithful God who maintains covenant loyalty with those who love him and keep his commandments,

CHAPTER TEN: JUDAISM AND CHRISTIANITY 1700 B.C.E.–1000 C.E.

10.1
10.2
10.3

How did Judaism
arise and what
are its evolving
beliefs?

to a thousand generations, and who repays in their own person those who reject him. (Deuteronomy 7:9–10)

- A God of history, whose power affects the destiny of individuals and nations:
  I am the Lord your God who brought you out of Egypt, out of the land of slavery. (Exodus 20:2–3)
- A community rooted in a divinely chosen family and ethnic group:
  Now the Lord said to Abraham, "Go from your country and your kindred and your father's house to the land that I will show you. I will make of you a great nation, and I will bless you, and make your name great, so that you will be a blessing." (Genesis 12:1–2)
- A specific, "promised," geographical homeland:
  When Abraham reached Canaan, God said to him: "Raise your eyes now, and look from the place where you are, northward and southward and eastward and westward; for all the land that you see I will give to you and to your offspring forever." (Genesis 13:14–15)
- A legal system to guide proper behavior: religious, familial, sexual, commercial, civic, ethical, and ritual. The introduction to this code was the Ten Commandments, revered as the heart of the revelation to Moses at Mount Sinai.
- A sacred calendar: Jewish religious leaders reconstituted earlier polytheistic celebrations of nature into a calendar of national religious celebration. A spring festival of renewal was incorporated into Passover, the commemoration of the exodus from Egypt; an early summer festival of first harvest was subsumed into Shavuot, a rejoicing in the revelation of the Ten Commandments at Sinai; and an early fall harvest festival became part of Sukkot (Succoth), a remembrance of the years of wandering in the desert. All these festivals were to be celebrated, if possible, by pilgrimage to the central, national temple in Jerusalem. Celebrations of nature, history, and national identity were fused together.

SOURCE

The Ten Commandments

The Torah contains legal codes governing many aspects of life, including family rules concerning marriage, divorce, and inheritance; civil laws regulating business practices and responsibilities; criminal law mandating rules of evidence and of punishment; rules commanding ethical and charitable behavior, especially toward the weak and helpless, strangers, orphans, and widows; and extensive rules concerning ritual practices of prayer, sacrifice, food, and priestly behavior. At the center of the codes are the Ten Commandments, given, according to the Torah account, directly by God to Moses atop Mount Sinai amidst terrifying thunder, lightning, clouds, and trumpet blasts. These commandments dictate behavior toward God, parents, and fellow humans. They also proclaim the importance of observing a Sabbath day once a week.

I am the Lord your God who brought you out of Egypt, out of the house of slavery.
You shall have no other gods before me. You shall not make for yourself an idol, whether in the form of anything that is in heaven above, or that is on the earth beneath, or that is in the water under the earth.
You shall not bow down to them or worship them; for I the Lord your God am a jealous god, punishing children for the iniquity of parents, to the third and fourth generation

of those who reject me, but showing steadfast love to the thousandth generation of those who love me and keep my commandments.
You shall not make wrongful use of the name of the Lord your God, for the Lord will not acquit anyone who misuses his name.
Remember the Sabbath day, and keep it holy. Six days you shall labor and do all your work. But the seventh day is a Sabbath to the Lord your God; you shall not do any work—you, your son or your daughter, your male or female slave, your livestock, or the alien resident in your towns. For in six days the Lord made heaven and earth, the sea, and all that is in them, but rested the seventh day; therefore the Lord blessed the Sabbath day and consecrated it.
Honor your father and your mother, so that your days may be long in the land that the Lord your God is giving you.
You shall not murder.
You shall not commit adultery.
You shall not steal.
You shall not bear false witness against your neighbor.
You shall not covet your neighbor's house; you shall not covet your neighbor's wife, or male or female slave, or ox, or donkey, or anything that belongs to your neighbor.

(Exodus 20:2–17; see also Deuteronomy 5)

10.1

10.2

10.3

How did Judaism
arise and what
are its evolving
beliefs?

To ground the mystical beliefs and forge the Jewish people into a "kingdom of priests and a sacred nation," rules issued in the name of God forbade intermarriage with outsiders; prohibited eating animals which do not have cloven hooves and chew their cud, and fish that do not have scales and fins (Deuteronomy 14 and Leviticus 11) (included in the rules of kashrut, "keeping kosher"); and centralized worship in the hands of a priestly aristocracy. Animal sacrifices were to be offered, but only by the hereditary priests and only in a single national temple in Jerusalem.

The Later Books of Jewish Scripture

The later volumes of the TaNaKh, the books of Nevi'im and Ketuvim, carry an account of the history of the Jewish people from about 1200 B.C.E. to about the fifth century B.C.E. God continues as a constant presence in these narratives, but he intervenes less openly and less frequently. These later records can generally be cross-checked against the archaeology of the region and the history of neighboring peoples, and they seem generally consistent.

The Book of Joshua begins the story about the year 1200 B.C.E., as the Jews returned to Canaan, or Israel, the land promised to them, and made it their home. This Biblical account tells of continuous, violent, political and religious warfare between the invading Jews and the resident Canaanite peoples. Modern scholarship suggests, however, that the number of Jews who had been enslaved in Egypt was not nearly so great as the Torah states (Egyptian records do not mention Jewish slaves at all) and that reentry into the land of Israel was a gradual process, with fewer, more localized battles and considerably more cultural borrowing among all the groups in the region.

Rule by Judges and by Kings. Arriving in Canaan, the Jews first organized themselves in a loose tribal confederacy led by a series of "Judges," *ad hoc* leaders who took command at critical periods, especially at times of war. Despite warnings that a monarchy would lead to increased warfare, profligate leaders, extortionate taxes, and the impressment of young men and women into royal service, the Jews later anointed a king. For three generations (c. 1020–950 B.C.E.), strong kings, Saul, David, and Solomon, are said to have ruled and expanded the geographic base of the people. They established a national center in Jerusalem, where they united political and religious power by building both palace and temple, exalting both king and priest. The earlier warnings against royal excesses, however, proved prescient. Unable to sustain Solomon's legendary extravagances in expenditure and in his relationships with 700 wives, many of them foreign princesses, and 300 concubines, the kingdom split in two, the kingdom of Judea and the kingdom of Israel.

Moses, mosaic in San Vitale, Ravenna, Italy, sixth century C.E. After he had led the Israelite slaves out of Egypt by the miracle of parting the Red Sea, Moses ascended Mount Sinai. There he received from God the Torah, or sacred teachings, beginning with the two tablets of the Ten Commandments. He led his quarrelsome people across the Sinai Desert but died at the border of the promised land.

The Teachings of the Prophets: Criticism, Morality, and Hope. Continuing despotism by their kings and greed on the part of their wealthier citizens ripped apart the social fabric of the two splinter kingdoms. A group of prophets emerged, demanding reform. In powerful and sublime language, these men called for a reinstitution of justice, compassion, and ethics. Speaking in the name of God and of the people, they cried out against the hypocritical misuse of religious and political power.

The prophet Isaiah, in the eighth century B.C.E., led the charge:

> When you stretch out your hands, I will hide my eyes from you; even though you make many prayers, I will not listen; your hands are full of blood.
> Wash yourselves; make yourselves clean; remove the evil of your doings from before my eyes; cease to do evil,
> Learn to do good; seek justice, rescue the oppressed, defend the orphan, plead for the widow. (Isaiah 1:15–17)

A century later, Jeremiah continued in the same spirit of moral outrage, rebuking the rulers and people of Judea, the southern kingdom:

> You keep saying, "This place is the temple of the Lord, the temple of the Lord, the temple of the Lord!" This catchword of yours is a lie; put no trust in it. Mend your ways and your doings, deal fairly with one another, do not oppress the alien, the orphan, and the widow, shed no innocent blood in this place, do not run after other gods to your own ruin. (Jeremiah 7:4–6)

Map of the world by Heinrich Bunting, 1585. Many peoples believed that their capital city was the cosmo-magical axis of the universe. This map, shaped like a clover leaf, places Jerusalem at the center, at the crossroads of Africa, Asia, and Europe.

10.1
10.2
10.3

How did Judaism
arise and what
are its evolving
beliefs?

So even at the time that Israel and Judea developed into powerful kingdoms, the prophets remembered that the beginnings of the Jewish people were in slavery and that a significant part of its mission was to identify with and help the downtrodden. When destruction came, the prophets interpreted it as punishment not of their God, as earlier peoples had often done, but *by* their God. Destruction of a corrupt nation indicated not the weakness of its God, but God's ethical consistency.

Finally, the prophets not only harangued, blamed, and condemned, they also held up visions of a future to inspire their listeners. They saw God transforming human history. He offered rewards as well as punishments. He offered hope. Micah's prophecy in the eighth century B.C.E. is one of the most exalted, and perhaps utopian:

> He shall judge between many peoples, and shall arbitrate between strong nations far away; they shall beat their swords into plowshares, and their spears into pruning hooks; nation shall not lift up sword against nation, neither shall they learn war any more; but they shall all sit under their own vines and under their own fig trees, and no one shall make them afraid; for the mouth of the Lord of hosts has spoken. (Micah 4:1–4)

Micah closed with a vision of great Jewish religious commitment, balanced by equally great appreciation for the diversity of others:

> For all the peoples walk each in the name of its god, but we will walk in the name of the Lord our God for ever and ever. (Micah 4:5)

The Evolution of the Image of God

The Torah portrays God as an evolving moral force in dialogue with humans. In God's early interactions with humans, his nature is still malleable. Disgusted at human disobedience, he destroys almost all humankind through a flood, but he then pledges never to be so destructive again, creating a rainbow as a kind of treaty of peace with humanity (Genesis 6–8). Still fearful of the collective power of humanity, God confounds their intercommunication by dividing them into separate language groups at the Tower of Babel (Genesis 11). While deciding the fate of the sinful cities of Sodom and Gomorrah, God listens to Abraham's plea for the defense: "Far be it from thee to do this—to kill good and bad together; for then the good would suffer with the bad. Far be it from thee. Shall not the judge of all the earth do what is just?" (Genesis 18–19). God apparently bans child sacrifice when he stops Abraham from killing his son Isaac. (The Muslim Quran reports this to be Abraham's son Ishmael.)

When asked by Moses to identify himself by name, God replies enigmatically and powerfully, "I am who I am" (Exodus 3:14). The Hebrew designation for God's name is YHWH, "Being." English-speaking readers have usually rendered it either Jehovah or Yahweh.

In Jewish theology, God is almighty but still directly accessible to every human being through prayer and even through dialogue. Indeed, humans and God come to understand each other by arguing with one another in a process that the contemporary rabbi Arthur Waskow has called "Godwrestling." If Jews are to be God's people and to follow his will, he, in turn, is expected to be a compassionate and attentive ruler.

This view challenged the polytheistic beliefs in self-willed gods, but it left Judaism with no strong answer to the eternal problem of evil in the universe: If there is a single God, and if he is good, why do the wicked often prosper and the righteous often suffer? One Biblical response is found in the Book of Job (*c.* 600 B.C.E.). To the questions of the innocent, suffering Job, God finally responds with overwhelming power:

Crossing the Red Sea, c. 245 C.E. Fresco, synagogue at Dura Europos, Syria. The fresco depicts the Biblical story of the exodus of the Hebrew people from slavery in Egypt. Here, the Red Sea parts, allowing the Hebrews, led by Moses, to escape on dry land, and then returns to its place, drowning the Egyptians who attempt to pursue them. The Dura Europos synagogue is one of the oldest in the world. Its frescoes demonstrate that, despite the Bible's apparent prohibition of visual images, painting flourished, even in synagogues. (National Archaeological Museum, Damascus, Syria)

How did Judaism arise and what are its evolving beliefs?

10.1

10.2

10.3

Who is this whose ignorant words cloud my design in darkness?
Brace yourself and stand up like a man; I will ask the questions, and you shall answer.
Where were you when I laid the earth's foundations? Tell me, if you know and understand.
Who settled its dimensions? Surely you should know …
Is it for a man who disputes with the Almighty to be stubborn?
Should he that argues with God answer back? (Job 38:2–5; 40:2)

But while God lectures Job for his brashness in questioning his authority and power, he understands Job's anguish at the apparent injustice in the world and ultimately rewards Job with health, a restored family, and abundance for his honesty in raising his questions.

📖 Read the Document: Book of Job and Jewish Literature on MyHistoryLab

Patriarchy and Gender Relations

The Torah grants women fewer civil and religious rights (and obligations) than men. By conventional interpretation, women were expected to be responsible for nursing and child-care, tasks that know no time constraints, and they were therefore freed

311

10.1 How did Judaism arise and what are its evolving beliefs?

10.2

10.3

JEWISH FESTIVALS AND FAST DAYS

Hebrew date	Gregorian date	Name of festival
1–2 Tishre	Sept–Oct	Rosh Hashana (New Year)
10 Tishre	Sept–Oct	Yom Kippur (Day of Atonement)
15–21 Tishre	Sept–Oct	Sukkot (Feast of the Tabernacles)
22 Tishre	Sept–Oct	Shemini Atzeret (Eighth Day of the Solemn Assembly)
23 Tishre	Sept–Oct	Simchat Torah (Rejoicing of the Law)
25 Kislev–2–3 Tevet	Nov–Dec	Hannukah (Feast of Dedication)
14–15 Adar	Feb–Mar	Purim (Feast of Lots)
14–20 Nisan	Mar–Apr	Pesach (Passover)
5 Iyar	Apr–May	Israel Independence Day
6–7 Sivan	May–Jun	Shavuot (Feast of Weeks)
9 Av	Jul–Aug	Tisha be-Av (Fast of Ninth Av)

from all ritual obligations that had to be performed at specific times, for instance prayers at certain times of day.

The regulation of sexuality is fundamental in Biblical Jewish law, as it is in most religions. Women are regarded as ritually unclean each month at times of menstruation, and in childbirth. Men may be ritually unclean as a result of wet dreams or sexual diseases (Leviticus 15), but these occurred with less regularity. Marriage is regarded as the norm, with a strong emphasis on bearing children. Homosexual behavior is strongly rejected. (Today, however, many branches of Judaism have revised gender rules and discarded prohibitions on homosexuality.)

Jewish scriptures credit a few women with heroic roles. Sarah, Abraham's wife, forced him to choose her son as his proper successor, and she gained God's approval (Genesis 16). Jewish midwives in Egypt continued to deliver healthy male babies despite the Pharaoh's decree and death sentence against these children. Deborah led Israel in peace and war during the period of conquering the land of Israel (Judges 4–5). Ruth, a convert, taught the importance of openness to the outside world; she became an ancestor of King David and, therefore, in Christian belief, of Jesus (Book of Ruth). Esther was married to the Persian king and used her position to block the attempts of a court minister to kill the Jews of the Persian Empire (Book of Esther). Although none of these stories can be authenticated externally nor dated exactly, they speak to the significance of individual, exceptional women at turning points in Jewish history, and in the collective mind of the Jewish people.

Defeat, Exile, and Redefinition

Jews represent both an ethnic community and a universal religion. This dual identity became especially clear when foreign conquerors exiled part of the Jewish population from Israel as part of a plan to encourage their assimilation and to open the land to foreign immigration. This dispersion of Jews to various lands ruled by other peoples is known as the **diaspora**.

First, Sennacherib of Assyria dispersed the Jews of the northern kingdom of Israel in 721 B.C.E. These exiles drifted into assimilation and were subsequently referred to as the "**Lost Ten Tribes** of Israel." In 586 B.C.E., Babylonian conquerors destroyed the temple in Jerusalem and exiled thousands of Jews from the southern kingdom of Judea to Babylon, but these Jews remained loyal to their unique identity as a separate community, remembering their homeland:

KEY TERMS

diaspora A dispersion of peoples. Most commonly used to refer to the dispersion of Jews among the gentiles, which began with the Babylonian captivity of the sixth century B.C.E.

Lost Ten Tribes Ten tribes of Israel were exiled from their homeland in 721 B.C.E. They totally assimilated into their new surroundings, lost their Jewish identity, and were lost to history. Periodically, groups in remote areas today claim that they are the Lost Ten Tribes.

By the rivers of Babylon—there we sat down and wept when we remembered
   Zion …
Our captors asked us for songs: "Sing us one of the songs of Zion!"
How could we sing the Lord's song in a foreign land?
If I forget you, O Jerusalem, let my right hand wither!
Let my tongue cling to the roof of my mouth if I do not remember you, if I do not
   set Jerusalem above my highest joy. (Psalm 137)

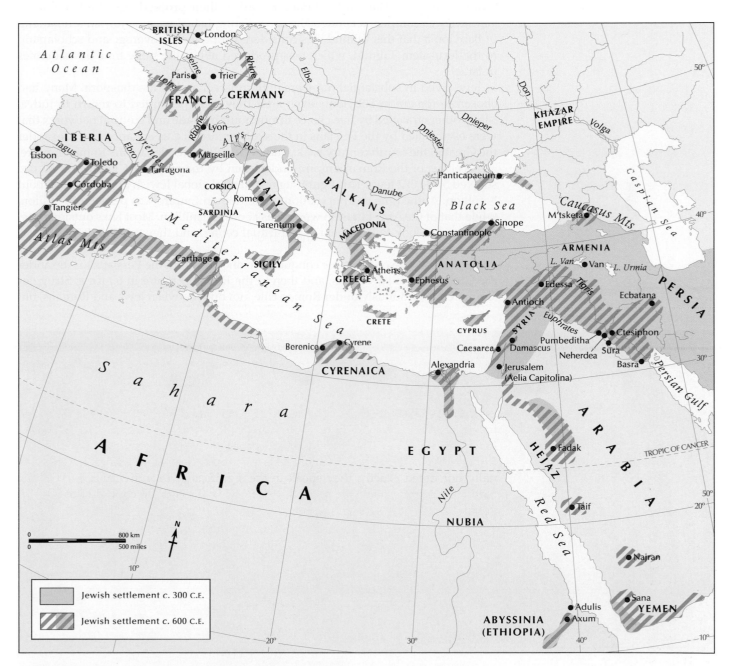

The Jewish diaspora. Following the Jewish Revolt in 66 C.E., the Roman destruction of the temple in Jerusalem in 70, and the defeat of the Bar-Cochba revolt in 135, the Roman government expelled the Jews from Judea. Their subsequent migrations spread Judaism north into Mesopotamia and Anatolia, followed trade routes throughout the Mediterranean and the Red Sea, and eventually resulted in the establishment of Jewish communities as far afield as northwest Europe and Ethiopia.

10.1
10.2
10.3

How did Judaism arise and what are its evolving beliefs?

When the emperor Cyrus permitted the Jews to return to Judea some 60 years later, many Jews left Babylonia, returned to Judea, rebuilt their temple, and reconstructed national life. But many did not. Those who remained did not assimilate into Babylonian culture, however. Instead, they reconstituted their religion, replacing the sacrificial services of the temple with meditation and prayers offered privately or in synagogues. They replaced the hereditary priesthood with teachers and rabbis, positions earned through study and piety. In academies at Sura and Pumbeditha, towns adjacent to Babylon, rabbis continued the study of the Torah. They interpreted and edited Jewish law, and elaborated Jewish stories and myths, which often conveyed moral principles. The multivolumed record of their proceedings, the Babylonian Talmud, was completed about 500 C.E. So distinguished was the Jewish scholarship of Babylonia that this Talmud was considered superior in coverage and scholarship to the Jerusalem Talmud, which was produced about the same time in academies in Israel.

Jews lived in substantial numbers both in Israel and in the diaspora. Many had chosen to remain in Babylonia even after they were permitted to return to Judea. Many others traveled by free choice throughout the trade and cultural networks that were established by the Persians in the sixth century B.C.E., enhanced by Alexander the Great in the fourth century B.C.E., and eventually extended by the Roman Empire.

A census of the Roman Empire undertaken by the emperor Claudius in 48 C.E. showed 5,984,072 Jews. This figure suggests a total global Jewish population of about 8 million. At the time, the population of the Roman Empire was perhaps 60 million, while that of the Afro-Eurasian world was about 170 million. Most Jews outside Israel continued to look to Jerusalem as a spiritual center, and they sent funds to support the temple.

Judea itself passed from one conqueror to another, from the Persians to Alexander the Great and his successors, and then to the Roman Empire in 63 B.C.E. Struggles simmered continuously under Roman rule, not only between Jews and Romans, but

Menorah procession, Arch of Titus, Rome, c. 81 C.E. The Romans put down the Jewish revolt of 70 C.E. by recapturing Jerusalem, destroying the temple, and looting its sacred objects. This relief from Emperor Titus' triumphal arch shows Roman soldiers carrying off the temple menorah, a seven-branched candelabrum, which today serves as an official emblem of the state of Israel.

also among Jewish political and religious factions. Three major revolts broke out and Roman authorities responded with overwhelming force in suppressing them. In 70 C.E. they destroyed the Jewish temple in Jerusalem, exiled all Jews from the city, and turned it into their regional capital. In 135 C.E. they dismantled the political structure of the Jewish state and exiled almost all Jews from Judea.

Unlike earlier exiles, this Roman dispersion fundamentally and permanently altered Jewish existence, removing all but a few Jews from the region of Israel until the twentieth century. This final exile established the principal contours of Jewish diaspora existence from then on: life as a minority group; dispersed among various peoples around the world; with distinct religious and social practices; united in reverence for sacred texts and their teachings, as interpreted by rabbi-scholars; usually dependent on the widely varying policies of the peoples among whom they lived; and sometimes forced to choose between religious conversion, emigration, or death. Jews preserved their cohesion through their acceptance of the authority of the TaNaKh and the importance of studying it, and their persistence in seeing themselves as a special kind of family even in dispersion.

Minority–Majority Relations in the Diaspora

In general, Jews remained socially and religiously distinct wherever they traveled. This identification was imposed partially from the outside by others, partially by internal discipline and loyalty to the group, its traditions, and its laws. Jewish history

How did Judaism arise and what are its evolving beliefs?

10.1

10.2

10.3

Western Wall, Jerusalem. The wall is the last remaining segment of the Second Temple of the Jewish people. All the rest was destroyed following their exile by the Romans in 135 C.E. It is the holiest shrine in Judaism. Just beyond the wall, on the hill on which the Second Temple once stood, and the First Temple before it, rises the Dome of the Rock, the third most sacred shrine in the Muslim world. The proximity of the shrines, and their claims over the same spaces, has often been a source of tension between the two religious groups.

◉ Watch the Video: Old City of Jerusalem on MyHistoryLab

10.1

10.2

10.3

How did
Christianity
emerge and
evolve?

becomes a case study also of tolerance and intolerance of minorities by majority peoples around the world.

In some civilizations, Jewish life in the diaspora survived and even flourished. For example, Rabbi Benjamin of Tudela, Spain, visited Muslim Baghdad in 1160–70 C.E. and reported: "In Baghdad there are about 40,000 Jews, and they dwell in security, prosperity, and honor under the great Caliph, and amongst them are great sages, the heads of Academies engaged in the study of the law. In this city there are ten Academies …" (Andrea and Overfield, Vol. I, p. 245).

There were contrary examples, however. The Book of Esther, written about (and probably during) the Persian diaspora, 638–333 B.C.E., captures the vulnerability of minority existence. A royal minister sees his chance to advance his career and profit, and argues to the king:

> There is a certain people, dispersed among the many peoples in all the provinces of your kingdom, who keep themselves apart. Their laws are different from those of every other people; they do not keep your majesty's laws. It does not befit your majesty to tolerate them. If it please your majesty, let an order be made in writing for their destruction; and I will pay ten thousand talents of silver to your majesty's officials, to be deposited in the royal treasury. (Esther 3:8–9)

The king agrees: "The money and the people are yours; deal with them as you wish" (Esther 3:11). On this occasion, according to Jewish traditions, the actions of Esther saved these Jews from destruction. But the Biblical account captures a pattern of official xenophobia and greed on the part of the majority, repeated frequently in Jewish history—and in the history of many minorities.

📖 **Read** the **Document**: **Expulsion of the Jews from France** (12th Century) on **MyHistoryLab**

Christianity

10.2   How did Christianity emerge and evolve?

While Judaism remained a religion of a relatively small group of people, it gave birth to the most populous religion in the world, Christianity. Here we trace the steps of Christianity's evolution: from the teachings of Jesus, a Jewish preacher and miracle worker who his followers believed to be the son of God, literally; to his disciples who began to spread the word of his teachings, and to transcribe them into writing; to Paul of Tarsus, who took Jesus' message to the broader world of the Mediterranean; to Emperor Constantine, who reversed centuries of persecution of Christians and began the process of making the Roman Empire Christian; to the division of the Catholic Church into Eastern and Western (Roman) branches; to the widespread institution of monasteries and convents throughout the remnants of the Roman Empire, the conversion of the barbarians, and the attempt to construct a new Christian Empire, the Holy Roman Empire.

📖 **Read** the **Document**: **Excerpt from the Gospel According to Luke** on **MyHistoryLab**

Christianity Emerges from Judaism

At the height of Roman rule over Judea, a splinter group within the Jewish people was forming around the person and teachings of Jesus of Nazareth. The times were turbulent and difficult. As a colony of the Roman Empire, Judea was taxed heavily and suppressed economically and politically. The Romans also demanded emperor worship from a people who were devoted to monotheism. Religious and political antagonisms were closely intertwined in an explosive mixture. The Jewish prophets of the Old Testament had promised a final end to such anguish, and many of Jesus' followers believed that he was the "servant" who had been promised to lead them into a brighter future.

In the face of Roman colonialism, the Jews were divided into at least four conflicting groups. The largest of these, the Pharisees, identified with the masses of the population in resenting the Roman occupation, but, seeing no realistic alternative to it, found some comfort in keeping alive and reinterpreting Jewish religious traditions. The more elite Sadducees, the temple priests and their allies, had become servants of the Roman state and preached accommodation to it. A much smaller, militant group of Zealots sought, quixotically, to drive out the Romans through violence. A fourth, still smaller group, the Essenes, lived a prayerful existence by the shores of the Dead Sea, stayed aloof from politics, and preached the imminent end of the world as they knew it.

Into this volatile and complex society, Jesus was born to Joseph, a carpenter, and Mary, his betrothed, about the year 4 B.C.E., in the town of Bethlehem, about 10 miles southwest of Jerusalem. (The year of Jesus' birth is not recorded. The Christian calendar places it at the beginning of the year 1, but it must have taken place no later than 4 B.C.E., for Herod, king at the time of Jesus' birth, died that year.) Biblical accounts report little about his early life, except that his parents took him to Jerusalem to celebrate the Passover holiday when he was 12 years old, and he entered there into probing discussions of religion with teachers sitting in the temple, astonishing onlookers and his parents. Jesus next emerges, at about the age of 30, as a powerful preacher, attracting multitudes to his sermons, which are filled with allegories and parables concerning ethical life, moral teachings, and predictions of the future.

In his calls for rapid and radical religious reform, Jesus found himself in opposition to the more conservative Pharisees, whom he frequently referred to as hypocrites. Like the Essenes, he spoke often of an imminent day of divine judgment of the whole world. He promised eternal life and happiness to the poor and downtrodden people of colonial Judea if only they would keep their faith in God. Similar predictions had also been common among the Jewish prophets centuries before, and Jesus' emphasis on the coming of the kingdom of God resonated strongly with the earlier voices as well as with the Essenes. Jesus' message, however, stressed a future not on earth during people's lifetimes, but in heaven after their deaths. In this he differed from most Jewish beliefs of his time. In addition to his preaching, according to Biblical accounts Jesus also performed exorcisms and miracles, fed multitudes of people, cured the blind and lame among his followers, and even brought the dead back to life. He pursued his unorthodox search for truth in the Galilee, the beautiful and lush northern region of Judea, only recently converted to Judaism. There he continued his preaching, angering both the Roman imperial government, which feared the revolutionary potential of his rabble-rousing, and the Jewish religious establishment, which viewed him as a heretic. Jesus said that he had come "not to abolish the Jewish law but to fulfill it," and his followers accepted much of the moral code of Jewish teachings. But they

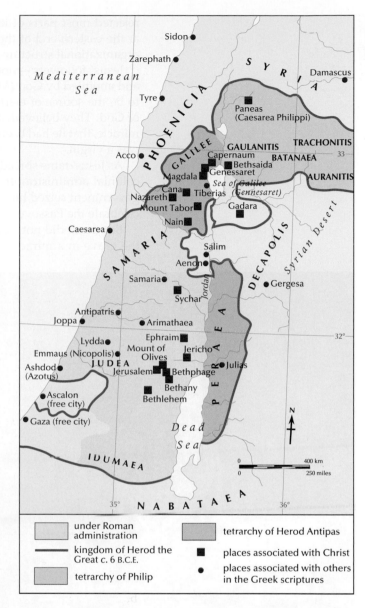

Palestine at the time of Jesus. Christianity first emerged as a sect within Judaism when Roman control of Palestine was increasing. Shortly before Jesus' birth, Rome had granted Herod the Great the Kingdom of Judea as a client ruler. Upon his death in 4 B.C.E. the kingdom was divided among his sons, and Judea itself came under direct Roman military rule.

10.1

10.2

How did Christianity emerge and evolve?

10.3

rejected most parts of its legal and separatist covenant. Beginning in a few towns at the eastern end of the Mediterranean Sea, Jesus' followers built an entirely new organizational structure for sustaining and spreading their new faith.

Jesus' followers—mostly common people—revered him as one specially chosen and anointed by God (*Messiah* in Hebrew, *Christos* in Greek). They proclaimed Jesus to be the source of eternal life and accepted him as a miracle worker and the son of God. They believed, according to the Biblical accounts, that his birth had been a miracle, that he had been conceived by the Holy Spirit of God and born to Mary, who was a virgin.

As Jesus' fame spread, the fears of the Jewish religious authorities and the Roman colonial administrators increased. To prevent any potential rebellion, the Roman government seized him when he once again returned to Jerusalem to preach and to celebrate the Passover, and executed him by crucifixion when he was 33 years old.

But death did not stop Jesus' message. His followers believed that he arose from the grave in a miraculous resurrection and triumph over death, and ascended to heaven to join God the Father. Their belief contained equal measures of admiration for his message of compassion and salvation and for his ability to perform miracles. Jesus' disciples took his message of compassion, salvation, and eternal life to Rome. The proud upper classes of Rome scoffed at first, but more and more of the simple people believed. Despite early persecution under several Roman emperors, Christianity increased in influence, until, in the fourth century, it became the official religion of the empire.

Spread through the networks of the empire, the Christian Church ultimately became the most important organizing force in post-Roman Europe. The message of Christianity and the organization of the Church expanded throughout the world. Today more than two billion people, one-third of the world's population, distributed among numerous different churches and denominations, declare themselves followers of Jesus, the simple preacher from Judea.

Jesus' Life, Teachings, and Disciples

Whatever the reality of the miracles associated with Jesus, clearly a new religion, Christianity, emerged from earlier Jewish roots, and, in this process, a number of adaptations and innovations took place.

Adapting Rituals to New Purposes. As we have seen, newly forming religions often adapt rituals and philosophies from existing religions, as, for example, Buddhism adapted the concept of *dharma* from Hinduism. This borrowing and adaptation can be attractive to members of the existing religion who wish to join the new one, for it assures them that their spiritual customs will be maintained. At the same time, a new interpretation gives the ritual a new meaning for the new faith. Jesus' form of prayer and much of his preaching were fully in accord with Jewish tradition. When he accepted baptism from the desert preacher John the Baptist,

Silver crucifix from Birka, Sweden, *c.* 900 C.E. The cross—signifying Christ's crucifixion—was adopted by Christians as a symbol of their faith as early as the second century. Making "the sign of the cross" was believed to be powerful in warding off evil, and, in later centuries, crusaders were said to "take the cross" when they set off on crusade (a word itself derived from the Latin for cross, *crux*). (Historiska Museet, Stockholm)

HOW DO WE KNOW?

The Search for the Historical Jesus

The only records of Jesus' life are the four Gospels, "the good news accounts," the first four books of the New Testament, which is the second section of the Christian Bible. Named for their authors—Matthew, Mark, Luke, and John—the Gospels are neither unbiased nor contemporary. Mark, probably the oldest of the four, dates to 70 C.E., some 40 years after Jesus' death. As with the early literature of Hinduism, Buddhism, and Judaism, the Gospels represent written recordings of oral traditions. They bring together traditions surrounding Jesus' life as they were transmitted among his followers. Although individual names are associated with them, the actual authors of the Gospels are unknown. Mark, for example, was the most common name in the Roman Empire at the time. Moreover, it appears that they were written for different audiences and therefore tell their stories somewhat differently. Mark, for example, addressed his beliefs in a future life to Christians who were being persecuted in Rome.

Fifty-two additional texts, called by scholars the Gnostic gospels, were discovered near the town of Nag Hammadi in upper Egypt in 1945, and have been subject to intense study ever since. Scholars believe that these texts were transcribed at about the same time as the four Gospels of the Christian Bible, but that they contain accounts of Jesus' teachings that were inconsistent with them and that they were therefore banned by Church leaders and hidden away.

According to the most important of the Gnostic gospels, the Secret Gospel of Thomas, Jesus taught that each individual could find the light of God within himself, or herself, without the necessity of belief in Jesus. "The kingdom is inside of you, and it is outside of you. When you come to know yourselves, then you will become known, and you will realize that it is you who are the sons of the living father" The search for meaning is most important: "Jesus said, 'Let him who seeks continue seeking until he finds. When he finds, he will become troubled. When he becomes troubled he will be astonished, and he will rule over all.'"

The Gnostic gospels also give a greater place to women in the search for religious truth, and they suggest that Jesus had some measure of physical relationship with Mary Magdalene, a prostitute whom he brought back to respectable society. These somewhat mystical gospels, with their message of a greater sexuality for Jesus, were suppressed as heresy in the wake of theological struggles within the Church in the late second century C.E.

The four Biblical Gospels themselves also present additional problems for historical analysis. They begin with the story of the birth of Jesus told as a miracle. According to the Gospels, Jesus was the son of God, born miraculously through Mary, a virgin betrothed to Joseph, a carpenter from Nazareth in the region of the Galilee. Believers certainly accept such an account, but it is not subject to historical verification. Moreover, despite the Gospels' accounts of Jesus' multitudes of followers, and his political and religious influence, neither Roman nor Jewish records of the time take note of his life or his teachings. Tacitus, although scornful of the early Christians, does take note of Jesus' death.

Modern scholars who have attempted to reconstruct the life of Jesus have reached very different conclusions about his essential character, depicting Jesus as political revolutionary, magician, Galilean charismatic, Galilean rabbi, proto-Pharisee, Essene, prophet of the end of days, exorcist, miracle worker, and marginal Jew. All the research, however, no matter how scholarly and how inventive, remains inconclusive. The four Biblical Gospels, despite their richness as religious teachings, have serious shortcomings as religious texts, and the historical validity of the Gnostic gospels is clouded by their official suppression.

- What are the shortcomings of the Gospels as historical texts for understanding the life of Jesus? What are their strengths?
- Historians attempting to characterize the life of Jesus have reached very different conclusions. What kinds of sources do you think they used?
- If the Gnostic gospels had not been suppressed by powerful theologians, do you think the Church might have developed differently? If so, how? If not, why not?

---

however, Jesus prepared the way for adapting an existing practice and giving it new meaning for his followers. A minor practice within Judaism, baptism would later become in Christianity a central **sacrament** of purification enjoined on all members.

Another example of adaptation is Jesus' "last supper," a Passover ritual meal. Jesus ate unleavened, flat bread as a symbol of slavery in Egypt, and he drank the wine that accompanies all Jewish festivals as a symbol of joy. Then he offered the bread and wine also to his disciples with the words, "This is my body ... this is my blood." Thus he transformed the foods of the Passover meal into the **Eucharist**, or Holy Communion, another central sacrament, a mystery through which Christians believe the invisible Christ grants communion to them.

Overturning the Old Order. In his teachings, Jesus also addressed political and social issues, staking out his own often ambiguous positions in relationship to the different and competing philosophies of the day. When Jesus, following John the Baptist, taught, "Repent; for the kingdom of heaven has come near" (Matthew 4:17), he was

KEY TERMS

sacrament In Christian theology, a rite or ritual that is an outward sign of a spiritual grace conveyed on the believer by Christ through the ministry of the Church.

Eucharist From the Greek *eucharistia*, "thanksgiving." The central sacrament and act of worship of the Catholic Church, culminating in Holy Communion, the eating of a sanctified wafer and drinking of sanctified wine as a reminder of Jesus' life, and, in Roman Catholicism, representing the actual act of partaking in his body and blood.

SOURCE

The Beatitudes from the Sermon on the Mount

Jesus' teaching—powerful in direct address, in parable, and in allegory—established his identification with the poor and oppressed, his disdain for the Roman authorities, and his scorn for the Jewish religious leadership of his time. He sounded much like a latter-day Jewish prophet calling his people to reform. The Beatitudes, a list of promises of God's rewards for the simple, righteous people, the first of Jesus' great sermons recorded in the New Testament, was delivered from the top of a hill in Galilee, northern Israel:

Blessed are the poor in spirit, for theirs is the kingdom of heaven.
Blessed are those who mourn, for they will be comforted.
Blessed are the meek, for they will inherit the earth.
Blessed are those who hunger and thirst for righteousness, for they will be filled.
Blessed are the merciful, for they will receive mercy.
Blessed are the poor in heart, for they will see God.
Blessed are the peacemakers, for they will be called children of God.
Blessed are those who are persecuted for righteousness' sake, for theirs is the kingdom of heaven. (Matthew 5:3–10)

10.1
10.2
10.3

How did Christianity emerge and evolve?

not explicit in describing that kingdom or its date of arrival. But in metaphor and parable he preached that life as we know it on earth would soon change dramatically, or even come to an end.

Jesus' words must have been especially welcome to the poor, as he spoke repeatedly of the "Kingdom of Heaven" in which the tables would be turned:

It will be hard for a rich person to enter the kingdom of heaven. Again I tell you, it is easier for a camel to go through the eye of a needle than for someone who is rich to enter the kingdom of God. (Matthew 19:23–24)

Jesus declared that the most important commandment was to "Love the Lord your God with all your heart, and with all your soul, and with all your mind," and the second was "Love your neighbor as yourself," both directly cited from the TaNaKh (Deuteronomy 6:7 and Leviticus 19:18). Indeed, he projected these principles into new dimensions, declaring "Love your enemies and pray for your persecutors" (Matthew 5:44). But he also warned that the coming apocalypse would be violent:

Do not think that I have come to bring peace to earth; I have not come to bring peace, but a sword. (Matthew 10:34)

Jesus and the Jewish Establishment. The gospels depict Jesus' attitude toward Jewish law as ambivalent but often condescending, and his relationship toward the Jewish religious leadership as confrontational. He scoffed at Jewish dietary laws: "It is not what goes into the mouth that defiles a person, but it is what comes out of the mouth that defiles" (Matthew 15:11). He constantly tested the limits of Sabbath restrictions, declaring that: "The Sabbath is made for man, not man for the Sabbath" (Mark 2:27). He restricted divorce, announcing that: "If a man divorces his wife for any cause other than unchastity he involves her in adultery; and anyone who marries a divorced woman commits adultery" (Matthew 5:32). Many of his teachings may have reflected his desire to return to earlier beliefs in faith and spirituality and his belief that the future lay in heaven, not on earth.

Miracles and Resurrection. The gospels describe Jesus' ministry as filled with miracles—healing the sick, restoring sight to the blind, feeding multitudes of followers from just a few loaves and fishes, walking on water, calming storms, and even raising the dead. Reports of these miracles, perhaps even more than his ethical teachings, brought followers flocking to him. The gospel narrative of Jesus' suffering on the cross, presenting him at the final moment of his life as both human and divine in one personage, and, finally, his miraculous resurrection from the grave, his appearances

10.1

10.2

10.3

How did
Christianity
emerge and
evolve?

to his disciples, and his ascent to heaven, complete the miracle and the majesty of his life and embody his promise of eternal life for those who believe in his power.

The stories of Jesus' life and death, message and miracles, form the basis for Christianity, at first a new sect located within Judaism. Although different followers attributed more or less divinity and greater or lesser miracles to him, apparently all accepted Jesus as a new, reforming teacher. Many saw him as the long-awaited "Messiah," a messenger and savior specially anointed by God. His apostles, especially Paul of Tarsus (d. 67 C.E.), now refocused Jesus' message and built the Christian sect into a new, powerful religion. The apostles' preaching, organizational work, and letters to fledgling Christian communities fill most of the rest of the New Testament.

The Growth of the Early Church

At first, the followers of Jesus functioned as a sect within Judaism, continuing to meet in synagogues and to identify themselves as Jews. Peter, described in the Gospels as Jesus' chosen organizational leader, first took the Christian message outside the Jewish community (Acts 10). Declaring circumcision unnecessary for membership, he welcomed gentiles (people who were not Jewish) into the new Church. James, Jesus' brother and leader of the Christian community of Jerusalem, abrogated most of the Jewish dietary laws for the new community (Acts 15). These apostles believed that the rigorous ritual laws of Judaism inhibited the spread of its ethical message. Instead, they chose to emphasize the miraculous powers of Jesus and his followers. They spoke little of their master's views on the coming apocalypse but stressed his statements on the importance of love and redemption.

Paul Organizes the Early Church. Tensions continued to simmer between mainstream Jewish leaders and the early Christians. One of the fiercest opponents of the new sect was Saul from the Anatolian town of Tarsus. Saul was traveling to confront the Christian community in Damascus when he experienced an overpowering mystical vision of Jesus that literally knocked him to the ground. Reversing his previous position, Saul now affirmed his belief in the authenticity of Jesus as the divine Son of God. In speaking within the Jewish community, he had preferred his Hebrew name, Saul. Now, as he took his new message to gentiles, he preferred his Roman name, Paul. Jewish by ethnicity and early religious choice, Roman by citizenship, and Greek by culture, Paul was ideally placed to refine and explicate Jesus' message. He became the second founder of Christianity and dedicated himself to establishing it as an independent, organized religion.

To link the flourishing, but separate, Christian communities, Paul undertook three missionary voyages in the eastern Mediterranean, and he kept in continuous communication through a series of letters, Paul's "Epistles" of the New Testament. He advised the leadership emerging within each local church organization: the *presbyters*, or elders; the deacons above them; and, at the head, the bishop. He promised eternal life to those who believed in Jesus' power. He declared Jewish ritual laws an obstacle to spiritual progress (Galatians 5:2–6). Neither membership in a chosen family nor observance of laws or rituals was necessary in the new religion. Paul proclaimed a new equality in Christianity:

> There is no longer Jew or Greek, there is no longer slave or free, there is no longer male or female; for all of you are one in Christ Jesus. (Galatians 3:28)

Paul formulated a new concept of "**original sin**" and redemption from it. Jews had accepted the story told in Genesis of Adam and Eve's disobedience in the Garden of Eden as a mythical explanation of some of life's harsh realities: the pain of childbirth, the struggle to earn a living, the dangers of wild beasts, and, most of all, human mortality. Paul now proclaimed that Adam and Eve's "original sin" could be forgiven. Humanity could, in a sense, return to paradise and eternal life. Jesus' death on the

KEY TERMS

presbyter In early Christian usage, a member of the governing body of a church.

original sin First understood as the disobedience of Adam and Eve in the Garden of Eden as they ate the forbidden fruit of the Tree of Knowledge. Later understood as the sexual relations between Adam and Eve. In Christian belief, Jesus' death atoned for these sins—for those who believed in him.

321

cross atoned for original sin. According to Paul, those who believed in Jesus and accepted membership in the new Christian community would be forgiven by God and "saved." Although they would still be mortal, at the end of their earthly lives they would inherit a life in heaven, and, much later, would even be reborn on earth (Romans 5–6).

The Christian Calendar. Like other religions, Christianity established a sacred calendar. People had long celebrated the winter solstice; in the fourth century Christians fixed the observance of Jesus' birth, Christmas, at that time of year, although no one knew the actual date of his birth. Good Friday, at about the time of Passover, mourned Jesus' crucifixion and death; three days later his resurrection was celebrated in the joyous festival of Easter. Corresponding to the Jewish holiday of Pentecost, the anniversary of receiving the Ten Commandments 50 days after the Passover, Christianity introduced its own holiday of Pentecost. It commemorates the date when, according to Acts 2, the "Holy Spirit," the third element of the Trinity along with God the Father and Jesus the Son, filled Jesus' disciples and they "began to talk in other tongues, as the Spirit gave them power of utterance," enabling them to preach to the various peoples of the world. (Modern-day Christian Pentecostals "**speak in tongues**," praying and uttering praises ecstatically, healing through prayer and laying on of hands, and speaking of experiencing spiritual miracles.)

KEY TERM

speaking in tongues A mode of praying and preaching emphasizing ecstasy and even an entering into trances, such that the words of prayer and preaching may not be understood, but are meaningful nonetheless.

Paul's missionary journeys. Following Jesus' trial and crucifixion, about 29 C.E., his disciples, notably the Roman convert Paul, set out to convert non-Jews, or gentiles. Paul's journeys took him throughout the Greco-Roman east Mediterranean, and beyond. These journeys and the epistles Paul wrote began to weave struggling Christian groups into a new religious organization, the Christian Church. Paul died in Rome, apparently a martyr to the emperor Nero.

Over time, special saints' days were designated to mark the lives and deaths of people who helped to spread the new religion. The new Christian calendar, which has become the most widely used in the world, fixed its first year at the approximate date of Jesus' birth. The Jewish Sabbath, a weekly day of rest and reflection, was transferred from Saturday to Sunday.

Gender Relations. Jesus attracted many women as followers, and women led in the organization of several of the early churches. Paul welcomed them warmly and treated them respectfully at first, but women gradually lost their influence as Jesus' disciples institutionalized the Church. Although they taught spiritual equality, early Christians allowed gender and social inequalities to remain. Paul had proclaimed that in Jesus "There is no longer male or female," but he seemed to distrust sexual energies. Like Jesus, he was unmarried. He recommended celibacy and, for those unable to meet that standard, monogamous marriage as a means of sexual restraint:

> It is well for a man not to touch a woman. But because of cases of sexual immorality, each man should have his own wife and each woman her own husband. The husband should give to his wife her conjugal rights, and likewise the wife to her husband. (1 Corinthians 7:1–3)

Paul's discomfort with sexuality continued to haunt Christianity. One result was the decision, by about the sixth century, to proclaim marriage as one of the Church's seven sacraments. Marriage would no longer be a contract that a man and woman could enter—or leave—on their own, but a ritual performed by a priest, in the name of Jesus, binding the man and woman forever in an unbreakable bond. For people seeking greater sanctity through celibacy, Church leaders established hundreds of monasteries and convents throughout the Christian world hosting thousands of unmarried, celibate men and women dedicated to the mission of the Church (see below). Many clergy who were not monks, however, continued to marry. In 1139, the second Lateran Council (named for the Pope's Lateran Palace in Rome, where it convened) declared all clerical marriages not only unlawful but also invalid (MacCulloch, p. 373). Despite the protests of many priests, especially those who had married, and despite breaches in practice, the Council's decision prevailed as the law of the Church.

Paul moved to subordinate women, first at home:

> I want you to understand that Christ is the head of every man, and the husband is the head of the wife … he is the image and reflection of God; but woman is the reflection of man. Indeed, man was not made from woman, but woman from man. Neither was man created for the sake of woman, but woman for the sake of man. (1 Corinthians 11:3–9)

Then in church:

> Women should be silent in the churches. For they are not permitted to speak, but should be subordinate, as the law also says. If there is anything they desire to know, let them ask their husbands at home. (1 Corinthians 14:34–35)

Paul had also declared that spiritually "There is no longer slave or free," but in practice he accepted slavery, saying, "Slaves, obey your earthly masters with fear and

MAJOR CHRISTIAN FESTIVALS

January 6	Epiphany
February–March	Shrove Tuesday, or Mardi Gras (day before Ash Wednesday)
February–March	Ash Wednesday (first day of Lent)
February–April	Lent
February 2	Candlemas Day
March–April	Easter
March 25	Feast of Annunciation
April–June	Ascension (40 days after Easter)
May–June	Pentecost/Whit Sunday (50 days after Easter)
May–June	Trinity Sunday (Sunday after Pentecost)
November–December	Advent
December 24	Christmas Eve
December 25	Christmas Day

10.1

10.2

10.3

How did Christianity emerge and evolve?

trembling." He did urge masters to be kind to slaves and to "stop threatening them for you know that both of you have the same Master in heaven, and with him there is no partiality" (Ephesians 6:5–9). These contrasting statements would later be invoked to justify both Christian approval and disapproval for the institution of slavery (see the chapter entitled "Political Revolutions in Europe and the Americas").

From Persecution to Triumph

Having established the central doctrines of the new religion and stabilized its core communities, both Peter and Paul moved to expand its geographical scope. They saw Rome as the capital of empire and the center of the international communication network of the time, and they traveled there to preach and teach. Tradition holds that both were martyred there in the persecutions of the emperor Nero, about 67 C.E., and that both are entombed and enshrined there.

In this capital of empire, Christianity appeared as one of several mystery religions, all of which were based on beliefs in supernatural beings. They included the religion of Mithra, a Persian sun god; Demeter, a Greek goddess; YHWH, the god of the Jews; and an eclectic mixture of beliefs called Gnosticism. Romans seemed to be in search of a more inspiring, otherworldly faith than paganism provided, but at the time of the deaths of Peter and Paul, Christianity was still a relatively weak force.

The first Christians, Jews by nationality, were scorned as provincial foreigners. Some Roman authorities thought that Christian beliefs in resurrection and an afterlife undermined pride in citizenship and willingness to serve in the army. About the year 100, the historian Tacitus wrote of:

> a class of persons hated for their vices whom the crowd called Christians. Christus, after whom they were named, had undergone the death penalty in the reign of Tiberius, by sentence of the procurator Pontius Pilate, and the pernicious superstition was checked for a moment only to break out once more, not only in Judaea, the home of the disease, but in the Capital itself, where everything horrible or shameful in the world gathers and becomes fashionable. (Tacitus, *Annals* XV:44)

Paradoxically, because they refused to worship the emperor or to take oaths in his name, official Rome viewed Christians as atheists. Their emphasis on otherworldly salvation and their strong internal organization were seen as threats to the state's authority. Roman leaders also mocked the sacrament of the Eucharist, in which Christians consumed consecrated wafers and wine as the body and blood of Christ, as a sign of cannibalism. Official treatment of Christianity was erratic but often marked by severe persecution. Nero (r. 54–68) scapegoated the Christians, blaming them for the great fire in 64, apparently executing both Peter and Paul among his victims, and sending hundreds of Christians to die in public gladiatorial contests and by burning. Edicts of persecution were issued by emperors Antoninus Pius (r. 138–61), Marcus Aurelius (r. 161–80), Septimius Severus (r. 193–211), Decius (r. 249–51), and Diocletian (r. 284–305). In 257 Emperor Valerian (r. 253–60) was prepared to launch a major persecution of Christians, but he was captured in battle by Persians. In these early years of persecution, thousands of Christians suffered martyrdom.

Despite the scorn and the persecution, Christianity continued to grow. Its key doctrines and texts were written, edited, and approved by leaders in the network of Christian churches. After years of debate, Christian leaders and scholars agreed on the contents of the New Testament by about the year 200, and by 250 the city of Rome alone held about 50,000 Christians among its million inhabitants. Most were of the lower classes, attracted by Jesus' message to the poor, but middle- and upper-class Romans had also joined. In particular, Christianity proved attractive to the wives of Roman leaders, who often contributed to their husbands' conversions. By the reign of Constantine, estimates reported that one out of ten inhabitants of the Roman Empire was Christian.

HOW DO WE KNOW?

Explanations for the Spread of Christianity

Many historians of our own time accept the thrust of Gibbon's explanations (see below), but tend to emphasize more the importance of community within the Church.

"From the outset, the major goal of the Jesus movement was to call into existence a new kind of inclusive community that might arch over all the ordinary human distinctions of race and religion," writes Howard Clark Kee (1991, p. 2). Kee analyzes five different kinds of community that were active in the Roman world during the first two centuries of the Christian era, and suggests that Christianity developed an appeal to each of them: The community of the wise, seeking special knowledge of the future; the community of the law-abiding, seeking appropriate rules of guidance in the present; the community where God dwells among his people, seeking assurance that it was specially selected and cared for; the community of mystical participation, influenced by the mystery religions of the time; and the ethnically and culturally inclusive community, outsiders seeking a place of belonging. Different aspects of the Christian message, developed by different Church leaders, spoke to each of these communities and succeeded in drawing them in.

The historical sociologist Michael Mann cites the psychological and practical rewards of the growing Christian "ecumene," the worldwide community of the Church, with its comprehensive philosophy for living and organizing. Although much of

Christianity's message targeted the poor, Mann notes that the religion also drew a large following of urban artisans, whom the aristocratic Roman Empire devalued. Excluded from political power, these working-class people were in search of a comprehensive and welcoming community. They wanted to recreate an earlier, simpler, more participatory era, and they became Christians. As imperial power became increasingly centralized, remote, insensitive, and, later, unstable, "In many ways Christianity represented how Rome liked to idealize its republican past" (Mann, p. 325).

- Jesus and St. Paul promised life after death to Christians. Do Kee and Mann cite this as a reason for Christianity's success in winning new adherents? If so, what terms do they use to indicate this promise? If not, why do you think they omit it?
- Gibbon suggests that a large part of early Christianity's appeal was the miracles that Christ and his disciples were said to have performed. Kee and Mann do not emphasize miracles. Why?
- Both Kee and Mann suggest that different groups were attracted to Christianity for different reasons. Based on what you know of people's motivations for joining religious groups, with which of their reasons would you agree? Disagree?

The Conversion of Constantine. In 313, Emperor Constantine (r. 306–37) had a vision in which a cross and the words *in hoc signo vinces*, "in this sign you will be victorious," appeared to him the night before he won the critical battle that made him sole emperor in the Western Empire. He immediately declared Christianity legal. He funded Christian leaders and their construction of churches, while withdrawing official support from the pagan churches, making Christianity the *de facto* official religion of the Roman Empire. On a personal level, Constantine encouraged his mother, Helena, to embrace Christianity, which she did enthusiastically. Helena had churches built in Asia Minor and the Holy Land, and traveled to Jerusalem seeking the cross on which Jesus died. After her death, she was canonized as a saint in the Catholic Church.

As emperor, Constantine took a leading part in Church affairs. He sponsored the Council of Nicaea in 325, the largest assembly of bishops of local Christian churches up to that time. He convened the council primarily to establish the central theological doctrines of Christianity, but it also established a Church organization for the Roman Empire, a network of urban bishoprics grouped into provinces, with each province headed by the chief bishop of its largest city. In 337, on his deathbed, Constantine accepted baptism.

In 392, Emperor Theodosius I (r. 379–95) declared Christianity to be the official religion of the Roman Empire. He outlawed the worship of the traditional Roman gods and severely restricted Judaism, initiating centuries of bitter Christian persecution of both traditions.

How Had Christianity Succeeded? How had Christianity, once scorned and persecuted, achieved such power? Christian believers attributed the success to divine

How did Christianity emerge and evolve?

10.1

10.2

10.3

How did
Christianity
emerge and
evolve?

assistance. Historians seek more earthly explanations. Let us consider one of the major historians to tackle the topic, Edward Gibbon (1737–94).

In 1776, Gibbon began the publication of his six-volume masterpiece, *The History of the Decline and Fall of the Roman Empire*. A child of the Enlightenment philosophy of his time, which rejected supernatural explanations (see the chapter "Migration"), Gibbon rather sarcastically presented five reasons for Christianity's victories. But beneath his sarcasm Gibbon revealed the profound strengths of the new religion:

- Its "inflexible and intolerant" zeal, derived from its Jewish roots.
- Its promise of resurrection and a future life for believers, soon augmented by the threat of eternal damnation for nonbelievers.
- Its assertion of miraculous accomplishments.
- The austere morals of the first Christians. The Christian search for spiritual perfection, a monogamous sexual code, the rejection of worldly honor, and a general emphasis on equality attracted many converts. In the extreme case, martyrdom won admiration, sympathy, and followers. Later commentators noted that the simplicity and self-sacrifice of the early Christians reminded some Romans of the ideals of the early Republic.
- The Church gradually generated a state within a state through the decentralized leadership of its local bishops and *presbyters*, the structure Paul had begun to knit together. As imperial structures weakened, Christianity provided an alternative community. This Christian community distributed philanthropy to needy people, Christian and non-Christian alike. It also publicized its message effectively—in Greek, the language of the eastern part of the empire.

Many later commentators noted that the Christian community included a local church in which to share the joys and sorrows of everyday life, celebrate life-cycle events, and commemorate major events in the history of the group. At the same time it provided membership in a universal Church that extended to the entire known world, and suggested participation in a life that transcended earthly concerns altogether.

Doctrine: Definition and Dispute

As it grew after receiving official recognition, institutional Christianity refined its theology. The most influential theologian of the period, St. Augustine (354–430), bishop of Hippo in North Africa, wrote *The City of God* to explain Christianity's relationship to competing religions and philosophies, and to the Roman government with which it was increasingly intertwined.

Despite Christianity's designation as the official religion of the empire, Augustine declared its message to be spiritual rather than political. Christianity, he argued, should be concerned with the mystical, heavenly City of Jerusalem rather than with earthly politics. Although Augustine encouraged the Roman emperors to suppress certain religious groups, some elements of his theology supported the separation of Church and state.

Augustine built philosophical bridges to Platonic philosophy, the dominant system of the Hellenistic world of his time and place. Christianity envisioned Jesus, God's son, walking the earth and suffering for his people. He was, literally, very down-to-earth. God, the Father, had more transcendent characteristics, but they were less emphasized in Christian theology at the time. Plato (*c.* 428–348 B.C.E.) and later **Neoplatonic** philosophers, however, provided the model of a more exalted, more remote god, a god that was more accepted among the leading thinkers of Augustine's time. According to Augustine, Plato's god was:

> the maker of all created things, the light by which things are known, and the good in reference to which things are to be done; … we have in him the first principle of nature, the truth of doctrines, and the happiness of life. (Augustine, p. 253)

KEY TERMS

Neoplatonic A philosophical system founded by Plotinus (205–70 C.E.) and influenced by Plato's theory of ideas. It emphasizes the transcendent, impersonal, and indefinable "One" as the ground of all existence and the source of an eternal world of goodness, beauty, and order, of which material existence is but a feeble copy.

heresy A belief that is not in agreement with, or that even conflicts with, the official orthodoxy of its time and place. Heretics, those who espoused heresy, were often persecuted.

In addition, Plato's god existed in the soul of every person, perhaps a borrowing from Hinduism (see chapter "Hinduism and Buddhism").

Augustine married these Platonic and Neoplatonic views to the transcendent characteristics of God in Christian theology. This provided Christianity with a new intellectual respectability, which attracted new audiences in the vast Hellenistic world. He also encouraged contemplation and meditation within Christianity, an important element in the monastic life that was beginning to emerge among Christians (as it had among Buddhists). Augustine himself organized a community of monks in Tegaste (now Souk-Ahras), the city of his birth.

In his earlier *Confessions* (c. 400), Augustine had written of his personal life of relatively mild sin before his conversion to Christianity. Now he warned Christians that Adam and Eve's willfulness had led to original sin; sin had unlocked the forces of lust, turning the flesh against the spirit; and lust had called forth a death sentence on all humans in place of the immortality originally intended for them:

> As soon as our first parents had transgressed the commandment, divine grace forsook them, and they were confounded at their own wickedness ... They experienced a new motion of their flesh which had become disobedient to them, in strict retribution of their own disobedience to God ... Then began the flesh to lust against the Spirit ... And thus, from the bad use of free will, there originated the whole train of evil ... on to the destruction of the second death, which has no end, those only being excepted who are freed by the grace of God. (Augustine *City of God*, pp. 422–23)

For Augustine as for Paul, and thus for early Christianity, sexuality was perilous and woman suspect. In early Christian theology, profane flesh and divine spirit confronted each other uneasily.

Augustine also believed that Christians should subordinate their will and reason to the teachings and authority of the Church. Although it is usually associated with the development of Protestant religions much later, the idea of predestination—that is, that individuals could do nothing through their own actions to obtain salvation and entrance to heaven—dominated Augustine's theology. Some Christian theologians, such as Pelagius (c. 354–after 418), rejected Augustine's argument about original sin and taught that human beings could choose between good and evil to determine their own fate. They feared that the growing acceptance of Augustine's beliefs would devalue both public service for the poor and private initiative by less disciplined Christians. Ultimately, Augustine's views prevailed, and popes at the time labeled those of Pelagius **heresy**.

Battles over Dogma. Some theological disputes led to violence, especially as the Church attempted to suppress doctrinal disagreement. The most divisive dispute concerned the nature of the divinity of Jesus. The theologian Arius (c. 250–336) taught that Christ's humanity limited his divinity, and that God the Father, wholly transcendent, was more sacred than the son who had walked the earth. The Council of Nicaea, which Constantine convened in 325 to resolve this dispute, issued an official statement of creed affirming Jesus' complete divinity and his indivisibility from God. The Arian controversy continued, however, especially on the fringes of empire, where Arian missionaries converted many of the Gothic tribes to their own beliefs. Wars between the new Arian converts and the Roman Church ensued, until finally Arianism was defeated in armed battle. Of these struggles,

St. Augustine, Piero della Francesca, 1454–69. Augustine emphasized spiritual rather than worldly issues, encouraged contemplation and meditation, and incorporated Platonic and Neoplatonic concepts of a transcendent god into Christianity. Piero della Francesca's painting captures the austerity and dedication of the saint himself along with the sumptuous and colorful robes he wears, in his capacity as Bishop of Hippo, depicting scenes relating to the life of Jesus. (National Museum of Ancient Art, Lisbon)

10.1

10.2

10.3

How did Christianity emerge and evolve?

327

10.1

10.2

10.3

How did
Christianity
emerge and
evolve?

the historian Ammianus Marcellinus (*c.* 330– 95) wrote: "No wild beasts are such enemies to mankind as are most of the Christians in the deadly hatred they feel for one another."

In the eastern Mediterranean, too, bitter and violent conflicts broke out among rival Christian theological factions, again over the precise balance between Jesus' divinity and his humanity. Persecution of dissidents by the Orthodox Church in Carthage, Syria, and Egypt was so severe that the arrival in the seventh century of

Monastery of St. Catherine, Mount Sinai, 557 C.E. According to the Torah, Moses received the tablets of the law from God on Mount Sinai. For this reason the Byzantine emperor Justinian I (r. 527–65) chose to found the monastery of St. Catherine in the place believed to be the Biblical Mount Sinai. The remote beauty of the place also made it ideal for spiritual meditation.

Muslim rule, which treated all the Christian sects equally, was often welcomed as a respite from the struggles.

By the sixth century, Christians far surpassed Jews in numbers, geographical spread, power, and influence. Christian missionaries continued their attempts to convert Jews, often by coercion. In 576, for example, a Gallic bishop gave the Jews of his city the choice between baptism and expulsion, a pattern that was repeated periodically, although Jews had not yet immigrated into Western Europe in large numbers.

10.1

10.2

10.3

What was the role of Christianity in the Roman Empire?

Christianity in the Wake of Empire

10.3 What was the role of Christianity in the Roman Empire?

Christianity spread to Western and northern Europe along the communication and transportation networks of the Roman Empire. Born in Judea under Roman occupation, Christianity now spread throughout the empire, spoke its languages of Greek and Latin, preached the gospel along its trade routes, and constructed church communities in its cities. Thanks to official recognition and patronage, the Church grew steadily. As the Roman imperial government weakened, it enlisted the now official Church as a kind of department of state. While the empire weakened and dissolved, Christianity emerged and flourished.

📖 Read the Document: Perpetua, *The Autobiography of a Christian Martyr* on MyHistoryLab

The Conversion of the Barbarians

During the first millennium C.E., bishops in the Western Church came "from the ranks of the senatorial governing class … they stood for continuity of the old Roman values … The eventual conversion of the barbarian leaders was due to their influence" (Matthew, p. 21). "None of the major Germanic peoples who entered the Roman provinces in the fourth and fifth centuries remained pagan for more than a generation after they crossed the frontier" (Mann, p. 335). About 496, Clovis, chief of the Merovingian Franks, rejected Arianism and converted to Roman Christianity, the first barbarian to accept the religion of the empire. He established his capital in Paris and had thousands of his tribesmen converted, for, in general, followers accepted the religion of their leader. Clovis' acceptance of Christianity brought him the support of the Roman ecclesiastical hierarchy, including the pope, and insured the triumph of this version of Christianity in Gaul.

Decentralized Power and Monastic Life

In Western Europe, Christianity developed a multitude of local institutions. Churches, monasteries, and convents were established, and leadership was decentralized. In regions that lacked organized government and administration, local Church leaders and institutions provided whatever existed of order, administration, and a sense of larger community. For several centuries, "Christendom was dominated by thousands of dedicated unmarried men and women" (McManners, p. 89), living in monasteries throughout the Christian world. Missionary activity continued enthusiastically, but now turned northward toward the Vikings and the Slavs, as other geographical doors had been forcibly shut by the victorious Muslim armies emerging from Arabia.

Pope Gregory I (r. 590–604) saw the usefulness of the monasteries and monks in converting and disciplining the barbarians, and he began to encourage the monastic movement. By the year 600 there were about 200 monasteries in Gaul alone, and the

Icon of Mary, Jesus, and SS. Theodore and George, St. Catherine's Monastery, Mount Sinai, sixth to seventh century C.E. The dispute over the use of icons in worship divided the Eastern Orthodox Church for more than a century, 726–843, between iconoclasts who wanted them banned and iconodules who continued to venerate them.

10.1

10.2

10.3   What was
the role of
Christianity in the
Roman Empire?

first missionaries dispatched by Rome arrived in England *c.* 597. By 700 much of England had been converted. In the ninth, tenth, and eleventh centuries, missionary activity was directed toward the "Northmen," the Vikings from Scandinavia, who raided and traded for goods and slaves from North America and Greenland, through the North Sea and the Baltic, down the Volga River, across the Caspian Sea, and on as far as Baghdad. The Vikings came into the Christian fold with only a tenuous link to Rome and a strong admixture of pagan ritual.

Although the pope in Rome had nominal authority over Christian affairs in the West, the Church's power was, in fact, fragmented and decentralized between 500 and 1000. Christianity spread in urban areas through its bishops in their large churches. In rural and remote areas, monks, acting as missionaries, carried the message.

Monasteries, which were small, isolated communities, each under the local control of a single abbot, modeled the spirituality and simplicity of the earliest Christian communities. Because sexual activity was ruled out, monasticism became as accessible to women in convents as to men in monasteries, and was equally valued by both. Many monasteries contained both men and women, each living in celibacy.

The most famous of the early monastics, St. Benedict (*c.* 480–547), founded a monastery at Monte Cassino, about 100 miles southeast of Rome. The writings of Pope Gregory I give us the most detailed information on the life, regulations, and discipline of that exemplary institution, although each monastery had its own variations in administration and practice.

Through a variety of educational institutions, the churches, monasteries, convents, and bishops kept Rome's culture alive in northern and Western Europe. In much of rural Western Europe, local authorities valued the monks not just as the only literate people in the region but also as the most capable in administering land and agriculture. These authorities also sought an alliance with the prestige and power of the Church. They granted land and administrative powers to nearby monasteries, transforming them into important local economic forces. (Compare the administrative roles of Hindu priests and Buddhist monks in south and Southeast Asia in the chapter entitled "Hinduism and Buddhism.") Monks became courtiers and bishops as well as missionaries as they expanded the geographic, social, and economic dimensions of the Church. Until the Fourth Lateran Council (1216) under Pope Innocent III (r. 1198–1216), monasteries could form and dissolve at local initiatives, so we have no record of their exact numbers in the early centuries.

A history of the very decentralized Church of this time would have to be written from the bottom up. The Church in the West was decentralized partly because the Roman Empire was decentralized, having lost its administrative power. There was no longer an emperor in Rome. The Church and what was left of the government in Western Europe groped toward a new mutual relationship.

📖 **Read** the **Document: Rule of St. Benedict (6th c.) by St. Benedict of Nursia** on **MyHistoryLab**

The Church Divides into East and West

In the far more literate and sophisticated Byzantine Empire, political leaders did not relinquish their power to Church authorities. Indeed, the emperor at Constantinople served as administrative head of the Church, a pattern that had been set by Constantine when he presided over the Council of Nicaea, outside Constantinople.

Today, Eastern Orthodoxy and Roman Catholicism share the same fundamental faith and scripture and maintain official communication with each other, but they developed many historic differences over Church organization, authority, and language. Doctrinally, at the Council of Chalcedon (451) both Eastern Orthodoxy and the Roman Church accepted the belief that Jesus was simultaneously an historical person and one with God. Organizationally, however, the Eastern Church remained far more urban. The West had so few roads and so little trade that it was held together

10.1

10.2

10.3

What was
the role of
Christianity in the
Roman Empire?

Icon of the "Triumph of Orthodoxy," Constantinople, late fourteenth/early fifteenth century C.E. In 843 the Empress Theodora restored the use of icons, an event that is still celebrated in the Eastern Church on the first Sunday in Lent. (British Museum, London)

KEY TERM

see The geographical home of a Church authority: the Vatican in Roman Catholicism, four separate locations for the Eastern Christian churches.

organizationally by its military and ecclesiastical strongholds. The Council of Chalcedon recognized four centers of Church organization, or *sees*, in the East—Antioch, Jerusalem, Alexandria, and Constantinople—with Constantinople predominating and having the same leadership role in the East as Rome had in the West. Rome, once one of

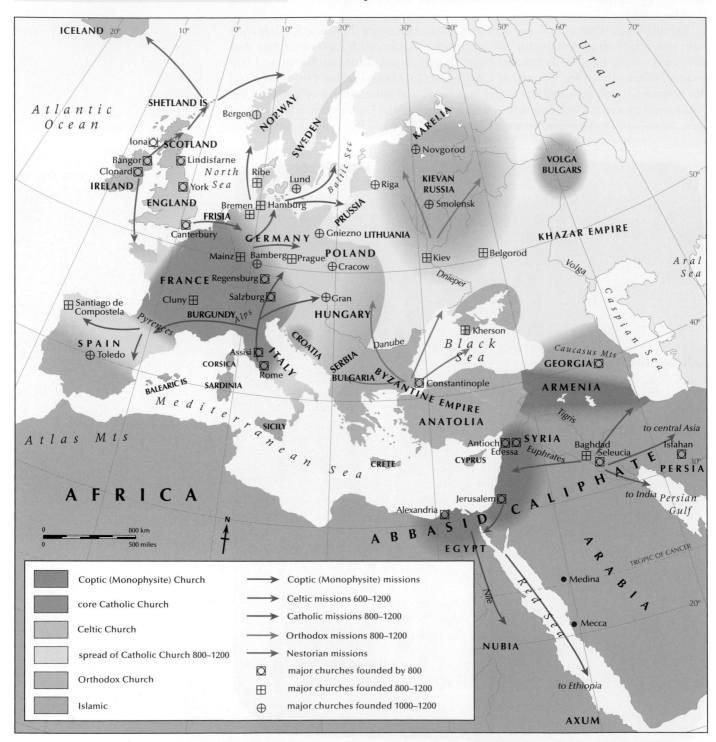

The spread of Christianity. The disciples and early missionaries established Christian communities in southwestern Asia, Greece, Italy, North Africa, and India. On the other hand, Roman persecution, the decline of western Rome, and the rise of Islam hindered its dissemination. The Orthodox Church of Constantinople converted eastern Europe, penetrating Russia; Rome became reestablished as a powerful center; and Celtic missionaries traveled throughout northwest Europe.

What was
the role of
Christianity in the
Roman Empire?

the patriarchates, and the only one in the West, was now deemed an entirely separate administrative center, still under its own emperor and with its own bishop.

The Split Between Rome and Constantinople. Rome and Byzantium have remained divided over the authority of the bishop of Rome to the present. From the sixth century, he has claimed to be pope, *papa*, father of the (Roman) Catholic Church and the direct organizational successor of the apostle Peter. Eastern Orthodox Christianity, however, has never recognized the pope's claim to preeminent authority, accepting as their principal authority the patriarch or bishop of Constantinople. Also, unlike the Roman practice, all but the highest clergy in Eastern Orthodoxy are permitted to marry, so here again the two clergies have not accepted each other's authority. The language of Rome is Latin, while the East uses Greek and the various Slavic languages of eastern Europe.

When Leo IX became pope in 1048, he aimed to expand his influence over all of Europe and sponsored the writing of a treatise that emphasized the pope's power. He sent one of his more zealous reformers to Constantinople to argue against the patriarch of Constantinople's claims to be independent of Rome's control. After failed negotiations, the reformer excommunicated the patriarch; in response, the patriarch excommunicated the reformer. Through this mutual rejection, called the Great Schism of 1054, the two Churches divided definitively into the Latin (later Roman Catholic) Church, which is predominant in Western Europe, and the Greek Orthodox Church, which prevails in the East. Friction between the two groups has waxed and waned over time, with the most direct confrontation coming in 1204, when crusaders dispatched by Rome to fight against Muslims in Jerusalem turned northward and sacked Constantinople instead.

New Areas Adopt Orthodox Christianity. As in the West, monastic life flourished in the Byzantine Empire, with exemplary institutions at remote, starkly beautiful sites such as Mount Sinai and Mount Athos. The greatest missionary activity of the Orthodox monks came later than in the West. Hemmed in by the Roman Church to the west and by the growing power of Islam to the east after about 650, Byzantium turned its missionary efforts northward, toward Russia. The brothers St. Cyril (*c.* 827–69) and St. Methodius (*c.* 825–84) translated the Bible into Slavonic, creating the Cyrillic alphabet in which to transcribe and publish it. When Russia embraced Orthodox Christianity in the tenth century, it also adopted this alphabet. In the late fifteenth century, after the fall of Constantinople to the Turks (1453), Moscow began to refer to itself as the "Third Rome," the spiritual and political heir to the Caesars and the Byzantine Empire.

In other regions of east-central Europe, Rome and Byzantium competed in spreading their religious and cultural messages and organizations. Rome won in Poland, Bohemia, Lithuania, and Ukraine; the Orthodox Church in Bulgaria, Romania, and Serbia. Other

Christ triumphing over evil, Frankish terra-cotta plaque, *c.* 500–750 C.E. It was not unusual for Western Europeans to represent Christ in contemporary local costume. Here, dressed as a member of the German warrior nobility, he treads the serpent, an emblem of the devil, underfoot. (Musée des Antiquités, St-Germain-en-Laye, France)

10.1

10.2

10.3   What was
the role of
Christianity in the
Roman Empire?

national Churches also grew up beyond Rome's jurisdiction, including the Coptic in Egypt, the Armenian, and the Ethiopian. They also asserted their independence from Constantinople, creating a pattern of distinct national Churches that the Protestant Reformation would later adopt.

Christianity in Western Europe

The abrupt, dramatic rise of Islam throughout the Middle East and into the Mediterranean, which we will examine in the next chapter, had an immediate and profound influence on Christianity. By the year 700, Muslim armies had conquered the eastern Mediterranean and the north coast of Africa, key regions of both Christianity and the former Roman Empire. The Muslim Umayyad dynasty pushed on into Spain and crossed the Pyrenees. Stopped in southern France by the Frankish ruler Charles Martel (c. 688–741) at the Battle of Tours in 732, the Umayyad forces withdrew to Spain. Muslim troops captured segments of the southern Italian peninsula, Sicily, and other Mediterranean islands. These Muslim conquests cut Christianity off geographically from the lands of its birth and early vigor. As a result, Christianity became primarily a religion of Europe, where many of its members were recently converted "barbarian" warrior nobles.

📖 Read the Document: Social Conditions in the Ninth Century on MyHistoryLab

The Pope Allies with the Franks. In Rome, the pope felt surrounded by the hostile powers of Constantinople and Islam to the east and south, and several Gothic kings to the north and west. Seeking alliances with strong men, he turned to a Frank, Charles (Carolus) Martel, who gave his name to the Carolingian family. As we have seen, Martel had repulsed the Muslims at Tours in 732. In 754 his son Pepin III (r. 751–68) answered the call of Pope Stephen II (r. 752–57) for help in fighting the Lombards, who were invading Italy and threatening the papal possessions. Pepin secured a swath of lands from Rome to Ravenna and turned them over to papal rule. In exchange, the pope anointed Pepin and his two sons, confirming the succession of the Carolingian family as the royal house ruling the Franks.

Charlemagne Revives the Idea of Empire. Pepin's son Charles ruled between 768 and 814, achieving the greatest recognition of his power when Pope Leo III (r. 795–816) crowned him Roman Emperor on Christmas Day, 800. In spite of this seeming unity of interests, Charles, who became known as Charles the Great or Charlemagne, rejected the title throughout most of his life and was often at odds with the various popes as he sought to expand an empire of his own. To achieve his goal, Charlemagne spent all his adult life in warfare, continuing the military expeditions of his father and grandfather. He reconquered the northeastern corner of Spain from its Muslim rulers, defeated the Lombard rulers of Italy and relieved their pressure on the pope, seized Bavaria and Bohemia, killed and looted the entire nobility of the Avars in Pannonia (modern Austria and Hungary), and subdued the German Saxon populations along the Elbe River after 33 years of warfare. Himself a German Frank, Charlemagne offered the German Saxons a choice of conversion to Christianity or death.

With Charlemagne's victories, the borders of his kingdom came to match the borders of the dominance of the Church of Rome, except for the British Isles, which he did not enter. The political capital of Western Europe passed from Rome to Charlemagne's

THE CAROLINGIAN DYNASTY

751	Pepin III "the Short" becomes King of the Franks
755	Franks drive Lombards out of central Italy; creation of Papal States
768–814	Charlemagne rules as King of the Franks
774	Charlemagne defeats Lombards in northern Italy
800	Pope Leo III crowns Charlemagne
814–40	Louis the Pious succeeds Charlemagne as "emperor"
843	Treaty of Verdun partitions the Carolingian Empire
870	Treaty of Mersen further divides Carolingian Empire
875–950	New invasions of Vikings, Muslims, and Magyars

10.1

10.2

What was
the role of
Christianity in the
Roman Empire?

10.3

SOURCE

Charlemagne and Harun-al-Rashid

Charlemagne spent his life fighting in the name of the pope and on behalf of Christianity. In 777 he invaded Muslim Spain, and by 801 he had captured Barcelona. (His campaigns in Spain gave rise to the epic poem *The Song of Roland* about the defeat of his rearguard in the pass of Roncesvalles. This became the most celebrated poem of medieval French chivalry.)

Yet Charlemagne carried on a valued diplomatic friendship with the most powerful Muslim ruler of his day, Harun-al-Rashid, Caliph of Baghdad (r. 786–809). Charlemagne's adviser, friend, and biographer Einhard (c. 770–840) describes the friendship:

With Harun-al-Rachid [sic], King of the Persians, who held almost the whole of the East in fee, always excepting India, Charlemagne was on such friendly terms that Harun valued his goodwill more than the approval of all the other kings and princes in the entire world, and considered that he alone was worthy of being honoured and propitiated with gifts. When Charlemagne's messengers, whom he had sent with offerings to the most Holy Sepulchre of our Lord and Saviour and to the place of His resurrection, came to Harun and told him of their master's intention, he not only granted all that was asked but even went so far as to agree that this sacred scene of our redemption should be placed under Charlemagne's own jurisdiction. When the time came for these messengers to turn homewards, Harun sent some of his own men to accompany them and dispatched to Charlemagne costly gifts, which included robes, spices and other marvels of the lands of the Orient. A few years earlier Harun had sent Charlemagne the only elephant he possessed, simply because the Frankish King asked for it. (Einhard, p. 70)

Einhard does not note what gifts Charlemagne might have sent to Baghdad in return, nor does he comment on the political benefits of this interfaith diplomacy between the two great empires—empires that flanked, and confronted, the Byzantine Empire lying between them.

own palace in Aachen (Aix-la-Chapelle) in modern Germany. Although Charlemagne was barely literate, he established within this palace a center of learning that attracted Church scholars from throughout Europe, initiating what historians call the Carolingian Renaissance.

Charles persuaded the noted scholar Alcuin of York, England (c. 730–804), to come to Aachen as head of the palace school and as his own personal adviser. The goals of the school were Christian and basic: reading and writing of Biblical texts in Latin, chanting of prayers, knowledge of grammar and arithmetic. This training would prepare missionaries for their work among the peoples of northern Europe. Scribes at the school prepared copies of prayers and Biblical texts for the liturgical and scholarly needs of churches and scholars. In the process they created a new form of Latin script that forms the basis of the lower-case (small) letters we use today. Charlemagne also fostered the arts by bringing to his capital sculpture from Italy and by patronizing local artisans and craftspeople. Alcuin himself had the ear of the emperor, criticizing him for using force in converting the Saxons and convincing him not to repeat the practice by invading England.

Charlemagne's coronation challenged the authority of the Eastern emperor in Constantinople, but during the next years Charlemagne managed, through negotiation and warfare, to gain Constantinople's recognition of his title. There were once again two emperors, East and West.

The Attempt at Empire Fails. The Carolingian family remained powerful until about the end of the ninth century. But then they could no longer fight off the new invasions of the Western Christian world by Magyars (Hungarians), Norsemen, and Arabs. Regional administrators, emboldened by the weakness of the Carolingian emperor, began to act independently of his authority. Only after yet another century would militarily powerful leaders begin once again to cobble together loosely structured kingdoms in northwestern Europe. Meanwhile, political leadership in Europe was generally decentralized in rural manor estates controlled by local lords.

Bronze and gilt statuette of Charlemagne, c. 860–70 C.E. Charlemagne's ceaseless warfare spread Christianity and Frankish rule across Western Europe, while repelling barbarian intruders and enemies of Rome. In 800 C.E. Pope Leo III showed his gratitude by crowning Charlemagne Roman Emperor. (Louvre, Paris)

Religious leadership in the cathedrals, churches, monasteries, and convents filled the gap, providing a greater sense of overall community and order. In this era, 600–1100 C.E., the Church gave Europe its fundamental character and order. The Magyar and Norse invaders, like the Germans before them, converted to Christianity. By the end of the eleventh century, the Roman Church, as well as the political authorities of Western Europe, were preparing to confront Islam.

Judaism and Early Christianity: *What Difference Do They Make?*

A small group of people, represented in the Bible in the stories of Abraham and his family, brought to the world the concept of monotheism, that one God created and cared for the entire world. As this group of people grew, and became known as the Jewish people, it told the melancholy story of its descent into slavery followed by the sequel of its escape from slavery through the intervention of its God, a story that has inspired oppressed peoples for thousands of years. Then, for about 1,200 years the Jews lived as a politically independent people, although often divided into tribes, with their own governments, on land that they claimed as sacred to them, given to them by their God. During those years, their prophets taught that ethics and morality could prevail in human relations, but only through dedication and hard work, and that unjust rulers should be confronted, whether they were their own rulers or foreign rulers.

Living at a geographical crossroads of people and ideas, the Jews were frequently conquered by other peoples and sometimes exiled from the land they claimed. Nevertheless, in their diaspora in Babylonia, they demonstrated that they could remain cohesive and culturally creative, even far from home. After the Romans exiled the Jews almost completely from their land, they dispersed throughout the world, especially the Roman world. They drew on their earlier experiences to create institutions based on the leadership of their rabbis and allegiance to their law codes and religious customs that enabled them to endure despite the lack of a common home and a cohesive political structure. Even so, life in exile took its toll through oppression and assimilation. At the height of the Roman Empire, there were an estimated eight million Jews in the world. Two thousand years later, there are not quite double that number, 15 million, while Christianity, which grew from Jewish roots, today has more than two billion members.

Christianity originated in Judea and spread throughout Europe. It began with a single Jewish teacher whose message was preached by a handful of disciples and institutionalized through the zeal of a single missionary. It began with a membership of downtrodden Jews, added middling-level gentiles, attracted some of the elites of Rome, and finally converted multitudes of Europe's invading barbarians. It had expanded its own organizational establishment via the network of transportation, communication, and trade put in place by the Roman Empire. Within that empire, it flowered into two separate, far-flung Church hierarchies and several localized structures. When that empire dissolved and contracted, the Church maintained and consolidated its position within the remains of those old Roman administrative and market centers.

As European society became more rural, Christian monasteries and convents were founded in the countryside and often took on administrative and developmental roles alongside their spiritual missions. In short, the Church, like the empire, was much transformed. By the year 1000 it had become the most important organizational and cultural force in Western Europe.

The transformations of both the Christian religious world and the European political world continued after 1000 with extraordinary developments in crusading vigor, trade and commerce, urbanization, intellectual and artistic creativity, and religious reform. We will explore these transformations in the chapter entitled "Establishing World Trade Routes." First, however, we turn to equally startling and revolutionary developments that had created another world religion, originating in the Arabian peninsula only a few hundred miles from the birthplace of both Judaism and Christianity. By the year 1000 it had spread across North Africa, northward into Spain,

Laon Cathedral, west front, c. 1190–95. Gothic architecture, first fully expressed in several cathedrals in northern France, including this one in Laon, was the dominant style in Europe after the twelfth century. Gothic churches were built to communicate, proclaiming the glories of heaven through their confident mastery of space and light and, at the same time, heralding the wealth and power of the Church. Laon's wide façade, monumental doorways, pointed arches, and numerous windows, some with gorgeous rose-hued stained glass, topped by two huge towers, is one of the earliest and best examples of this upward-reaching style.

throughout the Middle East, and on through Iran and Afghanistan into India. Our study of Islam in the chapter called "Islam" will complete our introduction to the origins and early life of the three major monotheistic religions.

CHAPTER REVIEW

JUDAISM

10.1 How did Judaism arise and what are its evolving beliefs?

To a world in which people believed in many gods, who sometimes fought with each other and interfered capriciously in human life, the Hebrews introduced the idea of a single God whose rule was just and orderly. This was a new kind of God, above nature, all-powerful, all-caring, and actively intervening in human history to reward righteous behavior and punish wrong-doing. From its beginnings, Judaism has claimed its origins in a single, select family that suffered centuries of slavery followed by centuries of political independence in a geographical location assigned to it by God. Earlier emphasis on priestly rituals was replaced with prophetic concerns for universal moral issues.

CHRISTIANITY

10.2 How did Christianity emerge and evolve?

Christianity emerged as a sect within Judaism. It began with a Jewish preacher named Jesus, whose followers believed him to be the son of God. He preached a message of compassion, salvation, and eternal life in a world dominated by Jewish ritual and Roman imperialism, and the Romans crucified him. Jesus' disciples, believing in his resurrection, transcribed and spread his message, first to the wider Mediterranean world and eventually across the Roman Empire. Later missionaries carried it around the world. It is today the most populous religion in the world.

CHRISTIANITY IN THE WAKE OF EMPIRE

10.3 What was the role of Christianity in the Roman Empire?

Christianity spread across Europe along the networks of the Roman Empire. Christianity spoke the empire's languages (Greek and Latin), preached its gospel along the empire's trade routes, and constructed church communities in the empire's cities. Christianity emerged and flourished even as the empire weakened and dissolved. In light of its origins and structures, the central Christian organization referred to itself as the Roman Catholic Church.

Suggested Readings

PRINCIPAL SOURCES

Brown, Peter. *The Rise of Western Christendom* (Malden, MA: Blackwell Publishers, 1996). Brown brings to bear expertise on the Roman Empire at the time of Christ to provide context for early Christianity.

Carroll, James. *Constantine's Sword: The Church and the Jews* (Boston, MA: Houghton Mifflin, 2001). Movingly written, often tragic story of the 2,000-year relationship between Christianity and Judaism.

Crossan, John Dominic. *The Historical Jesus: The Life of a Mediterranean Jewish Peasant* (San Francisco, CA: HarperCollins, 1991). One of the clearest interpretations of Jesus in his time.

Kee, Howard Clark, *et al. Christianity: A Social and Cultural History* (New York: Macmillan, 1991). Excellent, scholarly analysis and narrative of early Christianity.

MacCulloch, Diarmaid. *A History of Christianity: The First Three Thousand Years* (New York: Viking Penguin, 2010). A world history of Christianity, beautifully written, comprehensive, insightful, challenging.

The New English Bible with the Apocrypha, Oxford Study Edition (New York: Oxford University Press, 1970). Clear, readable, authentic text produced by an interfaith team of scholars.

Pagels, Elaine. *The Gnostic Gospels* (New York: Random House, 1979). Clear, concise explanation of the significance to our understanding of early Christianity of the Gnostic manuscripts discovered at Nag Hammadi in 1945.

Smart, Ninian. *The World's Religions* (Cambridge: Cambridge University Press, 1989). Useful general survey, clearly written.

Smeltzer, Robert M. *Jewish People, Jewish Thought* (New York: Macmillan, 1980). Excellent general history.

ADDITIONAL SOURCES

Andrea, Alfred, and James Overfield, eds. *The Human Record*, Vol. I (Boston: Wadsworth Cengage Learning, 7th ed., 2012). Superbly chosen selections.

Armstrong, Karen. *A History of God* (New York: Knopf, 1993). Concise history of the evolution of the three major monotheistic religions.

Augustine. *The City of God*, trans. Marcus Dods (New York: Modern Library, 1950). A central work of Christian theology from the late Roman Empire.

Baron, Salo Wittmayer. *A Social and Religious History of the Jews*, Vol. I (New York: Columbia University Press, 1952). First in a multivolume series by one of the leading Jewish historians of his time.

de Lange, Nicholas. *Atlas of the Jewish World* (New York: Facts on File, 1984). Excellent text, helpful maps, beautiful illustrations.

Einhard and Notker the Stammerer. *Two Lives of Charlemagne*, trans. Lewis Thorpe (Harmondsworth, Middlesex: Penguin Books, 1969). The standard primary source on Charlemagne.

Gibbon, Edward. *The History of the Decline and Fall of the Roman Empire*, 3 vols., abridged by D.M. Low (New York: Washington Square Books, 1962). The classic from the age of the Enlightenment. Follows and projects the story through the fall of Constantinople to the Turks.

Grant, Michael. *History of Rome* (New York: Charles Scribner's Sons, 1978). Readable, basic text.

——. *Jesus: An Historian's Review of the Gospels* (New York: Touchstone, 1995). Does the best he can to reconstruct Jesus' life and teachings based on the Gospels.

Halpern, Baruch. *The First Historians: The Hebrew Bible and History* (San Francisco, CA: Harper and Row, 1988). Attempts to demonstrate the extent to which Hebrew stories from the Bible can be authenticated.

Holy Bible. New Revised Standard Version (Grand Rapids, MI: Zondervan Publishing House, 1989). Another excellent, standard translation.

Honour, Hugh, and John Fleming. *The Visual Arts: A History* (Englewood Cliffs, NJ: Prentice Hall, 4th ed., 1995). Excellent textbook approach to the history of art.

Kaufmann, Yehezkel. *The Religion of Israel* (Chicago, IL: University of Chicago Press, 1960). Fascinating analysis of Biblical Judaism, stressing the inability of the early Jews even to comprehend the significance of images in worship.

Kee, Howard Clark. *Who Are the People of God? Early Christian Models of Community* (New Haven, CT: Yale University Press, 1995). Kee stresses the importance of the community of believers in the success of the early Christian Church.

Mann, Michael. *A History of Power from the Beginning to A.D. 1760* (Cambridge: Cambridge University Press, 1986). Mann searches for the success of early Christianity in its sociological composition and appeal.

Matthew, Donald. *Atlas of Medieval Europe* (New York: Facts on File, 1983). Excellent text, useful maps, beautiful illustrations.

McManners, John, ed. *The Oxford Illustrated History of Christianity* (New York: Oxford University Press, 1990). Outstanding set of basic introductory articles by major scholars, highly illustrated.

Meier, John P. *A Marginal Jew: Rethinking the Historical Jesus*, 2 vols. (New York: Doubleday, 1991, 1994). Meier emphasizes Jesus' abilities as a magician and exorcist in attracting followers.

Momigliano, Arnaldo. *On Pagans, Jews, and Christians* (Hanover, NH: University Press of New England for Wesleyan University Press, 1987). Compares the attractions of each of these perspectives, and their confrontations with one another in the early years of Christianity.

Pagels, Elaine. *Beyond Belief: The Secret Gospel of Thomas* (New York: Random House, 2003). Pagels' analysis of the most significant of the Gnostic gospels, and its meaning for her.

Pritchard, James B., ed. *Ancient Near Eastern Texts Relating to the Old Testament* (Princeton, NJ: Princeton University Press, 3rd ed., 1969). Basic compendium of the most important documents. Indispensable for the subject.

Rosenberg, David, and Harold Bloom. *The Book of J* (New York: Grove Weidenfeld, 1990). Analyzes the four major editorial strands in the composition of the Torah, stressing the one that refers to God by his Hebrew name of JHWH.

Rubenstein, Richard L. *When Jesus Became God* (New York: Harcourt Brace, 1999). An account of the armed battle and victory of the Roman Church over the theologian Arius, who declared that Christ's human nature diminished his divine nature.

Sand, Shlomo. *The Invention of the Jewish People* (London: Verso, 2010). Highly controversial book on the origins and evolution of the Jewish people. Early section on Biblical criticism is especially useful here.

Smart, Ninian, and Richard D. Hecht, eds. *Sacred Texts of the World: A Universal Anthology* (New York: Crossroad Publishing, 1982). Useful selection of religious texts.

FILMS

National Geographic. *When Rome Ruled the World: Rise of Christianity* (2011; 50 minutes). From scorned and persecuted mystery religion to a new religious empire arising out of Rome. Includes new research.

BBC. *History of Jerusalem: Making of a Holy City* (2013; 59 minutes). Narrated and presented by Simon Sebag Montefiore, based on his recent, highly acclaimed book. Archaeological and urban perspective on religious history. Part of a trilogy that continues through Muslim and crusader invasions up to the present.

Heritage: Civilization and the Jews (1984; eight parts of one hour each). History of the Jews and their place in the world from earliest times to the present. Narrated by Abba Eban, former foreign minister of the State of Israel.

Documentaries on early Judaism and Christianity abound, many from such excellent producers as the BBC, National Geographic, PBS, and the History Channel. New ones continue to be produced. To review and watch them, check YouTube.

See also "Crash Course in World History" (2012), also available on YouTube. These forty-two 10–12-minute frenetic "lessons" are set more at the high-school than the college level, but can be fun and useful. Episode 11 is "Christianity from Judaism to Constantine."

11 Islam

Submission to Allah: Muslim Civilization Bridges the World

570 c.e.–1500 c.e.

slam, in Arabic, means "submission." Islam teaches submission to the word of God, called "Allah" in Arabic. Muslims, "those who submit," know God's word primarily through the Quran, the Arabic book that records the teachings of God as they were transmitted to the Prophet Muhammad (570–632). Stories of Muhammad's life, words, and deeds, carefully collected, sifted, and transmitted over many generations, provide Muslims with models of the righteous life and how to live it. According to the Quran, Muhammad was the most recent, and final, prophet of God's message of ethical monotheism. Devout Muslims declare this belief in prayers, which are recited five times each day: "There is no God but God, and Muhammad is his Prophet."

Niche (*mihrab*) with Arabic calligraphy. Muslims pray in the direction of Mecca, and every mosque is marked by a *mihrab*, a niche in the wall, which indicates that direction. This *mihrab* is elegantly ornamented with floral designs and Arabic calligraphy of verses from the Quran, which frame it and mark its center. The color green is traditional and favored in Islam, perhaps referring to the lush vegetation of paradise in the world to come. (Metropolitan Museum, New York)

LEARNING OBJECTIVES

11.1	11.2	11.3	11.4
Tell the history of Islam, its origins and beliefs.	Understand the history of Islam after Muhammad's death.	Describe the flowering of Islam outside the Arab world.	Discuss Muslims' relationship with non-Muslims.

  Listen on **MyHistoryLab**

For Muslims, the teachings of the Quran and of Muhammad's life can be fulfilled only with the creation of a community of believers, the *umma*, and its proper regulation through political structures. Through its early centuries, Islam established administrative and legal systems in the areas to which it spread: Arabia, western Asia, northern Africa, and Spain. As Islam spread later to eastern Europe, central Asia, south Asia, and sub-Saharan Africa, it arrived sometimes with government backing, sometimes without. After the twelfth century, Islam won converts in China and Southeast Asia as a religious and cultural system without government support.

Islam is considered here as a world religion. Because it often unified government and religion into a single system, it may also be compared with the materials in

KEY TERM

umma The community of believers in Islam, which transcends ethnic and political boundaries.

AT A GLANCE: ISLAM

DATE	POLITICAL/SOCIAL EVENTS	LITERARY/PHILOSOPHICAL EVENTS
500 c.e.	• Muhammad (570–632)	
600 c.e.	• Hijra (622), flight to Medina • Muslim conquest of Mecca • Orthodox or Rightly Guided Caliphs (632–61) • Muslim conquest of Iraq, Syria, Palestine, Egypt, western Iran (632–42), Cyprus (649), and Persian Empire (650s) • Umayyad caliphate (661–750); capital in Damascus • Muslim conquest of Carthage (698) and central Asia (650–712) • Husayn killed at Karbala (680); Sunni–Shi'a split	• Revelation of the Quran to Muhammad (610) • Persian becomes second language of Islam
700 c.e.	• Muslim conquest of Tunis (700), Spain (711–16), Sind, and lower Indus valley • Muslim defeat at Battle of Tours (732) • Muslims defeat Chinese at Battle of Talas River (751) • Abbasid caliphate (750–1258) • Baghdad founded (762)	• Biography of Muhammad by Ibn Ishaq (d. 767) • Formulation of major systems of Islamic law
800 c.e.	• Divisions in Muslim Empire (833–945) • Fez founded (808)	• al-Tabari, *History of Prophets and Kings* • al-Khwarazmi develops algebra • Abbasid caliphate establishes "House of Wisdom" translation bureau in Baghdad • Sufi *tariqa*
900 c.e.	• Persians seize Baghdad (945) • Cairo founded (969)	• Ferdowsi, *Shah Nama* • al-Razi, *Encyclopedia of Medicine* • Turkish becomes third language of Islam • Mutazilites challenge Islamic orthodoxy
1000 c.e.	• Seljuk Turks dominate Abbasid caliphate (1038) • Almoravid dynasty in North Africa and Spain (1061–1145) • Battle of Manzikert (1071) • First Crusade (1095–99)	• Ibn Sina (Avicenna), philosopher, produces "Canon of Medicine" • al-Biruni (d. 1046) writes on mathematics and astronomy
1100 c.e.	• Almohad dynasty rules North Africa and Spain (1145–1269) • Second Crusade (1147–49) • Salah al-Din (Saladin) recaptures Jerusalem (1187) • Third Crusade (1189–92)	• al-Ghazali (d. 1111), Muslim philosopher and theologian • Ibn Rushd (Averroes; 1126–98) • Maimonides (1135–1204), Jewish physician, philosopher, and theologian
1200 c.e.	• Fourth Crusade (1202–04) • Sultanate of Delhi (1211–1526) • Children's Crusade (1212) • Fifth to Eighth Crusades (1218–91) • Crusaders driven from west Asia (1291) • Fall of Baghdad to Mongols (1258); end of Abbasid Caliphate	• Jalal-al-Din Rumi, *Mathnawi* • al-Juvaini, *History of the World Conquerors* • Rashid al-Din, *World History*
1300 c.e.	• Mansa Musa's pilgrimage to Mecca (1324) • Conversion of Malayans and Indonesians to Islam	• Ibn Battuta (1304–c. 1368), traveler • Ibn Khaldun, *Universal History*
1400 c.e.	• Ottoman Turks conquer Constantinople (1453) • Christians capture Granada, complete *reconquista* (1492)	

11.1 What is the history of Islam, its origins and beliefs?

11.2

11.3

11.4

"Turning Point: From City-states to Empires" on the expansion of world empires. In this chapter, we trace the growth and spread of Islam as a religious, governmental, and cultural system. We shall also examine its encounters with other religions and empires.

The Origins of Islam

11.1 What is the history of Islam, its origins and beliefs?

Islam emerged in the Arabian peninsula, an area largely inhabited by nomadic Bedouin tribes. The Bedouins organized themselves in clans. Inhabiting the desert, they lacked the sources of water so crucial for the emergence of cities and civilizations in the ancient world; nevertheless, a few cities, such as Mecca, grew up alongside major oases. Mecca flourished as a trading center in the seventh century, but the region in general lacked the governmental institutions and the powerful emperors that supported the emergence of major religions elsewhere. Religiously, the region was polytheistic, worshiping many gods. Mecca held a prominent role in this worship. It held the Ka'aba, a rectangular building that housed a cubical black stone structure, and the sacred tokens of all the clans of Mecca and of many of the surrounding tribes as well. Serving as a center of pilgrimage and trade, Mecca brought enormous economic benefits to the traders of the Quraysh tribes who controlled the city and its shrine.

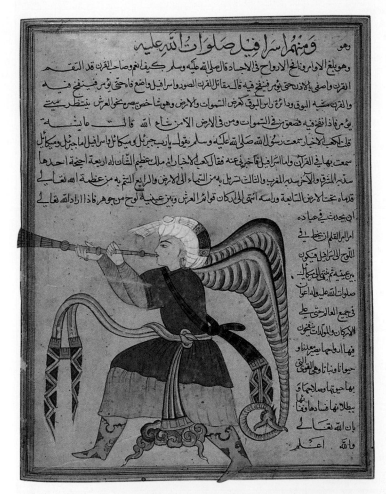

Trumpet call of the angel Gabriel. Muhammad's religious meditations were interrupted by the angel Gabriel, who commanded him to recite what became the first *surah* (section from the Quran) revealed to humanity. Here the encounter is symbolized by Gabriel's blowing on a trumpet. (British Library, London)

The Prophet: His Life and Teaching

Born in 570 to parents eminent in the Quraysh tribe, Muhammad was orphaned at an early age, and he was raised by his grandfather and later his uncle. He became a merchant, employed by a wealthy widow named Khadija. When he was 25 years old, he married her and they had four children together.

Muhammad was a deeply meditative person, retreating regularly to a nearby hill to pray and reflect. In 610, when he was 40 years old, his reflections were interrupted, according to Islamic teachings, by the voice of the angel Gabriel, who instructed him: "Recite: In the name of the Lord who created Man of a blood-clot." Over the next two decades, according to Islamic theology, God continued to reveal his messages to Muhammad through Gabriel. Muhammad transmitted these revelations to professionals whose task it was to commit them to memory. The verses were also transcribed on palm leaves, stone, and other material. Soon after Muhammad's death, scribes and editors compiled the entire collection of written and oral recitations into the Quran, which in Arabic means recitations. An officially authorized edition of the Quran was issued by Uthman (r. 644–56), the third ruler of the Islamic community.

Approximately the length of the Christian New Testament, the Quran is considered by Muslims to be the absolute, uncorrupted word of God. Composed in poetic form, the Quran helped to define the literary standards of the Arabic language. Muslims chant and study its text in Arabic, considering each syllable sacred. Even today many Muslims reject translations of the Quran into other languages as inadequate.

In the next century, new technologies led to broader dispersion of the Quran. During the mid-eighth century, as Arab armies defeated Chinese forces in central Asia, the Muslim victors learned from their prisoners-of-war the technology of paper-making. By the end of the eighth century Baghdad had a paper mill; Egypt had one by 900; Morocco and Spain by 1100. Turks brought the art of papermaking to northern India in the twelfth century. One use of paper was, of course, in the administration of the government bureaucracy. Another, perhaps even more important, was in the copying and diffusion of the Quran.

◘ View the Closer Look: The Quran on MyHistoryLab

The Five Pillars of Islam

The Quran reveals the "five pillars" of Islam, the five ritual expressions that define orthodox Muslim religious belief and practice:

- Declaring the creed, "There is no god but God, and Muhammad is his Prophet."
- Praying five times daily while facing Mecca (2:144), and, if possible, praying also in public assembly at midday each Friday.
- Giving alms to the poor in the community, especially to widows and orphans (2:212 ff.), later recommended at approximately 2½ percent of wealth.
- Fasting each day during the month of Ramadan, the ninth month of the lunar year, although eating is permitted at night, with a major feast marking the month's end (2:179–84).
- Making the *hajj*, a pilgrimage to Mecca, at least once in a lifetime, if possible (2:185 ff.).

Jihad, or sacred struggle, is sometimes called a "sixth pillar" of Islam. It was less stringently required and has been interpreted in different ways. Some scholars interpret *jihad* as a call to physical warfare to preserve and extend the ***dar al-Islam***, the "abode of Islam," the lands under Muslim rule, or, later, the lands in which Islam could be practiced freely, even if not under Muslim political rule. Even in this interpretation, however, *jihad* should be practiced only in self-defense, for "God loves not the aggressors" (2:187). Other scholars understand *jihad* as a personal call to the individual, internal, spiritual struggle to live Islam as fully as possible. The Quran gives a capsule description of this proper life:

> True piety is this: to believe in God, and the Last Day, the angels, the Book, and the Prophets, to give of one's substance, however cherished, to kinsmen, and orphans, the needy, the traveller, beggars, and to ransom the slave, to perform the prayer, to pay the alms. And they who fulfil their covenant, and endure with fortitude misfortune, hardship and peril, these are they who are true in their faith, these are the truly godfearing. (2:172–3)

Finally, the Quran promises repeatedly that those who observe Islam faithfully will find their reward in paradise, described as "gardens underneath which rivers flow ... a shelter of plenteous shade" (4:60). On the other hand, those who reject the opportunity to fulfill the teachings of Islam will burn in a fiery Hell forever. Humans must choose between doing good and evil, but the Quran asserts that ultimately free will is limited: "God has power over everything" (4:87).

The Quran emphasized many of the same principles as Judaism and Christianity, including the importance of worshiping a single God and the obligation of the rich to help the poor. As in Christianity, the Quran taught that there would be a final

11.1
11.2
11.3
11.4

What is the history of Islam, its origins and beliefs?

KEY TERM

dar al-Islam The literal meaning of the Arabic words is "the abode of Islam." The term refers to the land of Islam, that is, territories in which Islam and its religious laws (*shari'a*) may be freely practiced. Some interpreters argue that the rulers themselves must be Muslims and that they must institute *shari'a* law, others argue that freedom for Muslims to follow Islamic practice is the only requirement. Also, sometimes, *dar as-Salam*, "the abode of peace."

The Ka'aba in Mecca, with pilgrims. For Muslims the most sacred space on earth, the very center of the center of holiness, is the black stone, the Ka'aba in Mecca. This is the physical destination of the *hajj* pilgrimage, which every Muslim is called upon to undertake, if possible. Tens of millions of *hajjis* from all parts of the world make the pilgrimage each year.

11.1 What is the history of Islam, its origins and beliefs?

11.2

11.3

11.4

Judgment Day. Many of the Quran's practices, too, were consistent with the existing rituals of Christians, Jews, and Zoroastrians living in Arabia at the time, and this made acceptance of the new religion easier. For example, regular prayer times and recitals of creed were also central to Judaism and Christianity, as was institution-alized charity. Animal sacrifice was a part of pagan and Zoroastrian religions, and had once been central to Judaism as it was now to Islam. Ritual slaughter of animals for food mirrored Jewish practice, as did male circumcision. Ritual washing before public prayers was also practiced by Zoroastrians.

Responses to Muhammad

In Mecca, Muhammad created the nucleus of the *umma* as people accepted his message. Some were successful businesspeople, some slaves, some tribeless people, some were family members. His wife Khadija became his first disciple; his cousin Ali seems to have been the second.

Most Meccans, however, found Muhammad's moral teachings too demanding, and, when he told them of the physical state—resembling an epileptic fit—in which he received some of the revelations from the angel Gabriel, many questioned his stability. On more practical grounds, they feared that his teachings threatened their own beliefs, especially the idol worship in their homes and in the Ka'aba. Some

HOW DO WE KNOW?

Sources on Early Islam

Much of the historical writing on Islam is based on orthodox Islamic sources or, conversely, on the writings of their opponents. Such sources are not unbiased. In addition, several key documents were written down long after the events they describe, allowing possible alterations in the text. The Quran itself, for example, was compiled some 50 years after Muhammad received his first revelation. Muhammad Ibn Ishaq (c. 704–67) wrote the first Arabic biography of the Prophet more than a century after his death.

Moreover, Islam suffered three civil wars in its first 120 years and considerable internal fighting thereafter; many of the "official" histories were prepared in support of one position or another. Finally, as Islam confronted other religious civilizations, the accounts of its history were frequently tendentious, again supporting one side or another.

In their search for unbiased information, recent historians have made use of sources that were not recorded as historical narratives but that provide data from which history can be written:

The new generation of historians thus uncovered an impressive variety of sources: commercial documents, tax registers, official land grants, administrative seals, census records, coins, gravestones, magical incantations written on bowls, memoirs of pilgrims, archeological and architectural data, biographical dictionaries, inscriptional evidence, and, more recently, oral history. (Eaton in Adas, p. 4)

From these records has emerged a deeper understanding of the culture of Muhammad's homeland in Arabia and of the adjacent Byzantine and Sassanid Persian empires. These records suggest that Islam did not develop within a national vacuum. It incorporated religious, cultural, and social structures that were already present among its neighbors. As it grew and expanded, it incorporated aspects of Arab, Greek, Roman, and Persian civilizations.

- What are some issues in the early history of Islam that have led to the creation of primary source documents with conflicting interpretations?
- What use are tax registers, official land grant documents, and census records in interpreting the early history of Islam?
- If you were to study the degree to which Islam adopted practices from either the Greco-Roman or Persian civilizations, what primary sources would you seek?

Meccans were already monotheists, especially the Jews and Christians who lived in the city, but most of them also rejected his message for they did not believe that their own religions needed the purification that Muhammad proposed. Despite this intense opposition, including apparent threats on Muhammad's life, his family and his branch of the Quraysh tribe stood by him, including some who did not accept his message but trusted his integrity.

After Khadija and some others of his early supporters died, however, Muhammad's position in Mecca became more precarious. Some members of the Muslim community began to leave Mecca in search of a home more accepting of the new teachings.

The *Hijra* and the Islamic Calendar. Largely rejected by his own tribe and the inhabitants of Mecca, Muhammad, too, sought a place that would be more receptive. He welcomed an invitation from the elders of the city of Medina to come with his followers to their oasis city some 200 miles to the north to adjudicate bitter disputes that had arisen among local tribes and to take the reins of government. Muhammad may also have been attracted because Medina had a large Jewish population. As monotheists, they shared the central principle of his faith, and he may have thought that he could ultimately convert them.

Known as the *hijra*, Muhammad's flight under pressure to Medina became a central moment in Islamic history. As Christians begin the year 1 of their calendar with an event in the life of Jesus—his birth—so Muslims begin theirs with the *hijra* and Muhammad's assertion of governmental leadership in Medina, a year that corresponds to the year 622 on the Christian calendar.

Although he failed to convert many Jews, Muhammad found many other inhabitants of Medina who did accept his religious message. This allowed him to consolidate a unified religious community of Muslims. He believed that for Islam to survive, he needed to create a *dar al-Islam*, a government under which Islam could be practiced freely, legally, and securely. In Medina he promulgated codes of business

What is the history of Islam, its origins and beliefs?

11.1
11.2
11.3
11.4

KEY TERM

hijra The "migration" or flight of Muhammad from Mecca, where his life was in danger, to Medina (then called Yathrib), where he was welcomed as a potential leader in 622 c.e. The Islamic era (a.h.: After Hijra) is calculated from this date.

HOW DO WE KNOW?

Gender Relations in Islam

Although many readers might consider the relationships between men and women a private matter, in fact in each religion—and empire—that we have studied some official doctrines attempted to regulate gender relationships. In general, they placed women under the authority of men and granted men more legal rights than they accorded to women. Although they often gave women greater importance than men in the private realm of house and hearth, they vested more public power and responsibility with men. Islam also follows this general pattern. The Quran states:

> Men have authority over women because God has made the one superior to the other, and because they spend their wealth to maintain them. Good women are obedient. They guard their unseen parts because God has guarded them. As for those from whom you fear disobedience, admonish them and send them to beds apart and beat them. Then if they obey you, take no further action against them. God is high, supreme. (4:34)

According to the Quran, women are to satisfy men's sexual desires and to bear children:

> Women are your fields: go, then, into your fields when you please. (2:223)

As in Judaism and Hinduism, sexual intercourse is forbidden during a woman's menstrual period:

> Keep aloof from women during their menstrual periods and do not touch them until they are clean again. (2:222)

It might appear that men are the initiators of sexual relations, but women are considered sexually seductive, and the Quran therefore urges the Prophet to:

> Enjoin believing women to turn their eyes away from temptation and to preserve their chastity; to cover their adornments (except such as are normally displayed); to draw

Divorce proceedings. A scribe records the accusations of a husband and wife as they petition for a divorce in front of a *qadi*, or judge. A woman had limited rights to divorce her husband, but a man could divorce his wife without stipulating a reason, although in practice matters were rarely that simple. A *qadi* would bring to bear the combined wisdom of scriptural knowledge, local custom, and his own judgment in making an adjudication. (Bibliothèque Nationale, Paris)

their veils over their bosoms and not to reveal their finery except to their husbands, close relatives, and the very old and very young. (24:31)

As witnesses in legal matters, the testimony of two women equals that of one man (2:282). Similarly, in matters of inheritance, "A male shall inherit twice as much as a female" (4:11). Despite these regulations that apparently limit the status of women, some modern scholars assert that Islam actually introduced "a positive social revolution" (Tucker, p. 42) in gender relations. Compared to what came before, Islam introduced new rights for women and gave them greater security in marriage. Islamic law, *shari'a*, safeguarded the rights of both partners in marriage through contractual responsibilities: it insisted on the consent of the bride; it specified that dowry, or bridal gift, go to the bride herself and not to her family; and it spelled out the husband's obligations to support his wives and children, even wives that he might divorce. Although men were allowed to take up to four wives, the Quran added, "But if you fear that you cannot maintain equality among them, marry one only or any slave-girls you may own. This will make it easier for you to avoid injustice" (4:3); so, in practice, only one wife was normally permitted.

These scholars note also that in the life of Muhammad, three women played exemplary roles: his first wife, Khadija, who supported him economically and emotionally when the revelations he received brought him scorn from others; Aisha, the most beloved of the wives he took after Khadija's death; and Fatima, the daughter of the Prophet and wife of the fourth caliph, Ali. Nevertheless, these women drew their importance from their service to prominent men, and were criticized when they attempted more independent roles.

Other scholars, by contrast, have argued that Islam made the plight of women worse than it had been. These scholars argue that in pre-Islamic Arabia, women could initiate marriage, they could have more than one husband, they could divorce their husbands, they could remain in their parents' home area and have their husbands come to live with them, and they could keep custody of their children in case of divorce. In pre-Islamic Arabia, some women, such as Allat, al-Uzza, and Manat were worshiped with great honor, suggesting that there was considerable respect for females.

Of those scholars who feel that the position of women declined under Islam, some put the blame on Islam itself, but others suggest that the teachings of Islam were actually comparatively liberal. These scholars argue that it was contact with the Byzantine and Sassanid empires that reduced women's status. They argue that tribal, nomadic Arabia had treated women with relative equality, but the neighboring empires, with their settled, urban civilizations, veiled women and kept them mostly at home under male domination. The Arabs adopted these practices. In effect, this group of scholars is also saying that the more liberal Quranic rules regarding women were reinterpreted after contact with societies outside Arabia. Whatever the rules of the Quran, in practice gender relations varied widely in different parts of the world of Islam.

Ibn Battuta (1304–c. 1368), a famous Berber (North African) traveler whose adventures took him to much of the known world of Africa and Asia, learned his concepts of gender relations in the Arab heartland of Islam. As he traveled, he was often astonished, and sometimes shocked, by the status of women in other Islamic countries. In the Turkish and Mongol regions between the Black and Caspian seas, wives of local, ruling khans (sultans) owned property. When the senior wife appeared at the khan's residence, Ibn Battuta observes, the khan

> advances to the entrance to the pavilion to meet her, salutes her, takes her by the hand, and only after she has mounted to the couch and taken her seat does the sultan himself sit down.
>
> All this is done in full view of those present, and without any use of veils. (Dunn, p. 168)

In the Maldive Islands, in the Indian Ocean, Ibn Battuta was even more scandalized:

> Their womenfolk do not cover their heads, not even their queen does so, and they comb their hair and gather it at one side. Most of them wear only an apron from their waists to the ground, the rest of their bodies being uncovered. When I held the qadiship [position of judge] there, I tried to put an end to this practice and ordered them to wear clothes, but I met with no success. No woman was admitted to my presence in a lawsuit unless her body was covered, but apart from that I was unable to effect anything. (McNeill and Waldman, p. 276)

In Mali, West Africa, female slaves and servants went publicly into the ruler's court completely naked. When Ibn Battuta found a scholar's wife chatting with another man, he complained to the scholar. But the scholar quickly put Ibn Battuta in his place:

> The association of women with men is agreeable to us and a part of good conduct, to which no suspicion attaches. They are not like the women of your country. (Dunn, p. 300)

Ibn Battuta left immediately and never returned to the man's home.

- In terms of gender relationships, to what degree is Islam concerned with regulating sexual relations and the offspring that may result? Family relationships? Social and legal relationships outside the family? How do regulations in Islam compare with those in other religions?
- What is the evidence that Islam in its early years was more egalitarian toward women than were either the other groups in Arabia or the Byzantine and Sassanid empires outside Arabia? What is the evidence that it was less egalitarian?
- Ibn Battuta was surprised that the treatment of women varied quite widely in the various lands of Islam. Are you surprised? Why or why not?

11.1

11.2

11.3

11.4

What is the
history of Islam,
its origins and
beliefs?

ethics as well as family laws of marriage, divorce, and inheritance, all based on the
teachings of the Quran.

Muhammad Extends his Authority. After establishing his authority in Medina, Muhammad sought to gain converts in Mecca and ended up in skirmishes with the Quraysh
tribes that opposed him. In 624 he and his followers successfully raided a large Meccan
caravan train in the Battle of Badr, reducing Mecca's prosperity by cutting important
trade routes and winning local fame for themselves. In 625 the Meccans fought back,
defeating Muhammad and his forces at Uhud. In 627 the two sides fought to a draw at
the Battle of the Ditch, but Muhammad's reputation grew as he stood up to the powerful Meccans. In 630, following a dispute between the tribes of the two cities, Mecca
surrendered to Medina. Muslims gained control of the Ka'aba, destroyed the Meccan
idols, and turned the building with its sacred black rock into an Islamic shrine. By the
time he died in 632, Muhammad was well on his way to creating from the warring
tribes an Arabia-wide federation dedicated to the faith and the political structure
of Islam.

Connections to Other Monotheistic Faiths. According to the Quran, Muhammad
was only a messenger of God, not the originator of a new doctrine. Indeed, he was
not even the founder of Islam: several prophets, including Adam, Noah, Abraham,
Ishmael, Moses, and Jesus had prepared the way:

> Say (O Muslims): We believe in Allah and that which is revealed unto us and that
> which was revealed unto Abraham, and Ishmael, and Isaac, and Jacob, and the
> tribes, and that which Moses and Jesus received, and that which the prophets re-
> ceived from their Lord. We make no distinction between any of them, and unto Him
> we have surrendered. (Quran [Pickthall] 2:136)

Muslims claim the Hebrew Abraham, whom Jews see as the father of Jewish
monotheism, as the first Muslim: "Abraham in truth was not a Jew, neither a
Christian; but he was a Muslim and one of pure faith" (3:60). For this reason,
Muslims often refer to Jews, Christians, and Muslims collectively as "children
of Abraham."

The teachings of each of the earlier prophets, Muslims believe, were corrupted
over time by their followers. Muslims challenge the Christian belief in Jesus as the
son of God, and maintain that the Christian doctrine of Jesus' divinity conflicts with
the fundamental concept of pure monotheism. The Quran deplores this heresy,
declaring: "It is not for God to take a son unto Him" (19:36). The Jews' error was in
refusing to accept the Quran as a revised and updated version of the truth already
given to them:

> And when it is said unto them: Believe in that which Allah hath revealed, they say:
> We believe in that which was revealed unto us. And they disbelieve in that which
> cometh after it, though it is the truth confirming that which they possess. (2:91)

Muhammad and his followers came to believe that the revelations he received were
final, uncorrupted, and true. Muhammad did not formulate this message; he only
transmitted it as received. For Muslims, in the chain of prophets, Muhammad is the
last and final link.

Christian Arabs remained largely aloof from Muhammad's alliances, while some
Jews actively opposed his political goals and rejected his claims to religious prophecy.
Disappointed in his wish to unite the members of the two monotheistic religions of
the region under his leadership, and especially infuriated that some Jewish families
had joined his Meccan enemies in war, Muhammad had the Jewish men of the Banu
Qurayza clan executed, and the women and children enslaved. Elsewhere in Arabia,
however, Jews and Christians, though subject to a special tax, were free to practice
their religion.

Successors to the Prophet

11.2 What happened to Islam after Muhammad's death?

What happened
to Islam after
Muhammad's
death?

11.2

11.3

11.4

When the Prophet died leaving no male heir, the Muslim community feared that the *umma* and its political organization would break up. To preserve them, the Muslim leadership elected Abu Bakr (r. 632–34), one of Muhammad's closest associates and the father of his wife Aisha, as **caliph**—that is, successor to the Prophet and head of the Muslim community. The next three caliphs were similarly elected from among Muhammad's relatives and companions, but amidst much more dissension.

Abu Bakr mobilized to prevent Muslims from deserting their new religion and the authority of its government, attacking those who tried. Arabia was convulsed in tribal warfare. The contending tribes fought for power and looted one another, as they had traditionally. Their battles spilled over the borders of the Arabian peninsula, as did their search for allies. The Byzantine and Sassanid empires saw the Arab troops encroaching on their territories and fought back, but at the Battle of Ajnadayn (634) in southern Palestine, the Arab clans combined to form a unified army and defeated the Byzantine army. With this victory, the Arab warriors were no longer simple raiders in search of plunder. They were now at war for the control of settled empires.

Conquest followed conquest—Damascus in 636, Jerusalem in 638—but the north-ward march stopped as Byzantine troops held fast at the borders of the Anatolian peninsula. The Byzantine Empire defended its Anatolian borders for another four centuries, and its Balkan territories for eight. But the Sassanid Empire collapsed almost immediately. In 637 Arab armies defeated the Persians in battle, seized their capital, Ctesiphon, and forced the last emperor to flee. Meeting little opposition, Arab armies swept across Iraq, Iran, Afghanistan, and central Asia. Other Arab armies now turned toward northern Africa, taking Egypt in 641–43 and Tripoli in 643.

The second caliph, Umar I (r. 634–44), established the early principles of political administration, as a "rightly guided" caliph, in the conquered territories. The troops were not to interfere with the way of life of the conquered populations. The early caliphs did not encourage conversion to Islam, lest the political and social status of conqueror and conquered become confused. Also, since Muslims were exempted from land taxes and poll taxes, the conversion of conquered peoples would cause considerable loss of tax revenue to Umar's government.

To prevent the armies and administrators from interfering with the economy and the social traditions of the newly conquered territories, Umar ordered the occupiers to live somewhat apart from the conquered populations. Muslim armies built new garrison cities, such as Basra, Kufa, Fustat, and Merv, and added new neighborhoods to existing cities for their troops and administrators. They largely left local systems of taxation and administration in place, and incumbent personnel often kept their jobs, but the new government confiscated lands that had been owned by the state and its officials and claimed them for itself.

These new arrangements proved unstable. In the new garrison cities, conqueror and conquered lived side by side, and they could not effectively be segregated socially and culturally. In addition, the troops soon argued that their pay was not adequate. Their incomes lagged, even as the new conquests enriched the top-level administrators. What had become of Islam's call for a more egalitarian society? In essence, the imperial aims of the ruling class and the religious goals of Islam were pulling in opposite directions.

Civil War: Religious Conflict and the Sunni–Shi'a Division

The jockeying for power among various political, economic, tribal, and religious interest groups precipitated a series of civil wars. A contingent of Arab troops from Egypt assassinated the third caliph, Uthman (r. 644–56), complaining that under his

KEY TERM

caliph The spiritual head and temporal ruler of the Muslim community.

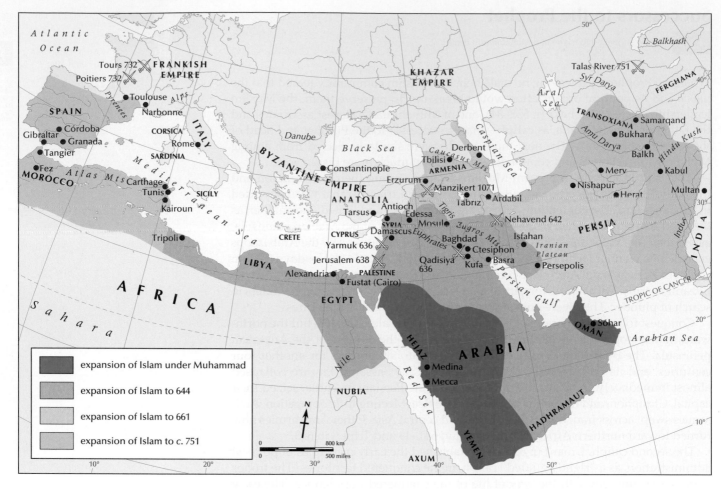

The expansion of Islam. The Muslim faith spread with astonishing speed from its center at Mecca, exploiting the weakness of the Byzantine and Sassanid empires. Within a century of the death of the Prophet Muhammad in 632, Arab armies had reached the Atlantic coast in the west, and the borders of India and China in the east.

KEY TERMS

Shi'a Short form for *shiat Ali*, "follower of Ali." In choosing a successor to Muhammad, the shi'a argued for Ali, his cousin/son-in-law, his closest male relative. From that time on, they remained a separate sect within Islam, representing about 20 percent of all Muslims worldwide, and a majority in countries such as Iran and Iraq.

Sunni From the Arabic *sunna*, the words and acts of Muhammad, as recorded in *hadiths*. The Sunni are the majority group in Islam, representing just over 80 percent of the total. They differed from the Shi'a in choosing Uthman as the first successor of Muhammad, and argued that they were following the wish and example of the Prophet.

administration their local governors were cruel, their pay was inadequate, and class divisions were destroying Arab unity.

Uthman's successor, Ali (r. 656–61), was elected despite considerable opposition. Supporting his election most strongly was the *shiat Ali*, "the party of Ali," usually referred to simply as the **Shi'a** or Shi'ites. This group felt that the caliph should be chosen from the family of the Prophet. They had opposed the election of the first three caliphs. Ali, as the cousin and also the son-in-law of Muhammad, having married his daughter Fatima, was the first caliph to fit their requirement. In opposition, members of Uthman's family, the Ummayad clan, preferred one of their own. They argued for acceptance of the first three caliphs as legitimate since they were chosen by the *umma* and reflected the *sunna*, or example, of the Prophet. They and their followers called themselves **Sunnis**. Finally, a third group, who had long opposed the Umayyad for their own reasons, feared that Ali might reach an accommodation with their rivals, and assassinated him.

After Ali's assassination, the Umayyad leader, Mu'awiya (r. 661–80), declared himself caliph. Moving the capital out of Arabia to Damascus in Syria, Mu'awiya distanced himself from the original Muslim elite of the Arabian peninsula. He opened Islam to more cosmopolitan influences and a more professional style of imperial administration.

11.1

What happened
to Islam after
Muhammad's
death?

11.2

11.3

11.4

Tension remained high among the various religious and tribal factions, however, and civil war broke out again on Mu'awiya's death in 680. His son Yazid I (r. 680–83) claimed the caliphate, but Husayn, son of the assassinated Ali, took the field against him. When Husayn was killed in battle at Karbala, Iraq, in the year 680, he joined his father as the second martyr of the Shi'a branch of Islam.

The Shi'as stressed the importance of religious purity, and they wanted the caliph to represent Islam's religious principles rather than its imperial aspirations. They felt that Ali, in addition to his heritage as a member of the family of the Prophet, represented that purer orientation, and they would recognize only descendants of Ali as **imams**, religious leaders who were also rightful caliphs. From 680 onward, Shi'as went into battle for the appointment of their imams to fill the position of caliph.

One after another, all of the first 11 Shi'a imams are believed to have died as martyrs, either in battle or through assassination. After the death of the eleventh, in 874, and the disappearance of his son, the hereditary line ended. From that time onward, "twelver" Shi'as have looked forward to the reappearance of the "hidden" twelfth imam, referred to as the *mahdi*, or "rightly guided one," a messiah, to usher in a new age of Islam, truth, and justice. Meanwhile, they have usually been willing to accept the authority of the current government, while stressing matters of the spiritual rather than the temporal world.

The great majority of Muslims, however, regarded the caliph as primarily a political official, administering the empire of Islam. They accepted the rule of the Umayyads, based on Sunni teachings and the importance of the *umma* in making political decisions.

The division between Sunni and Shi'a, which began over the proper succession to the caliphate, has continued to the present—long after the caliphate ceased to exist—as the principal sectarian division within Islam. Some 83 percent of the world's Muslims today are Sunnis, 16 percent are Shi'as. The split is largely geographical, with Shi'as forming 95 percent of the population of Iran and about 60 percent of that of Iraq.

The Sunni–Shi'a division is the most significant in Islam, but it is not the only one. At the death of the sixth imam, in 765, there was another conflict over acceptance of the seventh. The majority chose the imam's younger son, but a minority followed the elder son, Ismail. The Ismailis, a branch of Shi'as, proselytized actively and led frequent rebellions against the caliphate. Later the Ismailis also divided. One branch lives on today, mostly in Pakistan and India, revering the Aga Khan as its leader.

The Umayyad Caliphs Build an Empire

After the succession struggle on Mu'awiya's death, the Umayyads consolidated their rule and embarked on wars of imperial conquest. To symbolize their imperial power, the Umayyad caliphs constructed elegant, monumental mosques in Jerusalem in 691 (the Dome of the Rock); in Medina, 706–10; Damascus, 706–14; and, again, Jerusalem (the al-Aqsa Mosque), 709–15. They also began to create an imperial bureaucracy that owed its allegiance to the state rather than to the current ruler personally.

Life in the cities eroded the solidarity of tribal society. A new social structure was developing that was dividing the Arab upper and lower classes while mixing the Arab and non-Arab elites. The Umayyad caliphs looked to Islam as the glue that could hold the splintered society together. They sought actively to convert the conquered peoples and assimilate them into a single Muslim *umma*. By the middle of the eighth century, conversions to Islam were increasing among the urban populations, as was the use of Arabic as the language of administration, literature, and everyday speech.

The Umayyads quickly expanded their empire through a series of enormously successful imperial conquests. Arab armies conquered the entire northern coast of Africa by 711. In North Africa, after initial resistance, most of the conquered Berber

KEY TERMS

imam In Islam, a title for a person whose religious leadership or example is to be followed.

mahdi According to Islamic tradition, this messianic leader will appear to restore justice, truth, and religion for a brief period before the universal Day of Judgment.

The exterior of the Dome of the Rock, Jerusalem, first constructed in 692. The first Umayyad caliph, Abd al-Malik (r. 685–705), built this shrine as the first major monument in Islamic history. It celebrates the triumphal conquests of the Umayyad dynasty as it emerged from Arabia and defeated both the Byzantine and Persian empires to carve out a new empire of its own.

11.1

11.2

11.3

11.4

What happened
to Islam after
Muhammad's
death?

tribes converted to Islam. At one extreme, conversion was accompanied by intermarriage, and some of the Arab conquerors and Berber peoples intermingled to the point where it was no longer possible to distinguish among them ethnically. In other cases, whole tribes converted. They became part of the Islamic world but remained in their tribal groupings. Often they conducted their own internal administration as if they were a small state. Other Muslim armies marched eastward, capturing large parts of central Asia, and raiding repeatedly in the Indus valley region of Sind.

Between 711 and 756, Arab and Berber forces crossed the Straits of Gibraltar and completed the conquest of Spain. Muslim raiders also moved into France, but Charles Martel and Frankish armies pushed them back south of the Pyrenees in 732 after the Battle of Tours.

Muslim governments continued to rule at least parts of Spain for seven and a half centuries, until 1492. During those years the relationship between Muslims, Christians, and Jews was sometimes strained. Sometimes, however, they were very fruitful.

The Umayyads copied the imperial structures of the Byzantine and Persian empires: wars of imperial conquest, bureaucracy in administration, monumentality in architecture, and regal opulence at court. They used Arabic as their language of administration, and encouraged conversion to Islam.

However, Umar's successors were not as committed to the program of equality under Islam as earlier caliphs had been. Their implementation was inconsistent, and various interest groups were frustrated by the vagaries of their changing fortunes. Many Sunni religious leaders, although pleased with the new emphasis on Islam, were offended by the imperial pomp of the Umayyads and their use of religion for blatantly political purposes. Many Shi'as continued to nourish the hope that one of their imams would displace the Umayyads and take his rightful place as caliph. In Kufa, Iraq, Shi'as revolted in 740, but the revolt was suppressed, and its leaders were executed.

The Ummayads had raised conflicting expectations. Non-Arab Muslims, whose taxes were not lowered or were lowered only temporarily, railed against the government for not delivering on its promises. Arabs were unhappy that their own taxes were being raised to compensate for the reductions offered to others.

The Umayyad armies, which were overextended and exhausted, began to lose major battles. The Turks drove them from Transoxiania in central Asia; the Khazars stopped them in Armenia in 730; Charles Martel halted the Umayyad advance in France in 732; the Greeks destroyed a major Muslim army in Anatolia in 740; in North Africa Berber rebels, although defeated in 742, destroyed an Umayyad army of 27,000 in the process. Umayyad forces did win the critical Battle of the Talas River in 751, halting the advance of Chinese forces westward and opening central Asia and its silk routes to Islamic religious and cultural missions, but they did not push forward. Military advances stopped. Pulled in many conflicting directions, without the strength to reply, the caliphate was drawn into a third civil war.

The Third Civil War and the Abbasid Caliphs

The Abbasid clan in northern Iran—descended from an uncle of Muhammad named Abbas and also claiming support from descendants of the line of Ali—revolted against the Umayyads. Supported by Arab settlers in Iran who were protesting against high taxes, by Shi'as who were seeking their own rule, and also by a faction from Yemen, the Abbasid clan overthrew the Umayyad caliphate. In 750, Abu al-Abbas al-Saffah initiated the new Abbasid caliphate, which ruled in reality for a century and a half but held power in name until 1258. Signaling new policy directions, the Abbasid caliph built a new capital at Baghdad, 500 miles east of Damascus, along the banks of the Tigris River, in the heart of the historic Fertile Crescent.

The Abbasid caliphs continued the tasks of the Umayyads in trying to bring order and unity to an empire of heterogeneous peoples, and they followed many of the principles set forth by Umar II. They used Arabic as a unifying language of official communication and administration, and continued to urge non-Muslims to convert. They recruited widely among all the peoples of the empire to fill administrative and military positions, and as the bureaucracy expanded, Nestorian Christians, Jews, Shi'as, and numerous ethnic groups became prominent in the Abbasid administration.

For a century the Abbasids succeeded—to a surprising degree—in solving the problems of administering large empires. They kept their administration cosmopolitan and centralized, yet at the same time in touch with local communities. They rotated their officers so that none could become entrenched and semi-independent in a distant posting. They regularized taxes. They employed spies as well as troops of soldiers and armed police. They also attempted to maintain good relations with local notables, such as village headmen, large landowners, *qadis* (judges), officials of local mosques, religious teachers, money-lenders, accountants, merchants, and family patriarchs, who were the critical sources of information and power in the villages and towns.

The Weakening of the Caliphate

Inevitably, however, the Abbasid caliphate, too, encountered difficulties. The process of choosing a successor to the caliph remained unresolved. At the death of Caliph

Clay figurine of a female slave from Khirbat al-Mafjar, Syria, *c.* eighth century. Female slaves had their place in the world of the Umayyad dynasty and beyond. Often the objects of passionate love, many were accomplished singers and highly educated.

11.1

11.2

What happened to Islam after Muhammad's death?

11.3

11.4

KEY TERM

qadi A judge in Islamic legal practice.

11.1

11.2

11.3

11.4

What happened
to Islam after
Muhammad's
death?

Portrait of Mahmud of Ghazni, from Rashid al-Din's *World History*, 1306–07. Mahmud (998–1030),
a Sunni Muslim prince, is shown putting on the traditional diplomatic gift of a robe of honor, bestowed
by the Abbasid caliph. Regional rulers sometimes declared their independence from central control, but
Mahmud of Ghazni was careful to include the caliph's name on his coinage, thereby presenting himself
as a loyal subject. The variety of headdresses, clothing, and facial types gives evidence of the immense
geographical extent of the Abbasid caliphate. (Edinburgh University Library)

Harun-al-Rashid (r. 786–809), his two sons fought for the throne, provoking a fourth
civil war. Recruiting troops proved an even bigger problem. Throughout the empire,
local strongmen were invited to ally their troops to the caliph's armies, but these
military contingents naturally owed their allegiance not to Baghdad but to the local
potentate.

The caliphs expanded sharply the use of slave troops in their armies. Slave troops,
mostly from central Asia, were often poorly disciplined, and sometimes various contingents turned on one another. At the same time the civilian bureaucracy became
more corrupt and more distant from the general population, and tax collection was
increasingly turned over to exploitative, semi-independent **tax farmers**. Corruption
and reliance on slaves isolated the caliphs from their own civilian populations—the
more imperial the caliphate, the more distant it became from the original Islamic
ideals of equality and simplicity.

The Emergence of Quasi-independent States. As a consequence, revolts struck the
caliphate. In 868 a Turkish commander established a virtually independent dynasty
that included Egypt and Syria, until the caliph regained them in 905. The slaves in the
salt mines of southern Iraq waged a successful revolt for 15 years, from 868 to 883. In
867, frontier troops in central Iran revolted and won control of southern and western
Iran. Ismaili and Shi'a religious leaders organized revolts throughout the empire.
Denying the legitimacy of Abbasid claims to rule and highlighting the exploitation of
the village and tribal masses by the distant and corrupt administration in Baghdad,
they won many victories in the name of their own views of Islam. Inspired by the
Ismailis, peasant and Bedouin raiders attacked Mecca, briefly carrying away the
sacred Ka'aba stone, the most venerated shrine in the holy city.

The Fatimid clan, claiming to be the rightful successors of the Prophet, conquered
Egypt and much of northern Africa. They broke openly with Baghdad, declaring
themselves the legitimate caliphs. In Iraq, other rebels took control first of the regions
around Baghdad and then, in 945, of Baghdad itself. The caliph was permitted to continue to rule in name, but in effect the empire as a unified, centralized administration

KEY TERM

tax farmer An official entrusted
with collecting taxes. The total
amount to be collected was fixed
by the government, and any
collection exceeding that amount
belonged to the tax farmer. The
system encouraged exploitation
of the taxpayer.

was finished. The unity of the Abbasid state dissolved, although the nominal authority of the caliph was still accepted everywhere.

Turkic-speaking Peoples and their Conquests. Meanwhile, in the seventh and eighth centuries, the consolidation of the Tang dynasty in China had revived the pressure on the pastoral, nomadic peoples of inner Asia, pushing them westward, just as the Han had done centuries before. This time the pastoral nomads encountered peoples who had converted to Islam. As a result of contacts with Muslim scholars and mystics, many of the nomadic peoples converted as well.

One of these groups, the **Turkic**-speaking Qarluq peoples, gained control of Bukhara (992) and Samarqand (999) in modern Uzbekistan. They propagated Islam and began to sponsor the development of the Turkish language and a Turkish–Islamic civilization.

Another Turkic-speaking group, led by the Seljuk (or Saljuq) family, entered central Asia, conquered Afghanistan and Iran, and seized Baghdad in 1055. In Baghdad, the Seljuk Turks kept the Abbasid caliph on his throne and ruled in his name. They titled themselves sultans, claiming authority over the secular side of government, while leaving the administration of religious affairs to the caliph.

The Mongols and the Destruction of the Caliphate. In the twelfth century, a new threat destabilized empires from China to Europe, including the areas under Muslim rule. In Karakorum, Mongolia, Temujin (c. 1162–1227), later called Chinggis (Genghis) Khan ("Universal Ruler"), forged a confederation of Mongol and Turkish peoples, who rode outward, east and west, creating the largest land-based empire in history. The story of the Mongol expansion is told in "Establishing World Trade Routes."

> **KEY TERM**
>
> **Turkic/Turkish** Turkic languages are a family of related languages spoken by peoples of central Asia and their descendants. The most widely spoken of these languages is Turkish.

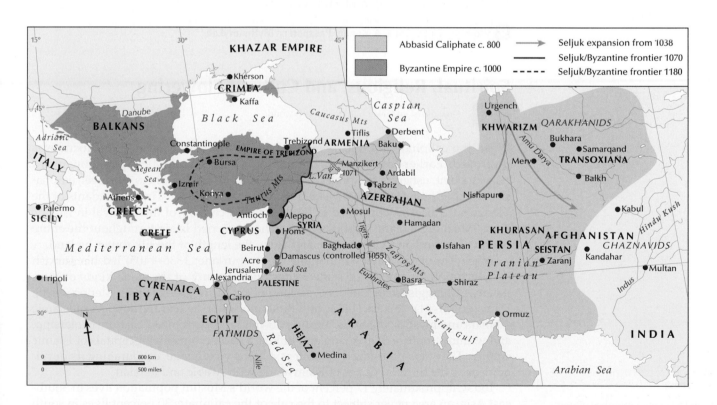

Byzantium and Islam. The Byzantine Empire remained the bastion of Christian political power in Asia Minor for 1,000 years after the fall of Rome in the West. A powerful new force for Islam, the Seljuk Turks, appeared out of central Asia in the eleventh century. After invading Persia and Syria, they defeated a Byzantine army at Manzikert in 1071 and began to infiltrate the Byzantine heartland.

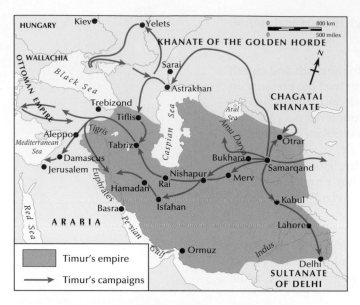

The empire of Timur, c. 1360–1405. The final stage of Mongol power was inspired by Timur's ambitions. Originating in Samarqand, his armies struck southeast to India, north to the Khanate of the Golden Horde, and west against the Ottoman and Egyptian Mameluke empires. The empire fragmented after Timur's death, but his descendants patronized Islamic culture in the capital cities of Samarqand and Bukhara.

11.1

11.2

11.3 How did Islam flower outside the Arab world?

11.4

KEY TERM

Sufi In Islam, a member of one of the orders practicing mystical forms of worship that first arose in the eighth and ninth centuries C.E.

Muslims whose lands the Mongols conquered felt devastated. An eyewitness observer, Ibn al-Athir, records his despair in the face of the early waves of invasions in 1220–21:

> For some years I continued averse from mentioning this event, deeming it so horrible that I shrank from recording it … To whom, indeed, can it be easy to write the announcement of the death-blow of Islam and the Muslims, or who is he on whom the remembrance thereof can weigh lightly? O would that my mother had not borne me, or that I had died and become a forgotten thing ere this befell … These [Mongols] spared none, slaying women and men and children, ripping open pregnant women and killing unborn babes. (McNeill and Waldman, pp. 249–51)

In 1258, Chinggis's grandson Hülegü (c. 1217–65) conquered Baghdad and executed the caliph, ending the Abbasid Empire. The Mongols might have continued further on their conquests in western Asia, but the death of Hülegü's brother in China diverted their attention. Meanwhile, the sultan in Cairo defeated the Mongol troops at the Battle of Ain Jalut, near Nazareth (1260), ending their threat of further advance. Mongol rule in west Asia continued, however, until 1336. Significantly, even after it lost its political power to the Mongols, Islam continued to expand and gain converts.

🔍 **View** the **Closer Look**: **A Mongol Passport** on **MyHistoryLab**

Spiritual, Religious, and Cultural Flowering

11.3 How did Islam flower outside the Arab world?

When the caliphate fell, the *umma* seemed to fall with it. Its political focus was destroyed. Earlier historians have therefore characterized 1258 as a downward turning point, ushering in a protracted decline. More recent writers, however, emphasize the continuing growth of Islam outside the Arab world. The descendants of the Mongols themselves converted to Islam within a century of their arrival in Islamic lands. Muslim scholars, mystics, and merchants carried Islam throughout the entire region of the Indian Ocean by sea, and along the length of the silk routes by land.

When Timur the Lame (Tamerlane or Tamburlane; 1336–1405) led his Turkish invaders along many of the same routes and in many of the same kinds of campaign as Chinggis Khan had done, sacking or capturing Delhi (1398), Aleppo (1400), Damascus (1401), Ankara (1402), and Bukhara (1402), he had the support of Islamic scholars and mystics, the **Sufis**. Timur's descendants patronized Islamic scholarship, and within a century Samarqand and Bukhara had become major capitals of Islamic culture. They also patronized Turkish as a literary language, encouraging its development as the third language of Islam along with Arabic and Persian.

Today, approximately 17 percent of the world's Muslim population lives in Southeast Asia, an area never subject to the rule of the caliphate; 30 percent lives in south Asia, where conversion took place almost entirely after its fall; 12 percent lives in sub-Saharan Africa, again virtually untouched by the caliphate. In short, some 60 percent of today's Muslims are descended from peoples who had no connection to the Abbasid caliphate in Baghdad. In the following pages we consider the factors that enabled Islam to flourish and spread as a religion and a civilization even after its historic political center collapsed.

📖 **Read** the **Document**. **A Contemporary Describes Timur** on **MyHistoryLab**

11.1
11.2
11.3   How did Islam flower outside the Arab world?
11.4

Islam Reaches New Peoples

The end of the caliphate did not mean the end of the spread of Islam; quite the contrary. Regional rulers, finding themselves more independent, pursued policies of political and military expansion while proclaiming the religion and culture of Islam as their own.

India. A Muslim government run by slave soldiers who had earned their freedom established itself in Ghazni, Afghanistan, as early as 962. From that base, Muslims launched raids into India and established their rule over the Punjab. In 1211, the Muslim general who conquered Delhi declared himself an independent sultan, initiating a series of five dynasties, which are known collectively as the Sultanate of Delhi (1211–1526). By 1236 they controlled northern India; by 1335, almost the entire subcontinent.

Delivering a lecture. A traditional saying—"Kings are the rulers of the people, but scholars are the rulers of kings"—indicates the esteem in which learning is traditionally held by Muslims. Moreover, the transmission of knowledge was deemed a major act of piety. A well-stocked library serves as the backdrop for a lecture, in which a teacher would first dictate a text, then discourse upon it. (Bibliothèque Nationale, Paris)

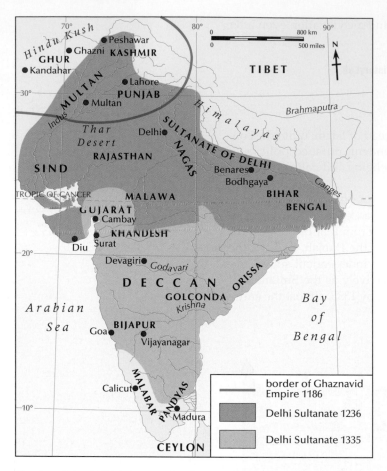

The rise of the Delhi Sultanate. The Muslim Afghan Ghaznavid Empire was the first of a number of Afghan and Turkic powers who, exploiting divisions among local Hindu rulers, established their hegemony in northern India. Based at Delhi, six successive Muslim dynasties commanded varying territorial extents, but only briefly, in the mid-fourteenth century, did they completely control the Deccan.

11.1

11.2

11.3 How did Islam flower outside the Arab world?

11.4

When Delhi's power dimmed, numerous Muslim rulers controlled other regions of India. These regional governments, in particular, stayed close to their subjects, encouraged the development of regional languages, and provided new opportunities to Sufis (Muslim mystics and teachers) to introduce and practice Islam in new areas. In 1526, temporarily, and in 1556, more permanently, a mixture of Mongol and Turkish Muslim invaders conquered India, heralding the start of a new era, the Mughal (from Mongol) Empire.

Most, but not all, of the Muslim rulers recognized the importance of a respectful religious accommodation with the overwhelming Hindu majority. The first Muslim invaders in Sind in the eighth century extended a protected status to Hindus usually granted only to monotheists. They argued that behind the many forms of god in Hinduism there was just one reality. They also recognized that warfare against so large a majority of Hindus was impossible. They allowed Hindus to practice their own religion as long as they accepted Islamic rule. Usually they protected Hindu temples, although in some instances they defaced shrines as a means of asserting their own supremacy. For example, they destroyed the famous Shaivite temple at Somnath, western India, in 1024. The Turkish forces occupying Bengal and Bihar also destroyed the last remaining libraries and monasteries of Buddhism in that region, delivering the final death blow to a religion that had already seen most of its following in India disappear.

The Muslim conquest of India opened the subcontinent to Persians, Afghans, Turks, and Mongols seeking jobs with the new governments. This immigration brought a variety of Islamic practices to India, where no single orthodoxy prevailed. Diverse Muslims coexisted with diverse Hindus, venerating some saints and sharing some devotions in common. India's population became 20–25 percent Muslim. Many were descendants of Muslim immigrants near the top of the social hierarchy; others were converts, escaping untouchability at the bottom of the caste system. The vast majority of India's population, however, remained Hindu.

Southeast Asia. The beginning of mass conversions of Southeast Asians to Islam came in the fourteenth and fifteenth centuries, and today, Malaysia and Indonesia are overwhelmingly Muslim. Ocean traders and Sufis from India seem to have accomplished most of the missionary work. The traders offered increased economic opportunities to those local people who would adopt Islam, while the Sufis and the regional kings of Southeast Asia exchanged support for one another in a familiar pattern of interdependence between religious and political leaders.

Sub-Saharan Africa. As in Southeast Asia, Islam was first carried to sub-Saharan Africa by traders and Sufis. They came from three directions: from Mediterranean North Africa across the Sahara to West Africa; from Egypt up the Nile to East Africa; and from India and Arabia across the Indian Ocean to the coast of East Africa.

The Arab conquest of North Africa in the seventh and early eighth centuries set the scene for increasing contact between Arab and Black Africans. As traders, and

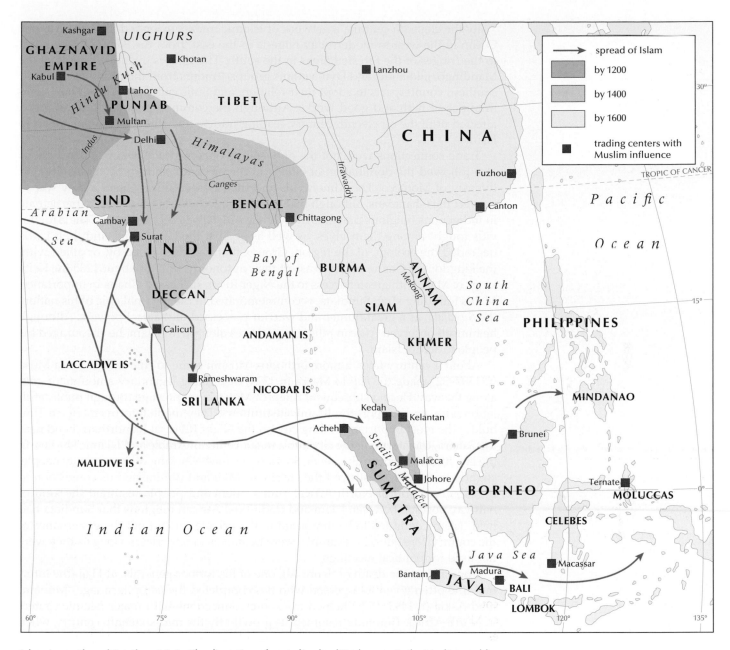

Islam in south and Southeast Asia. The disruption of centralized political power in the Muslim world did not stop the expansion of Islam in Africa and southern Asia. Arab maritime traders carried their faith to the shores of India and onward throughout maritime Southeast Asia. The Indian heartland was conquered by successive waves of Muslim invaders, who, by 1400, secured the key Indo-Gangetic plain.

11.1

11.2

How did Islam flower outside the Arab world?

11.3

11.4

sometimes as warriors, the Arabs began to cross the Sahara. When they reached the southern "shore" of the Sahara [the sahel], they found flourishing kingdoms in place, their power derived from control of the desert trade routes and the taxes they imposed on this trade. Founded (according to legend) in about 300 C.E., Ghana was the largest of these sub-Saharan kingdoms. (This Ghana is located approximately in the area of modern Mali, and is not to be confused with modern Ghana, to the southeast.) By the ninth century Ghana was both a partner and a rival of the northern Berbers for control of Saharan trade. Along these routes, gold, slaves, hides, and ivory were transported northward in exchange for copper, silver, metal goods, horses, dried fruit, cloth, and salt transported southward.

11.1

11.2

11.3

11.4

How did Islam
flower outside
the Arab world?

By the eleventh century, a network of Islamic traders extended from the Atlantic Ocean in the west to modern-day Nigeria in the east, from the Sahara in the north to the fringes of the forested areas in the south. The traders included people of the Mandingo, Jakhande, and Dyula ethnic groups. Traders from the north invited their southern counterparts to adopt their religion, and Sufis came to establish new communities of faith and good works. Although the common people were not much affected until the nineteenth century, leading traders and rulers began to convert to Islam.

Trade connections were not the only source of converts. A wave of conversions also followed the domination of Ghana in the eleventh century by the Almoravid dynasty of Morocco. The Almoravids and their Berber allies waged a holy war to convert the Ghanaians, although many of the new converts continued to participate in indigenous religious practices even while officially accepting Islam. The Almoravids fought among themselves, as well as against the Ghanaians, and their cattle degraded the ecology of the region. Groups that had been ruled by, or allied with, the kingdom of Ghana began to assert their autonomy, until in about 1235 the Keita kings of Mali, with greater access to the Niger River, surpassed Ghana in importance. Mali's founding king, Sundiata, is commemorated in the national epic of his nation, the *Sundiata*, as a great hunter and warrior possessed of magical powers. Although he himself observed African religious practices along with Islam, he encouraged his people to accept Islam.

About a century later, a more orthodox Muslim came to rule Mali. Mansa Musa (r. 1307–32) made the *hajj* to Mecca in 1324, disbursing legendary amounts of gold along the way. He and subsequent rulers of Mali sought prestige through public affiliation with, and support for, Islamic institutions. They made improvements in Timbuktu, the most important trading city on the Niger River, at its northern bend near the Sahara, transforming the city into a major center of Arabic and Islamic studies. In the late fifteenth century, however, Sonni Ali (r. 1464–92), king of the Songhay people, slightly to the east, destroyed the empire of Mali and diminished its connection to the Islamic world of North Africa. Mali's rulers and people resumed the kind of halfway position between Islam and traditional African religions that Sundiata had held. Islam continued to be important in the private life but not the governance of the country. Mosques, for example, were treated as sanctuaries, so long as they were not used for political meetings.

Ironically, at the death of Sonni Ali, one of his former generals, al-Hajj (the informal title often given to a person who has completed the *hajj* pilgrimage) Muhammad Askia (r. 1493–1528) helped to restore connections with major Islamic centers in North Africa. Timbuktu resumed its growth. By the mid-sixteenth century, when it was under the rule of Songhay, Timbuktu held between 150 and 180 Quranic elementary schools, which, in turn, laid the foundations for more advanced education. Timbuktu's scholarship matched that of Morocco, and leading scholars of Morocco came to learn from Timbuktu's leading scholar, Ahmad Baba (1556–1627). In 1591, however, the power of the city and its trading networks was undercut by the conquest of the region by Moroccan forces. Although the Moroccans were also Muslims, they acted as conquerors rather than as members of the same religious community, and the status of Muslims actually declined.

From Ghana, Mali, and Songhay, Islam was spreading eastward across Africa. For example, at the beginning of the twelfth century, the king of Kanem converted to Islam, made a pilgrimage to Mecca, and constructed a religious school in Cairo for students from Kanem. His subjects followed him in converting to Islam. When his Saifawa ruling dynasty was forced militarily to leave Kanem in the mid-fourteenth century, it reestablished its Muslim state in nearby Bornu. Islamic influences from Kanem and Bornu, in turn, reinforced the religious message brought by the scholars accompanying traders from Mali to the neighboring Hausa people in Kano in modern northern Nigeria. In these lands, too, Islamic practices and local religious practices often blended, with the people choosing whichever seemed most efficacious in their personal lives. Kings often responded similarly, following the practices that seemed most associated with their military victories, and abandoning those that seemed to accompany defeats.

Still farther east, the upper Nile valley had been mostly Christianized by the time Muslim traders, gold miners, and slave traders arrived. As Muslim governments in Egypt began to push southward, however, they defeated the Nubian Christian kingdom and Islam began to take root, with the first Islamic states in Nubia dating to around 1500. The state of Sinnar, ruled by the Funj dynasty, became the most important of these states, in part because its subjects were expected to accept the Islamic religion of its rulers, and it gave special privileges to Islamic holy men and scholars.

By the eighth century, Islam arrived on Africa's east coast. As it crossed from Arabia and Yemen into East Africa, it met fierce resistance in Ethiopia, which had become staunchly Christian. Nevertheless, about 1630, a Portuguese missionary estimated that Muslims made up one-third of Ethiopia's population. A mosque at Shanga, off the east coast of Kenya, dates to about the beginning of the ninth century. At about the same time, al-Masudi, an Arab historian and sailor, reported Muslim settlers on the east coast of Africa. Much larger growth appeared in the thirteenth century, and by the fourteenth century more than 30 communities had built their mosques along the East African coast. Kilwa, in southeastern Tanzania, was the most important settlement and port, and modern archaeologists have been busy excavating its medieval remains along with those of other coastal towns. Philologists also study the interaction between the Arabic language of the overseas traders and the Swahili language of the African coast as trading necessities brought the two languages—and the two peoples—together.

Islam in Africa. Islam entered sub-Saharan Africa as a result of trade. Trans-Saharan caravans from Egypt, Libya, and Morocco gradually introduced the faith overland among the trading kingdoms of West Africa, while the Arab traders of the Indian Ocean carried the message south by sea along the east coast of the continent.

Law Provides an Institutional Foundation

One of the central features of Islamic society that survived the fall of the caliphate was the law. The legal systems of Islam, *shari'a*, lived on and flourished. For Muslims, as for other populations, law expresses in formal terms the standards of proper conduct. Law supports the fundamental Islamic duty of *hisba*, "to promote what is right and to prevent what is wrong" (Musallam in Robinson, p. 175). Muslims encounter their legal system in the regulation of public life; in family matters of marriage, divorce, parental responsibilities, and inheritance; and in the *shari'a*'s advice on such daily activities as eating, dressing, and housekeeping.

As the early caliphs and the Abbasids began to confront legal questions, they appointed to resolve them. The *qadis* searched the classical texts of the Quran, the **hadith** (quotations from Muhammad), and biographies of the Prophet for their core teachings, and then relied on a combination of local custom and their own deliberation and judgment (***ijtihad***) in rendering final decisions.

Seeking to overcome wide differences in local practices, four great legal scholars of the eighth and ninth centuries formulated the major systems of Islamic law that

How did Islam flower outside the Arab world?

11.1

11.2

11.3

11.4

KEY TERMS

hadith Traditional records of the deeds and utterances of the prophet Muhammad, and the basis, after the Quran, for Islamic theology and law.

ijtihad A method of Quranic interpretation based on text, local custom, and the personal judgment of the *qadi*, or judge.

How did Islam
flower outside
the Arab world?

endure today: the system of Abu Hanifah (699–767), in use mostly in the Arab Middle East and south Asia; of Malik ibn Anas (*c.* 715–95) in North, central, and West Africa; of Muhammad al-Shafii (767–820) in East Africa, southern Arabia, and Southeast Asia; and of Ahmad ibn Hanbal (780–855) in Saudi Arabia. Although most localities have followed one or another of these systems since about the tenth century, the existence of multiple systems has allowed flexibility in interpretation. Under certain circumstances, local legal experts have the option of drawing on any of the four texts. Because Shi'ites maintain different traditions of authority, encompassing the teachings of Ali and the early imams, they have also developed different schools of law. The most widespread is that of Jafar al-Sadiq (d. 765).

The personnel of the legal system are the ***ulama*** (singular *alim*), the religiously trained scholars of Islam who interpret and implement the law. The *ulama* constitute a class that includes *qadis* and their assistants, Quran reciters, prayer leaders, and preachers. The *ulama* are sometimes trained in formal theological schools or, more frequently, are simply apprenticed to senior *ulama*. Islam has no formal hierarchical, bureaucratic institution of *ulama*—indeed, it has no official Church. Informal networks of respected *ulama* have provided cohesion, stability, and flexibility within Islam, regardless of the changing forms of government.

Ideally, *ulama* and ruler worked together to decide and implement religious policy, but when Caliph al-Mamun (r. 813–33) proclaimed that he had the right to give authoritative interpretations of the Quran, the *ulama* mobilized the population of Baghdad against him. He responded with an inquisition to root out these opponents. The only major leader who stood up to him was Ahmad ibn Hanbal, the greatest *hadith* scholar of his generation, who argued that only the scholars had the authority to interpret Quranic text. The people supported him, and to escape the continuing popular protest, Caliph al-Mutasim (r. 833–42) moved his capital from densely populated Baghdad to Samarra, 60 miles away.

In 848–49, Caliph al-Mutawakkil (d. 861) withdrew the claim of caliphal authority in religious matters. The *ulama* had won, but the battle had so embittered relations between caliph and *ulama* that their spheres of influence were forever separated: the caliph had authority over matters of state; the *ulama* over matters of religion. The caliphs came to represent the imperial aspirations of the state, while the *ulama* represented the everyday needs and wishes of the people. Over time, such departures from popular accountability cost them the caliphate. But the *ulama* endured, in touch with the people, serving as their religious guides and frequently providing welfare services as well.

Sufis Provide Religious Mysticism

Law brings order to life. It makes concrete the responsibilities of one individual to another and to society in general. In Islam it also fixes the formal obligations due to God. The *ulama* conveyed and interpreted this message, carrying it to people in vastly different societies. Sufis also spread Islam to many parts of the world, but they were much less interested than the *ulama* in strict religious doctrine and emphasized devotion to Allah instead.

📖 **Read** the **Document**: Sufi Poetry: Hafez, from the Diwan on **MyHistoryLab**

The Role of Mysticism. As the Umayyad Empire weakened, many people inhabiting it began to reject the materialism of its leaders and turned to a pious asceticism. For these spiritual seekers, Sufis revealed Islam's inner, mystical path to God. Early Sufis found and transmitted the inner discipline of mind and body and the purification of the heart that enabled their followers to feel that they experienced God directly as the ultimate reality. They usually disdained worldly pleasures. One of the earliest of the Sufis, Hasan al-Basri (643–728), concluded: "This world has neither worth nor weight

KEY TERM

ulama The theologians and legal experts of Islam.

with God, so slight it is" (Esposito, 1991, p. 102). Although most Sufis were men, some, like Rabi'a al-Adawiyya (d. 801), were women. Rabi'a, the Hindu Mirabai, rejected marriage in order to devote herself to God: "Love of God hath so absorbed me that neither love nor hate of any other thing remain in my heart" (Embree, p. 448).

As we have seen throughout this part, every theistic religion has an aspect of devotional love of God, expressed through spontaneous prayer, private meditation, fasting, and asceticism, and, often, through physical disciplines, music, dance, and poetry. In Islam these aspects were adopted by the Sufis, who also absorbed influences from the mystics of other religions, especially monasticism from Christianity and Buddhism, and ecstasy in prayer from Hinduism.

Through their lives of exemplary devotion to God and people, the Sufis enhanced the message of Islam. They attracted people through the simplicity of their piety, their personal love of God, and their dedication to the needs of others. Some developed a reputation for magical powers. The mosques where they lived and prayed, and the mausolea in which they were buried, were revered as sacred shrines. A sixteenth-century folk ballad of eastern Bengal tells of one such Sufi saint:

> At that time there came a Mahomedan pir [Sufi] to that village. He built a mosque in its outskirts, and for the whole day sat under a fig tree ... His fame soon spread far and wide. Everybody talked of the occult powers that he possessed. If a sick man called on him he would cure him at once by dust or some trifle touched by him. He read and spoke the innermost thoughts of a man before he opened his mouth ... Hundreds of men and women came every day to pay him their respects. Whatever they wanted they miraculously got from this saint. Presents of rice, fruits, and other delicious food, goats, chickens, and fowls came in large quantities to his doors. Of these offerings the pir did not touch a bit but freely distributed all among the poor. (Eaton in Adas, pp. 21–22)

Individual mystics appeared in Islam from its earliest days, drawing their inspiration directly from the Quran. Centuries later, they began to form *tariqas*, or mystical

How did Islam flower outside the Arab world?

11.1
11.2
11.3
11.4

Whirling dervishes. Sufism represents the mystical, contemplative strand of Islam—a strand that is captured vividly by this example of "whirling dervishes," the Mawlawi religious order closely linked to the teachings of the thirteenth-century Persian poet Jalal-al-Din Rumi. Their slow, revolving dance helps to create higher states of consciousness, while being a ceremonial ritual in its own right.

KEY TERM

tariqa In Islam, a generic term meaning "path," referring to the doctrines and methods of mysticism and esoterism. The word also refers to schools or brotherhoods of mystics, which were often situated at a mosque or the tomb of a Muslim saint.

SOURCE

Al-Ghazali, the "Renewer of Islam"

The more solemn *ulama* and the more emotional Sufis were often suspicious of one another. Deeply disturbed by the tension between the two perspectives, the revered scholar Abu Hamid Muhammad al-Ghazali (1058–1111) finally formulated a synthesis of the intellectual and mystical sides of Islam that has proved satisfying to Muslims ever since.

Born and educated in Iran, al-Ghazali was appointed at the age of 33 to teach philosophy at the leading *madrasa*, or theological institute, in Baghdad. During four years there, Ghazali began to doubt the importance of rationality in life, and searched for more holistic ways of experiencing the world. Torn between holding his prestigious tenure at the *madrasa* and giving it up to pursue new roads toward truth, Ghazali was on the verge of breakdown:

> For nearly six months … I was continuously tossed about between the attractions of worldly desires and the impulses towards eternal life. In that month the matter ceased to be one of choice and became one of compulsion. God caused my tongue to dry up so that I was prevented from lecturing. One particular day I would make an effort to lecture in order to gratify the hearts of my following, but my tongue would not utter a single word nor could I accomplish anything at all. This impediment in my speech produced grief in my heart, and at the same time my power to digest and assimilate food and drink was impaired; I could hardly swallow or digest a single mouthful of food. (al-Ghazali, p. 57)

In 1095 Ghazali resigned his post. He traveled to Damascus, Jerusalem, and Mecca, and then returned to his home town, where he lived the monastic life of a Sufi mystic for ten years:

> I learnt with certainty that it is above all the mystics who walk on the road of God; their life is the best life, their method the soundest method, their character the purest character. (p. 60)

During his time of contemplation, Ghazali wrote a great number of philosophical and theological works, including the influential *Revival of the Religious Sciences*, exploring the relationship between religion and reason. He asserted the importance of mystical experience and a direct, personal understanding of God, while at the same time defending the doctrine and authority of the Islamic faith.

In 1106 Ghazali was persuaded to return to teaching, now proclaiming the complementarity of Sufism and rationality:

> Just as intellect is one of the stages of human development in which there is an "eye" which sees the various types of intelligible objects, which are beyond the ken of the senses, so prophecy also is the description of a state in which there is an eye endowed with light such that in that light the unseen and other supra-intellectual objects become visible. (p. 65)

By the end of his life, Ghazali's reconciliation of Sufism and rationality within Islam had earned him the title "Renewer of Islam."

11.1
11.2
11.3
11.4

How did Islam flower outside the Arab world?

brotherhoods, often located at the mosque or mausoleum of an especially revered saint. Some *tariqas* emphasized ecstatic practices; others were more sober and meditative. The *tariqa mawlawiya* was founded by Jalal-al-Din Rumi (1207–73) in Konya, Turkey. Rumi is most famous for his expression of ecstatic worship through the dance of the "whirling dervishes." Rumi's Persian language text, the *Mathnawi*, expressed in rich and evocative lyrics his love of God: "The result of religion is nothing but rapture" (Rumi, *Mathnawi* 1:312, Vitray-Meyerovitch, p. 83).

Intellectual Achievements

As the *ulama* provided order to the social structures of Islam, and the Sufis spread its spiritual powers, other intellectuals further enriched its cultural depth.

History. The historian and theologian al-Tabari (*c.* 839–923) introduced formal historical writings with his *History of Prophets and Kings*. The segment on prophecy recorded the contributions from Abraham through Muhammad; the record of kings covered rulers from Biblical times to his own and included eyewitness reports of relatively recent events.

With the conquest of Iran in the mid-seventh century, Persian became the second language of Islam. (The arrival of the Turks in 923 introduced Turkish as the third.) The Persian poet Ferdowsi (940–1020) wrote an epic poem on the mythical origins of the Persian peoples, in which one of his central themes is the tragedy that befalls "a good man whose king is a fool."

The Mongols also supported historical writing, including al-Juvaini's (1226–83) *History of the World Conquerors*, which told of Chinggis Khan's conquests, especially in Iran. Rashid al-Din (1247–1318) wrote *World History*, which many regard as the first attempt at a history of humanity, as it integrates Chinese, Indian, European, Muslim, and Mongol history into a single cosmopolitan perspective.

How did Islam flower outside the Arab world?

11.1
11.2
11.3
11.4

Although others, notably Rashid al-Din, had attempted to write comprehensive, narrative histories, Ibn Khaldun (1332–1406) of Tunis is often viewed as the first to apply social science theory to the study of history. His *Universal History* stressed a cyclical theory of history, in which vigorous nomadic peoples regularly conquered urban peoples who were settled, cultured, and contented, took over their cities, settled into lives of luxury, and then themselves fell prey to the next round

Mihrab in the Great Mosque, Córdoba, Spain, *c.* 961–76. Under the Umayyads, Córdoba grew to be by far the most prosperous city in Western Europe, second only to Baghdad in the Islamic world. At its height, the city is said to have contained some 300 public baths and 3,000 mosques within its walls. Shown here is the most important surviving mosque. Great attention was lavished on the decoration of the Great Mosque, and the *mihrab*, a small domed chamber indicating the direction of Mecca, is considered unique for its horseshoe-shaped doorway, a stylistic innovation of the Muslims in Spain.

of invasion from more robust nomads. The theory seemed to fit the comings and goings of nomadic invaders from Arabia, Mongolia, and central Asia that characterized his times. Among Ibn Khaldun's other interpretive themes that still seem insightful today are: "The differences between Easterners and Westerners are cultural [not innate]" (p. 51); "The differences between peoples arise principally from the differences in their occupations" (p. 80); and, perhaps, "Scholars are of all men those least fitted for politics and its ways" (p. 64).

Philosophy. Theology and philosophy had been regarded as inferior to revelation in early Islam, but as Muslims came into contact with the philosophies of the Hellenistic and Indian worlds, they were drawn to concepts of Platonism and Neoplatonism in particular. The caliphate established in Baghdad a "house of wisdom," a translation bureau under Hunayn ibn Ishaq (803–73). In the next 200 years some 80 Greek authors were translated, including Aristotle, Plato, Galen, and Euclid. So, too, were writings from Syriac, Sanskrit, and Persian.

A group of Islamic philosophers, called Mutazilites, "those who keep themselves apart," began to challenge orthodox Islamic belief, arguing that the attributes of God in the Quran were not literal but metaphorical, that human actions and life were not predetermined, and that the Quran had not existed eternally. Al-Farabi (c. 870–950) argued that philosophical knowledge gained through study and thought was of higher value than revelation from God. Similar notions of the supremacy of philosophy were expressed by al-Kindi (d. 870), Ibn Sina (Avicenna; d. 1037), and Ibn Rushd (Averroes; 1126–98). Such philosophical speculation was marginal to mainstream Islamic thought, and actually found more resonance among Christian and Jewish philosophers of the time.

Christian thinkers in Europe were indebted to the Muslims for keeping alive the Hellenistic traditions, for with the fall of the Roman Empire in the West the intellectual traditions and resources of the European Classical world had been neglected and forgotten. Now, thanks to Arabic translations and Islamic thought, Christian and Jewish philosophers grappled both with the original texts from Greece and India, and with the newer concepts introduced by Muslim thinkers.

Mathematics, Astronomy, and Medicine. The intersection of intellectual traditions also enriched mathematics, astronomy, and medicine. Indian scholars brought their texts on astronomy to Baghdad as early as 770. The caliph had them translated into Arabic, which was becoming the common language of scholarship throughout the empire. Arabs adopted and transmitted Hindi numerals and the decimal system, including the zero, throughout the empire and into Europe, where they were (mis) named "Arabic" numerals. A few decades later, al-Khwarazmi (d. c. 846) used Indian texts in conjunction with scholarship from Greece and Iran to develop algebra (from the Arabic al-jabr, "restoration"). (The word algorithm comes from al-Khwarazmi's name.) Al-Biruni (d. 1046) wrote extensively on number theory and computation, and later scholars developed the trigonometry we study today.

Al-Biruni also wrote al-Qanun al-Mas'udi, a compendium of Islamic astronomy, which incorporated findings from throughout the empire. Arabic mathematical and astronomical theories apparently informed Copernicus' sixteenth-century theories of a **heliocentric** universe.

Medical wisdom and herbal remedies were transmitted from one end of the empire to the other. Al-Razi (Rhazes; c. 865–c. 935) compiled an encyclopedia of medicine giving the views of Greek, Syrian, Indian, Iranian, and Arab writers on each disease, and including his own clinical observations and opinions. Ibn Sina, noted above for his contributions to philosophy, produced the even more encyclopedic Qanun fi'l-tibb ("Canon of Medicine"), which included volumes on the pharmacology of herbs, the functioning of organs, fevers, and surgery. The Qanun was translated into Latin and dominated medical thinking for 300 years.

KEY TERM

heliocentric A system in which the sun is assumed to be at the center of the solar system—or of the universe—while Earth and the other planets move around it.

11.1

11.2

11.3

11.4

How did Islam
flower outside
the Arab world?

The Extension of Technology

By 751, at the end of the Umayyad dynasty, Islam served as a network of communication that linked all the major civilizations of Eurasia. For example, as we noted above, Muslims learned papermaking from the Chinese and transmitted the technology throughout their domain. European Christians learned the art from Muslims in Spain.

Exchanges of information on agriculture and crops also enriched the world of Islam. Between the eighth and tenth centuries, Arabs brought from India hard wheat, rice, varieties of sorghum, sugar cane, bananas, sour oranges, lemons, limes, mangoes, watermelon, coconut palm, spinach, artichokes, eggplants, and the key industrial crop, cotton. All these crops were introduced throughout the empire, wherever climatic conditions were favorable. This may well have been the largest agricultural exchange in world history up to that time. Because most of these crops from India were warm-weather crops, many of them facilitated summer cropping in areas that had previously lain fallow in that season. To replicate the monsoon climate of India, Muslim officials improved existing forms of irrigation (underground water canals and water-lifting mechanisms) and invented new ones (certain kinds of cistern). Agricultural productivity diversified and increased, encouraging population increase in general and urban growth in particular.

City Design and Architecture

Muslim governments built great cities and adorned their public spaces lavishly and often exquisitely. The largest of the cities were the political capitals. Baghdad was built on the west bank of the Tigris River in 762 to serve as the capital of the Abbasid dynasty, and it served that purpose for almost 500 years. In the ninth century, with between 300,000 and 500,000 people in 25 square miles, Baghdad became the largest city in the world outside China.

As the caliphate declined, and Baghdad with it, regional capitals grew in importance: Bukhara, Nishapur, and Isfahan in the east, and Cairo, Fez, and Córdoba in the west. The Fatimid rulers of Egypt began their administration in Fustat and expanded that existing city into al-Qahira (Cairo) in 969. In Morocco, King Idris II (r. 791–828) built Fez in 808 as the capital of the Idrisid dynasty, which had been founded by his father. A later dynasty, the Almoravids, built their capital Marrakesh in 1070. In Andalusia, southern Spain, the Umayyads developed Córdoba into one of the most cosmopolitan cities of the Islamic world. It achieved its greatest splendor in the mid-tenth century, but was sacked by Berbers in 1013 and never fully recovered. The architecture of these cities proclaimed the splendor of Islam and the power of the Muslim rulers.

Although the daily prayers in Islam may be performed privately, Friday noon prayers require collective assembly, so all cities and most neighborhoods within cities also constructed mosques for public services. Wealthy rulers proclaimed their power and piety by building monumental central mosques, as they did early on in Jerusalem, Medina, and Damascus. The Abbasids constructed an enormous central mosque in Baghdad, and during the years that Samarra served as their capital (848–52) a huge mosque was constructed there, too. Great mosques were also built at Qayrawan in Tunisia, Fez in Morocco, and Córdoba in Spain.

As the Seljuk Turks conquered and then joined the world of Islam, they built an especially monumental mosque at Isfahan in the late eleventh century, and then rebuilt it 50 years later after Ismaili Shi'as burned it down. Ottoman architects, most notably Hoja Sinan (1490–1578), constructed magnificent mosques, such as the Selimiye at Edirne and the Sulaymaniye in Istanbul, and other public buildings that incorporated Byzantine and Islamic forms. When Islam crossed the Sahara Desert, a new architectural form developed: the Sahelian mosque (see the chapter entitled

The Great Mosque and minaret of al-Mutawakkil, Samarra, Iraq, 848–52. Although now only a shadow of its former glory, this 1,150-year-old mosque remains the largest of its kind in the world. Essential elements of simple mosque architecture emerge clearly through the ruins: a central courtyard or atrium, and a minaret, or tower, from which the *muezzin* (crier) summons the community to worship.

11.1

11.2

11.3 How did Islam flower outside the Arab world?

11.4

"Establishing World Trade Routes"). When Mansa Musa returned from his trip to Mecca in 1325, he brought with him an Arab architect to supervise the construction of mosques and *madrasas* (theological schools), especially in Timbuktu.

Because Islam teaches that all the dead should be honored, and some believe that the saintly among them could confer blessings, mausolea have a special significance and sanctity. The followers of Timur (Tamerlane), for example, built an enormous tomb for him at Samarqand in 1405. Some burial shrines reveal extraordinary personal love and devotion. In 1632–49 Emperor Shah Jahan built perhaps the best known of all Islamic buildings, the Taj Mahal in Agra, India, as a mausoleum for his wife Mumtaz Mahal, who died giving birth to their fifteenth child. At a more humble level, simple tombs of local holy men are found throughout the Islamic world, attracting followers, especially women, who pour out their hearts in prayer, trusting that the sanctity of the saint will carry it to God.

The public architecture of mosques, mausolea, and, to a lesser extent, the royal and governmental buildings that frequently adjoin them anchored the formal religious and political institutions of the Islamic city. The bazaar, or market area, was home to business activities. Business in Islam was an honored profession. Muhammad himself had been a caravan operator, and his first wife had been a businesswoman. Even today, mosques often control the land immediately adjacent to them and lease it to businesses so that the rents can support the mosque.

Islamic cities were, in effect, nodes on international trade routes linking the Islamic world to Europe and China. These trade routes enabled the movement not only of goods but also of people and ideas from one end of Eurasia to the other. The *hajj* to Mecca was also instrumental in creating a communication network among the regions and peoples of Islam.

The *Rihla*, or travelogues, of Ibn Battuta demonstrate the opportunities for travel open to a person of culture. In 30 years of traveling from his home in Tangier, he traversed approximately 73,000 miles of territories that today belong to some 50 different countries. Thanks to his mastery of Arabic and his knowledge of *shari'a*, Ibn Battuta found a welcome reception, and frequently temporary employment and gifts of wives and wealth in the lands he traversed. Muhammad Tughluq, sultan of Delhi, appointed him a *qadi* and, later, his envoy to China.

11.1
11.2
11.3
11.4

How did Islam flower outside the Arab world?

The Taj Mahal, Agra, India, 1632–48. Built by India's emperor Shah Jahan for his beloved wife Mumtaz Mahal, who died in childbirth, this mausoleum complex is considered the finest example of Mughal architecture, blending Indian, Persian, and Islamic styles. One of the most beautiful buildings in the world, the Taj was designated a UNESCO World Heritage site in 1983.

Bronzesmith, Isfahan bazaar, Iran. In Islam, religion and business are integrally linked, in that the land adjoining mosques is often leased to market traders whose rents support the buildings and their activities. Closest to the mosque are the "noble trades," such as books, perfumes, and religious objects. Here, a bronzesmith works outside his shop in the bazaar at Isfahan, which has been thriving since the third century.

Ibn Battuta's tales of adventure reflect the unity of the Islamic world. Despite its diversity, this world was held together by reverence for the Quran, the *shari'a*, the Arabic language (supplemented by Persian and Turkish), the political officials who ruled in its cities, and the scholars and merchants who traveled through them.

Relations with Non-Muslims

11.4 How did Muslims interact with non-Muslims?

Early Islamic governments spread their worldly power by the sword. As a result, popular belief in the West has held that the religion of Islam spread in the same way. Although conversion by force was practiced occasionally (just as it was by Christianity), by and large forced conversion to Islam was unusual. For example, the early "rightly guided" caliphs and the early Umayyads did not seek to convert the people they conquered. They preferred to rule as Arab Muslim conquerors over non-Arab, non-Muslim subjects. Only when the later Umayyads feared that they could not continue minority rule over so large a majority did they decide actively to seek conversion of, and alliance with, the conquered peoples.

Dhimmi Status

From the earliest days of Muslim conquest, non-Muslims were offered three options. The first was to convert to Islam. The second was to accept "protected," *dhimmi*, status as worshipers of one God who accepted Muslim rule. All the monotheistic "peoples of the book"—Christians, Jews, and Zoroastrians—were eligible for this status. Later, Islamic governments in India also extended *dhimmi* status to Hindus. The *dhimmi* were often required to pay a special tax, but they could follow their own religion and their own personal law regarding marriage, divorce, and inheritance, and they were to be protected by the Muslim government. The third option was to fight against the Muslim state, an option that few chose.

The status of the *dhimmi* was spelled out in "The Pact of Umar," a document ascribed to Umar I, the second caliph. It prescribed second-class status for the *dhimmi*. They were not to build new houses of worship nor to reconstruct old ones. They were not to convert anyone to their religion. They were not to wear the same clothing as Muslims, but to wear distinguishing garments. The sounds of their prayers, their calls to prayer, and their funeral processions were to be muted. Their houses were not to be higher than the houses of Muslims. The special tax on the *dhimmi*, however, was not mentioned in this document. Perhaps designed to encourage non-Muslims to gain first-class citizenship by converting, these rules were nevertheless not crippling to life, and, indeed, they were often unenforced. Travelers throughout the Muslim

KEY TERM

dhimmi Translates as "protected." A term applied to Jews, Christians, Zoroastrians, and others who were accepted as monotheists, like Muslims, and therefore eligible for protection that allowed them to practice their faith, but required them to pay a special tax.

world noted that Jews and Christians often held some of the highest positions in public and private life, and were self-governing in their religious life.

A principal goal of conquest, however, remained the creation of a *dar al-Islam*, a land with a government under which Islam could be practiced freely. This did not mean that the people of the land were forced to become Muslims, only that the Muslims among them must have the freedom to practice their religion and sustain their culture.

Later, when many Muslims lived under non-Muslim governments, the *ulama* declared that any government that permitted freedom of religion to Muslims could be a *dar al-Islam*. The alternative was a *dar al-Harb*, an "abode of war," which had to be opposed because it restricted the practice of Islam.

11.1

11.2

11.3

How did Muslims interact with non-Muslims?　11.4

The Crusades

At opposite ends of the Mediterranean, Muslims and Christians fought each other in war for centuries. The goals, for both combatants, were victory in the name of god and religion, but also political control and economic profit. For the Church, the centerpiece of this warfare was a series of campaigns, usually numbered as eight, fought between 1095 and 1291, in the name of recovering for Christians and Christianity lands in the Middle East that had fallen under Muslim control, especially the "Holy Land" where Jesus had lived and died. The participants, mostly men, but many women, too—mostly non-combatants, but also fighters; wives and sisters of male crusaders; and prostitutes accompanying the armies of the faithful—were called "crusaders" because they wore the emblem of the cross on their clothing. The Church promised them indulgences, formal promises of speedy forgiveness of sins, and swift entry into heaven after death.

After Arab armies captured Jerusalem in 638, they built new, glorious mosques to proclaim their own dominance, but they allowed Christians to continue their religious practices without hindrance and permitted Jews to return to Jerusalem officially for the first time since their exile by the Romans in 135. Centuries later, after Muslim Turkish armies won the Battle of Manzikert in 1071 and opened Anatolia to conquest, the Byzantine emperor Alexius I called on Pope Urban II to help roll back the Muslim advance and recapture Jerusalem and the Holy Land. The pope seized this opportunity to unite Western Europe and its various rulers under his own banner in the name of religion. He promoted the crusades and promised indulgences to those who fought. On a more earthly level, the pope promised that the property and assets of the crusaders back home would be protected in their absence. Many pious Christians responded to his call: rich and poor, men and women, old people and children. Christian rulers, knights, and merchants joined in, driven by religious inspiration as well as political and military ambition, and by the promise of trade opportunities that might accompany the establishment of a Latin kingdom in the Middle East. In the course of the first four crusades—the major crusades—more than 100,000 people participated.

At first, the European Christian crusaders were successful—and brutal. In 1099 they captured Jerusalem, killing about 3,000 of its Muslim residents, men, women, and children, and many Jews as well. They turned the Dome of the Rock into a church and the adjacent al-Aqsa Mosque into an official residence. The savagery of the crusaders—reported in both Christian and Muslim sources—ushered in centuries of confrontation far more bitter than ever before. At the time, however, Muslim leadership in the region was divided, and did not respond. Then Salah al-Din (Saladin; c. 1137–93), who had established a new dynasty in Egypt, organized his armies and recaptured Jerusalem in 1187. In the key battle on the way to Jerusalem, the Battle of Hattin, Saladin killed thousands of Christian soldiers and then beheaded the members of the Knights Templar and Knights Hospitaler who had survived. More crusades followed. When Richard I of England, called the Lion-Heart (r. 1189–99),

THE CRUSADES

First Crusade (1095–99)	Proclaimed by Pope Urban II, the crusade was motivated by the occupation of Anatolia and Jerusalem by the Seljuk Turks. The crusaders recaptured Jerusalem and established several Latin kingdoms on the Syrian coast.
Second Crusade (1147–49)	Led by Louis VII of France and the Holy Roman Emperor, Conrad III, this was a disaster from the crusaders' point of view.
Third Crusade (1189–92)	Mounted to recapture Jerusalem, which had been retaken by Salah al-Din (Saladin) in 1187. Personal rivalry between the leaders, Philip II Augustus of France and Richard I of England, undermined the crusaders' unity.
Fourth Crusade (1202–04)	This crusade against Egypt was diverted, at the instigation of the Venetians, to sack and divide Constantinople, which led to half a century of Western rule over Byzantium.
Children's Crusade (1212)	Thousands of children crossed Europe on their way to Palestine. Untold numbers were sold into slavery in Marseilles, France, or died of disease and malnutrition.
Fifth Crusade (1218–21)	King Andrew of Hungary, Cardinal Pelagius, King John of Jerusalem, and King Hugh of Cyprus captured, then lost, Damietta, Egypt.
Sixth Crusade (1228–29)	The Holy Roman Emperor, Frederick II (r. 1212–50), led the crusade that, through negotiation with the sultan of Egypt, recovered Jerusalem. The city was finally lost in 1244.
Seventh Crusade (1249–54), Eighth Crusade (1270–91)	Both led by the French king Louis IX (r. 1226–70), who was inspired by religious motives, but both were personal disasters. Louis died during the Eighth Crusade. He was later canonized.

captured Acre on the Mediterranean coast in the Third Crusade (1189–92), he massacred thousands of its men, women, and children. By 1291, however, Muslim forces had reconquered Acre—in an equally bloody victory—and all other crusader outposts. Although four additional crusades followed, none succeeded in capturing and holding any outposts in the Holy Land.

The crusader soldiers themselves were inspired by religion, but they also attacked many in their path for their own profit. As early as 1096, *en route* overland to Jerusalem on the First Crusade, crusaders paused to slaughter and plunder Jews, who were now seen as a threat to Christianity even closer to home than the Muslims of the Middle East. In 1204, during the Fourth Crusade, Roman Catholic armies, acting against the direct orders of the pope, attacked the city of Zara in Croatia, and Constantinople, the capital of the Byzantine Empire (their presumed ally). Instead of uniting Christianity and defeating the Muslims, these crusaders further divided an already splintered Christianity, and ultimately lost out to Muslims. Older research often terminated its study of the crusades at the end of the Eighth Crusade, in 1291, but more recent scholars see rivalry and battles between Christians and Muslims preceding the crusades for the Holy Land, and continuing for centuries after them. Many include under the term "crusades" additional battles in the name of the Roman Catholic Church against nonbelievers and non-Catholics throughout Europe. Sometimes they include campaigns of colonization in the name of the Church, such as the military conquest of South America. On the other hand, in 2000, Pope John Paul II publicly apologized for "violence in the service of truth" that sometimes characterized the Church's

Illustration of the Second Crusade (1147–49). Lance-bearing Christian forces face a Muslim army in this scene from the Second Crusade. The fleur-de-lys emblem, here sported on his shield by the French king Louis VII, was adopted at almost the same time by his opponent, the ruler of Aleppo. (British Library, London)

relations with others—especially Muslims and Jews—throughout the centuries. The very word "crusade" continues to carry powerful connotations of religious missions backed by armed force.

11.1

11.2

11.3

11.4

How did Muslims
interact with
non-Muslims?

A Golden Age in Spain

At the other end of the Mediterranean, in Spain, Islam flourished and coexisted with the Christian and Jewish communities of the peninsula. Through a century of immigration, conquest, administration, and intermarriage, beginning in 711, Umayyad and Berber invaders brought Islam to a central position in Spain. They also revitalized trade by breaking the Byzantine monopoly over the western Mediterranean, and they introduced new crops and new irrigation techniques from western Asia. Abd al-Rahman III (r. 912–61) asserted his independence from the Abbasids by declaring himself a caliph rather than just a sultan. A series of rulers expanded the ornate mosque at Córdoba, making it one of the architectural showcases of Islam.

Eastern scholars of law and philosophy immigrated to the flourishing court. Poets developed new styles, based in Arabic but also influenced by local Spanish and Latin forms. Greek philosophical and medical treatises were translated into Latin as well as Arabic, thus opening intellectual communication with the educated classes in Christendom. Although some Christians revolted against Islamic and Arabic inroads, and were killed in battle (850–59), many more adopted Arabic lifestyles.

By 1030, the caliphate in Spain had disintegrated. Various armed struggles had broken out between the provinces and the capital, between townsmen and rural Berber immigrants, and between converts and Arabs. The conflicts did not, however, impede the spread of Islam. As in the eastern Mediterranean, provincial administrations replaced the central caliphate and brought the culture of their courts closer to the general population. Sufis spread their ascetic and devotional teachings.

The vacuum in the central government did, however, provide an opening for various Christian forces to begin the *reconquista*, the Christian reconquest of Spain. In 1085 Alfonso VI (r. 1065–1109), king of León—then king of León and Castile—captured Toledo. By the mid-thirteenth century all of Spain, with the exception of Granada, was in Christian hands.

During the years of the *reconquista*, culture continued to flourish. Until the mid-thirteenth century, Christian rulers in Spain patronized the rich, hybrid culture. They translated the Bible, the Talmud, and the Quran into Castilian. Arabic texts on astrology and astronomy, and the philosophical works of Muslim thinkers, including al-Kindi, al-Farabi, and Ibn Sina, were translated into Castilian and Latin, as was the philosophy of the Jewish thinker Moses Maimonides and his codification of Jewish religious law. Spain was the entryway into Western Europe for classical writings and their reworking through the prism of Islamic civilization.

With the fall of Seville to the Christian *reconquista* in 1248, Granada remained as the only Islamic kingdom in Spain. Nestled on a spur of the Sierra Nevada mountains in the south, the city flourished thanks to an influx of talented Muslims fleeing the advancing Christian armies, and the enterprise and vigor of its rulers. Two of the kings of the Nasrid dynasty, Yusuf I (r. 1333–54) and Muhammad V (r. 1354–59, 1362–91), built a complex of buildings called in Arabic *Qalat al-hamra*, or the Alhambra. This red citadel served as their home, a city within a city. Their legacy is today the best-preserved palace of medieval Spain. (See illustration, overleaf.)

By the fourteenth century, Christianity had become triumphal and intolerant. Jews and Muslims were forced to accept baptism and convert to Christianity, although many of them continued to practice their original religions in secret. In 1478, at the request of the Spanish rulers, the Roman Catholic Church established the Spanish Inquisition to hunt down those suspected of being insincere converts, whether Jews (called Marranos) or Muslims (called Moriscos). The first Grand Inquisitor, Tomás de Torquemada, began his work in 1483, and brought people to trial not only for

The Court of Lions, Alhambra Palace, Granada, fourteenth century. The elegance of this courtyard, with its central fountain and a dozen stone lions whose mouths are waterspouts, testifies to the power and aesthetic taste of the last Islamic kingdom left in Spain, until the Christian *reconquista* was completed in 1492.

apostasy and heresy, but also for sorcery, sodomy, polygamy, blasphemy, and usury. Under Torquemada's direction, about 2,000 people were burned at the stake, making his name a watchword for the fanatical misuse of religious authority.

Granada fell in 1492 to the Catholic rulers Ferdinand and Isabella. Muslim rule in Spain was broken. In 1492 Ferdinand and Isabella expelled the Jewish population from Spain. After the unsuccessful revolt of 1499–1500, Muslims, too, had to choose between exile and conversion to Christianity. In 1566 use of the Arabic language was banned in Spain. The golden age of religious tolerance and cultural exchange was over.

View the **Closer Luuk: A Cordovan Ivory Jar** on **MyHistoryLab**

Judaism, Christianity, and Islam: *What Difference Do They Make?*

Judaism, Christianity, and Islam share many common ancestors. They are all monotheistic religions and believe in divinely given written scriptures. They observe many similar rituals and practices. These include encouraging regular prayer, providing charity for the poor, and valuing pilgrimage to sacred places. Each also promises that behavior will receive its proper rewards and punishments in the future, on earth and in an afterlife. Finally, all three balance and integrate strands of mysticism, legalism, and pious devotion. Given these commonalities, the three religions would appear to be naturally suited to coexistence and even to mutual reinforcement. And, indeed, at times, notably in Spain for many years, the three faiths have coexisted and gladly learned from one another. But such warm, reciprocally beneficial coexistence has been the exception rather than the rule.

Perhaps two factors can explain the friction that has often characterized the relationships among these religions. First, all three have been proselytizing religions—although Judaism abandoned this practice early in the Christian era—and their very closeness has made them bitterly competitive. Each has had some feeling that it has come the closest to the essential truths of God and the world, and that the others have failed to recognize this. Both Christianity and Islam, for example, accuse Judaism of stubbornly refusing to accept later revelations that modify and update its original truths. Both Judaism and Islam accuse Christianity of a kind of idolatry in claiming that God begat a son who was actually a form of God and who walked the earth in human form. Both Judaism and Christianity reject the idea that God gave a special, final revelation to Muhammad. In each case these religions have looked at one another and said that, despite elements of deep commonality, there exist also fundamental differences. Indeed, within each of these religions, at various times, internal divisions have turned one group against another amid cries of heresy and calls to armed opposition. Truth was to be maintained, asserted, and defended through the force of arms. (Religions with less insistence on doctrinal correctness, such as Hinduism and Buddhism, have had fewer, and less violent, religious wars.)

HOW DO WE KNOW?

Conversion and Assimilation

Only in the last two decades has serious research been done on conversion to Islam, asking exactly how the process worked. For example, Nehemia Levtzion edited a set of studies, *Conversion to Islam*, in 1979, examining the motives of converts. Levtzion argued that "assimilation" was a better term than "conversion" for describing the process of becoming a Muslim. People in conquered areas, especially, were not so much overwhelmed by political conquest as they were impressed with the richness of the culture that Islam brought to them. They found that their lives were enriched by the rituals, philosophy, art, and sense of belonging to a world system that came with joining the *umma*, the Islamic community.

Richard Bulliet's *Conversion to Islam in the Medieval Period: An Essay in Quantitative History* (1979) demonstrates that conversion took place at different rates in each of the six societies he examines: Arabia, Egypt, Iraq, Syria, Iran, and Spain. He notes the problems of finding data to understand the process, since "medieval Islam produced no missionaries, bishops, baptismal rites, or other indicators of conversion that could be conveniently recorded by the Muslim chronicler" (p. 4). For data, Bulliet examines the speed of adoption of Muslim names in each of the six societies. He concludes that rapid acceptance of Islam went hand in hand with a breakdown in central political rule. As centralized Islamic rule fragmented, paradoxically, Sufis carried the word of Islam more freely and with more backing from local governments.

We also know of the very large-scale assimilation to Islam by the Mongol successors of Chinggis (Genghis) Khan and of the followers of Timur the Lame (Tamerlane or Tamburlane). These ruling groups were assimilated by Islam because the new civilization they encountered offered them cultural, political, social, economic, and spiritual rewards that were not available in the religions and cultures of their birth.

Finally, the great assimilation that took place outside the heartlands of Islamic conquest, in sub-Saharan Africa and Southeast Asia, was carried by traders and later supported by Sufis and *ulama*. In both these huge areas, the trade networks by land and sea were so densely worked by Muslims that indigenous traders began to assimilate Islam into their lives, either from religious conviction or from the promise of trade advantage. They stayed to join one of the world's richest and most widespread civilizations, the *umma* of Islam.

- Nehemia Levtzion prefers the term "assimilation" rather than "conversion" to describe the process by which people adopted Islam. What does he mean by each term? Do you agree with his argument? Why or why not?
- Besides political rulers, what other groups successfully encouraged large numbers of people to accept Islam? In what geographical regions of the world were they most effective?
- What was the problem faced by Richard Bulliet in determining how many people accepted Islam? How did he attempt to solve this problem? Do you think his solution appropriate? Why or why not?

Second, as each religion developed, it sought the support of government. It often sought to *be* the government. Truth was to be reinforced by power. Basic competition over spiritual and philosophical truths spilled over into competition also for tax monies, office, land, the public acceptance of specific ritual and architectural symbols, and suppression of opposition. When they could, these religions marched through the world armed. Until recently, in the lands where they predominated, the state and religion were usually intimately bound up with each other, and in many places the leader of the state expected that his subjects would accept his religion as their own, or at least give it preferential treatment.

Historically, Christianity came to dominate the European lands formerly held by the Roman Empire and traveled with its European faithful to the New World. Islam dominated North Africa and the Asian lands formerly held by the Persian and Alexandrine empires, and it traveled with armies, saints, and traders to India and Southeast Asia. This identification of different religions with particular geographical parts of the world was typical also of Hinduism, identified with India and, to a much lesser extent, with Southeast Asia; and of Buddhism, identified with the Indian subcontinent, East and Southeast Asia, and the routes connecting them. Judaism, which lost out to its younger successors both in numbers and in gaining the support of governments, remained everywhere a minority religion, dependent on the tolerance of others, preserving the memory of its ancient homeland in Israel.

Nevertheless, amid the carving up of the world into zones of religious dominance backed by supportive governments and frequent warfare among religious groups, there were also times of mutually beneficial coexistence, sharing of cultures, and recognition of the commonalities of these religions and of the common humanity of their faithful. In many regions, such as the Middle East, and in cities along the various trade routes all over the world, members of different religions lived side by side, often developing mutual understanding, respect, and trust. And always the voice of the mystic, like that of Jalal-al-Din Rumi, called out for recognition of the oneness of God and the unity of God's universe:

> What is to be done, O Moslems? for I do not recognize myself.
> I am neither Christian, nor Jew, nor Gabr [Zoroastrian], nor Moslem.
> I am not of the East, nor of the West, nor of the land, nor of the sea;
> I am not of Nature's mint, nor of the circling heavens.
> I am not of earth, nor of water, nor of air, nor of fire;
> I am not of the empyrian, nor of the dust, nor of existence, nor of entity.
> I am not of India, nor of China, nor of Bulgaria, nor of Saqsin;
> I am not of the kingdom of Iraqain, nor of the country of Khorasan.
> I am not of this world, nor of the next, nor of Paradise, nor of Hell;
> I am not of Adam, nor of Eve, nor of Eden and [the angel] Rizwan.
> My place is the Placeless, my trace is the Traceless;
> 'Tis neither body nor soul, for I belong to the soul of the Beloved.
> I have put duality away, I have seen that the two worlds are one;
> One I seek, One I know, One I see, One I call.
>
> (McNeill and Waldman, p. 242)

CHAPTER REVIEW

THE ORIGINS OF ISLAM

11.1 What is the history of Islam, its origins and beliefs?

Islam, arising in Arabia, especially in the cities of Mecca and Medina, teaches submission to the word of God, which Muslims know primarily through the Quran, the book that records the teachings of God as they were transmitted to the Prophet Muhammad. Along with the Quran, stories of Muhammad's life, words, and deeds provide Muslims with models of the righteous life and how to live it. According to the Quran, Muhammad (570–632) was the most recent, and final, prophet of God.

SUCCESSORS TO THE PROPHET

11.2 What happened to Islam after Muhammad's death?

When Muhammad died, Muslims feared that the *umma*, the community of believers in Islam, would break up. Muhammad had been both the religious and political leader of the new Islamic community, and to preserve that organization, the leadership appointed one of Muhammad's close associates as his successor. The succession was disputed, however, and a series of civil wars was fought between rival factions.

SPIRITUAL, RELIGIOUS, AND CULTURAL FLOWERING

11.3 How did Islam flower outside the Arab world?

Even after the consolidated political leadership of Islam—the caliphate—fell to Mongol invaders, Islam continued to grow and spread. Descendants of the Mongols converted to Islam, as did many of the peoples of south and Southeast Asia. Muslim scholars, mystics, and merchants carried Islam throughout the Indian Ocean and the length of the silk road; trade caravans introduced Islam to sub-Saharan Africa. Today, virtually 60 percent of Muslims are descended from peoples who had no connection to the caliphate.

RELATIONS WITH NON-MUSLIMS

11.4 How did Muslims interact with non-Muslims?

From the earliest days of Muslim conquest, non-Muslims had three choices: convert to Islam; accept "protected," or *dhimmi*, status as worshipers of one God (Christians, Jews, Zoroastrians, and later Hindus); or fight against the Muslim state (few chose this option). A principal goal of conquest, however, remained the creation of a land with a government under which Islam could be practiced freely. This did not mean that the people of the land were forced to become Muslims, only that the Muslims among them must have the freedom to practice their religion and sustain their culture. Periods of fighting among the monotheistic religions alternated with periods of peace and mutual support.

Suggested Readings

PRINCIPAL SOURCES

Donner, Fred. *Muhammad and the Believers: At the Origins of Islam* (Cambridge: Harvard University Press, 2010). Discusses the innovations Islam introduced against the background of existing local practice.

Esposito, John. *Islam: The Straight Path* (New York: Oxford University Press, 1991). Clear, basic exposition of the development and significance of Islam by a lifelong, non-Muslim scholar.

——, ed. *The Oxford History of Islam* (New York: Oxford University Press, 1999). Brings together an array of clear, well-illustrated essays by outstanding scholars on the origin and evolution of Islam, including materials on law, society, science, medicine, technology, philosophy, and Islam and Christianity.

Hodgson, Marshall G.S. *The Venture of Islam*, 3 vols. (Chicago, IL: University of Chicago Press, 1974). Hodgson's classic reinterpretation of Islam, seeing it not only in alliance with political power, but also as an attractive global culture.

Keddie, Nikki R., and Beth Baron, eds. *Women in Middle Eastern History* (New Haven, CT: Yale University Press, 1991). Presents a wide variety of feminist perspectives on women in Islamic cultures.

Lapidus, Ira M. *A History of Islamic Societies* (Cambridge: Cambridge University Press, 2nd ed., 2002). A comprehensive, even encyclopedic account by a single scholar.

Lewis, Bernard, ed. and trans. *Islam from the Prophet Muhammad to the Capture of Constantinople*, 2 vols. (New York: Oxford University Press, 1987). Outstanding anthology of primary sources, grouped as politics, war, religion, and society.

McNeill, William H., and Marilyn Robinson Waldman, eds. *The Islamic World* (Chicago, IL: University of Chicago Press, 1983). Outstanding anthology of primary sources.

Watson, Andrew. *Agricultural Innovation in the Early Islamic World* (Cambridge: Cambridge University Press, 1983). An account of the major crops of India transplanted westward to the very ends of the Islamic world. A kind of precursor to the later Columbian Exchange.

ADDITIONAL SOURCES

Adas, Michael. *Islamic and European Expansion* (Philadelphia, PA: Temple University Press, 1993). Contains excellent interpretive historiographic articles on Islam in world history.

Ahmed, Leila. *Women and Gender in Islam* (New Haven, CT: Yale University Press, 1992). Demonstrates the variety of practices chronologically around the world.

Andrea, Alfred J. *Encyclopedia of the Crusades* (Westport, CT: Greenwood Press, 2003). A single volume brings together a brief, cogent introduction with entries on people, places, battles, concepts, and activities of the crusades, including the *reconquista* in Spain.

Bulliet, Richard W. *Conversion to Islam in the Medieval Period: An Essay in Quantitative History* (Cambridge, MA: Harvard University Press, 1979). An innovative assessment of the rate of conversion through a study of name change.

Costello, E.J., trans. (from Gabrieli Francesco, trans. from Arabic). *Arab Historians of the Crusades* (Berkeley, CA: University of California Press, 1969). Through the eyes of Arab historians, the crusades appear less religious, more brutal and cruel, and much more concerned with money, than in most Western accounts.

Dunn, Ross E. *The Adventures of Ibn Battuta* (Berkeley, CA: University of California Press, 1986). An interpretive study of the great Muslim traveler as an introduction to the culture and lands of his travels.

Eaton, Richard M. "Islamic History as Global History," in Adas, *op. cit.*, pp. 1–36. Brings new social-science sources to bear in interpreting the rise and significance of Islam.

——. *Essays on Islam and Indian History* (New York: Oxford University Press, 2000). Important revisionist views of Muslim–Hindu interaction, usually emphasizing the achievement of accommodation.

Embree, Ainslee T., ed. *Sources of Indian Tradition, Volume I: From the Beginning to 1800* (New York: Columbia University Press, 2nd ed., 1988). The outstanding anthology of primary sources.

Ferdowsi. *The Legend of Seyavash* (London: Penguin Books, 1992). Classic tales of the early rulers of Persia.

al-Ghazali. *The Faith and Practice of al-Ghazali*, trans. W. Montgomery Watt (London: Allen and Unwin, 1953). Tells of the tribulations of the master as he painfully sought a synthesis between legalism and mysticism in Islam.

Grabar, Oleg. *The Alhambra* (Cambridge, MA: Harvard University Press, 1978). A beautiful, scholarly account of the architectural marvel.

Hodgson, Marshall G.S. *Rethinking World History: Essays on Europe, Islam, and World History*, ed. Edmund Burke III (Cambridge: Cambridge University Press, 1993). A reassessment of Hodgson's classic scholarship on Islam to demonstrate its relevance to world history.

Ibn Khaldun. *An Arab Philosophy of History*, ed. Charles Issawi (London: John Murray, 1950). An abridgment of Khaldun's *Universal History*, the fourteenth-century classic of contemporary social science.

The Koran, trans. N.J. Dawood (London: Penguin Books, 1990). Probably the most readable translation.

The Koran, trans. M. Pickthall (New York: Alfred A. Knopf, 1930). An early translation into contemporary English created by a convert to Islam.

The Koran Interpreted, trans. A.J. Arberry (New York: Macmillan, 1955). The translation most acceptable to Muslim scholars.

Levtzion, Nehemia, ed. *Conversion to Islam* (New York: Holmes and Meier, 1979). Argues that conversion to Islam was

at least as much a cultural process of assimilation as a sudden change in belief.

——. "Islam in Africa to 1800s: Merchants, Chiefs, and Saints," in Esposito (1999), pp. 475–507. Very useful overview of many of the states and regions of sub-Saharan Africa.

Lewis, Bernard. *Islam and the West* (New York: Oxford University Press, 1993). Basic but controversial interpretive account of cultural and political interaction, by a master.

Maalouf, Amin. *The Crusades through Arab Eyes* (London: Al Saqi Books, 1984). Brings together accounts written by Arab historians and contemporary observers from 1096 to 1291.

Morony, Michael. *Iraq after the Muslim Conquest* (Princeton, NJ: Princeton University Press, 1984). Account of the conquests of Chinggis (Genghis) Khan, his successors, and their legacies.

Niane, D.T. *Sundiata: An Epic of Old Mali* (Harlow, Essex: Longman, 1965). The classic epic of the founder-ruler of Mali.

Riley-Smith, Jonathan., ed. *The Atlas of the Crusades* (New York: Facts on File, 1991). Some 80 maps, each prepared by an expert, chart the campaigns in Europe as well as in the Mediterranean and the Middle East, to 1571.

Robinson, Francis, ed. *The Cambridge Illustrated History of the Islamic World* (Cambridge: Cambridge University Press, 1996). Beautifully produced, one-volume scholarly introduction to the Islamic world, lavishly illustrated.

Trimingham, John S. *Sufi Orders in Islam* (Oxford: Oxford University Press, 1971). An account of several different Sufi *tariqas*, their leadership, history, and commitments.

Tucker, Judith. "Gender and Islamic History," in Adas, *op. cit.*, pp. 37–74. A succinct, provocative historiographical assessment of various interpretations of the status of Muslim women through the ages and around the world.

Vitray-Meyerovitch, Eva de. *Rumi and Sufism* (Sausalito, CA: Post-Apollo Press, 1987). Basic introduction to Rumi, his poetry, and his place in the Sufi movement.

FILMS

The Alhambra and the Reign of Queen Isabella of Spain (2006; 53 minutes). Slow-moving, but remarkable in showing the power of Isabella, her choice to be buried in the Islamic Alhambra, and good views of Islamic architecture and art.

Cities of Light: The Rise and Fall of Islamic Spain (2007; 2 hours). Explores the relationships among Muslims, Christians, and Jews, revealing a golden age, followed by ages not so golden. Tracks the development and transfer of knowledge and philosophy. Fascinating and comprehensive.

PART FIVE

TURNING POINT: TRADE

1300–1700

Trade Routes Connect the Continents

Many westerners, and especially Americans, begin the study of modern history with the voyages of Christopher Columbus. Historians often refer to this story, beginning with Columbus, as the "master narrative" because it has dominated the study of world history for many years and because it has been perpetuated by the "masters," the heirs of Columbus' voyages and conquests, the people who have benefited from them.

There are good reasons for identifying Columbus' four expeditions, between 1492 and 1504, as the turning point that ushers in the modern age in world history. They transformed the Atlantic from a moat that separated the eastern and western hemispheres into a bridge that joined them. They inspired Ferdinand Magellan (c. 1480–1521) to explore the Atlantic and the Pacific, bringing the entire globe into touch. The consequences were immense, and immensely different for different peoples. No sooner did Europeans "discover" the New World than they conquered much of the land and many of its peoples. European kings, merchants, and priests grew rich, powerful, and proud on the basis of the gold and silver they brought from the New World, the land they seized and cultivated there, the laborers they forced into servitude, and the souls they claimed for Christianity. Columbus opened the door.

The *Santa Maria* (front) versus a Chinese junk (behind). This illustration of the difference in size between the Santa Maria, Christopher Columbus' flagship in his voyage across the Atlantic in 1492, and a Chinese junk of the same time period, suggests the difference in commercial power between the Chinese and the Europeans. It was the desire to enter more fully into the vast Asian trade that led the Europeans, and Columbus, to attempt to find new routes to China and India.

Despite these dramatic and powerful changes introduced by Columbus' discoveries, more recent narratives frame the story differently. They start out with Columbus' goals; he landed in the Americas, but he had set sail in search of new sea routes to China and India. The lucrative Indian Ocean trade, from which Spain felt excluded, was his intended target. So the newer narratives begin with an account of the trade networks of this earlier period, usually from about 1300. By that date the sea routes were fully operational. Even the land routes, the silk routes across Asia, were functional once again, protected by their Mongol conquerors.

Newer narratives also underline the continuing independence of the great Asian nations, in particular India and China. Like Latin America, Asia succumbed to significant European control, but only centuries later, and with much more limited consequences for their cultures. The British conquest of India dates only to 1757. China's loss of some of its sovereignty to Europeans came later still, after the Opium War of 1839–42. From this Asian perspective, 1492 appears less compelling as a turning point. The newer narratives do not question the significance of Columbus' voyages in creating a new world geography, magnifying the power of the Spanish throne, and transforming South America into Latin America through the introduction of Christianity and the cultures and languages of Spain and Portugal. They do, however, consider these transformations in the larger context of the history of the entire world.

Our account of trade in world history follows these more recent interpretations. We begin in the period around 1300, when trade in the Indian Ocean was flourishing but Spain and Portugal were blocked from participating by the restrictions imposed by the pope, the power of the Ottoman Empire, and the economic dominance of the ships and traders of Venice. Sailing for Spain, Columbus attempted to outflank all these blockages and to enter that lucrative trade network through the back door, by way of the Atlantic. (Simultaneously, the Portuguese, facing the same obstacles, were also attempting to find an alternate route—by sailing around Africa.)

In the chapter "Establishing World Trade Routes," we study the geography of the principal pre-Columbian trade

King Edward I Returns from Gascony, anon., 1470. Miniature. This is an example of a ship with triangular lateen sails. Europeans adapted these sails from Arab models because they enabled ships to tack against the wind as well as run with it. (British Library, London)

routes by land and sea. They were not yet unified, or global, but they were capable of linking Western Europe, most of Africa, and Eastern Asia. We explore the role of traders and their relationship with political rulers from 1300 to 1500. Long-distance merchants coordinated delivery of goods from one end of Afro-Eurasia to the other. Through the thirteenth and fourteenth centuries Mongol descendants of Chinggis Khan provided security along central Asia's silk routes, opening them after hundreds of years of abandonment. Traders and travelers including Marco Polo and Ibn Battuta explored these routes; we read about a few of their adventures.

"The Opening of the Atlantic and the Pacific" chapter turns to the Atlantic and Mediterranean coasts of Europe, remote from the world's main trade routes, but developing on their own. As Viking sailors forsook their raiding expeditions and began to settle down in their northern lands, commercial shipping began to ply the waters between ocean and sea in greater safety. Shipping increased as Europe grew wealthier from improvements in agriculture and renewed urban growth. Epidemics sometimes accompanied trade missions. The devastating "Black Death" wiped out more than one-third of the population in many places from China to Western Europe, with relationships of wealth and power dramatically restructured in its wake. The businessmen and artisans of newly prospering European cities developed new institutions, such as guilds; supported new inventions, such as the printing press; and accepted new philosophies of business, such as early capitalism, based on free markets, risk-taking, and the principles of

Siege of Vienna by Turks on July 14, 1683, Frans Geffels, 17th century. Oil on canvas. The Ottoman Empire began in central Asia and extended most of the way across North Africa and well into Europe. In 1529, led by Suleiman the Magnificent, and again in 1683, Ottoman armies set siege to Vienna, Austria, but this was as far as they were able to reach. Subsequently, forces led by the Habsburg empire pushed them eastward. (Wien Museum)

supply-and-demand economics. Religious philosophy, too, was evolving to accommodate more earthly desires for personal profit.

Christian Europe was changing, in part, because it was learning from its Muslim Arab neighbors in Spain and on the Mediterranean's southern shores. Europeans incorporated into their fleets the caravel ships and triangular lateen sails used by Arab sailors. Christian scholars and artists began to reclaim the cultural heritage of the ancient Greeks and Romans, which they had forgotten, relearning them from the Muslims and Jews who had kept them alive. They called the culture that emerged a *renaissance*, a rebirth of humanistic creativity that had been lost for more than 1,000 years. Both the Church and prosperous businessmen supported the new forms of cultural expression.

Western Europe's economic growth was blocked, however, by Arab, Ottoman, and Venetian control over trade routes in the eastern Mediterranean and beyond. Portugal, situated on the Atlantic, set out to circumvent these obstacles by circumnavigating Africa; in 1488 Bartolomeu Dias rounded the Cape of Good Hope and showed that the venture was feasible. In 1492, when Columbus promised the new rulers of Spain that he could find yet another, competitive, new route to the riches of the East by crossing the Atlantic, and win new converts to Christianity into the bargain, they agreed to finance his risky venture.

Columbus' voyages did initiate new chapters in world history, as we see in the chapter "The Unification of World Trade." They opened vast new resources of wealth—in land, gold, silver, and captive labor—for Europe to exploit (or develop, depending on the point of view). They heralded the destruction of powerful Native American empires and the deaths of millions of Native Americans, through warfare and disease. They made South America into Latin America, by introducing and imposing the languages, culture, and religion of Spain and Portugal. The "Columbian Exchange" of crops enriched diets and nutrition throughout the world, but the exchange of microbes, especially smallpox, killed millions, especially Native Americans.

The Portuguese pushed on with their voyages around the coast of Africa; Vasco da Gama reached the west coast of India in 1498. They attempted to assert control over Indian Ocean shipping, and to tax it; local peoples viewed these impositions as a form of piracy. The Portuguese also sought to convert souls to Christianity, sometimes threatening death as the alternative.

In the longer run, northern Europeans in the Netherlands, England, and France, more devoted to commerce than were the Iberians, reaped still greater profit from the new, global opportunities. At about the same time, many of the northern Europeans accepted the Protestant Reformation, rejecting Catholicism in favor of new denominations. This conversion provoked a lasting historical debate over the relationship between commercial success and religious affiliation.

Other world empires responded to these developments in varied ways. Alarmed by the new power of the Western Europeans, Russia tried to catch up militarily and commercially, although the Russian monarchy jealously preserved its political powers. The Ottoman Empire was strong enough militarily to lay siege to Vienna in 1529 and to battle again to take the city in 1683—both times unsuccessfully—but its commerce slipped into the hands of foreigners, especially the French, and the empire began its long descent. The Mughals ruled India effectively from 1556 until the early 1700s, but then, as Mughal power faltered, Europeans began to expand from their small trading fortresses along the coasts deep into the interior of the country. The Chinese and the Japanese excluded most European commerce throughout this period, although Jesuit priests won hundreds of thousands of converts. India and China would ultimately succumb to European control, but only after centuries of internal decay that left them vulnerable.

The expansion of world trade and transportation also brought vast migrations. Millions left Europe in search of economic, and sometimes religious, opportunity. They founded "New Europes" in the Americas, South Africa, Australia, and New Zealand, as well as colonial outposts around the world. Millions of Asians migrated from one region of that immense continent to another. The armies of the Ottomans conquered and occupied Turkey; the Mughals conquered and occupied India; and the Safavids conquered and occupied Persia. Millions of Chinese migrated northward as they drove the Mongols out of China's walls and as hardy crops from the Columbian Exchange opened these new territories to fruitful cultivation. Urban concentrations increased as new dynasties and rulers constructed new capitals. Two of the most devastating changes in history also marked this period: the death of tens of millions of Native Americans, the victims of warfare and disease; and the forced transportation of some ten million people taken as slaves from Africa, mostly to work the sugar plantations of the New World. The chapter "Migration" introduces demography as a means of following the lives of these migrants, mostly common people, mostly illiterate, who left no written records. The individual stories of the migrants are lost, but the statistical methods of the demographers help us to recover their collective experience.

Turning Point Questions

1. Why have the expeditions of Christopher Columbus been identified as a turning point?
2. Where were the existing trade networks in Columbus' time, and who participated in them?
3. How important were the demographic changes of this period? Describe them.

12 Establishing World Trade Routes

The Geography and Philosophies of Early Economic Systems

1300–1500

Today, long-distance, international trade forms a substantial part of the world's commerce and includes even the most basic products of everyday food and clothing. In earlier times, however, long-distance trade represented only a small fraction of overall trade, mostly supplying such luxuries as silks, gold, and spices for the wealthy. Because these goods were extremely valuable relative to their weight, merchants could carry them over thousands of miles and still sell them for handsome profits. Some commercial goods, such as raw wool and cotton, were traded over intermediate distances of a few hundred miles. The transportation costs of such raw materials were justified by the **value added** during further processing into finished goods after importation.

Trade in the Gulf of Cambay, Boucicaut Master, India, 1410. Vellum. As the main port of northwestern India, Cambay excited the wonder of painters and artists in far-off Europe. This illustration from the *Livre des Merveilles* (*The Book of Wonders*) of 1410 represents Cambay's ships and traders in European guise—not surprisingly, because the artist had never been to the city. (Bibliothèque Nationale, Paris)

LEARNING OBJECTIVES

12.1 ((	12.2 ((	12.3 ((	12.4 ((	12.5 ((	12.6 ((
Understand the ways in which societies regulate trade.	Describe Asia's extensive trading networks.	Understand how the Chinese focus on internal trade affected its culture.	Understand the legacy of the Mongol Empire.	Know the goods that were traded across the Sahara.	Describe trade in the Americas before Europeans invaded.

((Listen on **MyHistoryLab**

How do societies regulate and control trade?

12.1

12.2

12.3

12.4

12.5

12.6

By far the largest share of trade before 1500 was local: food crops traded for local hand manufactures or raw materials. These goods were necessities, but they had little value in relationship to their weight. Often, they were bartered in exchange for other local goods rather than sold for money in more distant markets. This local exchange of goods is a fundamental part of local and regional history, but the study of world history focuses on long-distance trade and its importance in knitting together distant regions of the world.

World Trade: A Historical Analysis

12.1 How do societies regulate and control trade?

Historians studying world trade seek to understand its social as well as its economic consequences. What social benefits have been achieved by international trade? Who has benefitted? Who has been harmed? To answer these questions we must examine the rules and regulations of the various systems of trade. For example, was trade mostly open and free, allowing anyone to enter and take his or her place among the buyers and sellers, or was access restricted? Were prices negotiated directly between buyers and sellers, or did government or trade organizations or religious institutions fix prices and conditions of trade? What have been the trade-offs between benefit and harm under each system? These questions, of course, are not only historical. The present-day debate over the "globalization" of trade—the transformation of the world into a single marketplace—demonstrates their enduring relevance. Recurrent protests against the 159-member-nation World Trade Organization, as it seeks to expand and regulate international trade, vent the intense passions that continue to surround these questions today.

To what degree should governments regulate or control economic markets? In a completely **free-market economy**, conditions of trade would not be regulated; prices would vary only in terms of the relationship between the **supply** of goods and the **demand** for them, and people would be free to conduct business as they chose. Societies, however, do regulate trade. For example, governments that wish to ensure that everyone has food may declare that agricultural production should be expanded and industrial production limited. In wartime, governments may ration food and essential commodities to ensure that everyone has access to at least minimum quantities. By taxing some items at high rates and others at low rates, governments can selectively promote or limit production and trade. Business may be more or less regulated, but government never leaves it completely unregulated.

Even in the earliest societies, such as those of Egypt, Mesopotamia, and China, government officials, often in alliance with priests, had the power to regulate trade. Nevertheless, market economies based on private profit existed there as well. This trade for private profit was embedded in deeper political, social, religious, and moral structures of society. For example, governments intervened in civilian economies to ensure adequate supplies of war materials for their armies. Concern for the general welfare, or fear of civic unrest, encouraged other interventions to ensure adequate food and basic necessities for the poor; such scholars as Karl Polanyi and James Scott sometimes contrast this **moral economy** with the free-market economy. Governments, especially those not subject to democratic controls, can, of course, also be predatory, taxing their populations for the benefit of government projects and officials, without regard to the welfare of the people.

The Traders

To understand world trade, we must look not only at the systems of trade, their rules and regulations, but also at the traders themselves. Long-distance private trade

KEY TERMS

value added An economist's term for the increase in value from the cost of raw materials to the cost of finished products. It is the value added to the raw material by processing, manufacture, and marketing.

free-market economy An economic system in which the means of production are largely privately owned and there is little or no government control over the markets.

supply and demand In economics, the relationship between the amount of a commodity that producers are able and willing to sell (supply) and the quantity that consumers can afford and wish to buy (demand).

moral economy An economy whose goal is providing basic necessities for all members of a society before allowing any particular members to take profits; in contrast to a free-market economy.

KEY TERMS

KEY TERMS

trade diaspora A diaspora is a dispersion over far-flung territories of a group of people who have a common bond. Usually this is an ancestral bond, such as in the Jewish diaspora and the African diaspora. A trade diaspora refers to the network of international traders who relate to one another through the bonds of their trade.

silk route The set of rough roads or transportation links across central Asia carrying trade and cultural exchange as far as China, India, and the eastern Mediterranean.

flourished most profitably in major port cities around the world. The merchants who carried on this port-city trade were often foreigners, with some independence from local political and social structures. Although they might occupy marginal positions in their host societies, they held central positions in the international trade networks. These long-distance merchants encouraged and brokered trade between the society in which they were living and the far-flung networks of international merchants. They formed **trade diasporas**, networks of interconnected commercial communities living and working in major trade cities throughout Africa, Europe, and Asia. Trade diasporas appear in the archaeological record as early as 3500 B.C.E., and some endured for millennia.

During the height of the Roman Empire, for example, traders from Rome sailed the waters of the Mediterranean Sea and the Indian Ocean, on rare occasions all the way to China. Most of these traders were not ethnically Roman. Usually they were descendants of the major trading communities of the eastern Mediterranean: Jews, Greek-speaking Egyptians, and Arabs. Long after the sack of Rome, small religious communities of Jews, Christians, and Muslim Arabs persisted along the southwest coast of India, a legacy of these ancient diaspora traders. Typically, the merchants

AT A GLANCE: WORLD TRADE, GLOBAL (compare box in Chapter 13)

DATE	POLITICAL/SOCIAL EVENTS	TRADE DEVELOPMENTS	EXPLORATION
1050	• Almoravids destroy Kingdom of Ghana (1067)		
1100		• Age of Great Zimbabwe in southern Africa	
1150		• Papermaking spreads from Muslim world to Europe	
1200	• Foundation of first Muslim empire in India • Chinggis Khan establishes Mongol Empire (1206–1405) • Decline of Mayan civilization in Central America; rise of Incas in Peru • Rise of Mali, West Africa		
1250	• Osman I founds Ottoman dynasty in Turkey (1290–1326) • Emergence of Empire of Benin • Mongols fail to conquer Japan (1281)		• Marco Polo arrives in China (1275)
1300	• Height of Mali (Mandingo) Empire under Sultan Mansa Musa (r. 1307–32)		• Ibn Battuta's travels in East Asia and Africa (c. 1330–60)
1350	• Ming dynasty in China succeeds Mongol (Yuan) Dynasty (1368)		
1400	• Ottoman Turks establish foothold in Europe at Gallipoli • Aztecs form alliances controlling Central Mexico (1428)	• China reconstructs and extends Grand Canal • Zheng He's seven voyages (1405–33)	
1450		• Decline of Kilwa and Great Zimbabwe in southeast Africa (c. 1450)	• Bartolomeu Dias sails around the Cape of Good Hope (1488) • Columbus reaches the Americas (1492) • Vasco da Gama reaches India (1498)
1500	• Zenith of Songay Empire of the middle Niger region (1492–1529) • Hernán Cortés and Spanish conquistadores defeat Aztecs and seize Mexico (1519–21) • Francisco Pizarro and Spanish conquistadores defeat Incas and seize Peru		

who conducted trade were marginal to their host societies rather than citizens within them. They were not unregulated by the hosts, nor were they totally subordinated, but they were allowed to make profits in return for the economic benefits they brought to the port city.

In a world that had no international courts or legal systems, shared religion and ethnicity often formed the basis for conducting long-distance trade. For example, Jews were able to carry on international trade across the entire eastern hemisphere. Their religious diaspora in numerous distant points of settlement supported their trade diaspora. They were dispersed in small communities from China to Western Europe and Africa, and their common faith formed a bond of trust that enabled them to establish highly efficient trade networks. During the period of Tang–Abbasid control over the **silk route**—the eighth and early ninth centuries C.E.—Jews were a preeminent trading community along the trade routes linking Europe and China. Charlemagne's ninth-century European empire employed them to carry trade in southern Europe. Baghdad, astride many of the key trade routes in western Asia, held the most prominent Jewish community in the world at the time, and there were also notable Jewish communities in Calicut and Cochin in southern India and in Kaifeng, China. When the Portuguese explorer Vasco da Gama reached Calicut in 1498, a local Jewish merchant was able to serve as interpreter. Cairo, Egypt, one of the world's great trade centers, also sheltered a significant Jewish community, including many long-distance traders.

How do societies regulate and control trade?

12.1
12.2
12.3
12.4
12.5
12.6

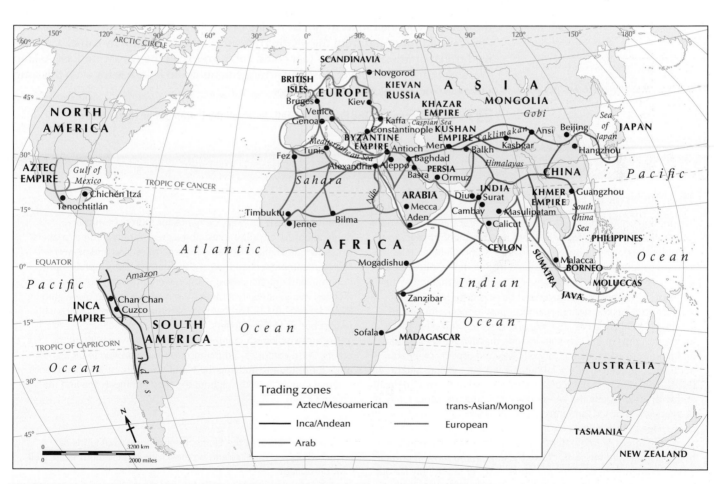

World trade routes. Between 1100 and 1500 a relay system of trade by land and sea connected almost all populous regions of Eurasia, as well as North and East Africa. Long-distance traders carried goods along their own segments of these routes, and then turned them over to traders in the next sector. The western hemisphere was still separate, and had two major trade networks of its own.

12.1
12.2
12.3
12.4
12.5
12.6

What were the
main Asian trade
networks?

Other groups of global traders also formed commercial networks on the basis of shared religion and ethnicity, although they were generally less extensive geographically, for example Christian Armenians, Jain and Hindu Gujaratis from western India, and Fukienese from the southeast coast of China. Like the Jews, these trading communities operated within their own social and religious networks, enjoying trade relations with local people, but not encouraging their religious conversion. On the other hand, overseas Muslim trade communities often sought to attract converts to Islam, as happened especially in Indonesia and Southeast Asia.

Asia's Complex Trade Patterns

12.2 What were the main Asian trade networks?

As the largest continent, with the largest population and the oldest civilizations, Asia contains trade networks that date back thousands of years. By 1250, a set of interlinked trade networks connected the main population and production centers of Asia, Africa, and Europe. The map "Trading ports and cities, Indian Ocean, 1200–1500 C.E.," opposite, illustrates the comprehensive geographic coverage of these networks. From east to west, Japan and China were linked by land routes to central Asia and by sea lanes to the Indian Ocean. Both land and sea routes continued westward to Arabia, western Asia, and on to the Mediterranean and Europe. Well-developed sea traffic linked also to the East African coast, where land routes extended into the African continent. North–south routes ran through China, central and western Asia, and Europe, and from the Mediterranean across the Sahara by camel. Centralized transportation companies that could carry goods all the way from East Asia to Western Europe did not yet exist, but arrangements could be made for even this long voyage to be completed stage by stage.

Read the **Document**: **The English in South Asia and the Indian Ocean (early 1600s)** on **MyHistoryLab**

HOW DO WE KNOW?

The Records in the Cairo Genizah

Information on Mediterranean cultures and their trade connections into the Indian Ocean, from the tenth through the thirteenth centuries, has come to historians from the Cairo Genizah (Hebrew for a repository of old papers), studied by Solomon Goitein from the 1950s through the 1980s. Jewish law requires that the written name of "God" not be destroyed but be stored for later burial; the Genizah was the storage point in Cairo for such documents for several centuries. Because paper was scarce and often reused, the manuscripts in the Genizah include massive bundles of notes and manuscripts on secular as well as sacred aspects of life: on trade and commerce, on social organization in general, and on the Jewish community in particular. Marriage contracts "state in detail and with great variety the conditions regulating the future relations of the newly married, and thus constitute a precious source for our knowledge of family life" (I:10). Wills and inventories of estates are "veritable mines of information" (I:10). Letters of correspondence, both personal and business, "form the largest and most important group [of manuscripts]. They are our main source not only for our knowledge of commerce and industry, but also for various other subjects, such as travel and seafaring" (I:11). "There are hundreds of letters addressed to various authorities containing reports,

petitions, requests for help, demands for redress of injustice, applications for appointments, and a great variety of other matters" (I:12). Religious responses are frequent, questions and answers between commoners and sages concerning religious philosophy, doctrine, and practice. Most women were illiterate, but they dictated many letters to scribes: "We hear the female voice guiding the male pen" (I:12). For the most part the writing is in Arabic, but transcribed in Hebrew letters.

Because the Jewish community was interwoven with all the others, these centuries-old manuscripts have proven to be a gold mine for historians studying the life of Cairo, its citizens, and their external connections throughout the Mediterranean Sea and the Indian Ocean.

- Given the nature of the Genizah repository, what kinds of record do you think would be most fully represented? Least well represented?
- How might records of family life and those dictated by women help to fill out the records of business transactions?
- How important was Cairo as a trade center at this time?

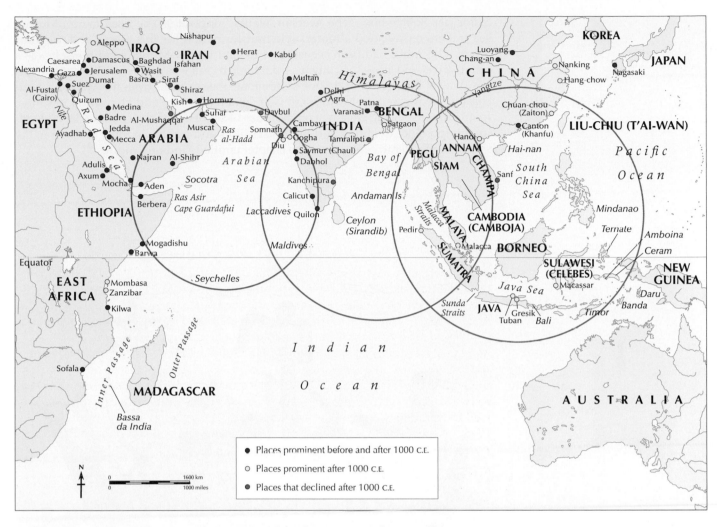

Trading ports and cities, Indian Ocean, 1200–1500 C.E. The Indian Ocean was the pivot of long-distance sea-borne trade from the Mediterranean to the South China Sea. Each of its port cities housed a rich diversity of merchants of many ethnicities and cultures. Trade goods did not travel on a single ship the whole length of this region. Rather, they would be loaded at a port in one of the three regions, offloaded and reloaded in the next for shipment to the third.

12.1

What were the main Asian trade networks?

12.2

12.3

12.4

12.5

12.6

The Indian Ocean

The great crossroads of the world's shipping lanes in the period 1300–1500 was the Indian Ocean. Its waters encompass three distinct geographical sectors, each with its own cultural orientation. The western sector—the Arabian Sea—extends from the East African coast across the ports of Arabia and continues to the west coast of India. From the time of Alexander the Great and the Roman Empire, Greek sailors plied these lanes. By the first century B.C.E. they had learned to use the monsoon winds to navigate these waters swiftly and efficiently. From the fourth to the eighth century, following the decline and fall of the Roman Empire, two new groups dominated this western region of the Indian Ocean: sailors from Axum (modern Ethiopia and Eritrea) and its Red Sea port of Adulis, and sailors from Sassanid Persia, a west Asian empire on the ascendant at the time.

Arab Traders. From the eighth to the sixteenth century, Arab Muslim traders and sailors became masters of the Arabian Sea, named for them, and the Indian Ocean sea lanes. This was the area made famous by the legendary exploits of Sinbad the

Sailor (see Source box, "The Arabian Nights," opposite). The rise of Arab Muslim sea traders represented a remarkable transformation for this ethnic and religious group. The Arabs had been accustomed to land trade—Muhammad himself was a camel driver and leader of caravans—but trade by sea was different. They took to this new way of life eagerly and came to dominate the sea lanes from the Mediterranean coast in the west all the way east to Guangzhou (Canton) and Hangzhou in China, frequently displacing existing communities of sailors. (For the commercial and cultural importance of Hindu and Buddhist sailors and traders in these areas from the seventh to the tenth century, see the chapter entitled "Indian Empires.")

Arab trader, illustration from the *Maqamat* of al-Hariri, twelfth century. Regional shipping routes linked into the oceanic, intercontinental routes. This ship, with Arab passengers and Indian, and perhaps African, crew, sailed the Persian Gulf connecting Mesopotamia and the Indian Ocean. (Bibliothèque Nationale, Paris)

SOURCE

The Arabian Nights

Arab Muslim traders of the Indian Ocean fill the pages of some of the best-loved tales of world literature. *The Thousand Nights and One Night* (also called *The Arabian Nights*), fables originally written in Persian during the years of the Abbasid Empire (750–1258), include the tales of the seven voyages of Sinbad (Sindbad) the Sailor, who won a fortune through a series of hazardous (if unbelievable) adventures at sea. The adventures—supposedly told night after night by Scheherazade to the emperor, Harun al-Rashid (r. 786–809), as a ploy to postpone her scheduled execution—are fanciful, but Sinbad's description of his departures on each of his voyages is based on the reality of Indian Ocean shipping. This translation from the beginning of the third voyage is by Richard F. Burton, who brought the complete tales to the English-speaking world in the late nineteenth century.

> I returned from my second voyage overjoyed at my safety and with great increase of wealth, Allah having requited me all that I had wasted and lost, and I abode awhile in Baghdad-city savouring the utmost ease and prosperity and comfort and happiness, till the carnal man was once more seized with longing for travel and diversion and adventure, and yearned after traffic and lucre and emolument, for that the human heart is naturally prone to evil. So making up my mind I laid in great plenty of goods suitable for a sea voyage and repairing to Bassorah [Basra], went down to the shore and found there a fine ship ready to sail, with a full crew and a numerous company of merchants, men of worth and substance; Faith, piety and consideration. I embarked with them and we set sail on the blessing of Allah Almighty and on His aidance and His favour to bring our voyage to a safe and prosperous issue and already we congratulated one another on our good fortune and bon voyage. We fared on from sea to sea and from island to island and city to city, in all delight and contentment, buying and selling wherever we touched, and taking our solace and our pleasure, till one day … [and here begin the fabulous adventures of the third voyage]. (*The Thousand Nights and One Night*, vol. 4, pp. 2031–32)

Islam encouraged trade. The *hajj* (pilgrimage to Mecca), required of every Muslim who could manage it at least once during his or her lifetime, necessitated travel, and international trade connections flourished as a result. A Muslim trade colony had operated in Sri Lanka as early as about 700 C.E. Arab traders sailed first to India, then to Southeast Asia, and some even on to the southeast coast of China. Muslim Arab traders also played critical roles in the development of African trade networks, by sea linking the East African coast to various ports along the shores of the Indian Ocean, and by land connecting north and south across the Sahara.

Lacking wood in Arabia, Arab sailors depended on others to build their ships, or obtained teak from southern India to build their own. For reasons that remain unclear, they did not use metal nails in the construction of their ships, but "stitched" the wooden planks together with coir—the fiber of coconut husks—or other fibers. Like the Greek sailors before them (and Malay sailors even earlier), they learned to sail with the monsoon winds. Catching the proper seasonal winds in each direction and using their **lateen sails** to maximum effect, sailors could complete a round trip from Mesopotamia to China in less than two years. The Arab Muslim Ahmad Ibn Majid included extensive recommendations on travel dates appropriate to the monsoon winds in his comprehensive fifteenth-century guide to navigation in the Indian Ocean.

Islam Spreads. Along with their trade goods, Muslims also conveyed their religious philosophies and practices. Distant merchants, who encountered Muslims in order to trade, often absorbed elements of Islam. In the thirteenth century, as the Muslim sultanate of Delhi came to rule northern India, many of the Hindu oceangoing traders, especially those along the west coast in Gujarat, converted to Islam. As they traded, they carried their new religion with them. In regions as distant as Malaysia and Indonesia, locals began to assimilate to the religion. Carried not by military power but by traders, Islam came to be the dominant religion in Indonesia (the most populous Muslim country in the world today), and to attract tens of millions of Chinese adherents. When the ruler of Malacca converted to Islam, about 1400, the trading circuit of Muslim merchants was complete. The entire length of the Indian Ocean littoral,

12.1

12.2

12.3

12.4

12.5

12.6

What were the main Asian trade networks?

KEY TERM

lateen sail A triangular sail affixed to a long yard or crossbar at an angle of about 45 degrees to the mast, with the other free corner secured near the stern. The sail was capable of tacking against the wind on either side. Lateen sails were so named when they appeared in the Mediterranean, where they were associated with Latin culture, although their origin was actually far away.

12.1

12.2

12.3 How did China's focus on internal trade affect its cultural growth?

12.4

12.5

12.6

from East Africa through India and on to Indonesia, housed a Muslim, largely Arab, trading diaspora.

Arabs did not sail into the Atlantic or Pacific oceans; they had no need. They sailed at will throughout the most lucrative seas of the world they knew. They had no problem of access. When Europeans explored new routes to reach the wealth of India and China in the fifteenth century, the Arabs were already there.

China: A Magnet for Traders

12.3 How did China's focus on internal trade affect its cultural growth?

By 1200 China was the world's most economically advanced region, a magnet for world trade. China is so huge, however, that its internal trade far outweighed its external trade. Others came to China to obtain its rich and varied products far more regularly than the Chinese traveled abroad in search of the products of others. China's policy towards trade varied during the centuries we are considering here, partly as a result of changes in imperial policy, partly in response to external pressure. Even though it possessed a highly integrated system of internal markets and reached extraordinary levels of agricultural and industrial productivity, the Song dynasty (960–1279) was overrun by Mongol invaders and had to abandon territory, relocate to the south, and reconstruct its economy. The Ming dynasty (1368–1644) overthrew the Mongols and undertook a series of spectacular ocean voyages. Then, in a reversal of policy, later Ming emperors forbade the Chinese to trade overseas. Nevertheless, merchants from abroad continued to pour in, eager to do business with the Middle Kingdom.

Internal Trade

When Marco Polo arrived in China from Venice in 1275, the splendor and wealth of the country overwhelmed him. He described its Mongol ruler, Kubilai Khan, as "the mightiest man, whether in respect of subjects or of territory or of treasure, who is in the world today or who ever has been, from Adam our first parent down to the present moment." Polo correctly reported that China in the late 1200s was the richest, most technologically progressive, and largest country in the world.

The foundations of China's wealth had been in place for centuries, its population, territory, power, and wealth growing through successive dynasties from Qin to Tang. Under the Song, China underwent an economic revolution. A revolution in agriculture underpinned the advance: better soil preparation and conservation; improved seeds that often allowed more than one crop per season; better water control and irrigation; and more local specialization of crops. The new techniques were implemented most intensively in the lower Yangzi valley, as the Song moved south from China's historic northern base around the Yellow River. Indeed, they maintained regional capitals, two of which also served as national capitals: Kaifeng in the north and Hangzhou in the south, near the mouth of the Yangzi. Thanks to the invention of woodblock printing in the ninth century under the Tang dynasty, ideas could spread rapidly. One of the first uses of print had been to conserve and spread religious concepts; the oldest printed book extant in the world is a copy of the Buddhist *Diamond Sutra* from 868. Now the new method of printing was put into the service of disseminating the new farming methods.

Agricultural improvements—plus China's traditional excellence in textile production and remarkable innovations in the most advanced coal and iron industry in the world—inspired a trade revolution. Common people became involved in the mass production of goods for sale. Domestically, this included the production of military goods for an army of over a million men. Trade became monetized, with copper

Going on the River at the Qingming Festival, Kaifeng, Zhang Zeduan, Song dynasty scroll. The multitude of Chinese junks on the Yellow River suggest the well-developed channels of trade in northern China. (National Palace Museum, Taiwan)

12.1

12.2

12.3

How did China's focus on internal trade affect its cultural growth?

12.4

12.5

12.6

as the principal currency. Chinese currency was so popular in Japan at this time that it became the most important medium of trade. In 1024, in Sichuan province, paper money was printed for the first time in the world. (Sometimes the government printed an excess of paper money, giving rise to inflation.) Merchants invented new credit mechanisms to facilitate trade. Government control of trade—quite marked under the Tang—was sharply reduced in favor of greater market freedom, and trade made up an increasing share of government revenue. Customs offices in the nine official ports, especially the largest, Canton and Zaitun (Quanzhou), collected import taxes of 10 to 15 percent of the value of goods. In 1128, maritime trade brought in 20 percent of China's total cash revenue. Merchants were valued for the taxes the state could collect from them. Those who paid the most were rewarded with official rank.

The international merchants were enjoying the peak of a highly integrated national system of trade and commerce, a system built on domestic as well as international water transport. To integrate the system of waterways, portage of goods was arranged at points of dangerous rapids and cataracts. To ensure smooth passage, double locks were installed on the man-made Grand Canal; this system helped to link the agricultural wealth of the south with the administrative cities of the north. Tugboats with human-powered paddle-wheels serviced the main ports. Chinese oceangoing ships, equipped with axial rudders, watertight bulkheads, and magnetic compasses, gained a reputation as the best in the world.

International Trade

As early as the fourth century C.E., the Chinese traded in the South China Sea and the Indian Ocean, although probably only as far west as present-day Sri Lanka (Ceylon). With the decline of the Tang dynasty in the ninth century, they largely withdrew from this oceanic trade and concentrated instead on inland issues, reflecting their geographical location in the Yellow River valley and the north. After 1127, however, they returned to oceanic enterprise, when the Song dynasty was driven from northern China by the invasions of the Tatars and other northern peoples. With various

12.1
12.2
12.3 How did China's focus on internal trade affect its cultural growth?
12.4
12.5
12.6

outside groups in control of the old overland silk routes, sea-borne trade was an obvious alternative. Thanks to their industrial innovations, the Song could supplement the traditional exports of silk and porcelain with products of iron and steel. To carry their expanding trade, the Chinese mastered the craft of building large ships, and Chinese merchants established new patterns of commercial exchange, including sophisticated credit systems. In addition to a merchant marine, China constructed a powerful navy.

The great luxury products of China—silk, porcelain, and tea—continued to attract thousands of foreign merchants. Many were Muslim Arabs; a few Lombards, Germans, and French also came to trade. They were treated as welcome guests, and special quarters in the port cities were set aside for them. In issues that involved no Chinese but only these foreigners, they could apply their own laws. Shops with foreign goods and foreign schools catered to their interests. Nevertheless, these merchants followed Chinese commercial rules, and many became quite Sinicized in their manners. When they ended their sojourn in China, they were often feted with large farewell feasts.

The Voyages of Zheng He. In the early years of the Ming dynasty, China's emperors adopted policies of expansionism by land and self-assertion at sea. The Ming emperor Yung-lo (r. 1402–24) dispatched a series of seven oceangoing expeditions under the Muslim eunuch Zheng He. The first voyage set out in 1405 with 62 large junks, 100 smaller ships, and 30,000 crew. The largest ships were 450 feet long, displaced 1,600 tons, and held a crew of about 500; they were the largest ships built anywhere up to that time. They carried silks, porcelain, and pepper. The first expedition sailed as far as Calicut, near the southwest tip of India. In six further missions between 1407 and 1433, Zheng He sailed to ports all along the shores of the Indian Ocean, at least twice reaching the East African ports of Mogadishu, Brava, Malindi, and Kilwa. Interested in exotic treasures that could not be found in China, Emperor Yung-lo seemed most pleased with exotic animals brought from distant lands, especially a giraffe sent to him by the sultan of Malindi on the fourth voyage, in 1416–19. These colossal expeditions demonstrated both the skill of Admiral Zheng He and the vision of Emperor Yung-lo. On the basis of these voyages, many historians believe that the Chinese would have been able to cross either the Atlantic or the Pacific Ocean—had they wished. But they did not push their expeditions any further and, in 1433, the Ming emperor terminated his sponsorship of the Indian Ocean voyages.

Why did the emperor end these voyages? Why did China not dispatch missions to Europe, and even to the western hemisphere? Why did the Chinese choose instead only to receive European shipping, beginning with the Portuguese in 1514?

Many answers seem plausible. The Ming turned their energy inward, toward consolidation and internal development. They pushed the Mongols out of China and beyond the Great Wall fortification along the northern border, but an invasion of Mongolia failed in 1449. Thereafter, the Ming limited their military goals. They rebuilt the Great Wall and restricted their forces to the defense of their land-based empire.

In 1411 the Ming reconstructed and extended the Grand Canal from Hangzhou in the south to Beijing in the north. The canal was a cheap, efficient means of shipping the grain and produce required by the northern capital. The man-made inland waterway also reduced the importance of coastal shipping, further enabling the Ming emperors to turn their backs on the sea. The faction of eunuchs, dedicated court servants such as Zheng He, who urged the government to continue its sponsorship of foreign trade, lost out to other factions that promoted internal development. International private shipping was also curtailed.

The Ming government limited contact with foreigners and prohibited private overseas trade by Chinese merchants. In 1371, coastal residents were forbidden to

CHAPTER TWELVE: ESTABLISHING WORLD TRADE ROUTES 1300–1500

12.1

12.2

How did China's
focus on internal
trade affect its
cultural growth?

12.3

12.4

12.5

12.6

A Chinese Junk, from *Jan Huyghen van Linschoten: His Discourse of Voyages into the East and West Indies*, Johannes Baptista van Doetechum, 1579–92. Engraving. Apparently first an invention of the Malay sailors of the South China Sea, and adapted by the Chinese, these ships could carry more than 1,000 tons of cargo and hundreds of sailors. (Private collection)

SOURCE

Chinese Ships in South Indian Harbors: An Account by Ibn Battuta

The fourteenth-century traveler Ibn Battuta (1304–c. 1368) did not usually comment on ships and sailors. He was far more interested in his encounters with people on land. In the south Indian port of Calicut, however, he was so impressed with the capacity and design of the Chinese ships that he gave a remarkable description. He notes that, while the Chinese allowed only Chinese ships to dock in their ports, the pilots and crew were not necessarily Chinese:

> We traveled to the city of Calicut, which is one of the chief ports in Malabar [the southwest coast of India], and one of the largest harbors in the world. It is visited by men from China, Sumatra, Ceylon, the Maldives, Yemen, and Fars [Persia], and in it gather merchants from all quarters … there were at the time thirteen Chinese vessels, and we disembarked. Every one of us was lodged in a house and we stayed there three months as the guests of the infidel [Zamorin ruler of Calicut], awaiting the season of the voyage to China. On the Sea of China traveling is done in Chinese ships only, so we shall describe their arrangements.
>
> The Chinese vessels are of three kinds; large ships called *chunks* [junks], middle-sized ones called *zaws* [dhows], and small ones called *kakams*. The large ships have anything from twelve down to three sails, which are made of bamboo rods

plaited like mats. They are never lowered, but turned according to the direction of the wind; at anchor they are left floating in the wind. A ship carries a complement of a thousand men, six hundred of whom are sailors and four hundred men-at-arms, including archers, men with shields and arbalests, who throw naphtha. Each large vessel is accompanied by three smaller ones, the "half," the "third," and the "quarter." These vessels are built only in the towns of Zaytun [Quanzhou] and Canton [Guangzhou]. The vessel has four decks and contains rooms, cabins, and saloons for merchants; a cabin has chambers and a lavatory, and can be locked by its occupant, who takes along with him slave girls and wives. Often a man will live in his cabin unknown to any of the others on board until they meet on reaching some town. The sailors have their children living on board ship, and they cultivate green stuffs, vegetables and ginger in wooden tanks. The owner's factor [representative] on board ship is like a great *amir* [nobleman]. When he goes on shore he is preceded by archers and Abyssinians with javelins, swords, drums, trumpets, and bugles. On reaching the house where he stays they stand their lances on both sides of the door, and continue thus during his stay. Some of the Chinese own large numbers of ships on which their factors are sent to foreign countries. There is no people in the world wealthier than the Chinese. (Ibn Battuta, pp. 234–36)

SOURCE

River Trade in China

China is such a huge country that most of its trade is internal; only a small fraction of local productivity makes its way to foreign markets. The vast and profitable trade in silk, both domestic and export, depended ultimately on the hard work of millions of spinners and weavers and their families. Similarly, river trade—some of which would ultimately be transshipped overseas—depended, at least partially, on the investments of common people. The four sources below support that assertion. The first is from Marco Polo, attesting to the abundance of river trade in China. The second is from Pao Hui, writing in the thirteenth century about the financing of overseas river trade. The third is a Song dynasty scroll illustrating the multitude of Chinese junks sailing on the Yellow River at Kaifeng. The fourth, a prose poem, describes the contribution of the women who produced and marketed the silk for which China was famous.

First, Marco Polo writes of the Yangzi River:

> I assure you that this river runs for such a distance and through so many regions and there are so many cities on its banks that truth to tell, in the amount of shipping it carries and the total volume and value of its traffic, it exceeds all the rivers of the Christians put together and their seas into the bargain. I give you my word that I have seen in this city [I-ching] fully five thousand ships at once, all afloat on this river. Then you may reflect since this city, which is not very big, has so many ships, how many there must be in the others. (cited in Elvin, pp. 144–45)

Then compare Pao Hui on the financing of river trade in Southern Song China:

> All the people along the coast are on intimate terms with the merchants who engage in overseas trade, either because they are fellow countrymen or personal acquaintances. Leakage [of copper currency] through entrusting occurs when the former give the latter money to take with them on their ships for the purchase and return conveyance of foreign goods. They invest from ten to a hundred strings of cash, and regularly make profits of several hundred per cent. (Shiba Yoshinobu, p. 33)

Third, examine Zhang Zeduan's twelfth-century scroll painting, *Going on the River at the Qingming Festival* (above). At this time, the city of Kaifeng, situated on the Yellow River and at the crossroads of some of China's most important canals, was the hub of water-borne traffic for all of northern China. Inland Kaifeng and Hangzhou, on the coast, were China's most important regional capitals. They formed the apex of a regional system of urbanization that unified the whole country.

Market towns sprang up throughout China, enabling almost every rural family to sell its products for cash and to buy city goods. In turn, the small market towns were linked to larger cities, which provided more specialized products and access to government administrators. Here, families could buy and sell, arrange a marriage, determine the latest government rulings, hear about new farming possibilities, and learn the dates and the results of academic examinations. These towns were so widespread that nearly every farm family lived within reach of one.

At the base were the rural families, struggling to survive by producing commodities demanded by the traders. Hand manufacture, especially of cotton and silk cloth, often supplemented farm production in rural areas. Invention made the process more productive. In particular, a reeling machine, invented around the eleventh century, drew several silk filaments at once from silkworm cocoons immersed in boiling water. It then drew the filaments through eyelets and hooks and finally banded them into silk thread.

The rural producers were integrated into the market system either through direct, personal access or through brokers who supplied raw materials and bought the finished product. Women were the chief producers in this supplemental rural industry. They also carried the finished product to market. Conditions of production and of marketing could be savage. Xu Xianzhong's "Prose Poem on Cotton Cloth," our fourth source, presents the harshness of both aspects. It is not clear whether the women in the marketplace are selling their cloth, or themselves, or both:

> Why do you ignore their toil? Why are you touched
> Only by the loveliness that is born from toil?
>
> Shall I tell you how their work exhausts them?
> By hand and treadle they turn the rollers of wood and iron,
> Feeling their fibre in between their fingers;
> The cotton comes out fluffy and the seeds fall away.
> The string of the cotton bow is stretched so taut
> It twangs with a sob from its pillar.
> They draw out slivers, spin them on their wheels
> To the accompaniment of a medley of creakings.
> Working through the darkness by candlelight,
> Forgetful of bed. When energy ebbs, they sing.
> The quilts are cold. Unheard, the waterclock flows over.
>
> When a woman leaves for market
> She does not look at her hungry husband.
> Afraid her cloth's not good enough,
> She adorns her face with cream and powder,
> Touches men's shoulders to arouse their lust,
> And sells herself with pleasant words.
> Money she thinks of as a beast its prey;
> Merchants she coaxes as she would her father.
> Nor is her burden lifted till one buys.
> (cited in Elvin, pp. 273–74)

12.1

12.2

12.3

How did China's
focus on internal
trade affect its
cultural growth?

12.4

12.5

12.6

Ink and watercolor print showing silk manufacture, Chinese, early seventeenth century. During the Song dynasty (960–1279), long-distance trade across central Asia dwindled. Maritime trade, with its very much safer and cheaper routes, now offered a viable alternative, and silk, along with porcelain and tea, continued to attract the merchants of the world. Unwinding filaments from silkworm cocoons in order to make yarn was considered women's work, as this Ming dynasty print suggests. (Victoria and Albert Museum, London)

travel overseas. In response to the smuggling that resulted, the government issued further prohibitions in 1390, 1394, 1397, 1433, 1449, and 1452. The repetition of this legislation reveals that smuggling did continue. Nevertheless, for the most part, private Chinese sailors were cut off from foreign trade. The government regarded the expeditions of Zheng He as political missions to exact tribute from outlying countries. Although products were exchanged on these voyages, trade was not their official purpose. So, while both private and government trade flourished in the interior of China, and while thousands of Chinese emigrated to carry on private businesses throughout Southeast Asia, China's official overseas trade came to a standstill. Zheng He's expeditions stand out as spectacular exceptions to the generally complacent and inward-looking character of the Chinese Empire.

The decision to limit China's international trade proved costly. Chinese society became introverted and, although economic growth continued, Chinese culture stagnated. Under the Song dynasty, Chinese technology had been the most innovative in the world. Creativity continued even under the Mongols, but by the beginning of the Ming dynasty, China was less imaginative. Military technology improved but

KEY TERMS

transhumance A pattern of seasonal migration.

yurt A portable dwelling used by the nomadic peoples of central Asia, consisting of a tentlike structure of skin, felt, or handwoven textiles arranged over wooden poles, simply furnished with rugs.

then it, too, stagnated. China had invented gunpowder before 1000 C.E., but used it only sporadically. In the early fifteenth century, Ming cannons were at least equal to those anywhere in the world, but metal was in short supply, and further development was limited. The Ming laid siege to few fortress cities, so they had little need for heavy artillery. In fighting against invasion from the north, the crossbow was the weapon of choice. At first, when China was much more advanced than its adversaries, decisions to limit further military innovation seemed inconsequential. Later, however, they would render the country vulnerable to distant, newly rising powers.

Central Asia: The Mongols and the Silk Routes

12.4   What is the legacy of the Mongol Empire?

The Song dynasty developed the waterways of China, but the great central Asian overland silk routes had declined after the ninth century along with the Tang dynasty that had protected and encouraged them. Under the Mongol Empire (1206–1405), the largest land empire ever known, traffic on the silk routes revived.

The two million Mongols who inhabited the plateau region of central Asia were divided into several warring tribes, each led by a *khan*, or ruler. The land was poor and the climate harsh. The Mongols shepherded their cattle, sheep, and goats in a circular pattern of migration called **transhumance**: in the brief summers they moved their herds northward to pasture; in winter they turned back south. They spent most of their waking hours on horseback and mastered the art of warfare from the stirrups, with bow and arrow as well as sword by their side.

Intercontinental Trade Flourishes

Cultural historians credit the Mongols with little permanent contribution because they were absorbed into other, more settled and sophisticated cultures. But they did establish, for about a century, the *Pax Mongolica*, the Mongolian Peace, over a vast region, in which intercontinental trade could flourish across the reopened silk routes. Reports from two world travelers, Ibn Battuta (1304–c. 1368) of Morocco and Marco Polo (1254–1324) of Venice, give vivid insights into that exotic trade route.

Ibn Battuta. During his 30 years and 73,000 miles of travel, Ibn Battuta commented extensively on conditions of travel and trade. For example, in central Asia he encountered a military expedition of Oz Beg Khan (d. 1341), the ruler of the *khanate*, or sub-empire, of the Golden Horde: "We saw a vast city on the move with its inhabitants, with mosques and bazaars in it, the smoke of the kitchens rising in the air (for they cook while on the march), and horse-drawn wagons transporting the people" (cited in Dunn, p. 167). The tents of this camp/city were Mongol **yurts**. Made of wooden poles covered with leather pelts, and with rugs on the floor, they could be readily disassembled for travel.

Later, Ibn Battuta was granted his request to travel with one of Oz Beg Khan's wives along the trade route as she returned to her father's home in Constantinople to give birth to her child. Ibn Battuta reported that the princess traveled with 5,000 horsemen under military command, 500 of her own troops and servants, 200 female slave girls, 20 Greek and Indian pages, 400 wagons, 2,000 horses, and 500 oxen and camels. They crossed from Islamic Mongol territory to Christian Byzantium.

Statuette of silk-route trader, Chinese, tenth century. Statuettes, found in tombs in China from the time of the Tang dynasty, record the presence of traders from Mediterranean regions who traversed the thousands of miles of the silk routes. From their features, scholars believe that they were Semitic peoples: Jews from the Fertile Crescent, Egyptians, and other Levantines. Some of them eventually settled along the trans-Asian routes. (Seattle Art Museum)

HOW DO WE KNOW?

The Mongol Empire

Because it was the largest contiguous land empire in history, understanding the entire Mongol Empire requires competence in the Mongolian, Chinese, Persian, Arabic, Turkish, Japanese, Russian, Armenian, Georgian, and Latin languages. No scholar can be expected to master all these, but serious scholars are expected to know at least one or two of them and to use others in translation. Surprisingly, Mongolian may not be the most important. Before Chinggis Khan, the language was not written and there are no archives of the Mongol Empire, at least none that have survived. The only major historical text in Mongolian is *The Secret History of the Mongols*, and, although some scholars think it inauthentic, it is our principal source for the biography of Chinggis Khan. Another text from his time, the *Altan Debter*, or *Golden Book*, is lost, but Persian and Chinese historians mention it, and their references show the book to be consistent with, although not the same as, *The Secret History*.

Chinese and Persian texts are the next most important, discussing Mongol rule over the two empires flanking, and captured by, the Mongol Empire. In China, the major text is the official dynastic history of the Yuan, or Mongol, dynasty. In Persia, several authors are important, most notably Rashid al-Din. Until his time, the Mongol conquest posed a problem for Muslim historians: the conquest of the Abbasid Empire was not supposed to happen. Muslims were to conquer others, as they had done with great consistency; they were not supposed to be conquered themselves. During Rashid al-Din's time, however, the Mongols converted to Islam. Rashid al-Din must have understood this well, since he himself had converted from Judaism. He wrote the history of the Mongol Empire, which, he said, marked a new era in world history. Later, he wrote *Jami' al-tawarikh* (*Collection of Histories*), recording the history of all the peoples touched by the Mongols from the Chinese in the east to the Franks in the west. It was the first example of the form of a world history. For the last 20 years of his life, until he was assassinated as the result of a court intrigue in 1318, Rashid al-Din served as principal adviser to the Il-Khan ruler of Persia.

In 1240 the Mongols captured and sacked Kiev, the most important city in Eastern Europe, and moved on into Poland and Hungary; a number of European sources discuss their conquests. These included such men as Giovanni de Piano Carpini, who was sent by Pope Innocent IV to visit the Khans, and William of Rubruck, who visited the Mongols at the behest of the king of France, Louis IX. The most comprehensive account is by Matthew Paris, who chronicled European reactions to the Mongol advances from his post at St. Albans, England. The most popular came from travelers, of whom the most famous was Marco Polo.

Reflecting on this array of European visitors, plus the Tunisian Muslim scholar Ibn Battuta, the Nestorian Christian Rabban Sauma, the Armenian king He'tun, the Chinese Confucian Zhou Daguan, and all the multitude of travelers who "journeyed along the traditional land-based Silk Roads … as well as the sea routes from West, South, and Southeast Asia to southern Chinese ports" (Rossabi, pp. 60–61), the historian Morris Rossabi concludes that "the Mongol period was the onset of global history" (p. 60).

- The most important biography of Chinggis Khan is in Mongolian, but Mongolian is not the most important language for the study of the Mongolian empire. How do you explain this paradox?
- Why are Chinese and Persian important languages for studying the Mongol Empire?
- Would you consider Rashid al-Din's *Collection of Histories* a history of the world? Why or why not?

Marco Polo. Marco Polo was a merchant in a family of merchants, and his account of his travels to and in China was particularly attuned to patterns of trade. His numerous descriptions of urban markets support the idea of an urban-centered trade diaspora. For example, consider his description of Tabriz in northwest Persia:

> The people of Tabriz live by trade and industry; for cloth of gold and silk is woven here in great quantity and of great value. The city is so favourably situated that it is a market for merchandise from India and Baghdad, from Mosul and Hormuz, and from many other places; and many Latin merchants come here to buy the merchandise imported from foreign lands. It is also a market for precious stones, which are found here in great abundance. It is a city where good profits are made by travelling merchants. The inhabitants are a mixed lot and good for very little. There are Armenians and Nestorians, Jacobites and Georgians and Persians; and there are also worshippers of Mahomet, who are the natives of the city and are called Tabrizis. (Polo, p. 57)

Central Asian routes challenged travelers and their animals. Despite the *Pax Mongolica*, merchants still had to be prepared to defend themselves from attack. As Marco Polo recounts,

12.1
12.2
12.3
12.4
12.5
12.6

What is the legacy of the Mongol Empire?

Among the people of these kingdoms there are many who are brutal and blood-thirsty. They are forever slaughtering one another; and, were it not for fear of the government ... they would do great mischief to travelling merchants. The government imposes severe penalties upon them and has ordered that along all dangerous routes the inhabitants at the request of the merchants shall supply good and efficient escorts from district to district for their safe conduct on payment of two or three groats for each loaded beast according to the length of the journey. Yet, for all that the government can do, these brigands are not to be deterred from frequent depredations. Unless the merchants are well armed and equipped with bows, they slay and harry them unsparingly. (p. 61)

For those merchants and statesmen who did reach Beijing, the *khan* maintained a massive service industry to provide hospitality. Polo noted, in particular, an army of prostitutes:

I assure you that there are fully 20,000 of them, all serving the needs of men for money. They have a captain general, and there are chiefs of hundreds and of thousands responsible to the captain. This is because, whenever ambassadors come to the Great Khan on his business and are maintained at his expense, which is done on a lavish scale, the captain is called upon to provide one of these women every night for the ambassador and one for each of his attendants. They are changed each night and receive no payment; for this is the tax they pay to the Great Khan. (p. 129)

Almost everything we know about Marco Polo's life is based on the colorful account he left us of his travels through Asia. Little is known of his childhood years in Venice or his education. Polo's father and uncle, both Venetian merchants, traveled from their home in 1260 on a trade mission as far as the northern end of the Caspian Sea. Then war broke out, and their route home was blocked. But the route eastward was open, so the brothers traveled on to Beijing, where Chinggis Khan's grandson Kubilai Khan (1215–94) ruled.

The Great Khan invited the men to return with more information on Christianity and a delegation from the pope. The information and delegation never materialized, but in 1271 the two brothers, bringing along the 17-year-old Marco, set out for China again. They arrived in 1275 and remained there for 17 years. How exactly they occupied themselves during this time is unclear from Marco's account, but it was not uncommon for foreigners to find employment in the Mongol state. Kubilai Khan, it appears, was so enchanted by Marco's tales of foreign lands that he sent him on repeated reconnaissance trips throughout the empire. The Polos eventually set off for home in about 1292, reaching Venice in 1295 and reuniting with relatives and friends who had believed them long-since dead.

Soon after his homecoming, Marco was captured in battle by Genoese sailors and imprisoned. He dictated the tales of his travels to his fellow prisoner Rustichello, a writer of romances. Europe now had its most complete and consistent account up to that date of the silk route and of the fabulous Chinese empire of Kubilai Khan. Marco's *Travels* was soon translated into several European languages, introducing to Christian Europe a new understanding of the world.

For seven centuries scholars have hotly debated the authenticity of Marco Polo's account. No original copy of *The Travels* exists, and scholars have been faced with some 140 manuscript versions that were copied in various languages and dialects from scribe to scribe before the invention of printing. In a book titled *Did Marco Polo Go to China?*, Frances Wood emphasizes the arguments against. Polo did not mention any of the phenomena that should have caught his attention during his reported time in China: Chinese writing, tea, chopsticks, footbinding, the Great Wall. Despite his claims to frequent meetings with Kubilai Khan, Marco Polo is not mentioned in any

Marco Polo, from *Li Livres du Graunt Caam, c.* 1400. The great world traveler is shown setting sail for China from Venice in 1271. Europe was eager for news of the Mongol Empire—potential allies against the Muslim enemy—and a steady stream of intrepid merchants and missionaries brought back amazing reports of the Khan's court. The exotic reminiscences of Marco Polo are by far the most famous. (Bodleian Library, Oxford)

Chinese records of the time. Wood concludes that Polo's work is actually based on materials gathered from others and that he himself never traveled beyond the Black Sea. As a travel narrative, Wood asserts, the book must be a fabrication, but as an account of what was known of China at the time, it is a rich and influential source of information. However, many commentators are equally adamant that Polo did complete all the travels that he claimed; the debate over the extent of his journeys continues.

📖 **Read** the **Document: Marco Polo on Chinese Society under the Mongol Rule (1270s)** on **MyHistoryLab**

12.1

12.2

12.3

12.4 What is the legacy of the Mongol Empire?

12.5

12.6

12.1

12.2

12.3

12.4   What is the
legacy of the
12.5   Mongol Empire?

12.6

Chinggis Khan and the Mongol Empire

The reopening and protection of the silk routes in the time of Marco Polo was the work of the Mongols, who emerged from Mongolia on a career of world conquest, led by Chinggis Khan. Temujin, later called Chinggis (Genghis) Khan, was born in about 1162 into one of the more powerful and more militant Mongol tribes. His father, chief of his tribe, was poisoned by a rival tribe. About three generations before Temujin's birth, one of his ancestors, Kabul Khan, had briefly united the Mongols, and Temujin made it his own mission to unify them once again. He conquered the surrounding tribes, one by one, and united them at Karakorum, his capital. Although skilled at negotiation, Temujin was also infamous for his brutality. Historian Rashid al-Din (1247–1318), writing almost a century after Temujin's conquests, reports his declaration of purpose, emphasizing women as the spoils of warfare: "Man's greatest good fortune is to chase and defeat his enemy, seize all his possessions, leave his married women weeping and wailing, ride his gelding, and use the bodies of his women as a nightshirt and support, gazing upon and kissing their rosy breasts, sucking their lips which are as sweet as the berries of their breasts" (cited in Ratchnevsky, p. 153).

Temujin defeated the Tartars and killed all surviving males taller than a cart axle. He defeated the rival Mongol clans and boiled alive all their chiefs. In 1206, an assembly of all the chiefs of the steppe regions proclaimed him Chinggis Khan—"Universal Ruler." He organized them for further battle under a pyramid of officers leading units of 100, 1,000, and 10,000 mounted warriors, commanded, as they grew older, by his four sons. Promotion within the fighting machine was by merit. Internal feuding among the Mongols ended and a new legal code, based on written and recorded case law, called for high moral standards from all Mongols.

Chinggis turned east toward China. On the way he captured the Tangut kingdom of Xixia, and from Chinese engineers he mastered the weapons of siege warfare: the mangonel and trebuchet, which could catapult great rocks; giant crossbows mounted on stands; and gunpowder, which could be launched from longbows in bamboo-tube rockets. In 1211, Chinggis pierced the Great Wall of China, and in 1215 he conquered the capital, Zhongdu (modern Beijing), killing thousands.

Chinggis departed from China to conquer other kingdoms. His officials and successors continued moving south, however, until they captured all of China, establishing the Yuan dynasty (1276–1368). They conquered Korea and large parts of Southeast Asia as far as Java, and attempted, but failed, to take Japan as well. The planned assault on Japan in 1281 was stopped by *kamikaze*, "divine winds," which prevented the Mongol fleet from sailing.

Chinggis himself turned west, conquering the Kara-Khitai Empire, which included the major cities of Tashkent and Samarqand. He turned southward toward India, reaching the Indus River and stationing troops in the Punjab, but he was unable to penetrate further. Turning northwest, he proceeded to conquer Khwarizm. In the great cities of Bukhara, Nishapur, Merv, Herat, Balkh, and Gurgan, millions were reported killed, surely an exaggeration, but still an indication of great slaughter. Chinggis went on to capture Tabriz and Tbilisi.

After Chinggis' death in 1227, his four sons continued the expansion relentlessly. In the northwest they defeated the Bulgars along the Volga and the Cumans of the southern steppes and then entered Russia. They took Moscow, destroyed Kiev, overran Moravia and Silesia, and set their sights on the conquest of Hungary. To the terrified peoples in their path, it looked as if nothing could stop the Mongols' relentless expansion. But in 1241, internal quarrels did what opposing armies could not: they brought the Mongol advance in Europe to a halt. During the dispute over succession that followed the death of Chinggis' son Ögedei (1185–1241), the Mongols withdrew east of Kiev. They never resumed their westward movement, and central and Western Europe remained untouched.

12.1

12.2

12.3

12.4

12.5

12.6

What is the
legacy of the
Mongol Empire?

Chinggis Khan in a book by Rashid al-Din, fourteenth-century. Ink and gouache on vellum. Most of the information we have on Chinggis Khan comes from the peoples he defeated, and they portray him as a brutal, bloodthirsty savage, but information from the Mongol perspective credits him with consolidating an array of local tribes into a unified nation, and introducing discipline, order, law, and careers open to talent. His conquests re-opened and protected silk routes that had been largely abandoned for almost a thousand years. (Bibliotheque Nationale, Paris)

In the southwest, under Chinggis' grandson Hülegü (c. 1217–65), the Mongols captured and destroyed Baghdad in 1258, ending the five-century-old Abbasid dynasty by killing the caliph. But in the next year, Möngke, Chinggis' grandson and the fourth and last successor to his title as "Great Khan," died while campaigning in China, and many of the Mongol forces withdrew to attend a general conclave in Karakorum to choose his successor. In 1260, Mongol forces were defeated by a Mamluk army at the

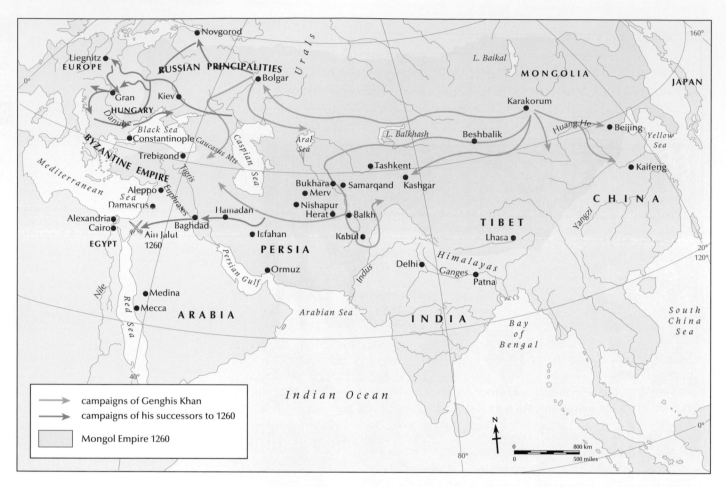

The Mongol world. The irruption across Eurasia of the Mongols, an aggressive steppe nomad people, remains one of the most successful military undertakings of all time. Within 30 years the campaigns of Chinggis Khan took the Mongol cavalry east to the Chinese heartland and west to Kievan Russia, the Caucasus, and Persia. His immediate successors consolidated China, entered Europe, and went on to establish a network of trans-Asian empires.

battle of Ain Jalut, in modern Jordan, ending forever their drive to the southwest (see map "The Mongol world," above).

📖 **Read** the **Document**: **The Mongols: An Excerpt from the Novgorod Chronicle, 1315** on **MyHistoryLab**

The End of the Mongol Empire

Mongol rule was extensive but brief. At their apogee, 1279–1350, the Mongols had ruled all of China, almost all of Russia, Iran, Iraq, and central Asia. The huge empire was administered through four separate geographical *khanates*, each under the authority of a branch of Chinggis Khan's family. Over time, central authority declined and the four *khanates* separated, each becoming an independent empire. Often they fought with one another.

The Mongols could not govern their empire from horseback, and they were soon absorbed by the peoples they had conquered. They intermarried freely with the Turks, who had joined them as allies in conquest. In Russia, Mongols and Turks merged with Slavs and Finns in a new Turkish-speaking ethnic group, the Tartars. In Persia and China they assimilated into local culture, converting to various

12.1

12.2

12.3

12.4 What is the legacy of the Mongol Empire?

12.5

12.6

12.1

12.2

12.3

12.4

12.5

12.6

What is the
legacy of the
Mongol Empire?

beliefs, including Christianity, Buddhism, and Confucianism. In most of the areas inhabited by Muslims, the Mongols and their Turkish allies typically converted to Islam.

As the four segments of Chinggis Khan's empire went their own separate ways, slowly they were driven from their conquests. By 1335, the male line of Chinggis and his grandson Hülegü died out in the Il-Khan Empire in Persia. The Ming dynasty defeated and evicted the Mongol rulers in 1368, ending the Yuan dynasty. The Chagatai *khanate* was destroyed after 1369 by Timur the Lame (Tamerlane, 1336–1405), a powerful Turkic leader who sought to recreate the empire of Chinggis Khan. In 1480, Russia's Ivan III defeated the Golden Horde (named not, as one might think, for their numbers, but for their tents, *ordu* in Turkish) and pushed them out of his territories, although the last Mongol state in the Crimea was conquered only in the eighteenth century.

The Mongol Legacy

The accounts of the merciless brutality of Chinggis Khan and the Mongols, recorded above, and earlier in "The Mongols and the Destruction of the Caliphate" in the chapter entitled "Islam," along with the claims of hundreds of thousands murdered and raped by their troops in war and revenge, present a picture of unchecked military sadism. But other accounts praise the Mongols for ultimately creating peace and stability in the lands they conquered, allowing the emergence of new economic institutions, technological innovations, and the flourishing of cultural, literary, and artistic creativity. The Mongols' tolerance also permitted various religious traditions to coexist. Even the historians, such as Rashid al-Din and Ata al-Mulk Juvaini, who write of the Mongols' merciless military devastations, credit them with allowing and encouraging humane administration, which took account of local traditions. This accommodation to local patterns of culture and governance became even more true in China under Kubilai Khan. While conquered women were treated savagely, Mongol women were highly valued as custodians of the homes and the herds of these nomadic warriors. Some, like Sorghaghtani Beki, Chinggis' war captive, daughter-in-law, and mother and teacher of four of the most powerful Mongol rulers—Möngke, Kubilai, Hülegü, and Arigh Böke—earned fame for their wisdom, power, and discretion.

Excavations in the Mongol capital of Karakorum, Shangdu (Xanadu), the summer capital of Kubilai Khan, and numerous Mongol sites in Russia have revealed exquisite artworks in gold, jade, silk, and porcelain, as well as frescoes. The Mongols may not have created these works, but they recognized their beauty and patronized their creators. Chinggis himself had a Uighur Turk scholar adapt the Turkic script for use as the first written language for Mongolian, although it was not widely accepted.

In terms of reopening the silk routes,

> Unprecedented contact between East and West was one of the most important Mongol contributions. The Pax Mongolica, or Mongolian peace, facilitated the exchanges of people, ideas, and technologies. The various Eastern and Western civilizations, which were exposed to foreign techniques and views, chose and modified whatever they borrowed from others to suit their own needs. Iranians introduced chickpeas, carrots, eggplants, and pasta to China; they translated Iranian medical texts into Chinese while a Chinese agricultural text was translated into Iranian, and Chinese motifs and techniques in porcelain influenced Iranian pottery. (Rossabi, p. 71)

The most famous travelers from the west to Mongol China are doubtless the Polo family, but their expeditions for trade followed earlier ones dispatched for religious reasons. After the Mongol victory at the Battle of Legnica in 1241, European leaders feared further invasion of Europe. Pope Innocent IV dispatched Giovanni de Piano

12.1

12.2

12.3

12.4

12.5

12.6

What goods were traded in sub-Saharan Africa?

Carpini to the Mongol Khans in 1245, to bring back more information and perhaps to negotiate some agreements. The mission ultimately led him to the Great Khan at Karakorum, but without any diplomatic or religious result. The king of France, Louis IX, sent William of Rubruck on a mission to Karakorum to convert the Great Khans to Christianity in 1253, again with no diplomatic or religious success. Nevertheless, links were created between Karakorum and Western Europe.

The Mongols were brutal, in the mold of empire-builders throughout history, but they were also creative, and they facilitated creativity in others. They valued trade and cultural exchange and they facilitated them as well, effectively reopening the silk routes that had lain unused for about three centuries.

From Mongol to Ming: Dynastic Transition

During the 90 years of Mongol rule, 1279–1368, China's population plummeted from a high of 100 million to just over 50 million. Despite the splendor of Kubilai Khan in his capital at Beijing, the Chinese economy did not serve everyone equally well. Marco Polo told of especially bitter poverty and class division in southern China, where the Han Chinese of the Southern Song dynasty experienced Mongol rule as cruel and exploitative: "In the province of Manzi almost all the poor and needy sell some of their sons and daughters to the rich and noble, so that they may support themselves on the price paid for them and the children may be better fed in their new homes" (Polo, p. 227). Revolution simmered until 1368, when the Ming dynasty overthrew the Mongols and ruled for almost three centuries, until 1644.

Under the Ming dynasty, the population increased sharply. By 1450 it had reached 100 million again, and by 1580 the population was at least 130 million. Plagues and rebellions caused the population to fall back to 100 million by 1650, but from that trough it rose consistently into present times. The population settled new territories as it grew. The origins of the Chinese Empire had been in the Yellow River valley in the north. At the time of the Han dynasty, more than 80 percent of the population of China lived north of the Yangzi valley. Under the late Tang dynasty, the population was divided about equally between north and south. Warfare with the Mongols in the north drove more migrants south, and at the height of the Mongol Yuan dynasty up to 90 percent of the population lived in the south. Economically, the south produced rice, cotton, and tea, three of China's most valuable products, not available in the northern climate. Closer to the sea lanes of Southeast Asia and the Indian Ocean, the south also developed China's principal ports for international commerce. The Song built a powerful navy and Chinese merchants carried on regular trade with Southeast Asia, India, and the Persian Gulf. After the Mongols were defeated, however, migration began to reverse. By about 1500, 25 percent lived in the north and movement back in that direction was increasing.

Trade in Sub-Saharan Africa

12.5 What goods were traded in sub-Saharan Africa?

Africa south of the Sahara was well integrated into extensive webs of trade relationships. In East Africa, traders along the coast procured gold and ivory from the interior of the continent and sold them to the seafaring merchants of the Indian Ocean. In far-off West Africa, traders dispatched caravans of goods on camelback across the Sahara, linking the merchants and rulers of the Mediterranean coast with the forest cultivators and miners in the south.

📖 **Read** the **Document: Strabo on Africa (1st c. CE)** on **MyHistoryLab**

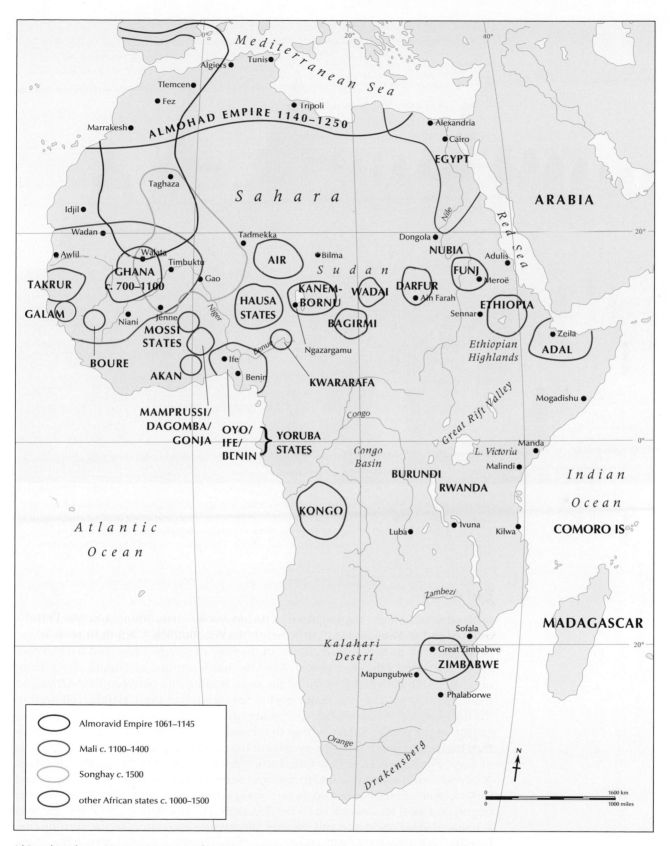

African kingdoms. Many states appeared in 1000–1500 in northern and western Africa, their power based on control over long-distance trade—gold, ivory, and slaves moving north; metalware, textiles, and salt carried south. Ghana, Mali, and Songhay are discussed in the text. These states, protected from marauders by the Sahara, could usually maintain their independence.

Mosque at Jenne, Mali, first built fourteenth century. The spectacular mud-brick mosques found in the major towns of the African savanna states, such as Jenne and Timbuktu, point to the acceptance of Islam by the merchant and ruling classes in the thirteenth and fourteenth centuries. The mud, which washes away in the rain, needs continual renewal—hence the built-in "scaffolding" of the structure.

East Africa

In the fourth century, the kingdom of Axum in Christian Ethiopia dominated the trade of the Red Sea and, to some extent, the Arabian Sea. With the rise of Islam, however, Arab traders gained control of the flow of merchandise, and Arab armies began restricting Ethiopian power. After the ninth century, and south of the Horn of Africa, Arab merchants provided the main trading link between East Africa and the Indian Ocean. The first major port to spring up had been Manda, followed in the thirteenth century by Kilwa. The ruling Arab dynasty along the coast also seized control of the port of Sofala further to the south. Through local African merchants they exchanged goods with the peoples of the interior, especially at the trading post of Great Zimbabwe. Here they found abundant supplies of such valuable metals as gold and copper (often cast into ingots) and animal products: ivory, horns, skins, and tortoise shells. Slaves were also an important commodity. Great Zimbabwe was the largest and most remarkable of all the developing towns. Architecturally, it featured a 100-acre stone enclosure and another 100 smaller enclosures in the surrounding region.

From these inland sources, goods were transported to the coastal ports and shipped onward to Arabia and India in exchange for spices, pottery, glass beads, and cloth. In the port cities of Africa's east coast, the Swahili language of the nearby

12.1

12.2

12.3

12.4

What goods were
traded in sub-
Saharan Africa?   12.5

12.6

Great Zimbabwe. The biggest and most celebrated of several stone enclosures in East Africa dating
from the tenth to the fifteenth century, Great Zimbabwe provided raw materials for trade at the coastal
settlements, especially gold, copper, tin, and iron, and was also a trading post for luxury goods—Islamic
pottery and cowrie shells were dug up at the site.

African peoples received from these Indian Ocean traders a strong admixture of
Arabic vocabulary, enriching Swahili and ensuring its place as the dominant language of the coastal trade.

📖 **Read** the **Document: Descriptions of the Cities of Zanj** on **MyHistoryLab**

12.1

12.2

12.3

12.4

12.5

12.6   How did
Americans trade
before 1500?

West Africa

The domestication of the camel in the second to fifth century C.E. opened the possibility of regular trans-Saharan trade. Oases provided the necessary watering points for caravans, as well as producing dates, a major commodity of trade. The first written records since Roman times of this trans-Saharan trade begin with the arrival of Muslim traders in the eighth century.

For the most part, African political units were local, but three large empires arose in succession around the northern bend in the Niger, near Timbuktu, where the sahel, the arid fringe of the desert, meets the vast Sahara itself. These three empires—Ghana (c. 700–c. 1100), Mali (c. 1100–c. 1400), and Songhay (c. 1300–c. 1600)—kept the trade routes open and secure. In contrast with most governments in other parts of the world, which amassed wealth and power by controlling land and agriculture, these empires of arid lands drew their power from control over trade, traders, and trade routes.

Gold, slaves, cloth, ivory, ebony, pepper, and kola nuts (stimulants) moved north across the Sahara; salt, dates, horses, brass, copper, glassware, beads, leather, textiles, clothing, and foodstuffs moved south. Gold was the central attraction. In the fourteenth century, the gold mines of West Africa provided about two-thirds of the gold used in trade in the eastern hemisphere. In 1324, when the Muslim emperor of Mali, Mansa Musa (r. 1307–32), passed through Cairo on his way to Mecca, he dispensed so much gold in gifts to court officials and in purchases in the bazaar that commodity prices in Cairo were inflated for years to come. A European map of 1375 showing a seated Mansa Musa as ruler of Mali is annotated as follows: "So abundant is the gold found in his country that he is the richest and most noble king in all the land."

There were many natural break-points for the north–south trade. From the Mediterranean coast to the northern fringe of the desert, trade was borne by packhorse; across the desert, via oases, by camel; across the arid sahel and the grassy savannah lands south of the Sahara again by pack animal; and, finally, through the tropical forest, impenetrable to larger animals and afflicted with the lethal tsetse fly, it was borne by human porters. For the most part, locally dominant trade groups carried the trade from one market center to the next in short relays. A few trading communities, however, notably the Soninke and, especially, their Mande-speaking Dyula branch, established trade diasporas that negotiated with the rulers.

📖 **Read** the **Document**: **Leo Africanus' Description of West Africa (1500)** on **MyHistoryLab**

Trade in the Americas Before Columbus

12.6   How did Americans trade before 1500?

The western hemisphere spawned two major trade networks. The northern network served primarily the area that is Mexico today, although in those years this region was dominated by several different groups. The southern network, in today's Ecuador, Peru, and northern Chile, ran north–south in two parallel routes, one along the Pacific Coast, the other inland along the spine of the Andes Mountains. East–west routes, linking the coastal settlements with those of the mountains, rose to altitudes of 15,000 feet. In both North and South America, goods were carried by pack animals and by humans; the American Indians had not invented the wheel. Boats were used on streams and rivers. Along the South American coast, near the equator, the Incas sailed boats constructed of balsa wood, while the Mayans of the Yucatán paddled canoes through their river systems. There was little traffic between North and South America and virtually none between the eastern and western hemispheres, except for rare voyages, such as that by Leif Eriksson, the Viking explorer who reached Newfoundland about the year 1000.

The Inca Empire

In the Andes Mountains of South America, a significant and long-lasting hub of civilization grew up after 600 C.E. A series of different peoples dominated the region, and by the time the Incas consolidated their empire in the early fifteenth century, these mountain peoples had built an extensive network of trade roads, connecting settlements over hundreds of miles north to south and linking some 32 million people (see map "Classic cultures of the Americas" in the chapter "A Polycentric World").

Inca trade was conducted up and down the mountainsides. With peaks as high as 20,000 feet, the Andes hosted several different ecological zones, encouraging product differentiation and trade. The valleys below produced sweet potatoes, maize, manioc, squash, beans, chile peppers, peanuts, and cotton. The hills above provided white potatoes, quinoa, coca, medicines, feathers, and animal skins. The highland people specialized in manufacture and crafts, including gold working.

The state controlled this trade between the ecological zones. Under Inca rulers, from the early 1400s until the Spanish conquest in 1535, many of the best of the 15,000 miles of roads through the Andes were open only to government officials.

Central America and Mexico

In the Yucatán peninsula of Mesoamerica the Mayan peoples had flourished from 200 B.C.E. to 900 C.E. Initially Mayan traders operated without interference, amassing a disproportionate share of wealth. Archaeologists suggest that the increasing wealth of the traders created social tension, and that ultimately the traders were brought under the control of the state, creating a new set of unequal relations dominated by kings rather than merchants.

By the time the Spanish arrived, in the 1520s, the Maya were in decline and the Aztecs dominated the valley of Mexico. The Spanish soldiers wrote vivid accounts of the great marketplace of the Aztec capital, Tenochtitlán, including this summary in a letter by the Spanish leader Hernán Cortés:

> This city has many squares where trading is done and markets are held continuously. There is also one square twice as big as that of Salamanca, with arcades all around … There are streets of herbalists where all the medicinal herbs and roots found in the land are sold. There are shops like apothecaries', where they sell ready-made medicines as well as liquid ointments and plasters. There are shops like barbers', where they have their hair washed and shaved, and shops where they sell food and drink. (Cortés, pp. 103–04)

The market met every fifth day, with perhaps 40,000 to 50,000 merchants swarming in, rowing their canoes across the lake to the island on which Tenochtitlán was built. In many ways, the market was like the great fairs of medieval Europe, drawing merchants from distant corners of the kingdom and beyond.

But how independent were these Tenochtitlán merchants? The Spanish described the city's market as being under tight government control. In addition to officers who kept the peace, collected taxes, and checked the accuracy of weights and measures, a court of 12 judges sat to decide cases immediately.

A guild of traders, called *pochteca*, carried on long-distance trade, which expanded steadily through the fifteenth century. They led trade expeditions for hundreds of

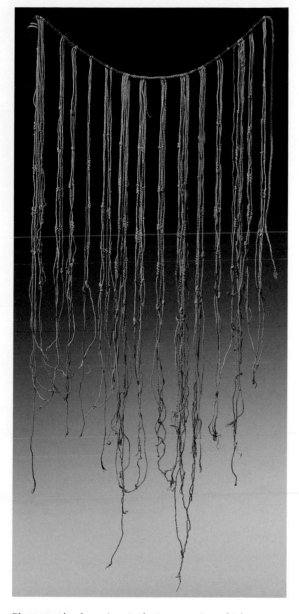

Photograph of a *quipu*. In the Inca empire, which extended from Ecuador to central Chile, trading was facilitated by an extensive road network. This *quipu*, a device of knotted string used to record dates and accounts, would have been a handy aid to the traveling South American businessman in the early 1400s. (Musée du quai Branly)

12.1

12.2

12.3

12.4

12.5

12.6

How did Americans trade before 1500?

La Gran Tenochtitlán, Diego Rivera. 1945. The great Mexican muralist Diego Rivera told the story of his people on the walls of several of Mexico City's most prominent civic buildings with a boldness that attracted casual passersby as well as art connoisseurs. His depiction of the Aztec capital, Tenochtitlán, before the arrival of Europeans, suggests the majesty of the city, but does not overlook the harshness of the life of many of its inhabitants. (Palacio Nacional, Mexico City)

12.1

12.2

12.3

12.4

12.5

12.6 How did Americans trade before 1500?

miles, exchanging city-crafted obsidian knives, fur blankets, clothes, herbs, and dyes for such raw materials as jade, seashells, jaguar skins, feathers from forest birds, and, in the greatest volume, cotton from the Gulf coast. The traders gathered both goods and military intelligence for the ruling Aztec families. Royal troops protected them and sometimes used attacks on traveling *pochteca* as a justification for punitive reprisals and the confiscation of land. The *pochteca* lived in their own wards in the towns, had their own magistrates, and supervised the markets on their own. They were to marry only within the guild and, although they remained commoners, they could send their sons to temple schools. Their main god, Yiacatecutli, resembles the Toltec god Quetzalcoatl, and this, too, suggests that they were to some degree foreigners living in a trade diaspora, with a high degree of independence from the state and temple.

The civilizational hubs in Mexico and in the Andes functioned independently of one another and both flourished, of course, prior to Columbus, and almost entirely isolated from the rest of the world. When Europeans arrived in the sixteenth century brandishing new weapons, commanding new military organizations, and transmitting new diseases, the Americans were unprepared for the challenges.

📖 **Read** the **Document**: **Tlaltecatzin of Cuauhchinanco: "Song of Tlaltecatzin" (14th c.)** on **MyHistoryLab**

World Trade Routes Before Columbus:
What Difference Do They Make?

The years around 1500 marked a turning point in world trade patterns. Before 1500, trading routes crisscrossed Africa, Europe, and Asia. These routes connected with one another, although they were not unified into a single system of trade. Long-distance trade goods would travel in stages, carried first by one set of traders and then transferred to another, as goods were transported to their final destination. The most important long-distance traders were the Muslim Arab sailors and merchants of the Indian Ocean routes and beyond to the ports of China. Chinese traders dominated the East Asian waterways and only occasionally sailed into the Indian Ocean. In the thirteenth and fourteenth centuries, Mongol rulers provided protection along the old silk routes, reopening these land passages through central Asia. At this time, however, few European traders ventured into eastern Asia.

Africa's west coast was fully integrated into these systems through Arabian Sea trade with Arabia and the west coast of India. The western regions of Africa were united among themselves, and with the Mediterranean coast, by caravan trade, especially after the domestication of the camel. The *hajj* pilgrimage assured that Muslim Africans, even from the western regions, would travel across that vast continent to reach Mecca; some would continue even beyond.

The western hemisphere had two sets of regional routes—mostly unconnected with each other—one centering on Mesoamerica, the other on the Andes Mountains of South America. The Americas remained separated from the rest of the world by the vast expanses of the Atlantic and Pacific oceans.

As European traders grew more active after 1500, they attempted to subordinate preexisting regional systems to their own centralized control from European headquarters. Within a single generation they seized control of the Americas. Asian countries, however, were much more powerful and tended to pay little attention to the newly arriving Europeans. Following early, problematic encounters, China and Japan mostly kept the visitors out. European control over global trade increased as northwestern Europe industrialized after 1750, after which the European traders and their governments, supported by new productivity at home as well as by new ships and new guns, began to assert themselves. They challenged the legacies of Arab and Chinese supremacy in the east, and Native American isolation in the west, and began to introduce new regimes of trade and domination into world history.

CHAPTER REVIEW

WORLD TRADE: A HISTORICAL ANALYSIS

12.1 How do societies regulate and control trade?

Networks of trade have flourished since at least 3500 B.C.E. Societies regulate trade in different ways, for instance by expanding or limiting production, or by taxing items at different rates. In wartime, governments may ration food and other commodities to ensure that everyone has access to minimum quantities. Sometimes governments trade through their own agents; sometimes they allow and encourage private trade; often they do both. They may allow anyone to trade, or they may restrict trading to only certain individuals or groups.

ASIA'S COMPLEX TRADE PATTERNS

12.2 What were the main Asian trade networks?

The main population centers of Asia, Africa, and Europe were connected by a set of interlinked trade networks that were thousands of years old. Japan and China were joined by land routes—the silk routes—to central and southern Asia and by sea routes to the Indian Ocean. Both land and sea routes continued westward to Arabia, western Asia, and the Mediterranean and Europe. Well-developed sea traffic linked to the East African coast, and land routes then extended into the African continent. The Mediterranean and sub-Saharan Africa were connected after about the second century C.E. by camel caravan routes across the Sahara Desert.

CHAPTER REVIEW (continued)

CHINA: A MAGNET FOR TRADERS

12.3 How did China's focus on internal trade affect its cultural growth?

Despite early years of oceanic exploration, later the Ming dynasty became inward-looking, and despite some policies of expansionism both across the Great Wall to the north and by ship across the Indian Ocean, by the sixteenth century the government limited its contact with foreigners and prohibited its merchants from trading overseas. Although economic growth continued, cultural growth stagnated. Where once Chinese technology had been the most innovative in the world—the Chinese invented gunpowder, woodblock printing, and many improvements in agriculture—it became less imaginative. Development of cannon work was limited, and Chinese soldiers even returned to the use of the crossbow.

CENTRAL ASIA: THE MONGOLS AND THE SILK ROUTES

12.4 What is the legacy of the Mongol Empire?

Although the Mongols are infamous for the stories of the brutality of their disciplined, horse-mounted armies, over time they created stability in the lands they conquered. This allowed for new economic institutions and technological innovations to emerge, and for cultural, literary, and artistic creativity to flourish. The Mongols tolerated different religious traditions; and they generally accommodated local patterns of culture and governance. Intercontinental trade expanded across the vast silk routes, which the Mongols reopened and protected. This unprecedented contact between east and west was one of the Mongols' most essential contributions.

TRADE IN SUB-SAHARAN AFRICA

12.5 What goods were traded in sub-Saharan Africa?

South of the Sahara Desert, African societies were well integrated into an extensive trade network. In East Africa, traders on the coast collected gold, copper, ivory, and slaves from the interior and sold the goods to merchants who carried them across the Indian Ocean. West African traders sent caravans of gold, slaves, cloth, ivory, ebony, pepper, and kola nuts north across the Sahara, and procured salt, dates, horses, brass, copper, glassware, leather, beads, foodstuffs, and textiles in return.

TRADE IN THE AMERICAS BEFORE COLUMBUS

12.6 How did Americans trade before 1500?

There were two major trading networks in the Americas: a northern network, which served the areas now known as Central America and Mexico; and a southern network, with two sectors, one that ran along the Pacific coast in the countries now known as Ecuador, Peru, and Chile, and another, parallel one, that ran along the spine of the Andes Mountains. Goods were carried by pack animals, by humans, and by boats on rivers. There was very little trade between north and south, but within each region trade, and trading cities, prospered.

Suggested Readings

PRINCIPAL SOURCES

Abu-Lughod, Janet L. *Before European Hegemony: The World System A.D. 1250–1350* (New York: Oxford University Press, 1989). A résumé of the principal trade routes around 1250. Unfortunately omits African routes.

Adas, Michael, ed. *Islamic and European Expansion* (Philadelphia, PA: Temple University Press, 1993). Key collection of historiographical essays on major topics in world history, 1200–1900. Articles by Richard Eaton and Judith Tucker on Islam and William McNeill on "gunpowder empires" are especially helpful for this unit.

Chaudhuri, K.N. *Trade and Civilization in the Indian Ocean: An Economic History from the Rise of Islam to 1750* (Cambridge: Cambridge University Press, 1985). A survey of goods, traders, ships, regulations, and competition among those who sailed and claimed to control the Indian Ocean.

Cortés, Hernán. *Letters from Mexico*, trans. from the Spanish and ed. Anthony Pagden (New Haven, CT: Yale University Press, 1986). Newest edition of Cortés' letters.

Curtin, Philip. *Cross-Cultural Trade in World History* (Cambridge: Cambridge University Press, 1984). Classical statement of the significance and ubiquity of trade diasporas.

Dunn, Ross. *The Adventures of Ibn Battuta* (Berkeley, CA: University of California Press, 1986). Dunn uses Ibn Battuta and his travels as the center-point of an analysis of Islamic life throughout the Islamic ecumene in the fourteenth century.

Elvin, Mark. *The Pattern of the Chinese Past* (Stanford, CA: Stanford University Press, 1973). Primarily economic history, focused heavily on the central questions of why China did so well economically until about 1700, and so badly after that time.

Mann, Charles O. *1491: New Revelations of the Americas before Columbus* (New York: Vintage Books, 2006). A popularly written survey, comprehensive and up to date. Also seeks comparisons between the past and the present.

Rossabi, Morris. *The Mongols: A Very Short Introduction* (New York: Oxford University Press, 2012). Immensely accessible, brief account by one of the leading scholars.

ADDITIONAL SOURCES

Bentley, Jerry H. *Old World Encounters* (New York: Oxford University Press, 1993). Survey of the range of crosscultural, long-distance encounters—especially through trade, religion, and culture—throughout Afro-Eurasia from earliest times to about 1500. Engaging.

Chaudhuri, K.N. *Asia Before Europe* (Cambridge: Cambridge University Press, 1990). Survey of the economic and political systems of Asia before the impact of colonialism and the Industrial Revolution. Comprehensive, comparative, and thoughtful.

Columbia University. *Introduction to Contemporary Civilization in the West*, vol. I (New York: Columbia University Press, 2nd ed., 1954). Very well-chosen, long source readings from leading thinkers of the time and place. Vol. I covers about 1000 to 1800.

Crosby, Alfred W. *Ecological Imperialism: The Biological Expansion of Europe, 900–1900*

(Cambridge: Cambridge University Press, 1986). The biological—mostly destructive—impact of European settlement around the world, a tragedy for native peoples from the Americas to Oceania.

Frank, Andre Gunder, and Barry K. Gills, eds. *The World System: Five Hundred Years or Five Thousand?* (London: Routledge, 1993). In this somewhat tendentious, but well-argued, account, globalization is nothing new.

Ghosh, Amitav. *In An Antique Land* (New York: Knopf, 1993). A novel, travelogue, historical fiction of Indian Ocean exchanges in the twelfth century and today. Captivating. Much of the tale is based on the research in Goitein's study, below.

Goitein, Shelomo Dov. *A Mediterranean Society: The Jewish Communities of the Arab World as Portrayed in the Documents of the Cairo Genizah*, 6 vols. (Berkeley, CA: University of California Press, 1967–83). Extraordinary research resulting from the examination of a discovered treasury of about 10,000 documents from about 1000 to 1300. Despite the title, gives insight into a variety of communities of the time.

Hanbury-Tenison, Robin. *The Oxford Book of Exploration* (New York: Oxford University Press, 1994). An excellent collection of primary sources on exploration.

Hourani, George Fadlo. *Arab Seafaring in the Indian Ocean in Ancient and Early Medieval Times* (Princeton, NJ: Princeton University Press, 1951, reprinted 1995). The standard introduction. Examines the trade routes and the ships before and after the coming of Islam.

Ibn Battuta. *Travels in Asia and Africa 1325–1354*, trans. from the Arabic and selected by H.A.R. Gibb (New Delhi: Saeed International, 1990). Selections from the writings of one of the greatest travelers in history.

Ibn Majid, Ahmad. *Arab Navigation in the Indian Ocean Before the Coming of the Portuguese*, trans., introduced, and annotated by G.R. Tibbetts (London: Royal Asiatic Society of Great Britain and Ireland, 1971). Translation of Ibn Majid's classic fifteenth-century guide for navigators, along with very extensive discussion by Tibbetts placing the author and work in context and discussing contemporary theories of navigation.

Komaroff, Linda, and Stefano Carboni, eds. *The Legacy of Genghis Khan: Courtly Art and Culture in Western Asia, 1256–1353* (New York: Metropolitan Museum of Art; New Haven, CT: Yale University Press, 2002). Lavishly illustrated catalogue of

blockbuster art exhibit, with numerous interpretive essays as well.

Levathes, Louise. *When China Ruled the Seas: The Treasure Fleet of the Dragon Throne, 1405–33* (New York: Oxford University Press, 1996). Scholarly study of the expeditions of Zheng He.

Menzies, Gavin. *1421: The Year China Discovered America* (New York: William Morrow, 2003). Menzies brings together many scraps of evidence in concocting the argument that Zheng He actually did sail to America. The evidence does not hold.

Polanyi, Karl, Conrad M. Arensberg, and Harry W. Pearson, eds. *Trade and Market in the Early Empires* (Chicago, IL: The Free Press, 1957). Fundamental argument by historical anthropologists that early trade was mostly regulated by rulers and priests.

Polo, Marco. *The Travels*, trans. from the French by Ronald Latham (London: Penguin Books, 1958). One of the most fascinating and influential travelogues ever written.

Ratchnevsky, Paul. *Genghis Khan: His Life and Legacy*, trans. and ed. Thomas Nivison Haining (Oxford: Blackwell, 1991). The current standard biography of the personally elusive Chinggis Khan.

Raychaudhuri, Tapan, and Irfan Habib, eds. *The Cambridge Economic History of India. Volume 1: c. 122–c. 1750* (Cambridge: Cambridge University Press, 1982). Collection of articles of fundamental significance.

Risso, Patricia. *Merchants and Faith: Muslim Commerce and Culture in the Indian Ocean* (Boulder, CO: Westview Press, 1995). Among the questions explored is "What difference did it make to be a Muslim?"

Schele, Linda, and David Freidel. *A Forest of Kings: The Untold Story of the Ancient Maya* (New York: William Morrow and Co., 1990). The story of the deciphering of the Mayan ideographs and the histories of warfare that they reveal, by two of the leading researchers.

Scott, James C. *Weapons of the Weak: Everyday Forms of Peasant Resistance* (New Haven, CT: Yale University Press, 1987). Peasants and the poor also have ways of resisting oppression. This eye-opening book shows how they work.

Shiba, Yoshinobu. *Commerce and Society in Sung China*, trans. Mark Elvin (Ann Arbor: University of Michigan, Center for Chinese Studies, 1970). Detailed, scholarly inquiry into the functioning of the Sung economy.

Shaffer, Lynda Norene. *Maritime Southeast Asia to 1500* (Armonk, NY: M.E. Sharpe, 1996). Useful survey on the voyages, trade goods, markets, towns, and government of the region—from earliest times.

Skinner, G. William. "Marketing and Social Structure in Rural China," *Journal of Asian Studies* XXIV, no. 1 (November 1964), pp. 3–43. Classic account of the interlocking structure of urban development in China from local market towns through national capitals of trade.

The Thousand Nights and One Night: A Plain and Literal Translation of the Arabian Nights Entertainment, 6 vols. in 3, trans. Richard F. Burton (New York: Heritage Press, 1946). These charming tales are set in a world of Arab sea trade.

Toussaint, Auguste. *History of the Indian Ocean*, trans. June Guicharnaud (Chicago, IL: University of Chicago Press, 1966). Broad historical sweep of exploration, trade, cultural exchange, fighting, and rule in and of the Indian Ocean from earliest times to the 1960s. Very useful survey.

Watt, James C.Y., and Anne E. Wardwell. *When Silk Was Gold: Central Asian and Chinese Textiles* (New York: Metropolitan Museum of Art in cooperation with the Cleveland Museum of Art; distributed by Harry N. Abrams, 1997). The catalogue of a blockbuster exhibit. See this and understand why silk was valued so highly. Available in pdf form on the museum website: metmuseum.org/research/ metpublications/When_Silk_Was_Gold_ Central_Asian_and_Chinese_Textiles.

Wood, Frances. *Did Marco Polo Go to China?* (Boulder, CO: Westview Press, 1996). One of the more recent, and lucid, statements of the controversy, by the head of the China Department at the British Library, London.

FILMS

Diego Rivera: Art and Revolution (1999; 11 minutes). A video news report from a Rivera exhibit in Los Angeles. Rivera's revolutionary proclivities appear in all his work, including his representation of pre-Spanish Mexico.

Secrets of the Silk Road exhibit, University of Pennsylvania Museum of Archaeology and Anthropology, 2010–11. Much of this remarkable exhibition is online, including a series of nine hour-long lectures by experts in the field. Begin at http://penn. museum/silkroad/events_lectures.php. The lectures, occasionally under different names, are also available on YouTube, but begin your access here.

The Vikings (2000; reissued 2011; 110 minutes). Demonstrates that the Vikings were much more than a nation of marauders and raiders. Impact on Europe, all the way to Russia and Byzantium. Up-to-date archaeological research.

13 The Opening of the Atlantic and the Pacific

Economic Growth, Religion and Renaissance, Global Connections

1300–1500

Until 1492, no continuous links connected the eastern and western hemispheres, although there had certainly been some voyages between them. The expeditions of Leif Eriksson and other Vikings from Scandinavia around the year 1000 are well documented and authenticated by the artifacts they left behind in their temporary settlements on the northeast coast of North America. Some of the foods of Polynesia—sweet potatoes and manioc—apparently came from South America, presenting evidence of contacts, even more fleeting, across the Pacific. However, permanent contact between the two major continental landmasses of the world was established only with Christopher Columbus' conquest of the Atlantic Ocean in 1492. The consequences for the people of both hemispheres were enormous.

French caravel, 1555. Watercolor on paper. The sturdy caravel, with its three masts and its array of both square and lateen (triangular) sails, was adapted by Europeans from the Arab ships of the Indian Ocean and became the ship of choice for oceanic exploration. Christopher Columbus and Vasco da Gama both sailed in caravels. By arming his caravel with cannons, Gama transformed it into a weapon of war.

LEARNING OBJECTIVES

13.1 ((•
Understand the changes that made the Atlantic voyages possible.

13.2 ((•
Describe the European economic and cultural rebirth, the Renaissance.

13.3 ((•
Describe the early world explorations of the Europeans.

((• **Listen** on **MyHistoryLab**

Oseberg Viking ship. The Vikings built magnificent ships that enabled them to sail the coasts of Western Europe, penetrate the Mediterranean Sea, trade on the rivers of northern Russia, and even cross the Atlantic, reaching North America. The Oseberg ship, named for the place in which it was excavated in 1904–05, was buried about 834, and remains one of the finest Viking ships still in existence. (Vikingskiphuset Museum, Bygdøy, Oslo)

We have seen that Arab traders and Chinese admirals (and Polynesian sailors) also had the capacity to cross the oceans before Columbus' expedition, but chose not to. Europeans, with the exception of the Vikings, also did not venture out into the oceans, so long as the ports of the Middle East provided access to the great markets of Asia. Only when that access was reduced and profits were curtailed, while their own economics and technologies grew stronger, in the fifteenth century, did they launch their voyages across the Atlantic. Even then, they were not exploring for new lands, but only for new routes to well-known markets. In a surprise that altered the history of the world forever, the attractions of Asian trade led, by accident, to the European discovery and conquest of entire continents, with their own civilizations, of which the Europeans had known nothing.

In order to comprehend the enormity of this turn of events, we briefly look backward in time to the economic and cultural transformations in Europe that made the Atlantic voyages possible, and then forward to the European economic and cultural **Renaissance**, or "rebirth," that accompanied and resulted from them. Developments in trade and commerce never take place in a vacuum, as these cultural changes make abundantly clear.

KEY TERM

Renaissance From the French for "rebirth," a period of cultural and intellectual creativity in Western Europe between 1300 and 1570. The artists and intellectuals who created the movement saw themselves reconnecting with the traditions of ancient Greece and Rome, thus giving a "rebirth" to European culture. The cultural rebirth was accompanied by an expanding urban economy, another rebirth.

415

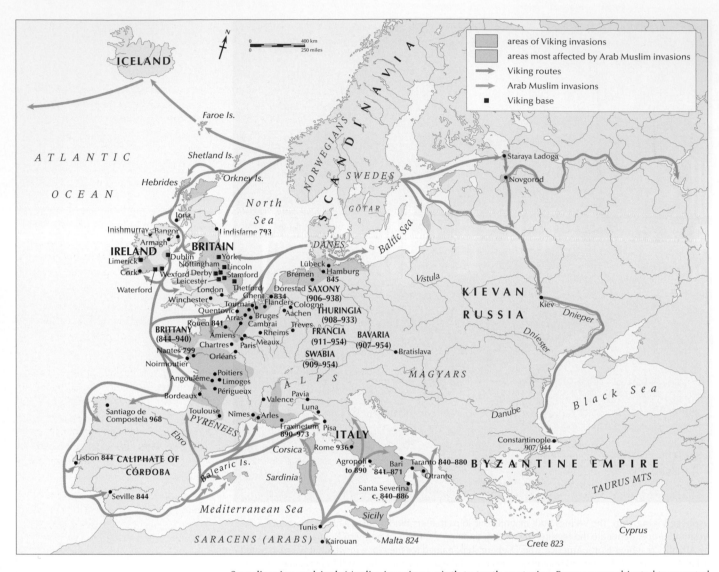

Scandinavian and Arab Muslim invasions, ninth to tenth centuries. Europe was subjected to repeated invasions that temporarily disturbed the continent but then increased its power. The Vikings, north Germanic peoples, settled and developed Scandinavia, and their interaction with the Slavs gave shape to Russia. The Muslims brought with them an understanding of the culture of ancient Greece and Rome that Europeans had forgotten. (Adapted from *The Times Atlas of World History*, 5th ed., London: Times Books.)

13.1
13.2 What changes in Western Europe made Atlantic explorations possible?
13.3

Economic and Social Changes in Europe

13.1 What changes in Western Europe made Atlantic explorations possible?

By the mid-1200s, Western Europeans were beginning to emerge from agrarian, manorial economies and from the localized political systems of administration and order that had marked the Middle Ages. As forests were cut down and additional lands were brought under metal-tipped plows pulled by horses with more efficient harnesses, agricultural productivity increased. Crop surpluses became available for sale to feed the craftsmen and merchants who began to migrate from the countryside into towns. Cities, which for centuries centered primarily on their churches, now increased the size of their marketplaces. Giovanni Villani describes the patterns of consumption in Florence, Italy, in 1338. Its population of about 100,000 made it the

HOW DO WE KNOW?

"Eurocentric" History?

As the study of world history moves toward modern times, a central question arises: How much attention, and what kind of attention, should we allot to the role of Europe? To what degree should world history be "Eurocentric"? The question has two dimensions: How significant were Europe's innovations, spread throughout the world by industrialization and imperialism? On balance, was Europe's influence beneficial or detrimental?

Europe usually gets more space than other regions in the modern world, because many innovations that have made the modern world what it is—capitalism, the nation-state, the Industrial Revolution, global imperialism—found first and deepest expression in the West. Some historians, such as David Landes, who is renowned for his studies in the history of economics and technology, therefore embraced a Eurocentric approach enthusiastically. "As the historical record shows, for the last thousand years, Europe (the West) has been the prime mover of development and modernity" (Landes, p. xxi). And, Landes argues, development and modernity have been for the best: "Some would say that Eurocentrism is bad for us, indeed bad for the world, hence to be avoided. Those people should avoid it. As for me, I prefer truth to goodthink. I feel surer of my ground" (p. xxi).

William McNeill, author of the influential world history *The Rise of the West* (1963), responded more cautiously. When his classic book was republished in 1991, he wrote a retrospective introduction, in which he regretted some elements of his earlier excessive "Eurocentrism": "I gave undue attention to Latin Christendom," he wrote (p. xviii); "My failure to understand China's primacy between A.D. 1000 and 1500 is particularly regrettable" (p. xix).

How had McNeill made these two interrelated errors? First, he explains, "*The Rise of the West* tends to march with big battalions, looking at history from the point of view of the winners—that is, of the skilled and privileged managers of society—and shows scant concern for the sufferings of the victims of historical change." Second, "in the years 1954 to 1963, when the book was being written, the United States was, of course, passing through the apex of its postwar capacity to influence others thanks to its superior skills and wealth." Looking for "winners," McNeill read the emerging American power—based on earlier European power—of his own day backward into the past. Nevertheless, McNeill presents not an abject apology for his earlier writing,

but an explanation: Winners do have disproportionate influence compared to victims; America's rise to power was a part of world history. Eurocentricity (including its American offspring) seemed a natural approach.

From his revised perspective, however, McNeill suggests an alternative to Eurocentrism:

"I should have made room for the ecumenical process. How this might be done remains to be seen. Somehow an appreciation of the autonomy of separate civilizations (and of all the other less massive and less skilled cultures of the earth) across the past two thousand years needs to be combined with the portrait of an emerging world system, connecting greater and greater numbers of persons across civilized boundaries" (p. xxii).

Many scholars have come to a similar conclusion and have chosen to emphasize the interconnections among peoples. In *Europe and the People without History* (1982), Eric Wolf, a historical anthropologist, writes:

"Following the global effects of European expansion leads to a consideration of the search for American silver, the fur trade, the slave trade, and the quest for new sources of wealth in Asia ... I then trace the transition to capitalism in the course of the industrial revolution, examine its impact on areas of the world supplying resources to the industrial centers, and sketch out the formation of working classes and their migrations within and between the continents" (p. 23).

Europeans may have initiated many of these changes, but each of the world's peoples responded in its own way.

The Indian-born, Western-educated historian and anthropologist Dipesh Chakrabarty takes Wolf's position a step further. He acknowledges the enormous contribution of the West to the modern world:

Concepts such as citizenship, the state, civil society, public sphere, human rights, equality before the law, the individual, distinctions between public and private, the idea of the subject, democracy, popular sovereignty, social justice, scientific rationality, and so on all bear the burden of European thought and history. One simply cannot think of political modernity

continued p. 418

fifth largest city in Europe, and every day its residents consumed "over 2,300 bushels of grain and drank in excess of 70,000 quarts of wine. Some 4,000 cattle and 100,000 sheep, goats, and swine were slaughtered each year to provide the city with meat" (cited in Brucker, pp. 51–52). The basis of Florence's wealth, like that of many cities in northern Italy and Flanders, in particular, was the manufacture of cloth. Villani reports that its textile industry employed 30,000 workers. As their manufacture and trade increased, Western Europeans felt increasingly aggrieved by the difficulty of doing business in the Middle East and the eastern Mediterranean.

What changes in Western Europe made Atlantic explorations possible?

13.1

13.2

13.3

View the **Closer Look**: **The Joys and Pains of the Medieval Joust** on **MyHistoryLab**

HOW DO WE KNOW? (continued)

"Eurocentric" History?

without these and other related concepts that found a climactic form in the course of the European Enlightenment and the nineteenth century. (Chakrabarty, p. 4)

But Chakrabarty cautions against the Eurocentric argument that European innovations would later be adopted wholesale by the rest of the world, "first in Europe, then elsewhere". Instead, like Wolf, he argues that peoples of other regions have adapted these innovations, each in their own way. One of his first examples is universal suffrage. Introduced first in the West, where literacy rates were relatively high, it was subsequently introduced more widely, including in countries, such as India, with very low levels of literacy. But India is not simply in the preliminary stages of developing European democracy. It is generating a new form of democracy, with different kinds of interest group, different methods of communication, and different kinds of relationship with the spirit world and ancestors, than those evolved in Europe. This is all right. Europe had its way of doing things; India and other countries have theirs. Europe is not the decisive guide and mentor to others; its way is not the only way. Chakrabarty titles his book *Provincializing Europe*.

The debate over the place of Europe in world history continues. It is difficult to envision a history of the modern world that does not give Europe an important place, because of its own cultural innovations and because of its globe-spanning industries and empires. But Europe is not itself unified; and, despite Landes' claims, not all its effects were positive. Each people created its own response to the Europeans, expressing its own unique character, which deserves its own separate study.

- Landes specializes in the history of technology; McNeill is a generalist; and both Wolf and Chakrabarty are trained in anthropology as well as history. To what extent do you think their specializations influence their attitudes toward Eurocentrism?
- With which of the four scholars do you most agree? Disagree? Why?
- Compare and contrast the accounts of Columbus' arrival in the New World as they might be written by a Eurocentric scholar and by one of the Taino people of the Caribbean who met him.

13.1

13.2

13.3

What changes in Western Europe made Atlantic explorations possible?

KEY TERM

guild A sworn association of people who gather for some common purpose. In the towns of medieval Europe, guilds of craftsmen or merchants were formed to protect and further their business interests and for mutual aid. Compare guilds in India, in the chapter "Indian Empires."

Workers and the Landed Gentry

As business increased, local traders and manufacturers formed trade organizations called **guilds**. These guilds regulated prices, wages, the quality and quantity of production and trade, and the recruitment, training, and certification of apprentices, journeymen, and masters. The guilds also represented their members in town governments and thus helped to keep industrial and commercial interests at the forefront of the civic agenda. Guilds were the principal means through which the commercial classes—merchants, artisans, and learned professionals—could counter the entrenched prerogatives of the landed aristocrats and win legal privileges for themselves, their businesses, and their cities. Guild members were mostly males, but widowed female heads of households and workshops were also included among the voting members.

Most guilds were organized within a single locality, but international traders organized international guilds corresponding to their commercial interests. The most famous and powerful of them was the Hanseatic League. More geographically dispersed and ethnically diverse, and therefore less closely knit, than a true guild, it was founded in the mid-thirteenth century to represent the interests of leading shippers of the cities of Germany and the Baltic and North Sea. From its headquarters in the city of Lübeck, the League established its own commercial trading posts as far west as London and Bruges (in modern Belgium), and as far east as Novgorod in Russia. Throughout the region, it lobbied for legal systems that favored its members. Sturdy cargo ships belonging to the League carried grain, timber, furs, tar, honey, and flax westward from Russia and Poland, and woolen goods eastward from England. From Sweden they carried copper and iron ore. In the fourteenth century about 100 towns were affiliated with the League. Nevertheless, as states such as the Netherlands (United Provinces), England, and Sweden grew powerful and asserted their control of the Baltic, the League began to die a natural death, after dominating the commerce of its region for almost two centuries.

Textiles and Social Conflict

In two regions of Western Europe, northern Italy and Flanders, the manufacture of textiles came to dominate the urban economies. In these regions early modern European capitalism was born. Capitalist entrepreneurs organized production, employed large numbers of laborers, and created markets for buying and selling, taking economic risks in hope of making profits. In Florence, between 200 and 300 workshops provided a livelihood for almost a third of the city's population, producing a total of 100,000 pieces of woolen cloth each year. Other cities of northern Italy, although smaller, had similar workshops.

The new organization of textile production created a complex class structure. Among the manual workers in the chain of production, guild masters and the aspiring journeymen and apprentices within the guilds held the best positions: shearing the sheep; fulling the cloth (that is, shrinking and thickening it by moistening, heating, and pressing it); and dyeing the wool. Weavers, carders, and combers were lower on the pay and social scales. The weavers, more skilled than the others, were better positioned to organize themselves into a guild.

Capitalist traders, in search of private profit, organized the manufacture in a **putting-out system**. They estimated the market demand for production and supplied workers with the raw materials and equipment necessary to meet it. Laborers then produced the finished products, sometimes in workshops but more typically in their own homes. Usually they were paid by the piece. An army of poor people washed, warped, and spun the wool. The additional income of female and child laborers, employed at even lower pay and in worse conditions than the men, enabled working families to survive.

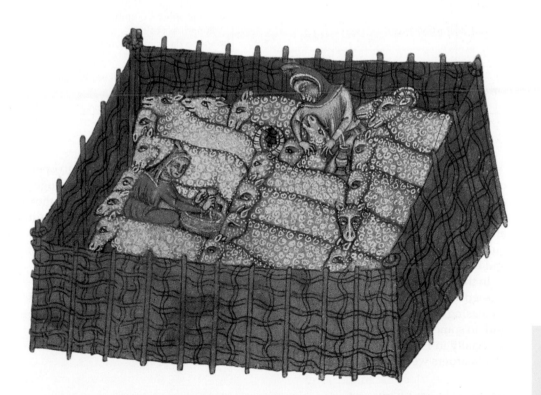

Sheep in pen being milked, Luttrell Psalter, fourteenth century. Woolen-cloth merchants had congregated in Flanders from an early stage. By the twelfth century the industry needed English wool to function to capacity. Before the fourteenth century, overland transport was so expensive that only small and valuable objects could be traded profitably over long distances; the emergence of sea routes lowered the transport costs of bulk goods, such as wool and grain. They could now be traded internationally, and profitably. (British Library, London)

KEY TERM

putting-out system In this system, employers provide employees with raw materials and the orders for turning them into finished products, which they then buy on completion. The employees carry out the work at home, thus reducing the production cost for the employer.

419

AT A GLANCE: WORLD TRADE, MOSTLY EUROPEAN (compare box in Chapter 12)

DATE	POLITICAL/SOCIAL EVENTS	TRADE DEVELOPMENTS	EXPLORATION
1150	• Salah al-Din (Saladin), sultan of Turkish Syria and Egypt, retakes Jerusalem (1187) • St. Francis of Assisi (1182–1226) • St. Dominic (1170–1221) • St. Clare of Assisi (1194–1253)	• Market fairs in Champagne region, France	
1200		• Rise of craft guilds in towns of Western Europe • Foundation of Hanseatic League (1241)	
1250		• Increasing Venetian links with central Asia and China (1255–95) • Revolt of craftworkers in Flanders	
1300	• Hundred Years War between England and France (1337–1453) • Black Death in Europe (1346–50)	• West Africa provides two-thirds of the gold of the eastern hemisphere	
1350	• Ghettoization of Jews in Western Europe • Ashigawa Shoguns dominate Japan (1338–1573)	• Revolts of urban workers in Italy and Flanders	
1400	• Ottoman Turks establish foothold in Europe at Gallipoli	• Great Chinese naval expeditions reach east coast of Africa and India under Zheng He	• Portugal's Prince Henry the Navigator sponsors expeditions to West Africa
1450	• Turks capture Constantinople (1453) • Printing of Gutenberg Bible (1455) • Wars of the Roses in England (1453–85) • Jews driven from Spain (1492) • Treaty of Tordesillas (1494)	• Medici family in Florence: Giovanni, Cosimo, Lorenzo	• Bartolomeu Dias sails round Cape of Good Hope (1488) • Christopher Columbus reaches the Americas (1492) • Vasco da Gama reaches the Malabar coast, India (1498)
1500	• Machiavelli, *The Prince* (1513) • Muslims in Spain forced to convert or leave	• Portugal sets up trading port of Goa, in India (1502); Portuguese ships armed with cannons	• Ferdinand Magellan's voyage around globe (1519–22)

13.1

13.2

13.3

What changes in Western Europe made Atlantic explorations possible?

KEY TERM

ghetto The part of a city to which a particular group is confined for its living space. Named originally for an area adjacent to an iron foundry (in Italian, *ghetto*) in sixteenth-century Venice where Jews were segregated by government order, the term has been used most often to designate segregated Jewish living areas in European cities. It is also used, more broadly, to indicate any area where specific groups are segregated whether by law, by force, or by choice.

Occasionally class antagonisms between employer and employee grew into open conflict. Revolts broke out in the Flemish cities of Douai, Tournai, Ypres, and Bruges at the end of the thirteenth century. The leaders were mostly craftsmen, and they usually demanded that guild members be allowed to participate in city government and thus have a voice in regulating the conditions of trade and manufacture. Workers outside the guild organizations could only hope that increased wages, shorter hours, and better conditions of work might trickle down to their level as well.

In the fourteenth century, such class antagonisms multiplied. Increasingly impoverished workers, suffering also from plagues, wars, and bad harvests, confronted increasingly wealthy traders and industrialists. Workers were forbidden to strike and, in some towns, even to assemble. Nevertheless, class unrest continued to grow, especially in Florence, the greatest industrial center of Western Europe. In 1345, ten wool-carders were hanged for organizing workers.

Business and the Church

In its efforts to establish its independent power, the urban business community confronted not only landed aristocrats and organizations of urban workers, but also an often hostile clergy. From earliest times, the Roman Catholic Church had taken a dim view of the quest for private profit and wealth. St. Augustine (354–430) perpetuated

Aerial view of present-day Delft, western Netherlands. Here, gabled medieval townhouses are seen surrounding the bustling market square in Delft. Since the late 1500s the town has been famous for its pottery and porcelain known as delftware. Dutch products began to compete in European markets with porcelain imports from China.

Painting of Hertogenbosch, Netherlands, 1530. Compare today's photograph of a medieval square on market day (left) with this view of a cloth market in another Dutch town, painted in 1530. The layout, construction, and function of the stalls are virtually identical.

the disdain. In the High Middle Ages (*c.* 1000–*c.* 1400) theologians seriously debated whether it was possible for a merchant to attain salvation.

Because the Church forbade Christians to take and give interest on loans, Jews carried out much of the business of money-lending. In fact, Jews were so much a part of the merchant classes in early medieval northern Europe that a traditional administrative phrase referred to "Jews and other merchants." Church laws forbidding Jews to own land also pushed them into urban life and commerce. By the end of the thirteenth century, Christian rulers forced Jews to live in **ghettos**, specific areas of the cities to which they were confined each night. In European society, Jews were stigmatized four times over: alien by religion, foreign by ancestry, money-lenders by occupation, and segregated by residence. Nevertheless, Jews were tolerated as an economically vital trade diaspora until local people mastered the intricacies of business. After that, Jews were often persecuted, sometimes murdered, and repeatedly exiled—from England in 1290, from France in 1394, from Spain in 1492, and from many German cities.

As commerce increased, the Roman Catholic Church began to revise its opposition to business and businessmen. St. Thomas Aquinas (1225–74) addressed the issue directly in his *Summa Theologiae*. Justifying commerce, he wrote: "Buying and

What changes in Western Europe made Atlantic explorations possible?

13.1

13.2

13.3

13.1 ¡What changes in Western Europe made Atlantic explorations possible?

13.2

13.3

selling seem to be established for the common advantage of both parties." Aquinas wrote of a "just" price, determined by negotiation between buyer and seller. Profit was allowed if its uses were deemed appropriate: "Nothing prevents gain from being directed to some necessary or even virtuous end, and thus trading becomes lawful." Traders were allowed compensation for their labor, and businessmen were allowed to charge interest on commercial loans.

Plague and Social Unrest

Europe's growing economy was undermined in the fourteenth century by extraordinary disasters: famine, civil upheavals, and, worst of all, a plague that killed one-third of the population. Until recently, the plague, called the Black Death, was believed to be the bubonic plague, but research in the twenty-first century suggests that it may have been a different, undetermined, form of plague. Whatever it was, the disease apparently followed the Mongols from central Asia into China in 1331. China's population, estimated at 123 million in 1200, dropped to 65 million in the census of 1393. (Part of the decrease was caused by warfare between the Chinese and the Mongols, but a large part must also have been caused by the plague.) The plague reached Crimea in 1346. There, plague-infested rats boarded ships, disembarking with the disease at all the ports of Europe and the Near East. Within the next five

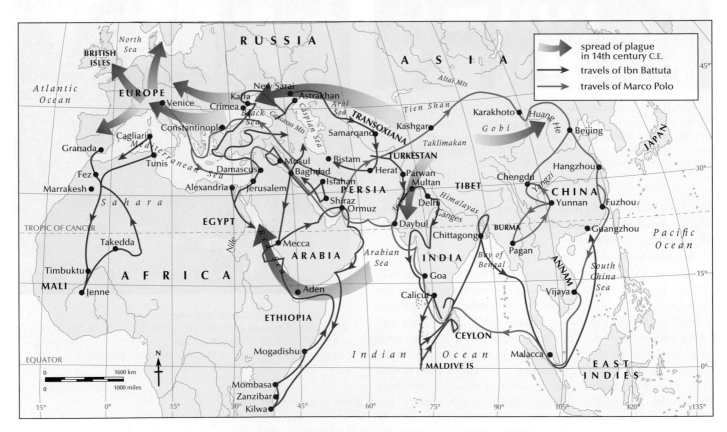

The routes of the plague. The central and eastern Asian stability imposed by Mongol rule—the "Mongol Peace"—brought mixed benefits. Trade flourished, and travelers, such as Ibn Battuta and Marco Polo, were able to write remarkable accounts of the lands they visited. At the same time, however, vectors for other travelers, such as the rats that carried plague, also opened up. The Black Death, which originated in central Asia, was one of a succession of plagues that followed the trade routes by land and sea, decimating parts of Europe and China.

View the **Map**: **The Spread of the Black Death and Peasant Revolts** on **MyHistoryLab**

SOURCE

Giovanni Boccaccio Describes the Black Death

Giovanni Boccaccio (1313–75) captured the horror of the Black Death in the introduction to his otherwise droll and humanistic classic of the era, *The Decameron*:

> In the year of Our Lord 1348 the deadly plague broke out in the great city of Florence … At the onset of the disease both men and women were afflicted by a sort of swelling in the groin or under the armpits which sometimes attained the size of a common apple or egg. Some of these swellings were larger and some smaller, and all were commonly called boils. From these two starting points the boils began in a little while to spread and appear generally all over the body. Afterwards,

the manifestation of the disease changed into black or livid spots on the arms, thighs, and the whole person … Neither the advice of physicians nor the virtue of any medicine seemed to help … almost everyone died within three days of the appearance of the signs—some sooner, some later …

> The calamity had instilled such horror into the hearts of men and women that brother abandoned brother, uncles, sisters, and wives left their dear ones to perish and, what is more serious and almost incredible, parents avoided visiting or nursing their very children, as though these were not their own flesh. (xxiii–xxiv)

years the plague killed one in three people, reducing Europe's population from 70 million in 1300 to only 45 million in 1400.

The catastrophe reshuffled the social classes. Peasants who survived benefited from the labor shortages that followed, gaining higher wages and access to more land, freedom from labor services, and geographical mobility. They began to form a new class of property-owning farmers. Together with urban industrial workers and guild members, they rioted more frequently and boldly against kings and nobles who attempted to raise taxes to fund their wars.

In urban areas, too, workers became scarce, and those who survived demanded higher wages, better working conditions, and more civic rights. In Florence, for example, the Ciompi (the lowest class of workers, named for the neighborhood in which they lived) revolted, supported by lower-level artisans. In 1378 they presented their demands to city officials: open access to the guilds, the right to unionize, a reduction of worker fines and punishments, and the right "to participate in the government of the City." They gained some of their goals, but Florence's powerful business leaders ultimately triumphed. By 1382 the major guilds were back in control, and soon a more dictatorial government was in power. Similar revolts occurred in Flanders, but on a smaller scale and with no more success.

In the aftermath of the Black Death the dissolution of the norms of everyday life, and of the certainties of the class structure, inspired Europeans to reassess their fundamental values and institutions. People's belief in God and their own future were shaken to their foundations. Some kind of new culture, some kind of renaissance, was waiting to be born.

 **Read** the **Document**: Black Death on **MyHistoryLab**

The Triumph of Death, French, 1503. This sixteenth-century work recalls the enormous loss of life caused by the plague of 1348. Brought back from East Asia by Genoese merchants, the disease is estimated to have killed between 20 and 50 percent of Europe's inhabitants. Contemporary medicine was impotent in the face of the disease, the onset of which meant almost certain death. (Bibliothèque Nationale, Paris)

The Renaissance

13.2   What was the European Renaissance?

The new economy underpinned the European Renaissance—a rebirth of Classical ideals in European thought, literature, art, manners, and sensibilities. Many of the wealthier merchants became patrons of the arts, encouraging an outpouring of painting, sculpture, architecture, poetry, and prose. They identified with their cities, sponsoring creative town planning to increase their efficiency as markets and their beauty as artistic designs, and hiring superb architects to enhance their visual splendor. Both patrons and artists were usually devout members of the Church, and an increasingly

The Renaissance in Italy, 1300–1570. From 1300 to 1570 in Italy, artists and intellectuals worked to fuse the Christian tradition (originating in antiquity but developed during the Middle Ages) with the Greco-Roman tradition in a movement fundamental for the later evolution of the modern civilization of the West: the Renaissance. This map shows the principal places that are associated with the names of important figures.

wealthy Church became one of the greatest patrons of the arts. Nevertheless, the creativity of the Renaissance gave a new orientation to religious expression, more earthy, more fleshy, more this-worldly than it had been throughout **medieval**—"middle period"—European times. Scholars of the fifteenth century already drew this three-part division of time into the ancient, medieval, and Renaissance worlds. They saw the Renaissance as a reconnection with the culture of the ancient world of Greece and Rome, across a thousand years of medieval time, and they praised themselves and their colleagues for making the great leap backward in time.

The Roots of the Renaissance

When so great a transformation as the Renaissance takes place, however, affecting economics, technology, religion, culture, aesthetics, and social and political structures, it is not usually possible to determine exactly what is cause and what is effect, nor to specify an exact date of its initiation. Some historians do attempt to show that a single cause predominates—some, for example, stressing economics, others political or social influences—but most see the various transformations as intertwined. For example, even when historians emphasize one aspect or another of the Renaissance, as we have done with trade, they identify its roots in other aspects of life as well. They detect glimmerings of the Renaissance in a shift in religious as well as secular values toward a more worldly and rational, less ascetic, less spiritual outlook. They date the beginnings of this shift, as we have seen in the chapter entitled "Islam," at least as early as the mid-eleventh century. At that time, contact with Arab Muslim civilization reacquainted European scholars with ancient Greek philosophy, which Arab scholars had kept alive. These changes in philosophic values supported the opening to trade, just as trade later gave support to new directions in philosophy.

Christian Scholars. Christian scholars, especially in Spain (where Christians, Muslims, and Jews lived side by side), began the systematic translation of Arabic texts into Latin. They sought to reestablish the link with the ancient Roman and Greek texts that the Arabs had preserved and developed, and that the Christian world had lost. The works of the Muslim philosophers Avicenna (Ibn Sina) (980–1037) and Averroes (Ibn Rushd) (1126–98) and the Jewish philosopher Maimonides (1135–1204) helped to restore the emphasis on logic and philosophy that Aristotle had taught. In the eleventh century, Church leaders began to suggest that pure faith was not enough to attain salvation. St. Anselm (1033–1109) stressed the need for an intellectual basis for faith while Peter Abelard (1079–1142), emphasized the need for a rational approach to the interpretation of texts.

Meanwhile, the new wealth and power of their Church offended some Roman Catholics, and they challenged the Church to live up to its early ideals of compassion for the poor and simplicity in everyday living. New orders of priests and nuns began to form as a way of returning to these early ideals: Franciscans followed the teachings of St. Francis of Assisi

13.1
13.2
13.3

What was the European Renaissance?

KEY TERM

medieval The "middle period." Europeans of the Renaissance period, who felt that they were, at last, reconnecting with the glories of ancient Greece and Rome, called the ten centuries between the end of the Western Roman Empire and the beginning of the Renaissance "the medieval period." They used the term pejoratively. More recent scholars see that very long period as far more complicated and diverse, and analyze it by specific geographical regions and into much smaller periods of time.

Avicenna, French School, eighteenth century. Oil on canvas. Ibn Sina, called Avicenna by Christian Europeans, was one of the foremost Islamic students of Aristotle's work. He influenced Church scholars, who relearned Greek scholarship through him. (Bibliothèque de la Faculté de Médecine, Paris)

425

St. Francis, Simone Martini, *c.* 1320. Fresco. St. Francis of Assisi gave
away all his possessions to the poor. When his father disowned him,
he stripped naked and, cloaked in a robe given him by the bishop of
Assisi, went from place to place begging for food, offering service, and
preaching. The religious order that he founded became the largest in
Europe. (S. Francesco, Assisi, Italy)

(1182–1226), Dominicans followed St. Dominic (1170–1221), and the "Poor Clares,"
an order of nuns, followed St. Clare of Assisi (1194–1253).

Universities. Universities were founded to preserve, enhance, and transmit knowledge. Most emphasized practical disciplines: medical studies at Salerno, legal studies
at Bologna, theological studies at Paris—all founded before 1200. Later, students and
professors from Paris crossed the English Channel and founded the University of
Oxford about 1200, with Cambridge University following shortly afterward. By 1300
there were about a dozen universities in Western Europe; by 1500, nearly a hundred.

Curricula centered on theology, but also included grammar, dialectic, rhetoric,
arithmetic, music, geometry, and astronomy. The theology curriculum, in particular,
required the approval of the Church. This could be problematic, as is illustrated by
the career of St. Thomas Aquinas, the greatest Christian theologian of his age, who
paved the way for the new ideas of the Renaissance. Contentiously, he also welcomed the systematic rationality of Aristotle. While many Church leaders rejected
Aristotelian logic as contradicting the teachings of the Church, Aquinas declared
that logic and reason, as taught by Aristotle, and faith, as taught by the Church, were

Theological lecture at the Sorbonne, Paris, fifteenth century. Manuscript illumination. Sponsored by the Church, universities were founded primarily for the study of theology, but some included specializations in medicine and law. All the students were male and most were quite serious-minded. (Bibliothèque de Troyes, France)

What was
the European
Renaissance?

13.1

13.2

13.3

complementary. In places where they did appear to conflict, he conceded that divine truths must take precedence: "Some divine truths are attainable by human reason, while others altogether surpass the power of human reason." Although Aquinas gave divine revelation precedence over human reason, on the eve of the Renaissance he opened the door of the Church to the importance of reason in all human endeavors.

Aquinas was ahead of his time. For more than 50 years, the Franciscan order of priests banned the reading of his works, and the universities of Paris and Oxford condemned many of his doctrines. But within a century, his synthesis of logic and faith, of Aristotle and the Church, became the new standard orthodoxy of Roman Catholicism.

In addition to modifications in official theology, the coming together of dozens of exuberant young male students in the universities (no matter how rigorous the rules and regulations) led to quests for individual expression and challenges to authority. The "Golliard Poets" took their name from the Biblical Goliath, a kind of early antichrist. These poets reveled in the pleasures of youth and ridiculed the conventions of sobriety, solemnity, and sanctity. They wrote parodies that were usually irreverent and sometimes obscene, for example, a *Drunkard's Mass*, a *Glutton's Mass*, and an *Office of Ribalds*. They mocked the most sacred beliefs of their time, declaring, "I believe in dice … and love the tavern more than Jesus." They declared their blessings for one another: "Fraud be with you."

Such turmoil in religious and philosophical attitudes, both official and unofficial, helped to pave the way for the transformations of the Renaissance.

HOW DO WE KNOW?

Islamic Influences on the European Renaissance

Arab thinkers, their translations of Classical Greek works, and their comments on them helped to inspire the European Renaissance. Averroes' Arabic translations of and commentaries on Aristotle revealed that philosopher's works to Western Europeans who had lost contact with the originals. In addition to his philosophy, Avicenna's *Qanun* (Canon) of medicine remained central to European medical thought for centuries. Al-Khwarazmi's work in mathematics remained influential for centuries, and lives on in our lexicon today in the word *algorithm,* which is based on his name. From the tenth to the twelfth century, Arabs, Christians, and Jews lived in such proximity, and even harmony, in parts of Spain—the home of these three scholars—that linguistic borrowing back and forth became common. Poetic and prose forms were also borrowed, especially from Arabic literature to Latin and the Romance languages. European scholars, such as Gerard of Cremona, sought out the best in Arabic thought in order to translate it. We have also seen that Europeans adapted Arab technology, such as the caravel, which gave them access to the oceans of the world.

Despite this rich harvest of culture and technology from the Arab world, we have the harsh, even hysterical judgment of Petrarch (1304–74), one of the greatest Italian poets of the Renaissance, often called "the father of humanism":

> I implore you to keep these Arabs from giving me advice about my personal condition. Let them stay in exile. I hate the whole lot … You know what kind of physicians the Arabs are. I know what kind of poets they are. Nobody has such winning ways; nobody, also, is more tender and more lacking in vigor, and, to use the right words, meaner and more perverted. The minds of men are inclined to act differently; but, as you used to say, every man radiates his own peculiar mental disposition. To sum up: I will not be persuaded that any good can come from Arabia. (Cassirer *et al.*, p. 142)

What has happened between the early welcome given to Arabic learning and its bitter, summary rejection by Petrarch? Several interpretations are possible. First, Arabic influence was always greatest in Spain, where Muslims ruled much of the country for centuries, in some regions for almost eight centuries. Other European countries, such as Petrarch's Italy, were influenced less. Even in Spain, as Christians began to reconquer the country, they

began to focus on Muslims as political and religious enemies rather than as cultural colleagues. A similar change occurred over time throughout the Christian world as the launching of the crusades, after 1095, crystallized a new political antagonism between the two religious communities. The passing of time also brought new cultural currents to Europe, as the development of new vernaculars, especially in the Romance languages (such as Spanish, Italian, and French), broadened and deepened the base of culture, making it more nationalistic. The Western Europeans also developed their own intellectual competences and institutions, reducing their reliance on others. The European Renaissance took Western Europeans in new directions. Meanwhile, Islam, which suffered severe political and military defeats in Spain and in Baghdad (1258), became less open to new intellectual currents.

Scholars sometimes designate three different periods as "renaissances" in Western Europe. The first was the Carolingian Renaissance, initiated by Charlemagne about 800; the second was the Renaissance of the High Middle Ages, about the middle of the eleventh to the middle of the thirteenth century, significantly influenced by Muslim scholarship and learning; the third was the best known, and most influential, the Renaissance of the mid-fourteenth to the mid-sixteenth century. Each of the later renaissances built on the earlier ones, but also discarded some of their qualities. In Petrarch's dismissal of Arabic poetry and of Arabs generally we see a dramatic transformation in the attitudes of Christian thinkers, as their own religious and philosophical traditions became less open, and more hostile, to the influences of other cultures.

- The fourteenth-century Renaissance took place primarily in Italy and in northwestern Europe. Why do you think it did not take place in Spain, where so much earlier cultural development took place?
- Petrarch turned against Arabic learning, but not against the early Greek philosophers. Would such a division have been possible in twelfth-century Spain? Why or why not?
- Arabic learning could be seen as more successful because it continued to adhere to traditional paths, whereas Western Christian scholarship could be seen as a failure for turning in new directions. Would you accept such a characterization?

Humanism

KEY TERM

humanism Cultural movement initiated in Western Europe in the fourteenth century deriving from the rediscovery and study of Greek and Roman literary texts. Most humanists continued to believe in God, but emphasized the study of humans.

The Renaissance began in the cities of Italy, where thriving economies provided an economic foundation, the Church provided an intellectual foundation, and both the Church and the commercial elite provided patronage to artists and intellectuals. Italy was also the heartland of the Roman Empire, a natural place in which to forge a reconnection to that ancient world. The central motivating philosophy of the Renaissance was **humanism**, the belief that the proper study of man is man. Asserting the importance of the individual, humanism challenged the monopoly of the Church over the interpretation of cultural life. Renaissance humanism held strongly to a belief in God, but assigned him a less overwhelming, less intimidating role in human

13.1

What was
the European
Renaissance?

13.2

13.3

life and action. In his *Oration on the Dignity of Man*, Giovanni Pico della Mirandola (1463–94) places in the mouth of God himself the most succinct statement of this humanistic perspective of the Renaissance:

> I have given you, Adam, neither a predetermined place nor a particular aspect nor any special prerogatives in order that you may take and possess these through your own decision and choice. The limitations on the nature of other creatures are contained within my prescribed laws. You shall determine your own nature without constraint from any barrier, by means of the freedom to whose power I have entrusted you … I have made you neither heavenly nor earthly, neither mortal nor immortal so that, like a free and sovereign artificer, you might mold and fashion yourself into that form you yourself shall have chosen.

According to this typical Renaissance perspective, God gives humankind the power to shape its own destiny.

New Artistic Styles

Renaissance art continued to emphasize religious themes, but it also began to reflect the influence of humanist and commercial values. Masaccio's painting *Trinity with the Virgin, St. John, and Donors* (1427) demonstrates the evolution of geometric perspective in painting, revealing not only a new artistic technique but also a new, objective interrelationship of individuals with the world.

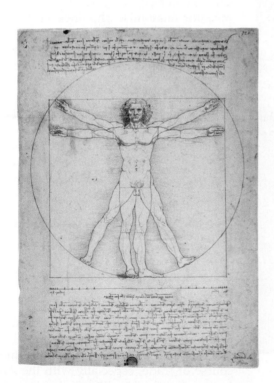

Vitruvian Man, Leonardo da Vinci, *c.* 1492. Pen and ink on paper. Renaissance artists studied the proportions of the human body carefully and represented it accurately. Leonardo's drawing suggests the geometric perfection of the body, relating it both to the circle and to the square, and thus to a perfect and harmonious cosmos. (Galleria dell'Accademia, Venice)

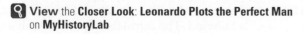
View the **Closer Look**: **Leonardo Plots the Perfect Man** on **MyHistoryLab**

Trinity with the Virgin, St. John, and Donors, Masaccio, 1427. Fresco. During the Renaissance, people began to rethink their relationship with God and the world around them; at the same time, artists were developing a new means of depicting reality. According to some art-history scholars, Masaccio's monumental fresco is the first painting created in correct geometric perspective (the single vanishing point lies at the foot of the cross). (S. Maria Novella, Florence, Italy)

What was
the European
Renaissance?

By the fifteenth century, religious, commercial, and artistic sensibilities appear joined together. Portraiture flourished as major artists depicted their patrons, frequently the elites of the Church and of commerce. *The Arnolfini Wedding Portrait*, painted in 1434 in Flanders by Jan van Eyck, presents the marriage of an international businessman, probably an Italian stationed in Flanders. Simultaneously, Van Eyck signaled the economic success of his subject through the elegance of the physical setting of the marriage and his religious concerns through the symbolism of the dog (Fido?), representing fidelity; the removed clogs indicating that the ground is sacred; and the mirror suggesting the all-seeing eye of God.

The richest fruits of Renaissance creativity matured in Florence, where the illustrious Medici family provided lavish patronage. The family's fortune had been built by the merchant banker Giovanni de' Medici (1360–1429), and was enhanced by his son Cosimo (1389–1464) and great grandson Lorenzo (1449–92). In this supportive environment, creative artists developed and expressed their genius. They included Filippo Brunelleschi (1377–1446), who designed and completed the dome of the Cathedral of Florence, the greatest architectural and engineering triumph of his time; Michelangelo Buonarroti (1475–1564), the sculptor of such masterpieces as the *David*, which is in Florence, and the painter of the Sistine Chapel ceiling in Vatican City; Leonardo da Vinci (1452–1519), scientific inventor, anatomist who drew *Vitruvian Man* (see above), and painter of the *Mona Lisa* (also known as *La Gioconda*); and Niccolò Machiavelli (1469–1527), author of *The Prince*, a harsh and hard-nosed philosophy of government. At the same time, the general population of the city of Florence enjoyed high standards of literacy and expressiveness. Michelangelo's subsequent move to Rome, where he sculpted the statues of *Moses* and the *Pietà*, and painted the Sistine Chapel, reminds us that the Church, too, remained a great patron of the arts.

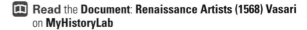

📖 Read the Document: Renaissance Artists (1568) Vasari on MyHistoryLab

Developments in Technology

Creativity flourished in the practical arts as well as the fine arts, and contributed substantially to the rise of merchant power. Local techniques were enhanced by innovations encountered in the course of trade, especially with the Arab world. Improvements in sailing technology included a new design for the ships themselves. In the thirteenth century the caravel of the Mediterranean, with its lateen sails, used mostly by Arab sailors, was blended with the straight sternpost and stern rudder of northern Europe. The caravel could also be rerigged with a square sail for greater speed in a tailwind. The astrolabe, again an Arab invention,

The Arnolfini Wedding Portrait, Jan van Eyck, 1434. Oil on oak. Giovanni Arnolfini, an Italian merchant living in Flanders, commissioned this pictorial record of his marriage. On the far wall, Van Eyck has written in Latin "Jan van Eyck was here," much as a notary would sign a document. Art historians assure us that although the wife may look pregnant on her marriage day, in fact this is simply what women looked like in the large-hooped skirts of the day. (National Gallery, London)

📖 Read the Document: The Office and Dutie of an Husband (1529) Juan Luis Vives on MyHistoryLab

Basilica di Santa Maria del Fiore, Florence. The dome that sits atop the Cathedral (Duomo) of Florence, and dominates the skyline of the city, was built by Filippo Brunelleschi and completed in 1436, 142 years after the design of the cathedral was approved. The dome was and remains the largest masonry dome in the world, built of 37,000 tons of materials, including 4 million bricks. Brunelleschi's unparalleled structural innovations were matched by his creation of hoisting machinery to put it all into place.

Sistine Chapel ceiling (post-restoration), Michelangelo Buonarroti, 1508–12. Fresco. Renaissance humanism praised the ability of human beings to be creative and original, yet it continued to be anchored in religious imagery. Pope Sixtus IV commissioned Michelangelo to use his imagination in painting the ceiling of the Sistine Chapel in the Vatican, Rome, with Biblical scenes. (Musei Vaticani, Rome)

The cannon. From the 1450s, innovations in weapons changed the nature of warfare. The most dramatic changes affected the cannon, as shown here in *Four Books of Knighthood*, 1528.

13.1

13.2 What was
the European

13.3 Renaissance?

helped sailors to determine their longitude at sea. The rediscovery in the early fifteenth century of Ptolemy's *Geography*, written in the second century C.E. and preserved in the Arab world, helped to spark interest in proper mapping. (An error in longitude in Ptolemy's map led Columbus to underestimate the circumference of the globe by about one-third. This error emboldened him to set out across the Atlantic and, later, to believe mistakenly that he had reached East Asia.)

Cannons, especially when mounted on ships, gave European merchants firepower not available to others. Although the Chinese had invented gunpowder centuries before, the Europeans put it to use in warfare in the fourteenth century and became the masters of gun making. By the early 1400s they were firing cannonballs. The Ottoman Turks employed Western European Christians to build and operate the cannons they used in 1453 to besiege and conquer Constantinople. The Turkish rulers of Persia also employed European gunners and gun manufacturers, and copied their works. By the late 1400s European warring powers were energetically competing in an "arms race" to develop the most powerful and effective cannons and guns. Leonardo and others worked on the mathematics of the projectiles. When Portuguese ships began to sail into the waters of the Indian Ocean after 1498, claiming the right to regulate commerce, their guns and cannons sank all opposition. Some historians have called this era the Age of Gunpowder Empires.

The Chinese had also invented the principle of movable type and the printing press, but, again, the Europeans surpassed them in implementation. Movable type was better suited to Europe's alphabetic languages than to Chinese ideographs. By 1455, in Mainz, Germany, Johannes Gutenberg (c. 1390–1486) had printed the first major book set in movable type, the Bible. By the end of the century at least 10 million individual books in some 30,000 different editions had been produced and distributed.

The Chinese also created clocks centuries before the Europeans, as early as the eleventh century, although they were apparently turned by waterwheels and regulated by an elaborate escapement mechanism. European cities recognized the need to announce the passage of time, but at first did it simply by ringing bells in public, imprecisely. Around 1300, Europeans invented their first mechanical clocks, about the same time as they invented cannons and spectacles. No one knows exactly who did it or where. A church in Milan installed a clock made of iron in 1309. The Milanese were also the first to erect a public clock to strike the hours, in 1335. It had no hands, only a bell that rang once for one o'clock, twice for two o'clock, and so on. Perhaps the inspiration for the new invention came from China, but in any case, as the historian Alfred Crosby points out in his study of the importance of quantification for the economic development of urban Europe, "Hours were of central significance to city dwellers, whom buying and selling had already initiated into the vogue of quantification" (Crosby, 1997, p. 76).

In fourteenth-century Italy, two centuries after the decimal system had been absorbed from India via the Arab world, businesspeople began to develop double-entry bookkeeping. This facilitated the accurate accounting of transactions and the efficient tracking of business profits and losses. In 1494 Luca Pacioli (c. 1445–c. 1514), a Franciscan friar and mathematician, published the method in systematic form.

By the end of the fifteenth century, some people in Western Europe were ready for new adventures. The Renaissance brought new energy not only through its humanist philosophy and art, but also through its technological inventions. Newly emerging political rulers and urban businessmen in Western Europe were also inspired. One of their more practical goals was very specific: to gain direct access to the wealth of the Indies and China. They did that. In the process they also discovered a new world.

A New World

13.1
13.2
13.3

Where did the
early European
explorers go?

13.3   Where did the early European explorers go?

During the centuries after the demise of the Roman Empire, the Mediterranean Sea and its coastline had gradually devolved into three cultural and political spheres: Muslim, Byzantine, and Roman Catholic. By about 950, Muslims had established their dominion by land along the eastern and southern coasts of the Mediterranean and held parts of southern Italy as well as major islands in the Mediterranean: Cyprus, Crete, and Sicily. The southern and southeastern Mediterranean had become a "Muslim lake." Even so, the Byzantine Empire continued to control the northeastern shores, while various Frankish and Germanic Christian powers held the north-central coast. (See map "Byzantium and Islam" in the chapter entitled "Islam.")

These divisions had three results. First, the Mediterranean became a war zone. Warfare between the Christians of southern Europe and the Muslims of the Middle East and North Africa persisted from the eighth century until 1571, when the naval Battle of Lepanto, in Greek waters, fixed generally accepted zones of control between them. Second, trade stability oscillated in response to Europe's internal economy and warfare in the Mediterranean. Third, and most important to our story here, the European merchants felt hemmed in. The valuable merchandise and profitable trade coming from the Indian Ocean basin—the spices of India and Indonesia; the silk and porcelain of China; and the gold, ivory, and slaves of East Africa—were controlled by Middle Eastern Muslim traders.

This last, the eastern Mediterranean trade blockage, is often seen as a religious confrontation, but in fact trade opportunities often trumped religious rivalries. The crusades, beginning in 1096, which brought Christians and Muslims into armed conflict, simultaneously brought new opportunities for commerce across the Mediterranean to Middle Eastern ports and increased demand for the merchandise that arrived there from Asia. Although on several occasions popes forbade Catholics to trade with

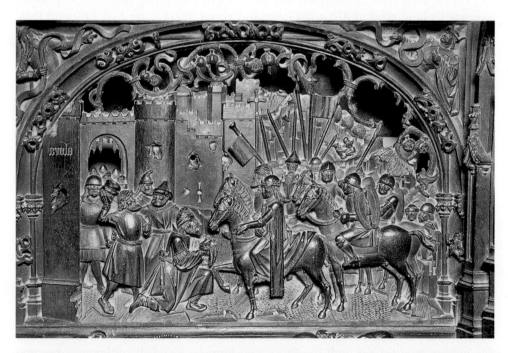

The Conquest of Granada on January 2, 1492, Rodrigo Aleman, Toledo Cathedral, late fifteenth century. The conquest of Granada by the Catholic king Ferdinand II and Queen Isabella I of Spain marked the final victory of the *reconquista*, the Christian recovery of all of Spain from Muslim rule. Here, the Moorish king Boabdil is handing over the keys to the town.

13.1

13.2

13.3

Where did the
early European
explorers go?

Muslims, these prohibitions were generally disregarded. Religious and ethnic differences may have compounded the tensions, but the main contest was the competition for profits among the very diverse groups of traders.

European merchants and princes began to seek alternative routes to the lucrative products of the Indian Ocean. This search took on special intensity in Western Europe, which was geographically farther from the Middle East and closer to the Atlantic. Beginning in 1277, a maritime route between Italy and Spain in the Mediterranean and England and Flanders in northwestern Europe brought regular trade to Europe's north Atlantic coast. By the early fifteenth century, European trade generally was picking up, as the continent recovered from the devastation of the Black Death. Increasingly prosperous, and bold, Western Europeans were prepared to attempt two new routes to Asia: one south around the coast of Africa and then east to India; the other west across the Atlantic.

Most of the dynamism of Western European trade through the fifteenth century emanated from the relatively secular city-states of Flanders and Italy, but in the Iberian peninsula Portugal and Spain created a powerful new merger of the missionary desire to spread Catholicism with the economic desire for wealth. The Portuguese crown dispatched sailing expeditions along the African coast that ultimately reached the Cape of Good Hope, turned north into the Indian Ocean and onward to India, and were poised to continue to China. The newly unified government of Spain commissioned Christopher Columbus to sail westward in search of a new route to the Indies. Instead Columbus discovered a "New World."

The Early Explorers, 800–1000

There had been some excursions onto the waters of the Atlantic Ocean before Christopher Columbus made his famous voyage in 1492. From the eighth until the twelfth century, the European North Atlantic was primarily the province of marauding raiders from the north. These Vikings, the ancestors of today's Norwegians, Swedes, and Danes, were colonizers, fishermen, and traders. One group from Norway began to settle Iceland around 870 and Greenland about 982. Under Leif Eriksson they reached Newfoundland in North America about 1000 and established a settlement there as well, but it did not endure. Danes and Norwegians plundered along the entire Atlantic coast of Europe. In 859 they sailed through the Strait of Gibraltar and attacked ports along the Mediterranean. Arabs from North Africa and Spain were launching similar attacks in the Mediterranean at about the same time.

The Vikings were also traders and colonizers who often fostered urban development in the places they conquered. (See map "Scandinavian and Arab Muslim invasions," above.) They founded the town of Dublin, in Ireland, in 841, and they conquered much of northern England, establishing the kingdom of York in the 870s. Vikings also conquered the French territory of Normandy in the late eighth century, from where in 1066 their leader, William of Normandy (William the Conqueror), conquered England. The Normans, as these "Northmen" came to be known, also founded a kingdom in southern Italy and Sicily and established a principality in Antioch.

👁 **Watch** the **Video**: **Who Were the Vikings?** on **MyHistoryLab**

The Swedes turned eastward across the Baltic Sea and founded trading cities along the river systems of Russia, establishing their capital first at Novgorod in the early ninth century and then in Kiev in 882. They proceeded all the way south to the Black Sea, where they traded with the Byzantine Empire. Swedish settlements became catalysts for the formation of the political and economic organization of the Slavic people in whose midst they were established. Kiev became the capital of the first Russian state; its people were called the "Rus." By about 1000 the Vikings became more peaceful, and their raids ceased as their home regions in Scandinavia developed into organized states and accepted Christianity. They lost interest, as well, in further exploration westward across the ocean.

Earlier voyages across the North Atlantic other than those of the Vikings are not recorded historically, and are unlikely to have occurred. There is no known crossing of the South Atlantic. Africans carried on only limited coastal shipping, and Europeans were leery of the hazards of the West African coast, especially south of Cape Bojador. In addition, they recognized that the prevailing winds on the African coast blew from north to south, and they feared that, while they might be able to sail south, they might not be able to return north.

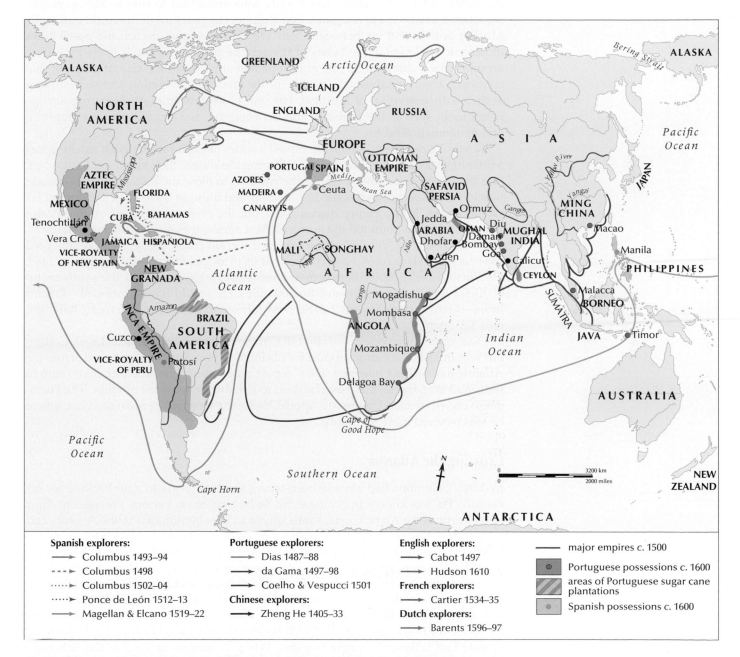

Spanish explorers:
→ Columbus 1493–94
--→ Columbus 1498
····→ Columbus 1502–04
·····→ Ponce de León 1512–13
→ Magellan & Elcano 1519–22

Portuguese explorers:
→ Dias 1487–88
→ da Gama 1497–98
→ Coelho & Vespucci 1501

Chinese explorers:
→ Zheng He 1405–33

English explorers:
→ Cabot 1497
→ Hudson 1610

French explorers:
→ Cartier 1534–35

Dutch explorers:
→ Barents 1596–97

— major empires c. 1500
Portuguese possessions c. 1600
areas of Portuguese sugar cane plantations
Spanish possessions c. 1600

World exploration, 1450–1600. Spanish and Portuguese explorers and traders had established settlements in South America and the Caribbean by 1600, and commercial depots on the coasts of Africa, India, the Pacific islands, China, and Japan—at a time when English, Dutch, and French explorations of North America had just begun.

Where did the
early European
explorers go?

Down Africa's Atlantic Coast

Portugal was particularly well situated geographically to explore the Atlantic coast
of Africa as the opening step in finding an alternative route to India, despite the fears
of the unknown. In 1415 Portugal captured Ceuta on the Moroccan coast of North
Africa, one of the major points of the trans-Saharan trade in gold and slaves and
under the control of Muslims. Then, to get closer to the sources of supply, Portuguese
ships, under the direction of Prince Henry (1394–1460), later called the Navigator,
sailed down the coast of West Africa.

Henry had two goals. He wanted to defeat Muslim power over African trade
routes. Inspired by legend, he sought to establish contact and a military alliance with
the mythical Christian king Prester John, sometimes said to rule in Mesopotamia,
sometimes in Africa. He imagined that together the two kingdoms could defeat the
Muslim powers that lay between them. Henry also wished to test the possibilities
of oceanic exploration. He believed it might be possible to reach India by sailing
around Africa, although no one in Europe had any idea of the size or shape of that
continent. Henry established a center for the study of navigation and shipbuilding
at the southwestern tip of Portugal. His staff of experts employed existing naviga-
tional tools, such as the astrolabe and the compass, and created new geographical
and mathematical tables.

Slowly, Prince Henry's men attempted a series of explorations, each reaching just
a little further down the African coast. Fearing the shoals, they sailed out to the west,
into the ocean, and allowed the northern winds to blow them south. On an expedition in 1444 they captured some 200 Africans and brought them back to Portugal for
sale as slaves. Prince Henry died in 1460, but the project continued. As the Portuguese expeditions rounded the hump of West Africa, they proved their profitability.
They reached what the Portuguese called the grain coast, the ivory coast, the gold
coast, and the slave coast—each named for its principal exports to Portugal. In 1488,
the Portuguese explorer Bartolomeu Dias (c. 1450–1500) reached the southern tip
of Africa and turned northward for 300 miles. He would have continued—toward
India—with his two caravels, but his crew refused to go further. The route, however,
now lay open.

Dias' career intersected with that of Christopher Columbus (1451–1506). Columbus was in Lisbon seeking support for his intended exploration westward across the
Atlantic just as Dias returned. Dias' report made clear that an alternative route to
India had been found; there was no need to risk the transatlantic attempt. The Portuguese crown rejected Columbus' appeal, and so he went to the Spanish court, where
he was received more favorably.

Crossing the Atlantic

By 1488, Columbus had already been trying for three years to gain backing for his
venture. He was known in Portugal, for he had sailed on various Portuguese ships
as far north as the Arctic Circle, south almost to the equator, east to the Aegean, and
west to the Azores. Finally, in Spain he received the backing he needed from the
newly merged thrones of Ferdinand of Aragon and Isabella of Castile. In his voyage
in 1492, Columbus depended on two geographical estimates, and he got both wrong.
He underestimated the total circumference of the earth and he overestimated the total
east–west span of the Eurasian continent. The globe was bigger than he thought, and
so was the oceanic distance that he had to traverse. Nowhere in his figures was there
the space for two continents of which he and the people of Europe knew nothing,
despite Leif Eriksson's earlier voyages. When Columbus arrived in the Bahamas,
he thought he had reached islands off the eastern coast of Asia. Although he found
only a little gold, he believed—and promised his patrons—that an abundance of it
yet awaited him. He promised also a virtually limitless supply of cotton, spices and

SOURCE

The Journal of Columbus' First Voyage to the Americas

Columbus kept a day-by-day journal of his first voyage. The original has been lost, but fortunately the priest Bartolomé de Las Casas (1474–1566) prepared an abstract, which he used in writing his own *Historia de Las Indias* (1875). Columbus' leading biographer in English, Samuel Eliot Morison, calls the abstract "The most important document in the entire history of American discovery." This account of what Columbus saw and how he related to it is written sometimes in the first person of Columbus, and sometimes in the third person, as the voice of Las Casas. Note especially the overwhelming importance given to religion:

> **Prologue:** Your Highnesses, as Catholic Christians and Princes devoted to the Holy Christian Faith and the propagators thereof, and enemies of the sect of Mahomet and of all idolatries and heresies, resolved to send me, Christopher Columbus, to the said regions of India, to see the said princes and peoples and lands and the disposition of them and of all, and the manner in which may be undertaken their conversion to our Holy Faith, and ordained that I should not go by land (the usual way) to the Orient, but by the route of the Occident, by which no one to this day knows for sure that anyone has gone …

> **12 October 1492:** At two hours after midnight appeared the land, at a distance of two leagues … Presently they saw naked people, and the Admiral went ashore in his barge, and [others] followed. The Admiral broke out the royal standard, and the captains [displayed] two banners of the Green Cross, which the Admiral flew on all the vessels as a signal, with an F and a Y, one at one arm of the cross and the other on the other, and over each letter his or her crown … and said that they should bear faith and witness how he before them all was taking, as in fact he took, possession of the said island for the King and Queen …

> **15 October:** It was my wish to bypass no island without taking possession, although having taken one you can claim all …

> **22 October:** All this night and today I was here, waiting to see if the king here or other people would bring gold or anything substantial, and many of this people came, like the others of the other islands, as naked and as painted, some of them white, others red, others black, and [painted] in many ways … any little thing I gave them, and also our coming, they considered a great wonder, and believed that we had come from the sky …

> **1 November:** It is certain that this is the mainland and that I am before Zayto [Zaytun] and Quisay [Hangzhou] [two great port cities of China], 100 leagues more or less distant the one from the other …

> **6 November:** If they had access to devout religious persons knowing the language, they would all turn Christian, and so I hope in Our Lord that Your Highnesses will do something about it with much care … And after your days (for we are all mortal) … you will be well received before the eternal Creator …

> **12 November:** Yesterday came aboard the ship a dugout with six young men, and five came on board; these I ordered to be detained and I am bringing them. Afterwards I sent to a house which is on the western bank of the river, and they brought seven women, small and large, and three boys. I did this because the [Indian] men would behave better in Spain with women of their country than without them …

> **27 November:** Your Highnesses ought not to consent that any foreigner does business or sets foot here, except Christian Catholics, since this was the end and the beginning of the enterprise …

> **22 December:** The Indians were so free, and the Spaniards so covetous and overreaching, that it was not enough that for a lace-tip or a little piece of glass and crockery or other things of no value, the Indians should give them what they asked; even without giving anything they [the Spaniards] wanted to get and take all, which the Admiral had always forbidden …

> **23 December:** In that hour … more than 1000 persons had come to the ship, and that all brought something that they owned, and that before they come within half a crossbow shot of the ship, they stand up in their canoes with what they brought in their hands, saying "Take! Take!" (cited in Morison, pp. 41–179)

aromatics, timber, and slaves. He characterized the people of the lands he had come upon as ready for conversion to Christianity. He reported all these observations in a letter to Ferdinand and Isabella (see "Source" box, above).

Six months later, Columbus embarked on a much larger expedition with 17 ships, 1,200 men (including six priests to carry on the work of conversion), and enough supplies to establish a permanent settlement. The expedition, however, yielded no serious commercial gains, and it took Columbus two years to gain support for a third expedition, in 1498, with only six ships. For the first time, he landed on the

13.1

13.2

13.3

Where did the early European explorers go?

Vasco da Gama, Portuguese School, *c.* 1524. Gama's expedition in 1497–99 on behalf of the Portuguese crown completed the sea link from Europe around Africa to India. On his next voyage, in 1502–03, he established the policy of using military force to create Portuguese power in the Indian Ocean. (National Museum of Ancient Art, Lisbon)

continental landmass, in what is today Venezuela. Even at the end of his life, after yet another, fourth, voyage that brought him to Central America, Columbus recognized neither the enormity of his mistake nor the enormity of his discovery. He never realized that he had not found China, Japan, India, or islands off the coast of Asia. Nor did he realize that he had discovered a "New World."

Amerigo Vespucci (1454–1512) of Florence was the first person to recognize Columbus' error and his success. In 1499, sailing with a Spanish fleet after Columbus' third expedition, Vespucci traveled some 1,200 miles along the coast of South America. He recognized clearly that this was a continental landmass, but he did not yet realize which one. In a second voyage, 1501–02, this one under the flag of Portugal, he traveled some 2,400 miles down the coast of South America. He reported carefully on all that he saw: humans and their customs and tools, animals, plants, and hints of great treasures. Unlike Columbus, however, Vespucci was cautious: "The natives told us of gold and other metals and many miracle-working drugs, but I am one of those followers of Saint Thomas, who are slow to believe. Time will reveal everything" (cited in Boorstin, p. 250). On his return to Spain, Vespucci was asked by Queen Isabella to establish a school for pilots and a clearinghouse for information brought back from the New World. In 1507 the clergyman and mapmaker Martin Waldseemüller published a new map of the world as known at the time, and on it he named the new western areas "America." In 1538, Gerardus Mercator published his large and influential map of the world, designating the two new continents as North America and South America. Vespucci himself died in 1512 of malaria, contracted on his voyages.

Crossing the Pacific

Only the eastern coast of the Americas was known to Europeans when the Spaniard Vasco Nuñez de Balboa (1474–1517) followed the guidance of one of his Native American allies, crossed the Isthmus of Panama, climbed a peak, and, in 1513, became the first European to see the Pacific Ocean from the east. Four years later, Balboa was falsely accused of treason against the king of Spain, and was beheaded. With the recognition that the Americas were continental in size, and that another ocean lay between them and Asia, Charles V of Spain commissioned Ferdinand Magellan (*c.* 1480–1521) to sail west, find a passage around the southern tip of South America, proceed across the Pacific—no matter how long the voyage—and reach the Spice Islands of East Asia. Magellan set out in 1519 with five ships and about 250 sailors from several different European countries. The voyage became the first circumnavigation of the globe, yielding the first accurate picture of the full magnitude of the planet and completing the picture of most of its main contours. It took just 12 days less than three years. Only 18 men completed the trip. Magellan himself was killed in a skirmish with Mactan tribal warriors on the Philippine island of Cebu. Europeans became aware of Australia and its peoples in the 1500s, but did not map it carefully until the late 1700s.

13.1
13.2
13.3 Where did the early European explorers go?

Legacies to the Future:
What Difference Do They Make?

Voyages of exploration, trade, conquest, and settlement evoke a sense of wonder at the skill and daring of the captains and sailors who embarked for the unknown with so few and such small ships and such limited equipment, and the foresight of the governments and businesspeople who organized and financed them. Each participant was called by a different set of values: the desire to chart the unknown; the pressure to find a new home; the quest for profit; the urge to proselytize; the lust for conquest; the competition for national superiority. Often, many of these motives were mixed together. The legacy of these people is the achievement of a geographically known and integrated globe. It is not, however, a single, simple legacy, but a variegated set of mixed legacies that includes competition, greed, self-righteousness, and violence. Few participants prepared for oceanic voyages with the greater good of the entire world at heart. Most, instead, sought benefits for themselves, their region or nation, or their religious group. They looked out on a huge and diverse world from relatively narrow and often self-interested perspectives.

By 1521 European traders had established a permanent connection between the eastern and western hemispheres for the first time, following Columbus' voyages across the Atlantic and Magellan's circumnavigation of the world. Meanwhile, inspired by the early explorations of Henry the Navigator along the west coast of Africa, Portuguese sailors rounded the Cape of Good Hope and opened new routes into the Indian Ocean. These explorations followed centuries of Western European economic expansion, national consolidation, and intellectual renaissance. Explorers were motivated by their mixed desire for knowledge, profit, national aggrandizement, and Christian proselytizing.

CHAPTER REVIEW

ECONOMIC AND SOCIAL CHANGES IN EUROPE

 13.1   What changes in Western Europe made Atlantic explorations possible?

In the 1200s, Western Europeans were emerging from agrarian, manorial economies. Productivity increased as new lands were opened and new innovations introduced. Crop surpluses were available to feed the merchants and craftspeople who established themselves in greater numbers in the cities. Cities, formerly centered on their churches, now increased the size of their marketplaces. As their own economies and technologies grew stronger, Western Europeans began to look for new routes to the great markets of Asia.

THE RENAISSANCE

13.2   What was the European Renaissance?

The Renaissance was a nearly 300-year period of cultural and intellectual creativity in Western Europe, beginning about 1300. The artists and writers who created the movement saw themselves as reconnecting to the traditions of the ancient Greeks and Romans, and thus producing a renaissance, or "rebirth," of Classical ideals in thought, literature, art, and sensibilities. With their increasing success in trade and manufacture, urban businessmen became patrons of the arts, and creativity flourished.

A NEW WORLD

13.3   Where did the early European explorers go?

Seeking routes to the lucrative Asian markets, Western Europeans tried two new directions: the Portuguese headed south along the western coast of Africa until they could turn east toward India; the Spanish headed west across the Atlantic Ocean. By 1600, Portuguese and Spanish explorers and traders had established commercial depots along the coasts of Africa, India, China, Japan, and the Pacific Islands. Westward, they had established settlements in South America and the Caribbean. The English, Dutch, and French had begun also to explore North America.

Suggested Readings

PRINCIPAL SOURCES

Adas, Michael, ed. *Islamic and European Expansion* (Philadelphia, PA: Temple University Press, 1993). Key collection of historiographical essays on major topics in world history, 1200–1900. Articles by Richard Eaton and Judith Tucker on Islam and William McNeill on "gunpowder empires" are especially helpful for this section.

Boorstin, Daniel J. *The Discoverers* (New York: Random House, 1983). Extremely well written, engaging history of four kinds of invention and discovery. One is maritime, mostly European explorers and cartographers 1400–1800.

Chakrabarty, Dipesh. *Provincializing Europe: Postcolonial Thought and Historical Difference* (Princeton, NJ: Princeton University Press, 2000).

Chaudhuri, K.N. *Trade and Civilization in the Indian Ocean: An Economic History from the Rise of Islam to 1750* (Cambridge: Cambridge University Press, 1985). A survey of goods, traders, ships, regulations, and competition among those who sailed and claimed to control the Indian Ocean.

Crosby, Alfred W. *Ecological Imperialism: The Biological Expansion of Europe, 900–1900* (Cambridge: Cambridge University Press, 1986). The biological—mostly destructive—impact of European settlement around the world: a tragedy for native peoples from the Americas to Oceania.

Curtin, Philip. *Cross-Cultural Trade in World History* (Cambridge: Cambridge University Press, 1984). Classical statement of the significance and ubiquity of trade diasporas.

Landes, David S. *The Wealth and Poverty of Nations: Why Some Are so Rich and Some so Poor* (New York: W.W. Norton, 1999). Credits the Western European world with creating the institutions that made its economic growth flourish.

McNeill, William H. *The Rise of the West: A History of the Human Community, with a Retrospective Essay* (Chicago, IL: University of Chicago Press, 1991). Reopened the professional field of modern history. Analyzes the basis of power, and those who created it, in global perspective, in each time period.

Wolf, Eric R. *Europe and the People without History* (Berkeley, CA: University of California Press, 1982). Laments history's emphasis on the powerful, and attempts to correct the imbalance by bringing into the historical record peoples who have been left out.

SECONDARY SOURCES

Aquinas, St. Thomas. *Summa contra Gentiles* and *Governance of Rulers* (excerpts) in Columbia University, *Introduction to Contemporary Civilization in the West,* cited below. Aquinas defined the field

of thirteenth-century Roman Catholic theology—and beyond.

Bloch, Marc. *Feudal Society,* 2 vols. (Chicago, IL: University of Chicago Press, 1961). Classic, if dated, comprehensive view of the workings of feudalism in Western Europe.

Boccaccio, Giovanni. *The Decameron,* trans. Frances Winwar (New York: Modern Library, 1955). Delightful tales, set against the background of the Black Death, which raged through Western Europe in the 1340s.

Braudel, Fernand. *Capitalism and Material Life, 1400–1800,* trans. Miriam Kochan (New York: Harper and Row, 1973). Comprehensive survey of the beginnings of the modern capitalist system in Europe.

———. *The Mediterranean and the Mediterranean World in the Age of Philip II,* trans. Sian Reynolds (New York: Harper and Row, 2 vols, 1973). Magisterial work that introduces Braudel's concept of three complementary time frames in the study of history: short range, middle range, and *longue durée.*

Brotton, Jerry. *The Renaissance: A Very Short Introduction* (New York: Oxford University Press, 2006). Excellent, concise survey. Credits Islamic learning with helping to inspire the Renaissance.

Brucker, Gene. *Renaissance Florence* (Berkeley, CA: University of California Press, 1969). Older, but still classic account.

Cassirer, Ernst, Paul Oskar Kristeller, and John Herman Randall, Jr. trans. and eds. *Philosophy of the Enlightenment* (Chicago: University of Chicago Press, 1956).

Chaudhuri, K.N. *Asia Before Europe* (Cambridge: Cambridge University Press, 1990). Survey of the economic and political systems of Asia before the impact of colonialism and the Industrial Revolution. Comprehensive, comparative, and thoughtful.

Cipolla, Carlo. *Clocks and Culture, 1300–1700* (New York: W.W. Norton, 2003). Presents the technology of early clocks, and then credits them with increasing people's sensitivity to the importance of time, especially in the world of work.

Cohn, Samuel K., Jr. *The Black Death Transformed: Disease and Culture in Early Renaissance Europe* (London: Arnold, 2002). Studies and summarizes the research on the nature of the Black Death and its longer-term effects.

Columbia College, Columbia University. *Introduction to Contemporary Civilization in the West,* vol. 1 (New York: Columbia University Press, 2nd ed., 1954). Very well-chosen, long source readings from leading thinkers of the time and place. Vol. I covers about 1000–1800.

Crosby, Alfred. *The Measure of Reality: Quantification in Western Europe, 1250–1600* (Cambridge: Cambridge University Press, 1997). By quantifying the processes of work and productivity, people gained greater understanding and control of them, and increased their efficiency.

Fernandez-Armesto, Felipe. *Columbus* (New York: Oxford University Press, 1991). Careful, sensitive biography of the man and his times.

Frank, Andre Gunder, and Barry K. Gills, eds. *The World System: Five Hundred Years or Five Thousand?* (London: Routledge, 1993). In this somewhat tendentious, but well-argued, account, globalization is nothing new.

Gabrieli, F. "The Transmission of Learning and Literary Influences to Western Europe,' in Holt, P.M., Ann K.S. Lambton, and Bernard Lewis, eds., *The Cambridge History of Islam,* vol. 2B: *Islamic Society and Civilization* (Cambridge: Cambridge University Press, 1970), pp. 851–89. Comprehensive summary of the influence of Islamic learning on Europe. Especially good on contrasting different time periods.

The Hammond Atlas of World History, ed. Richard Overy (Maplewood, NJ: Hammond, 1999). Excellent, standard historical atlas.

Havighurst, Alfred F., ed. *The Pirenne Thesis: Analysis, Criticism, and Revision* (Lexington, MA: D.C. Heath, rev. ed. 1969). Well-selected pieces from Pirenne, his critics, and supporters. Well introduced, supported, and summarized, although mostly European in orientation.

Hohenberg, Paul M., and Lynn Hollen Lees. *The Making of Urban Europe, 1000–1950* (Cambridge, MA: Harvard University Press, 1985). Brief but comprehensive text on the significance of cities to the history of Europe. Special attention to the social development of cities and their residents.

Huff, Toby. *The Rise of Early Modern Science* (New York: Cambridge University Press, 2nd ed., 2003). Controversial analysis of how Western European Christians developed early science, and why Arabs and the Chinese did not.

Levenson, Jay A. *Circa 1492: Art in the Age of Exploration* (Washington, DC: National Gallery of Art, 1991). Catalogue of an astounding art exhibit, covering the arts in all the major regions of the world at the time of Columbus' voyages.

MacCulloch, Diarmaid. *Christianity: The First Thousand Years* (New York: Penguin, 2009). Thoughtful, incisive, lucid.

Morison, Samuel Eliot, trans. and ed. *Journals and Other Documents on the Life and Voyages of Christopher Columbus* (New York: The Heritage Press, 1963). The crucial documents.

Pirenne, Henri. *Medieval Cities: Their Origins and the Revival of Trade,* trans. Frank D. Halsey (Princeton, NJ: Princeton University Press, 1925). Classic statement of the importance of free merchants to the rise of commercial cities and the development of the modern world. Dated, and more limited than claimed, but pathbreaking and enormously influential.

———. *Mohammed and Charlemagne,* trans. Bernard Miall (New York: W.W. Norton, 1939). Key revisionist text citing the Islamic victories in the Mediterranean as the end of Roman Europe and the beginning of rebirth in the north under Charlemagne.

Polanyi, Karl, Conrad M. Arensberg, and Harry W. Pearson, eds. *Trade and Market in the Early Empires* (Chicago, IL: The Free Press, 1957). Fundamental argument by historical anthropologists that early trade was mostly regulated by rulers and priests.

Reynolds, Susan. *Fiefs and Vassals* (Oxford: Clarendon Press, 1994). Scholarly, influential examination of "feudalism," arguing that the word is used to cover too wide a variety of regional and temporal patterns.

Subrahmanyam, Sanjay. *The Career and Legend of Vasco da Gama* (Cambridge: Cambridge University Press, 1997). The most thorough available account of the man, his contributions, and the historical puzzles surrounding them, presented in overwhelming scholarly detail.

Tuchman, Barbara. *A Distant Mirror: The Calamitous Fourteenth Century* (New York: Knopf, 1978). Engaging history of a century filled with war and plague.

Wills, John E., Jr. "Maritime Asia, 1500–1800: The Interactive Emergence of European Domination," *American Historical Review* XCVIII, no. 1 (February 1993), pp. 83–105. Survey of European entrance into and domination of Indian Ocean and Chinese sea lanes.

FILMS

The Battle of Lepanto (2012; 30 minutes). Reveals not only the diverse forces arrayed on each side, but also the technology of naval warfare and the treatment of the sailors.

Forgetting the Arabs: Europe on the Cusp of the Renaissance (1999; 27 minutes). Argues that after the fall of Baghdad in 1258, the Muslim world rejected new ideas and thinking, while European Christians expanded their personal intellectual freedom.

Italy, Age of Architects (2007; 1 hour 25 minutes). Uses Leonardo as a touchstone to examine many aspects of the Italian Renaissance, especially engineering, architecture, and city planning.

The Medici: Godfathers of the Renaissance, 4 parts (2003; 2 hours). Comprehensive, engaging account of 300 years of European history seen through the experiences of a single family.

GLOSSARY

adivasis "Original inhabitants." The aboriginal peoples of the Indian subcontinent, who are outside the caste system and live somewhat separately from the rest of society, generally in remote places. Previously referred to as "tribals," they are today sometimes referred to as *vanvasis*, or forest dwellers.

agora A central feature of ancient Greek town planning. Its chief function was as a town market, but it also became the main social and political meeting-place. Together with the acropolis, it normally housed the most important buildings of the town. Later, the Roman forum fulfilled this function.

assimilation The process by which different ethnic groups lose their distinctive cultural identity through contact with the dominant culture of a society, and gradually become absorbed and integrated into it.

atman The soul of each individual person, identical in its substance to Brahman, the universal power. Thus each individual soul is part of the great soul of the universe.

B.P. Before the Present. Archaeologists frequently use this notation, especially for dates before about 20,000 B.C.E.

balance of power In international relations, a policy that aims to secure peace by preventing any one state or alignment of states from becoming too dominant. Alliances are formed in order to build up a force equal or superior to that of the potential enemy.

barbarians The Greeks first used the term "barbarous" to designate foreign and uncivilized peoples, those whose languages sounded to Greek ears like the sound *bar-bar*, rather than like Greek. Today, "barbarian" continues to refer to persons who are considered foreign and uncivilized, and may, in the extreme, also refer to people who are violent, uncontrolled, and, perhaps, uncontrollable.

bas-relief In sculpture, relief is a term for any work in which the forms stand out from the background. In bas- (or low) relief, the design projects only slightly

from the background and the outlines are not undercut.

Bhakti Devotion to god; a personal dedication to and worship of god, often through meditation, music, chanting, dance—different from more formal rituals.

bodhisattva A "being of wisdom" worthy of entering *nirvana*, but who chooses to stay on earth, or be reborn, in order to help others. In Mahayana Buddhism, the Buddha himself is considered also to be one of the *bodhisattvas*.

bread and circuses Provision by the government of free food and entertainment, designed to divert the masses, and especially the poor masses, from engaging in political action.

Caesar Augustus "Caesar" and "Augustus" are both titles of the emperor Octavian. Caesar means ruler or emperor, and the word comes down to the present in the title czar or tsar. Augustus means dignified, even majestic. It was sometimes used in place of Octavian's given name. The words could also be reversed as Augustus Caesar.

caliph The spiritual head and temporal ruler of the Muslim community.

caste A hierarchical ordering of people into groups, fixed from birth, based on their inherited ritual status and determining whom they may marry and with whom they may eat.

centuries The smallest units of the Roman army, each composed of some 100 foot soldiers and commanded by a *centurion*. A legion was made up of 60 centuries. Centuries also formed political divisions of Roman citizens.

consul Under the Roman Republic, one of the two magistrates holding supreme civil and military authority.

cuneiform A writing system in use in the ancient Near East from around the end of the fourth millennium to the first century B.C.E. The earliest examples are in Sumerian. The name derives from the wedge-shaped marks (Latin: *cuneus*, a wedge) made by pressing the slanted edge of a stylus into soft clay.

dar al-Islam The literal meaning of the Arabic words is "the abode of Islam." The term refers to the land of Islam, that is, territories in which Islam and its religious laws (*shari'a*) may be freely practiced. Some interpreters argue that the rulers themselves must be Muslims and that they must institute *shari'a* law, others argue that freedom for Muslims to follow Islamic practice is the only requirement. Also, sometimes, *dar as-Salam*, "the abode of peace."

deme A rural district or village in ancient Greece, or its members or inhabitants. The demes were a constituent part of the polis but had their own corporations with police powers, and their own cults, officials, and property.

dharma The duty of each person, determined in large part by his or her caste.

dhimmi Translates as "protected." A term applied to Jews, Christians, Zoroastrians, and others who were accepted as monotheists, like Muslims, and therefore eligible for protection that allowed them to practice their faith, but required them to pay a special tax.

diaspora A dispersion of peoples. Most commonly used to refer to the dispersion of Jews among the gentiles, which began with the Babylonian captivity of the sixth century B.C.E.

dictator In Roman times, a leader elected at a time of crisis by the Senate of Rome for a short term, usually six months, and vested with extraordinary powers to deal with the situation.

diffusion The spread of ideas, objects, or traits from one culture to another.

dominance The imposition of alien government through force, as opposed to hegemony.

ecumene A Greek word referring to the inhabited world and designating a distinct cultural-historical community.

Eucharist From the Greek *eucharistia*, "thanksgiving." The central sacrament and act of worship of the Catholic Church, culminating in Holy Communion, the eating of a sanctified wafer and drinking of sanctified wine as a reminder of Jesus' life, and, in Roman Catholicism, representing the actual act of partaking in his body and blood.

free-market economy An economic system in which the means of production are largely privately owned and there is little or no government control over the markets.

ghetto The part of a city to which a particular group is confined for its living space. Named originally for an area adjacent to an iron foundry (in Italian, *ghetto*) in sixteenth-century Venice where Jews were segregated by government order, the term has been used most often to designate segregated Jewish living areas in European cities. It is also used, more broadly, to indicate any area where specific groups are segregated whether by law, by force, or by choice.

guild A sworn association of people who gather for some common purpose, usually economic. Guilds of craftsmen or merchants were formed in order to protect and further the members' professional interests and for mutual aid.

hadith Traditional records of the deeds and utterances of the prophet Muhammad, and the basis, after the Quran, for Islamic theology and law.

hegemony The predominance of one unit over the others in a group, for example, one state in a confederation. It can also apply to the rule of an empire over its subject peoples, when the foreign government is exercised with their substantial consent.

heliocentric A system in which the sun is assumed to be at the center of the solar system—or of the universe—while Earth and the other planets move around it.

heresy A belief that is not in agreement with, or that even conflicts with, the official orthodoxy of its time and place. Heretics, those who espoused heresy, were often persecuted.

hieroglyphs The characters in a writing system based on the use of pictograms or ideograms. In ancient Egypt, hieroglyphics were largely used for monumental inscriptions. The symbols depict people, animals, and objects, which represent words, syllables, or sounds.

hijra The "migration" or flight of Muhammad from Mecca, where his life was in danger, to Medina (then called Yathrib), where he was welcomed as a potential leader in 622 C.E. The Islamic era (A.H.: After Hijra) is calculated from this date.

Hominid Any of a family (Hominidae) of erect bipedal (two-legged) primate mammals, which includes humans and humanlike species.

Homo erectus The most widespread of all prehistoric hominids, and the most similar to humans. Evolved about two million years ago and became extinct 100,000 years ago.

Homo sapiens Homo, "human," is the genus in which modern humans are placed; sapiens means "wise."

Homo sapiens sapiens The first human being of the modern type.

hoplite A heavily armed foot soldier of ancient Greece, whose function was to fight in close formation, usually in ranks of eight men. Each soldier carried a heavy bronze shield, a short iron sword, and a long spear for thrusting.

humanism Cultural movement initiated in Western Europe in the fourteenth century deriving from the rediscovery and study of Greek and Roman literary texts. Most humanists continued to believe in God, but emphasized the study of humans.

iconoclast An "image-breaker," or a person who rejects the veneration of icons, on the grounds that the practice is idolatrous.

ideogram (alternative: ideograph) A character or figure in a writing system in which the idea of a thing is represented rather than its name. Languages such as Chinese use ideograms.

ijtihad A method of Quranic interpretation based on text, local custom, and the personal judgment of the *qadi*, or judge.

imam In Islam, a title for a person whose religious leadership or example is to be followed.

Indo–Aryan A subgroup of the Indo-Iranian branch of the Indo-European group of languages, also called Indic, and spoken in India, Sri Lanka, Bangladesh, and Pakistan. The Indo–Aryan languages are descended from Sanskrit, the sacred language of Hinduism.

innovation The explanation that similar cultural traits, techniques, or objects found among different groups of people were invented independently rather than spread from one group to another.

janapada A large political district in India, beginning about 700 B.C.E.

kami In Japanese thought, the powers and spirits inherent in nature.

karma The doctrine that actions have their own appropriate consequences. A person's actions carry their own rewards

(or punishments) because they set the directions of his or her life.

lateen sail A triangular sail affixed to a long yard or crossbar at an angle of about 45 degrees to the mast, with the other free corner secured near the stern. The sail was capable of tacking against the wind on either side. Lateen sails were so named when they appeared in the Mediterranean, where they were associated with Latin culture, although their origin was actually far away.

Legalism A school of Chinese philosophy that came into prominence during the Period of the Warring States and had great influence on the policies of the Qin dynasty. Legalists took a pessimistic view of human nature and believed that social harmony could be attained only through strong government control and the imposition of strict laws, enforced absolutely.

Lost Ten Tribes Ten tribes of Israel were exiled from their homeland in 721 B.C.E. They totally assimilated into their new surroundings, lost their Jewish identity, and were lost to history. Periodically, groups in remote areas today claim that they are the Lost Ten Tribes.

magistrate An official elected by the Senate of Rome to administer the Republic under the supervision of the Senate. There were many different ranks of magistrate, serving different functions. At the end of their term of office they became senators themselves.

mahdi According to Islamic tradition, this messianic leader will appear to restore justice, truth, and religion for a brief period before the universal Day of Judgment.

mandala A symbolic circular diagram of complex geometric design used as an instrument of meditation or in the performance of sacred rites in Hinduism and Buddhism.

Mandate of Heaven A concept in China: the ruler had moral authority so long as the heavenly powers granted it to him on the basis of his good character. A well-functioning government was evidence that the ruler possessed the Mandate of Heaven. A poorly functioning government, especially when accompanied by such natural disasters as flood or drought, showed that the Mandate had passed away.

mantra A formula of words and sounds that are believed to possess spiritual power, a practice of both Hinduism and Buddhism.

mastaba A low, rectangular, benchlike structure that covered a grave. The architectural forerunner of the pyramid.

master narrative The conventional, widely accepted view of the historical record.

maya Illusion. The manifest world in which we appear to live is only illusion; there is a reality beyond what we experience here on earth.

medieval The "middle period." Europeans of the Renaissance period, who felt that they were, at last, reconnecting with the glories of ancient Greece and Rome, called the ten centuries between the end of the Western Roman Empire and the beginning of the Renaissance "the medieval period." They used the term pejoratively. More recent scholars see that very long period as far more complicated and diverse, and analyze it by specific geographical regions and into much smaller periods of time.

moral economy An economy whose goal is providing basic necessities for all members of a society before allowing any particular members to take profits; in contrast to a free-market economy.

mudra A hand gesture with specific meaning or significance in Indian classical sculpture and dance. One specific *mudra*, for example, indicates teaching, another fearlessness, another revelation, etc.

myth An interpretive story of the past that cannot be verified historically but may have a deep moral message.

Neolithic "New Stone Age," the last division of the Stone Age, immediately preceding the development of metallurgy and corresponding to the ninth to fifth millennia B.C.E. it was characterized by the increasing domestication of animals and cultivation of crops, established agricultural communities, and the appearance of such crafts as pottery and weaving.

Neoplatonic A philosophical system founded by Plotinus (205–70 C.E.) and influenced by Plato's theory of ideas. It emphasizes the transcendent, impersonal, and indefinable "One" as the ground of all existence and the source of an eternal world of goodness, beauty, and order, of which material existence is but a feeble copy.

nirvana In Theravada Buddhism, the blissful nothingness into which a soul that had lived properly entered after death, and from which there would be no further rebirth. In Mahayana Buddhism, *nirvana* became an abode of more active bliss, a kind of heaven, filled with heavenly activities.

nome An administrative district in ancient Egypt.

original sin First understood as the disobedience of Adam and Eve in the Garden of Eden as they ate the forbidden fruit of the Tree of Knowledge. Later understood as the sexual relations between Adam and Eve. In Christian belief, Jesus' death atoned for these sins—for those who believed in him.

paleoanthropology The study of the earliest humans and their environments.

paterfamilias The head of a family or household in Roman law—always a male—and the only member to have full legal rights. The *paterfamilias* had absolute power over his family, extending to life and death.

patrician Born to a family with long-standing residence and prominence in Rome, a patrician was an aristocrat. About seven to ten percent of Rome's population were patricians.

patron–client relationship In a patron–client relationship, the patron offers protection and, often, employment, while the client offers obedience, labor, and services in exchange. Sometimes these relationships are formalized under law. More frequently they exist in place of law, in situations where legal structures are weak or nonexistent. Patron–client relationships are common throughout world history.

Pax Romana The "Roman peace," that is, the state of comparative concord prevailing within the boundaries of the Roman Empire from the reign of Augustus (r. 27 B.C.E.–14 C.E.) to that of Marcus Aurelius (r. 161–180 C.E.), enforced by Roman political and military control.

pictogram (alternative: pictograph) A pictorial symbol or sign representing an object or concept.

plebeian A citizen of ancient Rome who was not a member of the privileged patrician class. Beginning in the later Republican period, the term "plebeian" implied low social class.

praetor In ancient Rome, the term was originally applied to the consul as leader of an army. In 366 B.C.E. a further praetor was elected with special responsibility for the administration of justice in Rome, with the right of military command. Further praetors were subsequently appointed to administer the increasing number of provinces.

prehistory Everything that occurred before the invention of writing.

presbyter In early Christian usage, a member of the governing body of a church.

publicans or **tax farmers** Collected taxes on behalf of the government, paying in an agreed sum but keeping for themselves any surplus they could extort. The system was extremely oppressive to those who were taxed.

putting-out system In this system, employers provide employees with raw materials and the orders for turning them into finished products, which they then buy on completion. The employees carry out the work at home, thus reducing the production cost for the employer.

qadi A judge in Islamic legal practice.

Renaissance From the French for "rebirth," a period of cultural and intellectual creativity in Western Europe between 1300 and 1570. The artists and intellectuals who created the movement saw themselves reconnecting with the traditions of ancient Greece and Rome, thus giving a "rebirth" to European culture. The cultural rebirth was accompanied by an expanding urban economy, another rebirth.

republic A state that is ruled not by a hereditary leader (as in a monarchy) but by a person or persons appointed under the constitution.

sacrament In Christian theology, a rite or ritual that is an outward sign of a spiritual grace conveyed on the believer by Christ through the ministry of the Church.

samsara The process and cycle of living, dying, and being reborn.

satrapy A province or colony in the Achaemenid or Persian Empire ruled by a satrap or governor. Darius I completed the division of the Empire into provinces, and established 20 satrapies with their annual tributes. The term "satrapy" can also refer to the period of rule of a satrap.

see The geographical home of a Church authority: the Vatican in Roman Catholicism, four separate locations for the Eastern Christian churches.

shaman In the religious beliefs of some African, Asian and American tribal societies, a person capable of entering into trances and believed to be endowed with supernatural powers, with the ability to cure the sick, find lost or stolen property, predict the future, and protect the community from evil spirits. A shaman may act as judge or ruler, and, as a priest, a shaman directs communal sacrifices and escorts the souls of the dead to the next world.

Shi'a Short form for *shiat Ali*, "follower of Ali." In choosing a successor to Muhammad, the shi'a argued for Ali, his cousin/son-in-law, his closest male relative. From that time on, they remained a separate sect within Islam, representing about 20 percent of all Muslims worldwide, and a majority in countries such as Iran and Iraq.

silk route The set of rough roads or transportation links across central Asia carrying trade and cultural exchange as far as China, India, and the eastern Mediterranean.

sinicization The adoption and absorption by foreign peoples of Chinese language, customs, and culture.

sophist An itinerant professor of higher education in ancient Greece, who gave instruction for a fee. The subjects taught, which included oratory, grammar, ethics, mathematics, and literature, had the practical aim of equipping pupils for successful careers. The sophist professor taught his students to argue all sides of every question, regardless of their merit. **Sophistry** is this kind of clever argumentation, regardless of merit.

speaking in tongues A mode of praying and preaching emphasizing ecstasy and even an entering into trances, such that the words of prayer and preaching may not be understood, but are meaningful nonetheless.

state Several definitions; sometimes used for the total political organization of a group of people controlling their own territory.

Sufi In Islam, a member of one of the orders practicing mystical forms of worship that first arose in the eighth and ninth centuries C.E. Some Muslims see Sufis as fulfilling the mission of Islam; others criticize them as not adhering strictly enough to the formal laws and practices of Islam.

Sunni From the Arabic *sunna*, the words and acts of Muhammad, as recorded in *hadiths*. The Sunni are the majority group in Islam, representing just over 80 percent of the total. They differed from the Shi'a in choosing Uthman as the first successor of Muhammad, and argued that they were following the wish and example of the Prophet.

supply and **demand** In economics, the relationship between the amount of a commodity that producers are able and willing to sell (supply) and the quantity that consumers can afford and wish to buy (demand).

syllabary A writing system in which each symbol represents the syllable of a word, in contrast to ideogram.

syncretism refers to the merging of different traditions from different origins into a single unified practice. The term is also used to refer to hybridity in other areas, such as art, music, philosophy, and religion.

TaNaKh A Hebrew term for the books of the Bible that are written in Hebrew. The word is composed of the initial letters of the words Torah (first five books of the Bible, traditionally attributed to Moses), Nevi'im (the books of the Prophets), and Ketuvim (additional historical, poetic, and philosophic writings). These are the three sections of the Hebrew Bible.

tariqa In Islam, a generic term meaning "path," referring to the doctrines and methods of mysticism and esoterism. The word also refers to schools or brotherhoods of mystics, which were often situated at a mosque or the tomb of a Muslim saint.

tax farmer An official entrusted with collecting taxes. The total amount to be collected was fixed by the government, and any collection exceeding that amount belonged to the tax farmer. The system encouraged exploitation of the taxpayer.

teleology The philosophical study of final causes or purposes. Teleology refers especially to any system that interprets nature or the universe as having design or purpose. It has been used to provide evidence for the existence of God.

theme A theme was originally a military unit stationed in one of the provinces of the Byzantine Empire, but it later applied to the large military districts that formed buffer zones in the areas most vulnerable to Muslim.

trade diaspora A diaspora is a dispersion over far-flung territories of a group of people who have a common bond. Usually this is an ancestral bond, such as in the Jewish diaspora and the African diaspora. A trade diaspora refers to the network of international traders who relate to one another through the bonds of their trade.

transhumance The practice of shifting residence and livestock between mountains and valleys according to the season of the year, or more generally a pattern of seasonal migration.

tribune In ancient Rome, a plebeian officer elected by the plebeians and charged to protect their lives and properties, with a right of veto against legislative proposals of the Senate.

tributary status The relationship of a low-ranking state to a more powerful one, recognized formally by the regular payment of tribute.

triumvirate Literally, an association of three strong men. An unofficial coalition of Julius Caesar, Pompey, and Crassus formed in 60 B.C.E. After Caesar's murder in 44 B.C.E., a triumvirate including his heir Octavian (later Augustus), Mark Antony, and Marcus Lepidus was appointed to maintain public order.

Turkic/Turkish Turkic languages are a family of related languages spoken by peoples of central Asia and their descendants. The most widely spoken of these languages is Turkish.

tyrant A ruler with absolute power, sometimes granted through election in times of crisis, sometimes seized through force of arms.

ulama The theologians and legal experts of Islam.

umma The community of believers in Islam, which transcends ethnic and political boundaries.

value added An economist's term for the increase in value from the cost of raw materials to the cost of finished products. It is the value added to the raw material by processing, manufacture, and marketing.

vassal A low-ranking political ruler or state that is subordinate and pays homage to a more powerful one.

yurt A portable dwelling used by the nomadic peoples of central Asia, consisting of a tentlike structure of skin, felt, or handwoven textiles arranged over wooden poles, simply furnished with rugs.

ziggurat A temple tower of ancient Mesopotamia, constructed of square or rectangular terraces of diminishing size, usually with a shrine on top built of blue enamel bricks, the color of the sky.

zimbabwe (zim-bahb-way) Stone-walled enclosure or building built during the African Iron Age in the region of modern Zimbabwe and Mozambique. The structures were the courts of local rulers. They have been associated with foreign trade, integrated farming and animal husbandry, and gold production. The Great Zimbabwe is the ruins of the former capital of the Monomatapa Empire, situated in Zimbabwe and occupied from around the thirteenth to the sixteenth century C.E.

PICTURE AND LITERARY CREDITS

Picture credits

Literary credits

For permission to reprint copyright material the publishers gratefully acknowledge the following:

Introduction
(p. I-19): from *Christianizing the Roman Empire (A.D. 100–400)* by Ramsay MacMullen (New Haven, CT: Yale University Press, 1984).

Chapter Two
(pp. 57–58): from *The Epic of Gilgamesh*, translated with an introduction by N.K. Sandars (Penguin Classics, 1960, Third Edition 1972), Copyright © N. K. Sandars, 1960, 1964, 1972, reproduced by permission of Penguin Books Ltd; **(p. 60):** from *The Sumerians: Their History, Culture, and Character* (Chicago, IL: University of Chicago Press, published 1963), by Samuel Noah Kramer. Copyright © 1963 by The University of Chicago. All rights reserved. Reprinted by permission of University of Chicago Press.

Chapter Three
(pp. 65, 70): "Hymn to the Nile," and "The Harper's Song for Inherkhawy," both from *Ancient Egyptian Literature: An Anthology*, translated by John L. Foster (University of Texas Press, 2001), copyright © 2001, by permission of the author and the University of Texas Press; **(p. 73):** "The Egyptian Book of the Dead and the 'Negative Confession'," from *Ancient Near Eastern Texts Relating to the Old Testament*, Third Edition With Supplement, edited by James B. Pritchard (Princeton University Press, 1969) © 1950, 1955, 1969, renewed 1978 by Princeton University Press, reprinted by permission of Princeton University Press; **(p. 77):** "Si-nuhe," from *Ancient Near Eastern Texts Relating to the Old Testament*, Third Edition With Supplement, edited by James B. Pritchard (Princeton University Press, 1969) © 1950, 1955, 1969, renewed 1978 by Princeton University Press, reprinted by permission of Princeton University Press.

Chapter Four
(p. 93): from *The Book of Songs*, translated by Arthur Waley (London: George Allen & Unwin, 1936), copyright © by permission of The Arthur Waley Estate; **(p. 106):** "Great-Jaguar-Paw: Mayan King of Tikal" from *A Forest of Kings: The Untold Story of the Ancient Maya*, edited by Linda Schele and David Freidel (William Morrow, 1990), © 1990 by Linda Schele and David Freidel; **(p. 108):** from *Popul Vuh: Sacred Book of the Quiché Maya People* (Norman: University of Oklahoma Press, 2007), translation and commentary by Allen J. Christenson. Reprinted by permission of University of Oklahoma Press and O Books, John Hunt Publishing.

Chapter Five
(p. 140): "Hector Returns to Troy", from *The Iliad* by Homer, translated by Robert Fagles, translation copyright © 1990 by Robert Fagles. Used by permission of Viking Penguin, a division of Penguin Group (USA) LLC; **(p. 140):** "Book 22: Slaughter in the Hall", "Book 23: The Great Rooted Bed" from *The Odyssey* by Homer, translated by Robert Fagles, translation copyright © 1996 by Robert Fagles. Used by permission of Viking Penguin, a division of Penguin Group (USA) LLC; **(p. 145):** from *The History of the Peloponnesian War* by Thucydides, translated by Rex Warner, with an introduction and notes by M. I. Finley (Penguin Classics 1954, Revised edition 1972). Translation copyright © Rex Warner, 1954. Introduction and appendices copyright © M. I. Finley, 1972. Reprinted by permission of Penguin Books Limited. Reproduced with permission of Curtis Brown Group Limited, London on behalf of The Estate of Rex Warner. Copyright © Rex Warner, 1954; **(pp. 146, 148):** from *The Collected Dialogues of Plato*, Including the Letters, by Edith Hamilton. © 1961 Princeton University Press, 1989 renewed. Reprinted by permission of

Princeton University Press; **(p. 150):** from *The Reign of the Phallus: Sexual Politics in Ancient Athens* by Eva C. Keuls. Reprinted by permission of University of California Press; **(pp. 150–151):** from *Worshiping Women: Ritual and Reality in Classical Athens*, edited by Nikolaos Kaltsas and Alan Shapiro (Alexander S. Onassis Public Benefit Foundation in collaboration with National Archaeological Museum, Athens, 2008). Reprinted with permission; **(p. 156):** from *Alexander of Macedon* by Peter Green (Berkeley, CA: University of California Press, 1991). Reprinted by permission of University of California Press.

Chapter Six
(pp. 185): from *The Aeneid* by Virgil, translated by Rolphe Humphries (Charles Scribner's Sons, 1951) © 1951 Charles Scribner's Sons, reprinted by permission of Pearson Education Inc; **(p. 193):** Sima Qian, from *First Emperor: Selections from the Historical Records*, translated by Raymond Dawson (2007). By permission of Oxford University Press.

Chapter Seven
(p. 205): from *The Book of Songs*, translated by Arthur Waley (London: George Allen & Unwin, 1936), copyright © by permission of The Arthur Waley Estate; **(pp. 210, 211, 212, 220):** from *Sources of Chinese Tradition* Volume I, Second Edition, edited by William Theodore de Bary and Irene Bloom (Copyright © Columbia University Press, 1999), reprinted by permission of the publisher; **(pp. 210–211, 213, 220):** Sima Qian, from *First Emperor: Selections from the Historical Records*, translated by Raymond Dawson (2007). By permission of Oxford University Press; **(p. 217):** "A Woman's Hundred Years" from *Chinese Civilization: A Sourcebook*, Second Edition, edited by Patricia Buckley Ebrey (The Free Press, 1993), copyright (1993) by Patricia Buckley Ebrey, reprinted by permission of The Free Press, a division of Simon & Schuster, Inc. **(p. 229):** Du Fu, "Autumn Meditation" from *The Selected Poems of Du Fu*, translated by Burton Watson (Copyright © Columbia University Press, 2002), reprinted by permission of the publisher; **(p. 231):** Du Fu, "Ballad of the Army Carts" from *Three Chinese Poets: Translations of Poems by Wang Wei, Li Bai, and Du Fu*, edited by Vikram Seth (HarperCollins Publishers, 1993), translation copyright © 1992 by Vikram Seth, reprinted by permission of the publisher and Irene Skolnick Literary Agency.

Chapter Eight
(p. 249): from *Asoka and the Decline of the Mauryas* by Romila Thapar (1998). By permission of Oxford University Press, USA; **(p. 254):** "A King's Double Nature" and "Harvest of War" from *Poems of Love and War: From the Eight Anthologies and Ten Long Poems of Classical Tamil*, translated by A.K. Ramanujan (Columbia University Press, 1985) © 1985 by Columbia University Press, reprinted by permission of the publisher.

Chapter Nine
(p. 272): from *Sources of Indian Tradition* Vol. I (From the Beginning to 1800), edited by Ainslee Embree (New York: Columbia University Press, 2nd ed., 1988) (translations of *The Rigveda*). Copyright © 1988 Columbia University Press, reprinted by permission of the publisher; **(p. 276):** from *Bhagavad-Gita*, translated by Barbara Stoler Miller (Bantam Books, 1986), translation copyright © 1986 by Barbara Stoler Miller, used by permission of Bantam Books, a division of Random House, Inc.; **(pp. 280, 281):** from *The Wonder that Was India* by A. L. Basham (New York: Grove Press, 1954), St Martin's Press; **(p. 288):** "A Woman's Hundred Years" from *Chinese Civilization: A Sourcebook*, Second Edition, edited by Patricia Buckley Ebrey (The Free Press, 1993), copyright (1993) by Patricia Buckley Ebrey, reprinted by permission of The Free Press, a division of Simon & Schuster, Inc.

Chapter Ten
(p. 325): from *Who Are the People of God? Early Christian Models of Community* by Howard Clark Kee (New Haven, CT: Yale University Press, 1995); **(pp. 326, 327):** from *The City of God* by Augustine (New York: Modern Library, 1950); **(p. 335):** from *Two Lives of Charlemagne* by Einhard and Nokter the Stammerer, translated with an introduction by Professor Lewis Thorpe (Penguin Classics, 1969). Copyright © Professor Lewis Thorpe, 1969.

Chapter Eleven
(pp. 343, 346–347, 348): from *The Koran* (With a Parallel Arabic Text), translated with notes by N.J. Dawood (London: Penguin Books, 1990). Copyright © N.J. Dawood, 1956, 1959, 1966, 1968, 1974, 1990; **(p. 347):** from *The Islamic World*, edited by William H. McNeill and Marilyn Robinson Waldman (Chicago, IL: University of Chicago Press, 1983) (OUP); **(p. 348):** from *The Koran*, translated by M. Pickthall (New York: Alfred A. Knopf, 1930).

Chapter Twelve
(p. 393): Ibn Battuta, from *Travels in Asia and Africa 1325–1354*, translated and edited by H.A.R. Gibb (The Hakluyt Society, 1958). By permission of David Higham Associates; **(pp. 397, 398, 404):** from *The Travels of Marco Polo*, translated with an introduction by Ronald Latham (Penguin Classics, 1958), Copyright © Ronald Latham, 1958, reprinted by permission of Penguin Books Ltd; **(pp. 397, 403):** from *The Mongols: A Very Short Introduction* by Morris Rossabi (2012). By permission of Oxford University Press, USA.

Chapter Thirteen
(p. 423): from *The Decameron* by Giovanni Boccaccio, translated by Frances Winwar (New York: Modern Library, 1955). Reprinted by permission of MBI Inc.

Every effort has been made to obtain permission from all copyright holders, but in some cases this has not proved possible. The publishers therefore wish to thank all authors or copyright holders who are included without acknowledgment. Pearson Education Inc./Laurence King Publishing Ltd apologizes for any errors or omissions in the above list and would be pleased to incorporate any corrections in the next edition.

INDEX